NEWSWEEK CONDENSED BOOKS

SHANA ALEXANDER

KURT HALBRITTER

JONATHAN KWITNY

MARGARET TRUDEAU

GARY CARTWRIGHT

ANYONE'S DAUGHTER

HALBRITTER'S ARMS THROUGH THE AGES

VICIOUS CIRCLES

BEYOND REASON

BLOOD WILL TELL

NEWSWEEK BOOKS, New York

NEWSWEEK CONDENSED BOOKS

Herbert A. Gilbert, Editor
Mary Ann Joulwan, Art Director
Elaine Andrews, Associate Editor
Danielle Woerner-Bobrick, Assistant Editor

Alvin Garfin, Publisher

CONTENTS

ANYONE'S DAUGHTER

A Condensation of the book by

SHANA ALEXANDER

*Patty Hearst as "Tania." Patty was kidnapped,
sexually abused, threatened with death, and became
a bank robber, revolutionary, and fugitive from justice.*

AP

We could be anyone's daughter,
son, wife, husband, lover, neighbor,
friend. . . .
                    —*the "Tania Interview"*

OPENING REFLECTION

Long before Patty Hearst's trial, even before her disappearance, her flight into the wilderness, before the awful incineration in the burning house in Los Angeles, before she stuck up the bank, even before she joined her captors and denounced her parents as "the pig Hearsts" and said, "I have chosen to stay and fight"—possibly while she was still in the closet in the hideout on Golden Gate—I became captive of Patty Hearst and her story, whatever that story might turn out to be.

I understood her because in some way she was the girl I had been, and in some way I was also her mother. I understood that a mother-daughter struggle was close to the core of her story, something similar to what had happened to me and my mother, and to myself and my own daughter, whom I was losing now. (When Patricia Hearst was kidnapped, I was the anxious, guilt-ridden mother of one unhappy twelve-year-old daughter, who, due to the divorce of her parents and attendant alarums and excursions over many years, was temporarily homeless and had just been reluctantly packed off to boarding school.) One of these daughters was taken entirely by accident. But all three were in rebellion and revolt.

I understood the peculiar attraction and tension between the kidnappers—seven young white university dropouts, five of them

9

women, and one black escaped convict—and the shadowy legion of imprisoned black men in "Fascist Amerikkka," for whom the Symbionese Liberation Army felt such unbounded, uncritical compassion.

I understood the central role of the media in the entire event, all the way from Grandfather William Randolph Hearst, who invented tabloid journalism, down to the modern hysteria that was taking place in California and around the world over Patty Hearst.

I understood that none of the characters in the story understood any of the others. Everyone was talking at once, and each was speaking a different language: the anguished parents, the defiant militants, the California authorities, the hot-breathing press, the psychiatric establishment, the lawyers—the whole Tower of Babel—and I felt sure that long after the case was over, we would all be talking about it still.

Early in March 1974, I was in Los Angeles, driving to meet a friend for lunch. Patricia Hearst had been missing for five weeks. My car radio was tuned to the twenty-four-hour news to which I had become addicted. The radio droned incessantly about the case, which already had captured the fancy of the nation and, in particular, the shallow, capricious fancy of California's freeway-trapped audience. A sharp physical sensation occurred as the revelation hit: Patty was *my* story. It felt as if a light bulb had switched on over my head, the way they used to in comic strips, and simultaneously a rubber-tipped arrow had struck me in the breast. As time passed and my life went along as a journalist, as a mother, and as a daughter, I lost confidence at various times in everything but one thing: I understood this story.

The problem for a long time was not substance but form. "How can you begin to write the story when you don't know how it ends?" people used to ask. Another difficulty was that my central character was offstage, so to speak; no one even knew whether she was alive. A more serious problem, technically speaking, was that the Hearst case was an interesting story about a fundamentally uninteresting girl. What happened to Patty and what then happened to America are akin to what happens when a pebble is tossed into a pond: the pebble disappears, the pond ripples. I was attracted by the ripples, not the stone.

When she was kidnapped, this unremarkable young woman had become the object of world scrutiny, focused through the media's compound, unblinking eye. Not just one world but the separate worlds of law enforcement and psychiatry; the tremulous eyes of many parents besides her own; the hard eyes of revolution; the wary-stary eyes of fugitives, prisoners, psychopaths, terrorists, and self-proclaimed outsiders of every stripe; and the professional attentions of the best lawyers and doctors money could buy—all these were trained on Patricia Hearst. Yet she was invisible all the while, a pebble in dark waters.

To me, the story was not just the tabloid bonanza of all time, evolved directly from the billion-dollar formula that Grandfather Hearst had invented. It was a California event, reflecting the people, the dynasties, the patterns, the attitudes of that fevered, rootless state. It was a linguistic event in which all the main characters spoke different languages. It was a newfangled media event in which the characters captured the reporters, in which the Symbionese Liberation Army (SLA) in effect took hostage the press, forcing it to print each of its mad communiqués in full. It was a criminal event in which the outlaws acted from new compulsions, unmellow motives. The money demanded for Patty's release was not to enrich the kidnappers but to help the poor: a Robin Hood ransom—America's first. But all of it, the $2 million spent by the victim's parents on the People in Need free-food-distribution program, and the $4 million they put into escrow to await their daughter's return, was set up beforehand as a charitable foundation. Tax-exempt ransom money! Surely another first in the annals of crime. It was a family event, occurring at a time when the family as an institution was in disunion and despair, when real families withered and shattered, and pseudofamilies thrived. The SLA was itself a pseudo-family, as well as a homegrown American terrorist band that prefigured the Palestine Liberation Organization and Italy's Red Brigades. It was a fiercely female event, woman-created and woman-driven. It was a pathological event, sickening in its violence, frightening in its new formulations of old concepts of responsibility, free will, crime, and punishment. It was a mythological event, crowded with uniquely American figments—Bonnie and Clyde, Perry Mason, and the Lindbergh baby all come to mind; and it was a descendant of much older archetypal myths about evil dragons and captive maidens. It was not just any one of these, it was all of them; it was, to me, a kind of all-American pie. Then, just about the time I got all this figured out, something disconcerting happened. The pebble reappeared. The real Patricia Hearst, the actual flesh-and-blood girl, was captured by the FBI in San Francisco. But even after she was tried for bank robbery and convicted, she remained, or some part of her remained, an enigma to all the world, and quite possibly to herself. I was never allowed to meet her, and though I sat only a few feet away from her in court every day, I was unable to read what I saw there.

By the time Patricia Hearst was brought to trial, two years to the day after she had been kidnapped, her disordered story had acquired a certain shape. A baroque sequence of what had once seemed random events had arranged themselves, I thought, into the classical three acts. The drama even had a name: HERNAP, FBI teletype code for the case.

Act I begins on the evening of February 4, 1974, when a college girl is dragged half-naked and screaming out of the anonymity of her private life and deposited, like a bone, onto the front pages of the world. Offstage, in a burst of machine-gun fire, she becomes "Tania," girl guerrilla. Then she disappears. Nineteen months pass, which become known as the Missing Year.

In Act II she is locked in jail, invisible and incommunicado for four and a half months, seeing no one but her millionaire parents, her big-time psychiatrists, and her celebrity lawyers.

Act III is Patty's trial for having taken part in the armed robbery of the Sunset branch of the Hibernia Bank of San Francisco more than twenty-one months before.

By the end of Act II I knew that much more than the defendant would soon be put on trial: four of our most powerful gods also would be weighed in the balance—the blessed American family, the sanctified free press, the holy men of modern psychiatry, and the almighty jury system, which has been an indispensable element of our concept of justice for nearly a thousand years. By the time the curtain rose on Act III, I had determined to cover and write about that event in full. The *device* of the trial would enable me to deal with much more than the trial; ordered by a trial's classic unities of time and space, the courtroom doings could serve as a kind of prism through which to refract the whole.

WEEK ONE

Monday, January 26, 1976

United States of America v. Patricia Campbell Hearst is scheduled to begin today in the United States District Court for the Northern District of California, the Honorable Oliver J. Carter presiding. The defendant is charged with two violations of the U.S. Criminal Code: armed bank robbery and use of firearm to commit a felony. Each count carries a maximum sentence of twenty-five years and a $100,000 fine. In the corridor outside the nineteenth-floor courtroom, the chief defense counsel, F. Lee Bailey, is dragging deeply on a cigarette and scanning an advance copy of the latest *Newsweek* with Patty's picture on the cover. In all, the magazine will publish ten Patty Hearst cover stories, and each one will break all previous records for newsstand sales. The public may detest Patty, but they cannot get enough of her. She is this year's girl you love to hate.

Bailey wears a new pearl-gray suit, fine pink linen, and a tie of gray silk damask. The hand holding the magazine trembles slightly. The stiff attire of Bailey's pudgy sidekick, codefense counsel J. Albert Johnson, vaguely suggests a military uniform; a Marine Corps insignia adorns his lapel. Reporters jam the corridor. More than three hundred journalists are here to cover this trial. Judging by the weight of international media manpower assembled in San Francisco, we are about to witness the biggest news event since World War II. The sixty-three of us fortunate enough to have a guaranteed seat pass one by one through an airport-style metal detector operated by stone-eyed federal marshals and take our assigned places. From *her* assigned seat at her lawyers' table, the defendant smiles wanly at her parents and sisters, who are sitting in the front row, and she signals them a quick, secret wave. Below the table at which Patty sits, emerging from a tailored sleeve, five pink and perfectly enameled fingers flutter like the frilly fin of a Siamese fighting fish.

Patty is costumed today in a jaunty navy pants suit and white bow-neck blouse, and looks very different from the first time I had seen her. That had been in this very same courtroom, at the arraignment the day after her arrest. Her parents had entered first that day, followed by three of their five daughters. Then a tiny figure had appeared, slouched in front of the high bench, one hand hooked in the back pocket of the corduroy trousers. Nothing to see from the back but a defiant posture, a soiled lavender T-shirt, and chopped and dyed red hair. When she took a seat we could see that Patty wore heavy horn-rims, like her father; and that though stick-skinny, at odd moments she looked matronly, like her mother. Who was she, this skinny girl who looked plump? This kid who looked old? This debutante who looked like a stoned-out doper? Today, five months later, she looks every inch the proper Hillsborough girl. One still doesn't know what she is.

Comes a sharp *rap-rap* of the gavel. "Everybodypleaserisethecourtof thehonorableoliverjcarterisnowinsessionpleasebeseated." Then one loud *rap*. From the bench: "It is now time to swear in the jury."

They fill the entire spectator section of the courtroom. A deep rumbling sounds as they rise, humanity getting to its feet. Two hundred and fifty strong, they are the largest panel of prospective jurors ever called in a federal trial here. The narrow-faced judge has black-rimmed spectacles and thin hair. Running through the familiar boiler-plate instructions to the prospective jurors, he seems firmly in command. He advises them they can expect a trial lasting four or five weeks, five days a week, from ten to noon and one-thirty to four, with a ten-minute recess in midmorning and midafternoon. "Because of the nature of this case and the amount of publicity, this is going to be the most fully covered case that I know of."* The pressure of public interest makes it practically impossible in a big case for a juror to keep an open mind, so to protect them from such pressure, this jury will be sequestered. "You will be in the custody of marshals at all times." No radio, no television, no phone calls out or in except for emergencies, and all calls to be monitored. "Hotel rooms have been reserved for you. . . ." Friends and relatives may bring things on weekends, but no visits will be permitted alone in the rooms. There will be a common room with *monitored* television and radio. "If some of you wish to go to church, the marshals will escort you, and you may read censored newspapers." The defendant is charged with two things only: armed bank robbery and use of a firearm to commit a felony. "That's all. She's not charged with any other offense in this court at this time. Now, I'm going to go through you alphabetically and ask: are you able to perform the service of a juror under the conditions of sequestration which I have described?"

"Marian T. Abbe," the clerk intones. She is a pretty, young airline stewardess and appears to be part Hawaiian or Japanese.

"Are you able?"

"Yes, sir. I can get leave from work."

The clerk goes down his list. Aiken? I feel I am able. Anderson? Yes, Your Honor. Aragon? Yes, sir. As the questioning drones along it becomes obvious that Judge Carter is deaf, and soon I begin to wish I were, too. My mind floats, drifts away.

---

*A note on punctuation. In a trial manuscript of this length, traditional punctuation would have required a *pointillist* profusion of quotation marks of no conceivable value. I have therefore eliminated quotation marks wherever, as is more often than not the case, I have condensed or paraphrased a speaker's actual words. But wherever this system might risk misconception or ambiguity, traditional quotation marks do appear. In the further interest of clarity, I have refrained from the use of paraphrase in presenting the all-important final arguments of the prosecution and defense attorneys. However, these passages have been substantially condensed, although the conventional ellipses do not appear.

F. Lee Bailey is strolling back into the courtroom. The first round of jury eliminations is over. More than half the panel has been excused.

Carter reads the indictment aloud. Potential jurors must fully understand the nature of the charges. "A presumption of innocence clothes and covers the defendant throughout this proceeding. It is up to the government to prove that her plea of not guilty should be overturned beyond a reasonable doubt and to a moral certainty. I will define for you reasonable doubt at the conclusion of this trial." He asks Patty to stand and show herself to the prospective jurors. On her feet, she looks pitifully frail. Attorney Al Johnson steadies her bony elbow. The judge has some general questions for the panel as a whole. "One, are any of you, as far as you know, acquainted with the defendant or members of her immediate family?" He asks the Hearsts to rise. Randolph, Catherine, Ginna (Mrs. Jay Bosworth), Vicki, and Anne stand up and turn toward the prospective jurors, all five executing a right about-face with parade-ground precision, five profiles as expressionless as carvings on an Egyptian tomb. One hundred pairs of eyes gaze back. No, they are not "acquainted" with these people, whose faces, after two years of constant media exposure, must be nearly as familiar as their own. More questions. "Are *all* of you willing to give the defendant the presumption of innocence?" No one moves. These one hundred people seem to want more than anything in the world to be on this jury. Then a few speak out. A man from Oakland says his wife's brother was nearly beaten to death. "I'd hate to say so, but I think subconsciously I'd be tilted against . . ." An angry-looking black woman says her son was involved in a crime. "I did not attend his trial," she adds, scowling at Catherine Hearst. They are excused, and when the clerk again calls the roll, we are down to seventy-four potential jurors and Carter is still asking questions. Does anybody discredit witnesses with beards, long hair, or both? Finally, Carter announces that tomorrow he will draw thirty-six names by lot; the rest will be standbys. Looking at the would-be jurors, I think them all alike, each one desperate to be *in on* it.

It is not just the jurors who long to be in on it. So do the judge and prosecutor, and neither man has been reluctant to make his feelings known. Oliver Carter, sixty-five, has recently been in poor health with serious coronary problems, and the weekend before the trial, he was forced to submit to emergency surgery to repair a broken blood vessel in his neck. Chief United States Attorney for the Northern District of California James R. Browning, Jr., forty-three, is a Nixon appointee who has not tried a case in seven years. Both men see this case as the capstone of a long career in government service. Sad to say, their visions are accurate. Three months after the trial ends, and before passing final sentence, Judge Carter will suffer a fatal heart attack, and the task of determining the extent of Patricia Hearst's punishment will fall to a man who has never even seen her, Judge William H. Orrick. At about the same time, Browning's government career will quietly end when President Carter, despite preelection promises to keep politics out of the Justice Department, replaces him with a Democratic appointee.

The canons of judicial ethics require a judge to "abstain from public comment about a pending or impending proceeding in any court." But a few days after Judge Carter was assigned to the Hearst case, an extraordinary interview appeared in the *New York Times*. Speaking with unusual, if not unprecedented, frankness for a sitting judge on a pending case, Carter said, "Legally, it boils down to a question of whether you believe her, and how much you believe her. The tales she tells are very horrible. It's kind of like—not to be facetious—you don't know whether to cry or to vomit."

Tuesday, January 27

The Federal Building's large Ceremonial Courtroom, reserved for show trials, is veneered in executive teak. Bench, counsel tables, jury boxes, entrance, and exits—all are as formally arranged as an Elizabethan stage. Only the drama is shapeless, at least to those of us who have never seen a trial before. We see only random movements, sequences, comings and goings, no form or agenda apparent. To us the action is less like watching a play than watching an aquarium.

The bailiff raps his gavel twice. We rise as if he were tapping on the glass. Feeding time. Otherwise, we sit passively attentive, watching. The big fish is Bailey, a grouper or sheepshead bass, all massive head and strong shoulders. Perhaps later he will become a shark, swim upside down, and attack. But for now he is benign. Browning is a pipefish, reed-slim, long-legged, brushed, and bespectacled. The twelve jurors and four alternates who will occupy the jury box are a school of fish, two rows moving as one, sixteen pairs of eyes, sixteen heads, turning back and forth from lawyer to witness stand, shifting gaze at the tap of a pointer from the giant movie screen to the artist's easel on which various pieces of evidence are displayed. The press box for top-rank reporters, exactly across the courtroom from the jury box, holds a similar school of fish—sixteen reporters who mirror the jurors' every twist and turn. For forty-six court days the witnesses—individual marine exotica, no two alike—will enter, testify, and exit. Shoals of spectators—marshals, stenographers, the regular courthouse herring—drift in and out, changing shifts at regular intervals.

Patty's team of lawyers sits at the big oak defense table, stage left, led by Bailey and cocaptained by dear, sentimental Fat Albert, packed like a blowfish into his belt-in-the-back bus-driver suit.

The prosecutors at their matching table, stage right, wear suits of no-wrinkle fiber, thin-rimmed spectacles, thin mouths. *Do not underestimate these men,* I scrawl in my notebook. Dead center and motionless, sitting so still he might be barnacled to the back wall of the tank, hangs the black-robed judge.

Al Johnson has arranged a special seat for me this morning, only a few feet from the Hearsts. I watch Catherine, a mother strikingly more beautiful than any of her five daughters, swivel clear around in her seat and fix a gimlet eye on each potential juror as he or she stands up to answer the standard questions. All morning I have avoided meeting Catherine's gaze. The situation between us is awkward. Although I interviewed Patty's father many times during the Missing Year, her mother and I have not met. We did have one brief telephone conversation, but it ended abruptly and mysteriously with Mrs. Hearst's saying, "I don't think I care to talk to you," and hanging up the phone. I have been watching her this morning out of the corner of my eye. She looks brightly Lana Turnerish, yet also strangely Chinese because of the tilt of her eyes and the full skin of her eyelids. But now, suddenly, just before the bailiff raps, Randy smiles, beckons to me, then formally introduces his wife. She smiles at me and we shake hands. "Come home, all is forgiven," she says, mysterious as ever.

"These benches sure are hard on the tail," says Randy.

Wednesday, January 28

The jury lottery is well under way. As each name is called, that person is asked to rise and go sit in or alongside the jury box. The box fills in and overflows with faces: black, white, old, young, male, female.

"Has anybody *not* heard about this case? I don't think it's physically possible to live in this world and not have heard about it, so I'm going to speak to each one of you privately." Carter sounds like an emcee on a quiz show explaining the rules of the game that is about to begin. Swiveling abruptly from the jury box to face the press box, he announces, "We are going into another, adjoining courtroom, to interrogate these jurors individually. The marshals are not going to allow *you* to charge *that* courtroom, or you will be thrown out bodily!" With that he skedaddles through a side door. This judge may appear bumbling and in poor health, but he has just managed, very deftly, to box out the press. In the granite Siberia of the corridor, the outraged reporters mutter darkly about the First Amendment. I dismiss myself from this silly stakeout and go to my rented apartment.

WEEK TWO

Monday, February 2

In all, jury selection at the Hearst trial will grind along for four and one half court days. During these *voir dire* proceedings, fifty-six prospective jurors are interrogated in detail by judge and counsel behind closed doors. Both to gain perspective on Patty and to keep my court-reporting hand limber despite the press lockout in Judge Carter's courtroom, I decide briefly to leave town. Today I cross to the other side of the Golden Gate and drive north to Marin County Courthouse. Inside, for several months, the trial of the so-called San Quentin Six has been taking place behind a bulletproof plastic shield. The Six, all black convicts, are charged with multiple counts of murder and conspiracy growing out of the 1971 prison uprising in which the legendary George Jackson and five others were killed. The legal maneuverings leading up to this trial have been going on ever since. Long after Patty's case has been decided, these six defendants will be sitting here, chained and shackled into their chairs.

Wednesday, February 4

At last, today, at ten o'clock, Patty's trial begins. People have been lined up in the street since seven. Many in the 150-person queue are young lawyers eager to study the defense tactics of the master; others are psychologists, kids, housewives, students, and the usual courthouse eccentrics. Inside, reporters outnumber spectators by eight to one. We sit in absolute silence in our assigned and numbered press seats for a full quarter hour until suddenly Catherine Hearst jumps to her tiny feet. Only then do I hear the two sharp raps of the gavel and see Judge Carter enter upstage right, his narrow head poking out of his robes like a turkey caught in a black sack. Two years to the day from the day she was kidnapped, Patty Hearst's trial is finally under way.

First comes the yo-yoing of the peremptory jury challenges. In silence, as if a tennis match were in progress, the clerk carries a list of jurors' names back and forth between the two teams of lawyers. Huddled over the list of prospects, Patty, Bailey, and Johnson look like three horseplayers handicapping the big race. The twelve jurors and four alternates who have survived the legal choose-up are the least memorable citizens on the original panel. Blacks and oddballs have disappeared. One female juror is part Oriental. One man has a beard. The others are entirely unremarkable, average even in height and weight, almost aggressively neutral. Seven are women; five are men. Just now they look a bit stunned as the clerk swears them in and the judge instructs them.

"Remember, you are not to discuss . . ." the judge says, wagging a schoolmasterish finger before sending the jurors out of the courtroom so the lawyers may argue some last-minute motion. Nervous, Patty begins to pour water into Styrofoam cups and pass them around the table to her lawyers, as if she were a hostess at a sorority tea. Carter administers to the press a stern and patronizing rebuke. In future, reporters are not to rush up to the counsel when recess is declared. There will be no press conferences in his courtroom, and no whispering. I feel humiliated, and grateful the jury is not present. Everybody in the courtroom feels on trial—lawyers, spectators, press, judge, and jury.

Bailey argues that the second count of the indictment—use of firearm to commit a felony—is "duplicitous," which turns out to mean not "deceptive" but "doubled." He wishes to exclude certain other matters and to prohibit the prosecutor from bringing up events in his opening statement before the evidence itself can be presented and dealt with by the defense.

"I understand what you are saying, Mr. Bailey. As we say upcountry, you can't unring a bell."

"You can't get a skunk out of a courtroom once you bring it in," Bailey replies.

In the defense view there are four skunks. Skunk One is Patty's boast on the sixth SLA tape that she robbed the bank. Bailey claims that Patty was forced to make the tape and that one of the kidnappers, Angela Atwood, wrote out the actual words.

Skunk Two would be testimony that more than a month after the robbery, Patty sprayed Mel's Sporting Goods store in Los Angeles with machine-gun fire in order to rescue her SLA companions Bill Harris and his wife, Emily. Such testimony would indicate that Patty was familiar with the use of automatic weapons, as well as loyal to the SLA.

Skunk Three would be testimony from Tom Matthews, the Los Angeles youth whom Patty and the Harrises have been charged with kidnapping. During the night Matthews spent with Patty and the Harrises in their van driving aimlessly around Los Angeles, Patty told him she had taken part willingly in the Hibernia Bank robbery. Bailey contends she was forced to say this by the Harrises under threat of being "blown away." Further, the very presence in this trial of Tom Matthews would bring up evidence of other crimes (his own kidnapping) not related to the bank robbery.

Skunk Four is the notorious "Tania Interview," a purported autobiography written many months after the bank robbery and discovered by the FBI in a locked closet in the Harrises' apartment. In it Patty again says, partly in her own handwriting, that she was a willing participant. Once more, Bailey contends that Patty was coerced, and he has a battery of psychiatrists standing by to prove it.

The government, for its part, sees all of the proposed psychiatric testimony as one great big skunk and asks the judge to exclude mention of it from Bailey's opening statement on the grounds that Patty's defense is not *insanity*. It is *duress*: she did what she did because there was a gun at her head. "A psychological or psychiatric *explanation* ought not to be a psychiatric *justification*," says David P. Bancroft, the prosecution's expert on psychiatric testimony, and he speaks of the "circus atmosphere" already created by the defense, especially in the media.

I lunch by myself in the courthouse cafeteria. How slow I am to get the hang of all this! I turn out to be a trial illiterate, a courtroom primitive without the slightest concept of ordinary criminal procedures, let alone the particularities and subtleties of this special case. What to do? I do not take shorthand, nor can I afford to buy the daily trial transcript that the court reporters sell at a dollar a page to the lawyers and to the big news outfits like the *New York Times*. Besides, the official transcript provides both more and less information than I require. But I do have a guaranteed press seat, center section, third row, on the aisle. So long as I occupy this seat every day, nobody can throw me out. I will manufacture my own transcript, homemade, to suit my own needs.

I walk around the corner to a stationer and buy a couple of large pads with blue covers. Eventually my homemade transcript will fill seven and a half of these reassuringly legal-looking, fifty-page pads. To hell with court stenographers. My home-baked, one-person transcript will be, for my purposes, an improvement on the original. It could even be more truthful, as a painting is more truthful than a photograph. I will force myself actually to *write*. I will be impressionistic and put down what interests *me*. I prefer this plan on journalistic grounds (no reporter tells the whole truth; he tells the parts he thinks important) as well as on artistic ones.

After lunch, when court resumes, I notice the defense table is sprinkled over with cough drops. Bailey's team is obsessed by bad breath; they consume mountains of lozenges, Clorets, deodorizers. Johnson carries a tiny vial of spray breath freshener. As he prowls about the courtroom he employs it discreetly, but with relish, like a man with a solid-gold toothpick.

The judge denies each lawyer's motion to limit the other's opening statement. Evidence will be admitted at the proper time, he says, provided the proper foundation is laid. Warning both sides they "proceed at their peril," he sends for the jury and smiles thinly, visibly eager to begin. "An opening statement is a narrative preview . . . a bird's-eye view of what the case is all about," he tells the jury.

The pattern of a criminal trial seems to be very like the formula for organizing a long magazine article. As my first editor explained it years ago, "First you provide a menu. You tell 'em what you're gonna tell 'em. Then you tell 'em. Then you tell 'em what you told 'em." This corresponds to the legal sequence we shall follow: opening statements, prosecution's case, defense case, prosecution's rebuttal case, defense surrebuttal, prosecution's closing argument, closing defense argument, prosecution's final final. The prosecution gets the last word because it has the burden of proof. All the defense must do to win its case is raise a reasonable doubt of the defendant's guilt in the jurors' minds.

U.S. Attorney James Browning is well suited to offer a bird's-eye view. Balanced on storklike legs, he inclines his head toward the jury, clears his throat, unrolls his menu. "Ladies and gentlemen, my purpose in speaking to you at this time is to acquaint you with the evidence. The evidence will show that on April 15, 1974, at 9:40 A.M., the Hibernia Bank was held up by five persons, one male and four females, one of them the defendant, who had been kidnapped ten weeks prior by one or more of these same people . . . the group called itself the Symbionese Liberation Army. . . . The government will call various witnesses to this bank robbery—customers, bank employees, and passersby." Clumsily, he hoists some large pasteboard maps onto an easel and picks up a pointer. He indicates the location of the bank, the position of its two surveillance cameras, check desks, and tellers' counters, the positions of various bank personnel and customers, the two getaway cars parked outside.

The bank opened at 9:00 A.M. At 9:40 customer James Norton came in, leaving his mother in the car outside. He was followed through the door by customer Zigurd Berzins and then, almost immediately, by five bank robbers, who have been identified by the FBI as Nancy Ling Perry, who entered first, followed in order by Patricia Hearst, Camilla Hall, Patricia Soltysik, and Donald DeFreeze. Four carried sawed-off carbines; Soltysik had a handgun. Patty's gun was the only one with a straight clip. The other automatic rifles had curved "banana" clips, which hold more bullets. For the benefit of those jurors who know nothing about guns, Browning explains that the clip is the thing that contains the bullets, which are forced out of it and into the firing chamber by a spring mechanism.

Browning indicates the bank guard's position with his pointer and says, "You will hear the bank guard, Mr. Shea, testify that he saw the defendant approach him with her weapon and say, 'The first person who moves gets his M-F head blown off!' You will hear a second witness testify that he heard the defendant say something like 'Get on the F floor. We are not fooling around!' You will hear a third witness testify he saw DeFreeze near the safe-deposit counter and saw Patricia Hearst pointing her weapon directly at a Mr. Ryan. The whole robbery lasted two, maybe two and a half minutes total, and most of it was recorded by the surveillance cameras. Perry was between the entryway and the manager's desk. Soltysik you will see clearly in the film leap over the teller's counter and go toward the vault. DeFreeze stands at the corner of the wall and the left, or west, end of the counter. Camilla Hall is to the east. Patty Hearst is between them in the middle area of the counter.

"Each camera took four hundred frames of film. A regular movie camera goes at a rate of twenty-four frames per second. If you reprint each bank frame six times, therefore, you can make a kind of jerky movie which is true in time to actual events. We will show you such a movie and tell you how it was taken. We will show it both in full speed and in slow motion. You will see DeFreeze, Perry, and Patty Hearst turn their weapons toward two new customers coming into the bank. Nancy Ling Perry fires at and wounds the two customers. You will see the ejected shell casings fall from Perry's weapon. You will see the defendant, Patty Hearst, looking at her watch. You will see her checking her weapon. You will see that her fingers are in the area of the trigger. You will see her hand move freely on the weapon. Various employees and customers in the bank will tell you they heard things like 'SLA! SLA!' 'This is a robbery!' 'This is Tania!' or 'This is Patty Hearst!' One person heard 'I am Patty Hearst!' "

During this recital I glance at Patty. She appears to be reading a book in her lap.

"Witnesses outside the bank will testify that the robbers exited in the following order: Hall, Soltysik (carrying the money), Perry, Hearst, DeFreeze. One shot was fired outside the bank. One witness thinks Patty fired the shot; another witness thinks it was DeFreeze."

Now comes the first mention to the jury of the disputed SLA tapes. Browning says that on April 24, nine days after the robbery, a cassette was found taped to the steps of Woodrow Wilson High School in San Francisco. The jury will hear Patricia Hearst's voice on this tape. They will hear her say, "Greetings to the People. This is Tania. On April 15 my comrades and I expropriated $10,660.02 from the Sunset branch of the Hibernia Bank. . . . My gun was loaded and at no time did any of my comrades intentionally point their guns at me."

Browning shifts his story to events that occurred one month later, in Los Angeles, during a shoplifting incident at Mel's Sporting Goods store. At about 4:15 on the afternoon of May 16 a security clerk heard "the sound of cellophane being stuffed into a coat" and looked up to see Bill Harris stealing a pair of socks. He managed to get one handcuff on Harris as they scuffled. Emily Harris tried unsuccessfully to intervene. The clerk will identify a 1970 Volkswagen van parked across the street. He will describe how he saw Patricia Hearst lean out of the van's front window, on the driver's side, and fire a volley of shots at him.

Patty, eyes downcast, sits absolutely motionless as Browning describes how she sprayed the area with lead, how the Harrises ran to the van and they all drove off, how the clerk gave chase in his car, and how, as the van was stopped in traffic, he saw Patty leap out and commandeer another car, the Pontiac in which the three of them then disappeared.

Browning says that markings on the shell casings recovered from Mel's match one of the weapons later found in the closet of the San Francisco apartment where Patty was arrested.

At 7:00 P.M. on May 16 the fugitives passed a Ford van with a "For Sale" sign in its window and persuaded its owner, eighteen-year-old

Thomas Matthews, to get into the van with them. He was held captive for twelve hours. They tried at several places to buy a hacksaw and, when they found one, removed the handcuff from Harris' wrist.

"You will hear Matthews testify that Patricia Hearst told him that she had been a voluntary participant in the Hibernia Bank robbery and that it had been carefully planned and rehearsed . . . that each person in the robbery was instructed to move his weapon only a few degrees, so as not to shoot one another accidentally. She also told him how she had fired her weapon at Mel's that afternoon. She said she felt lucky to have glanced up from her newspaper when she did and have seen the Harrises in jeopardy."

The next morning at 7:00 Matthews was abandoned along with his van. He went home and at first didn't mention to the authorities that he had seen Patty Hearst. The Harrises had warned him not to, and besides, he had received good treatment from his abductors. But the following day, after watching the SLA's televised death by fire in a burning house, and after hearing the newscasters say that the Hearsts still did not know whether or not their daughter had been burned alive, Matthews went to the FBI.

Seventeen months later, Browning continues, on September 18, 1975, the defendant and the Harrises were arrested separately in San Francisco. The Harrises occupied an apartment at 288 Precita Avenue. The defendant was living at 625 Morse Street, more than a mile away. A number of documents were found at the Harris apartment, both typewritten and handwritten, including a series of questions and answers, some in the defendant's handwriting. *Why did you rob the bank?* "Because we wanted to illustrate that Tania Hearst was alive." *Why did you choose this bank?* "Because of the bank cameras." A typewritten diary, also found at Precita Avenue, with interlineations in Patty's handwriting, states that the perpetrators of the bank robbery intended it to be "well-planned and flamboyant."

So much for the government's opening argument. It is 2:55 P.M. as we file out. In the corridor I note Catherine's black dress, black pumps, black stockings, black crocodile handbag. It appears to be the same outfit Patty had begged her on the second SLA tape not to wear because it made her feel her mother considered her already dead.

It is now time to hear the defense's opening statement. Tension hangs across the courtroom like a trapeze net. Brick-faced, with Brillo sideburns, dressed in a formal dark-blue suit, Mr. F. Lee Bailey approaches the jury and begins to speak quietly and without notes.

"Ladies and gentlemen, ninety percent of what Jim Browning has told you is not in dispute."

In a low, intimate tone of voice and the simplest possible language, the lawyer tells a story. In 1973 a man was assassinated in Oakland. He was Dr. Marcus Foster, superintendent of schools, "and the following day, the world heard for the first time of an organization of terrorists that called themselves the Symbionese Liberation Army. . . . On January 10, 1974, Joseph Remiro and Russell Little were arrested after a shoot-out with the police [near] their apartment in Concord, whereafter the building was burned. On the following day, an arson warrant was issued for Nancy Ling Perry, who was identified as an SLA member, and who was the person that in August of 1973 rented that very same apartment.

"Patricia Hearst was then nineteen years of age. She had led, as it pertains to this case, a most ordinary life. She was a completely apolitical creature: She had no interest in radical politics, causes, or anything of the like, did not attend meetings, or get involved in projects of this sort. She was living in Berkeley with Steven Weed and somewhat concerned about the security of her apartment, to which end a burglar-alarm system had been installed.

"On the evening of February 4, two years ago tonight, a form showed up at the door. And although Miss Hearst's first inclination was to advise Mr. Weed not to take the chain off, before she could make a decision or articulate her concern, the door was opened, and a young lady was talking about an auto accident and a need to get to a phone. Very shortly thereafter, there burst in by force Donald DeFreeze and William Harris, who threw Miss Hearst to the floor and held her down, at the same time disabling Mr. Weed, who was subsequently beaten rather badly. . . .

"This was the SLA terrorist group. As they yanked Patty Hearst forcibly from her home she began to resist, and they clouted her hard in the cheek with the butt of a rifle, causing her a serious injury." Neighbors came out, and anyone who showed curiosity was fired upon. The prisoner was placed in the trunk of an automobile "and taken to an apartment, she knew not where. She was blindfolded at all times and thrown into a closet in which there was no light. . . ."

Miss Hearst spent the next six to nine weeks in a closet. We don't know precisely how long. The SLA had several purposes in kidnapping her: One, it gave them bargaining power to negotiate for the release of Little and Remiro. Two, these crazy people actually thought that if they could put food on the street for poor people and thus earn the support of the have-nots, they could overthrow the United States of America. Three, they wanted to show the Establishment that they could convert one of its own members to their terrorist beliefs.

Until World War II, torture was the traditional way one got prisoners to change their minds. Now there is a new technique, variously called brainwashing, coercive persuasion, mind control. "Donald DeFreeze, you will learn, who gave himself the grandiose name General Field Marshal Cinque, had read some books in prison about mind control." In Miss Hearst he thought he had a vulnerable prospect, a nineteen-year-old girl who could rather easily be persuaded that she had been abandoned by society, abandoned by her parents and by the representatives of law enforcement. He could convince her these people were now her enemy and would kill her if she tried to escape. Furthermore, if she were compelled to become an outlaw, he need be even less concerned with the possibility of her attempting to flee. And so, "for perhaps the first time in the history of bank robbery, a robber was told to identify herself during the commission of the act," and she was also told that if she messed up in any way, she would be blown to bits.

The first warrant issued for Patty's arrest named her only as a material witness. But the SLA wanted her *charged* as a bank robber, so they told her to confess publicly to her voluntary participation in the robbery, and she did. But the jury will be shown that Angela Atwood wrote the words Miss Hearst spoke on the tape.

In fact, says Bailey, every single one of Patty's taped messages was read from a draft written by others. But after William Saxbe, the Attorney General, told the press, "She is nothing but a common criminal," the SLA shrewdly told Patty, "You have been *defined as a criminal*" by the government of the United States. Now you can never convince an American jury that you did *not* want to get into that bank." A month later, on May 17, when Patty watched on live TV as the police burned and shot to death all the other members of the SLA, it confirmed to her in the most vivid possible way that everything the SLA had told her was true.

Bailey's story so far has been simply and powerfully told. Unquestionably the jury is impressed. When he arrives at the moment of his client's arrest, in the apartment on Morse Street, his rich voice deepens, slows. Miss Hearst had been so conditioned to the idea that *FBI* was synonymous with *"Kill! Kill Patty Hearst!"* that upon hearing the shout at her doorstep *FBI!* "the degree of her terror mounted to the point which is probably the highest that a human being can stand without passing out, and"—here his voice drops dramatically—"she became incontinent."

26

For twenty months, Bailey continues, Miss Hearst had been kept literally a prisoner of war. She had every opportunity to escape "but also every opportunity to believe she had nowhere to go." We will hear testimony from three distinguished medical specialists in the field of brainwashing, experts either originally appointed by the court or persons who have since agreed or even asked to testify for her defense. All these experts agree that Miss Hearst's is a classic case, a textbook example of the type of coercive persuasion undergone by American prisoners of war in Korea and in Vietnam. Against these intolerable pressures, Patty held out longer than one could expect of a combat-trained male, but inevitably her will was broken. It broke while she was still held captive in the closet. "Her terror was real. But for the kidnapping of Patricia Hearst, there would have *been* no bank robbery," Bailey concludes, "and she would not be here today."

Spectators and journalists alike have been deeply moved by this spare, eloquent, even elegant summary of the case. Two of Patty's sisters and several reporters leave the courtroom in tears.

When a court day ends, I am usually too tired to do more than watch the television re-cap of the trial, eat, and fall onto the hard, rented bed. But this evening, when Al Johnson telephones, I invite him to stop by for a drink. Over the months Patty has been in jail, her defense lawyers and I have developed a wary friendship. Occasionally we dine together, eating and drinking splendidly on the Hearst tab.

The man F. Lee Bailey would most like to have been, had he not had the extreme good fortune to be F. Lee Bailey, is Hildy Johnson, the savvy, wisecracking reporter in *The Front Page*. The famous trial lawyer vastly enjoys the hard-drinking, swaggering company of newspapermen. He understands their fears, and he gives them what they need: colorful quotes, gaudy facts, quantity and quality bullshit, and, often, truth. Bailey takes risks with reporters. He dares to be indiscreet; he takes chances on their honor. If he can ever find time and bread enough to quit practicing law for a while, Bailey knows just what he would do: become a full-time writer. He has written a bestseller, *The Defense Never Rests*, about his big cases, but he longs to attempt a novel.

Bailey's sidekick, Al Johnson, is damp-eyed, overworked, smart, shy, complicated, and, like his childhood friend, Boston Irish. Al is as tough as Lee, but he lacks the flamboyance. Whereas Bailey's personality can be grating, Johnson's tends to have a soothing effect on almost everybody. By the time the trial got under way Johnson had logged several hundred hours visiting Patty in jail, sitting knee to knee with her in a small, airless room—"the iron phone booth"—where attorneys and clients meet privately and face to face, without the bulletproof glass, television monitors, and bugged telephones that separate prisoners from their other visitors.

Johnson was the pivotal figure in HERNAP's Act II. During this crucial four-and-a-half-month period, the defense managed an arpeggio of medico-legal-propaganda delays, arguing on each occasion that the client simply was not yet ready to stand trial because she was still, in Johnson's oft-repeated refrain, "incapable of cooperating in her own defense." Johnson's assignment was to restore that capacity, which is to say, to preside over the demise of Tania and make sure the defiant girl guerrilla of the Missing Year was dead and buried before the trial began. Whoever Patty Hearst may be right now, Al Johnson knows better than anyone else in the world.

The last time I had seen either of Patty's lawyers outside of court was last Friday, at a final pretrial lunch of soft-shell crabs and hard-sell Bailey in the dining room of the Mark Hopkins Hotel. Johnson, as usual, was with Patty down at the jail, thirty miles away. Bailey had told me then that the government's two psychiatrists were feuding, and that the defendant was in such poor emotional shape that even the prosecutors were losing their stomach for the coming trial.

"Jim Browning told me last week, 'Plead guilty to *anything*, and I'll dismiss the case,'" Bailey had said. "I told him, 'Dismiss *all* the charges, then I'll talk to you.' Jim said, 'You know I can't do that. The American people won't put up with it.' And I said, 'You're damned right they won't.'" Bailey also emphasized that Patty's life was in considerable danger. Terrorists, counterterrorists, and assorted crackpots all wished her ill. "You wouldn't *believe* the threats that are coming into the jail," he said.

As with his previous big cases, Bailey was planning to write about his new client. The novel would have to wait a little longer. Income from other, extralegal activities had become especially important in recent years. He also presided over a TV talk show and published a magazine. He gave frequent public lectures, at good fees, as well as legal seminars for trial lawyers. He was franchising the helicopters manufactured by the Engstrom Helicopter Company, which he owned. Its manager was a one-time client, former Marine captain Ernest Medina, of My Lai-massacre fame. Himself a former Marine fighter pilot, Bailey today flies himself around his busy world in one or another of his own aircraft.

His rise to the top had been, as the press frequently pointed out, "meteoric." Barely three months after being admitted to the bar, he won his first case when the jury acquitted an auto mechanic accused of chopping up his wife. A year later, Bailey, then thirty-two, found glory in the Sam Sheppard case: He argued before the Supreme Court that Dr. Sheppard had not had a fair trial because of the judge's failure to insulate the jurors from the vicious anti-Sheppard campaign in the *Cleveland Plain Dealer*. Bailey won a landmark eight-to-one decision and later an easy acquittal for Sheppard. He went on to defend a spectacular series of cases, and won most of them. Dr. Carl Coppolino, an anesthesiologist, was acquitted of murdering his mistress's husband (though later convicted of killing his wife). Albert DeSalvo, the alleged Boston Strangler, was convicted of robbery and other offenses but not of the string of sex murders of which he was accused. Bailey got four alleged plotters off scot-free in the Massachusetts $1.5 million Great Plymouth Mail Robbery. In Medina's court-martial the captain was acquitted so briskly that the panel of officers voted to smoke an extra cigarette before announcing their verdict, to make it look better.

But despite this series of Alpine peaks, Bailey had been in a valley for the past couple of years. He had become too enthusiastic about one of his clients, Glenn Turner, the cosmetics franchiser and "Dare to be great!" man, and when the government indicted Turner for mail fraud, Bailey was indicted, too. After an eight-month trial, which ended in a hung jury, the government dropped the charges against Bailey, but during this harrowing period the lawyer had had to borrow $400,000 just to stay afloat. His practice plummeted, and he had to disband a legal stable of twelve attorneys. Fortunately, his boyhood chum J. Albert Johnson was around to keep Bailey's Boston office open.

A month after the charges against Bailey were dropped, an emergency call from Randolph Hearst reached Bailey at the state penitentiary in Jackson, Mississippi, where he was visiting a woman on death row. Hearst thought his daughter, who had been represented since her capture, a week earlier, by young Terence Hallinan, under the guidance of his eighty-one-year old father, Vincent, needed new or additional counsel right away. Bailey said his plane was parked nearby, and he told Hearst he would fly to San Francisco at once. He paused just long enough to call his buddy Johnson, who was on a first-degree murder case in Niagara Falls. Then, each at the controls of his own plane, both lawyers headed west. By week's end Bailey had met Patty at the jail, won her approval, and concluded his arrangements with her original counsel and with her parents, who would be paying the bills. His agreement with the Hearsts called for him to defend Patty in at least two trials: the charge of bank robbery in federal court in San Francisco, and the California case in Los Angeles, where Patty was a codefendant with the Harrises for the shoot-up at Mel's Sporting Goods and related offenses. For the Hibernia Bank case he would charge the Hearsts only $125,000 plus expenses, which of necessity would be vast.

"Did *Patty* accept you and Al as her lawyers right off?" I had asked over lunch at the Mark Hopkins.

"She said she did. What you need most is the confidence and trust of the client. A lawyer has two obligations: One, I've got to be good, but two, she's got to believe I'm good."

"In this case," Bailey continued, "the key issue will be how the jury is instructed. Because Patty is a kidnap victim, the ordinary rules don't apply. Ordinarily the robbers' presence in the bank proves their intent to rob the bank. But if the accused is a kidnap victim, and there is un-broken custody by the kidnappers, there can be no inference she was there intentionally. Just as likely she was there unintentionally."

One of Bailey's expert witnesses would be a quadruple-threat man, Dr. Martin Orne, a psychologist and a psychiatrist who is also a hypnotist and polygraph expert. Bailey himself knows a great deal about hypnosis and has taught courses in its legal aspects. Patty had already weathered a three-day test on Bailey's favorite item of detective hardware, the polygraph, and "she did real well."

The afternoon was late. At the door of the suite, Bailey smiled. "By the way, I think I can get Catherine to see you now." This was startling news.

"How is she holding up?" I asked.

"Mrs. Hearst is a terrible pessimist. Deep down she thinks that despite the apparent genius of counsel, her daughter will go to jail."

Al Johnson is pale and splotchy when he arrives for a drink after court, bearing a present from Lee. It is a copy of the master cassette, so that I can listen to the entire sequence of the seven SLA messages. But he has bad news. "Catherine has changed her mind again. Now she won't talk to you. She says you wrote that Patty smoked pot at school."

"Al, you know I didn't write that! She just doesn't trust me."

I mention a rumor that before the kidnapping Patty and Steve Weed had not been getting along. "That's putting it mildly. She hated him! For six months she'd been thinking about suicide, she wanted so desperately to get out of that marriage."

"Why not just call it off?"

"She was weak. Her mother was out buying china. The wedding juggernaut was rolling, and she didn't know how to stop it."

Al is upset because an extract of Weed's book, *My Life with Patty Hearst,* had just appeared in a magazine, despite all of Bailey and Johnson's warnings. "It may influence the jury. Besides, it's a lie. He says she seduced *him,* that she initiated the pot and sex experiments."

Before he leaves, Al offers to get me an official front-row seat at the trial, on the Hearsts' own bench, and urges me please to "use our office anytime, the secretaries, the Xerox, whatever you need. Tomorrow I'll bring you the transcript of today's hearings." Then, with a whiff of Vitalis and a shy smile, he is gone.

It is difficult not to believe Al has been sent over to leak some of this. But which was the important part? How much was leak, how much truth? Is he sure himself? For me, the stunner is his admission that Patty had been desperate enough to get out of her coming marriage to consider suicide, for if this is true, disturbing questions arise. Was she desperate enough to get herself kidnapped? Even if she did not actually engineer her own abduction, would not the SLA's abrupt intervention in her life seem like a blessing in disguise? If Patty was always, by nature, the weak person with no will of her own whom Al has just described, what becomes of the notion that Cinque regressed and brutalized her until he *destroyed* her strong will? What becomes of the famous brainwashing premise, on which her entire defense rests?

Thursday, February 5

In court Patty looks terrible. She is dressed in a dowdy brownish wrapper over an orange turtleneck, which emphasizes her pallor, and she looks like an inmate in a 1930s' prison movie. The government's first witness is the bank manager who pushed the burglar alarm which automatically activated the cameras.

The second witness, Vernon L. Kipping, is an FBI photography expert. He explains how the bank's automatic cameras work, slipping easily into worn, photography-lecture cadences.

I hate technical explanations of how things work, and my attention wanders toward the figure on the bench, the quizzical face and birdlike head above the robes. Carter parts his thin hair in the old style, straight down the middle, like his decisions. He enjoys an even contest in his courtroom. Lawyers have told me that if one side appears to him stronger than the other, Carter will tend in his rulings to favor the weaker side. Well-matched opponents make a better ball game, but I'm not sure I like to find the sports mentality on the high bench. He appears now both benevolent and irritable, first a pixie, then a fussbudget. He is meticulous and frail. He scratches his head. He peers over his glasses. He closes his eyes to rest them; sometimes he falls asleep.

Comes now our first glimpse of Bailey's famed skills at cross-examination. "Mr. Kipping, the second version of the film you showed us hones in on the center section. *Why did you crop out the rest?*"

"To show the expression and demeanor of the subject."

"You were aware, as you made the edited version, that there were serious questions about whether the defendant was covered at all times by people carrying weapons?"

The witness appears not to understand, and Bailey repeats, as if speaking to a slightly retarded person, "At the time you made the film, you were aware there was a serious question whether she was covered at all times by the others' weapons?"

KIPPING (*deliberately misunderstanding*): I had no knowledge she was in fact covered.

BAILEY (*hard*): Are you learning for the first time today, Mr. Kipping, that there is a question about whether she was covered in the bank?

KIPPING: I saw no evidence that she was under the gun.

BAILEY (*airy*): Was it your purpose, when you made the edited version, to blank out evidence that she *was* under the gun?

"Absolutely not!" says the witness. But the lawyer has successfully raised doubt in the jury's mind about whether and, if so, to what purpose the government has meddled with this crucial film.

After lunch, spectators find that an enormous movie screen, the size of an outdoor billboard, has been set up in the left rear corner of the courtroom, between the press box and the bench. The jury will now see the bank film for the first time, as narrated by Tom Padden, the senior FBI agent on the case.

The lights dim, and enormous, ten-foot-high figures rush onto the screen—huge, lurching shadows carrying automatic weapons. First Nancy Ling Perry dashes in, then DeFreeze in his floppy Abzug hat, then Camilla Hall, and now Soltysik vaults over the counter in a single bound and soon flies wildly back toward the camera with a sack of money in her fist. The gigantic phantoms skitter across the bank floor. Twice the specter of Patty in black coat and wig looks back over her shoulder at DeFreeze. Her movement is ambiguous. The jury must decide whether she is seeking instruction from a cohort or cowering under the gun.

The courtroom twilight lasts for a long ninety seconds. During this time the real Patty watches the screen Patty intently. Her mouth is open, and she is swallowing hard, licking her lips, holding the table edge with whitening knuckles. When the lights go up, her eyes are wet.

The government next calls the clerk, who testifies that on the morning in question she "heard metallic noises." Browning reaches behind the court clerk's desk and fishes up a semiautomatic carbine with a big manila FBI identification tag dangling from the webbing strap. In two quick strides, he is across the courtroom and beside the jury, pulling back the bolt and ramming it home. *Tock!* "Was it similar to this sound?"

"It could have been."

The next witness, the bank guard, is an elderly man with a shaky voice, thick glasses. He "saw four men . . . four persons . . . in a doorway . . . four abreast. . . . They stepped forward and divided, two and two. . . ." His testimony is impossible to follow.

Carter says, "I want to know which was male and which was female."

"It appeared to be a female wearing pants."

"What did she say?" The judge is becoming crotchety.

"She said, 'First person puts up his head, I'll blow his motherfucking head off!' " So the dread words have been uttered. In the old man's quavery, dry hole of a mouth, they really do sound obscene.

"Is the person who spoke those words now here in court?" Browning asks.

"She's over there. . . . You want her name?"

Bailey rises to cross-examine, cream dripping from his whiskers. He asks Shea to repeat his description of the female bandit. What comes out is hodgepodge.

"Miss Hearst, would you rise, please?" She stands up, pink-polished fingertips braced against the table top to steady herself, perhaps ninety-five pounds, the size-six dress hanging on her frame like a shroud.

"Now, Mr. Shea. What would you say is the height and weight of this lady?"

"'Bout five foot six, hundred and twenty pounds."

"Mm-hmm. Thank you. Now, would you go to the chart and point out to the jury the *position* of the female bandit you were describing." The decrepit Mr. Shea marches out of the witness box and points to an orange sticker marked F. "Have you been informed, Mr. Shea, that position F was occupied by Nancy Ling Perry and not by the defendant?"

It is time for recess. Outside, in the corridor, the defense is feeling good. Round One is theirs. Randolph Hearst lights a cigarette and giggles. "I wouldn't put any money in that bank, if I were you."

The next important witness is James Norton, a hospital therapist, who was making a deposit when he saw the bank guard suddenly shoved against the wall by the black man in the floppy hat, and next found himself looking straight down the barrel of a gun held by a woman who ordered him to lie on the floor or she would blow his fucking head off. He identifies Patty as the woman.

Inside this courtroom the press is sequestered as much as the jury. During lunch we discover that the day's big Patty Hearst story is not even in San Francisco. The *Chicago Tribune* has just published huge chunks of the notorious "Tania Interview," and in response, the Harrises have released a statement accusing Patty of selling them out in order to free herself. The two stories underscore the double nature of the trial. Patty is being judged simultaneously in this courtroom, where she remains cloaked in her "presumption of innocence," and in the media, where her cloak was torn to shreds long ago.

Patty was never *not* on trial in the media; she was suspected from the beginning of plotting her own abduction. Despite denials by everybody, including the U.S. government, public skepticism persists. That Patricia Hearst was a genuine kidnapping victim is as difficult for many Americans to believe as the notion that President Kennedy was the victim of Lee Harvey Oswald acting alone. It may be that no matter whom Patty and her parents had chosen to represent her, her lawyers would have had no choice but to run two defenses concurrently: one before the judge, for the jury and the record; the other an "instant replay" before the television cameras, for the press and the public. Lest it be imagined that the U.S. government is any less anxious than the defense to try its case in the media, it is well to remember that the "Tania Interview" was leaked the same week Patty was captured, but it was so damning, the papers refrained from printing it. The instant the jury was locked up, however, the papers rushed into print with Patricia Hearst's "innermost thoughts" during her time with the terrorists:

> After a couple of weeks, I started to feel sympathy with the SLA. I was beginning to see what they wanted to accomplish was necessary, although at the time it was hard for me to relate to the tactic of urban guerrilla warfare.

My comrades were willing to help me learn the political and military skills that I was lacking as long as I was willing to struggle to become a guerrilla soldier. . . . What some people refer to as a sudden conversion was actually a process of development, much the same as a photograph is developed. . . . When the members of the unit decided I could stay with the cell, the decision was unanimous. . . . Like someone said . . . I'd been brainwashed for twenty years, and it only took the SLA six weeks to straighten me out.

Tania's comments about her parents are extraordinarily bitter:

I told Cin right away that I didn't think my parents would cooperate—that they had no love for me, and I had none for them. I'm glad it turned out the way it did because, if I'd been closer to my family, I would have been a different kind of person. . . . My decision to join the SLA would have been a lot harder. . . . I would have been much more prone toward developing into a Fascist rather than a freedom fighter.

Patty's description of herself as a "freedom fighter" is no more persuasive, at least on the face of this document, than is Donald DeFreeze's grandiose deisgnation of himself as a "Field Marshal." SLA rhetoric is loonily overblown. Yet amid the lush verbiage, one paragraph of the "Tania Interview" rings with the faint, clear bell of truth: "What you have to understand is that if I'd been a different person, a typical 'rich bitch,' 1 would have been treated a lot differently. Nobody would have wanted to talk to me after about a week." Right there, perhaps, might be the kernel of it all.

Once more it is time for the ritual twice-daily plunge for the elevators and the scramble down to the television press room on the seventh floor. Here each day, and sometimes twice a day, the lawyers reenact the trial upstairs, staging a condensed instant replay for the benefit of the cameras. Bailey relishes these sessions; they give him a second chance to score points and wisecrack with the press.

"Mr. Bailey, are you satisfied you demolished Mr. Shea?"

"He did not go writhing to the floor in Perry Mason fashion . . . but I'm satisfied the jury has some questions about his accuracy."

Friday, February 6

When Bailey rises to cross-examine James Norton, canary feathers are

35

hanging out of his mouth. His purpose is to get Norton to waver on his earlier identification of Patty as the female bandit who ordered him onto the floor. The film is to be run again, this time in slow motion. Twenty-seven seconds into the film, Norton identifies the lady, "but not *where* I first saw her." Bailey's trap is about to spring. "Mr. Norton, I would like you to examine this document." In his original FBI interview, the day after the robbery, Norton had identified a different lady at a different location. Bailey stands patiently, one hand resting lightly on the edge of the witness box, his eyes turned heavenward. It is a long, long wait. Then: "There is *no mention in that document* of Patty Hearst threatening you or using obscenities. . . . Mr. Norton, do you recognize John McNally?" Bailey's ace investigator, the burly ex-NYC cop, beams like a seraph over at the defense table. "Did you not tell Mr. McNally that you believed Patty is guilty and that nothing could convince you otherwise?"

After the recess court resumes with a third running of the film—this time cropped to show the defendant only, in extreme close-up, so that she appears as a monstrous, gun-toting automaton, the Patty balloon in Macy's Thanksgiving Day Parade. Twice, the huge head half turns toward Cinque, behind her, and appears to speak. The government contends we are seeing Patty tell Mr. Norton to get on the fucking floor. The defense claims Patty said only what the SLA told her to say: "This is Tania Hearst!" The second set of mouth movements is not speech at all, but Patty's gasps as she hears the sound of gunfire. Save for the tick-tick-tick of the projector, the darkened courtroom is deadly quiet.

The remainder of Friday is given over to various witnesses to the robbers' getaway. Bailey has no difficulty pointing out discrepancies between their testimony today and what they told the grand jury nearly two years before, his implication being that the prosecutors had assisted the witnesses in making their identification.

When we adjourn, Catherine Hearst precedes her husband and daughters down the aisle, still impeccably groomed and coiffed after a full day in court. "Flawless!" a press photographer exclaims. "Catherine Hearst is the most perfect woman I've ever seen . . . and I once spent a weekend with Grace Kelly."

Patricia Hearst and her misadventures had been the focus of my professional life for nearly two years. Now, at the end of her first week on trial, I had much to ponder, beginning with my own complex relationship with the defendant, her parents, and her attorneys. I had been working on my own book for eighteen months before Bailey entered the case. Indeed, by that time mine was one of more than a dozen Hearst-books-in-embryo, and three Patty books already had been published. But my project had the tacit approval at least of Randolph Hearst, as well as of the family lawyer, William Coblentz, an old acquaintance of mine. It was Coblentz who had originally introduced me to the Hearsts, saying that since Patty books were inevitable, it might be wise for the family to cooperate with one more-or-less respectable journalist. Patty's mother emphatically did not agree, but Randolph Hearst had remained ever affable, ever available. Each time I saw him, however, he made the point that "the real story is Patty, not me." Although I thought then that the "real story" was everything but Patty—as I expressed it at the time, "I want to write the doughnut, not the hole"—nonetheless, her reentry on the scene, complete with a lawyer who was also a would-be biographer and who controlled all access to the client, had set up a certain literary conflict of interest.

Bailey faced the conflict, if that is what it was, with characteristic bravura. Throughout the pretrial months he had given me repeated assurances that I would see Patty "when she was ready." This moment never occurred, but on the very last weekend before trial, Bailey had made me an offer I couldn't refuse. Certain critical documents existed by that time that shed light on the emotional state of Patricia Hearst before her capture and after. One of these was the "Tania Interview." But an even more interesting one was a confidential psychiatric report, 162 pages long, prepared by two of the four doctors who had originally examined the prisoner, within days of her capture, at the request of Judge Carter. The purpose of these examinations was to determine whether the defendant was legally capable of standing trial. Carter was obliged to call for such examinations, he said, because Patty's first attorneys, the Hallinans, had themselves raised the whole issue of Patty's mental health in spectacular fashion. Five days after her arrest, the Hallinans had filed the damnedest bail affidavit anybody around San Francisco had ever seen. It said that after she was kidnapped, Patricia Hearst was held for weeks in a tiny closet, bound, blindfolded, and in the dark. During her first ten days "she was unable to dispose of her body wastes." Nobody spoke to her except Cinque, and he told her "she would be executed unless the ransom demands were complied with." During this period,

she felt as if she were on some LSD trip; everything was out of proportion, big and distorted. She heard constant threats against her life . . . was told by her captors that her parents had abandoned her . . . that [if the FBI found the SLA hideout they] . . . would bust into the house with drawn guns . . . and she would undoubtedly be killed in the general massacre. After a month of this sort of treatment, she was in such a condition that she could stand for only 60 seconds or so, and would then fall to the ground. . . .

. . . She was taken to the bank . . . given a gun . . . told that . . . if she made one false move . . . she would be killed instantly. . . .

Finally, under the pressure of these threats, deprivations of liberty, isolation and terror, she felt her mind clouding, and everything appeared so distorted and terrible that she believed and feared that she was losing her sanity, and unless soon freed, would become insane. . . . A short while before her arrest, she began to experience lucid intervals in which her sanity briefly reappeared, and during one of these she began to doubt that her parents were involved in any plan for her destruction . . . but when the FBI agents appeared, she thought that she would instantly be killed. When this did not happen, her mind began to clear up again, but the first full realization that she had been living in a fantasy world whose terrors could be resolved by merely returning to her family or even consulting the law officers, occurred when her mother, her father and her sisters hugged and kissed her.

The troubles to flow from this lurid affidavit were terrible and manifold. Set aside for a moment the fact that the document conflicted with previously disclosed information on Patty's actions after her kidnapping, and that it made no reference to numerous documents in the government's possession in which Patty in her own handwriting described how she had willingly, enthusiastically joined the SLA, forsworn her parents and even denied her own identity as Patricia Hearst; how she had stuck up one bank and, at the very least, made detailed plans to rob others; and how she had joyfully joined the revolution. Although the public was not yet aware of the nature and extent of these documents, Patty and her attorneys surely knew that the FBI had carted off boxloads of this incriminating stuff and had also recovered an arsenal of weapons from her apartment, including some of the guns used in the Hibernia Bank robbery.

The Hallinans' affidavit violated basic rules of legal strategy: It disclosed Patty's defense in detail and bound her to it; it left her lawyers almost no room to maneuver. Less than a week after her capture, Patricia Hearst's legal position appeared to be as messy as her mental state and her public image.

Upon receiving the astonishing affidavit, Judge Carter had appointed a panel of doctors to examine Patty. Until Carter received the medical report, he said, he would continue to refuse bail.

A preliminary psychiatric report was filed on October 4 by Carter's panel of doctors. It said Patty was legally sane but somewhat diminished in her capacity to cooperate in her defense because of her emotional state, a consequence of the severe stress of the past twenty months. Not surprisingly, the doctors recommended that Patty would benefit from some pretrial psychiatric treatment, assuming there was to be a trial, and it gave the court a list of possible treatment facilities. Finally, the doctors promised Judge Carter that "detailed reports to the Court will be provided by us individually within the next ten days." All this was a professional way of saying that while the doctors could not agree on what, or how much, was the matter with the girl, some immediate treatment certainly couldn't hurt.

Two of the subsequent individual reports were one page long. The third one was a collaborative effort by Louis Jolyon West, MD, chief of psychiatry at UCLA, and Margaret Thaler Singer, PhD, a clinical psychologist from the University of California at Berkeley, who was brought in at Dr. West's request to administer a full battery of psychological tests. It went on for 136 pages, plus bibliography, footnotes, and *curricula vitae* of its authors.

Carter accepted all the reports and then ordered the trial to proceed within ninety days under the terms of the Speedy Trial Act. He declared the reports confidential and inadmissible as evidence. Only three copies existed, and all three were placed under court seal. Anyone who revealed the contents to anybody save the judge or one of the attorneys risked prosecution for contempt of court. Eventually the hefty West/Singer psychiatric report would turmoil the trial of Patty Hearst just as much as the Hallinans' bail affidavit. Indeed, it was these two remarkable documents—each intended with the purest of motives to help a girl in deep trouble—that set the law and psychiatry on their collision course and guaranteed the sustained shambles that was to take place over eight grueling weeks in Judge Carter's courtroom.

Just a week ago, on the Friday evening before trial, a few hours after I had left Bailey and Johnson at the Mark Hopkins, my apartment doorbell rang. Standing in the hall was one of Bailey's young men, and he was holding an enormous liver-colored legal envelope. This was the offer I couldn't refuse. The envelope contained the entire confidential West/Singer report, as well as the twenty-seven-page "Tania Interview."

In showing me both documents, Bailey had acted with characteristic audacity, and had faced me with the same dilemma he intended to lay out for the jury: Which version of Patty Hearst do *you* believe, the doctors' or the SLA's?

It took the entire weekend to read it all. At the competency hearing Carter had called the West/Singer report "verbose." This turned out to have been an understatement. The report was an extraordinary document that swiftly became irritating on its reiteration of the obvious and amplification of the minimal. Its table of contents listed ten chapters and seven "attachments," one of them a ten-page single-spaced listing of the authors' vast professional credentials.

The doctors said Patty had undergone several personality changes. They had described a case of multiple personality in which there were four separate defendants:

A. Patty   February 20, 1954—February 4, 1974
B. Tania   February 4, 1974—May 17, 1974
C. Pearl   May 17, 1974—September 18, 1975
D. Pat   September 18, 1975—to present time

"Patty" had seemingly metamorphosed into "Tania" the instant she was kidnapped. After the fire in Los Angeles, the Harrises began to call Tania "Pearl" because it was too risky to address Tania in public. But when the jail interviewing began, none of the prisoner's three previous names seemed quite right to the doctors, so they settled on "Pat."

Dr. West describes his patient's fourth personality, "Pat," in this manner:

> Pat was a painfully constricted, tearful, bewildered and deeply regressed young woman. . . . She could hardly talk about her nineteen months in the hands of the SLA. This reticence is not seen in a normal person who returns from a prolonged, unusual, even terrifying experience and who can hardly wait to pour out the story. Pat resembles, more than anything else, a returned prisoner of war, one who has endured an experience that cannot be revealed for fear that the unbearable emotions of that ordeal will return and tear the fragile survivor apart.

Dr. West then goes over and over the same material like a pants presser. The verbosity becomes amazing as he rehashes it first in Chapter V, "Present Illness," and then a third time in three more chapters, entitled "Psychiatric Diagnostic Formulation," "Medico-Legal Formulation," and "Discussion."

I turned next to the "Extended Report," by Dr. Singer, a separate document from her psychological-test findings. Despite her professional objectivity, Dr. Singer's maternal instincts seemed to have been stirred by the plight of this unfortunate, multiply-abandoned, multiply-misunderstood girl. Among Singer's test findings, Patricia's answers to a sentence-completion test were particularly affecting.

"The underlined words below are the sentence starters," Singer writes. "The responses suggesting the 'immediacy' of her associations are as follows:"

Much of the time	"I smoke"
If I	"was out of here I'd like it"
My clothes	"don't fit me"
My greatest trouble	"is the present and the past, and I guess the future, too"
I envy	"people who are free"
My chief worry	"is this case"
The future	"doesn't look like much"
I suffer	"in silence"
There are times	"when I feel like dying"
Most men	"are assholes"
I feel	"death"
Many of my dreams	"I try not to remember"
I cannot understand	
what makes me	"cry"
Secretly	"I am depressed"
I feel most proud	"of nothing"

Dr. Singer's "Extended Report" moves beyond the ordinary presentation of test findings to include small essays on such subjects as "Ms. Hearst's attitude toward being examined" (docile, cooperative, troubled), "Ms. Hearst's conversational style during the examining period" (long pauses, dislocations, and discontinuities of space and time), and "Ms. Hearst's susceptibility to coercive persuasion." The last was particularly informative, despite its windy style, because it was the basis of the defense.

MS. HEARST'S SUSCEPTIBILITY TO COERCIVE PERSUASION

Included among the factors that contributed to making Patricia Hearst particularly susceptible to being coerced into "cooperating" with her captors were . . .

1. *Uncertainty About Self*

   a. During Patricia's childhood, she had a prolonged period of significant close contact with a harsh governess upon whom she was very dependent and who frequently told her that she was a child unwanted by her parents. Cinque, upon whom she also found herself dependent, also told her that her parents rejected her, punctuating his message with threats of pain and with actual brutality. Cinque's technique rekindled her old childhood doubts about her self-worth.

   b. As a schoolgirl, Patricia had a poor opinion of herself and was more vulnerable to feeling put down by her classmates and associates than would be someone who felt secure about her own worth and proud of her accomplishments.

   c. At the time of her capture, Patricia was mildly depressed. She was unsure of her plans for the future . . .

   d. During the first two days of testing, Patricia behaved at times as though she considered herself guilty of some sort of serious transgression. Her manner was that of a pathetic little girl who had done something terribly wrong or one characteristic of prisoners of war who have been browbeaten by their captors.

2. *Ambivalence Towards Her Parents*

   a. Patricia developed a feeling of some alienation from her parents. As she grew older, she particularly felt unable to make contact with her mother other than on a shallow, surface level.

   b. During her formative years, particularly in adolescence, Patricia had often felt herself to be a "prisoner" of the Hearst family tradition.

   c. As a young adult, Patricia was [making] . . . a natural move toward independence. Her new life with Steven Weed was a statement of her willingness to deviate from the life-style exemplified by her family. . . .

3. *Characterological Lack of Inner-Directedness*

   a. Patricia's school history is noteworthy for its pattern of discontinuity. Although some of her moves from school to school were made for understandable reasons, others appear to have been based on caprice. At no time was her choice of a school predicated upon some carefully thought-out long-range plan for acquiring an education.

b. In comparison with some of her more studious, thoughtful classmates or with the more mature friends whom she met through Steven Weed, Patricia was not an intellectual, a deep thinker, or a conceptualizer. She was not inclined to explore issues with depth or logic, nor was she given to introspection or to dwelling on inner psychological processes. Furthermore, Patricia was politically naive and unconcerned with the political issues that absorbed many of her contemporaries. Therefore, when faced with a barrage of intense political propaganda from Cinque and his followers, Patricia had no inner frame of reference that would enable her to understand their behavior or put her experience into some perspective. . . .

c. Patricia's trait of responding to the immediacy of situations is demonstrated in her adjustment to life in jail. . . . As an example, she showed the examiner her cell with the demeanor of a little child proud to show off her very own special place.

4. *Psychological Suggestibility*

a. Patricia was always prone to take on the ways of those around her. As a child, she adapted more "responsibly" to the demands of her parents than did her four sisters. As a young woman, taking her first tentative steps toward independence by living with Steven Weed, she adapted swiftly to the style of life he provided.

b. Patricia's natural style of talking can best be described as informal, and is typical of the casual form of communcation currently in vogue among the young. Her way of phrasing ideas is elusive and her reference points are non-specific. In sharp contrast to this is the language style she used on the tapes she was required by Cinque to make for propaganda purposes. The passages marked by crisp wording, clear phrasing and a rehearsed manner were written out for her beforehand, disclaimers to the contrary notwithstanding.

c. During psychological testing Patricia reported that her subjective experience resembled what she had felt when she was interacting with Cinque, namely that he knew everything she was thinking.

The weekend's reading left me stunned, sad, and embarrassed. Going over the doctor's reports, I felt like a Peeping Tom staring into the emotional boudoir of the young woman who for so long had intrigued me from afar. But I also felt a new rush of maternal concern and of empathy for her ordeal. The psychobabble of these doctors was far more

43

affecting than the florid rhetoric of the Hallinans. The creature the doctors described appeared to be a classic shell-shock victim; that much was clear from—or perhaps clear despite—all the grandiose verbiage. But then how was one to deal with the other document, Tania's purported "autobiography"? The two documents read like a photographic double-exposure. Superimposed on the doctors' picture of the pathetic shell-shock victim was Tania's first-person self-image of a young girl strongly impressed by a very idealistic and brave set of values. As Tania saw it, the objectives of the SLA were admirable. She could not see that the methods proposed to achieve them were psychopathic. The SLA, it appeared, had invented a new formula for compounding insanity.

WEEK THREE

Monday, February 9

This morning Patty will take the stand for the first time. But the jury will not be present. Only the larger jury of the media will be on hand when Judge Carter considers a defense motion that Patty's various statements about being a willing participant in the bank robbery should not be admitted into evidence because they were not made voluntarily. Bailey is still fighting hard to keep the skunks out of the courtroom.

Alone and palely loitering at the bare oak table, the defendant looks beautiful for the first time. Her long white throat rises out of a Byronic collar of salmon-pink silk, spread out over a velvet jacket the color of port wine; pale and perfect skin, aquiline features, charcoal smudges for eyes, the whole softly framed by fine, coppery hair. When she moves into the raised, pulpitlike witness box, one of the sketch artists lends me his close-up glasses, and the powerful lenses make a corona of gold light around the edges of the cream, auburn, and copper girl. The aquarium has found its mermaid.

Bailey is brisk. Who was with Patty when the tape in which she describes taking part in the bank robbery was made?

In a faint monotone: "Donald DeFreeze, Nancy Ling Perry, Patricia Soltysik, Camilla Hall, William and Emily Harris, William Wolfe . . ." A long pause here. The voice trails off, she appears to go blank, and Bailey has to prompt her. How about Angela Atwood? Oh, yes . . . and Cinque said they were going to make a tape to show I participated in it . . . so everybody sat down on the floor, and Angela Atwood wrote out some words. Cinque took Patty into the closet, and she read by flashlight while he operated the tape recorder.

Bailey reads from a transcript of that tape: " 'I am obviously alive and well. As for being brainwashed, the idea is ridiculous to the point of being beyond belief. . . . ' Was that your language or the language of Angela Atwood?"

"Angela Atwood."

And if she had refused to say those words, what would have happened?

Patty's cheeks redden. Her eyes fill with tears. "I was told that—I'd be killed."

So much for the taped confession. Now the oral one, the Matthews boy. What kind of van were they riding in? Well, it had benches in the back. Emily was driving, and William Harris said to Matthews, "You recognize her, don't you? That's Tania."

From the moment she was kidnapped until this moment, how many times had Patty been threatened with death? Her answer is inaudible, and the judge asks her to speak up. Soft but clear now: "Hundreds of times."

Now, the written confession. We are told that the "Tania Interview" is entirely untrue, that she was forced to help write the "autobiography" because the fugitives were running short of funds.

Browning rises to cross-examine and thumps down onto the witness stand a monumental pile of photographs. The girl's eyes widen; she shrinks in fear. Lillian Gish could not do it better, but in Patty's circumstances, the exaggerated reactions of a silent-movie heroine are believable.

"Is this the closet where you were held?"

Patty looks, closes her eyes for a moment. Then: "Yes." She was in this closet until sometime early in March and was then tied inside a garbage can and transported to another closet in another apartment.

The bail affidavit describes Patty's imprisonment "in the closet." "But you say now there were *two* closets," Browning prods. Patty admits she signed an incorrect affidavit, knowing it was incorrect.

How about the "I have chosen to stay and fight" tape of April 3? She closes her eyes; a long blink, a slight frown. Again she looks scared. She doesn't recall making that tape and doesn't know who composed it. "They would bring in a sheet of paper, and I would read it."

Browning's questions get tougher. Is it not correct that just before making this tape, the SLA told Patty she was free to leave? Well, DeFreeze told her, first, that they had decided that she could either join the SLA or be killed. Later, when they told her she had a different choice—join or go home—"I didn't believe them."

Browning reads from the SLA's final tape: " 'Neither Cujo [William Wolfe] nor I had ever loved an individual the way we loved each other, probably because our relationship wasn't based on bourgeois values. . . .' Do you recall those words?"

"Could I see them?" It is apparent that Miss Hearst has been well prepared by her lawyers. She knows not to answer a question until she understands what she is being asked; she always asks to see the documents on which the government is basing its questions; she looks the prosecutor in the eye. This "voluntariness" hearing is giving Patty an excellent chance to accustom herself to the stress of the witness box and to develop stamina under cross-examination before facing the jury.

"*Do* you, in fact, recall those words?" Browning repeats.

"No."

"Miss Hearst, did you participate in other activities with Mr. and Mrs. Harris with respect to banks?"

"*Objection!*" Bailey is on his feet, quivering. "That question goes far beyond the scope—"

"Sustained."

Browning, unperturbed, asks the witness if she recognizes a two-page typewritten document headed "Bakery." She shakes her head. "How about this one? A diagram headed 'Bank of America, Marysville'?"

Bailey is on his feet shouting, "Object! This is a fishing expedition, not a hearing! It is a violation of my client's constitutional rights! She demands a recess. It is not *right* to force her to incriminate herself."

Judge Carter is calm. "I want you to tell me what your point is. If you have one, state it."

"My point is that you're forcing her to answer questions which could expose her to further charges, and I will not permit her to do it."

Carter is becoming testy. "Tell me the nature of the charges, so that I can rule. Are these state charges or federal charges?"

Browning interrupts to say that Bailey waived his client's right against self-incrimination when he allowed her to take the witness stand.

Carter is exasperated. "You *can't* waive a constitutional right!"

The questioning resumes. Browning asks about fingerprints on the "Bakery" document. Bailey insists that his client is instructed *not* to answer the question on fingerprints.

"Objection sustained."

In courtroom skills Mr. Browning appears outclassed, but he has other resources. He has twenty-seven typewritten pages of the "Tania Interview," with revisions in Patricia Hearst's handwriting, describing the kidnapping, the revolutionary politics behind it, the SLA's views on military action, and the terrorists' reaction to subsequent events. There is also a grimly detailed autobiographical description of the childhood, education, and family background of Patricia Hearst, as seen from Tania's new, revolutionary perspective.

In the history of terror, in the history of crime, surely no group suffered such excesses of literary manufacture as the Symbionese Liberation Army. They were terrorists with the habits of graduate students. After the arrest, the FBI hauled more than seven hundred cartons of documents out of the Hearst and Harris apartments. The previously discovered SLA hideouts were similarly littered. They left a paper trail behind them so wide that one might imagine that they were seeking rather desperately to be found out and stopped. One item found in the half-burned SLA safehouse in Concord, amid the rubble that Nancy Ling Perry set afire the day after Remiro and Little were arrested and the terrorist cadre went into still deeper cover, was a green spiral notebook. It contained a list of twenty possible future victims to follow Marcus Foster. Some persons on the SLA hit list were alerted by the authorities; inexplicably, Patricia Hearst was not, and neither were her parents. The Hearsts never forgave the FBI for neglecting to tip them off, and the failure looks now like inexcusably sloppy police work.

The SLA wrote, sorted, classified, and revised, manufacturing its revolution as it went along, working with the diligence of aardvarks. Night and day, without letup, it was busy formulating what it believed were original political coalitions—the great new symbiosis of all radical thought, the grand amalgam of every scheme ever invented to alleviate the suffering of the oppressed people on earth. The architects burned to put the theory to the test. The necessary time for theory to cure and mellow, to translate and modulate into action, simply did not exist. The SLA members lived on instant terror, instant politics, brewed like instant coffee, fast-frozen, and shot from guns. Their "politics" offered instant gratification to any rebellious impulse, no matter how half-cocked or half-baked. They were very American. The paper detritus they left behind, the laundry lists of potential assassination victims indiscriminately mixed in with *real* laundry lists, the scratch-pad notations of "cat food" and "sink stopper" scrawled on the back of the same envelope as the maps of banks and diagrams of homemade pipe bombs, did not indicate a shortage of scratch paper but a hopeless confusion of trivia and terror, of theory and action, a lost ability to discriminate between violent, rage-based revolutionary fantasy and reality.

Of all the captured documents, none is potentially more damaging to the defense than this "Tania Interview." Bailey will fight like hell to keep the jurors in innocence of it. Prosecutor Browning reads aloud from the incriminating manuscript:

> Q. The media has at times put across the theory that you were being brainwashed. . . . How do you feel about that?
>
> A. I think that that kind of cheap sensationalism is all you can expect from the media. From the moment I was kidnapped they consistently attempted to discredit the revolutionaries. After the first communiqué was received, the pigs reacted by hauling out "stress machines" [which] indicated that I was being tortured and kept awake 24 hours a day. I couldn't believe that anyone would come up with such bullshit! I was furious. I refuted their lies in the next communiqué and announced that I was going to stay with the SLA.

"You say this material was dictated by the Harrises. Was anybody else forcing you to write those words? Was Wendy Yoshimura* helping you?"

Patty's eyes open wide. "Oh, no!" The two words convey the only passion she has shown so far.

Browning wonders why Patty didn't try to escape. After the group returned to San Francisco, were they not living in separate apartments, more than a mile apart? Yes, but "they knew where I was."

Couldn't she have gone to the police?

Almost whimpering: "I thought they would kill me. Or the FBI would . . ."

How about the incident in Los Angeles seventeen months before? Patty had been alone reading the paper when she looked up and saw the Harrises scuffling with the store clerk. Why grab a machine gun and open fire? Why not simply drive off?

"Where would I have gone?"

BROWNING: Did you prefer staying with the Harrises, who had

---

*Ms. Yoshimura, a three-year fugitive from justice, was living with Patty when they were arrested together at 625 Morse Street. Steven Soliah, Patty's lover and also a resident of the apartment, was arrested the same day at another location. He was later tried for and acquitted of a bank robbery in a Sacramento suburb in which a woman was killed.

threatened to kill you, to simply walking away from them when you had the opportunity? You could have walked away, could you not? [*Scornful.*] You *rescued* the Harrises!

PATTY (*resigned to not being believed, and somewhat scornful herself*): If I had walked away, the other members of the SLA would have come looking for me . . . and the FBI would, too.

Browning shows Patty a transcript of the tape in which she says she has "decided to stay and fight." Did DeFreeze force her to make such statements? "He said that I'd be killed." She is biting her lips now and seems on the verge of tears.

Browning leads Patty through an account of her escape from California at the height of the most extensive manhunt in FBI annals, of her hegira to Pennsylvania and then back to Las Vegas. She was driven cross-country from Oakland by Jack Scott and sheltered by Scott's parents. By naming the senior Scotts, Patty is laying them open to prosecution for aiding and abetting a kidnapping and harboring a fugitive. She is putting into effect the defense strategy imposed by Bailey and Johnson from the moment they took over the case. Six months ago, sitting in the sweaty, smoke-filled "iron phone booth" at the jail, Johnson had told Patty, "You're gonna have to dump it all out, honey."

On the way back from Pennsylvania to Las Vegas, Patty and Jack Scott traveled alone, staying in motels. Could Patty have left *then*? "Where would I have gone?"

A clerk whispers something to the judge, who abruptly announces the noon recess, although it is only eleven-thirty. In the corridor we learn the reason: the New World Liberation Front has just called the courthouse and said that somewhere in the twenty-story building a bomb is ticking.

After lunch the daughter flashes the mother a tiny, private smile just before climbing back up into the witness box. Mom's response is to fire back a wide-open grin of a Miss America contestant.

Browning is leading Patty through the "Tania Interview." "After a few weeks I started to feel sympathetic with the SLA." Did Patty write *those* words? No. How about this? "My mother appeared at press conferences dressed in black to urge me through her racist tears to 'Keep praying honey. . . . God will bring you home.'" Are those Patty's words? No.

"You don't recall speaking about a 'black dress'?"

"No."

I glance over at Mom. Again today she wears a black dress, with black shoes and bag, and a folded black coat lies across her lap.

Now a passage about Catherine Hearst's behavior as a regent. " 'People like the Berkeley student body president would come over to the house to talk to her during the '60s, and her way of dealing with the situation was to direct them to the swimming pool and send out sandwiches. She always prided herself on how much the students liked her. . . .' " The rest of the typewritten paragraph has been crossed out and in Patty's hand is written, " 'when in fact they thought she was a corrupt right wing little bitch.' "

Randy Hearst leans forward, elbows on his knees, staring at the floor. Browning now switches to the bail affidavit: Did you know it contained errors? Yes. Then why did you sign it? Because the lawyers told me to sign. Then another switch. In the robbery rehearsals were you positioned so that the bank surveillance cameras would see you? Yes. Now a critical question: During the robbery was your weapon loaded? "I was told it was loaded."

Browning asks the clerk for people's exhibit number 19 and crosses jauntily to the witness box. Its FBI identification tag flutters like a pennant from the green webbing strap of the M-1 semiautomatic rifle. He hands the weapon to Patty, asks her to examine it, break the bolt, inspect the clip. Her tiny hands know precisely what to do. They look like the hands of an educated bank robber. Patient Dad watches his favorite daughter handle the weapon as a plumber would a wrench.

On redirect, Bailey questions Patty about another part of her testimony.

Okay, now you were asked by Mr. Browning whether or not a statement made by you . . . in June 1974 is true, particularly as to your alleged affection for William Wolfe. Did you, in fact, have any such affection . . . ? No. Did William Wolfe ever do anything offensive to you? Yes, he assaulted me sexually. Was he the only one? No. Was it in the closet? Yes.

Is it not a fact that the SLA told you that if your hideout were discovered, the FBI would kill all the people in the house? Yes.

Where were you, Miss Hearst, on the evening of May 17, 1974? The defendant was in a motel in Anaheim, across the street from Disneyland, watching on television the fire in which six of her comrades were burned alive. Although the police and everybody else at the time believed that Patricia Hearst, too, was trapped inside the house, they had continued shooting, had held back the firemen, and let the house burn to the ground.

On re-cross-examination, Browning inquires if the Hallinan affidavit is not again incorrect when it says "that you were made to lie in your own body wastes." Patty in her tiny voice and Bailey in his ringing Papa Bear tones exclaim simultaneously, *"It doesn't say that!"*

The prosecutor picks up a sheet of paper and reads, " '. . . was given food but was unable to eat any for a period of about ten days, and for all that period was unable to dispose of her body wastes.' What does that mean, Miss Hearst?"

Small voice, eyes lowered: "It means when they took me to the bathroom I was unable to use it."

So much for what an imaginative lawyer can do with an ordinary case of constipation. It is time for midafternoon recess.

The mermaid's song has been long and moving. By the time she leaves the stand a half-dozen of the toughest sob sisters in the American press are cluck-clucking, dabbing their eyes.

When court resumes, we meet two important new characters: David Bancroft, thirty-four, the soft-spoken Justice Department lawyer who will handle all the psychiatric testimony; and Professor Margaret Thaler Singer. After Dr. Singer completed her psychological tests for Dr. West, she undertook an elaborate linguistic analysis of the seven SLA tapes and has now concluded that although Patty was the speaker, she was not the author of the words.

Tall and fiftyish, Dr. Singer takes the stand and testifies that her analysis of Patty's language style is based on more than twenty-four hours of personal interviews with the defendant, as well as on a careful study of the SLA tapes, Patty's old school papers, and some old letters on tape that Patty mailed to Steve Weed during a trip to Europe. Singer can identify the stylistic language pattern of each SLA member. Even before Patty and Bailey told her that the language on the portion of the tape in which Patty confessed to the robbery was written by Angela Atwood, Dr. Singer had concluded that the passage was written, not spontaneous, speech. Singer listens for pauses and for the sound of pages turning. When one reads aloud, the pauses tend to follow written punctuation; in spontaneous speech the pauses emphasize the meanings of individual words. One also uses a simpler style in speech, a more complex style when writing. But the tape on which Patricia admits to having participated in the bank robbery resembles neither her written *nor* her oral style.

Cross-examining, David Bancroft wonders how Dr. Singer explains Patty's having given her occupation to the jail matron as urban guerrilla. Because Emily Harris, whom she feared, was present in the room. And why did Patty tell her friend Trish Tobin during a jail visit that, were she to issue a public statement, it would be made from a "revolutionary feminist perspective"? Because Patty had been coached by her captors to talk in those terms.

Citing Dr. Singer's written report to the court, Bancroft asks, "Is there any possibility that *your questions* suggested the answers given by Miss Hearst?"

"No. Miss Hearst was in such a state of tension and difficulty that I had to ask questions again and again, to make very sure I had correctly understood her very brief remarks . . . and to let her know I was offering her an opportunity to correct herself."

Well, doesn't that itself suggest that possibly the kindly Dr. Singer was leading or coaching the girl into giving "correct" responses? Singer stands firm. The language of the confessional tape is "heavy and convoluted . . . not in the style you yourself heard her talk in today, before I came on the stand. She speaks in very short, simple sentences." The prosecutor persists until the witness dismisses him with school-marmish finality. "The trouble is, Mr. Bancroft, that I'm talking about her style, and you're talking about her content."

It is 4:05 P.M. *I* think Dr. Singer has scored heavily, but the judge may not be so impressed. "I have an appointment now with my doctor— who is an MD, not a PhD," he harrumphs, rising from his chair.

Tuesday, February 10

Last night there was another bomb scare. Today the voluntariness hearing continues. It is our second day without a jury. Anthony Shepard, the young man on the witness stand, was the clerk at Mel's, and he is studying to be a cop. Browning leads him through his story. Shepard caught William Harris shoplifting a pair of socks and "attempted to put handcuffs on the gentleman. Emily Harris was on my back, attempting to protect Mr. Harris." Still struggling out on the sidewalk, Shepard had managed to snap on only one handcuff when "we were fired upon from across the street by an unknown vehicle." When he "saw an unknown suspect hanging out of the van window with a weapon, I proceeded to shimmy out of the street, behind a light stand. . . ."

The Harrises dashed across the street into the van and took off. The clerk gave chase in his own car. When both vehicles got stuck in traffic, someone jumped out of the van and approached Shepard with an automatic rifle held at port-arms position. It was "an individual with shoulder-length hair."

"Do you know who that person was?"

He knows it was not William or Emily Harris.

"No questions," Bailey snaps.

"Whew!" Shepard shakes his head, glad to avoid cross-examination.

Tom Matthews steps into the box, and we get our first look at the young man whom Patty and the Harrises are accused of kidnapping. He wears an open shirt, a half smile, and a shock of hair over his forehead. In contrast to this open-faced young man, Patty looks so—I search for a word—"so dead," I write, though that is not quite the word I want.

Matthews testifies that after he got into the van, he was told that one of his companions was Patricia Hearst.

"Do you see that person here today?"

"She's sitting right next to Mr. Bailey," says Matthews.

The Matthews boy, arms folded across his chest, is cheerfully describing how the SLA told him they needed money because it was expensive to be engaged in guerrilla warfare. Matthews likes everybody, including Patty. During the night in the van, "she kept patting me on the head, under the blanket, and asking me if I was all right."

Did she ever ask you to get a message to her parents? No. Ever talk about the shoot-up at Mel's? She said it was "a good feeling" to see her two comrades come running back across the street.

Bailey's cross-examination is brisk. Did Patty express concern as to whether he was comfortable? Yes. Thank you, that's all.

As we rise for the lunch break Vicki Hearst suddenly opens her hand and flashes her sister a Day-Glo-orange rabbit's foot. The defendant's vacant, *dolorosa* face breaks into a startled grin, and for an instant Patty is beautiful again. But the grin vanishes, and I find then the word I have been searching for all morning: embalmed. Patty looks not dead, but rather as if she is being made up for her courtroom appearance by cosmeticians from Forest Lawn.

After lunch the jury returns briefly to hear testimony by FBI experts about the various cars and false identification papers used by the robbers.

Home from the trial, I find Al Johnson waiting in the lobby. He has stopped by for a drink and to watch the news. Jack Scott is reportedly close to being indicted in Pennsylvania. Al looks at his watch. "Time to call the jail. Don't make any noise. She doesn't like it if she thinks anybody else is with me."

He dials, and after some banter with the warders, Patty comes on the line. "So what's going on in the can? . . . Oh, *you* just called *me*? No, I wasn't in my room. I just came in here now, and I'm going right out again. Did you have supper?" She tells him what was served at the jail. He lights a cigarette, loosens his collar, and asks how many mouthfuls of it she was able to eat. Al is a genial fairy godfather. A bizarre "friend" for a girl like Patty, but these days her only one. With Patty, as with everyone, Al is unfailingly patient, cheerful, and entirely himself. They slip into a conversation they've had many times: planning Patty's coming-out party. "Have you been working on the menu, like I told you? . . . Good. By the way, whaddya gonna wear? . . . Naw, get something new. Better be a gown, a long gown. You'll have a lot to celebrate. . . ."

Poor girl. If she can exist at this simpleminded level, she must be well and truly lost. She might as well join her semiinvalid sister, who works at a convent, and live out her life as an impaired creature, a medieval recluse, embroidering, manicuring her nails, doing good works.

Having spooned into Patty her evening's ration of applesauce, we go downstairs for dinner.

"How do you get Patty to eat?" I ask.

"Choo-choo."

"Huh?"

"You know, like you feed a kid. You say, here comes the choo-choo train. Open up now, food's going in."

Wednesday, February 11

This is a critical day. If Judge Carter rules to admit the enormous amount of evidence in Patty's own words that she was a willing participant in the bank robbery, Bailey must then show that all of it—taped, spoken, and written in her own hand—was forced out of her while she was under immediate fear of death or great bodily harm; further, he must show that this immediate danger lasted from the moment she was kidnapped until the moment of her capture, more than nineteen months later. The defense is *duress,* but the duress was physical only up to a point. Once she joined the SLA it became mental, and was imposed jointly by her captors and by Patty Hearst herself because she had come to believe whatever they told her. Browning's task may not be easier than Bailey's, but it is certainly simpler. To win his case, he must convince twelve jurors beyond a reasonable doubt that Patricia Hearst is a liar.

Bailey finds it unseemly at best "and in my view a flat violation of the rights of the defendant [for the SLA] to create evidence against [her in order] to isolate her from the society from which she came and to which she might otherwise return—and then to have that [manufactured] evidence admitted in a court of law." A ruling to admit the "manufactured" evidence would encourage and even inspire other radical groups to attempt similar kinds of terrorist actions, he says. "To allow an American jury to carry out [the SLA's] predictions that, if she were to return, she would be cast in jail, because of evidence *they* had forcibly created, is an outrage. And I ask Your Honor to exclude that evidence." Bailey's speech is full of menace.

The prosecutor's argument runs just as Bailey had told me it would. Normally, the burden of proof would be on the government to prove that Patricia had acted voluntarily, not under duress. However, "no government agency was involved in the alleged involuntariness because private individuals made these threats," not cops or overeager district attorneys. The evidence that force and intimidation were used is in the possession of the defense. Therefore, it should properly bear the burden of proof. This fugue in double negatives makes my head spin.

Now Browning shifts to simpler logic. "The real question is whether the defendant may be believed. . . . The evidence submitted here does not suggest she was in fear of great bodily injury or death." Does Patty look in fear of injury or death in the film? She does not. Patty had enough time alone with Matthews to ask him for help; why didn't she? She could have escaped when she was alone in the van, across from Mel's; why didn't she? Unless the Harrises trusted Patricia, why did they permit her to remain alone in the van with a weapon? Why on earth, if the defendant were in fear of her life, would she rescue the very comrades she claims to have been so afraid of?

If the jury were present to listen to the government's damning list of questions, the case would be all over. But they are not present, and to them Patricia is still clothed in the presumption of innocence that Judge Carter spoke of. It will be Bailey's job throughout the remainder of this trial to answer Browning's last question: He must make the jury understand that *rescuing the very comrades she lived in fear of* is precisely what "brainwashing" is all about.

The problem must be decided carefully, Carter says, "because it brings the Fifth Amendment into play" [the right of the defendant against self-incrimination by involuntary statements] and he declares a recess so he can consider the matter.

I am on a corridor telephone when a herd of reporters comes thundering down the marble hallway, *Front Page* style, racing for the bank of phones. Carter has just denied Bailey's motion to suppress the evidence. He will let all four of Bailey's skunks into his courtroom, because he finds "by a preponderance of the evidence that . . . the statements made by the defendant after the happening of the bank robbery, whether by tape recording or by oral communication or in writing, *were* made voluntarily."

It is a severe blow for the defense. The jury files back, and the morning drones along with tedious FBI testimony documenting the chain of custody of the bullets, the begats of criminal testimony. The judge yawns openly. At his noon press conference Bailey is appealingly candid: Carter's ruling did not catch him unawares. Since the damaging materials had already been permitted in the government's opening statement, the only alternative to this morning's ruling would have been to throw the case out of court.

Thursday, February 12

Patty appears unusually energetic today, talking rapidly, gesturing as if she were speaking in sign language, pointing animatedly at photographs of the closets, as if in some perverse way she is happy to see these awful old homes once more. Possibly late this afternoon, certainly by tomorrow, the defense case will begin. So this morning two of the biggest guns in academic psychiatry are drawn up on the defense side of the courtroom. The ruddy man is Dr. Louis Jolyon West. The handsome, saturnine fellow in the tweed jacket is Yale's Robert Jay Lifton, MD. Later a large, rumpled, European-looking couple will arrive from the University of Pennsylvania—Dr. Martin Orne and spouse. Bailey can hardly wait to rip the canvas off his three cannons and blow the government out of the water.

Now a parade of jargon-talking FBI agents identifies incriminating evidence found in the two SLA apartments. "This particular weapon was first observed by myself on the upper portion, more specifically, on the *shelving,* of the closet. . . ."

During the noon recess reporters learn with a shock that there has been still another terrorist bombing. This time the target was San Simeon, William Randolph Hearst's castle-fortress, now the top tourist attraction in the California State Parks system. SLA sympathizers are suspected; later the New World Liberation Front will take credit for the explosion in which two small outbuildings were destroyed. Randolph Hearst says he is "shocked and outraged," but to hear his weary voice is to feel that there is no shock or outrage left in the man.

The FBI's droning identification of various weapons continues after lunch. The carbines and M-1s seem unreal as they are handed about, like stage props in a war play. It is important to know whether or not Patricia had a weapon *capable* of being fired.

In cross-examination, Bailey demonstrates that Patty's weapon has a tendency to "hang up," to jam, and when this happens, "you could pull the trigger all day long and it wouldn't fire!" With a snort, he turns on his heel and walks off in disgust. The point has been to suggest to the jury that Patty's gun was possibly not even in working order, that she had deliberately been issued a faulty weapon because the SLA didn't trust her with an operative one.

FBI agent Tom Padden has been dozing. Now Bailey calls him to the stand to identify the all-important SLA tape no. 6, Patty's confession. Although only her portion of the tape has been transcribed, Bailey insists the jurors hear all the voices, including Cinque's long, ravening, paramilitary introduction. He wants the SLA wildness loud in the jurors' ears before they hear Tania herself speak. Browning is willing, and we hear Cinque's extraordinary monologue begin:

> Greetings to the People. And all sisters and brothers, behind the walls and in the streets. Greetings to the Black Liberation Army, the Weather Underground, and the Black Guerrilla Family, and all combat forces of the community. This is General Field Marshal Cin speaking.

Booming out over the silent courtroom, the gently cadenced, powerful voice makes my skin prickle.

Patty's voice comes on the tape:

> Greetings to the People. This is Tania. On April 15, my comrades and I expropriated $10,660.02 from the Sunset Branch of the Hibernia Bank. . . . My gun was loaded, and at no time did any of my comrades intentionally point their guns at me. . . . For those people who still believe I am brainwashed or dead, I see no reason to further defend my position. I'm a soldier in the People's army. *Patria o muerte . . . Venceremos.*

As Tania's amplified voice fills the courtroom we can watch Patty's eyes moisten, then rapidly scan the jury, searching each face as they listen to her words. Tears begin to run down her cheeks. She sips water, strokes her hair from her brow; the ivory pallor of her face blotches red.

The day ends with agent Padden describing the arrest. Looking in a kitchen window, he saw two females, one white and one Oriental. He yanked open the door and shouted, "FBI—freeze! Freeze or I'll blow your head off!"

"Would you have blown her head off?" Browning asks.

"No, sir."

"Did she freeze at that time?"

"Yes, sir, she did."

In the corridor the women reporters huddle to compare notes on how many tears Patty shed.

Friday, February 13

Sometime today the defense case is to begin, with Steven Weed expected as the first witness. The prospect has drawn additional mobs to the Federal Building. It is impossible to keep one's feet; one just moves with the human current toward the banks of elevators.

Today Patty is wearing a smart apricot silk shirt and gray flannels. But the girl herself looks terrible. The circles under her eyes are darker, her skin is grayer, her body thinner, her lips almost blue.

Bailey is easygoing in his cross-examination of agent Padden. "In any kidnap case it is rather important for the investigator in charge to attempt to psych out what the captors are doing and what might trigger them to kill the victim, right? This is an, ahem, a matter of continuing concern to the Bureau?"

"The safety of a hostage, the victim, is paramount," says Padden.

Bailey reviews the SLA's bloody history, rooted in the assassination of Marcus Foster. "So you were aware they would not stop short of murder." And, of course, the witness also recalls that Miss Hearst was considered a prisoner of war, to be exchanged for Remiro and Little? He does. Now the big point. The grizzled Padden has been involved in thousands of bank robberies. "Did you *ever* hear of a bank robber identifying himself by name?"

Padden acknowledges that Miss Hearst made little effort to conceal her identity, though she did wear a wig, and DeFreeze wore a funny hat. Is there some question in Padden's mind that she might have been under the gun of several of the others at the time? Yes, there is. Has Padden ever heard of prisoners of war turning against their own country? Yes. Is he aware of the existence of a fairly extensive U.S. government library on the subject? Yes. Did anybody in the FBI attempt to gain access to those materials? No. What was Patty's reaction to being arrested? She wet her pants. Have you ever had any others—among *all* the ones you have arrested at gunpoint—who reacted in that fashion? No, sir.

Bailey has sketched a face-off between a veteran FBI man, gun in hand, and two young women suspects, one of them so terrified she pees in her pants. It looks like a strong finish to his cross-examination until Browning, on redirect, asks the veteran agent if he has "ever heard of a prisoner of war who had been converted, and then committed a violent act" and gets exactly the same soft reply, "No, sir."

Just before the noon recess the government rests its case, having presented thirty-two witnesses in seven court days. Over lunch we learn there has been still another extortion demand: The New World Liberation Front now wants a quarter of a million dollars from the Hearsts to finance the defense of William and Emily Harris—or else.

Court resumes ten minutes late. The room is tense, anticipating Weed's appearance. The lovers will see each other for the first time in two years. A bailiff waits at the door of the witness room, one hand on the knob. Patty is tight-lipped. "Mr. Bailey, you may call your first witness," Carter says.

"We call Steve Suenaga," says Bailey, and to the astonishment of all, a chubby, cheerful Japanese in glasses and a sweater comes hurtling through the door, shoved into the courtroom by investigator McNally. Weed's absence is not explained.

On the night of February 4, 1974, Suenaga, a student neighbor in Berkeley, returned from dinner in Chinatown and "saw a black gentleman in front of Patty's window." Suenaga ventured closer. The black man had a rifle, and he ordered Suenaga inside the apartment and told him to lie on the floor, next to Weed. What happened next? "The gentleman who was there proceeded to tell a young lady to tie me up. He told Patty Hearst to shut up or they would have to knock her out. The female said, 'No, they've seen us. We've gotta kill 'em.' " Suenaga heard a shotgun blast and heard Patty crying. "She was frantic. Weed looked bloody and beat up. He said, 'Call Randolph Hearst.' " Browning has no questions.

The next witness was studying in Mrs. Reagan's apartment, across the way from Patty's, when he heard screams, looked out the window, and saw two men stuffing a girl in a car trunk.

The third student eyewitness heard Patty beg "please" and noted she was blindfolded. He ran after the kidnappers and was shot at by people following in a backup car. A fourth student saw Cinque standing with a machine gun at the head of the stairs and then a flash of blue, which she recognized as Patty's robe.

These witnesses move with crisp dispatch. Next comes Mrs. Reagan herself, an old woman, walking painfully to the stand on crutches. "I used to see her painting her furniture, washing her little rug," Mrs. Reagan says. "One of the nicest girls I ever met. I wish we had more like her." This is the first representative of the American public to utter a kind word for Patty since the bank robbery.

When Mrs. Reagan heard the shooting, she thought people were celebrating the Chinese New Year. Then she looked out her window and saw two black boys carry Patty down the walk and shove her into a car trunk. The prosecutor having no more questions, Mrs. Reagan hobbles from the stand. Halfway across the courtroom, the old lady pauses on her crutches, smiles merrily at the defendant, and waves a green handkerchief. Barry Fitzgerald never made a finer exit. Patty begins to weep. Bailey suggests a recess.

In the corridor the lawyer snorts and snarls. He is furious at Weed for holding a press conference that very morning to plug his new book, in which he says he believes Patty was "coerced," not brainwashed. Johnson says that at the press conference Weed "seemed insincere. We were afraid he'd impress a jury the same way."

The moment has arrived for the defendant to take the stand in front of the jury for the first time. Bailey helps her walk across the courtroom, leaning gently on his arm, and the jurors watch the small, composed, but terrified-looking young woman give details of her family and school history. She was born in Los Angeles on February 20, 1954, the third of five sisters. She attended Marymount School in Los Angeles, a school in San Mateo, then St. Matthew's, Sacred Heart, Crystal Springs, and Santa Catalina in Monterey. After a year at Menlo College, she went on to the University of California at Berkeley.

Patty was aware of the Foster murder and the SLA prior to her being kidnapped. "Black friends of Steven Weed" had told her about them. Coming to the evening of February 4, "while you were watching TV did something unusual happen?" Yes. Someone knocked at the door; three people forced their way in. One was Angela Atwood, one was Donald DeFreeze, and one was William Harris.

"What did they do?"

"Um [sigh] . . . um . . . Angela Atwood put a pistol in my face and told me to be quiet." Harris tied her hands. She was blindfolded and gagged but bit down on the gag "so they couldn't put it in as far as they wanted. Steve Weed was screaming—" Patty has begun to cry. Regaining her composure, she testifies that she heard firing and more screaming, was pulled to her feet and struck by a gun butt, "right here"—she points to her cheek—and briefly lost consciousness. She begins to cry again as she describes how she was dragged downstairs and stuffed into the car trunk, then transferred to a station wagon and shoved onto the floor, between the seats. Emily Harris drove; Nancy Ling Perry rode shotgun.

How would Patty describe her own situation? Swallowing hard to maintain her precarious control, she says, "I was bound, blindfolded, and gagged. They drove around for an hour or two."

"Did Cinque say anything?"

"He just said, 'Bitch, you better be quiet or I'll blow your head off. If you make any noise, we'll kill you.'"

How did Patty feel when she was put in the closet? "I just was real scared."

Catherine Hearst looks over at the jury to see how they are taking her daughter's description of the dirty closet, its walls covered with old carpet. They looked concerned but deadpan.

Patty's cheek was sore; she had no wristwatch and only the blue bathrobe to wear. An hour or two passes, she thinks, before they opened the door.

Who opened it? Cinque. Was he the only black person in this group? Yes. What did he say to you? He said that they were the SLA and that I was going to be held as a prisoner of war. I'd be safe as long as their comrades Remiro and Little were. He said if I made a noise they would hang me from the ceiling. Nancy Ling Perry and Angela Atwood were standing outside the closet. They said I was a bourgeois, and it didn't matter if I got killed or not.

But of course the real bourgeois was not Patricia Hearst; it was the SLA itself. Of the group's eleven known members (including Remiro and Little), all were white and all were in their mid-twenties except for Donald DeFreeze, who was thirty-one. Only Joe Remiro, Mexican-Italian from San Francisco, could conceivably be termed working class. DeFreeze was really underclass. Again with the exception of DeFreeze, all were highly educated, although Remiro's education after high school had taken the form of on-the-job training in Vietnam, where he had acquired invaluable practical experience as a combat grunt in a long-range reconnaissance platoon, engaging in one-to-one killing and taking part in numerous search-and-destroy missions during two combat tours. But all of the others, save Willie Wolfe, were at least college graduates—several held advanced degrees—and Wolfe was a prep-school–educated National Merit Scholarship finalist who had abandoned his studies in astronomy and archaeology to work full time for the cause of prison reform.

DeFreeze was a product of the black ghettos of Detroit and Los Angeles, but all the others came from suburbs and small towns. Their parents were professional people from traditional, stable families in which the mother was homemaker; the father, provider. Angela Atwood was the daughter of a New Jersey Teamster official. She had originally come to California from Indiana University, along with Emily and William Harris. Harris was another Vietnam vet and the son of a career army officer. The former Emily Schwartz was the daughter of an Illinois insurance executive. Russell Little, from Pensacola, Florida, was the son of a middle-level aerospace executive. Nancy Ling Perry was the daughter of a furniture dealer in Santa Rosa, California, and a former high-school cheerleader and Goldwater girl. Patricia Soltysik was the daughter of two pharmacists from Goleta, California, and bisexual. One of her lovers was DeFreeze. Another was Camilla Hall. Willie Wolfe (*Cujo*) was a doctor's son from Pennsylvania and, at twenty-three, the youngest of the group.

The young of the human species take longer to mature than any other animal, and a nest is needed in which to rear them. The best nest is the family, nuclear or extended, and marriage stabilizes the nest. By the mid-1970s unprecedented numbers of Americans were on the loose. Makeshift nests were needed, and almost anything would do. The proliferation of communes, counterculture families, intense brother-hoods such as the Moonies, and depraved grotesqueries like the Manson Family—all were expressions of the need to create substitutes for the crumbling nest. One substitute was a style of intense communal living long practiced in Berkeley, which produced the SLA.

Assuredly the SLA was an extended family. Its members cared for one another in a multitude of changing patterns. Their shared and shifting love was something far more important and integral than merely having to "take care of one another's sexual needs within the cell," as one of their interminable writings had it. It was love on the run, love on the lam, love in a pressure cooker, love on the barricades, love all mixed up with political passion and suicidal despair, love born of broken hearts and cracking minds—for all of them the most intense emotional experience of their short lives.

Certain parallels with the Manson Family suggest themselves. In each case a group of women is clustered around a sexually hyperactive male. In each there is a tinge of diabolism, or at any rate cobra worship. Both groups were preparing for the Apocalypse. Both anticipated race war and attempted in different ways to precipitate it—the Manson Family by initiating what they called "helter-skelter," killing whites and trying to make it appear as if it had been done by blacks in order to bring down reprisals, and the SLA by killing a respected black civil-rights leader, a deed that by some pathological political miscalculation they thought would cause the ghetto people to rise up.

A striking difference between the Manson girls and the SLA women was that whereas the Manson girls were strays and family rejects, the bewildered SLA mothers and fathers all were remarkably supportive, loyal, and loving parents.

Although there is no doubt that Manson led his family, there has been considerable speculation about the role of Cinque. He was the leader of the whites but also their captive. He was their pet nigger as well as their essential nigger. Yet he made the tactical decisions, which were invariably disastrous as well as weird. After the robbery, when it became necessary to "break out of the massive pig encirclement" in the Bay Area, the Field Marshal moved his group to his home turf—Los Angeles. No other SLA member would have led them to that dead end.

Patty had been in her closet about twenty-four hours, she is saying, when Cinque returned and told her she was in People's prison. Patty is breathing with difficulty, panting for air, as she says, "They accused my parents of crimes against the People. They said I could be tried for the crime of my parents."

The Court of the People was going to try you for the crimes of your folks, is that it? Yes.

Did Cinque interrogate you? Yes. The conversation lasted several hours. What kinds of things did he want to know? About my family. ". . . the names of my sisters, where they lived, where my parents owned property, how old they were, about the Hearst Corporation . . ."

Patty, did you know very much about the structure of the Hearst Corporation or your parents' holdings at the time you were kidnapped? No.

Golden Gate, which was actually the SLA's second hideout, although we went there first, the jurors saw a closet five feet long, one foot seven inches deep, and seven feet high. Each juror went inside it and examined the rest of the apartment as well. Unfortunately the place had been renovated after the SLA left it in a rubble of dirt, slime, graffiti, and cockroaches, and the landlord had replaced the closet door, removed the doorknobs, and repainted. In Daly City they saw the closet off the rear bedroom, two feet deep and five and a half feet long, where Patty lived for the first month. Each juror again went inside the closet and then viewed the bathroom. This was all the jury saw, presumably because it was all that Patty saw during her confinement. Patty had been reluctant to go on the tour at all and started crying as soon as she saw the first closet.

Tuesday, February 17

Today will be Patty's worst ordeal yet. She will have to tell all the rest of her story again, this time to the jury. Over the three-day weekend, Bailey has flown his jet to Seattle and Los Angeles, addressed a meat-packer's convention, and conducted a legal seminar. He cannot relax, cannot slow down. He is smoking maybe forty Benson & Hedges a day and drinking maybe ten highballs—usually scotch and sodas at night, Bloody Marys or margaritas at noon. His weight worries him, and he puts saccharin in his morning coffee. His belly bulges more than he likes over the waistband of the eight brand-new suits he has brought to San Francisco. But in court his tension does not show at all.

On the witness stand, Patty is explaining why in her very first taped message she warned authorities not to rush in and try to rescue her. By then the SLA had told her that the FBI had stormed a house in Oakland looking for her, and that if the SLA *had* been inside, Patty would already be dead.

It is time now to play the second tape, received four days later. Johnson throws the switch, and we hear, "I would like to emphasize that I *am* alive. I'm well. I'm fine. It's not a racial issue, it's a political issue. . . . I am being held as a prisoner of war. . . . I am not being starved, beaten, or tortured. . . ."

The real Patty looks as if she were now suffering all three of these abuses. She dabs at her eyes with Kleenex. "Mom should get out of that black dress. As long as the FBI doesn't come busting in on me . . . that is my biggest worry . . . I think I can get out of here alive."

Bailey reminds us that the tape's "not unreasonable" demands—$70 worth of free food for every poor person in California—add up to $400 million. He asks Patty about the circumstances under which the tape was made. "Cinque came into the closet. . . . He had notes. . . ." She has again begun to weep.

Can Patty remember anything of significance that occurred between the making of the second and the third tapes? She looks briefly bewildered and upset; then she understands the question. "Okay. They got real mad because my father was going to give two million dollars. They said he was just playing with my life. They said he could just write it all off."

On February 20, on a third tape, Cinque said that Hearst's $2 million was "an act of throwing a few crumbs to the people and forcing them to fight over it." The jury hears Cinque list the Hearsts' holdings: a silver mine and thousands of acres of land in Mexico, land in Hawaii, 70,000 acres of timberland in northern California, a cattle ranch near San Luis Obispo, orange groves in Florida, rice paddies near Sacramento, and homes in Hillsborough, New York, and San Diego, each valued at well over half a million dollars. Then comes the personal stock portfolio—large interests in IBM, Exxon, Safeway Stores, United Airlines, Hughes Airways, drug companies, paper companies, lumber companies, cattle ranches. There is a huge collection of antique paintings, Cinque says, in addition to Chinese screens and Greek pottery, including a group of twenty-four vases valued at $10,000 each; a collection of valuable Oriental rugs given Hearst by his friend the Shah of Iran; other gifts from friends like Howard Hughes. . . . The Hearst Foundation is a tax loophole for the Hearst fortune. The $1.5 million that by now has been promised to the SLA from the foundation is but 50 percent of what the foundation is legally required to give away anyhow in order to maintain its tax-exempt status.

Can any of this be believed? I don't know. Now Cinque begins to list the assets of the Hearst Corporation: "Annual profits of $78 million a year from *Cosmopolitan* magazine," for example. *That's* absurd, I know. But how about the next part? "Mr. and Mrs. Hearst have a personal fortune of hundreds and hundreds of millions of dollars." Is this whole tape an absurd Ali Baba fantasy, or is it at least partly true?

Sixteen years after Grandfather Hearst's death, *Forbes* magazine estimated the total assets of his estate as "well over the $500 million mark, and approaching $1 billion in the estimable future." It was to protect all this from the depredations of the tax men and the possible folly of his heirs that the Pharaoh of San Simeon invented the Hearst Family Trust, a sort of charitable foundation run by thirteen trustees, of whom no more than five—according to the terms of the will—may be members of the Hearst family. Randolph Hearst is chairman of the Hearst Family Trust; his brother William is president. The trust holds all the voting stock of the Hearst Corporation; the trustees elect the corporation's board of directors, largely from their own ranks. Until the trust is dissolved, upon the death of the last surviving son or grandchild who was alive in 1951 (when the Pharaoh died), the will states, the trustees are independently in control of the fortune and family members are employees of the trust. The corporation, run by professional managers, owns and controls the great wealth, not the individual Hearsts. In sum, the whole thing is a tax shelter more gorgeous than San Simeon itself, and as its assets continue to multiply in near-perfect fiduciary hygiene, they could guarantee the Hearst heirs the largest family fortune in history. The arrangement led the SLA to claim that Patty's parents were figures of Midas-like wealth, and it led the Hearsts, equally afflicted with tunnel vision, though looking down a different tunnel, to claim they didn't really have very much money at all and were not a great deal better off than their Hillsborough neighbors.

In the courtroom the tape continues to spin. Cinque is now demanding a total of $6 million in ransom, all of it to be used for the purchase of top-quality food at wholesale prices. No supermarket must make a profit off the poor. Cinque sounds passionate but stoned. The jury seems numb. Judge Carter appears to be fast alseep.

This tape was made after Patty had been in the closet about fifteen days, she says, with little hope of getting out. "I mean, I mostly thought I would be killed."

The SLA told her it intended to demand a prisoner exchange with Remiro and Little. "Did you have any hope the authorities would release these men?" asks Bailey.

"I hoped they would, but I knew they wouldn't."

You've told us you were blindfolded at all times except when you were allowed to bathe. How often was that? "I think once a week." When her blindfold was removed, the light hurt her eyes. Her hands looked huge and distorted. The bath mat seemed to be moving. As she describes this Patty's hands flutter rapidly, as if she were doing a newscast for the deaf.

One day Cinque told Patty that the War Council was thinking about offering *her* a chance to fight for the People, too. Her alternative? To die. Here Patty's voice breaks, and she is unable to continue.

The third tape was made on the day before Patty's twentieth birthday. After it was received and broadcast, the prisoner was told repeatedly that "my parents weren't doing anything except trying to humiliate people and trying to provoke the SLA to kill me. . . . They were throwing the food at the people, distributing garbage. . . ."

It is now time to play the fourth tape. The SLA has been thinking of putting Patty into a "strip cell" like the ones in which Remiro and Little are confined on death row in "San Quentin Concentration Camp." Saxbe's statement that the FBI should burst in and get Patty, even if it meant killing her, "was no slip of the tongue, but was in reality a prematurely exposed government policy decision."

When it is Patty's turn, one hears a new firmness and bitterness in her voice. On this fourth tape one seems to hear the personalities of Patty and Tania speaking almost in fugue:

> The SLA are not the ones who are harming me. . . . It's the FBI, along with *your* indifference to the poor. . . . I can't believe you are doing everything you can. . . . If it had been you, Mom, or you, Dad, I know that I and the rest of the family would do *anything* to get you back. . . . I'm sorry to think no one is concerned about me anymore. . . . I no longer seem to have any importance as a human being.

This part of her statement, at least, is manifestly true even now. The real Patty stares down at the tabletop, and Judge Carter snoozes as the amplified, disembodied voice booms out of the loudspeakers across the quiet courtroom.

> I hope you will not think that I have been brainwashed into saying this. Please listen to me because I am speaking from my heart. . . .

By now nearly all the reporters watching her believe Patty's story. The tears, the gaunt face, make disbelief impossible. But for some reason— perhaps the reporters are being overly "objective," struggling too hard to keep their copy clean of emotional contamination—the public still believes she's lying.

After lunch Patty describes the shotgun the SLA gave her to defend herself with. It had a cut-down barrel, a sawed-off stock, and no ammunition, and Cinque gave her lessons on how to break it down and clean it. Her only previous experience with shotguns was on a shooting trip with her father when she was thirteen.

"Did there come a time when one of the women came to you and talked to you about getting it on with someone?" Bailey asks. Yes, Angela Atwood. Where? In the closet. "She said that in the cell everybody had to take care of the needs of other people. She said I was gonna sleep with Willie Wolfe." The corners of Patty's thin mouth turn down, and she begins breathing heavily. "So I did." Wolfe came into the closet that same night.

What did he say and do? I don't remember. Did he take you out of the closet? No. He came into the closet, and he closed the door and . . . Patty's chest heaves; her breath comes in convulsive gasps, so that for a moment she cannot speak.

"Did he make you lie down on the floor?"

"Yes."

"And then what did he do?"

"Had sexual intercourse."

And one week later, did someone else come to the closet for the same purpose? Yes. Who was it? It was Cinque.

During this testimony Catherine Hearst has first covered her eyes with her hand and then, in a gesture almost Japanese in its suggestion of abject submission to grief, bent forward and buried her face in her lap. Randolph just stares woodenly ahead.

A short while later, the SLA decided to move to a new hideout, and the blindfolded prisoner was tied inside a garbage can and loaded into the trunk of a car. "Then they took it out of the car and dropped it a couple of times." "It" is Patty; she has become an object, not a human being. When they opened the garbage can, she couldn't stand up. "Then they put me in another closet." Once more she begins to weep. She remained in the second closet a few weeks, until about April 1. Patty is crying uncontrollably.

Shifting focus, Bailey takes her back to the making of the fourth tape. Did she really believe then that the FBI would murder her and blame the SLA? No, she then believed only that she might be killed accidentally in a shoot-out.

When at last Patty was brought out of the closet and her blindfold was removed, "they were all sitting around in a circle"—here Patty draws a circle on the desk top with one dainty fingertip. Camilla Hall said we needed money. Cinque said we were going to rob a bank. . . . I couldn't believe they were really going to do it."

Cinque sent people out to case banks, and when they decided on the Hibernia Bank, Patty was afraid to mention that its president was the father of her best friend, Trish, because she feared "they might kill someone just because it was the Tobins' bank."

Patty's normal weight is 105 pounds. She lost about fifteen pounds in the closet, and when she was let out, her legs were too weak for her to stand. What had you been eating? Patty furrows her brow like a little girl; she can't quite remember . . . beans and rice . . . water, coffee, tea.

Does Patty know why that particular bank was chosen? It was on a corner. It had cameras and a guard. Cinque said the guard meant the bank was less likely to have good security; his mere presence would be depended on to frighten off thieves. The cameras were important "so that everyone would know that I'd been robbing the bank." She was also "supposed to say my name and give a speech: *This is an expropriation. The money is going to be used for the Revolution.*"

Bailey now asks the court's permission to play the fifth tape, received April 3. It contains as full out a revolutionary statement from Patty as we ever get: ". . . I wrote what I am about to say. It's what I feel. I've never been forced to say anything on tape, nor have I been brainwashed, drugged, tortured, hypnotized, nor in any way confused." Because we know that Patty's entire defense is based on the opposite contention— that she *was* brainwashed—these phrases sound like code, as if Patty were deliberately attempting to suggest the opposite of what her words in fact say. "Mom, Dad, I would like to comment on your efforts to supposedly secure my safety." As the voice on tape accuses the Hearsts of deception one can see the face in the witness box literally turn gray. Gray with shame, I wonder, or in dread of what is to come?

> I have been given a choice of being released in a safe area or joining the forces of the Symbionese Liberation Army and fighting for my freedom and the freedom of all oppressed people. I have chosen to stay and fight.

The voice rolls on. Before us sits a classical image of suffering, dolorous beyond belief. Our lady of sorrows, gray lids downcast.

> Dad . . . tell the poor and oppressed people of this nation what the corporate state is about to do . . . Tell the people, Dad, that all lower class and at least half the middle class will be unemployed in the next three years and that the removal of the . . . unneeded people has already started. Tell them how the law-and-order programs are just a means to remove so-called violent—meaning *aware*—individuals in the community . . . in the same way that Hitler controlled the removal of the Jews from Germany.

71

The connection of these words to the weeping, suffering child in the witness box is absurd. The rhetoric is all Tania now, and she is rallying the black prisoners.

> If I'm feeling down, I think of you. . . . We are learning together, I in an environment of love, and you in one of hate in the belly of the fascist beast. . . . Greetings to Death Row Jeff, Al Taylor, Raymond Scott [three black convict SLA sympathizers]. . . . We share a common goal as revolutionaries! It is in the spirit of Tania that I say: *Patria o muerte. Venceremos!*

Watching the defendant listening to the paranoid and pivotal fifth tape has been extremely painful because Patty's suffering is so apparent.

Cinque planned the robbery. Emily Harris and Camilla Hall rented the cars. The robbers had a number to use when communicating with one another. "Cinque was number one, Patricia Soltysik was number two, number three was Nancy Ling Perry, four was William Harris, five was William Wolfe, six was Emily Harris, seven was Angela Atwood, eight was Camilla Hall, and I was number nine." Bailey and Johnson must have carefully rehearsed this part of her testimony. It is important that in the jurors' minds every bit of responsibility for planning and carrying out the crimes with which she is charged be placed firmly on shoulders other than her own.

"Okay. Did Cinque tell you why he wanted you inside the bank?"

Her answer sounds like a country-and-western song title. "He Wanted Me to Be Wanted by the FBI."

Patty has a cold and speaks in a soft, hoarse monotone. When she got out of the closet, Patty saw that the other SLA members were always armed and that the apartment had a large closet chock-full of weapons, gas masks, ammunition, and wigs and disguises of all kinds. Patty was shown the guns and taught how to "field strip," clean, and fire the carbine she would carry. It is as startling to hear this delicate young woman talk knowingly about weaponry as it had been earlier to hear her speak with authority about radical politics.

Bailey has asked Patty and the jury to watch the bank film again. So once more we see the defendant and her comrades skitter silently across the polished marble floors. Bailey directs the witness's attention to film frames 19 and 20, where Patty is squarely positioned in front of Camera A. What were Patty's instructions? To get into a crouch, move around, keep my balance, shift from leg to leg, and "if anybody in the area moved, to shoot to kill."

Bailey now proposes to show the film in close-up and slow motion, and he will ask Miss Hearst to describe four of her actions in more detail: one, she looks at her wrist; two, she looks down at something; three, her mouth "comes open"; and four, can she identify the frame in the film where she says the word "Tania"? So we watch it all for the fifth time. Patty cannot explain the wrist motion; she doesn't remember if she was wearing a watch. Opening her mouth was a reaction to the gunfire. "I remember seeing the man get shot, his coat rip open—" She is very near to tears again. Bailey asks the clerk for exhibit 19, then walks over to the box to show Patty her own carbine, its bolt only half closed, the way it was in the film. Wet-eyed, the defendant stares down at the weapon. Bailey establishes that when the bolt is not fully closed, Patty's gun could not possibly have been fired. In a Perry Mason finish to the longest day yet, he carries the gun over to the jury and draws its attention to "this silver portion right here"—the telltale partially open bolt. But my own lingering impression of the day is of two wet, round, disbelieving eyes.

Wednesday, February 18

Patty is dressed in deep Renaissance velvets the color of plums, and Bailey wears a strange new pale-green pinstripe the color of a $10,000 bill. Patty describes the gang's escape from the bank and the dividing of the spoils. The cash was split into nine equal piles so that any member of the group who got cut off from the rest would have his own funds. After each SLA shopping expedition, the money was pooled again and redivided. A more equitable redistribution of wealth could scarcely be imagined; in fact, symbiotic banking.

Last week, just before the government rested its case, the jury listened to tape no. 6 in which Patty described the bank robbery. Does she recall the part where she says Steve Weed would be foolish to think that "once freed" she would want to go see him? Yes. Were those her own words, "once freed"? No, Angela Atwood wrote every word. Bailey grins as if he has just earned the price of his suit. To him, "once freed" is a critical SLA slip; it acknowledges that Patty was *not free* when she spoke the words. Bailey returns to the "once freed" point several times both during the trial and in the after-hours briefings he holds for the press, but I doubt whether the jury grasps its significance.

He moves along to another crucial piece of that construct. Was there any talk among the SLA members that the bank robbery had made Patty a criminal and any discussion of what that might mean to the official FBI view of the case? "Cinque said that I was wanted by the FBI . . . and that I'd be shot on sight if they found me."

"Did anyone talk to you about what would happen if you surrendered or were picked up?"

"That I'd be charged with bank robbery. And be tried for it." Bailey pauses to let that one sink in.

After the robbery the SLA moved from the racially mixed neighborhood of Golden Gate to an all-black area. The eight white SLA members, wearing black greasepaint and Afro wigs, moved by daylight, carrying all their guns and bullets with them. The racial fantasies were getting out of control; the entire SLA was playing nigger now.

Patty was no longer kept in a closet, but neither was she ever allowed to go out alone. All nine members of the band slept together in the front bedroom. Several weeks passed before Cinque suddenly decided the Bay Area was no longer safe. One evening he declared that they might actually, *right then*, be surrounded by FBI agents, and they left San Francisco that very night, driving south in a caravan of vans. One, a red-and-white Volkswagen, was the vehicle later used at Mel's. In Los Angeles everybody rendezvoused "in a park or something." Nancy Ling Perry and Patricia Soltysik rented a small, shabby house in an all-black neighborhood because "Cinque wanted to get busy doing what he called *search and destroys.*"

BAILEY (*languorous*): Search and destroys? Who was to be searched, and who was to be destroyed?

"Police."

"Police! Ah. And how was he going to go about that?"

"He was going to have everybody just go out and steal a car, and do the search and destroy, and then take over a house afterwards, and stay there. And every night do that . . ." Her voice trails off.

Was she, by this time, beginning to have hope that maybe she would survive, after all? "After I got through the bank robbery, I thought I might live." But escape "didn't seem realistic anymore." It seemed more realistic at the time that the FBI would kill her and blame the SLA.

Daily gun classes and drills in how to crouch, roll, and dive continued. All this was done in anticipation of open street warfare. "Everybody was talking about the search and destroys all the time. Willie Wolfe said he couldn't wait until we could become real urban guerrillas."

The purpose of the expedition to Mel's, she now explains, was to purchase boots and heavy clothing to wear on the search and destroys. They had plenty of money, and there had been no advance plan to shoplift anything from Mel's. But Patty had been trained "that if anybody ever got in trouble, that you were supposed to fire on the people that were attacking them and help them get away."

The Harrises each carried a handgun; two carbines, a shotgun, and another handgun were in the van. Patty had a clear shot through the open window, on the driver's side. Her response "was just like a reflex, it happened so fast." She aimed for the top of the building, to avoid hitting anybody. "I pulled the trigger. . . . The gun jumped out of my hand . . . bullets hit the bushes." She recovered the weapon, emptied the clip, then picked up the semiautomatic and continued to fire.

The instant Patty opened fire, the Harrises came flying across the street, and they all took off. William Harris was "yelling at me because I didn't shoot sooner," and Patty was rolling and bouncing around in the back of the van.

At the time she saw the Harrises struggling with the clerk, did the thought of escape cross her mind? No.

"Were the other members of the SLA, other than the Harrises, still at large?"

"Yes."

"What was the penalty for failure to rescue a comrade in trouble?"

"Death."

"After the Harrises did, in fact, escape, and you were driving away in the van, did you consider at all the opportunity that might have been before you and was now gone?"

"Yes . . . I mean, I just couldn't believe I'd done what I did."

During recess the courtroom has been set up for a multimedia extravaganza: A large rear-projection screen and two color television sets will show the jury the videotape of the burning house; extra microphones have burst into bloom. But first Bailey must clear up a few points. Patty explains that she smiled at Tom Matthews because the SLA had instructed her to smile at everyone, to make her look more like her well-publicized smiling pictures. But why did she tell Matthews that she had been in the bank voluntarily, that her hands were not tied under her pea jacket, that she had not been brainwashed, and that the bank robbers had practiced how to avoid shooting one another should it be necessary to open fire? To all these questions her answer is the same: She's sure she said it, if Matthews says so, but she doesn't know why.

At the drive-in movie they set up a prearranged distress signal—a paper cup upturned on top of the movie-speaker stand. But nobody showed up to rescue them. The next morning Bill ordered Patty and Emily to steal a car. "I said I didn't want to do it. They said: 'Too bad.'" Pretending to be hitchhikers, Patty and Emily commandeered a car and kept the driver captive while they drove around most of the day, listening to the radio. In the afternoon Emily was able to buy a car, and they turned their hostage loose in Griffith Park. The three fugitives then drove to a motel across the street from Disneyland. It was early evening. Emily rented a room, and as the trio entered, Bill flipped on the television set. The shoot-out between the SLA and the cops was appearing live on the evening news.

Backstage yesterday during recess, we learn, Patty had been shown the television tape of the shoot-out, to confirm that it is the same fiery footage she had watched in the motel room. Now it will be the jury's turn. The courtroom is darkened, the film begins—people running; cops crouching, ducking and pushing back black spectators; barefoot, open-mouthed children flattening themselves back against walls; smoke and flames upstaging the palm-treed sunset; the ever-present sound of gunfire; occasional glimpses of snipers on rooftops.

On the bench, Judge Carter is biting his fingernails. Expressionless in the dim light, Patty in rusty velvet and pink silk is a diminutive Borgia queen. Her coppery hair, now grown long, is spread over her shoulders. Her face is a grim cameo in profile, lit only by reflected light from the huge video screen. Flames rise from the house. The SLA is being burned alive, barbecued in the shabby house, by an army of police who behave like Vietnam commandos. The cops run one way through the smoke, the newsmen run the other way, each heavily laden with the gear of their trade, like teams of movie extras.

The morning after the fire, five bodies charred beyond recognition, gas masks melted onto their faces, were removed from the ruins, put into plastic body bags and delivered to the coroner's office. One female corpse was found eight feet outside the house; the woman seemingly had been trying to crawl to safety. By noon the coroner had made positive identifications from dental records. Only then did Catherine and Randolph Hearst learn that their daughter was not among the victims.

The last time Patty's parents saw this film, they believed their daughter was inside the house. But when the lights go up, the Hearsts appear entirely composed. Their daughter resumes her testimony.

During the evening of May 17 the trio in the Disneyland Motel continued to watch reruns and updates of the mass cremation, and Patty heard frequent speculation that she was inside the house, being burned alive by the cops and FBI—in short, that the SLA's prophecy had come true. Patty and the Harrises remained in the motel three days, then moved north to Costa Mesa, then to a Bay Area hotel for two days, and finally to an Oakland apartment.

In Los Angeles more than a hundred cops and FBI men were searching for Patty and the Harrises; it was the start of the biggest manhunt since the one for Dillinger. Numerous "sightings" eventually were reported, from Denver to Hong Kong, as if Patty were some sort of UFO, but there were no facts. The FBI was universally mistrusted. Nobody would talk. A 1970 Gallup poll had said that 84 percent of the public had a "highly favorable" opinion of the FBI. By the time Patty Hearst disappeared public confidence in the G-men was badly eroded; by the time she was arrested the figure was down to 37 percent. HERNAP's occurring when it did put the government's credibility squarely on the line, and for nineteen months FBI Director Clarence Kelley was asked about Patty at every single news conference. By the time the case came to trial *Newsweek* estimated the FBI had spent $5 million trying to find the missing girl.

In the courtroom, Patty is describing the start of the Missing Year. Because of her continually downcast, charcoal-smudge eyes, it looks from where I sit, thirty feet away, as if a blind girl occupies the witness box. After Cinque's death William Harris assumed the leadership of the three-man "army." "I was supposed to 'struggle' with them to rebuild the SLA and be sure the people who had died had not died in vain."

The time has come to play the final tape, the long euology to the slain, which was delivered to a Los Angeles radio station three weeks after the immolations. As the tape is threaded into the machine Patty really does close her eyes. The reason soon become apparent. This message is the most emotional of them all.

Comes the familiar, breathy, Jackie Kennedy voice:

> Greetings to the People. This is Tania. Cujo was the gentlest, most beautiful man I've ever known. . . . We loved each other so much. . . . Neither Cujo nor I had ever loved an individual the way we loved each other, probably because our relationship wasn't based on bourgeois, fucked-up values. . . .

On the witness stand, Patty looks acutely uncomfortable. The eulogies sound real. Of all the tapes she made, this one must be the most excruciating to listen to, and the one she is most ashamed to repudiate.

Now she is selling out the dead. She weeps again as we hear how

> Cinque loved the people with tenderness and respect. . . . He helped
> me to see that it's not how long we live that's important, it's how we live,
> what we decide to do with our lives. . . .

The taped voice states, "On February 4th, Cinque M'Tume saved my
life. . . ." It is hard to believe that Patty did not mean these words at the
time she spoke them. The girl in the witness box is breathing heavily,
gasping for air. The jury is staring at her openly as the voice says,

> It's hard to explain what it was like watching our comrades die . . . a
> battalion of pigs facing a fire team of guerrillas, and the only way they
> could defeat them was to burn them alive. . . . The pigs probably have
> the little Olmec monkey that Cujo wore around his neck. He gave me
> the little stone face one night. . . .

Patty looks so soft and vulnerable she is more like a blurry watercolor
portrait of herself than a flesh-and-blood being. Her mother is weeping
uncontrollably, but I look away. To stare now seems indecent.

We hear again, this time from the defense point of view, how the
terrified girl, disguised in glasses and a wig, was driven cross-country by
the Scotts. It must have looked like a scene from a Thornton Wilder
play: four average Americans, all wearing spectacles, riding in a
four-door sedan, kindly-looking John Scott driving, his wife beside him,
and, sitting up straight in the back seat, the bewigged Patty and Jack.

Emily was driven east by Phil Shinnick, a friend of Scott's. Then Jack
Scott returned to the West Coast to pick up William Harris while Micki
Scott hunted for the farmhouse in which they would write the book. The
place was to be "like a writers' retreat," Scott had said.

Before leaving California, Patty was given the new name Pearl. During
these car trips or at any time at the various hideouts back East, did Pearl
ever believe she had a chance to escape or to surrender to the FBI?
Never. She thought that if she tried she would be killed. She feared not
only the government but the Harrises, who had often said that
mysterious "friends" would kill her if she disobeyed them. Pearl and the
Scotts remained a couple of months in the Scotts' New York City
apartment. Then, with the Harrises, Pearl spent several weeks at the
farmhouse near Scranton, two more months at a farm near Jeffersonville, New York, and finally returned to Scranton before heading west
again. At the Scotts' apartment Wendy Yoshimura joined the group.

Work on Scott's proposed book got under way. It was to be partly Patty/Tania/Pearl's autobiography and partly a political discussion of the aims of the SLA, which Scott found admirable. Lists of questions and answers were prepared by the Harrises, reviewed by Patty, then tape-recorded. Once transcriptions were made, the Harrises had the tapes destroyed because Patty's voice sounded "forced," and her answers to the questions were "not radical enough." Patty helped type the manuscript, penciled in some corrections, and contributed some material "in her own language" to the final draft. But the part that described her relationship with her parents is in the Harrises' language only. Patty assures the jurors she "didn't have anything to say about" these particular sentences.

At the farmhouse, Patty testifies, she and Wendy and the Harrises spent their time jogging, practicing search and destroys, running obstacle courses, rehearsing rolls and dives, and training for armed combat, using weapons owned by the Scotts. In late September or October 1974 the group headed back west, first to Las Vegas, where Scott's parents operated a motel. A year later Patty was living in San Francisco with Steve Soliah and Wendy Yoshimura.

On the morning of September 18, 1975, when Tom Padden came up the back stairs, Patty was in the kitchen doorway. "FBI. Freeze!" he yelled. "Come out or I'll blow your head off!"

"When you first heard the words 'FBI,' what did you think?"

"I thought I was dead."

Patty was arrested and put in a cell next to that of Emily Harris, who told her she'd better not talk to her lawyers or the Harrises would be charged with kidnapping, "and that better not happen, or somebody would kill me." A woman deputy filling out forms asked Patty her occupation. "I just shook my head and said I didn't have a job." But the woman said, "We have to have an occupation," so Patty replied, "Urban guerrilla." She was brought into court almost immediately, wearing the same clothing in which she'd been arrested, and was photographed in the police car, grinning and giving a raised-fist salute. Why did she do this? "Because I . . . because I knew that's what I was supposed to do."

Patty's attorneys, the Hallinans, came to her with a bail affidavit based on information obtained "from Wendy and others," and although it was incorrect, Patty signed it at the Hallinans' direction.

"Do you know why no effort has been made to get you out on bail?"

"Yes."

"Why?"

*Above left, Steven Weed,
Patty's fiancé, in 1972.
Weed later turned against
her. Below left, the tiny
confinement closet where
Patty was held captive by the
Symbionese Liberation Army.*

MICHAEL ALEXANDER

We had to ~~smash~~ the dependencies created by monogomous sexual relationships, and to do this we had to destroy monogomy in the cell. Monogomy only serves to reinforce male supremacy and the oppression of women. Monogomy means that "the men wear the pants."
We had to destroy all the attitudes that make people think that they have to be monogomous; fear and passivity, false sense of seecurity, power-trips,

The writings above were from the months before Patty's capture, and were used during the trial to cast doubt on her avowals that she was always a terrified victim of the SLA. Below, left and right, two scenes shot by the surveillance cameras at the Hibernia Bank in San Francisco, robbed by the SLA in 1974. The FBI had no doubt that the gun-carrying woman shown in both photos was Patricia Campbell Hearst, who adopted the revolutionary name of Tania.

Above left, Patty gave a clenched fist salute leaving San Mateo County Jail. Her parents, above, show strain leaving their daughter's arraignment on 11 felony charges. Below, jurors return from lunch.

The prosecutor says the question is irrelevant. Bailey says his client's present state of mind is highly relevant, and Carter agrees.

BAILEY (*repeating his question*): Why?

PATTY: Because I'd be safer in jail.

Now Bailey is asking Patty to name the doctors who examined her at the jail. "*All* of them?" she says, and Carter permits himself a prim grin. But Bailey is after the name of the first person to whom she related the events about which she has been testifying. Doctors West and Singer, she says. Did Bailey or Johnson ever interrogate her about these events *before* the West/Singer psychiatric reports were filed with the court? No. Does Patty still fear the Harrises? "Yes. I think there is a good chance I could be killed, because—"

"May we approach the bench, Your Honor," Browning interrupts. Carter dismisses the jury in order to hear a motion on a matter of evidence. The government believes the defense is about to bring up the bombing two days ago at San Simeon, as well as more recent threats made against the life of Randolph Hearst. These are events of which the jury is, and should remain, unaware, as they have no bearing on the case.

The jury certainly *should* know of the newest threats, Bailey says. On the final SLA tape William Harris endorses the very same organization that made the threats, the New World Liberation Front. San Simeon *was*, in fact, bombed, and "the usual radical garbage" aside, the NWLF communiqué attempted to extort still another quarter-million dollars from Randolph Hearst, to pay for the Harrises' defense. It also warned Patty to "stop the lying that is designed to free Miss Hearst and bury the Harrises." What does this new threat have to do with testimony on matters that occurred two years ago? Carter asks, becoming testy.

It is a typical example of the sort of thing that has terrorized his client from the day she was kidnapped by "these same people."

What "same people"? snaps the judge.

The Harrises, of course!

Browning explodes. "Can you prove any connection between the Harrises and the bombing of San Simeon?"

Whether the threat is real or not is obviously not relevant, Bailey admits. But whether Patty believes it to be real and to have been issued at the request of the Harrises in order to continue their two-year terrorization of her and her family is most certainly relevant. Further, it tends to rebut the notion Browning is trying to sell to the jury: that Patty has no fear of the Harrises.

I find the argument persuasive, but Judge Carter does not. "Mr.

Bailey, I'm not going to have this blown up out of all proportion." He decides the jury should remain ignorant of the threats.

Since the jury is still out, Browning brings up another matter: his opportunity to cross-examine Patty is fast approaching, and Mr. Bailey's direct examination "leaves out a considerable amount of time," approximately a year, during which period Browning has documents that indicate Patty was living in Sacramento and was "out casing banks with the Harrises. I want to cross-examine her on that."

"You may *not!*" Bailey fairly shouts.

But Browning says once more that he has a two-page "laundry list" of how to rob a bank, which list bears Patty's fingerprints, and he also has a record in Patty's handwriting of the actual surveillance of a specific Sacramento bank. Surely such documents are relevant to a bank-robbery case. Bailey reminds Carter that he has already ruled to exclude these documents. Carter says he'll rule again, if necessary, when the time comes, but he will not prejudge.

The jury returns, and Bailey makes a few final points. Although Patty had no intention of using the many guns found in her apartment, she kept them cleaned and loaded in case William Harris should drop by. Otherwise, "he would have started yelling and screaming." In fact, however, Harris had not dropped in. Nor had Patty ever visited the Harrises' apartment.

"Thank you," Bailey says. "That concludes direct examination."

It is late Wednesday afternoon, two days before the defendant's twenty-second birthday, and James Browning rises to cross-examine. His manner is quiet, his mode humdrum. The defense lawyers watch Patty like new owners of a thoroughbred on a strange track. It is a fast track, and the filly looks good. Browning is inquiring about a sheaf of typed papers headed "Anarchism, Trotskyism, Marxism, Leninism, and Maoism," found in Patty's bedroom. She isn't positive who typed them, but believes it was Jim Kilgore. Before she can say more, Bailey rushes to the bench for another off-the-record conference, seemingly to deter any reference in the jury's presence to the Missing Year. While the lawyers whisper Patty flashes her sisters a near-invisible smile. And when Browning again inquires about Kilgore, there is a tiny bit of spunk to Patty's reply: "I told you. I met him in Berkeley. Before I met Jack Scott." By day's end Patty has implicated twelve persons, and laid the groundwork for authorities in Alameda County to charge the Harrises with kidnapping.

Browning questions the item-by-item details of the kidnapping as they are described in the "Tania Interview." Patty acknowledges that many statements of fact in the manuscript are correct, but "the whole tone is incorrect," she says, "because it was written to show that they were nice to me and that's why I joined them."

Next Browning reminds us of the unwisdom of asking a question to which one does not know the answer. Browning presumes Patty was allowed elementary hygiene. "You *were* given a toothbrush, I take it?"

"I think it was just the toothbrush that everyone used." A compassionate shudder sweeps the courtroom. How revoltingly un-American!

I am convinced to a moral certainty and beyond reasonable doubt that Patty is one of those rare people who never, ever lies. All her life, Patty has been a literal-minded girl, and bravely, even brazenly outspoken. The trouble is that though I know Patty never lies, I am not so sure about Tania or Pearl or Pat—and one does not really know who is sitting up there in the witness box. One must be alert for cues to the reality behind the mask. One such cue is contained in Patty's answer to Browning's next question: Do you know whether there was a lock on the closet door? Yes. How do you know? "Because I tried to turn the doorknob once."

Once! The tiny word conveys, in a way that reams of lurid testimony never can, the paralyzing dread and hopelessness this girl must have felt during the month she spent sitting blindfolded, in darkness, on the closet floor while on the other side of the door the revolutionaries clicked and fired unloaded weapons, rehearsing war.

The prosecutor is reading the Hallinans' bail affidavit aloud, pausing every couple of sentences to inquire whether the statements are, in fact, correct. Many things in the affidavit admittedly are untrue: that her mind clouded, that she could comprehend only that "we will kill you," that her recollection of the time between the holdup and her arrest, seventeen months later, is "as though in a fog," that she lived in perpetual terror and could not distinguish fantasy from reality, that it was her own decision to return to San Francisco. Nonetheless, she signed the affidavit despite the penalty of perjury, is that correct? Yes.

Browning moves toward deeper waters. Cinque's sexual torments and the brainwashing itself. But first, one question about another bodily function. Would it be fair to say that the kidnapping was a terrifying experience? Yes. Yet being kidnapped did not cause Patty to wet her pants, did it? No.

What does he mean? I would interpret the fact that she wet her pants when she was captured but not when she was kidnapped as evidence of emotional deterioration. But Browning has put the question so clumsily it is not clear what his point is. Possibly the prosecutor is trying to suggest that Patty was "in on" her kidnapping without actually saying it, since he has not a shred of evidence that such was the case.

Did Cinque pinch one or both of Patty's breasts? She really doesn't remember. Browning could be much tougher with Patty, pressing for more details. But the prosecutor is evidently as eager as Patty to get this part of his cross-examination behind him, for he sails into his next question with a Freudian slip that is almost a skid. "Now, at the time you made the first tape, Miss Harris," he begins, falters, starts again, and finally brings out that when the FBI issued a warrant for Patty as a material witness, she was not sure what the FBI might do to her, but she was *certain* the SLA would kill her. Under direct examination, the importance of these two threats had become reversed; Bailey had made it appear that the FBI was Patty's chief fear.

Browning is proceeding through his cross-examination like a novice downhill racer, ankles wobbling, poles twisting, skis crisscrossing, yet somehow staying on his feet and hitting all the important markers before coming to rest. He hits a crucial marker now—namely, the sixth tape, in which Patty confesses to the robbery and says, "As for being brainwashed, the idea is ridiculous to the point of being beyond belief." These were Angela Atwood's words, right? Yes. At no time did you believe you had been brainwashed? No.

"Do you now feel that you had, in fact, been brainwashed at any time, Miss Hearst?"

"I'm not sure what happened to me."

Truer words have not been spoken in this courtroom.

Outside, after lunch, blinking in the strong sun, I see the new *San Francisco Examiner* headline: PATTY TELLS OF SLA RAPES. Once more Bailey has scored in his "other trial": he has got the word "rape" into the headlines, and into the barroom and bus-stop debates about the case, without ever once using it in court.

The girl is going to need all the help she can get. This afternoon the moment everybody has been dreading will arrive: cross-examination on her activities during the Missing Year. First, a few preliminary questions. Browning establishes that the Hallinans got the information in the bail affidavit primarily from Wendy, but Wendy got it from the Harrises,

Patty says, not from her. Browning bears down harder. Patty has testified that when she was released from the closet, DeFreeze gave her a choice: stay and fight with the SLA, or be killed. But was it not, in fact, a choice to stay and fight with the SLA *or go home?*

"I said that's what he told me. But that was no *choice*." Patty in her frail way has acquired some of Bailey's own arrogance. "I wasn't given any *choice*. I mean, that wasn't a *choice!*"

"Why not?"

Tears again. She crumples. "Because they wouldn't have let me go."

"How do you know?"

With great bitterness: "Well, I mean, maybe I should have taken a chance." Her lawyer grins wickedly at his client's put-down of the prosecutor.

Patty's characteristic answer is monosyllabic. She almost never explains, justifies, amplifies, so when Browning asks if she contacted her parents during the Missing Year, her response is unexpected. "No. Because . . . because I felt if my parents—" Tears come stronger.

"Pardon me?"

"I felt my parents wouldn't want to see me again." This is said with tremendous pain.

Browning is cross-examining the witness like an angry parent trying to deal with a naughty child who refuses to admit wrongdoing. Finally, he forces out the truth. Patty feared that if she wrote to her parents, they would have notified the FBI, and if the Harrises in turn had found this out, they would have killed her. Now Catherine Hearst begins to cry—moved by compassion or remorse, one is not sure. The fact is, Catherine *did* notify the FBI at every turn.

Yes, Patty and Wendy had had a falling out with the Harrises and, no, Patty did not fear Wendy. Or Steve Soliah, with whom she was living at 625 Morse Street when she was arrested. Where had she been previously residing?

"Object!" Bailey is on his feet. Judge Carter invites the jury to leave.

Bailey says he has advised Patty not to discuss the events of the Missing Year because they might be used to incriminate her in another proceeding. "She has a right to refuse to answer to avoid incriminating herself . . . and I have asked for an order that the prosecutor not knowingly provoke the Fifth Amendment claim in the presence of the jury."

Carter offers the U.S. attorney an opportunity to interrogate the witness now, out of the presence of the jury, and the offer is quickly accepted. Browning asks Patty where she went after Las Vegas. Bailey advises her not to answer.

CARTER: On what grounds, Miss Hearst?

"On the grounds that it may incriminate me."

So there it is. The fatal words are out.

Browning attempts to frame his question in different ways, to no avail. Each time, she replies, "I refuse to answer on grounds I may incriminate myself." As the litany goes on, I reflect on what a relief it must be to a beleaguered witness *not* to have to think.

While the jury is out Browning would like to discuss other evidence the defense objects to. He has a huge mass of documents taken from the two apartments that he wishes to have marked for identification and put into evidence, pending Carter's ruling. He holds up a green notebook, "containing handwriting and a list of answering and mailing services." Does Patty recognize it?

"I refuse to answer on the grounds that I may incriminate myself."

With Bailey at her side to coach her, she says the same words eighteen more times as other notebooks, several money orders, hand-drawn maps, book lists, and so on are presented for her identification. "Refuse to answer . . . Refuse to answer." As the Fifth Amendment litany drones on, Patty begins to giggle. Finally, she is giving rote answers without even bothering to look at the government's captured documents.

Patty takes the Fifth on all but one—the cassette of her jail conversation with Trish Tobin, taped two days after her capture.

The judge doesn't believe he can examine all the evidence and rule on it before Monday. "You just threw a big package at me."

"The FBI threw a big package at *me!*" says Browning.

This irritates Carter, who sees it as a ploy to try to question Patty on the evidence before he has had time to examine and rule on it. "Stop playing ring-around-the-rosy! The buck stops here!" he barks. Still spluttering, Carter orders the jury brought back.

Browning now retraces Patty's movements that summer between the two farm hideouts, in Pennsylvania and upstate New York, and then the ride back cross-country to Las Vegas, emphasizing her many opportunities to call for help. But, when the prosecutor asks where in Las Vegas Scott dropped her off, Bailey lunges at the bench like a guard dog. Browning withdraws his question and moves to the matter of the final tape. " 'Cujo was the gentlest, most beautiful man I have ever known,' " he reads again. " 'Neither Cujo nor I had ever loved an individual the way we loved each other.' " Now, in fact, did you have a strong feeling for Cujo? In a way, yes. Did you love him? No. I believe that you testified that he raped you. That's right. When was that, Miss Hearst? While I was in the closet at the Daly City house, after I'd been there about a month. Was anybody else around aware of what was going on? In a flat voice: "As far as I knew, everybody was aware of it."

Was it a forcible rape? He gets no answer and repeats, "Was it a forcible rape? Did you struggle? Or did you submit because of fear?"

"I didn't resist. No."

"And why didn't you? . . . Was it because you were afraid?"

Bailey pounds his fist on the table. He finds this question outrageous. Browning says he merely wanted to get her fear on the record before inquiring whether she *later* developed a strong affinity for Wolfe. "You answered my earlier question, Miss Hearst, that it's sort of correct that you thought highly of him. Can you enlarge?"

"She didn't say that!" Bailey shouts, and simultaneously Patty says, "I didn't say that at all!"

"Well, what did you say?"

"I said I had a strong feeling for him."

"Well, what was that feeling?"

Browning has walked right into it. "*I couldn't stand him!*" Spectators gasp at Patty's audacity, her ferocity, and Browning's bum luck. Spasms of glee shake the defense table. Only in retrospect does it occur to me that Patty's outburst may have been a cheap Bailey plant, though I'm not sure how he could have set it up.

It has been a rough day for Jim Browning. Every Perry Mason fan knows that a lawyer never asks a witness a question to which he does not already know the answer. Browning has violated this rule with such abandon that he has frightened the defense. "He must have a couple of bombs we don't know about," mutters a young defense investigator as we adjourn.

Friday, February 20

When Patricia Hearst was kidnapped, she was nineteen years old. She spent her twentieth birthday bound and blindfolded in a closet. We don't know about the twenty-first birthday; that one occurred during the Missing Year. But this morning, when she awoke on the lower iron bunk of a bare cell in the San Mateo County Jail, it was her third birthday as a captive. At daybreak a bomb threat was phoned to the jail, so the jailers varied the routine and drove Patty to the courthouse an hour early. But at ten o'clock sharp the questioning gets under way as usual. Browning is still hammering at her many chances to escape or call for help. She cannot recall the names of towns or motels, whether Scott bought gas with cash or credit cards. She wasn't allowed to visit rest rooms. Yes, she was alone in the motel rooms while Scott shaved and showered. What places did they stop at on the return trip? "One was . . . I think . . . Cheyenne, Wyoming?"

Patty did guard duty at Golden Gate, just like the other SLA members, "so to a large degree, you *were* active. You *convinced* them you were a part of the SLA. . . . Are you a good actress, would you say?"

Bailey objects to the question, but is overruled.

"Are you good at acting, Miss Hearst?"

"Not particularly."

"Are you acting now?"

"*I object to that!*" Bailey yells. His sudden ferocity frightens me and scares hell out of his client, but the judge merely says mildly, "I'll sustain that objection. Proceed, Mr. Browning."

Comes now a discussion of the words scrawled on a wall at Golden Gate: PATRIA O MUERTE, VENCEREMOS. TANIA—"My country or death. We shall overcome." Yes, she wrote this, but only because she had been told to. That was the way the real Tania, the mistress of Che Guevera and a left-wing heroine, signed her letters.

You were acting the part of a bank robber, were you not? I did exactly what I had to do, sure. And you wanted to convince them, did you not, that you were one of them? I guess so, yes. Didn't they give you any extra ammunition? Well, I knew there was more ammo in the car outside. When you looked down at your weapon in the bank, you saw the bolt was open and turned, so that the gun wouldn't fire, didn't you? But you also knew, didn't you, that "in order to correct that condition, one would simply pull back the bolt and let it go forward?" Loud, metallic snap from exhibit 19.

Patty does not react to the sound, saying only, "I just wanted to get out of that bank." But *why* didn't she correct the half-open, inoperative position of the bolt? Wasn't she afraid of being punished if her weapon was in an inoperative state? "Because it didn't make any difference. I was in there just to get my picture taken. . . ." And if it had been necessary for you to fire some shots, too, as you did down in Mel's Sporting Goods in Los Angeles a month later, you would have had to do that, wouldn't you? No. No? Well, what was the difference?

Well, if anything had happened at that bank or any other time . . .

Patty stops to take a breath, then bursts out, "I was always their ticket to get out of anything!" Tears come from her in freshets. "I . . . was . . . a *hostage*."

Browning moves on to the mysterious subject of the wigs. If Patty was in the bank primarily to be recognized and have her picture taken, why did they first cut off her hair and then outfit her in a wig a different color from her own hair? Dully, she says she doesn't know.

Back to the captured documents, including one explaining why two bank customers were shot. "Because of our inexperience, we had some pretty rigid ideas about the amount of force necessary to control twenty or more persons inside a bank. Inflexibility is one of the hazards of inexperience." The last sentence is in Patty's handwriting.

Yes, Patty wrote it, but Emily dictated it. Why would she bother to dictate? . . . You wrote this on your own volition, now, didn't you?

"No. They asked me to write it."

Browning is dogged; he almost has the rabbit in his teeth. The captured document says the SLA had expected more trouble from the bank's employees than from its customers. "That part is true, isn't it?" Yes. And when the document moves into Q.-and-A. form and asks, "Why did you decide to rob a bank?" there is an interlineated answer, in Patty's handwriting, which Browning asks her to read.

"You want me to *read* it?" She is crying heavily now. Yes. " 'There were two reasons. We needed the money, and we wanted to illustrate that Tania was alive, and her decision wasn't a bunch of bullshit.' "

"Now, these words were written by you . . . and they are factual, are they not?"

"No, they're not."

Not factual! In what way are they not factual? The prosecutor is most puzzled. Amid floods of tears, Patty says, yes, it's her handwriting and, yes, the SLA needed money, but "talking about the fact that I'd made a decision to join the SLA" is not factual.

Mercifully, Judge Carter now says it's time for a recess.

When we return, we learn the fugitives spent two months at an abandoned creamery in Jeffersonville, making tapes for Scott's book. But after the tapes were made and transcribed, the tapes were burned because the Harrises decided they didn't like them, and the back sides of the original transcriptions were used as scratch paper. Presumably, these are the pages that contain evidence that Patty was the most militant of the three SLA survivors and of the new recruits they attracted—the group Bailey calls the Second Gang.

91

It is nearly noon, and Browning is asking for an early recess. The morning has passed with surprising swiftness. In the corridor Randy looks weary and defeated, but Catherine seems eager to talk, and buttonholes me. "My daughter is incredibly strong," she says. "If she weren't telling the truth, she couldn't be so strong. She's willing to testify against *all* those people! Why don't they indict the Harrises for kidnapping my daughter?"

This evening, on television, Catherine says she hopes that at least she and Patty can spend Patty's next birthday together and points out that her daughter has now spent ten percent of her life in custody.

The next big problem for the defense is the Trish Tobin tape, the one made while the two girls were smiling at each other through bulletproof glass. The buggers were within their rights; only attorney-client jailhouse conversations are privileged, and all jails are bugged. Whether the Hallinans failed to warn Patty or whether she was so glad to see Trish she didn't care what she said; whether she was foolish, or was a defiant and committed revolutionary, or was so "brainwashed," so self-destructive, or so traumatized by what had befallen her since her kidnapping, nineteen months earlier, that she was unaware of what she was saying—one doesn't know. But Patty said a great number of things to her friend that would be very damaging for this jury to hear, and her lawyers intended to try like hell to keep the Trish Tobin tape out of court.

First the jury is sent out, and then Al Johnson moves to exclude the Trish Tobin tape from evidence on two grounds: It is an unlawful invasion of his client's privacy, and an FBI report just filed with the court implies that the tape may have been tampered with. The prosecution has a counterproposal: Until the judge rules, Browning would just like to ask Patty *about* her conversation with Trish; he will make no reference in front of the jury to the existence of an actual tape. But Carter isn't buying. "Human memory is a frail thing . . . this is why we say the written document speaks for itself." He will rule Monday and meanwhile will brook no more argument from the government.

The jury is brought back, and Miss Hearst resumes the stand. After the fire the three SLA survivors stayed two nights in a hotel in the middle of San Francisco, then went to Oakland, and finally moved to an empty Berkeley flat. Patty describes a life of perpetual terror, lived among people who were always armed, dangerous, and on the run. She dared not make even an anonymous phone call. If she were rescued from the Harrises, unknown SLA sympathizers could have killed her.

The Harrises "weren't the only people running around who are like that. There were many others who could have picked up where they left off, and if they'd wanted me dead, all they had to do was say so."

What led you to believe the Harrises had this great power over your life? What caused you to believe that if they were safe in police custody—if you'd turned them in—they could simply, by the snap of their fingers, turn around and have you killed?

"It's happening like that now on the streets."

"What do you mean, Miss Hearst?"

Suddenly Browning sees the trap ahead and attempts to withdraw his question. Bailey is on his feet, shouting, "He's asked the question! Let's have an answer!"

Smiling thinly, the judge agrees.

PATTY (*exultant*): San Simeon was bombed! My life was threatened if I took the witness stand! My parents received a letter! *Their* lives were threatened if I took the stand! And they demanded a quarter of a million dollars for the Harrises' defense fund!

The courtroom is in an uproar. Our heroine has come through and done it all by herself. She has given the tightly sequestered jury just the news they need; she has told them what Bailey wants them to hear more than anything else in the world—that terrorists are still around, to this day, *still* bombing, blackmailing, destroying property, extorting money, threatening death, and striking fear into the hearts of decent citizens. Patty has just given herself her own best possible birthday present.

WEEK FIVE

Monday, February 23

This is a critical day. The judge has ruled that the government may question Patty about the entire period between her kidnapping and her arrest because Patty herself opened it up when she voluntarily took the stand and gave testimony about the events at both ends of that period. He has also ruled to admit the Trish Tobin tape. The law is clear, he says, that a person in jail has no right of privacy, and the tape itself bears evidence that Patty knew her conversation was being monitored. The effect on the defense is incalculable but vast—a terrible blow.

I take my assigned seat. Bailey is arguing that Patty took the stand only because Carter forced her to.

CARTER: Mr. Bailey, nobody made her take the witness stand.

BAILEY: If you are creating the rule that everybody who chooses to defend himself the only way he can in a charge must therefore incriminate himself *ad infinitum,* that is simply something we have to discover at a higher level.

CARTER: Mr. Bailey, don't argue about it. I have ruled.

Bailey drops back to his second line of defense: the physical jeopardy of Patty and her family, proved by fresh threats and extortion attempts within the past seventy-two hours.

Carter is losing patience. "Mr. Bailey, I will deny your motion. You can go to the Ninth Circuit, if you desire. Have at it!"

At 10:55 A.M. the jury is marched in, totally unaware that a big scene is about to begin. Carter directs Patty back into the witness box. Bailey is right beside her. Browning's questions begin. Where in Las Vegas did Jack Scott drop her off?

"I refuse to answer on the grounds that it may tend to incriminate me and cause extreme danger to myself and my family."

Physical danger is not a legal basis for refusing to answer, Browning says. Judge Carter warns that if Patty persists in her refusal, he will have to cite her for contempt of court. "You should answer," he says.

Where did Scott drop her off? I refuse to answer. Who met you there? I refuse to answer. How long were you in Las Vegas? I refuse to answer. She refuses to answer questions about what happened or where she lived after Las Vegas, who was with her, what her relationship was with James Kilgore, Steven Soliah, or Kathy Soliah. Were any of these people members of the New World Liberation Front? "I don't know." She is coached in all her answers by Bailey, at her side. Questions about a hospital visit for treatment of poison oak during the Missing Year. Refuse to answer. About various retrieved documents—phony identification cards, notebooks, manuscripts, money orders. Refuse to answer. Bailey and Johnson are both beside Patty now, three heads together. The jury for the first time is not afraid to look directly at the press, not afraid to smile. One fears that what animates them is the sniff scent of guilt in the chamber. In all, Browning asks more than sixty questions and gets forty-two refusals.

This part of the ordeal is at an end, but there is still the matter of Patty's conversation with Trish Tobin. Browning reads from the transcript of this tape, in which Patty tells her friend she will make no statements until she can get out on bail. But the tape itself is a statement and, for one in her circumstances, a colossal indiscretion. Upon her release, she will speak in "a revolutionary feminist perspective totally. . . . I guess I will just tell you my politics are real different from way back when. Obviously. [Laughter.] Right. And so this creates all kinds of problems for me in terms of a defense."

In redirect Bailey will attempt to demolish Browning's just-built palace of perfect guilt. Had Emily indicated to Patty what "posture" the group would take during their trial? Yes, lots of "jumping up, clench-fisting all over the place, shouting and defiance . . ." In other words, they would be revolutionaries to the end, right? And that's what Patty meant when she told Trish she was having difficulties with her defense? Yes. Furthermore, the transcript of the Trish Tobin tape is incomplete and Bailey manages to raise reasonable doubt, at least in my mind, about the integrity of the tape: It *may* have been doctored. Last Friday, Patty testified she was still in fear of the Harrises and others. "Do you know if the other people you fear are incarcerated?"

"No, they're not."

Bailey reminds the jury of the threats to the Hearsts and the bombing of San Simeon, and asks if there have been other bombings since. Browning demands the jury be sent out before Bailey makes his offer of proof. Then we learn of another explosion. Last night the New York City offices of the Hearst magazines were bombed. The jury is brought back and informed of the latest bombing. Browning and Bailey have another whispered bench conference with the judge. It is extraordinary how much of the script for this drama we are watching is known to the principals only—to Patty, the lawyers, and the judge. If I am as bewildered as I am, the jury must be utterly baffled.

No one can judge at this point how damaging Patty's Fifth Amendment pleadings have been or how much credibility Bailey will be able to recover when his battery of psychiatric big guns finally opens up.

One phase of this trial is at an end. The jury has heard most of the facts—what did, or did not, happen to Patty/Tania/Pearl/Pat—few of which are in dispute. Now we are to hear the important part, at least according to the defense: not the *whats* but the *whys*. It is time for Commodore Bailey to go into action with his big guns. The first of these is Louis Jolyon West, MD, the bulky, genial, fair-headed, fatherly-looking man who now rises, buttons his jacket, picks up his briefcase, and crosses gravely to the witness stand. His professional credentials fill ten pages in the monumental West/Singer report. Today he lists only the high spots, which is like listing the high spots of the Himalayas. Dr. West is professor of psychiatry at UCLA, chairman of his department and psychiatrist-in-chief of UCLA Hospitals.

Bailey's questions begin on a historical note. During the Korean War, he reminds us, a number of the American pilots shot down over North Korea broadcast on Chinese radio that they had been engaging in germ warfare. This was untrue, and as an Air Force medical officer Dr. West's assignment had been to learn how the Chinese had produced these results in the captured pilots and to figure out what could be done to help future airmen resist these techniques. Systematic torture, hypnosis, and drugs—the traditional means of persuading a captive to change his mind or his testimony—had not been used. Yet of fifty-nine pilots who got the full Chinese treatment—whatever it was—thirty-six broke down completely. Dr. West and his colleagues identified a new triple-threat technique, which they labeled DDD—debility, dependency, and dread. "Debility" meant that the subject was allowed to become physically weak and run down but not dangerously ill. His "dependency" was enforced by making him turn to his captors for every comfort, for food, for his toilet needs. His "dread" was compounded of his fear of torture and death, and fear of reprisals to his family. To get the DDD process off to a quick start, the Chinese used "forceful interrogation"—rapid-fire endless questions to which the interrogator already seemed to know the answers. Isolation was also a factor in this initial phase, intensified by darkness.

BAILEY: Doctor, have you ever heard the term "brainwashing"?
WEST: Yes, I have.

"Is that a term of any medical significance?" No. The literal meaning of brainwashing is "cleaning of the mind." Another common term is "thought reform," meaning political indoctrination accomplished without physical coercion. But the best term for forceful interrogation designed to produce compliant behavior is "coercive persuasion."

The signs that one has been subjected to coercive persuasion are "a marked degree of anxiety and pressure and an inability to deal with reality." Finally, Bailey says, "Dr. West, do you know the defendant, Patricia Hearst?"

Asking permission to refer to his notes, the psychiatrist says he first met Miss Hearst on September 30, 1975, and examined her thereafter for a total of twenty-three hours. His associate, Dr. Margaret Singer, whose experience also includes many Army studies on prisoners of war, spent seventeen hours with Patty. What were West's clinical observations of the defendant when they first met?

She was pale, very thin, with a strained facial expression, frightened and obviously on her guard. She had no complaints, however, and rather cheerfully showed the doctor her tiny cell. "But as soon as I asked her for any information about her previous nineteen-month experience, she would begin to cry, her eyes were downcast, her voice became almost inaudible, her pulse went up to a hundred and forty, she broke out into a clammy sweat, and she became pale around her nose and mouth." He believed he was watching "a person reexperiencing a profound fear. She could not remember things clearly. She had patchy amnesia."

Can Dr. West tell from a person's answers to a battery of standard psychological tests whether that person is trying to feign mental illness? Yes, he can, and Patty exhibited no such signs whatever. On that note we recess for the day.

Tuesday, February 24

West tells the jury that Patty's unusual degree of freedom previous to her kidnap made her more vulnerable to her subsequent confinement. Patty's transition to her life with her kidnappers was "about as violent a transition as I can imagine, or have ever seen, more violent than any military captive." Patricia Hearst suffered an abrupt and brutal "plunge into another world," which in its acute phase—between the kidnapping and the bank robbery—lasted about seventy days.

When Doctors West and Singer interviewed the defendant last September and October, they concluded that she was suffering from "a psychiatric illness which was misunderstood both by the patient and by those around her." Now Dr. West wishes to read some passages from the clinical diagnosis he filed with the court at that time. A hush falls over the room. The defendant, supporting her chin on her hand, seems thoughtful and serene. As Dr. West drones on, Judge Carter goes to sleep.

The doctor's best estimate of the amount of time Patty spent in the closet is fifty-seven days. He cannot evaluate the effects of so prolonged a period of blindness. There are no data. Even people who go down in caves do not suffer such severe blindness for so long a time. After the second week Patty's time distortions and confusions became severe. But by putting together her own recollections with the recovered documents provided by the government, Dr. West figures that five weeks had gone by when Cinque decided that the best way the SLA could use Patty might be to force her to join their group. Little by little, she was given to understand that joining up would mean she would get out of the closet, need no longer wear the blindfold, and no longer fear death, at least from them. It was a classic example of coercive persuasion.

As plans for the robbery developed, she became more and more numb. She was told that her part in it had a double purpose: to show the world that she had joined the SLA and to prove her own reliability. Cinque had told her that she was also free to leave. But for her the decision was not to stay or to leave. It was to live or to die. The bank robbery sealed her fate because it made her a common criminal. The Attorney General himself had said so.

Now Bancroft is on his feet, objecting that Dr. West is not just giving his psychiatric evaluation but, in effect, arguing the case. The judge reminds Bailey to "develop your thesis through question and answer," not narrative.

BAILEY: Doctor, how important is the human impulse to survive and not to die?

WEST: It's fundamental.

I'll say! Surely the impulse to survive is operating in this courtroom right now. If I were the prosecutor, I would ask Dr. West whether Patty's confinement in jail is not even more anxiety-provoking than the closet ever was, even more likely to make her willing to lie to the jury, betray her comrades, sell out, do anything to avoid *further* confinement?

"Doctor, what is the purpose of drilling in military situations?"

"To diminish the amount of thought prior to action." At Mel's, Patty did what she had been trained to do. She grabbed the heaviest weapon first, squeezed the trigger, and bullets flew out. When she dropped it, she grabbed it again, and more bullets flew. Then she grabbed a second weapon and began firing.

What was the defendant's first reaction when West asked her about the Hibernia Bank robbery? "After the usual tears and choking, her first words were 'It was like a dream.'" This sort of memory lapse is characteristic of the dissociated state brought on by terror and stress.

In making a medical diagnosis, the doctors took into account not only Patty's and Tania's history up to Mel's but "two more and longer phases" of her mutating personality: Pearl and Pat. Tania was her media name, but after the fire the Harrises and the others called her Pearl. She clung to the identity of Pearl even after she was arrested, as long as Emily Harris was around. Pearl grinned; Pearl clenched her fist; Pearl was the urban guerrilla. These acts were characteristic of a person with weak identity hanging on to her most recent personality until she was sure she was no longer in enemy hands. By the time Singer and West met the defendant, a few days later, she had been separated from Emily, and now was Pat, "a person sort of without any identity."

On the stand, Dr. West is clarifying his diagnosis: Patty's condition is not like the classic dissociations—dual personality, fugue states, or sleepwalking—but a *traumatic neurosis* (the trauma being the kidnapping) *with some dissociative features.* Dr. West ascribes this to being kidnapped 4 February 1974, battered, isolated, blindfolded, and confined to the small closet continuously for approximately fifty-seven days, tormented, reduced to a helpless and physically weakened state, threatened repeatedly with death, sexually molested and raped, humiliated in various ways, for example, literally shorn of her hair and so forth, rendered submissive and highly susceptible by the debility and dependency and dread, and finally left without hope of survival unless she gave the appearance of joining the group.

Despite the torrents of professional jargon, Dr. West seems to me a near-perfect witness; clear, modest, forthright. When he solemnly reports that despite her newfound anger, Patty still trembles whenever one mentions the SLA or Cinque or the Harrises; that when one mentions the closet, she turns pale, starts to sweat, and her pulse rate goes up by fifty percent; that she is still preoccupied with the danger of violent attack, you take the expert at his word. He is not the sort of man to indulge in hyperbole.

David Bancroft opens his cross-examination of this first expert witness with a solid punch. "Dr. West, do you recall who it was who said that 'perhaps the most insidious domestic threat posed by "brainwashing" is the tendency of Americans to believe in its power'?" Dr. West smiles and rolls away from the punch like a sportive porpoise. "It sounds like something I might have said myself."

Another punch. "Doctor, do you know of any case where by thought reform or coercive persuasion someone was indoctrinated so as to commit violent acts against their own kind?"

Another porpoise arabesque. "Oh, yes, Mr. Bancroft, many, many examples. Except that it didn't require what I would call brainwashing or coercive persuasion."

"No. That's why I asked it that way."

"There were literally tens of thousands of Chinese who had been in the Nationalist forces and, after a relatively short period of thought reform, joined the army of Mao Tse-tung and went back and were killing people in their own villages, even members of their own families."

"Has that been scientifically attributed to thought reform, Doctor?"

"That, in fact, is what it was attributed to."

Bancroft's technique is to festoon the courtroom with long strands of quotations from the doctor's writings and then attempt to strangle the witness with his own words. You have written, have you not, about "the absence of any ideological converts . . . in the POW camps . . ."? Yes. But you didn't include any such observations in your big, fat report on Miss Hearst, did you? No, because I didn't find that Miss Hearst had been ideologically converted. Would you say that again, Doctor?

"I did not find Miss Hearst had been ideologically converted."

Judge Carter is out cold.

Are there other possibilities than the so-called survivor syndrome that could account for Patty's symptoms? Yes, many. How about the anxiety produced by a situation in which a young woman from a prominent family who had previously scorned her parents, now facing multiple felony charges, after one of the most intensive manhunts in a decade, is sitting in jail with loyalties torn between previous comrades and the help necessary to get her out of a heck of a fix? Could that not account for someone feeling sorrowful and regretful, for the racing pulse and clammy hands, and for not having the best of memories?

Jolly West's blue eyes are very steady, and he includes the jury as well as Bancroft in his slow, sweeping gaze. "I approached this examination in as objective a fashion as I could. If I had found her to be, let us say, trapped between the expectations of her family and the expectations of her comrades, that is what I would have reported."

Yes, Dr. West has heard the tapes on which Patty spoke scornfully of her parents, but he didn't put much credibility in them. "I have heard too many taped confessions, Mr. Bancroft." At this, Patty turns and gives her mother a quick, full smile.

Why should Patty first identify herself as an "urban guerrilla," then change her story? Was it not just a matter of trying to get out on bail? "I don't think she had any idea of getting out on bail. I quickly discovered she had great fear of being released—even to go to a hospital for a medical examination. She only felt safe in jail."

Midafternoon recess. We straggle out reluctantly. The contest is a good one. From a spectator's viewpoint, West versus Bancroft is a far more interesting tennis match than Bailey versus Browning.

Cross-examination resumes with a long wrangle about whether Patty's hands were tied in front or in back, and how much pain she endured. The doctor notes that Patty said it didn't matter which way they tied her hands, though "it was better when they did it around the front." How on earth could he find *that* a "very significant" remark? Because nobody can lie in a closet for forty-eight hours with her arms tied behind her back and *not* experience great pain. POWs had told him the pain was "excruciating" after only a few hours. Even after allowing for differences in male and female anatomy, West was forced to conclude Patty was blocking out the pain she had felt. If she had been lying rather than blocking, she would have exaggerated the pain, not minimized it.

Dr. West admits Patty did not say much about the Missing Year. Then "how could you testify that when she was found she was suffering from survivor syndrome, without knowing exactly what happened to her in the previous year and a half?"

Excellent point, Holmes, I note on my yellow pad; the witness is unable to tell us what his survivor has survived. Bancroft bristles like a bloodhound catching the scent, and several times the judge must caution him against becoming argumentative. But the warnings are offered with barely suppressed glee; Carter enjoys a good fight.

Wednesday, February 25

Dr. West, were you aware when you took this case that Mrs. Hearst sits on the board of regents of the University of California and also hands out money for research proejcts? Bancroft asks the next morning. Calmly the witness says he was not aware, but it wouldn't have made any difference. When West came to UCLA he had $1 million available for research. Now he has $12 million, all from federal funds, not a penny from the state of California.

But now, suddenly, the prosecutor has changed horses. Do you remember Steven Weed's telling you that the defendant's capacity for sarcasm is unparalleled? Bancroft reads aloud some of the psychiatrist's own interview notes in which Weed is describing his former fiancée: "In many ways she was very immature. . . . She has a tendency to overstate things. . . . Her capacity to be sarcastic is unparalleled. . . ." Small wonder Bailey and Johnson were determined to keep this witness off the stand!

Bancroft is ready to sum up. "Is it your view, Doctor, that a person who was politically embarrassed by their family situation, oriented toward the surface aspect of things, whose characteristic mode of expression is deep sarcasm, and if that person—prior to their acquaintance with political matters—in addition felt depressed or trapped—

could that person not come to a sudden political expression of their own hostilities?" Damn good question.

West says the prosecutor has raised five points, and he wishes to answer them one by one. "By the way"—soft smile—"I assume we're talking about Patricia Hearst?"

A Halloween grin illumines Bancroft's face. "I certainly hope so."

West's reply to the extended question is an extended no, an archipelago of denial. She was not "depressed and trapped." She may have had personal, private reservations about marrying Weed, but "even her sisters didn't know about them."

My mind trails off. Private reservations, personal reasons. How unusual would it be for a young girl having rather commonplace second thoughts about her impending marriage to fling herself into terrorist political activities for private reasons? This is the question a psychiatrist *should* be answering. . . .

Doctor, you have examined the SLA tapes and the "Tania Interview." Don't you find expression in both places of Patty's desire to be considered as an individual and her resentment for not having been so considered previously?

I find nothing of the sort. I consider them unmitigated propaganda comparable to the statements made by American prisoners of war. Some of the phrases sound as if they were copied out of the same book.

In redirect, Bailey must deal with the fact, brought out in Bancroft's cross-examination, that despite all Patty's suggestions to the contrary, Emily Harris was indeed not present while Patty talked to Trish. So the last thing the jury hears from Dr. West is his opinion that for Patty, Emily Harris was "a presence" whether she was in the room or not.

"Thank you, Dr. West." Leaving behind him the spectral presence of Emily Harris hanging in the courtroom air, the first and biggest of Bailey's three big guns steps down from the stand at last.

"Dr. Orne, please." A rumpled, spectacled, mustached, well-fed son of Old Vienna waddles slowly toward the witness stand. Martin Theodore Orne, MD, is a research psychiatrist at the University of Pennsylvania, a graduate of Harvard and Zurich universities and of Tufts Medical School. He is both a psychiatrist and psychologist, and a lecturer in hypnosis as well. He has done a great deal of work for the Veterans Administration and much research for the Air Force in the field of "resistance training"—teaching men to withstand interrogation.

Dr. Orne was shown the findings of all the other doctors, and only then did he examine Miss Hearst personally and alone, in December. He was surprised to find that the by now famous "patchy amnesia" extended backward in time into the period before the kidnapping. This "didn't make any sense" in terms of the patches' being self-serving. "I found, much to my surprise, that this girl was very troubled and would be *trying* to relate the events that had transpired . . . but it was just impossible for her to talk about the closet." The doctor provided all sorts of booby traps, but "she just didn't pick up on cues. It was really quite remarkable. Miss Hearst simply *did not lie*."

Bancroft leaps to his feet, objecting, and Carter issues a solemn instruction to the jury: this witness has naively overstepped his province. He has stated that the defendant tells only the truth, but "that is *your* judgment. You and you alone have to make this ultimate decision, and no judge, and no psychiatrist, no lawyer, can do this for you."

Bailey thanks the court for making this critical distinction, and now he questions the flustered Dr. Orne more carefully, artfully shaping his questions to keep the bubbly Viennese, who has discovered this fountain of truth in a cell at the San Mateo County Jail, from pissing the case away. Once he has got his man quieted down, Bailey extracts the information that what Dr. Orne meant when he said Patty didn't lie was that "I couldn't sway her to tell me something by the way I asked the question."

Dr. Orne is now safely back under the control of the architect of this defense, F. Lee Bailey, and it is a good time to recess for the day. The law is concerned exclusively with facts; psychiatrists deal in "subjective truth." In Dr. Orne's testimony and the government's objection to it, we have witnessed exactly the head-on collision between psychiatry and the law that has been inevitable ever since this trial got under way.

Thursday, February 26

Dr. Orne's examination of the defendant lasted an hour and a half, he tells us, and he threw her his entire range of curveball questions. When Patty told him about being in the bank under Cinque's gun, he observed, "You must have been very scared"; to which she replied, "I don't know what I felt. It was like a dream." This is an inappropriate response from someone who is "simulating," the doctor says. What a downy word— "simulating"! A neutral psych-lab term, lacking any moral knobs or prickles, so different from "lying." Patty "didn't protect herself psychologically" or try to defend herself from the pain of his questions. "If I'd ask about the closet, she would immediately begin to cry. This was a terribly difficult thing to talk about. But she would answer anything I asked her, though clearly in anguish. This is unusual. Many times a psychiatric examination is not a pleasant experience because one must ask about very private things which the patient doesn't want to discuss. But despite the hurt, she showed no evidence of trying to push me away. She appeared to be in intense pain but continued to cooperate."

What is the meaning of "dissociation"? It means ceasing to be "yourself," and varies in degree from the common kind of dissociation we all experience at a cocktail party when we simultaneously talk to someone and think about something else to its most extreme form, "fugue," in which amnesia wipes out the original personality and a second personality becomes the "real" one. Dr. Orne's testimony, like Dr. West's, is becoming so boring that I, myself, begin to dissociate.

Patty is motionless, her long Egyptian eyes downcast and unblinking. Where is her mind? Is she dissociating now? There is never a smile, no facial response, no animation whatever. Bailey is ready to nail down his examination of Dr. Orne with a couple of solid final points. When did the dissociation begin? It began when Tania began. If she had been recaptured right after the robbery, there would have been no question about her behavior in the bank, and no trial. But the robbery made Patty an outlaw not only in the eyes of the law but in her own eyes. She knew it was a criminal act, and she knew there was no way back, so she was stuck with the role. As time passed, the role became more and more real. There was nobody to whom she could say, I am only *playing* this game.

Bancroft's counterattack is unexpected. How is it that Dr. Orne did not attempt to inform himself of the additional background information on Miss Hearst that was developed by the United States in the course of preparation for trial? Had not Dr. Joel Fort, an independent psychiatrist consulting with the government, suggested that Dr. Orne examine the government materials and also look into the legal definition of "coercion"? Yes, but their conversation seemed to Orne somewhat improper. Bancroft pushes for a better answer. Finally Dr. Orne says, "I was quite outraged by what had happened with the examination of Miss Hearst, and I did not feel I wanted to contact the government." Precisely what outraged him is not made clear, but Bancroft has successfully raised the question of whether Orne's Old World sense of punctilio might not have overwhelmed his scientific objectivity.

Bancroft presses on. Aren't there several reasons why people minimize what has happened to them? Yes. Throughout his cross-examination of the defense's expert witness, Dave Bancroft has been formulating the same question in different ways: Is there not a second, equally plausible commonsense explanation of the defendant's curious behavior? Why is it necessary to see her as a victim of something so fancy as "coercive persuasion"? Why can't the symptoms she has exhibited since her capture be seen simply as the normal reaction of a scared kid who knows she's done something wrong and is now in one hell of a jam? It scarcely takes a psychiatrist, he repeatedly implies, to see that this is the truth of the situation.

Suddenly it's lunchtime. It has been a particularly good show this morning. Bailey/Orne and Bancroft/Orne were both *mano a manos* worth watching, and everybody—with the possible exception of the defendant—appears to leave the courtroom in high spirits.

After lunch Dr. Orne is at pains to explain his thought processes. "I asked myself, Why would somebody rob a bank? There were only three reasons. One, she really needed the money, which I excluded in this instance." So either she was converted or coerced. In trying to make up his mind, the doctor had to add up many scraps of evidence rather than base his conclusion on any one thing.

Yes, says the prosecutor, but how could Patty's failure to resist the sexual advances of Willie Wolfe, for example, provide a basis for judging her truthfulness? Could not the fact that Patty described herself as "helpless" during her encounter with Wolfe equally be interpreted as self-serving? It could. But "usually when you have a girl who describes a rape she describes *some* resistance. At least she says, I *tried* to push him away."

When he asked specifically whether Wolfe had threatened to kill her, Orne couldn't even get an answer. "Her failure to make it a good story is what I found so impressive. She had a remarkable resistance to embroidering." Couldn't it be, Doctor, that she already had such a good story going?

It is Dr. Orne's view, in sum, that Patty was coerced at the time of the bank robbery, and thereafter a dissociation began that continued for a year and a half. The weight of the data is to him unequivocal. Is it not even *possible* that the facts could be interpreted in exactly the opposite manner? "Possible? Of course it's possible. I'm certain if it were not possible, we wouldn't be here, and I would never have been asked to see the defendant."

"Thank you, Your Honor," says Bancroft, deadpan.

Bailey calls Dr. Robert Jay Lifton to the stand. He has at least as many and as impeccable credentials as his two predecessors: Yale, Harvard, Ford Foundation grant for East Asian studies; Air Force psychiatrist at Walter Reed; author of twelve books on psychiatric subjects.

After Patty was arrested, Lifton got many calls from newsmen. "Of course, I would tell them I could not make any specific comments on the case itself," says the witness, beginning to seem somewhat pompous, "but they would say, *Could* it be some kind of brainwashing or thought reform?" and Lifton would reply with a guarded "yes."

There had also been a call from the government, asking if Dr. Lifton might be interested in consulting with the prosecution on the case—if there *was* a prosecution. But it was just a preliminary inquiry, and nothing came of it. Then, in December, Lifton got a call from Al Johnson, asking if he was willing to be a consultant for the defense. With the mutual reservation that nothing would be decided until Dr. Lifton had had an opportunity to examine Miss Hearst, the psychiatrist flew to San Francisco. He saw Patty in January for a total of fifteen hours and saw her again just last Saturday for two more hours.

This appears to be a convenient place to break for the day. Outside the courtroom, we learn of death threats today against five people connected with this trial: Judge Carter, F. Lee Bailey, Jim Browning, and the witnesses Tom Matthews and Anthony Shepard.

Friday, February 27

Bailey asks Dr. Lifton to list the steps in the process of coercive persuasion. The first requirement, Dr. Lifton tells us, is total control of all communication between the captive and the outside world. This makes the captors omniscient, so much so that even after their control ceases, the captive "still feels their presence inside." Thus the process begins with a terrific assault on the prisoner's sense of self.

The second element is the manipulation of guilt and blame so that the victim is held entirely responsible for his predicament. On the heels of guilt comes confession. Mandatory self-betrayal is critical to the coercive process because it cuts the victim off from his old roots and loyalties.

A feeling follows that one has reached the breaking point. This is a period of extreme anxiety about death, and in a sense, a kind of slow death has already overtaken these isolated, fearful, guilt-ridden people. Now comes a burst of leniency by the captors—the removal of the handcuffs or chains or the gift of a cellmate to relieve one's isolation.

Though the reward is small, the prisoner feels tremendous relief and a renewed eagerness to live. He begins to search for a sure path to survival. Then the clincher: group and peer pressure applied by fellow prisoners. To prove to his peers that he has reformed, the prisoner struggles the harder to effect that reform.

What Dr. Lifton has been describing, he says, is a combination of traumatic neurosis and survivor's syndrome. Reviewing the Hearst case in the light of his massive knowledge in this field, the doctor found that Patricia had had each of the eight experiences he has enumerated.

Could you document that, Doctor?

Lifton clears his throat. One, she was thrust into the totally controlled environment—the closet. Two, the SLA gave her the sense they were omniscient. Leaning forward, fixing the jury with his bespectacled eyes, the witness proceeds. "She told me, 'I confessed to anything, because they seemed to know everything about me anyhow.' She also—"

There is a loud thud. "Just a moment, Doctor!" Judge Carter says. ". . . a brief recess, please . . ."

The woman juror closest to Lifton has pitched forward and passed out cold at his feet. A bailiff helps her up, and the rest of the jury straggles out behind her, clucking sympathetically.

When court reconvenes, an alternate has taken the place of the stricken juror—a victim of a sudden intestinal attack—and the professor resumes his lecture. The defendant's sense of being totally controlled was present from the instant of her capture. "I felt like a 'thing' in the closet," she told Lifton. Patty's sense of guilt was very strong. She already felt guilty for being a Hearst and—Lifton turns directly to the jury—in addition, she felt the same guilt you or I would feel if we were put in a closet and accused. "Because all of us have a store of guilt. Not legal or moral guilt but psychological guilt," the mental capacity to experience oneself as bad or wrong.

Overwhelmed by primal guilt and a desire to appease her captors, Patty began telling the SLA all sorts of things that weren't true. This was the self-betrayal, the enforced burning of all the victim's bridges. In Patty's case it took the form of making propaganda tapes and denouncing her family, although "the ultimate act of self-betrayal" was the coerced bank robbery, further reinforced by the Attorney General's remark.

During her first two months of captivity Patty was threatened with death many times. Her very real fear was enhanced by the SLA's boasting about Foster's murder, the omnipresent guns, and her confinement in the closets, especially the tiny second closet, in which she feels "already dead." Cinque visits her here and says, "Fight or die." Unless she stays, she will be killed. Her struggle from then on is to convince them that she really wants to stay.

Now the moment of slight leniency, the opportunity to adapt to one's captors. One is shown a path. Patty is reborn as Tania, comes out of the closet, and her hair is shorn. After the robbery she actually feels her ties to her past have been destroyed.

The doctor now wishes to differentiate between compliance and ideological or political conversion. In his judgment, Patty was in a psychological state of "absolute compliance, but with virtually no ideological conversion." The witness was impressed by the speed with which the coerced ideology fell by the wayside as soon as Patty was arrested.

Dave Bancroft objects that Lifton's testimony is "not responsive to questions." And, indeed, for some time there have been none.

It is coming close to noon. Do you have an opinion, Doctor, from all you have observed? Yes, this is a traumatic neurosis—no doubt in Lifton's mind. By virtue of both her tender years, the importance of which cannot be overestimated, and the sheltered life she had led, Patricia Hearst was less well equipped to withstand what happened to her than any other person Lifton has ever interviewed.

Lifton may expect a rough cross-examination from Bancroft, and it begins, after lunch. Since Lifton is aware that before he got to Patty she had spent approximately forty hours with Dr. West and fifteen hours with Dr. Orne, and that she was receiving regular visits from her own psychiatrist, Dr. Richards, will he admit that all these many hours spent with lawyers and doctors might have caused a slight shift in her attitudes since her arrest? No, I will not. Doctor, how many kidnapping victims have you known? None. How many persons you have examined in jail have been fugitives on felony charges for at least two years? None. How many young women have you interviewed in jails who came from prominent families and got involved in terrorist groups? None.

Now, Doctor, do you know of anybody who went through the prisoner-of-war process who ever committed an overt act of violence against their own kind? An American pilot flying in formation with the Red Chinese or North Korean air force? A good question; it grabs the jurors' attention.

"My sense of what the Chinese were after was false confessions of germ warfare for propaganda purposes. And they got them." A straight answer, as good as the question, though not perhaps so effective with the jury.

One difference between psychology and the law is that in the mind two things can be equally true, and sometimes three or four. The mind is oceanic; the law is snug harbor. For the past week Bailey's three big guns have kept up their continuous offshore barrage. But until the smoke clears, there is no way to know how much damage they have done.

WEEK SIX

Monday, March 1

One alternate juror is down with the flu, and the jury is out again so that Bailey can argue the admissibility of Margaret Singer's testimony. The tall figure settles herself once more in the witness box. She has gone over the SLA tapes and Patty's other postkidnapping literary productions, and compared them with Patty's earlier writings. This morning she filed a report that corroborates Patty's own testimony that although she spoke the words, she did not write them.

Browning inquires about Patty's style on the Trish Tobin jail tape. He shouldn't have asked, because the question gives Dr. Singer a chance to say that the tape has been doctored, and she knows where the gaps are.

What is your opinion, Doctor, of tape no. 7?

A torrent of raw linguistic research floods the courtroom. "Okay. I laid out a count of complex versus simple sentence beginnings. And as you'll see, thirty-six percent, forty-six percent, and forty-five percent of the sentences Miss Hearst reads on tapes four, five, and six have complex starters." FBI agent Tom Padden is by now fully asleep. Although Patricia Hearst has never looked so content and pleased in court, Carter is not. "Mr. Browning, I would hope to conclude this."

"A very few more questions, Your Honor." Has Dr. Singer ever before been a witness in a court of law? No, but courts have sent writings to her for analysis, and she knows plenty of people in classified agencies of the government who do this kind of work all the time. "And they consult with me all the time."

Bailey mouths a silent "Hurrah." Patty laughs aloud. Browning doesn't seem to know what to do with this witness; he is a bird caught in a snare. A protracted wrangle between counsel ensues over the admissibility of Dr. Singer's testimony. It is one of the most difficult rulings Carter must make. On balance, he decides that her testimony would "add many hours without adding sufficient productive evidentiary value to make it worthwhile." Bang of gavel. Motion denied.

In that case, Bailey wishes to make an offer of proof and to put Dr. Singer's formal findings into the record, in view of a possible appeal. He would also like the right to cross-examine the government's witnesses as to *their* linguistic expertise when the time comes. Carter will do better than that. If the government's experts take the position that Miss Hearst not only spoke but authored all this material, the judge will not foreclose the possiblity of bringing Dr. Singer back at that time.

Back after lunch is Vernon Kipping, the FBI photography expert. This time, Johnson will examine. What he wants to know is whether the figure of Camilla Hall is not *substantially* different in the two versions of a photograph even though both sets of prints are made from the same negatives from the surveillance camera in the bank. In the five-by-seven prints Camilla Hall has been cropped out! And when she does appear, in the eight-by-tens, the muzzle of her weapon is pointed at Patty, is it not? Well, Kipping would prefer to say it is pointed in the general direction of the counter. In any case, the mistake was inadvertent. The automatic printer in the FBI's Washington laboratory masked the edges of the negative.

Did the movie as shown in this courtroom depict Camilla Hall or not? The witness is uncertain, so we must view the film yet again.

During the film Johnson points out more than once that we cannot see Camilla Hall's face. The movie was made from the cropped photographs. Johnson has saved his most damning point for last. He now draws from Kipping the admission that when the larger, eight-by-ten individual prints were trimmed, to remove the sprocket holes, Camilla Hall vanished from these pictures as well.

The debate over the photographs seems interminable. Browning cross-examines Mr. Kipping, then the same grainy ground is replowed a third time by Johnson on redirect and by Browning on re-cross-examination. I am half asleep when Bailey abruptly says, "If it please the court, that rests the case for the defense."

We have listened to twelve defense witnesses, including Patty, in eleven days. The purpose of the long wrangle over the film becomes clear when Carter asks the jury again to leave so that Mr. Johnson may make a motion out of their presence. The lawyer comes to dismiss all charges against Patty, on grounds that the government has withheld exculpatory evidence—namely, the seventy-three frames of bank film that fail to show Camilla Hall at the opposite end of the teller's counter from Donald DeFreeze. The newly discovered evidence, as the defense reads it, shows that Patty was in a two-gun sandwich between DeFreeze and Hall throughout the course of the robbery. "The government knew or should have known that exculpatory evidence was available. This has left the defense in the peculiar position of not being able to examine witnesses on what we now consider to be so vital." Even if the failure was inadvertent, its effect has been overwhelmingly prejudicial.

But it has all been a long run for a short slide. Judge Carter denies the motion to dismiss. The jurors return with a note to the judge. They find it difficult to examine photographs and listen to testimony at the same time. Then we shall have no more testimony today, Carter says, and the jurors may use the final fifteen minutes to study in silence the enigmatic stacks of pictures and ponder what they may or may not mean.

Outside, we learn of a stunning development. In Los Angeles a judge has ruled that the FBI lacked a proper search warrant when it broke into the Harrises' apartment. Not one speck of the voluminous evidence seized at 288 Precita Avenue can be used against the Harrises at their trial. What does this mean for Patty? Her trial is into its sixth week, and that same evidence has been used against her since day one.

Before the trial a big unanswered question was *When did Tania die?* Was it during the Missing Year, or did the defense lawyers have slowly to strangle the life out of her during those grim four and a half months in the "iron telephone booth"? The task was made immeasurably more difficult because before she died, Tania had written a detailed autobiography. Without the "Tania Interview," it would have been far less imperative to explain Tania; the psychiatrists might even have stayed home. The jury could have seen and judged a straight bank-robbery trial, rather than the psychiatric and at times psychedelic carnival now irrevocably under way. Alone, Tania's SLA tapes might have been dismissed as the coerced ravings of a kidnapping victim temporarily crazed by fear or under the gun of her fiendish captors. Bolstered by the "Tania Interview," the tapes have a written concordance; the manuscript means that Tania exists or, at least, that she once did. But Tania without her manuscript is a revolutionary without a text. And now it appears that the fatal text was seized by the government illegally.

Tuesday, March 2

The government's rebuttal case begins this morning. The first witness is a self-employed electronics technician, Zigurd Berzins. On the morning of April 15, Berzins was hurrying to the bank to make a deposit before going out on a service call. He vaguely noticed a car pull into a bus stop in front of the bank and saw some people get out. As Berzins pushed open the bank door he heard a metallic noise behind him and thought he had let the door hit someone. Turning, he saw a person down on one knee, just outside the half-open door, about eight or ten feet away from where he stood. A carbine lay across the figure's right knee. He saw a pair of hands trying to retrieve the dropped clips and noticed that one or two rounds of ammunition had also fallen. The kneeling figure wore a long, dark coat "draped to the ground," and he saw no face, only the hairline and the top of the head. The figure was female, with long, wavy auburn hair. Browning hands Berzins a carbine and asks him to demonstrate how the figure was holding the gun. It is apparent the witness knows weapons. We learn he is a three-year Vietnam combat vet. The government would like to show him a film and ask if he can identify the person he saw.

Berzins steps down from the box, the room is darkened, the film begins to click through the projector, and when Patty, or rather Tania, skitters back into view, bouncing on the balls of her feet, a flat voice says, "This is the person I saw."

A few hours after the robbery, the FBI showed Berzins mug shots of three women, and he thought he could identify Soltysik and Nancy Ling Perry as two women he'd seen inside the bank but not the "person down on one knee." That person had better get down on both knees, and soon, because Berzins now says that the next day, when the bank surveillance-camera pictures were published in the newspapers, the identity of "the person down on one knee" became clear to him. It was Patricia Hearst.

Browning puts the newspaper photographs into evidence. When Bailey shouts, "No objection!" we begin to sniff the blood that is to come.

It is time to cross-examine. Bailey executes a fast, brilliant passage of cross-examination flamenco, impossible to reproduce, in which the attorney stomps his heels, swivels his hips, beats a tattoo, and razzle-dazzles the witness until he scarcely knows what he is saying. Berzins by now has been interrogated by the FBI half a dozen times; his identifications varied somewhat; sometimes he made mistakes; sometimes the agents misquoted him; some but not all of the misquotations were later corrected and initialed in the FBI transcripts. At first Berzins appears to have thought that the kneeling figure in the doorway and the robber who shouted, "SLA! Get on the floor!" and the person who said, "This is

Tania Hearst," were all the same woman. Later, slowly, he sorted out his impressions. Bailey's rapid-fire questions are intended to flummox us all, and to a degree he succeeds. Yet Ziggy Berzins is holding up.

The defense plays its last card: Bailey reads aloud the entire report of Berzins' first FBI interview, made on the afternoon of the robbery, using his rich voice to underscore Berzins' many errors: The robbery lasted seven minutes . . . the dropped shells he saw on the sidewalk were .45 caliber . . . the person in the doorway was Patricia Soltysik. But Browning, too, has a hole card: *He* reads aloud the entire report of Berzins' second FBI interview, in which the witness revises his statement after having studied the newspaper photographs: The kneeling figure looked most like the pictures of the hatless Patricia Hearst. As Browning reads, Berzins is redeemed—once more a truthful man.

I had visualized a jail matron as a Bella Abzug figure wearing a belt of keys, but the next witness is a leggy blonde in a purple miniskirt. When Deputy Sheriff Stephanie Marsh first asked the new prisoner her occupation, she got no response. When she repeated her question, asking if she were a student or had ever had a job, the prisoner replied, "Urban guerrilla." What was the expression on her face? No real expression at all. What name did she give you? Patricia Campbell Hearst. When I asked her if she went by any other name, she said, "Tania."

I glance at the clock on the wall: 2:15 P.M. For some reason this moment feels like the exact fulcrum of the trial, a psychological balance point, which I note in my home-baked transcript. Up to now, I would have said the defense was clearly ahead. Up to now, not only has Bailey been outperforming Browning on the legal trampoline; the press and spectators have tended to believe Patty more than they do the government. Now, one senses, the balance may be starting to tip.

The jury is sent out so that the defense may now make a heroic attempt to piggyback on the good fortune and/or thorough legal work of the Harris lawyers in challenging the FBI search of the Harrises' apartment. If Carter agrees with the Los Angeles judge that the FBI broke into the apartment without a valid warrant, he will have to instruct the jury to disregard so much of what they have heard that there may be grounds for a mistrial. You can't unring a bell, you can't get a skunk out of a courtroom, and you can't count on anything in a criminal trial.

Wednesday, March 3

The two teams of lawyers have spent the morning and much of the

113

previous night together, studying the Los Angeles transcript. Bailey winks at me. Patty wears her half smile. Her parents and sisters look cheerful. The presence in this courtroom for the first time of FBI special agent in charge Charles Bates indicates the importance of any challenge to the FBI's search-and-seizure procedures. A charge of false arrest at this point would be disastrous to the FBI's already tarnished image.

Two elements are necessary to obtain a proper search warrant: a positive identification and probable cause to believe that the evidence is there. The government claims it lacked both in San Francisco until the actual moment of arrest. At that time Patty's lover was Steven Soliah, a house painter. FBI agents testify that they got on to the Harrises because they were keeping a very close watch on Steven Soliah and his sisters, Kathy and Josephine. Their interest in the Soliahs is not explained now. Only later do we learn the full chain of events that finally led the FBI to Patty Hearst: After Walter Scott put them on to his brother, Jack, the trail led to a Pennsylvania farmhouse, where a fingerprint found on a newspaper stuffed into a hole in a mattress matched the prints of the three-year fugitive Wendy Yoshimura. This, in turn, led the FBI to check back on Wendy's boyfriend, William Brandt, who was still doing time. Brandt's prison visitors included not only the Scotts but the two Soliah sisters. (Soliah's full-time house-painting partner, Jim Kilgore, had been one of the three men arrested in 1972 along with Brandt for the Oakland bomb plot. Kilgore later became Wendy's lover. Steven Soliah became Emily's. For a while Emily Harris and Kathy Soliah were lovers—a complicated and sad daisy chain.) The FBI agents went to Palmdale, a small desert town northeast of Los Angeles, and called on Martin Soliah, a high-school English teacher and track coach, ex-fighter pilot, Nixon supporter, and devoted father of five, and asked his help in tracking down the three of his children who were living in San Francisco.

The entrapment of the patriotic Martin Soliah into helping the FBI snare his own children is one of HERNAP's uglier bits of minor narrative. Soliah was told that the FBI wanted only to talk to his kids and was assured that the inquiry had nothing to do with the Hearst case. He was persuaded to come to San Francisco at FBI expense and, as Soliah put it later, become their "Judas goat." After he made contact with his children through a mail drop, he took the kids out to a five-hour family dinner, during which he told them the FBI had been around asking questions. His son and daughters assured him they had no connection with any radical activities. "That's what I told them!" said the father, much relieved, and went on back to his hotel. The FBI paid Martin

Soliah's hotel bill and reimbursed him with thirty pieces of silver to pay for the supper. They kept a tail on his three kids.

Two and a half weeks later, on the evening of September 17, the agents watching the Soliah sisters saw two people who they thought might be the Harrises walk into a Laundromat.

The day after the Laundromat encounter, while the Harrises were out jogging, FBI agents broke into their apartment through a window. Finding a locked closet, they broke into that, too, and saw guns, bomb parts, ammunition, and other contraband. They photographed the stuff without touching it, the agents testify, and only then went off to get a warrant. By then the Harrises had been under surveillance some thirty hours, plenty of time to get a proper warrant before breaking the window—or so it had seemed to the judge in Los Angeles.

Bailey is posing the "almost undecidable question I hear all the time," Judge Carter says, the critical matter of the sufficiency of the warrant. "From the government's point of view, you're damned if you do, and you're damned if you don't." If the warrant is insufficient, then the search is illegal, and the evidence seized will be thrown out of court. If you wait too long, the previous evidence may be destroyed. "I would say the answer is: Be sure—then get your warrant."

It is four o'clock. Carter smiles. "I think I will be able to decide this first thing in the morning."

Thursday, March 4

Before court opens, Judge Carter has filed his singularly evenhanded ruling: the government may show the jury *some* of the evidence found in the Harrises' apartment, including the "Tania Interview," but not the Bank of America floor plan, which is partly in Patty's handwriting and bears her fingerprints. During *voir dire*, several jurors had indicated an awareness that the defendant was under investigation for a bank robbery in the Sacramento area in which a woman was killed. "If you are talking about Sacramento banks, you are raising the flag of homicide," Carter says. "When you start talking about banks, you start ringing bells." Bells or skunks, the pity is that, though the defense may not be able to undo them now, it might have kept them out to begin with. Bailey's tone of voice is much muted this morning, and Mom is back in her funeral black dress.

Bailey would have asked for a change of venue, he protests, "but it was beyond my wildest dreams that you would admit *any* Sacramento evidence!" Then you admitted Mel's, on grounds that that wouldn't prejudice the jury because nobody got hurt in the store. "But there is a homicide in Sacramento. Some of the jurors know that. There is no way to wipe that from their minds. This is an invitation for them to speculate without guidelines." In his opinion, Carter's rulings up to now have so favored the government that Bailey has had, in effect, to try the Los Angeles case here. Even though he knows Carter will instruct the jury to disregard Patty's guilt or innocence on that charge, "I urge you not to let this case get dirtied up by this kind of evidence!"

Browning sputters, Bailey rails, Carter fusses but remains firm. He will admit the document labeled "Bakery," which Browning has described as a "laundry list," in Patty's handwriting, of instructions on how to rob a bank, but not the annotated floor plan of a specific bank. The press rushes out the front doors of the courtroom to phone in this important ruling just as the jury is marching back in through the rear doors.

Carter now orders the government to place in evidence various items taken from the Harrises' apartment: a green spiral notebook, money orders, old bills, shopping lists, maps, scraps of manuscript, a bankbook, a diagram of a restaurant, a document in Patty's hand headed "Consul General Of," another headed "American Revolution," and an envelope on which she has scribbled, "cat food, beef bouillon cubes, wine, hammer, screwdriver, stopper for tub." Johnson and Browning are quibbling over whether one side of a piece of paper may be put in evidence but not the other when suddenly Bailey is bent over me, whispering, "Have you got your copy of Fort's press release?" About a week ago Dr. Fort had sent a long letter to the court, with copies to every news organization in town, setting forth his view of the proper roles of the expert witness in criminal proceedings. The letter said he sought no personal publicity and would prefer, if possible, that his name not even be mentioned in press accounts of the Hearst trial. It is odd that Bailey lacks a copy. Again I am surprised by the seat-of-the-pants conduct of this defense.

Fort's lawyer arrives to plead his client's case for anonymity. Joel Fort, MD, who enters now through a side door, is shaven-skulled and wears a bold red-and-white-striped shirt, a mustache, and heavy glasses. He is grave and somewhat nutty-looking. Carter wants Dr. Fort to understand that this trial is governed by the Sixth Amendment guarantee of a speedy and public trial by jury. The doctor's curious request suggests he may think he has some right to privacy. He does not. He doesn't have to testify if he doesn't want to, but whatever he says on the witness stand is open to public scrutiny.

All that Fort is really after is protection from exploitation by the news media, his lawyer says. But there is one other matter, a document that has been subpoenaed, a manuscript—

"A book. It says '*book*.'" Bailey interrupts.

All right, a book. But there *is* no book, only an outline and some lecture tapes. Several publishers have been approached: One has some of the tapes; another has an outline for a book, "Expert Witness," prepared from Fort's past lectures and research, and submitted before Fort was called into this case. He does not want to expose it to the public now in its present form. He feels he has some right of privacy on this, perhaps a First Amendment right, perhaps a Fifth Amendment right—

Carter's high forehead pleats up like an accordion. "You mean he has a First Amendment right to something he hasn't written yet!" Even Catherine gives a whoop of laughter. Dr. Fort glowers silently.

Until now we haven't had any real heavies in this case, only real victims. After the fire in Los Angeles, the original villains all became martyrs and ascended to radicals' heaven. But over in a shadowed corner of the courtroom, slumped in a big leather chair, Joel Fort looks marvelously malevolent.

Bailey continues to snap away at Fort's lawyer until Carter, anxious to hurry this case along, intervenes. "Gentlemen, I am calling a halt to all these procedural delays! I am advising you, Mr. Browning, and you, Mr. Bailey, that tomorrow morning at ten o'clock in front of the jury we are going to start taking evidence!"

Friday, March 5

Joel Fort's testimony is prefaced by the usual catechism of credentials: medical degree from Ohio State University Medical School in 1954; PhD in clinical psychology; several years in the U.S. Public Health Service.

Fort speaks directly to the jury, his back half turned toward the bench and counsel tables, and the jurors pay him very close attention. Dr. Fort has been an expert psychiatric witness in twenty-two states and in six federal-court districts, he says, and has consulted and testified in more than two hundred criminal cases, about 60 percent of the time for the defense. In cases with multiple defendants, he has testified for both sides in the same trial. Fort was an expert witness in the Charles Manson trial; the Kemper and Mullin mass-murder trials in Santa Cruz; the trial of the two homosexual Houston murderers, Henley and Brooks, who tortured and killed twenty-seven young boys; the Timothy Leary drug trial; and the Lenny Bruce case. What a grotesque company in which to find the daughter of mild and humdrum Catherine and Randolph Hearst!

More credentials: Dr. Fort has taught courses at various branches of the University of California in sex and crime, drugs and crime, and rehabilitation of criminal offenders. He has made a number of educational films and tapes and has written books and contributed articles to numerous legal and medical journals. Dr. Fort is often asked to testify at congressional hearings, and he has been a consultant to the World Health Organization, the United Nations, and to the governments of Canada, Thailand, and Australia.

Now, Dr. Fort, Browning begins, what varieties of radicals have you dealt with? He has had extensive contacts with "the so-called hippie population" and with student radicals. In preparation for this trial he has done a special study of thirty-five kidnap victims, and, of course, he is familiar with the literature of urban guerrilla movements in other countries. He has consulted with CIA and Defense Department terrorism experts and has conducted perhaps fifty in-depth interviews with concentration camp survivors. He has also known many victims of rape, mugging, assault, and attempted murder. In 1963 he had some experience with Chinese thought reform while interviewing Chinese refugees on a trip to Hong Kong. In sum, Joel Fort's qualifications are more than sufficient.

Lunch is over but before Fort can begin his expert testimony, the defense challenges his qualification as an expert. Dr. Fort, you've indicated a rather large range of interests, Bailey says. Can you tell me in what capacity you were retained by the prosecution? General consultant. Are you an expert in psychiatry? Board-certified, for example? No. "Was it any part of your assignment from the prosecution, or your responsibilities as you understood them, *to give legal advice as to this case?*" A sudden, very ugly edge has come into Bailey's voice.

"It was not part of my assignment, and I did not specifically see myself as giving legal advice."

"Do you know Mr. and Mrs. Hearst, sitting in the front row?" Certainly. "Have you met and talked with them?" I certainly have.

"Did you go to them, Dr. Fort, and try to fix this case behind my back?" Suddenly Bailey is bellowing like a bull. "Did you go to Mr. and Mrs. Hearst and try to arrange a meeting with Jim Browning without my

knowledge and without my presence to try to dispose of this case? Did you advise Mr. Hearst how to go about avoiding a public trial?"

I raised one or two possibilities.

"Did you advise him to call a lawyer not retained by the defense?"

It was an attorney already retained by them—William Coblentz.

"Did you advise them to do that without telling me?" Bailey's voice shakes with fury.

"I *had* told you, Mr. Bailey, *and* Mr. Johnson *and* Mr. Browning *and* Mr. Bancroft. It was done with the full knowledge of all four of you, and as a matter of fact, you praised me and my motives for doing so." Fort's voice is as cool and flat as a sheet of glass.

"Did you say, 'The problem with this case is that Bailey likes to try cases and Browning wants to be a federal judge'?"

"I never said that. I'll tell you what I did say that you have considerably distorted."

"Oh! Tell me." Bailey burns with such scorn one can feel its heat.

"I said that often the needs of the defendant in any criminal case . . . get lost in terms of other motives that are sometimes a part of the background of attorneys on both sides."

"Did you encourage Mrs. Hearst to meet with Mr. Browning directly?"

"No, I encouraged her to call Mr. Coblentz and ask if he thought such a course would be helpful."

"Without the defendant's counsel's knowledge!"

"That is absolutely untrue. I talked to both Mr. Johnson and you, as I did to Mr. Browning and Mr. Bancroft."

"That's absolutely false, Dr. Fort."

"No. You're lying about it, Mr. Bailey."

So there we have it, head to head: psychiatrist and lawyer each trying to sink his teeth into the other's neck.

Dr. Fort, did you tell Mrs. Hearst that this case should be disposed of because a trial would be agony for her daughter, and if she pleaded guilty the worst sentence she could get as a kidnapping victim would be six months' probation?

"Mr. Bailey, for the third time, I told Mrs. Hearst and Mr. Hearst, and I told you and Mr. Johnson, and I told Mr. Browning and Mr. Bancroft that if there was any way possible, I thought it would be desirable to avoid a public trial. A public trial, I felt, would be destructive to the defendant, to her family, and to society. I said no more, and no less, than that." The fat is in the fire, the gauntlet thrown.

The prosecutor is at pains to bring out that he never urged Fort to say anything to the Hearsts, that he and Fort never discussed Browning's career aspirations and had never even met before this case. Dr. Fort suggested nothing in the least "under the table," no "fix," nothing beyond the proposition that a public trial might not be the best disposition of the case.

Can an expert be fooled, Dr. Fort? Certainly. What is mental illness? Swiftly, Judge Carter points out that the appropriate question to ask is what the term that has been used here—"traumatic neurosis with dissociative features"—means in relationship to the term "mental illness."

Okay. Dr. Fort, would a diagnosis of traumatic neurosis with dissociative features at the time the defendant was captured be retroactive? Would it indicate whether or not she'd had it fifteen months before? Absolutely not. If the person were seen in jail, what is called mental illness could in part or in whole be caused by the jail experience. You would also need to consider whether the illness was of the same intensity or severity now as then. Mental illness can be mild, moderate, or severe; sometimes it is continuous, sometimes brief and abrupt. Sometimes it is incapacitating; more often, it is not.

Dr. Fort, can psychological testing determine a person's past mental state? Absolutely not, nor is there any relationship between such tests and criminal responsibility.

Bailey says these questions are irrelevant; there is no plea of insanity in this case. Judge Carter cautions the prosecutor against going into the question of mental illness; it is a dangerous door to open. But Browning plows stubbornly ahead. Doctor, how do you go about determining mental illness?

What Dr. Fort's five-minute answer boils down to is that you make a complete analysis of the patient's history, put it together with the present symptoms, look for internal inconsistencies, and try to rule out alternative possible diagnoses. This last is important because studies have shown as much as 60 percent disagreement between two psychiatrists on any given diagnosis. When a third psychiatrist is brought in, the differential may fall to 45 percent.

"Mmmmmmm, when you come to a convenient place, Mr. Browning," says Carter.

"Suits me fine now."

"All right. We will take the afternoon recess." Bang of gavel. We all rise and, OD'd on facts, stagger into the corridor for a smoke.

But on the matter of Joel Fort's research, folks, you ain't heard nothin' yet. We learn after the recess that the doctor has gone over every word of the jail tapes made by Doctors West and Singer, in transcript form when possible. He spent several hours at the house in Daly City, including one hour alone inside the closet, turning a radio on and off and trying to determine how much sound could be heard under various conditions. He drove to the apartments where Patty and the Harrises were captured, in order to ascertain the distance between them. He visited the kidnapping site in Berkeley and the apartment on Golden Gate. He made four visits to the San Mateo County Jail. He examined the sheriff's logs and spent an hour or so interviewing Al Johnson. During his interviews with Patty, incidentally, Johnson was always nearby.

Then there was his background reading. Dr. Fort has boned up on attitude change; radicalism; feminism; guerrillaism; the youth culture; criminology; religious conversion; the Moonies, Jesus freaks, Zen Buddhists, and similar groups; concentration camps; Maoist thought reform, suggestibility, sensory deprivation, hypnosis, and other altered states of consciousness. He looked at more than 200 books and 125 articles, and put in a total of 300 hours' consultation over five months before finally writing his report.

Now Browning is ready to put the specific question. "Did the defendant at the time of the bank robbery charged have any mental disease or defect—traumatic neurosis with dissociative features or anything else—which substantially affected her capacity to conform her conduct to the law, or to appreciate the moral wrongfulness of participating in that bank robbery?"

Bailey objects. This is not an insanity defense!

But yes, indeed, in Dr. Fort's opinion Patty "had no mental disease or defect at that time that would in any way affect her functioning."

Did she lack the mental capacity or awareness to know what she was doing? Again Bailey objects, and Carter sustains the objection.

Browning's third question: In Dr. Fort's opinion, at the time the bank robbery was in progress was Patty under any threat of grave bodily injury or death? Bailey objects even more violently. "If that doesn't go to the merits of the case, I never heard anything that did! Your Honor, that's a jury question!"

"Mr. Bailey, calm down. . . . Ladies and gentlemen, your function is to determine intent. This witness may give his opinion, but you are not bound by it."

Bailey has still another objection: Dr. Fort has no expertise in whether or not Patty was under the gun in the bank.

BROWNING: Do we understand three defense psychiatrists can get up on the stand and give their opinions, but the government can't give one? If Bailey thinks Dr. Fort's testimony is improper, perhaps he would join in a motion that *all* psychiatric testimony be stricken?

Bailey will fight, at any cost, to prevent Joel Fort from expressing an opinion on whether Patty was in fear during the robbery because his case rests on her fear. If the jury finds the defendant in fear of death or bodily injury, they cannot find her guilty.

"Proceed, Mr. Browning."

In forming his opinion, did Dr. Fort use a single frame of reference, such as the POW experience, or more than one frame of reference? Multiple frames, of course. The doctor's level, bee-buzzing voice starts in again. One frame was all the elements that contribute to attitude-change—family life, education, the mass media, advertising and propaganda, peer-group relationships, business and organization relationships, religious experiences, psychotherapy experience, and legal and criminal and police relationships. Another frame was the defendant's prekidnapping attitudes, since "the most important ingredient in any kind of alteration of behavior is what you already are.

"The third thing I thought was extremely important was the total context of the SLA. Who were the eight other members? . . . We need to explain how these people became SLA members if we are to understand what happened to the defendant. Seven out of eight came out of white, middle-class, affluent, educated backgrounds, and five were women."

The fourth frame of reference was the physical environment in which change occurred. What was the closet like, the radio noise, the food and drink, the toilet privileges? Next frame: the experience of other kidnapping victims of similar backgrounds. Sixth frame: concentration-camp survivors and POWs, rape victims, and veterans of Chinese thought reform.

For myself, I find this information fascinating. Why is Patty paying so little attention?

The defendant is a Madonna *dolorosa,* a classic image of female suffering. She sits motionlessly, and tears fall from her eyes as in a Sicilian religious painting. Fine-featured, smooth-skinned, narrow, and pale, she is almost as white as the "Pietà" of Michelangelo. The corpse across her knees is the dead Tania, vibrant, defiant guerrilla girl. She has sat thus for six weeks, silently weeping, an Italianate image of agony. Strange! Despite its purity and classical lineaments, that agony has gone entirely unmentioned in this courtroom until the advent, some six weeks into the trial, of Dr. Joel Fort, a man whom the defense counsel sees as scoundrel-in-chief and devil incarnate, as the miscreant who went to the parents of the beleaguered madonna and tried simultaneously to "fix" the case, smear her counsel, and intrude himself ass-backwards into Patty's limelight. Shaven-headed, swarthy, lithe, intense, with piercing eyes behind silvery glasses, Dr. Fort sometimes looks the part he plays in Bailey's mind. Others see the doctor as a psychological pragmatist, concerned to deal bluntly with the case at hand, and to hell with the lace-handkerchief formalities of academic disciplines and the over-ripened niceties of the law. But to me, Dr. Fort is beginning to look like the little boy in Anderson's fairy tale, the one who pointed to the royal procession and said, "The emperor has nothing on!"

In his first day on the stand, he has given voice to three ideas that have been buzzing around in my mind for six weeks now, and presumably therefore in the minds of jurors as well, without having once been articulated in open court. The failure of either side to mention them is astounding, as they are so manifestly *there*, hanging like a scrim of reality between the audience of jury and press and the lawyers' and doctors' kabuki show taking place on stage. What are these heretofore-unuttered statements of the obvious? First, the defendant is in manifest agony, which it would have been desirable to avoid if possible. Why the needless public spectacle? Why the sensational trial, the ordeal-by-media? Why hold this form of twentieth-century exorcism if a way around it could have been found?

Second, the opinion of the defense psychiatrists may indeed, and understandably, have been somewhat skewed, not only by their professional interests but also by their unique relationship to the defendant. Office doctors and academics *would* be likely to see Patty not as a neutral subject to evaluate but as a patient, someone who evokes their natural wish to effect a "cure," a wish not diminished by the fact that they are at least temporarily in the service of the patient's powerful, and powerfully suffering, father.

Third is the striking but unremarked-on similarity between the defendant and the SLA women who captured and seemingly converted her. "Could this happen to *my* daughter?" America had asked itself for two years. It is the one question Bailey says he wants the jurors to ask themselves now. Fair enough. But, save for the kidnapping that preceded it, exactly this *did* happen to the daughters of a Goleta pharmacist, a Santa Rosa furniture dealer, a Midwestern minister, a New Jersey Teamster official, and a Chicago insurance man.

That these three vital matters have not been raised until Dr. Fort raised them may account for the charge of negative electricity sparking between Bailey and Fort now. I see three possible motivations for Bailey: He is trying to find a way to denounce the doctor *a priori* as a liar and fraud, in order to deflect the jury's attention from the damage Fort is about to do his client; or he wants certain things said in the course of this trial about Patty's ordeal, and the best way to do that is to put the words in Fort's angry, scornful, unbelievable mouth; or Bailey's ego is indeed as festering as it seems. Most likely all three explanations are true.

WEEK SEVEN

Monday, March 8

Today Judge Carter is ready to rule on whether to admit Joel Fort's expert opinion. "While the ultimate issue here is the defendant's intent at the time of the offense, the initial situation—the defendant's status as a kidnap victim and whether this would deprive her of the requisite intent—is very unusual and beyond the common experience of jurors," he begins. Diminished capacity may or may not be part of the defense—Carter does not intend to "get into labels"—but if you look at the testimony of the three defense psychiatrists, "you must conclude they were talking about coercion."

Now Judge Carter is saying that Dr. Lifton's testimony for the defense was loaded with suggestions, discussions, and flat-out assertions of coercion. Therefore Dr. Fort's opinions may also be heard. Bang of gavel, and Bailey suffers another nail.

Browning pops the big question. No, Fort thinks Patty "did not perform the bank robbery because she was in fear of her life. She did it as a voluntary member of the SLA." The jury has heard the dread words. Before the prosecutor can go on, the judge interrupts. "Ladies and gentlemen, let me repeat an instruction I have given you before. Only *you* can determine guilt or innocence. One of the issues in determining that is whether or not she was coerced and to what extent. The purpose of the psychiatrists' testimony is to advise you of their opinion. You will decide whether and how much of it to believe."

Fort is an excellent, practiced lecturer who uses no notes but never loses the thread. His testimony is like a copy of *Psychology Today* made into a talking book for the blind.

Dr. Fort has carefully researched and reconstructed the defendant's prekidnapping personality, and "My findings were that she was extremely independent, strong-willed, rebellious, intelligent, and well educated, but not especially intellectually inclined." He cites Patty's numerous fights with nuns at school, the fact that she had been sexually active since age fifteen, and was notably independent about rules in general. He mentions that once Patty wanted to get out of taking an examination, and so she told the teacher her mother had cancer, knowing it was not the sort of alibi the nun would attempt to check. The defendant, in short, is not only a liar but a calculating one.

Patty's jaw drops, and she turns toward her sister Vicki in open-mouthed disbelief. Her claim that she was coerced by the SLA makes Patty's veracity the key issue in this trial. But Fort does not see the dumb show. He is faced squarely to the jury, telling them how Patty's parents and sisters and Steven Weed felt about her. All of them described her as independent, assertive, and self-assured. Though she expressed ambivalent feelings about her parents to Dr. Fort and obviously had poor communication with them, other materials support the belief that she disliked or hated them flat out and felt only a desire to get away from the Hearst name and role. Fort would describe the prekidnapping Patty as very opinionated, sure of her attitudes, dogmatic, and authoritarian.

Judge Carter is asleep again. All psychiatrists bore him equally. He is interested in the law and in the adversary contest, not in this interminable, vague "science" that can explain things into the ground. I envy him as Fort delineates how Patty's "group interaction seemed to progressively increase" and "friendly contacts and mutual liking developed," especially with Atwood, Wolfe, and Perry. Who told you that, Doctor? Miss Hearst did, and it also comes across in some of the other accounts. The jurors look perplexed. Do they doubt what Patty told the doctor or what the doctor is telling them?

Browning moves on to the period on Golden Gate Avenue. When did the conversion begin, Doctor? It is difficult to pinpoint because all prisoners have a blurred time sense, but in the "Tania Interview," Patty writes that she felt an attraction to the SLA purposes within two weeks of her capture. Nothing magical or brutal was done to convert her. The change came about through admiration for her new comrades, their sense of commitment, their enthusiasm and motivation.

Oliver J. Carter is *still* asleep, but I am awake because I think Fort has just said it. The core of it, the Big Persuader for Patty, must have been the unusual commitment and belief she found in these young women and men in all other respects so like herself. On Golden Gate, Patty began to get out of the closet more, to take part in gun drills and political indoctrination, and to experience still more "group interaction." By about March 1, Fort believes, the defendant had voluntarily joined the SLA.

Carter has ordered Browning to "speed it up," and in the ensuing *rataplan* of question-and-answer, two of Fort's replies stand out.

Doctor, were the other SLA members experienced enough to conduct some sort of mind conversion with respect to the defendant? No. Their radical philosophy, "which I would summarize as a superficial blending of Marxism, Maoism, and terrorism," was still in its early stages. They were committed to violent social change as a general principle but lacked experience in converting others.

Doctor, would you comment, please, on the effect of the defendant's prekidnapping personality on the attitude change that occurred after her kidnapping? Yes. She had been a strong, willful, independent, bored, and dissatisfied person, in poor contact with her family, disliking them to some extent, dissatisfied with Weed after their three years together, missing a sense of purpose in life. . . .

In short, she sounded to me a lot like any kid her age, but Catherine Hearst smiles scornfully, for Joel Fort has just spelled out precisely the version of reality that she and her husband and the defense attorneys have steadfastly refused to accept.

Browning moves on to the date of the bank robbery. Did Dr. Fort find any evidence of mental illness or defect at *that* time—any traumatic neurosis, for example? No. To elude the bank's burglar alarms, the whole thing had to be pulled off in ninety seconds, and somebody debilitated by severe depression or anxiety probably couldn't even carry out the actions shown in the film.

Is there any evidence of mental disease or defect in Patty's behavior *after* the robbery—say, at the time of Mel's? Quite the opposite. Fort gets a picture of the defendant sitting alone in a van, reading a newspaper, "and upon finding that the Harrises are being arrested, putting down the newspaper, picking up a gun and shooting in order to rescue them, and then driving away with them after they joined her in the car." To carry out so complex a series of acts so successfully would indicate the absence of mental illness or stress.

"Doctor, what can you tell us, from a psychiatric standpoint, with respect to the claim that she fired the gun at Mel's almost involuntarily or instantaneously?"

"I find it unbelievable."

"Doctor, in your opinion, was the defendant a private in an army of generals?"

"No, I think she was a queen in their army. She brought them international recognition. It was an exciting thing for her, and for the rest of them, that the media responded to the group the way it did."

Did you see any signs of disease or mental defect at the time the defendant was in the San Mateo County Jail? She was certainly having what traditional psychiatry calls a depressive reaction, which is a long-winded way of saying she was kind of upset and discouraged and blue. But that's characteristic of anyone's first jail experience. What is the significance of the clenched fist, the guerrilla salute? I interpret it as a re-assertion of her SLA identity. It was different from the way POWs behave. Released concentration-camp victims do not say *"Heil Hitler!"*

During midafternoon recess the press is in high spirits. Joel Fort's delineation of the case has given a fresh twist to an old rag, and the headline he supplied is so catchy—QUEEN OF THE ARMY!—they'd forgive him anything. Journalistic juices rise in anticipation of the pleasure of writing today's file. Reporters clown around the corridors like kids at school recess, making up gag headlines: FORT CALLS HEARST CLOSET QUEEN! BAILEY HOLDS THE FORT! PATTY FRIGID AFTER DEFREEZE!

Recess over, the prosecutor is ready to wrap it up and tie the bow. "All right, Doctor, based upon all of your research and inquiries, is it still your opinion and conclusion, sir, that the defendant, Patricia Campbell Hearst, on April 15, 1974, was in the Hibernia Bank without immediate fear for her life or great bodily injury?"

"That is my opinion."

Bailey's re-cross-examination begins with an attempt to make Fort look like a profiteer or a publicity hound. By the time Dr. Fort interviewed the defendant for the government, in January, he knew that the three defense psychiatrists had already been chosen, so if Fort was to get on the stand at all, it would *have to be* for the prosecution, right? On the contrary, Mr. Bailey. It was my hope that there would *be* no expert testimony in this case. I think a jury can make up its own mind.

Tuesday, March 9

Bailey has to destroy the doctor's credibility because the jury must disbelieve Fort in order to believe Patty. It appears to me, watching the duel, that Lee Bailey is repeatedly hurling himself against Dr. Fort and losing, because it is a poor strategy to try to show up as a *poseur* a man who is obviously sincere. Bailey continues to threaten, bluster, and loom, but each time Bailey puffs with rage Fort grows quieter and more badgerlike.

When at last we debouch into the corridor, the reporters agree that the doctor is holding up remarkably. Fort is an accomplished counter-puncher, as is Bailey. But whereas Fort has one enemy—orthodoxy—which assumes multiple forms, Bailey has many. Bailey is against ambiguity, change, newness, stupidity, losing, boredom, inactivity, and anonymity. But the greatest of these is losing.

Wednesday, March 10

This morning another juror is excused, owing to a death in the family. Now only two alternates stand between us and a mistrial. Bailey asks Fort whether he has read the chapter on brainwashing in a standard textbook of psychiatry. "Will you look at it, please?"

"Will you let go of it for a minute?" So much for the flavor of the morning's dialogue.

"Dr. Fort, do you know of any cases you studied where the victim of the kidnapping was prosecuted?"

"No." It is the shortest answer to the best question of the week.

The end, however, is near. Bailey mentions Tania and asks, "What is the significance to you, Doctor, when somebody changes his name?" It commonly signifies a dissatisfaction with the previous name. It can also indicate an allegiance to a new group, as when Black Muslims take the name "X." Mmmm-hmm.

One feels as if Bailey for five days has been constructing some vast and elaborate trap for this witness that somehow has never sprung. "Does that conclude your cross-examination, Mr. Bailey?" Carter asks in dubious tones. Yes, says Bailey, already at the defense table, his face brick-red. One had not even noticed him sit down. The witness exits silently, swiftly, through a side door, a Kafka survivor of an inexplicable ordeal.

At 2:50 P.M. Dr. Harry Kozol is called to the stand. Patty's face is the dead-white color of a fish's belly. In a high voice and with a slight lisp, Dr. Kozol recites his credentials. Most of his work over the last twenty years has involved young people, and his primary interest is in violence. Why are kids marching in the streets, blowing up college labs, wrecking computers? He is not condemning these young people so much as he is concerned about his own children and grandchildren.

Dr. Kozol has appeared as an expert witness twenty to thirty times in thirty to forty years and has often served as a court-appointed psychiatrist. He has dealt professionally with Russian, German, Italian, Canadian, and Japanese war prisoners.

When Dr. Kozol was first asked by the government to consult on the Hearst case, he replied with the standard letter "that they had no assurance, and I made no commitment," as to his findings. What materials did you study, Doctor? Kozol's voice winds down to a truly excruciating slowness. Yes . . . he . . . also . . . has heard . . . all the psychiatric . . . testimony . . . in this courtroom and has filed his own sixty-three-page report. Kozol goes over the familiar ground.

Thursday, March 11

Patty is sick. Judge Carter announces that he will recess the trial until Monday and use the intervening time to handle matters that do not require the presence of the defendant.

Friday, March 12

With Patty still ill this morning, the lawyers meet informally with the judge to settle on his instructions to the jury. A skeleton crew of reporters is on hand, which means that Bailey can still get his message out to the public. Today's message is a broad hint that the client, if acquitted, will turn state's evidence against the Harrises and others.

Browning is worried because "I don't know how many people have come up to me on the street and asked, 'Why don't you put the Harrises and the Scotts on the stand?' " and the jury may be wondering the same thing.

"They also want to know why you haven't indicted them," Bailey shoots back.

"All in good time. As soon as we have a witness who will testify before the grand jury."

"She's sick right now!" Bailey snaps. Another part of his message is that had the trial been limited to events in the Hibernia Bank, he would have relied strictly on the bank film and not even put his client on the stand, let alone his battery of psychiatrists. His defense would have been that Patricia was a kidnapping victim and, if not literally under the gun in the bank, at least under imminent threat of death if she had failed to cooperate. But once the machine-gunning at Mel's and her confession to young Matthews were admitted, it took psychiatrists to explain them. Then came the "Tania Interview" and other documents, including descriptions of banks and notes on homemade explosives in Patty's handwriting. These materials strongly suggested that Patty was now in the business of robbing banks, and psychiatrists were required to explain that Ms. Hearst was kept in a *continuing* state of terror and fear for her life until the moment of her arrest, and that her irrational-seeming fear of the Harrises, the police, the FBI, and her parents was, in fact, a quite normal response to her abnormal situation.

WEEK EIGHT

Monday, March 15

After four days' recess, Dr. Kozol scampers into the witness box. Everybody else seems somewhat subdued. Patty looks terrible, paler than she has since the trial began.

Kozol now tells Browning that he had asked Patty about Willie Wolfe. "I told her that on the June seventh tape she had provided a eulogy in which she spoke of Cujo so lovingly, so tenderly, so movingly that she made it come alive.

"She seemed to get upset and said, 'I don't know how I feel about him!' deeply moved, as if sobbing inside. 'I don't know why I got into this goddamn thing! Shit!' Then she ran out of the room."

In the next interview, Patty told Kozol she had been assaulted twice. Catherine Hearst's eyes are again downcast as the fifth psychiatrist relates how Cinque pinched her daughter. Did you specifically ask her, Doctor, if he ever sexually assaulted her again? No, but my feeling was that this had not been a sexual assault but rather an angry assault that had a sexual connotation.

Today Kozol has abandoned his notes, making him a far more effective witness, but now Patty is scribbling furiously on a yellow pad.

What did she say about the Missing Year? Just that she was in Sacramento until two months before her arrest. Did you also discuss the Trish Tobin tape? Yes, I asked her if Miss Tobin knew Emily Harris personally, because she spoke of her as "Emily." "I'm not going to say *anything* about the Harrises," Patty replied. When Kozol asked the reason for her interest in revolutionary feminism, she said, "Because I am a woman." In relation to the person we have been watching for seven weeks, this answer is burlesque Garbo, not to be taken seriously.

Browning, the woodpecker of prosecutors, continues tapping away at his witness. Summing it all up, does the doctor have an opinion with respect to the defendant's mental state when she walked into the bank? Did she walk in voluntarily?

"Objection! Witness is not an expert on voluntariness."

"Overruled . . . with the same instruction to the jury. You have to determine intent in your own minds."

"I think she entered the bank voluntarily in order to participate in the robbing of the bank. This was an act of her own free will."

"Did you also form an opinion with respect to whether she joined her captors voluntarily?"

"Same objection!"

"Overruled."

"I have an opinion. I think she joined the people who had captured her some weeks before."

During this testimony Al Johnson and Lee Bailey look more glum than I have ever seen them. Dr. Harry Kozol may have seemed a fuddy-duddy once, but he is very believable right now.

"Doctor, do you know a man named Nicholas Groth?" Bailey asks.

Calmly: "Yes. This is a man I fired. A clinical psychologist . . . for misbehavior with a patient . . ."

Bailey develops and builds the story of Dr. Kozol and his underling Groth for another five minutes, perhaps ten, leading the increasingly agitated witness through interminable false starts and half sentences. Was Dr. Groth working at your facility the day Patricia Hearst was arrested? Yes. I fired him eight days later. Following the arrest, and while the publicity was front-page, did you say to Dr. Groth, "The Hearsts are disgusting and venal. Mrs. Hearst is a whore"?

"Ne-e-e-v-er! That is not my language! That is inconceivable and incredible! A misstatement and a lie, in exact keeping with some of the reasons I had to fire this man."

"Did you say, 'I understand Patty referred to her father as a pig. Well, they *are* pigs!'?"

"No, I didn't . . . oh, dear . . . I don't think I even knew what the word 'pig' meant until I got here. . . ."

At this moment Harry Kozol reminds one very much of the White Rabbit. Quite possibly he did say this. But so what? Bailey says a recess would be convenient at this time. The recess ended, Bailey digs in again, cross-examining like a Chinese Ping-Pong player, every question delivered with a spin, an edge, a twist, a curve.

From your broad view of the case, Doctor, tell us when you feel that her fear of the SLA and Cinque was dissipated. I think it dissipated gradually. She writes in the "Tania Interview" that they started leaving the closet door open after the first two weeks. I don't have a specific date. Fear doesn't drop off like a mantle. Nonetheless, by the time Patty made the April 3 tape she was "not a prisoner."

Hearing Dr. Kozol say these words, I realize that this is what I, too, have now come to believe—not from any single bit of testimony but from the drop-by-drop accumulation of the weight of the evidence, even though I cannot clearly remember the train of evidence that brought me to this conclusion.

Dr. Kozol believes Patty *was* free to go, just as Cinque said. "I would take the word of that dead black man."

"Despite the fact that he had served time for armed robbery, illegal possession of firearms, participated in the execution of Marcus Foster, kidnapped Patricia Hearst and publicly threatened her execution, and extorted one point eight million dollars out of her family and demanded four million more, and demanded the release of four killers—you would take that black man's word! Is *that* your testimony, Doctor?"

"I would, in respect to the promise that no harm would come to her. Because harm did not come to her. They didn't kill her."

"Is that the proof—that they did not kill her?"

"Well—did they?"

"Doctor, she is sitting in this courtroom today exactly as they planned! You know that, don't you?"

"Exactly as she chose, Mr. Bailey."

"Does the phrase 'Once freed . . .' in a confession of a supposedly free person have any importance to you, Doctor?"

"Not necessarily," Kozol replies. And he is right. This is the answer I have wanted to hear ever since Bailey first raised the obscure point.

The cross-examination of Harry Kozol is at an end. It is late, already 4:19 P.M. But the prosecutor begs for just twenty minutes more, in which to present three brief witnesses. First, Tom Padden returns to confirm that he was the arresting officer and to identify plaintiff's exhibits 176 and 177—the one an object, the other a photograph.

Bailey interrupts. "To save time we will stipulate that the stone objects around the neck in the photograph once belonged to Willie Wolfe, now deceased." But the items are produced, and Browning plods ahead. The photograph is a blowup of the SLA group picture recovered from the ashes in Los Angeles. Browning asks Padden where he found no. 176, the stone object. "I got it out of the purse of Patricia Hearst."

"So stipulated," Bailey barks.

The second brief witness is the Los Angeles police sergeant who examined the dead bodies in the ruins of the fire. Browning hands a small object—exhibit 178—to the police sergeant and asks him to identify it. This was found under the body of Willie Wolfe when the corpse was turned over. At the defense table, Patricia Hearst appears troubled.

"What is it?" Judge Carter asks, peering down.

"I'm sorry, Your Honor. A small figurine." Patricia Hearst takes a deep breath and assumes a queer half smile.

Browning's third brief witness is Clement Meighan, a UCLA professor of anthropology and archaeology, whose work deals with "prehistoric human remains in the New World."

The professor is frequently called upon to identify a certain category of ancient Mexican artifacts that are plentiful, easy to find, and generally called *monos*, which in English means "monkeys." Exhibits 176 and 178 are *monos*. Now Browning wishes to replay a bit of the SLA's final tape. Patty's voice says again, "The pigs probably have the little Olmec monkey that Cujo wore around his neck. He gave me the little stone face one night. . . ."

BROWNING: Professor, did you hear the voice on that tape saying "The pigs probably have the little Olmec monkey that Cujo used to wear around his neck"?

MEIGHAN: Olmec is a style named for a very early culture in Mexico for a particular class of archaeological artifacts.

These figurines are commonly sold in Mexico as authentic Olmec monkeys, but the professor thinks these two *monos* are both fakes. Poor Patty.

Does that conclude the government's case? Yes, the government rests, Your Honor. Then Mr. Bailey may begin his surrebuttal tomorrow morning.

The corridor buzz-buzz is louder than usual around the U.S. attorney, who is looking slightly pleased with himself. "You know, we didn't get onto that monkey thing until this very morning," Browning says. But he did, and so the trial of Patricia Hearst has wound up with a Perry Mason flourish, after all.

Tuesday, March 16

The jury is not present. Bailey is still trying to shoehorn Margaret Singer into this trial. This morning he has filed a brief citing as a precedent some twenty-year-old law-review articles on psycholinguistics.

Bailey's next couple of witnesses, a private detective and a lawyer employed thirteen years ago by the late Lenny Bruce, do nothing to elevate the tone of things. Bruce was attempting to overturn a Los Angeles conviction for narcotics possession, and he became frightened that these two men might quit the case when they saw so much drug paraphernalia at Bruce's home, even though the medication— Metheldrine—was entirely legal. To prove the drugs were legit, Bruce put the private eye on the telephone with the doctor who had signed one of the prescriptions, Joel Fort.

As long as he was able to get drugs and prescriptions from Dr. Fort, Bruce said, he could keep going and have a great time.

At this testimony, I feel my own heart lift. Surely now Patty will go free. Even though I think Fort and Kozol's interpretation of what happened was probably largely correct, I do not want Patty convicted, and the image of linking Dr. Fort to Bruce must be very damaging in the jurors' minds.

Bailey's next witness is Trish Tobin. The California Girl in rose-tinted glasses and flower-sprigged frock ascends the witness stand and settles herself with a shake of her shiny yellow hair.

Patricia Cooper Tobin and Patricia Campbell Hearst met at the Burlingame Country Club "in the summer after fourth grade." Would you describe yourself as being her best friend? "Yes, I would," says Trish, with a melting smile. What was her relationship to other members of her family? She had a very warm relationship with them. What were the defendant's political views? We never discussed politics. What were her views on revolutionary matters? Feminist matters? Radical matters? We never discussed any of those things. Trish maintains that her best friend has *no* views, on anything.

What was her friend like on the day after her arrest, when they talked on the jailhouse phones? Patty had no animation or vitality; she just droned along and sighed a lot. She looked terrible and "seemed really dazed." At times she didn't seem to understand what I was saying, and I couldn't follow her. I had no idea we were being taped. But later Dr. West had played the tape for her, and their conversation had been edited, of that she is certain. She recalls Patty saying things that are not on the tape, for example, a comment about the SLA that "these people are so *crazy* or *weird.* . . ."

Trish is trying too hard to help her friend; her testimony sounds overblown. One wonders who "prepared" Trish, and why the decision was made to put her on the stand. The bond between Trish and Patty is clearly one of utter loyalty, but it is girlish and mindless, the loyalty of midnight marshmallow roasts.

"Now, Miss Tobin, if I told you that yesterday Dr. Kozol indicated that, prior to her kidnapping, Miss Hearst was a rebel looking for a cause, how would you describe his comment?"

"As totally false."

"Thank you." With a nod to Browning: "You may cross-examine."

You told Patty Hearst you wished you were a lawyer so you could represent her, didn't you? Agreeing, the witness dissolves into attractive giggles, and the judge smiles. Trish had attended Patty's arraignment and bail hearing in disguise. All during the Missing Year, she maintained a special post-office–box letter drop on the chance her best friend might want to reach her. Her testimony has overtones of girls' adventure books; Patty and Trish could be characters in a mystery.

The government is now ready to play the Trish Tobin tapes for the jury. Patty sounds drugged. The judge cannot understand her. The tape player is faulty again. Repair the machine, Carter orders, and meanwhile, work from the transcript. Browning reads it aloud. The dialogue sounds almost subliterate. "I'll tell you that, well, God, once I get out of here, I'll be able to tell you like all kinds of stories that you just wouldn't even believe, man. [Laughter.]"

When Patty said, "I guess I'll just tell you like my politics are real different from, uh, way back when . . . so this creates all kinds of problems for me in terms of my defense . . ." Trish replied, "Right!" and later, "Yeah, it does. . . . That's the thing."

"What did you really mean by that?" Browning asks.

"It was just something to say."

Bailey's next witness is a surprise. "Call Mr. Hearst, please!"

What a relief, after all these little fish, to see Big Randy stand up and glide serenely over to the witness box. Patty's father has lost fifteen or twenty pounds during the trial. Did you see much of your daughter before the kidnapping? "Oh, sure," he says, in his giggly, Ed Wynn voice. We often had lunch together. What kind of a girl is she? "A very bright girl. Pretty. Strong-willed and fun to be with—*I* think."

A girl could not ask for a more devoted and sincere and adoring father. Randolph Hearst in the witness box appears relaxed, easygoing, *nice*. Yes, Joel Fort had come to the Hearsts' apartment to ask questions about their daughter, as had the other psychiatrists, and, yes, he said that a public trial would be very bad for Patty, that she was pretty run-down and depressed, and that the adversary system was bad. He suggested I inform myself about plea-bargaining, though I don't think he used that word.

In cross-examination, Browning asks, "Was it your impression, sir, that Dr. Fort was trying to fix the case?"

"I wouldn't say he was trying to fix it."

Bailey's next surprising witness is J. Albert Johnson. *Why* has Bailey put his partner on? To my surprise, he is still gnawing away at the Fort bone. The fat man explains that early on, Dr. Fort came around and told Bailey and Johnson he had grave doubts about whether he would testify for the government, in which case he would be available to them. The next thing Johnson knew, Fort had proposed to Catherine Hearst that she try to stop the trial.

Perhaps *this* is the fulcrum of Bailey's fury. It had been inconceivable to Bailey, from the beginning, *not* to try this case, just as it had been inconceivable to the Hearsts not to seek vindication of their good name. If the Hearsts had not wanted a big public trial, would they have hired F. Lee Bailey? Fort's off-the-wall proposal to avoid a trial, cop a plea, turn state's evidence, or plead guilty and throw herself on the mercy of the court would also have deprived a man widely regarded as America's greatest criminal lawyer of the capstone of his career. No wonder F. Lee Bailey hated Joel Fort.

Carter promises this case will be wrapped up tomorrow morning. After that, there will be no more witnesses. His assurance is welcome news. Bailey's attack on Joel Fort recalls the Los Angeles Police Department's response to the SLA—total, hysterical overkill. For more than a week the defense has been diverted and subverted into an all-out personal assault, a legal firefight, a ruthless search-and-destroy mission into the background and character of one little man.

Wednesday, March 17

The jury is brought in, and Bailey calls his last witness. Catherine Hearst, wearing a close-fitting pigeon-brown dress and pink scarf, walks very slowly to the witness box. What kind of girl was Patricia? Catherine flashes the Double-Mint smile. "A very warm and loving girl."

Was she sometimes strong-willed?

"She was. I wouldn't want anything I say make you think it is an easy job to raise five children, Mr. Bailey." Catherine says Dr. Fort told her that if Patty pleaded guilty, the worst sentence she could get as a kidnapping victim would be six months' probation. Fort told Mrs. Hearst the government would besmirch Patty's character and do everything it could to damage her reputation, including presenting evidence on sex and drugs. "They would say things that were very harmful to our family."

Our family. That is what it all seems to come down to in Catherine's mind. If our family must be protected at all costs, then Patty must shed her "bad girl" image; she must have been brainwashed if the honor of our family is to be preserved. But if our family must be protected, even at the cost of one's daughter, then Patty has lost, whatever the verdict.

Cross-examination is brisk. But the jurors are not very attentive to her testimony anyhow; this is the *mother*, after all. Bailey's use of her at all seems bizarre.

The evidence is now finally closed, Carter says, and we shall recess for the day. Final arguments are to begin the next morning, and the following morning, Friday, he will instruct the jury in the law. They will then retire, and their deliberations will take place in the judge's robing room, directly behind the Great Seal of the United States that hangs over his head.

Thursday, March 18

Patty is back in the navy blue with a white bow at the throat. Her skin is bone-white; you can see the skull beneath. The jury files in. It is 9:35 A.M. when Judge Carter begins to speak. "All traffic in and out of the courtroom during the closing arguments will be stopped. . . . Anyone who desires to leave may leave at this time. If not, we are going to lock the doors and start."

Browning's suit is wrinkled, his nose is red, he looks awful; the flu epidemic has hit him. Bailey, by contrast, is animated and well pressed in dignified dark blue. A new podium and microphone have been placed directly in front of and only a few feet from the jury box. Carter swivels to face it and speaks in his patient jury voice, as one would address a small child. Fourteen deadpan faces stare back, solemn as stone.

Ladies and gentlemen, arguments are a time-honored process, so you will understand—in the adversary system—the opposition views of the case. Out of that process usually develops truth. Counsel are skilled in this process, and you should give careful attention to their arguments.

Mr. Browning, on behalf of the United States, will make the opening argument. Mr. Bailey will make his one defense argument, and then there will be the closing argument of the United States by Mr. Browning, who knows that he must make a rebuttal argument only. Mr. Browning, you may proceed.

Sniffling slightly, the U.S. attorney steps up to the special podium. One does not expect much.

Ladies and gentlemen, we expect that Judge Carter will instruct you as to the elements of the crime of bank robbery. Essentially, there are four: One, the United States must prove that somebody took some money from a bank. Two, this was accomplished by means of force, violence, or intimidation. Three, it was accomplished by an assault or by the use of a dangerous weapon. Fourth, that the acts have been done willfully. There is no dispute in this case with respect to the first two elements.

As to the third element, there has been some question raised as to the operability of the defendant's weapon. We do not concede it was inoperable, but aiding and abetting others would be enough, under federal law. So the sole question it boils down to is whether the defendant was in that bank voluntarily and whether she acted willfully with criminal intent.

The burden is on the government to prove the case beyond a reasonable doubt. A reasonable doubt is a doubt based on reason. It is not a possible doubt.

Carter looks quiet, thoughtful, alert, and yes, judicious.

In judging this case, consider the evidence: motion pictures made in the bank, documents in her own handwriting. Rarely has so much evidence of apparent intent been available to a jury. But in addition to the evidence of apparent voluntariness and intent, I want to talk about some of the testimony of the witnesses and some of the circumstantial evidence. . . .

Bailey and Johnson take no notes, but watch the jury intently.

Let me comment on the film itself. The more you see that film, the more things you see in that film. You will see the defendant appear to glance at her watch. She immediately swings her weapon. She does not look over to Mr. DeFreeze or Camilla Hall to see whether she should swing it. You see her mouth open. She may have yelled an order to those customers—"Come in!" or "Get down!"—just before Nancy Ling Perry fired the shots. There is no evidence any of the other four were holding a weapon on Patricia Hearst.

But the evidence, ladies and gentlemen, does not depend only upon the witnesses and upon the film to establish the defendant's intent. You must also consider three other broad categories . . . circumstantial evidence, psychiatric testimony, and the credibility of the defendant.

In dealing with intent, we can't unscrew the top of a person's head and look in. You cannot take the person's word. There is too great a motivation to lie, if it means being convicted of a criminal offense. So we have to look at extrinsic factors. There is just no direct evidence that proves intent because there is no way of fathoming or scrutinizing the operations of a human mind. But you may infer intent from surrounding circumstances. Incidentally, the law makes no distinction, despite what laymen think, between direct evidence and circumstantial evidence. It is what convinces you, ladies and gentlemen, whether circumstantial or direct, that is important.

The most crucial segment of circumstantial evidence is the events at Mel's Sporting Goods store and the following day and night. Why? Well, first of all, I suggest that it is reasonable to believe that a person who is in fear of being killed by her captors does not, when confronted with an opportunity to escape from the captors, fire weapons in the direction of other persons in order to free the captors and does not fail to try to escape, given an opportunity. Can you, as reasonable people accept the story that they forced her to rob that bank when, one month later, she is spraying this area with machine-gun fire in order to free the very people she claims forced her to rob the bank? Finally, don't forget that the defendant told Tom Matthews that very same afternoon that it gave her "a good feeling" to see her comrades come running across the street.

Other items of circumstantial evidence would include the words "Patria o Muerte," written on the wall of the Golden Gate apartment in the defendant's handwriting. As I understand her testimony, they did not make her write it on the wall. They also trusted her enough to stand guard duty with a loaded weapon. Is it reasonable that the captors would entrust their safety to their hostage?

You can say, I suppose, the defendant simply put on a good act. Where does a good act leave off and voluntary participation begin? Consider the fact that after the bank robbery they all counted the money. And they split it up nine ways. If you, as a reasonable person, heard that a person in a bank with a weapon had helped count the money and had received an equal cut thereof, would you conclude that *it's reasonable to believe that that person participated willfully? I submit that you most certainly would. So there again is an item of circumstantial evidence for you to consider.*

Fourthly, I want to mention to you the concept of flight. Flight is a very old concept in American jurisprudence and in English common law, almost as old as the law itself, and it holds simply that a guilty person usually flees. Flight tends to indicate a consciousness of guilt. So does concealment of a defendant after a crime that is a fact. Here we have a defendant who was missing for some seventeen months after the bank robbery. You might say she didn't call us; we called her. She didn't turn herself in. And you may consider that she had opportunities to escape or at least to get some word back to the authorities; she did not do it.

I suggested to you earlier that the operability of a weapon bears upon her intent. I want to come back to that.

Browning steps over to Gene Driscoll, the court clerk, who hands him the carbine with its flapping tag.

If the defendant was in the bank with an operable weapon, it is more likely that she was there with willful intent, and not, as Mr. Bailey characterized it, as a "prize pig." In other words, if you're going to rob a bank and you're not sure about one person, you certainly don't give them an operable weapon with live bullets. You give them a simulated weapon that doesn't work. You recall she testified that she looked down and she saw that the bolt was turned. It's rather difficult to keep the bolt in that turned position, so that it is not all the way forward. You will recall when Mr. Sibert, the firearms expert, demonstrated, simply by tapping the gun against the corner of the table, that the bolt would slide forward by itself.

It is already ten-forty. The time is going by very fast.

Ladies and gentlemen, let me say a few words about this psychiatric testimony. It is not alleged that she has a mental disease or defect that causes her to lack the mental capacity to commit a crime. It is not an insanity defense. Under the instructions that you will receive from the judge, you will hear that you are free to accept or reject the opinion of an expert witness, a psychiatrist. The psychiatrists weren't there at the bank robbery; they weren't there at Mel's; they don't have any ability to unscrew the top of a person's head and look in and take a picture of what the intent was any more than you or I do. They are trained, yes. But I hope you decide this case on the facts because that is, frankly, where it's at.

A duress defense is what is being proposed in this case—that somebody was threatening to kill her unless she robbed that bank and that she was in imminent fear of death or great bodily injury as a result of those threats. You don't need a psychiatrist to tell you whether that is true or not. You can decide that just as easily as anybody else can. . . .

All the talk about mind control, psychological coercion, et cetera, et cetera, apparently was injected in this case by the defense in the hope that if duress does not stick to the ceiling, maybe something else will. I urge you not to be misled by that, because brainwashing and coercion are totally inconsistent concepts. If a person is brainwashed, there is no *necessity to coerce her physically. And the converse is equally true. Duress or coercion is a factual defense. It depends upon physical evidence that you yourselves can look at, that any individual who is familiar with human affairs is capable of evaluating. You don't need an expert.*

I want to ask you to bear in mind that the doctors who were called by the defense in this case are basically not experienced in examining persons who are charged with criminal offenses, as were Doctors Fort and Kozol. Every one of them referred to the defendant as "a patient," not as a subject or a defendant but as "a patient." Most of these doctors are used to working with individuals who come to them for treatment. There is a great difference between that type of relationship and one in which you are evaluating persons charged with criminal offenses.

Secondly, the psychiatric experts called by the defense are academicians. They are not forensic psychiatrists. They are apt to find in any subject a varying degree of the particular malady they happen to specialize in.

Thirdly, all the doctors, that is, defense and prosecution, seem to agree that the other members of the SLA came from similar white upper-middle-class backgrounds, and they all found that significant. Apparently something changed those other white upper-middle-class females; something made them become urban guerrillas or revolutionaries. What was it? Was each and every one of them brainwashed? And, if not, is it all that surprising that Patricia Hearst could have made the same voluntary conversion, attitudinal change? I submit to you that it is not.

We take a short midmorning recess. The reporters are subdued and impressed. The prosecutor has revealed himself as a fine carpenter who has built a solid case, and he is now hitting each one of his points squarely on the head. He tells us he doesn't intend to talk much longer. It is 11:04 A.M. when the marshals relock the doors.

Ladies and gentlemen, I know it's not easy to sit there and listen to a harangue for two hours, and I do thank you for your patience. You recall that Dr. West was the leadoff witness for the defense. But they all talked about brainwashing or thought reform, and they all took the SLA babble rather literally. They found, in effect, that they were an army, eight young middle-class people, college-educated, from professional backgrounds, filled with guilt, led by a black man but overwhelmingly female. This was the army. The SLA announced they were at war.

The SLA, in rather pompous rhetoric and to dazzle the media, called Patricia Hearst a POW. So the defense psychiatrists found that she was, in fact, a POW. And the conclusions followed not from an analysis, we submit, of hard evidence, but from a rather literary description of her. Once they find that Patricia Hearst was a POW, they conclude that everything she did was coerced—notwithstanding, ladies and gentlemen, that they are unable to cite to us a single instance of a POW ever committing an overtly violent act as a result of the mind control or brainwash. They conclude she couldn't escape during well over a year and a half, notwithstanding that she was not in a POW camp behind enemy lines and the fact that many of the POWs who were did undertake successfully to escape.

Browning's presentation is so orderly, so measured, I find I can write down almost every word in longhand.

What emerges from all of [this] ladies and gentlemen, is that psychiatrists and—just as Judge Carter said—lawyers as well have no corner on being able to tell when somebody is lying. The time-honored and tested commonsense way to look at these matters is for you to decide, based on the evidence, with your own collective intelligence and your own good sense.

Let me speak to a very, very important matter in this case, and that is the defendant's credibility as a witness. You may look to the substance of her testimony, that is, what she says, as well as how she says it, in determining what credibility to ascribe to her testimony. When a defendant makes some statement tending to show innocence, and this explanation or statement is later shown to be false, you may consider that falsity as circumstantial evidence pointing to a consciousness of guilt. In this connection, I urge you to consider the affidavit that Miss Hearst signed with respect to bail. We find in the affidavit not one reference to a second closet. We find in the affidavit that she heard "constant threats against her life and saw her captors armed with revolvers, shotguns, and other weapons." Later she admitted that was not a true statement because she was blindfolded. She states in the affidavit, "Meanwhile, one of her captors, armed with a gun which was kept pointed at her, had told her in advance [of the bank robbery] that if she did anything except announce her name, she would be killed immediately." But she testified she was supposed to make a speech in the bank. The affidavit was untrue again.

Does it surprise you ladies and gentlemen at all that this affidavit was signed two days after the conversation you heard yesterday, wherein Miss Hearst says to

Trish Tobin, "I can tell you things you wouldn't believe." I won't belabor you, ladies and gentlemen, but that affidavit was signed under penalty of perjury, just as the oath she took when she appeared as a witness in this case.

There is another matter that you should consider in gauging Miss Hearst's credibility, and that is the matter of her refusing to answer questions. The law holds that when a witness refuses to answer a question after being instructed by the court to answer, that fact may be considered by you in determining the credibility of the witness and the weight her testimony deserves. The court also will instruct you that fear of death is no legal privilege to take the Fifth.

There are some other matters bearing on the credibility of the defendant. She said she gave the clenched-fist salute and talked the way she did on the Trish Tobin tape because she feared the presence of Emily Harris. And yet we know now, pursuant to stipulation after the facts were checked, that Emily Harris was not in that visitors' room at the time of that conversation.

Now this claim about her fear of the Harrises. She was living at 625 Morse Street. She stated in her testimony that neither Harris—Emily nor William—had ever been to 625 Morse Street. And yet we are asked to believe that she had loaded weapons on those premises and a loaded pistol in her purse because she was afraid that William Harris might pop in sometime. Is that reasonable, ladies and gentlemen? I submit it is not.

And then we have the opportunities that the defendant had to escape, to make telephone calls, even to turn the Harrises in. Yet she didn't do it. . . .

Is this business of the haircutting reasonable? First to decide to put the defendant in the middle of a bank robbery as a "prize pig" to show her off, then to cut off nearly all her hair, and then have to find her a wig so she would look like herself again? I suggest it's more reasonable to believe that she wanted a wig to disguise herself. Persons who rob banks do often disguise themselves to make apprehension and identification more difficult.

All this sounds so reasonable, as Jim Browning lays it out, that one wonders, marvels even, at the easy, friendly trust we have held this girl in, in this courtroom—not only in the early weeks of trial, when she looked so wan, but also in later weeks as she began to look merely pale and familiar. *Nothing* is appealing about the defendant right now except her plight, which is heartrending.

Finally, ladies and gentlemen, I want to talk just a bit about the alleged forced sexual intercourse or rape by Willie Wolfe. . . . Consider Miss Hearst's testimony when I asked her what her strong feeling was about Willie Wolfe. Remember that? "I couldn't stand him," she said. "I couldn't stand him!" Of course, that was after she testified he raped her. Sure. And on the occasion of her arrest, a year and a half later, after he "raped her," she had this little stone face in her purse!

Browning turns out to be a surprisingly good mimic. He lifts his lanky arm and holds aloft the little monkey charm while rising slightly on his toes, like a matador, after the fancy capework, about to go in over the horns for the kill.

She "couldn't stand him." And yet there is this little stone face that can't say anything. But, I submit, it can tell us a lot.

In short, ladies and gentlemen, we ask you to reject the defendant's entire testimony as not credible. She asks us to believe she didn't mean what she said on the tapes. She didn't mean what she wrote in the documents. She didn't mean it when she gave this power salute, this clenched-fist salute, after her arrest. She didn't mean it when she told the San Mateo County deputy sheriff that she was an urban guerrilla. She says the Tobin conversation wasn't the real Patricia Hearst. The Mel's shooting incident was simply a reflex, ladies and gentlemen; the untruths in the affidavits were simply some attorney's idea. She was in such fear she couldn't escape in nineteen months, while she was crisscrossing the country, or even get word to her parents or someone else. The confession to Matthews was recited out of fear. She couldn't stand Willie Wolfe, yet she carried that stone face with her until the day she was arrested!

It's too big a pill to swallow, ladies and gentlemen. It just does not wash. I ask whether you would accept this incredible story from anyone but Patricia Hearst. And if you wouldn't—don't accept it from her, either.

It is 12:03 P.M. when the prosecutor sits down. He has talked for two hours and introduced 295 pieces of evidence in making his orderly, detailed, and factual argument.

The jury is sitting in its box after lunch, the spectators waiting, when the courtroom's rear door opens and F. Lee Bailey hurries down the aisle, his hair rumpled, his face flushed, a thick sheaf of notes in his hand. Asking Judge Carter's permission to use a hand microphone, he rises on his toes and detaches the podium mike from its cradle. In so doing, he leaves all his notes behind him on the table. No matter. Speaking in a low but vibrant voice, looking directly at the jury, holding the mike in his hand, he bends his body across the awkward, chest-high podium as if it were a rack. The crowd is tense.

The SLA was so right about so many things that I, as a citizen, am a little bit ashamed that they could predict so well what we would do. But I think an overview of this case is more appropriate than talking just about bank robbery. This is not a case about a bank robbery. It is a case about dying or surviving. How far can you go to survive? People eat each other in the Andes to survive. The big question is—and we don't have it in this case, thank God—can you kill to survive? We do it in wartime, but that is a different set of rules. We allow ourselves all kinds of special privileges when we fight the enemy. G. Gordon Liddy would have been an international hero if it was only the Russians who caught him instead of the reporters, and ultimately the Department of Justice. A novelist once wrote a most disturbing book—you may have heard about it. It was a best-seller and a movie. A man who was condemned to hang for killing his wife killed his executioner to survive, and then it was determined that he had not killed his wife. And a judge had to decide whether or not he could be tried for that second killing. Does one have an obligation at some point to die? We're all going to die, and we know it. And we're all going to postpone that date as long as we can. And Patty Hearst did that, and that is why she is here and you are here. And the manner in which she did it is the subject of this trial.

There has been much contradictory evidence of peripheral matters. I don't agree with Mr. Browning that we are in no better position to judge the truth than you are. We are skilled at this sort of thing. There are specialists in deception and simulation, and you were privileged to hear from one of the very best alive today, whose opinion you may accept or reject because, in the end, we come back to a nonperson.

Is this reference to Fort? Orne? Patty? One is not sure. Bailey's train of thought is erratic.

What happened in this case? We all know what happened and we watched it happen. The news media kept us informed of every detail. The interest of the news media in this case has been so intense that it was necessary to protect you from it. A young girl who absolutely had no political motivations or history of activity of any kind was rudely snatched from her home and taken as a political prisoner. She did rob the bank. The question you are here to answer is why. And would you have done the same thing to survive? Or was it her duty to die, to avoid committing a felony? This is all this case is about, and all the muddling and stamping of exhibits and the little monkeys and everything else that has been thrown into the morass don't answer that question.

Patty Hearst has a lot going against her. The escape that Mr. Browning and Dr. Kozol think she should have welcomed—she said, "I had nowhere to go"—

has resulted in only a change of captors. But at least now, as long as society is her captor, she does not have to worry about being killed. Freedom may be a more awesome alternative—but you are not here to decide that.

The SLA predicted this trial. They also predicted your verdict and persuaded her that coming back would get her twenty-five years. If we can't break the chain in their predictions, there are going to be other Patricia Hearsts.

This is the first of several implied threats that Bailey will make to the jurors in the course of an increasingly rambling and emotional appeal: if you find Patty guilty, you will be responsible for future Patty Hearsts.

The SLA said, this is a political prisoner, paying for the crimes of her parents. I don't perceive they committed any crimes. An enemy of the country perceived that, a bunch of crazy psychopaths that Harry Kozol had the unmitigated gall to delineate similar to the defendant. In what possible way? They killed people because they liked to kill people. They wanted to insult the world in which we live. They perceived us as bad, and some of them died for that belief. I ask you to rememeber that were it not for Mel's Sporting Goods, Patricia Hearst would be dead, too, and you wouldn't even have a body to try.

This case has to be tried. The public would not have stood still for its dismissal. It had to be tried. Joel Fort just tried to put together a deal so he could write another chapter in his book, the one to tell you how he saved Lenny Bruce.

Bailey drops his voice very low.

. . . You heard a little girl saying, "Please, please, do what they want! Don't come bombing in here like you did in Oakland. There will be gunfire and I will be the first one to get it. Don't do that. Be nice to them. Do everything they want." And she might as well have said, As I have done. And she did, and she survived. In every kidnapping case there are only two kinds of victims: those who survive and those who don't. But, as Dr. Fort discovered, while the government paid him to try to become the expert he pretended to be, all of the ones who survived do exactly what they are told to do when they are told to do it.

Patty Hearst robbed a bank. The case boils down to the fine line between whether she wanted them to believe she was voluntary—or really wanted to be there. Dr. Orne said there were three possibilities. First, she needed the money. Second, she wanted to be there as a rebel. And third, she had no choice.

When I considered defending the case, I had a great concern. I do not tolerate people who think a United States courtroom is the place to put on a show. Because when the court's orders are not obeyed, the system of which I am a part is failing. I said to myself, If I walk in and find this is a flaming revolutionary, who's going to insist on the right to jump up and protest and insult all and sundry from the witness box, I think I want no part of that—much as I grieve for the plight of Mr. and Mrs. Hearst.

The problem did not arise. You have the word of the court-appointed doctors as to what happened. When Tania's American operators were removed from the scene, the "urban guerrilla" died, gradually and slowly, and all that was left was fear—and hatred. A real fear, of undergoing this trial, and being told not to testify, by people who were now demanding $250,000 to save those who have destroyed your life, punctuated by a bomb that blows up a building with the name Hearst on it.

Patricia Hearst was not a bad girl. She is not famous for anything she did before February 4. She's famous for what happened to her afterward. And what did happen is up to you to decide. If—and this is a pretty far-out theory—if she really liked these people who kept her in the closet, the closet, the closet, the closet—the one Dr. Fort thought was reasonably comfortable, I gather . . . If you can be duped into believing the preposterous notion that Dr. Kozol said he believed, that when Cinque said, "She is with us," she really was . . . "I believe that black man," were Kozol's words. . . . You consider whether you would stand up to that closet. Not your daughters or your sisters but you, yourself.

Bailey steps out from behind his podium, walks right up to the jury box, grips the rail, and leans in, saying directly into the jurors' faces the words he pictures Cinque saying to Patty, "Either do what I say—or—I—will—blow—your—head—off." The moment is no less frightening for the words' being delivered in an almost inaudible whisper.

Once I have seated myself, my job is done, and I must be forever silent. Mr. Browning has the opportunity to answer any questions I may have raised, and you will get the court's instructions, and then you are on your own until you come back and give us a verdict. And that will either be the most horrible saying that Patricia Hearst has ever heard, in one word—or the symphony the SLA says we couldn't deliver, in two.

Bailey stops talking, but he doesn't move. Is this the end? Not quite.

This case is riddled with doubt. It always will be. Perry Mason brings perfect solutions to all cases. Real life doesn't work that way. No one is ever going to be sure. They will be talking about this case for longer than I think I am going to have to talk about it. But there is not anything close to proof beyond a reasonable doubt that Patty Hearst wanted to be a bank robber. What you know, and you know in your hearts to be true, is beyond dispute. There was talk about her dying, and she wanted to survive. Thank God, so far she has. Thank you very much.

Bailey turns away with tears in his eyes and straps his wristwatch back on. He has talked less than forty-five minutes. The court declares a short recess, and the lawyer trudges wearily out of the courtroom between the defendant's parents, one heavy arm thrown across the shoulders of each. When we return to our seats after recess, Browning promises his closing argument will last no longer than half an hour.

I am sorry Patricia Hearst was kidnapped. I am sorry when anybody is kidnapped. I wouldn't want to be kidnapped. Neither would you. But to make the assumption that she remained a kidnap victim for the next nineteen months strains credulity.

The bottom line here, ladies and gentlemen, is to use your good sense in arriving at a verdict in determining whether the person inside the Hibernia Bank on April 15, 1974, was a person who fired the guns down at Mel's in Los Angeles a month later. The person who gave the clenched-fist salute in this courthouse. The person who described herself as an urban guerrilla upon booking. The person who, time after time, failed to escape, to notify her parents. The person who spoke with Trish Tobin on the tape said she was pissed off about being arrested. The person who signed that affidavit. The person who, in short, the evidence shows had become a revolutionary and robbed the bank voluntarily.

We ask you to return a guilty verdict on both counts of the indictment.

Friday, March 19

Catherine Campbell Hearst comes down the aisle like a new-made widow, wearing on her crumpled face the Celtic certainty of disaster. She is leaning hard on Vicki's arm and weeping openly; even her chrysanthemum hairdo is wilted by grief. Judge Carter announces that the rules of reason have come down to us through the history of jurisprudence, and, he adds, smartly stacking a thick sheaf of papers on his desk top, the same principles will now be stated in varying ways.

What Carter is, in fact, doing is explaining the rules of the game retroactively, after the game has been played. It is six months to the day, less three and a half hours, from the moment Tom Padden crashed through the door of 625 Morse Street, shouting, "FBI! Freeze!" and causing one of the occupants to wet her pants.

This was to have been a weekend of entire, blissful escape. Nobody expected a verdict until at least the middle of next week. Late yesterday afternoon I drove an hour out of San Francisco to a glamorous, easeful ranch house in the wine country north of the city. I could not find a more perfect hospice. Except that after one candlelit dinner, one fitful night in the linen sheets, I am jumpy as a water bug. When I try to work on my blue notebooks, the jumpiness gets worse, so this morning, even before lunch, I slam notebooks, suitcases, and myself back into my rented Hertz without quite knowing why, startling myself and insulting my host, and then I barrel top speed back toward the city, country music blasting from the car radio and me singing along at the top of my lungs. As I make the turn onto Van Ness the disc jockey interrupts to announce that the jury in the Hearst case has just sent a message to the judge. My foot mashes the accelerator, and in ten minutes I have thrown my car into an empty lot and am back up on the nineteenth floor, breathless.

Johnson looks gray, Bailey waxen-faced; Catherine's Chinese face is perfectly composed; Randy's is set like cement. When we rise this time for Judge Carter's entrance, we all remain standing, as if awaiting the blessing in church. Patty stands up at her table, braced by her pink-enameled fingertips, mouth slightly open, cheeks hollow. The jury files in, staring straight ahead. Patty's mouth opens wider. My own heart batters my ribs with a force I would not have believed. Judge Carter bites a cuticle. The foreman hands a paper to the clerk. A split second before he reads it aloud, Patty sways toward Bailey and says one word in a low but clear voice: "Guilty."

"We, the jury, find the defendant guilty on the first count and guilty on the second count," the clerk reads. Then the jury is polled, and each person tonelessly repeats the word "guilty." But Patty said it first, and said it aloud, and right now that millisecond's lead in saying "Guilty" before everybody else says it, too, appears to be her only victory.

EDITOR'S NOTE

Patricia Hearst served fourteen months of her seven-year prison term, including her pre-trial detention, before she was released on $1.5 million bail in custody of her parents in November 1976. On February 1, 1979, President Jimmy Carter granted Patty a pardon and two and a half months later she was married to a former body guard, Bernard Shaw.

Introductory Note

What distinguishes this book from all other histories of
weaponry is that it principally examines an aspect of the
subject hitherto unexplored: design failure. And in
particular the failure in design of secret weaponry from
Antiquity to the present day.

The book has taken many years of extensive, privately
funded research, and though it cannot claim to be a catalogue
raisonée of all such weapons, it does aim to examine wherever
possible the basic prototype rather than its multitudinous
variants.

The author presumes that his readers do not wish to be bored
by measurements and specifications, nor by the quotation of sources.

An Introduction to the Secret Weapons of History

HALBRITTER'S ARMS THROUGH THE AGES

A Condensation of the book by

KURT HALBRITTER

The Spartan Ram, later The Rabbit Punch

Fortresses existed in ancient Greece and even then special devices were required to attack them. The Spartan Ram was popular because of its simple, inexpensive construction. During the Swabian War of 1499 the enemies of the Swabian Federation modelled their battering rams in the shapes of rabbits, after hearing that no animal struck more terror in the Swabian heart.

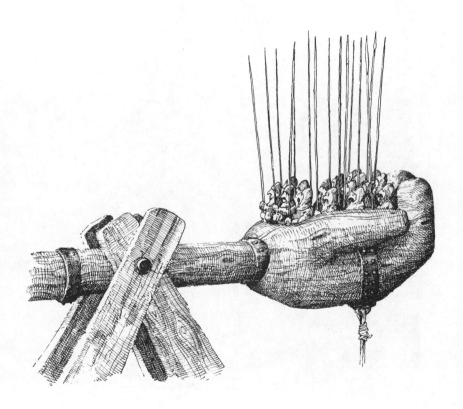

The Hand Grenade

The Hand Grenade was carved out of hard wood bound with iron bands and counter-weighted with a single granite boulder. It was much used in ancient times, but the Roman authorities phased it out because of the extraordinarily high injury rate amongst Hand Grenadiers.

The War Horse

This is one of the earliest known examples of mechanised weaponry. During the rule of the tyrants Hippias and Hipparch (527-514 B.C.) the War Horse was often used for street fighting. The complicated way in which it moved made daily exercises obligatory.

The Duck
Between 483 and 481 the Romans built and launched one
hundred and eighty amphibious craft. This was the first
historically-recorded fleet-building programme. Of course
this type of craft has antecedents in legend, one such exists
in the Old Testament (cf. The Book of Jonah.)

Grecian Hang Gliders

The account of the escape of Daedalus and Icarus from the
Labyrinth at Knossos was an inspiration to the weapons
industry of the day, despite the tragic outcome of Icarus's test
flight.
Flying Helmet F 104, shown above, was considered
extremely difficult to fly by those chosen to wear it.
Nevertheless, in battle the Grecian Hang Gliders were
thought to be unbeatable.
Double-spread illustration overleaf: manoeuvres, late
summer, 400 B.C.

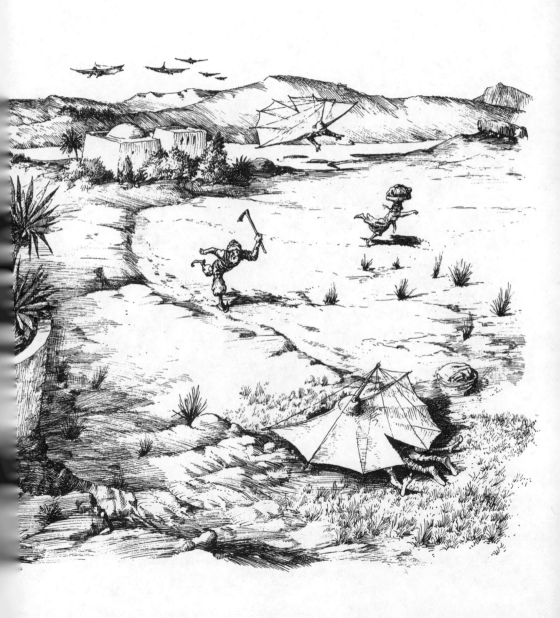

Disc-Throwers: Grecian and Roman

The technique of disc-throwing became famous throughout the Ancient World as Greek culture spread after the conquests of Alexander the Great. The music the spinning discs made when hurled into the air was particularly pleasing, and the legions of Rome could not resist lending an ear to its tunes.

An Athenian Missile Battery (With Homer Device)
The failure of the Athenians to liberate themselves from the
Macedonian occupying forces in 265 B.C. is, according to the
author's research, largely attributable to their dilettantish use
of missiles with untested and, as far as aim was concerned,
almost irresponsibly inaccurate warheads.

**A Stately Subquinquereme with Its Bamboo Snorkels
in the "Up" Position**

One of the little known facts of history is that the conquest of
Carthage in 146 B.C. was largely decided by the Subquinquereme. Surprisingly, one hundred years later this
miracle weapon was already obsolescent and only brought
out to intimidate visiting heads of state.

**The Carthaginian
Stork Squadron**

Carthaginian attempts to gain air
supremacy in the Spring Offensive of 146 B.C.
failed because of the unreliability
of the Stork Squadron.
The Squadron had to follow the migratory
pattern of its storks and scrambled
at no other time.

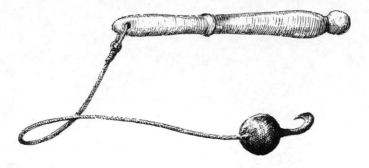

Kamikazi Catapulters

Caesar's legions came face to face with Kamikazi Catapulters for the first time when the Gauls led by Vercingetorix rebelled. They catapulted themselves over the walls of Roman fortresses by an ingenious, if suicidal, method.

The Baconeers

The decline and fall of the Roman Empire was considerably hastened by the Baconeers, most feared of all the northern hordes. To call the Baconeers a fighting unit is to presume they understood military discipline. They did not. Their only motivation was greed. Pillage and rape they regarded with keen anticipation. Therefore, although the Visigothic High Command appreciated their ferocity, it was continually at a loss to know how to keep the Baconeers in check. They had an unattractive habit of butchering anyone sent to command them.

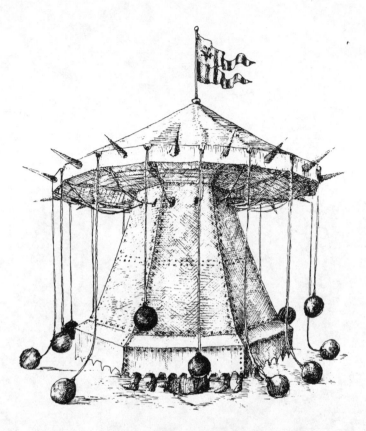

The Merry-Go-Wound

The effectiveness of this weapon depended upon the enemy
mistaking it for a harmless fairground Merry-Go-Round.
When it was approached to within striking distance,
mechanics hidden from sight inside the central core revolved
the Merry-Go-Wound at high speed. The iron balls suspended
from the deceptively ornamental canopy flew outwards and
severely wounded the enemy.
However, the weapon was extraordinarily expensive to
produce, not readily transportable, and its distinctive
appearance made avoidance a simple and wholly effective
tactic.

The Field Screw

The Field Screw was one of a number of weapons devised to pierce enemy defences. Under cover of night whole sections of palisade could be removed (see illustration), and sentries on guard duty were trained to listen out for the faint rhythmical squeak of an enemy Field Screw working its way into their wooden fortifications.

"My name is Brother Bertold Schwarz."

"What can I do for you?"

"Well, I've invented this powder."

"Oh yes, what's it for?"

Gunpowder

Just who it was who invented gunpowder is a subject much debated amongst historians, but recent research conducted by the author of this work proves conclusively that the inventor was a quiet, unassuming Bernardine monk called Brother Bertold Schwarz. Uncertain of what use he might make of his discovery, Brother Bertold took his powder to demonstrate to a fellow monk. The quotations are from a contemporary eye-witness account:

"Saltpetre, sulphur, charcoal,
 Saltpetre, sulphur, charcoal,
 Saltpetre . . ."

"Well, if you'll let me borrow your ink-pot
I'll give you a demonstration."

"I must say I'm curious to know what it does."

"Its use I dedicate to God."

"Fine, but what's the point of it?"

"Now, you hold it firmly while I make a
spark with my tinderbox."

"This is absolutely fascinating."

"Bang!"

The Invention of the Cannon

The cannon was invented accidentally by a simple
blacksmith called Frederick Wuchtel, who came from the
town of Eisenberg in eastern Germany. Wuchtel was in the
habit of keeping a quantity of powder in his smithy, sealed
inside a metal container. One day Wuchtel forgot to replace
the top. He realised his mistake almost immediately and
thrust it back, but he was too late. A spark from the forge had
ignited the powder and, with a violent explosion, the top of
the container was blown through the smithy roof. Wuchtel,
badly shaken, looked up to where his predecessor, an
Englishman, had engraved an inscription, part in English,
part in Latin: "Oh Lorde admitte meus fore I can non existe
sine teus". The missile had torn away the words "can non".
"Whatever it is that I have invented", said Wuchtel pointing
to the hole in his roof, "it shall henceforth be called the can
non".

The Muzzle-Loading Haversack Five Pounder

The demonstration of this new weapon was one of a number of festivities arranged to celebrate the coronation of Ferdinand I as king of Bohemia and Hungary. But the ballistics experts responsible for the design failed to take into account the effect of recoil; it was said at the time that had the gun not been blessed it might have dethroned the Emperor or worse.

Papal Galleons
These stately craft proclaimed the religious message of the
Papacy by their sheer size and impressiveness.

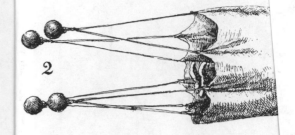

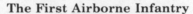

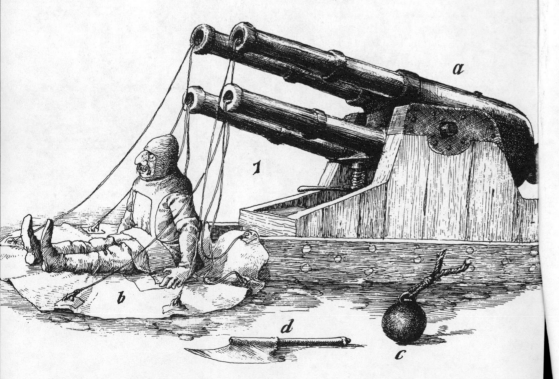

The First Airborne Infantry

The Italian painter and inventor Leonardo da Vinci discovered the principles governing both powered flight and the parachute, but the latter seemed to the arms industry of the High Renaissance to be pointless without the practical realisation of the former—i.e. a soldier had to be up in the air before he could hope to parachute down upon an enemy. The illustrations depict one ill-fated method devised to overcome this problem:

1. A four-barrelled cannon (a)
2. shot an infantryman (b) strapped into a weighted parachute (c) and armed with an axe with which to cut himself free (d) over enemy lines.
3. Landing was a nightmare which few survived.

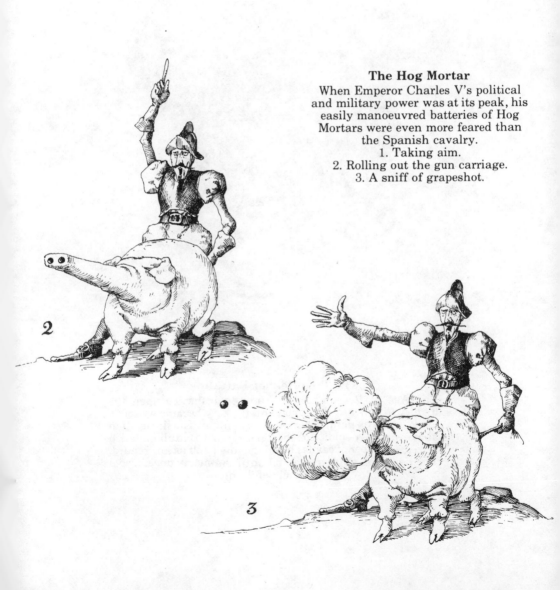

The Hog Mortar

When Emperor Charles V's political and military power was at its peak, his easily manoeuvred batteries of Hog Mortars were even more feared than the Spanish cavalry.
1. Taking aim.
2. Rolling out the gun carriage.
3. A sniff of grapeshot.

2

3

The Tree Helmet Battalion

The Age of Reason had a profound influence upon the
history of warfare: deception and trickery became weapons
as powerful as gunpowder and the cannon. The illustration
above shows a soldier of the Tree Helmet Battalion, which
seized a number of castles by disguising itself as an orchard.
The tactic remained successful until the enemy developed a
powerful defoliant.

Bladed Breastplates

A large number of officers went into the Thirty Years War in the belief that it would be over by Christmas 1618. At home their wives became more and more furious as the years passed by. By 1648 many officers simply could not face the anger of their spouses and returned home wearing Bladed Breastplates. These ensured that homecomings were brief and to the point and lengthy explanations superfluous.

The Scissor Stabber
The wives of soldiers fighting in the Thirty Years War had to rely upon the resourcefulness of their servants to protect them from the bands of marauding mercenaries who roamed throughout Europe. Out of everyday implements an astonishing variety of weapons were constructed (see above).

Some Seventeenth-Century Developments in the Science of Gunnery

The Up and Over Twenty Pounder

This cannon enabled armies to fire over walls and other major obstructions in the field. The Up and Over came with a number of different barrel lengths and a cunning modification which enabled it to fire round corners.

The Parthian Pounder

It has been said more than once that the best form of attack is defence, for an army is never more vulnerable than at the moment it senses victory. Disciplined formations are abandoned, the infantry rush forward impetuously and the Parthian Pounder comes into its own. It was a devastating weapon which more than once completely reversed the almost certain outcome of a battle. Note the more intimate Parthian Arquebus in the foreground of the double-spread overleaf.

Small Arms

The Spiral Musket

The spiralled barrel of this ingenious weapon gave it a
potent muzzle velocity and its periscopic sights
enabled a fusilier to fire from behind complete cover.
Much loved throughout the eighteenth century.

Small Arms

A Cross-Country Arquebus
Considerably less ingenious than the Spiral Musket,
the Cross-Country Arquebus was cumbersome and not
at all accurate.

The Blowpipes of St. Blaise

The legendary invincibility of alpine fortresses was in no small part due to the blowpipers of St. Blaise, who rained down volley after volley of steel-tipped darts upon their enemies. Subsequent generations of Swiss failed to understand that the St. Blaise blowpipe was a weapon of war and not a musical instrument.

VICIOUS CIRCLES

A Condensation of the book by

JONATHAN KWITNY

CHAPTER 1

THE MEAT THAT DIDN'T MOO

It was 1964, the first of thirteen frustrating years that Bob Nicholson and Lou Montello of the Manhattan district attorney's office would spend trying to break the Mafia's hold on the New York meat market. As much as 20 percent of all the meat in the country changed hands on the New York market, making it the world's largest. And the Mafia seemed to own it—the way the Mafia continues to own a lot of American marketplaces. In fact, more than a decade later, when Nicholson and Montello resigned from the police force in disgust, most of the major criminal figures in their original investigation were still in the meat business.

Back on November 14, they had planted a bug—a tiny wireless microphone and radio transmitter. The bug was in the office of Norman (Nat) Lokietz, the president and principal owner (if you didn't count the hoods on his back) of Merkel Meat Company, whose headquarters was seven or eight blocks from where Nicholson and Montello sat listening. Merkel had been an industry leader for more years than anyone could remember. The hoods brought Lokietz in to run it in 1963.

The cops had bugged Lokietz's office in an attempt to prove allegations that corruption in the meat industry was costing the public millions of dollars. But Nicholson and Montello were about to learn— with an explicitness that appalled them—that Mafia control of an industry robs the public of far more than just its money.

What Nicholson and Montello had expected to hear in the Merkel office was talk about the extortion activities of the leaders of Local 174 of the Amalgamated Meat Cutters and Butcher Workmen of North

America, AFL-CIO. Local 174 was the largest in the five-hundred-thousand-member butchers' union. It had grown out of a local founded in 1934 by a Mafia captain known as Little Augie Pisano (born Anthony Carfano) and his labor side-kick George Scalise. Scalise organized on the Mafia's behalf not only the butchers' union, but also the Building Service Employees Union, the Liquor Wholesalers and Distillery Workers' Union, the gasoline station attendants' union, and a Teamster local, among others. When the Mafia wants to control an industry, the union is usually the easiest place to start.

The officers of butchers' Local 174 had been mere fronts—well-paid fronts—for the Mob from the beginning. All this had been proven in court by the Manhattan District Attorney's Office back in 1940 when Thomas E. Dewey was running it. Scalise even went off to jail in the 1940s on account of his union work, but the system never changed.

Now, a generation later, Nicholson and Montello were working under the direction of D.A. Frank Hogan and his rackets chief, Alfred Scotti, who himself had worked on the Dewey investigations. In what they attempted and what they learned, Nicholson and Montello would go much further than Dewey's men ever did. Over thirteen years they would track the Mafia's power out of the union halls and into the executive suites of the great supermarket chains and finally to Iowa and Nebraska, and to the chief executive of the largest slaughtering and meatpacking company in the world. They would learn the power of a crime syndicate over much of a large industry, over the American diet and pocketbook, and sometimes even over law enforcement.

By the time the bug had been secreted inside Nat Lokietz's office in Queens, the two detectives were already six months into their investigation. Their long study of the meat industry had taught them that so-called "straight beef"—fresh-cut steaks, roasts, and chops—doesn't provide much kickback money unless there is very high volume or unless substantial upgrading is involved. The biggest kickback items are the so-called "specialty cuts," such as briskets, corned beef, and navels (which are ground into hamburger and sausage). As an admittedly corrupt meat buyer explained it, "On straight beef you can't hit 'em too hard, 'cause there's not enough money in it. Most of them [the wholesalers] work a half to a quarter cent a pound [profit]. They can't kick back too much on that." But on the small stuff, navels, briskets, he said, the price went up by six to eight cents a pound to account for bribes.

Based on what their informant told them, Nicholson and Montello began tailing A & P buyers in the New York area to secret lunch-time meetings with wholesale meat suppliers. Conversations were overheard. The cops learned that a supplier had sent $15,000 in U.S. savings bonds to the home of one A & P meat executive, Walter Kromholtz. When they faced him with this information, Kromholtz broke down and confessed that he was getting kickbacks from seven or eight suppliers, and that others at A & P were doing the same. He provided a list of givers and takers, and agreed to wear a hidden tape recorder in conversation with them. A considerable number of conversations with A & P men and with suppliers were successfully recorded before Walter Kromholtz decided he had had enough, locked himself in the garage and turned on the car engine. His wife and children found his body.

Most of the talk overheard among meat dealers, however, was not about kickbacks to the supermarket executives. A much bigger concern seemed to be something that Nicholson and Montello hadn't known about—extortion by the butchers' union. In fact, perhaps because 1964 was a contract renewal year, it seemed that whenever two meat executives got together the talk quickly turned to complaints about the bribes that had to be paid to union officers whenever a labor problem arose, and particularly at contract time.

It happened that Nat Lokietz's Merkel Meat Company had been working both sides of the street. Lokietz had been contributing at least $600 a month to the welfare of Walter Kromholtz and the A & P meat department to guarantee that Merkel products would be prominently displayed on the shelves of the giant supermarket chain. But Lokietz was also a prime mover in the behind-the-scenes payoffs to the leaders of Local 174 of the butchers' union.

Despite all the evidence of corruption among meat company and supermarket executives, the prime targets of the investigation were now the three top leaders of Local 174—Frank Kissel, Harry Stubach, and Karl Muller.

When they decided to plant their bug, Nicholson and Montello still didn't know that the Mafia itself was behind Merkel Meat. They did learn that Merkel had been built up over the years by a family of German immigrants, and then had fallen on hard times. Eventually the company was sold to Williams-McWilliams Industries Inc., a Texas-based manufacturer of heavy construction equipment looking to diversify. Evidently, it figured that Merkel's losses would provide immediate tax relief as an offset to the profitable construction equipment business, after which Merkel itself could be turned around through more efficient management. The problem at Merkel was the employees, many of whom were operating their own meat businesses on the side with Merkel merchandise. Logically enough, Williams-McWilliams reckoned to fire the troublesome employees and straighten Merkel out. But they reckoned without Local 174 of the Amalgamated Meat Cutters' union.

Williams-McWilliams had unwittingly put their diversification program in the hands of the shakedown artists at the New York butchers' union. Unwilling to pay the price for rehabilitating Merkel, Williams-McWilliams decided to get out of the meat business, and Merkel was sold to a corporation controlled by Nat Lokietz for $2 million. In a year's time Merkel proceeded to undersell other provisioners and greatly expand its share of the market, lining up all the major supermarket chains including A & P. Union problems vanished, the result, it was later learned, of a $15,000 bribe.

The real story, however, had stayed secret. Now Nicholson and Montello heard it from Lokietz's own bugged conversation. It seemed that the Mafia, for whom the butchers' union local was merely a branch office, had sized up the situation along with Williams-McWilliams, and apparently had decided to put a man of its own choosing into Merkel. For all of its profitability problems, Merkel still had tremendous cash flow, selling millions of dollars of meat to supermarkets, butcher shops, delicatessens, and government institutions. For a mobster, the bottom line on a profit-and-loss statement comes a lot higher than it does for legitimate businessmen. To a mobster, many of the costs of doing business can simply be dispensed with by not paying bills, so that the cash flow becomes the paramount consideration.

The particular gentleman who intervened in the Merkel case was Anthony "Tino" De Angelis. He was the architect of what has become known as The Great Salad Oil Swindle, one of the biggest frauds in history. In the press reports, books, and legal cases concerning the salad oil swindle, numerous attempts were made to substantiate rumors that Tino was in the Mafia. Associations were established, but the conclusions were all tenuous. He has never appeared on the lists of Mafia members produced by Congressional investigations. He has flatly denied being a "front" for others in the salad oil swindle, and in its investigations the Government never established that he passed loot from the swindle on up any chain-of-command. On the other hand, New York Police Department experts on the Mafia suspect that this is exactly what happened. They say they think Tino De Angelis is close to, or part of, the Mafia family headed by Joseph Bonanno.

By 1963, Tino had taken a corner on the international market for salad oil—or what the world thought was salad oil. Starting slowly, Tino began trading in futures contracts and IOUs in ever increasing amounts. He completely outfoxed the American Express Company, which, in exchange for his storage fees, practically turned over to him its huge warehousing facility in Bayonne, New Jersey. Soon Tino had sold literally hundreds of millions of dollars of salad oil for future delivery by American Express. According to some accounts, rumors that he had the Mafia behind him actually lured many legitimate investors into giving Tino their money.

This was the situation in 1963 when Tino began talking business with Nat Lokietz, who was running a Fourteenth Street-area meat concern known as Eagle Brand Products. At this point, Merkel was still owned by Williams-McWilliams. The Mob evidently respected Lokietz, who had developed a reputation over the years for being able to sell hot dogs, baloneys, and hams with an improbably high water content. That he bribed his government inspectors was assumed. Now, Tino, a big public success, was trying to persuade Lokietz to expand. At this point only Tino, a few top employees and possibly some Mafia associates knew the big secret: those storage tanks in Bayonne, the ones the financiers were counting on, contained water and air. There was only enough salad oil to give visitors an occasional peek. But Lokietz, like the financiers, didn't know this when Tino began trying to interest him in buying El Dorado, a meat company Tino owned.

Nicholson and Montello were listening not far away when Lokietz recounted the whole story to a friend over the telephone a year later: "He says, 'How would you like to own Merkel?'"

"I said, 'I'd love it.'"

"He says, 'You got it.' He was already dickering for Merkel and he was going to give it to us."

In the year between the time Tino made this offer and the day in early December 1964, when Lokietz was recounting it, his Allied Crude Vegetable Oil Company was bankrupted, and so was at least one large Wall Street commodities firm and the American Express warehousing subsidiary. The losses, believed to exceed $400 million, had reverberated throughout the financial world. Tino had been indicted for fraud, and every company Tino was associated with was suffering. Lokietz noted that except for a twist of fate, Merkel would have been bankrupted along with the rest of Tino's holdings. At the closing of the Merkel deal, Lokietz had been required to make an $833,000 down-payment to Williams-McWilliams. Tino had been supposed to provide the money, but there was a last-second argument over legal details. Lokietz came up with his own lender. The day of the closing, he recalled, "was the Saturday before the Monday this thing [the salad oil scandal] hit the papers."

The Tino De Angelis story was interesting, but the name that the detectives were listening for most intently was that of Frank Kissel, the secretary-treasurer of butchers' Local 174 and its most powerful officer. Kissel was a close friend of the mobster Lorenzo "Chappie the Dude" Brescia, former bodyguard for Lucky Luciano. Brescia's brother Frank, himself never identified as a Mafia member or convicted of wrongdoing, was (and still is at this writing) on Local 174's payroll as a business agent. Kissel's name came up soon after the bug was installed, but not in the context the detectives expected.

Lokietz was commiserating with another meat dealer who stopped by his office. The other dealer complained that he was being shoved out of the processed meats and sausage market by the expanding empire of Harry R. "Buddy" White, Sr., who (with his son) owned White Packing Company—and still does.

"He's in Grand Union," Lokietz said disgustedly of White. "He was bumped from Grand Union five times. I pick up the phone to talk to the chief buyer there, he says to me, 'I would like to get Buddy White out of here tomorrow. But my hands are tied.' He said orders come from headquarters." And why? "He's gonna be Kissel's brother-in-law," Lokietz said with obvious irritation. "Frank Kissel's son is marrying his [White's] sister-in-law."

Then there was the name of Charles "Charlie Callahan" Anselmo, a loan shark with an arrest record for bookmaking and a close friend of Tino De Angelis's. Anselmo, then thirty-eight, had moved in on the meat business through a trucking operation he started—something mobsters can do easily because the Syndicate controls the Teamsters' union. Meat dealers who accepted Anselmo's generous offers of credit soon found that it wasn't like taking out a charge card at Sears. At least one dealer, Seymour Ehrlich, was forced to turn over control of his business to Anselmo. Now, operating as Triangle Meats, a brokerage concern, Anselmo was supplying Lokietz with a lot of the meat that went into Merkel products.

Perhaps these purchases from Anselmo were some kind of quid pro quo to the Mob. Tino had put Lokietz into Merkel to start with, and the deal may have specified where the meat was to come from. At any rate, Anselmo's name was mentioned a lot more reverently than others around Lokietz's office. A separate detective crew was sent out to tap Anselmo's phone.

"Charlie Anselmo," Lokietz was saying over his own phone November 23. "It seems that they sent me out a [unintelligible] and they picked it up. It so happens that the company it went to found dirty meat. So fourteen boxes were left behind. It seems that—you know—fucking Anselmo's got people taking all over."

"Taking" was the street word for bribery.

"I wanted to grab the meat," Lokietz went on. "I understand he had the [unintelligible] on 'em. I got the whole information, and as long as I know, [then] I'm guilty of that, don't you understand? . . . I had to send back a trailerload of meat. He's got to pay for it, he knows that. . . . We had to open the meat up, put it into tanks, get rid of the boxes. I still got meat downstairs, twenty thousand pounds. Somebody coming up tomorrow to open them up. . . . I talked to Mr. Callahan, I said, 'Look, Charlie . . . little by little, we're going to try to get rid of it. Little by little . . . Chock Full O' Nuts . . . ShopRite . . . ' "

Dirty meat? What was going on? Moments later, Lokietz was on the phone with Herman Jukofsky, Merkel's plant manager and the son-in-law of Lokietz's junior partner, Samuel Goldman. "How much meat do you put in?" he asked Jukofsky. There was a pause, as if for an answer. "Eighty pounds of meat and twenty pounds of that stinger meat?"

Everybody knows that hot dogs and packaged meat patties often contain cereal and other fillers besides meat. But Lokietz seemed to be talking about something else. What was stinger meat?

Robert Nicholson was soon on his way to finding out, thanks to a chance investigation that was taking place coincidentally seven hundred miles away. A federal food inspector in Ohio—apparently one of those the Mafia hadn't bribed—walked into a meat warehouse and almost keeled over from the smell. The meat was traced to a plant in Wisconsin that was licensed to process animal food for mink ranches and zoos. The Agriculture Department began questioning the Wisconsin processor about what his meat was doing stinking up Ohio. The processor quickly passed on warning of the investigation to the customer who had ordered the shipment: Charles Anselmo. For the record, Anselmo had claimed to represent east coast zoos.

Anselmo knew—as the Wisconsin processor must have known, too, and as Nicholson would eventually find out—that the meat was being held over in warehouses en route east, often treated with formaldehyde to get rid of the stench and discoloration, then repackaged for human use. Formaldehyde is the chemical that morticians use to preserve human bodies. Eating it can make you sick, but, toxicologists say, it won't really kill you in small doses—unless you have a heart condition. Toxicologists also say that formaldehyde would be hard to trace in meat, even at dangerous levels, so that use of it could easily go undetected.

After the meat had been soaked in this toxic chemical, it was put in boxes and sealed with counterfeit Department of Agriculture stamps that said the meat had been inspected and approved for human consumption at the slaughterhouse of Hyplains Dressed Beef Company in Dodge City, Kansas. News of this would later distress Hyplains Dressed Beef Company, which had never heard of Charles Anselmo.

Typical of mobsters in business, Anselmo simply couldn't accept the fact that a businessman occasionally has to cut his losses. He wasn't going to let the forty thousand pounds go. As soon as he learned that his meat had been impounded in Ohio by the Department of Agriculture, he determined to steal it back under cover of night. He would bring it to his warehouse in New Jersey for whatever treatment and repackaging was necessary.

So Anselmo hired some men, who then broke into his Ohio warehouse at night, stole the meat from the Agriculture Department and hauled it away. But then Nicholson and Montello overheard talk of dirty meat at the Merkel plant, and learned that Anselmo had been discussing plans for the Ohio theft over his tapped telephone. So the detectives began comparing notes with the federal inspection service. With Anselmo's own telephone description of where the stolen shipment was to be taken, and with a little help from their noses, the Agriculture inspectors zeroed in on a warehouse in Pittsburgh where Anselmo's meat lay waiting for the next leg of its journey. Nicholson and a partner boarded the first plane west.

For nearly two days in late November, Nicholson and his partner sat in a cold car parked outside the freezer house where the meat was stored, waiting for action. From time to time they would get out and sniff. There was no doubt the meat was still there. Finally, on the morning of the second day, a truck pulled up and men began carrying the meat out of the warehouse and loading it—forty thousand pounds of stinking meat boxed in fifty-pound cartons.

Poised for a long drive, Nicholson and his partner began to follow the truck as it pulled out. The truck went three blocks, parked, and the driver went into a gin mill. It was after dark when the driver finally returned to his truck. He drove three more blocks, parked again and went to sleep.

The next day the detectives followed the truck to a parking lot in New Jersey's heavily industrial Hudson County. The trailer was detached and left behind as the tractor drove away. Some men came and loaded ice into the freezer truck as if preparing it for a long wait. Then they departed. Nicholson and his partner were exhausted. There was no one to relieve them, and it could be days before anyone came for the trailer. They took a chance and went home for a night's sleep. When they came back, the trailer was gone.

Nicholson returned dejectedly to Queens and the sounds of the Merkel bug. There were a lot of unanswered questions. What had happened to the vanished forty-thousand-pound shipment? If Anselmo was buying dirty meat, what was he using it for? Was this the meat he was selling to Lokietz for Merkel sausages? And if so, how were the federal meat inspectors letting it go through? Was Lokietz paying them off?

In the very first conversation that Nicholson and Montello had taped November 17, 1964, Lokietz had said to a man on the phone, "You gonna be here when they do the inspection? Well, when you come down, I'll explain it to you. I know how to rub the monkey."

Then, on December 4, the Merkel crowd apparently found out that the Agriculture Department was querying Anselmo about the forty thousand pounds of meat that had vanished. Lokietz and several other persons in the office sounded agitated, especially because of the coincidence of this new investigation and the pending arrival of Johnson, the new meat inspector.

Most of what the detectives heard was mundane, but on December 10, the recorder began to fairly sizzle.

Suddenly there were sounds of a group of men bursting into Lokietz's office, talking excitedly so that their voices could scarcely be distinguished.

"Nobody ever checked this stuff from them . . . sent it to a lab?"

"Nope."

"Don't worry about it," Lokietz said.

"But I don't want horsemeat. It could be publicized. There could be trouble. You better be careful. We're in the same boat."

Footsteps went away and a door closed. A phone was dialed and

Lokietz's clearly identifiable voice said, "Did you get any meat from Anselmo? Good. Today? What'll you need, one load?"

He dialed the phone again. He was calling Charles Anselmo. "Hello. . . . Listen, who do you *think* it is? . . . Yeah. Is your wire clear? Not tapped? This meat in Jersey, you know why they're looking for it? We just got the report. On the Q.T. Is this horsemeat? Well, I'll tell you, I'm going to check this one out myself. I'm going to do it my own way in a private lab. But if it is, we can't have any part of this thing. The other thing I don't give a shit about. ["The other thing" Merkel was using, as Nicholson and Montello would later learn, was meat from diseased cows, a far greater actual health hazard than the horsemeat was.] But," Lokietz continued, "this thing here definitely cannot come into this house, if this is what it is. You better be honest with me."

Anselmo was stalling him off. He still wouldn't be specific about whether it was horsemeat.

Lokietz finally posed the question this way: "Does it moo?"

"Well," said Anselmo, as his voice was picked up elsewhere over a wiretap, "some of it moos, and some of it don't moo."

At one point a secretary was told to make lunch, and apparently reached for the wrong package of hot dogs. "Oh, no, not those," came the horrified exclamation of men afraid to eat the product they were selling to the public.

Nicholson and Montello were not amused. They now knew how Merkel had turned around its financial fortunes in the past year. The supplies Merkel was buying had come a lot cheaper than clean, inspected beef. Nicholson and Montello also knew how little chance there was of the Agriculture Department's intervening to stop Merkel. The inspectors were more loyal to Merkel than to the government. And Lokietz was arranging to get rid of the evidence.

The detectives were in a terrible quandary. It was the end of the day, a Thursday, December 10, 1964. They knew where there was a load of illegal horsemeat and other uninspected meat—perhaps even the same stinking load Nicholson had followed east from Pittsburgh. They knew that the men who had this meat were eagerly stuffing it into various kinds of sausage for sale to the public through major supermarket and restaurant chains, and that these same men were desperately trying to unload the unused portion to any other wholesaler who would buy it.

The cops couldn't let this poisoning of the public go on. But on the other hand, if they raided the Merkel plant—if the police came in—then the cover would be blown on their entire operation. The evidence hadn't been developed to nail Frank Kissel and the other corrupt union leaders. There wasn't even enough explicit taped evidence to make payoff cases against particular meat inspectors. Anselmo's exact connections to the Mafia were still a mystery. But the detectives couldn't let Merkel send its sausages to market.

CHAPTER 2

THE MERKEL SCANDAL

It was early afternoon, the next day. Lokietz was out to lunch. But suddenly there were sounds of general consternation in the Merkel office. The words came in raspy shouts, loud enough to show panic, muted enough to show fear. Men from the city markets commission were raiding the cooler.

For several minutes, Nicholson heard the staff debating whether it would be illegal to flee. Before they could make up their minds, an agent found his way into the office and announced that the Merkel freezer was being put under seal and that no meat could be removed unless released by the markets commissioner.

As soon as Nicholson and his partner Louis Montello had overheard the previous afternoon that Merkel was grinding up horsemeat and other unapproved products to use in its sausages and hot dogs, they had taken the news to Al Scotti, the first assistant district attorney. Scotti could have told his detectives to get a warrant, raid the Merkel plant and arrest the operators. That would have guaranteed a lavish publicity coup for the D.A.'s office. But it also would have forced disclosure of the hidden bugs, and their purpose, and thus would have squelched the union bribery investigation.

Nicholson was sent to tell Markets Commissioner Albert Pacetta to check Merkel for contaminated meat. Pacetta wasn't told why the D.A.'s office was suspicious. The real cops didn't have enough respect for the markets commission to trust it. And their disdain was justified. Two years later, Nicholson would have occasion to burst into a New York meat plant immediately after a team from the markets commission had inspected it and pronounced it in apple-pie order; Nicholson found not only large quantities of rancid beef and chicken and mislabeled meat patties, and large quantities of a toxic chemical used to make rancid meat appear fresh, but he also found 116 bales of hot gingham cloth that had been stolen in a truck hijacking two weeks before. Then the owner of the plant blatantly tried to bribe him, giving him some indication of why the markets commission men might have overlooked all the violations.

In the Merkel case, Scotti figured that Pacetta would have to act decisively because there was pressure from the D.A.'s office. The meat would be impounded and the publicity would kill Merkel. The crooks would assume that the Agriculture Department, after finding a shipment of bad meat destined for Anselmo, had tipped off the commissioner of markets.

But if Pacetta's raiders were in the dark about what was really going on in the meat industry, Nicholson still knew very little of it himself. Soon after the commissioner's men had left the Merkel office, he began to hear evidence of new levels of criminality. He began to sense that the horsemeat scandal was not an isolated case, but part of a vast network of corruption.

Meanwhile, Lokietz ordered a quick inventory of how much suspect meat was on the premises. If there was exactly a full truckload—forty thousand pounds—he would say it was the first such shipment received and that none of it had been used. But the report came back that some of the latest truckload had already been put into the grinder, as Lokietz himself had instructed the day before.

Lokietz's first idea was to sneak the remaining 790 boxes of bad meat out of the cooler that night and replace them with good meat. The commissioner's men had already taken samples of the Anselmo shipment, but Lokietz knew that the horsemeat was carefully hidden in the middle of the boxes. The samples, taken from the outside, would probably turn out to be 100 percent beef. A switch would assure that any future samples would also pass inspection. He began calling friends in the business, beginning with Buddy White, the meat dealer who had married into the family of the head of the butchers' union. But apparently he couldn't cajole White or the others into opening their warehouses to the illegal meat.

Lokietz decided that a more extreme measure had to be tried. Bribery. They had to—in Lokietz's words—"reach Pacetta." Names were mentioned of people who might know Pacetta. None of them satisfied Lokietz. "We gotta get higher," he insisted.

Then a voice popped up: "We gotta get Herbie. Herbie knows somebody, don't you understand?"

"Moe Steinman," another voice agreed.

At the time, the names meant nothing to Bob Nicholson. He didn't know that "Herbie" was Herbert Newman, the business front man for Moe Steinman. And he had never before heard the name of Moe Steinman, the corruption kingpin of the New York meat market, the man who kept the butchers' union and the supermarket executives paid off and in the service of their true masters, the Mafia. Over the next dozen years, Moe Steinman would become to Robert Nicholson almost as the white whale was to Captain Ahab.

Moe Steinman, however, couldn't be reached that day. It was a Friday in December, a time Steinman often prefers to be on a golf course in Florida. So Lokietz and Anselmo resumed laying plans for a transfer of meat out of the Merkel plant by truck that night, while still looking for a political fixer. And soon they found that fixer, who really did reach out with the big bribe. He was the very next man on Lokietz's list of potential octopuses: Tino De Angelis, the great salad oil swindler who had set Lokietz up in business in the first place.

Tino had plenty of political contacts, including Congressman Cornelius Gallagher of New Jersey. Gallagher's district included Bayonne, where Tino had his phony oil storage tanks. According to a *Life* magazine exposé (which proved devastatingly accurate in every confirmable detail), Gallagher received $50,000 in legal fees from Tino during the time the salad oil swindle was in operation. After the scandal was exposed, *Life* reported, Gallagher engineered a $300,000 loan from a bank he was director of, to enable Tino's associates to start a tallow and lard business; that business then used phony merchandise receipts as collateral for big loans, just as Tino's salad oil business did.

When Nat Lokietz called, Tino De Angelis said he knew a Brooklyn lawyer who was counsel to a state legislative committee. He said he'd check with the lawyer and call back. A little while later Tino reported that J. Louis "Jack" Fox, an eighteen-term Democratic state assemblyman from Far Rockaway, Queens, was the guy who got Pacetta his job. Pacetta was also from Queens. Tino said he had arranged an appointment for Lokietz that Sunday at Fox's house.

Tino De Angelis was never charged with this bribery plot. The D.A.'s lawyers eventually decided that without a tape recording, there was no proof of what De Angelis and Fox had actually said to each other. But Nicholson knew there had to be a bribery case against someone in what he'd heard. On Sunday, December 14, he followed Lokietz to Fox's house, then followed him back to his own house and heard him call his partner Sam Goldman on the telephone—which Nicholson had wiretapped. Lokietz told Goldman that Assemblyman Fox would take care of Pacetta for $10,000. The first half was to be paid the following morning at ten o'clock in Fox's law office. The bribe would be split fifty-fifty between Fox and Pacetta. Armed with a tape recording of that conversation between Lokietz and Goldman, Nicholson got a judicial order on Sunday evening to bug Fox's office. Nicholson and a partner spent all night picking the lock, installing the microphone and transmitter, then locating and setting up a listening post. With the first rays of dawn they sat back to wait for ten o'clock, and, they hoped, the sounds of an indictable crime.

They heard Lokietz ushered in, and heard Fox say he had talked to "my people on Saturday afternoon . . . Unless the complaint originated from some other department, like the commissioner of investigations, or unless it came through the mayor's office," Fox said, the matter could be taken care of to Lokietz's satisfaction. "If it originated within his [Pacetta's] office, that's one thing. If it originated outside his office, that's another thing."

The explanation apparently satisfied Lokietz, for the sound of his response was the sound of shuffling currency.

There was a long pause, and then came the stupid, unthinking voice of greed, providing Bob Nicholson with the sure proof he needed. Assemblyman J. Lewis Fox said, "I'm short one."

"Count it again!" Lokietz demanded, answering the detectives' prayers for explicit conversation. There was more shuffling of bills and the unmistakable voice of Jack Fox counting, "one . . . two . . . three . . ."

No sooner was Lokietz out the door than Fox called in his secretary. "I have $5,000 in cash," he told her. "You don't have to count it. Just put it somewhere so that we know where it is."

Robert Nicholson was euphoric. He had the perfect bribery case on tape. The euphoria didn't last long, however. The laboratory report had come back on the meat samples that were taken from Merkel. The report said they were 100 percent pure beef. Nicholson was dumbfounded. He knew what was in those boxes. But how do you argue with science?

Nicholson sent Pacetta's men back to the sausage factory to take more samples. Once again the samples came back from the lab pronounced 100 percent pure beef, infuriating Nicholson. Determined to prove what he knew, Nicholson insisted on posing as a markets commission inspector and getting a third sample personally. So the detective went in with a band saw and sliced his way to the heart of the shipment. This time the laboratory confirmed the presence not only of horsemeat, but of another unidentifiable variety, possibly kangaroo.

With a new lab report, Nat Lokietz's worst dreams came true. On Friday, December 18, 1964, the headline that covered the top half of the front page of the New York *Daily News* read, "MOB FLOODS U.S. WITH FAKE BEEF—Find 20 Tons in Queens Plant." On page three was a picture of commissioner Pacetta standing grim-faced behind a table of raw meat. Pacetta was quoted as saying, "The people from whom Merkel bought this stuff are in a mob-operated enterprise. Obviously there is a bootleg meat fabricating plant where they bone, chop and package this meat. The ring has facilities for transporting and storing its product. It has to be on a national scale."

Though the D.A.'s office had no evidence that he was even offered any of the bribe money from Assemblyman Fox, Pacetta would continue to defend Lokietz. Pacetta took steps almost immediately to counteract the supermarket order cancellations that had forced Merkel to announce a shutdown. On Sunday, December 20, 1964, two days after the scandal broke and one week after Lokietz put in the fix with Fox, some two hundred butchers' and Teamsters' union pickets appeared outside Pacetta's home to protest the layoffs that would result from Merkel's closing. Pacetta welcomed representatives inside and half an hour later he emerged to read a statement emphasizing confidence in Merkel.

Finally, Merkel itself issued a press release saying that "as a result of Commissioner Pacetta's statement . . . public confidence has been restored in our company and its products and we are getting a number of orders. In fact, many who canceled orders have restored them." Merkel said it was rehiring the five hundred furloughed employees.

Merkel's revival lasted only a month, however, because regardless of what Commissioner Pacetta said, Nicholson and Montello were weaving an ever-tightening noose around Nat Lokietz's neck. Now that the fake beef case had erupted in public, the D.A.'s men could pursue it openly without blowing their still-secret bribery and extortion investigation.

The detectives found that adulterated meat had been coming in to Merkel regularly at least since December, 1963, shortly after Lokietz had taken the company over. The bad meat had been distributed not only to supermarkets, but to the New York City school system, state hospitals and prisons, the Army, the Air Force, restaurants, and hotels. It had been shipped to Merkel from two primary sources, one in Wisconsin, the other in Utica, New York.

Both sources were ostensible suppliers of food for mink ranches, and, fortunately for the mink ranchers, mink aren't very particular about what kind of meat they eat, so the ranchers can get away with buying the dregs that could never be approved for human consumption.

Bob Nicholson found abattoirs in Alma Center, Wisconsin, and Utica, New York, selling their product not only to local mink farmers, but also to Charles Anselmo. Prices were cheap because costs were minimal. Normally, a healthy cow will bring several hundred dollars to the owner. But the going rate for "downers"—old, sick, sometimes already dead, cows—was as follows:

If the cow was already dead, you could take it away free.

If the cow was sick and couldn't walk—three dollars.

Sick but could walk—six dollars.

Did the mink food dealers know when they sold to Charley Anselmo that he was feeding people instead of minks? At the very least, they had reason to be suspicious. The detectives located one of the dealers by grabbing a truck driver who hauled the meat east from Wisconsin. The driver, Joseph Hasenberg of Jim Falls, Wisconsin, was given a deal that he wouldn't be prosecuted if he would help get the goods on the mink food supplier, Orland "Buster" Lea of Alma Center, who had a firm called Lea Brothers. Hasenberg agreed to wear a hidden microphone to a meeting with Lea, which Lea then set for an abandoned truck stop in Mosston, Wisconsin, late at night.

A detective heard Lea argue that, as far as he knew, he was just selling food for eastern mink ranches and zoos. First he had sold to a man named Gasparello—who Nicholson later learned was Ralph Gasparello, a Boston meat dealer who sold meat to Anselmo. Later, Lea said, he had been approached by another friend of Anselmo's, who described himself as a mink rancher in Pennsylvania and who announced that he "was the big fish from now on—he made the deals."

Hasenberg earned his escape from prosecution by steering Lea into several tacit admissions. Lea evidently knew that the meat was going on to New Jersey from Pennsylvania, and that the deals were handled with haste, surreption, and cash. There were no records. He knew that higher than standard trucking rates were charged, and instructed Hasenberg not to tell the New York investigators about the higher trucking rates. And he admitted having met Charles Anselmo on a trip to New York after the hauling began—not only having met him, but having brought him sixty animal skins from Wisconsin as a present because Anselmo had said earlier he wanted a fur coat for his wife.

The other major supplier for the fake beef operation was Dominick Gerace of Utica, an area known for dairy farming, mink ranching, and an extremely high per capita level of Mafia activity. Nicholson and Montello tracked down Gerace with information from the Anselmo wiretap and evidence picked up during the raid on Anselmo's warehouse. The District Attorney's office said in court that Gerace had a "powerful underworld leader in the upstate area" as "a silent partner" in his Party Packing Corp. Party Packing regularly sold mink food to Charles Anselmo.

Nicholson went to Utica and with local and state police staged a surprise raid on Gerace's three plants there. They turned up the horsemeat and sub-par beef one would expect to find at an animal food factory. But they also turned up something one would not expect to find: counterfeit U.S. Department of Agriculture stamps saying that meat had been inspected and approved for human consumption.

Now the cops had a strong case against Lokietz, Anselmo, Lea, Gerace, a slew of truck drivers, and some of the other officers in the Merkel plant. The next logical step was to call in the federal meat inspectors who were supposed to prevent this sort of thing from happening. Presumably they were the monkeys whom Norman Lokietz was adept at rubbing. Six inspectors assigned to the Merkel plant and the assistant inspector in charge of the meat protection program in the New York area were brought before a grand jury January 6, 1965, and asked to sign a waiver of immunity—a voluntary surrender of their Fifth Amendment rights against self-incrimination.

All seven meat inspectors refused to sign the waiver. Among them was the man Nat Lokietz said had tipped him off to the pending investigation, allowing Lokietz to try to get rid of the evidence. District Attorney Hogan and his chief assistant, Al Scotti, fired off a report to the Department of Agriculture, expecting that the seven inspectors would be suspended from work and ultimately discharged if they still refused to talk. But the Agriculture Department kept all seven men on the job.

Since much of the criminal activity occurred outside New York, Hogan's office shared its information with the United States Attorney in Manhattan, Robert Morgenthau, who could prosecute interstate crimes. On February 23, 1965, Morgenthau's federal grand jury charged Anselmo, Herman Jukofsky (Lokietz's plant manager), Michael Sramowicz (a truck driver), and Madeline Bullard (the owner of a New Jersey trucking company) with interstate transportation of falsely labeled meat products. All but Jukofsky were also charged with conspiracy. At a press conference, according to the *New York Times*, Morgenthau credited the indictments entirely to the Department of Agriculture and to an intensive investigation by his own federal grand jury.

A day later, on February 24, Hogan's state grand jury voted indictments accusing Anselmo of conspiring with Gerace and Lokietz to cause the transportation and sale of improper meat, and six counts of actual sales. Then the D.A.'s office turned to the seven suspected meat inspectors who had refused to waive immunity. The mere fact that Lokietz or a colleague boasted on tape of having bribed an inspector was insufficient evidence of bribery. To permit a conviction, the inspector's own voice had to appear on the tape making an incriminating statement. Identifying the various voices from the jumble in Lokietz's office was difficult. But on March 10, 1965, inspectors Hyman Erdwein and David Fellner were charged along with Anselmo and Lokietz in a conspiracy to obstruct justice by plotting to remove meat from the Merkel plant the night after Commissioner Pacetta's men had seized it.

The D.A.'s team was anxious to throw everything it had at Lokietz. On April 20, 1965, the Walter Kromholtz tapes were dragged before the grand jury. Lokietz was indicted again, this time for the "corrupt influencing" of an A & P executive, by paying Kromholtz $150 a week to insure that A & P would stock Merkel products. The men who ran eight other wholesale meat concerns in New York were indicted along with Lokietz for also bribing Kromholtz, and the meat director for Dan's Supreme Supermarkets Inc., a local chain, was indicted for perjury before the grand jury.

In May, Morgenthau announced federal indictments against Anselmo, Gerace, and Buster Lea of Alma Center, Wisconsin, for transporting uninspected meat across state lines and for conspiring to do so. By the time the indictments were handed down, the evidence compiled by Nicholson, Montello, and others certainly seemed overwhelming.

Nevertheless, the prosecutors did not want to go to trial. It is a popular misconception that lawyers love to march into court and nail an opponent's hide to the wall in dramatic fashion before judge and jury. In truth, most prosecutors see their job as avoiding the costs of a trial wherever possible by getting the defendant to plead guilty. The problem is, this requires a concession from the prosecutor—a bargain. Sometimes it can be a good bargain for society, if there is at least one charge the criminal pleads guilty to that carries a stiff penalty.

Prosecutors argue that they have to allow a lot of bargain basement pleas because the cost of trials is great. But the cost of guilty pleas is often far greater; it just doesn't show up in dollars on an annual budget the way trials do. The cost of cheaply bargained guilty pleas is the perpetuation of crime.

The Merkel case is a perfect example. It involved dealing for testimony, the seamiest kind of plea bargaining. Deal making means giving a defendant lenient treatment not just to avoid trying him, but also because the defendant agrees to "cooperate"—to tattle on others. This is a deadly game. Sometimes it works, particularly against very well insulated Mafia bosses who have learned to evade taps and bugs, and who can't be nailed except by the testimony of associates. Even so, most of the really valuable witnesses from inside the Syndicate have talked only after they began serving very stiff sentences.

It was this kind of deal making, even more than simple plea bargaining, that kindled the disgust Nicholson and Montello felt when they resigned from the police force after the close of their long meat investigation. That would come more than a decade later, as they realized that despite all they had done, most of the same people were still providing America with its meat. But the very first deals, back in 1965, the detectives went along with.

Seymour Ehrlich's deal was relatively easy on the conscience. Ehrlich was a meat dealer who had fallen into debt to Charlie Anselmo, and consequently allowed Anselmo into his meat business. In the course of gathering evidence, Nicholson and Montello tracked Ehrlich down and, given the chance to talk and avoid prosecution, Ehrlich took it.

Ehrlich's role was to permit his company to be used as a cover for a dirty meat operation. Whatever meat Anselmo brought in, Ehrlich would box it, label it "boneless beef," and bribe an inspector to stamp it (or to give Ehrlich access to the stamp so he could stamp the meat himself). What happened after that, Ehrlich wasn't supposed to ask.

The business started small, and Ehrlich was able to mix the dirty meat in with greater quantities of good meat that was moving through his shop. The inspectors hardly noticed it. But by late 1963, Anselmo had begun shipping whole truckloads at a time, six to eight hundred cartons. Ehrlich said he had to make special arrangements with a federal inspector, paying up to $100 a day to "borrow" the inspector's stamping equipment.

At first they split the income fifty-fifty as Anselmo had promised.

Then Anselmo began to ask himself the question that all mobsters in "legitimate" business ultimately ask themselves: Why give up the other 50 percent? So Anselmo announced early in 1964 that from now on, Ehrlich wasn't a partner any longer. Ehrlich would get one and a quarter cents commission for every pound of meat he obtained a federal inspection stamp for, and an additional penny and a quarter for meat Ehrlich sold on his own. No percentages. By mid-year, Anselmo decided that even this arrangement was too generous. He cut the commission to half a cent a pound. Ehrlich said he couldn't take the risk for so little money. "Well, then, you can forget the deal," Anselmo told him. Ehrlich's business was now in the hands of Anselmo, lock, stock, and braunschweiger.

With Ehrlich in tow, the D.A.'s office would certainly seem to have had the Merkel Meat case pretty well wrapped up. But two more deals were made. First, Gerace came in to Morgenthau, the federal prosecutor, and offered to give information against Anselmo. The prosecutors took Gerace up on it. Anselmo was left holding the bag. The Mafia family he was believed to be connected to was in a period of decline, which may have had something to do with this. Anselmo's believed overlord, Joseph Bonnano, had been forced from his New York power base, while the family of Stefano Magaddino, which ruled upstate, was on the rise. When Gerace freely offered his testimony against Anselmo, it may well have been with the Mafia's blessing in an effort to cut its losses. We can't really know.

After Ehrlich and Gerace had been dealt with, there was still another test. Despite their commanding position in the Merkel horsemeat case, Nicholson and Montello still didn't have a word of usable evidence against Frank Kissel, Karl Muller, or Harry Stubach, the butchers' union leaders. They had indictments pending against eight wholesale meat company executives for bribing the A & P. All eight executives probably knew something about bribing the union, too, since it was all part of the same system. If the executives would testify, then they could break the case against the union. But seven of the eight were unlikely to cooperate for the simple reason that they were unlikely to suffer if they didn't cooperate. One of the eight, however, had a real reason to quake. He was Norman Lokietz, and he faced numerous charges. Lokietz certainly would be susceptible to a deal if the cops wanted to propose it. But how could anyone in conscience offer leniency to Nat Lokietz—the author of a despicable crime against whom the evidence was overwhelming?

Somehow, the D.A.'s men resolved whatever problems they had with their consciences.

Lokietz agreed to plead guilty. But he still refused to talk, even about his colleagues who were obviously involved in the Merkel scandal. It was one thing to plead guilty after being caught red-handed; it was another to testify against well-connected men like Charlie Anselmo. Then the D.A.'s office played its trump card; Lokietz's son, Sheldon, would be indicted, too. Only then did Nat Lokietz agree to a deal, and it provided that Sheldon would never see the inside of a cell.

A deal, however, meant that the D.A. had to inform Morgenthau's federal office, which also had charges pending against Anselmo, and which would have to consent to whatever was arranged. When the FBI insisted on interviewing Lokietz, Nicholson became leery, but Morgenthau's office and the FBI said they needed to talk to Lokietz before they could prosecute the corrupt federal meat inspectors. Their reasoning went this way: federal courts prohibited the use of wiretap evidence (prior to 1968). Lokietz had been wiretapped extensively. So Nicholson and his men would inevitably use the results of the wiretaps to elicit Lokietz's story, and thus his testimony might be poisoned as evidence in federal court. But if the FBI talked to Lokietz first, without benefit of the wiretap information, Lokietz's testimony in the federal case would remain pure.

Lokietz spent two weeks with the federal agents—a suspiciously long time to talk only about government meat inspectors. But the FBI agents assured Nicholson afterwards, he recalls, that Lokietz hadn't been asked for and hadn't given any information about other payoffs.

Then Nicholson, Montello, and Assistant District Attorney Frank Connelly, who was assigned to the case, began questioning the witness. To their utter amazement, he first denied knowing about labor racketeering or any bribery beyond the known outlines of the Merkel scandal. Finally, after several days, he tired of his own lies. "You guys tell each other everything anyway," he broke down. "I might as well tell you. I told the FBI about the fifteen thousand dollars I paid to the butchers' union."

The stunned questioners began a whole new series of interviews. It would lead to what became known as "The Kissell Case." Nicholson and Montello wanted to start immediately pursuing Lokietz's information—tailing suspects, throwing up wiretaps. But it would be more than a year before they could do so. There were too many outstanding charges still open on the Merkel scandal.

One peril of deal making is that it snowballs. Once a deal has been offered to a prominent figure in a case, it becomes difficult to refuse the same deal to co-defendants who are less culpable. So Sam Goldman, Lokietz's partner, and Goldman's son-in-law, Herman Jukofsky, the plant manager, were allowed in under the umbrella of prosecutorial grace. So were Michael Sramowicz, the truck driver, and Madeline Bullard, the trucking company owner.

Lokietz, Goldman, and Jukofsky gave up a meat inspector, as requested. But now, when it counted, they didn't mention the inspector who Lokietz earlier said had tipped him off to the investigation. Lokietz, Goldman, and Jukofsky now told the prosecutors that they had bribed an inspector named Robert Wilson, who had been assigned to Eagle Brand—Lokietz's old company—several years earlier. They said Wilson had been bribed from way back, and that it took only $25 to $100—depending on the size of the shipment—to get him to turn his head while the bribers used his inspection stamp on whatever unstamped meat Charlie Anselmo brought to town.

With this, the plea bargaining and deal making stopped. The remaining defendants were waiting for the opening trial to see exactly what evidence the prosecution had compiled. Thus 1966 dawned, with the curious teams aligned. On the prosecution side were Lokietz and the others who processed the meat, Sramowicz and Bullard who trucked it, and Dominick Gerace who sold it, standing shoulder to shoulder with Bob Nicholson, Lou Montello, Nicholas Scopetta (the prosecutor assigned to try the cases for the D.A.'s office), and Robert Morgenthau. On the other side, there were Charles Anselmo, Buster Lea, Lea's cattle ranching pal Thomas Barr, Ralph Gasparello (who originally approached Lea to supply dirty meat for Anselmo), Robert Dvorin (who ran an animal food plant in Elizabeth, New Jersey), and the three meat inspectors, Fellner, Erdwein, and Wilson.

The first scheduled trial was of Charles Anselmo, the biggest target on the list. The case was called May 6, 1966. It was over by lunchtime.

As soon as Anselmo heard Prosecutor Scopetta's opening description of the evidence and heard that Lokietz and the others had become state's witnesses, he began to huddle with his lawyer. Together, they went to Scopetta and agreed to call off the trial. Anselmo pleaded guilty to one count from each of two indictments, for which Scopetta agreed to drop all the other counts of the three state indictments pending against him. The counts all carried a maximum penalty of one year in prison, and Scopetta figured that a judge wouldn't string together more than two one-year sentences anyway. The federal prosecutor agreed to a settlement on similar terms.

Scopetta, relying on what Nicholson and Montello had learned, told the sentencing judge that Anselmo had sold Merkel more than one million pounds of meat for more than $500,000 in 1964 alone. Contradicting markets commissioner Pacetta, Scopetta said, "All of that meat was eventually processed to stores and supermarkets in New York City and we can assume it was consumed. It was sold as edible meat." Moreover, he noted, Anselmo had been arrested half a dozen times in connection with organized crime activities. "He brought a background of loan sharking and bookmaking to the meat business," Scopetta said, "and utilized those means to work his way into the meat business."

Judge Edward R. Dudley responded with the requisite pomposity. "The interests of the city, of our community, can only be protected if the sentence is both of a punitive and deterrent nature." He then proceeded to award Anselmo a sentence that was neither punitive nor deterrent: a total of eighteen months. A month later, on July 13, 1966, Anselmo appeared before Federal Judge Edmund L. Palmieri, pleaded guilty to two of the federal counts facing him, and got a duplicate eighteen-month sentence that could be served concurrently with the state sentence. Anselmo entered the federal correctional institution at Danbury, Connecticut, on August 24, 1967, and was paroled four and a half months later. He was scarcely out of the hoosegow before he had set up a new meat brokerage in the Fourteenth Street market, just a few doors from where he had done business before.

On June 15, 1966, Ralph Gasparello pleaded guilty to two counts of unlawfully transporting uninspected meat. He walked right out of court and back to his business, a free man.

Later, Robert Dvorin, the animal food manufacturer whose plant Anselmo had used in New Jersey, pleaded guilty to transporting horsemeat not conspicuously labeled. He served only eight and a half months before parole.

On August 15, 1966, Buster Lea and Thomas Barr pleaded guilty to two counts of illegally transporting uninspected meat. The plea was entered under federal Rule 20, which allowed them to be sentenced in their home district in Madison, Wisconsin, instead of in New York. Federal Judge James E. Doyle sentenced Lea to jail for six months. He was released in less than five. Barr got one month. They stayed on probation for two years. According to the chief probation officer in Madison, "Both remained in their respective businesses and were operating so" when their two-year probation was completed.

On September 28, 1966, Norman Lokietz pleaded guilty in state court to one count of conspiracy. As promised, prosecutor Scopetta was there to praise his cooperation, and Judge Mitchell Schweitzer gave him a six-month sentence with the added courtesy of a two-week grace period to prepare his affairs before turning himself in. Merkel, of course, had closed, but upon his release Lokietz went immediately to work buying and selling meats under the name Regal Provisions Company.

Lokietz's partner Sam Goldman pleaded guilty to second degree perjury for having denied to the grand jury back in December, 1964, that he had discussed uninspected meat with Nat Lokietz. Goldman got a six-month suspended sentence.

On November 18, 1966, Dominick Gerace was allowed to Rule 20-himself to Albany, where James Foley, then and now the chief federal judge of the Northern District of New York, put him on probation. He went right back to his meat packing plants without seeing a jail cell.

Charges against Sramowicz and Bullard, who trucked the meat, and Jukofsky, who helped mislabel and move it, were dropped as promised. This was their reward for having agreed to supply overkill testimony against Anselmo, who almost certainly could have been convicted on other evidence, and who served only four and a half months anyway.

All the meat inspectors who were at one time or another called into suspicion because of the horsemeat scandal either kept their jobs or qualified for their pensions. Apparently no meat inspector was penalized in the matter, though Erdwein and Fellner were suspended without pay while awaiting trial.

The other seven meat company executives (besides Lokietz) accused of bribing Walter Kromholtz, the A & P meat buyer, received mere fines.

Nicholson and his men came up with a clever ploy to trap J. Louis Fox, the long-time Queens assemblyman whom Lokietz had paid in order to "reach" Pacetta, the markets commissioner. Nicholson had the whole bribe recorded on tape, of course, but back in 1965 he didn't want the existence of the tape disclosed.

Fox was called before a grand jury and was asked a series of questions that would force him either to admit the bribery or commit perjury. He chose the deception, so on January 19, 1966, with Lokietz and the others ready to testify against him, Fox was indicted—not for bribery, but for perjury. That year he was defeated for renomination for the first time in his decades in office. On June 18, 1968, he pleaded guilty, and on October 14 Judge Joseph A. Sarafite sentenced him to probation for one year.

Pacetta himself went on to be indicted for grand larceny and bribery. A judge ordered his acquittal in 1976 on the grand larceny charge, which involved $10,000 in allegedly false insurance claims in connection with an automobile accident. The bribery charge, however, said he took $35,000 from a doctor to influence his vote as a member of the New York State Human Rights Appeals Board, to which he had been appointed. That, too, was scheduled for trial in 1976. Apparently, he beat the rap, but under a strange provision of New York State law, no one can find out what happened.

But Nicholson and Montello, for all their work, had one thing to console themselves with. The price was high, but they had bought a song from Norman Lokietz about the butchers' union. He gave quite a performance, and it resulted in what became known as the Kissell case.

CHAPTER 3

THE UNION, MANAGEMENT, AND THE MAFIA

By the Spring of 1965, Detective Robert Nicholson and the Manhattan District Attorney's squad had the witness who could unlock the mystery of the corrupt New York butchers' union. Nat Lokietz knew plenty about how the payoff system worked, and about the mobsters who were in control. This was his story:

The union had divided the wholesale meat industry in New York into two negotiating groups: the fresh beef companies, and the pork and processed meat companies such as Merkel. At every contract the groups were shaken down, and the contracts were staggered so the union leaders had a constant source of extra income. Lokietz professed to know only about his own group, called the Meat Trade Institute, whose contract with the union had last been renewed on July 1, 1964. The date was a crucial bargaining tool in the hands of the union, because the July 4 weekend was the biggest of the year in the picnic meats business. If the companies were shut down by a strike on the June 30 contract expiration date, tons of meat would rot.

And that, according to Lokietz, is exactly what the union bosses had threatened would happen if the Meat Trade Institute didn't make the customary payoff to the leaders of Local 174: Frank Kissell, Karl Muller, and Harry Stubach. In 1964, the ante was set at $60,000. The companies paid.

Convinced that Lokietz's story was the break they had been looking for, Nicholson was anxious to throw wiretaps around the butchers' union office to provide corroborative evidence, especially because the FBI might also be on the trail. Nicholson didn't want the federal agents to steal the case.

But until the Merkel case had been dispensed with, the lawyers in the office considered it essential that Nicholson and his men devote all their working hours to helping prepare for the upcoming trials. Someone had to go through the boxes of subpoenaed documents, accounting for all of them no matter how innocuous, and someone had to gather the records of all interviews done on the case no matter how tangential, so that full disclosure could be made to the defense.

Finally, in April, 1966, Nicholson was freed to go after the labor racketeers. Taps and bugs were authorized for the headquarters of Local 174 of the butchers' union. Once again, though, nothing seemed to happen quite as simply as might have been expected.

On the night of April 11, 1966, Nicholson led a troop of twenty men from the D.A.'s office to the union headquarters on East Eighteenth Street off Union Square. Extreme precautions were taken to wrap secrecy around the break-in that was necessary to plant the bugs.

Once inside the building, the break-in crew proceeded up the stairway—elevators made noise—to the union's office on the fifth floor. An electronics technician went to work on the switchboard. Moreover, by other wiring tricks, lines to the offices of Kissel, Muller, and Stubach, the top officers, could be thrown open so that the telephones in those offices would act as bugs without the use of additional microphones. If Kissel picked up his phone, his conversation would be overheard by the wiretap. When he put the phone back on the hook, everything that went on in his office would still be transmitted via the open line to the bug in the switchboard. (The phone system at Merkel hadn't permitted such wiring, and the microphone had to be planted in the room.) Finally, a big cable packed with fifty pairs of wires—to allow the monitoring of many conversations at the same time—was strung out the back of the union office, into the back of another office that the cops had rented.

Within an hour of the time the office opened the next morning, they knew they had made a terrible mistake the night before. As Kissel strolled out into the reception area, the switchboard operator called him over and said, "You know, a funny thing's been happening. Every time you go into your office and talk to somebody, I can hear everything you say over my headset."

Kissel was only briefly taken aback. It had been raining a lot recently, he noted. "All this dampness must have done something to the phone wires. If it doesn't clear up soon, we'll call the phone company."

The police shuddered at the idea that the telephone company might find out what they were doing with the company's equipment. So after a discreet interval, one of the cops called the union and identified himself as a representative of the New York Telephone Company. "Have you been having any trouble with your phones?" he asked.

Soon, another cop, in a telephone company uniform, appeared at the union office and went to work on the switchboard. He quickly disconnected the wire from Kissel's office. Lacking the necessary equipment, however, he left the job of rewiring it for another break-in crew to handle that night.

Thinking their job would be relatively simple—just hooking up one bug—Nicholson went back with only two other men that night. They made their way into the building easily, having done it before, and had just started up the stairs when from above them they heard a "thump . . . thump . . . thump . . ." As they proceeded up, the sound got louder. "Bang . . . bang . . . bang . . ." By the time they got to the fifth floor it was obvious that all the banging and crashing was coming from the union office.

The officers flashed their bright lights into the room and illuminated what Nicholson later recalled as "three of the biggest men I ever saw." They had lifted a six-foot, double-door steel safe off its legs and onto its side on the floor, and were attacking it with sledgehammers and crowbars.

"Police! Freeze!" an officer shouted.

The men around the safe looked up and saw nothing but a bright light. One of them threw a metal tool toward the light and started to take off in the opposite direction. The police drew their guns and opened fire. There was a shattering of glass, as windows in the office partitions were hit by the bullets.

"We give up! Don't shoot!" the men screamed.

At that point it would have been hard to say which trio of burglars were the most surprised—the ones with the court authorization to be there or the ones without it. The last thing the policemen wanted to do on their black-bag job was to stumble on a team of safecrackers. If they arrested the safecrackers, it could blow their secret operation. On the other hand, they couldn't very well tell the safecrackers to just go on home and forget about it.

The cops decided they would first take time to fix the switchboard, then call the local precinct with the following story: they had been off-duty and out drinking, just passing by on the street, and had heard some noise. So they had broken in to investigate, and had captured the safecrackers.

A squad from the local precinct arrived and was impressed by the story. "We've been looking for these guys for months. They've been breaking in everywhere in the neighborhood," one of the officers said.

So Nicholson graciously offered to let the local precinct men make the arrest. He explained that he and his friends had been with women that night and that if their names got on the arrest report, their wives might find out.

The D.A.'s men didn't know exactly how well their ruse had worked until on their bugs the next morning they heard an office manager explaining to Kissel what a wonderful job the local police had done.

The investigation into the butchers' union had begun. It would continue for a decade.

The Amalgamated Meat Cutters and Butcher Workmen of North America bargains for some 525,000 American workers. The union was founded in 1897 after a decade of unrest and protest among employees in the big midwestern stockyards. At the same time, local retail butchers were getting together in many eastern and some midwestern cities, and these organizations often affiliated with the Amalgamated. From the beginning, relations were strained between the packinghouse workers and the retail butchers because then, as now, their short-term economic interests seemed to diverge.

In 1921, the Amalgamated—dominated until then by the packing-house faction—put nearly all its chips on the table in an armageddon-type strike against the big packinghouses, including Swift, Armour, Wilson, and Cudahy. In the face of rising inflation and a generally anti-union mood in the country, the packinghouses had unilaterally reduced wages and nullified many work rules and grievance procedures that the union had won over the years. The strike merely proved that the companies had the power to do it. Government supported management. By the spring of 1922, the meat cutters were back in the packinghouses under pretty much whatever terms the packers cared to have them.

But the union still had a source of strength—the urban retail locals, whose members did cleaner, more highly-skilled work, and were much less affected by economic and political trends.

From 1922 on, this retail faction was predominant in the Amalgamated Meat Cutters' Union. And the retail butcher locals were increasingly under the domination of the Mafia. Butcher shops were part of the food distributing system, which naturally came under the influence of the Mob whether the food was meat, cheese, or olive oil. Food distribution involved two elements the Mafia thrives on: trucking, which has always been under the Mob's thumb through the Teamsters' union, and ethnic loyalty, which diminishes competition.

In Chicago, the retail butchers' local—perhaps the most powerful local in the Amalgamated—was controlled by Mike Kelly, who associated with Capone allies who controlled other local unions in the dairy, alcoholic beverage, and laundry and dry cleaning distribution systems. It was Kelly who installed as leader of the Amalgamated Patrick E. Gorman, the man who achieved and maintained the predominance of the retail locals over the next five decades.

Gorman was a strange creature in many ways, but the most curious trait his critics see in him is his support for the racketeers who have infiltrated his union and dominated large segments of it. He has allowed them to plunder at will, he has visited them in jail when they have been sent there, and he has welcomed them back into union office when they have gotten free. Why? Some critics say Gorman still owes a debt to the memory of Mike Kelly, who put him in office. Others say that while he never personally has been suspected of taking payoffs from employers, he may need racketeer support so he can continue to enjoy the supposedly legitimate perquisites of his office, including a $75,000-a-year salary, liberal expenses, and having his wife on the payroll at fees of up to $120,000-a year.

On September 13, 1940, a mobster named George "Poker Face" Scalise went on trial for grand larceny and forgery. He had stolen millions of dollars from members of the building employees' union and other unions he controlled. He shook down employers with threats. He padded union payrolls. His criminal overseer was Anthony Carfano, known as Little Augie Pisano, a top Mafia captain in New York.

District Attorney Thomas Dewey's star witness against Scalise in 1940 was a Mob labor lawyer, Louis Marcus, who had agreed to testify to save his own neck. The young prosecutor handling the case for Dewey was Murray Gurfein, now a federal judge. After guiding Marcus through a description of how Scalise had looted the building employees' union, Gurfein asked him, "Did you have any further contact with any other union at the instigation or direction of Scalise?"

MARCUS: I did. He told me that he would like to get a charter for the non-kosher butchers in the Borough of Brooklyn. At that time, I represented the butchers' union in New York and I told him that I would get a charter for the non-kosher butchers in Brooklyn—providing I know who was going to be in this union, because I told him that the butchers' organization will not have anyone but butchers in the organization. He mentioned the name of Max and Louis Block, both of whom I know to be butchers; and I said, "That's very good. I will get you the proper applications and you will fill them out, and I will do all that I can to get you this charter." I asked him who, if anybody, was going to finance this proposition, because I told him that the butchers' international would not advance any finances for organization, and he said, "Augie and myself."

GURFEIN: Augie and myself?

MARCUS: That's right.

GURFEIN: That was—was that the same man you referred to as Augie Pisano?

MARCUS: I believe so.

GURFEIN: Now, was a charter obtained for this non-kosher butchers' union in Brooklyn?

MARCUS: It was.

GURFEIN: [a few minutes later] Did you ever have any conversation with respect to any bosses' association of butchers at or about that time, with Scalise?

MARCUS: Yes. I believe several weeks later Mr. Scalise again called me to his office . . . and told me that he would like to form an association of Italian-American butchers.

GURFEIN: Employers, was that?

MARCUS: That's right.

The jury believed Marcus and convicted Scalise, who spent most of the 1940s in jail and then resumed racketeering.

Thus the Mafia wound up on both sides of the bargaining table in the meat industry, a situation that only extended itself in the years ahead. The local that Pisano and Scalise started through the Block brothers grew and merged, and remains today the central organization of the butchers' union in the New York metropolitan area. It bargains for one of every ten members of the Amalgamated Meat Cutters across the country, and one of every five members of the dominant non-packinghouse group.

Pisano and Scalise chose their lieutenants wisely. Max and Louis Block remained in office through two generations of Mafia leadership. As Jewish immigrants from Europe, they knew other European Jews in the meat business who went on to executive positions in the supermarkets. Through the Blocks, Poker Face Scalise and other mobsters were brought to the same restaurant tables with top officials from such major chains as Bohack, Waldbaum's, Daitch-Shopwell, Big Apple, Finast, and A & P.

Pisano's star was at its zenith in the 1930s. Under his patronage, Scalise held control of at least seven unions including the beauty operators, the garbage workers, the ashcan handlers, the building employees, the elevator operators, and the distillery workers as well as the butchers. Membership in these unions increased in multiples under the Mafia's strong-arm organizing tactics. The more members, the more dues, and the more pension and welfare contributions there were; according to testimony, the Pisano-Scalise cut was as much as 50 percent of everything that came in.

Scalise lived in a twenty-seven-room mansion on an eighteen-acre estate, with a lake, in Ridgefield, Connecticut. The estate was bought with straight cash, almost certainly union cash. Off and on in the 1940s, Scalise also lived in New York state prisons at Ossining and Dannemora, and the federal penitentiary at Atlanta. His power faded somewhat, but in the mid-1950s he still was able to engineer the theft of $540,000 from the welfare fund of the distillery workers and whiskey wholesalers' union.

Pisano's power had faded as well. While Al Capone was in his glory days, Pisano shared in the wealth from the Cuban casinos and Florida race horses. His gambling and liquor distribution rackets in New York were protected by his father-in-law, Jimmy Kelly (real name John di Salvio), a powerful Democratic political figure. Pisano's companies handled beer deliveries to Tammany Hall political clubs both during and after prohibition. His goons had access to police badges and uniforms in case they needed cover for their dirty work. His beer trucks had access to genuine police when necessary to protect them from the occasional competitive instincts of rival Mafia families. He owned nine limousines and had two rum boats. But by the mid-1940s, links to Kelly and Capone were of small benefit. Pisano's income kept flowing, though, from lingering union and political connections. For example, he and Vincent Rao, consigliere of the Lucchese Mafia family, were associated in a firm called Ace Lathing Company, which presumably had an easy time dealing with Local 404 of the Lath Hoisters Union. Joseph Vento, a soldier in the Lucchese family, was president and treasurer of the local. In about 1967, Ace Lathing received a contract to renovate state-controlled Yonkers Raceway for $200,000; the work was entirely subcontracted at a total cost of $150,000, producing a $50,000 profit.

Finally, the night of Friday, September 25, 1959, fate caught up with Little Augie. He and a frequent companion—a blonde former Miss New Jersey—went out for drinks at the Copacabana and dinner. On the way home, Pisano's new Cadillac jumped a curb on a residential street in Queens and came to rest against a utility pole. He and the beauty queen were found dead in the front seat, three bullets in his head, two in hers.

Such were the friends of Max and Louis Block, who ran the butchers' union in New York for twenty-five years, accumulating enormous wealth and influence. Max became an international vice-president, one of the three or four most powerful men in the international butchers' union. The Blocks had arrived in New York from Poland in 1915 with their mother and three sisters. While Mom opened a grocery store in the Brownsville section of Brooklyn, the boys tried prize fighting. Max apparently confined his pugilism to the ring, but Louis was convicted in 1932 of beating up a policeman in Brooklyn; he got a suspended sentence despite two other arrests. Then came the brothers' butcher shop and the call from Little Augie Pisano to head the union.

At least as important as what the Blocks did at union headquarters was the socializing they did on the outside. On an almost nightly basis, the Blocks brought together the meat industry and the underworld. To accommodate their varied friends, and their own taste for the sweet life, the Blocks acquired a steakhouse in New York, which they dubbed the Black Angus, and a country club in Connecticut, the Deercrest. Scalise and Pisano were regular diners at the Black Angus, as were many other ex-convicts, Mafia murderers, meat dealers, and supermarket chain executives who stopped by the restaurant to greet friends and make payoffs.

Another who showed up at the Black Angus on occasion was the late Senator Joseph R. McCarthy, the Communist witch-hunter the Blocks successfully wooed. Like some other corrupt labor leaders, notably in the Teamsters, the Blocks jumped on the anti-Communist bandwagon of the 1950s as a way of winning public sympathy and knifing their honest opposition.

Though the corrupt system survived and prospered, the Blocks personally got their comeuppance at the hands of Robert F. Kennedy and the McClellan Committee in 1958. Kennedy showed how the Blocks financed their private country club in Connecticut with "loans" and contributions from employers. For example, the chief negotiator for the rendering industry chipped in $25,000 for the country club in return for a nine-month delay in the effective date of a wage increase for the workers. More money came in from the owners of Daitch-Shopwell—one of whom was Moe Steinman—in return for which Daitch was given a one-year respite from making any contributions to the union pension fund. Food Fair bought a similar deal, and Connecticut General Insurance Company ponied up a $350,000 mortgage to the Blocks' club in return for some of the union's insurance business.

Extensive testimony was given about the organization in 1952 of ten thousand A & P clerks. The clerks were agitating for representation, and the Retail Clerks' International Association and other unions were threatening to come in, so A & P wisely went to Max Block for help. Dissident officials of Bronx and Westchester butchers' locals testified that the Blocks had "really rigged" an organization election, "betrayed" the workers and arranged a "sweetheart deal . . . a backdoor deal" for a "company union." According to Fred Cornelius, a former aide to the Blocks, forgery was the source of most of the application cards that A & P and the Block brothers claimed were from workers petitioning to join the Amalgamated. The result: ten thousand workers were committed by a new contract to a forty-five-hour work week when clerks in rival stores were winning a forty-hour week. Worse, the A & P workers were never told that an additional agreement had been signed guaranteeing the forty-five-hour week for five years.

The testimony landed on front pages all over the country. Gorman stood by the Blocks at first, and to this day defends them morally. But within two weeks, when the furor wouldn't die down and government action appeared likely, the international accepted the resignations from the local and international offices of both Block brothers. The Blocks got full pensions, however, and held on to the Deercrest Country Club and the Black Angus.

The Blocks' biggest locals were placed in trusteeship by the international. To run them, Gorman appointed Irving Stern, who in 1976 would go to prison for income tax evasion as a result of Nicholson's continuing investigation of bribery and corruption. A reorganization of the New York area locals ensued, with Stern remaining in control of the main supermarket local. New "elections" were held to select leadership for a wholesaling and processing local. The logical leadership candidate was Karl Muller, a veteran practicing butcher who was popular with others in the trade. Muller was no angel; he had been a friend and supporter of the Blocks, and events later showed that he was not adverse to seeing money passed around and taking some for himself. But the Mafia considered him inadequately connected to its own power structure—not obligated enough—and so it injected its own man for the number one job of secretary-treasurer, while Muller took the number two job of president.

The Mafia's main man on what became the official slate for the election was Frank Kissel, long a buddy of Chappy Brescia and Johnny Dio, the mobsters, and Moe Steinman. Like them, Kissel frequented the Black Angus. He had been associated with Mob meat dealers in Yonkers. Brescia's brother, Frank Brescio (they spell the name with different vowels at the end), went on the payroll of the Kissel local as a business agent, where he remains to this day.

With the replacement of the Blocks by Frank Kissel, the corrupt system flowed on. This continuity, despite the overthrow of individuals would be seen again in the years ahead.

CHAPTER 4

THE KISSEL CASE

Nat Lokietz had rented an apartment on Twenty-Third Street, a short walk from the Fourteenth Street meat district. There, the bribers and bribees in the New York meat business could come for card games, or visits with girl friends. If a meat buyer didn't have a girl friend, a meat supplier would bring him up a prostitute. After bugging the union headquarters, Bob Nicholson put a bug in the apartment.

Shortly after the listening devices had been fixed at the union headquarters, Kissel got a call there from Johnny Dio, and Nicholson bolted up when he heard it. Kissel said the FBI had been around to see him about payoffs from Lokietz. Ironically, Nicholson and Dio came to the same realization at the same moment: Lokietz had told the FBI in great detail about the payoff system, and now that Lokietz had been publicly identified in court as an informant (in the horsemeat case), the bureau was following up.

The FBI didn't know it, but the New York Police Department was now using bugs and wiretaps to monitor federal agents as they broke their promise and began investigating a local bribery case that the police had developed. Apparently no prosecution resulted from the FBI interviews. But the police were learning a lot from the physical surveillance and hidden listening devices. These are some of the things they saw and overheard:

Johnny Dio and other mobsters passed money to Kissel, sometimes in front of Pete's Tavern, around the corner from the butchers' union office. Almost every night the mobsters and the union boss met at the Black Angus, where Steinman and the Block brothers (supposedly long out of union office) joined in. Kissel, in turn, paid off Muller, but customarily cheated him; Muller apparently never realized he was being short-changed.

As the police tape recorders wound on, a grand jury investigation into the bribery was opened. Most of the witnesses, of course, came from the meat industry. Eventually the questions asked by the prosecutors became so specific—"Did you pay $1,000 to Frank Kissel on such-and-such a day?"—that the union officers heard about it and began to suspect that their phones were tapped. Kissel ordered all his officers to go buy radios. "As soon as you come into the room, turn the radio on," he directed.

Chappy Brescia called Kissel and asked him what he thought the grand jury investigation was driving at. "I know what they're after," Kissel replied. "They're after me. I expected this for a long time and I'm prepared for it." Kissel vowed he would never squeal—and he never did.

Then one day the bartender from Pete's Tavern, a Kissel subordinate known as Billy, called. "Tell [Kissel] you definitely got somebody on your phones. Be careful on your phones," the bartender instructed. After that, telephone conversations by the butchers' leaders grew circumspect. But the bug, which monitored conversations in the office, had long been the most productive device anyway. Then, two weeks later, on September 13, 1966, the bartender called Kissel and told him the exact location of the police listening post. To protect their thousands of dollars of eavesdropping and tape recording equipment, and also for their own safety, Nicholson and his men immediately pulled all the equipment out of the union office and the listening post.

The end of the bugging and tapping operation left Nicholson and his men with some inferior but still viable investigative techniques. Thanks to Lokietz, the cops knew who the dealers were, and there was reason to believe they would be willing to talk if the proper guarantees for their protection could be arranged. The reason was that Kissel and his colleagues had offered a particularly bad proposition to the dealers in 1964. It was extortion pure and simple. So, given protection, the employers might talk.

But while their testimony would nail Kissel, it wouldn't produce the case Nicholson ultimately wanted to make. To connect Kissel to the higher-ups in the corruption system without secretly recording their conversations, the cops required something of a miracle. As long as Kissel and the bosses wouldn't talk, some third party would have to see or overhear a transaction between them and then testify about it.

The one productive incident during this period was a conversation Nicholson observed at the Black Angus in November 1966. Kissel and Brescia sat down together at a table with Irving Grossman, the head of Local 88 of the Retail-Wholesale Department Store Workers Union in Brooklyn. It looked obvious that Grossman was not the one who had asked for the meeting, and in fact clearly would rather have been someplace else. Nicholson and a partner edged closer. Grossman was being intimidated by Brescia—and who wouldn't be! In the 1930s he had served as personal bodyguard for Lucky Luciano. Then he graduated to chief enforcer for a taxicab medallion racket.

Now Brescia glowered across the table at Grossman, while Frank Kissel bawled Grossman out. What was the disagreement about? A wiretap was put on Grossman's phone to see if he would tell anyone. Conversations revealed that Grossman had been organizing in the meat industry, and Kissel and Brescia didn't like it. At the Black Angus, Kissel declared that Grossman had been warned before and he wouldn't be warned again. Then Brescia himself had said, "I don't want you in the meat business. Get out or I'll kill you."

Grossman was called before the grand jury. He denied ever having a conversation with Brescia or Kissel in the Black Angus, or being threatened. He was indicted for perjury in 1967. Six times his lawyers requested delays while he stayed on as head of the union. He underwent cancer surgery. Finally, in 1973, he pleaded guilty, and with lawyers still raising the cancer issue, Judge Burton B. Roberts let him off with a $1,000 fine. He remained president of the union local, and sole union trustee of its pension and welfare funds. When the federal pension reform act (ERISA) took effect in 1975, it became illegal for Grossman to continue as fund trustee because five years had not elapsed since his conviction. He appealed to the U.S. Parole Commission for a waiver. Nicholson personally went to court in 1977 and persuaded an administrative law judge to deny the waiver. So Grossman can't run the pension fund, though he remains president of Local 88.

Chappy Brescia also was called before the grand jury and jousted with it, trying to avoid testifying. The prosecutor—at this point Nicholas Scopetta—foreclosed Brescia's effort to take the Fifth Amendment by offering him immunity from prosecution. If Brescia talked, he could explain how the whole racket worked. But he wouldn't. On May 25, 1967, he began serving two consecutive thirty-day jail sentences for contempt of court. Sixty days later he went free, having successfully refused to answer all questions.

Though thirty or sixty days meant little to a professional criminal like Brescia, it was still a sobering penalty in the eyes of the meat dealers who had bribed Kissel. Lokietz had turned the dealers' names over to the D.A., and now they were being subpoenaed. They faced a real dilemma. They couldn't lie—thirty days for contempt was bad, but seven years for perjury was worse. On the other hand, telling the truth wasn't a promising course, either.

It's commonly thought that the Mafia has only one weapon to keep its charges in line—the weapon usually referred to as a cement overcoat. In fact, the murder of outsiders is resorted to rarely by traditional mobsters. The butchers' union, which the Mafia controlled, could destroy a business that had taken a lifetime to establish. Long after the grand juries had been disbanded and the prosecutors and detectives had gone on to other jobs, Frank Kissel or someone else the Mob appointed would still run the union, and the meat company owners would have to deal with him. What guarantees, they wanted to know, could the district attorneys give them that if they testified, their businesses wouldn't be ruined, either now or a few years from now?

So the District Attorney promised that the dealers would testify as a group, one after the other. That way the union couldn't retaliate against them without destroying the whole industry. No one dealer would be forced to testify unless all agreed to testify. And they would be given immunity from prosecution.

One dealer, Irving Berger, president of Mogen David Kosher Meats Products Corp., still refused to cooperate. He insisted before the grand jury that he had never spoken to the three union leaders—Kissel, Muller, and Stubach—about a bribe. Berger was indicted for perjury. Eventually the case was dismissed, but Berger's indictment—along with the one pending against Grossman—evidently had its effect on the other meat dealers, who all told their stories to the grand jury. On August 1, 1967, Kissel, Muller, and Stubach were arrested and arraigned on an indictment for extortion. The charges were limited to the payment of $60,000 in bribes by a group of pork wholesalers in 1964 in exchange for the union's promise not to strike. The statute of limitations had expired on all bribes paid before that.

There were the usual delays, but finally, on March 10, 1969, a jury was impaneled. The first important witness was Lester Levy, president of Plymouth Rock Provision Company. Levy said he had met Karl Muller nearly forty years before, when Muller was working as a ham boner for another provisions company. Frank Kissel was a more recent acquaintance. But Levy was a member of the Meat Trade Institute negotiating committee, so in the spring of 1964 he found himself face to face with Kissel at a negotiating session. There, he testified, Kissel took him aside and told him the meat dealers would have to come up with a $60,000 payoff to avert a strike.

There hadn't been a strike in the New York processed meat industry since 1930, Levy said. "It was just before the Fourth of July, which is one of the busiest weeks of the year. We had two, three hundred thousand dollars of perishable inventory and no freezers." He recalled going to his old friend Muller and complaining about the size of Kissel's demands.

Kissel later said he'd be around to collect Levy's $6,000 share of the payoff. Levy told his controller, John Gevlin, to make the payment in cash.

Gevlin, the next witness, told how one crime had been compounded into another to facilitate the payoff. Levy's Plymouth Rock Provision Company bought many of the meats it cured from Stoll Packing Company. In a normal week, Stoll would bill Plymouth Rock from $3,000 to $5,000 for these meats. But Stoll, like Plymouth, was a member of the Meat Trade Institute and was involved in the payoff problem. So Gevlin arranged for Stoll to overbill Plymouth Rock some $6,000. Plymouth Rock paid the extra $6,000 to Stoll with checks, and then Stoll cashed the checks and returned the money as cash to Plymouth Rock. This made the bribe tax-deductible because it was added to the cost of the meat. Gevlin put the cash in the office safe.

"One morning our receptionist advised me that Frank Kissel was outside to see me," Gevlin recalled. So Gevlin went out, escorted Kissel into his private office and gave him the money in an envelope. Kissel took it and left. Not a word was said by either man the whole time, Gevlin testified.

The next witness, Fritz Katz, was the owner of Stoll Packing—and also of Smokemaster Inc., a ham-maker; Pitchal Packing Corp., a bacon-maker; and J. L. Frederick Corp., an importer-exporter of pork. Katz employed 250 to 280 butchers. He was fifty-six years old and had been in the meat business since he was thirteen. In the course of his career he had been convicted of bribing a meat buyer and of shipping mislabeled meats.

Katz recalled to the jury that Lester Levy of Plymouth Rock had taken him aside and told him, "You know what they want? They want sixty thousand dollars. And they want it before the contract is signed and there is nothing we can do about it."

So Katz and Kissel's brother-in-law Buddy White made a list of pork dealers, and by a rough estimate of their size and financial strength determined who would pay what share. The biggest packers, like Merkel and Plymouth Rock, were stuck for 10 percent or $6,000. Stoll and White were at the next level, $4,000, and so on down the line.

Katz testified that he set up a meeting with Kissel at the Old Homestead, a beef house at the edge of the wholesale meat district. Just before departing, he reached into his office vault, pulled out $4,000 cash and later slipped it to Kissel in the men's room.

In his testimony, Buddy White said that when word of the investigation leaked out in 1967, Kissel met him in bars several times and urged him not to talk to the grand jury.

Defense lawyers then suggested through their questions on cross-examination that the state's case was built around the blackmail of prosecution witnesses. The lawyers already had established that the after-hours party apartment Lokietz had rented on West Twenty-Third Street was bugged. Now they suggested that the only reason White had testified was that the D.A.'s men had threatened to tell White's wife what White had been doing in the apartment. Nicholson and the detectives on his team insist to this day that no such tactics ever became part of the investigation.

The defense never denied that the payoffs took place. It merely argued that the employers had conspired to bribe the union bosses rather than the union bosses having conspired to extort money from the employers. The evidence, however, was so overwhelming that the jury's verdict of guilty was no surprise. What surprised people was Judge Abraham J. Gellinoff's sentencing, which actually would have approached a realistic punishment if it had been carried out. Kissel drew seven-and-a-half to fifteen years, Stuback five to ten years and Muller—

who was sixty-six years old and in ill health—three to six years.

Less than two weeks after the union bosses were imprisoned, another judge ordered them free on the ground that there was probable cause their appeal would be upheld. Upset, the D.A.'s office unveiled its reserve weapon: a new indictment charging the same three union leaders with a similar extortion scheme against the fresh beef side of the industry during the same period. The new indictment named eleven additional meat companies that were forced to cough up $65,000. Before the case could go to trial, however, the appeal of the first case was denied, and the men went back to Sing-Sing on May 27, 1970. Muller was paroled less than two years later, and discharged from supervision in May, 1976. Stubach was paroled in September, 1973, and died the following spring. Kissel did four years of hard time, then went on a work-release program until his parole May 2, 1975. Records of the State Department of Correctional Services show that Kissel was out working for a Bronx firm that can't be located now. Nicholson insists Kissel was brokering meat in Yonkers while serving his sentence. In the meantime, all three men had pleaded guilty to the second extortion indictment and had received sentences concurrent with their original ones.

CHAPTER 5

A BLOODY TALE OF CURDLING

Until the hoods moved in quietly about 1966, Alburg, Vermont's, 520 residents managed to eke a living out of their ragged dairy farms, supplemented in the summer by catering to the needs of a few vacationing campers on nearby Lake Champlain. Then came the Great Mafia Cheese Caper. In 1974, the hoods moved away, but several years later the economy of Alburg still hadn't fully recovered from the devastation. Meanwhile, the cheese caper had come and gone from such other unlikely crime capitals as Luxemburg, Wisconsin, and Hayfield, Minnesota.

The caper works this way: milk is bought on credit; cheese is made from the milk and sold; then nobody pays for the milk. Thousands of dairy farmers have been stuck with millions of dollars in unpaid bills in recent years, and at least one large farmers' cooperative outside of Alburg has been driven out of business. Yet the price of cheese for the consumer doesn't go down under the Mafia plan. It goes up.

The cheese caper really is just a new wrinkle in an old racket—control of the pizza industry. When an American orders a pizza, the Mafia expects a slice of the pie, and usually gets it. The Mafia, of course, has a predilection for making money off retail industries by cornering the market on some essential ingredient or process. One ingredient of pizza, mozzarella cheese, comes from a relatively few factories in dairy centers like Vermont and Wisconsin. Control them, and nobody's going to make a true pizza without you. So a lot of old-line Mafia families entered the cheese business early in this century.

The Great Mafia Cheese Caper that devastated Alburg, Vermont, and other dairy communities around the country grew out of a merger that took place in the late 1930s and early 1940s, combining eastern and midwestern Mafia cheese interests. The organization of Joseph "Joe Bananas" Bonanno of Brooklyn, which is near a lot of Italian cheese stores, teamed up with the old Capone organization in Chicago, which is near a lot of cows. The Capones controlled the Milk Wagon Drivers' Union and at least two large dairy companies, and the Bonannos were major food distributors. While Capone, of course, is long dead, Bonanno is considered by many authorities to be the top Mafia boss in the country at this writing.

In 1941, the Capone-Bonanno combine began muscling into the Grande Cheese Company, which had addresses in downtown Chicago and Lomira, Wisconsin. Grande is now called Grande Cheese Products Inc., and is based in Fond Du Lac, Wisconsin. It remains a major producer of mozzarella cheese, and is still managed by descendants or in-laws of the Mafiosi who took it over in the forties.

In Grande's first years under Mafia influence, at least six persons intimately connected with the company, its prior ownership or its competition, met with pronounced misfortune. In 1943, Thomas O. Neglia, whose name appeared on Grande's incorporation papers, was murdered in a barber's chair. The next year, cheeseman Sam Gervasi was killed in a repair shop, and James V. De Angelo, who had claimed an earlier interest in Grande, was found in the trunk of his wife's car with his skull crushed. In 1945, Anofrio Vitale, whose name was on the Grande incorporation papers, was an unexpected product of the Chicago sewer system, and Vincent Benevento, who had been known till then as "the cheese king," was shot five times in West Bend, Wisconsin. Finally, in 1947, Nick DeJohn, who blundered into the mozzarella field unauthorized, was found in the trunk of a car in San Francisco, and the Bonanno-Capone grip on the cheese business had solidified.

It was philosophically, if not geographically, appropriate that Grande's labor ties were to Teamster Local 138 of Vineland, New Jersey, later identified as a branch office for Murder Inc.

Grande was a major national supplier of mozzarella. Evidently it was unable to meet the growing demand, because John DiBella and his brother and sister went on to found Kohlsville Cheese Company of Fond Du Lac, Wisconsin, in 1947; Gourmay [sic] Cheese Company Inc., also of Fond Du Lac, in 1954; and Cloverdale Dairy Products Inc., of Fairwater, Wisconsin, in 1957. By the time of the famous raid on the Apalachin, New York, Mafia gathering in 1957, Joe Bonanno's cheese empire had spread to manufacturing plants in Michigan, Colorado, California, and Canada. He also owned a laundry, two coat companies, and a very unusual funeral parlor. History may record Joseph Bonanno as the mortician who invented the duplex coffin. That is, one with a false bottom and a secret compartment, where his family's hit victims could be laid to rest underneath the displayed body of record.

While the notorious Joe Bananas made this feeble attempt to lead a respectable second life, John DiBella, the cheese tycoon, made a successful attempt. Though he was Bonanno's friend, follower, and possibly relative, DiBella apparently had no criminal record. In 1964 he died a respected citizen, with a proper funeral attended by colleagues both Mafia and legitimate. Some are still in the food industry today. Carlo P. Caputo was there, and so were law enforcement agents who described Caputo in their notes as head of the Wisconsin Mafia.

Already, however, forces were in motion that would alter control of the Italian cheese industry in the United States. As with control of many other large enterprises, control of the Italian cheese industry was merely an auxiliary prize in a much larger power struggle for control of a Mafia family. The cheese industry was merely a spoil in the Banana War. Yet it illustrates how products that we use every day may hang on the outcome of Mafia violence.

On the night of October 20-21, 1964, two men grabbed Joe Bonanno as he and his lawyer were approaching the lawyer's apartment building. The men hustled Bonanno into a car and he wasn't seen in public again until he unexpectedly strode into the U.S. Courthouse in Manhattan May 17, 1966. Reporters and law enforcement officials have offered numerous guesses as to what had happened. Bonanno had been scheduled to testify before an investigative grand jury in New York the day after he disappeared, and perhaps other Mafiosi were afraid he might talk. Or perhaps Bonanno arranged his own kidnapping to avoid the grand jury's questions. Then a story came out that Bonanno had let contracts for the murder of four rival godfathers, which would have been about the heaviest single hit list in history. According to this story, the appointed gunman (Joseph Colombo) betrayed the murder plans to the national commission, which then ordered Bonanno's kidnapping (and arranged for Colombo's meteoric rise to boss of his own family as a reward).

Finally, on June 10, 1969, the Justice Department submitted in open court the transcribed product of its bug on the office of Sam the Plumber DeCavalcante, the New Jersey Mob boss whom the national commission had appointed in 1964 to mediate certain disputes with Bonanno. DeCavalcante's taped conversations make clear that for several months before Bonanno disappeared, the commission had been summoning him to come explain himself.

Sam the Plumber, after talking with other members of the commission, told his underbosses in the bugged office that Bonanno had staged his own kidnapping, although Sam couldn't figure out why. DeCavalcante mentioned nothing about a mass murder plot. But he cited two other grievances against Bonanno. First, Joe had promoted his son Bill to the high post of *consigliere*, over the heads of more veteran hoods whose noses were put out of joint. Second, Joe Bonanno had been invading the territories of other Mob bosses—in California and in Canada.

Giuseppe Saputo & Sons Ltd., Montreal, is today a major Canadian cheese maker, as it was back in 1954 when Joseph Bonanno was allowed to buy 20 percent of the stock for a mere $8,000 (Saputo explained at the time that Bonanno had "been very helpful to us over the years advising us," and therefore merited the bargain investment). John DiBella's son Pino went to work for Saputo. Giuseppe Saputo and his sons Emmanuel and Francesco have run several cheese making and distributing companies whose products are now widely available in American stores and supermarkets. The Saputos also run companies in Montreal that distribute olive oil, salami, and other Italian foods, and in 1978 announced plans to build a large cheese plant in Vermont.

In 1963, the year before Bonanno disappeared, a cheese war broke out in Montreal when a man named Santo Calderone went into business in competition with Saputo. According to police reports, Calderone's trucks and equipment were bombed, burned, and vandalized, and acid was dropped in his fermenting milk; he closed up shop. In 1971, the

it. By filing certain legal papers, the Falcones made the Alburg cheese operation independent from its Brooklyn parent. The new corporation, Creamery Inc., continued to ship mozzarella primarily to Falcone Dairy Products in Brooklyn, but instead of its being an internal transfer of merchandise as before, Alburg Creamery began to bill Falcone Dairy.

By 1971, the first Vermont dairy cooperative had sued Alburg Creamery for lack of payment for milk. The suit was settled, but Alburg kept falling further behind. By early summer, 1973, the creamery owed well over half a million dollars to several cooperatives, including nearly $400,000 to the Milton (Vermont) Cooperative. There were more lawsuits. The jig was up.

What happened next was exactly what you might expect to happen at a Mafia-run plant that is faced with going out of business: there was a suspicious fire that reduced the plant to rubble and destroyed books and records. The creamery, incidentally, was directly across a two-lane street from the Alburg Volunteer Fire Department.

Questioned before a grand jury, Joseph Falcone acknowledged that he was in Vermont the day of the fire, but offered a staunch alibi witness. The witness, interestingly, was Thomas Ocera, whose family ran two businesses that distributed Falcone merchandise to Long Island restaurants, and who fronted for the Falcones in operating a large Long Island restaurant.

The fire cost Alburg's insurer, Lumbermen's Mutual Casualty Company, $350,000. It would have cost Lumbermen's a lot more except for the alertness of some U.S. border guards. According to government sources, two big truckloads of stinking, rancid mozzarella cheese had been shipped from Canada the day before the fire, destination Alburg Creamery. If the guards hadn't turned the cheese back because of its condition, the cheese would have been burned up in the fire, and presumably reported as an insurance loss worth about $80,000. The cheese came from Giuseppe Saputo & Sons.

The local bank that held the mortgage on the Alburg factory had a direct claim on the first $100,000 from Lumbermen's Mutual. That still left $250,000 in additional insurance money. The Falcones were never able to ease their pain with this money, however. Before a penny of it was paid over by Lumbermen's, Alburg's big creditors—three farmers' cooperatives—forced an involuntary bankruptcy, freezing the insurance money.

The $250,000 should have provided close to enough to satisfy the creditors, because on paper the Alburg Creamery was only marginally insolvent. It still had as assets several hundred thousand dollars in accounts receivable from Falcone Dairy Products, to which Alburg was shipping about $1.6 million a year in mozzarella. Theoretically, the farmers, as creditors in bankruptcy, could sue Falcone Dairy for the money they owed.

But the mozzarella mob was ready for them. In January, 1974, just as the court was sinking its teeth into the bankruptcy case, Joseph Falcone and Joseph Curreri made a bookkeeping switch. They suddenly remembered that back in the fall of 1971, about half the cheese that the Alburg Creamery had shipped—four hundred thousand pounds of it—had been rancid. So they put retroactive credits on the books, which turned Falcone Dairy from Alburg's biggest debtor into a $48,709.31 creditor. In other words, Falcone Dairy claimed that it had suffered losses because of the rancid cheese, and was entitled to additional money just as the farmers were.

Unfortunately for Falcone Dairy, Albert O. Axten, the FBI's resident agent in Montpelier, had been watching the Alburg Creamery ever since the investigation of the suspected arson. When he saw the Alburg bankruptcy papers, he sensed fraud in the way Falcone Dairy had escaped without paying its bills, and he persuaded the Justice Department to bring charges against Joseph Falcone and Joseph Curreri.

The Falcone-Curreri trial was held in Burlington in 1976. Key testimony was provided by J. Leo Laramee, the hired cheesemaker, who said that he didn't recall anyone mentioning anything to him about half the cheese he made being rancid. Once again, Joseph Falcone needed witnesses to support his story. There were plenty of witnesses. They were Falcone Dairy's customers—Brooklyn-based wholesalers who service New York-New Jersey area pizzerias. And they were willing to offer documents or testimony asserting that Falcone Dairy had indeed been supplying a lot of bad cheese and had been forced to give refunds for it.

The jury in the Falcone-Curreri case chose not to believe the self-serving testimony of the distributors, however. It convicted both Curreri and Joseph Falcone of bankruptcy fraud, and the judge sentenced them to three years in prison. They stayed free on appeal well into 1977.

Meanwhile, if J. Leo Laramee was really making rancid cheese at the Alburg factory, the stink evidently didn't bother the Falcones very much. Right after the fire, Joseph Falcone flew to Vermont to enlist Laramee's services in another mozzarella venture. Accompanying Falcone was the man who some observers think is the real Big Cheese: Thomas Gambino.

There are two important Tommy Gambinos. Neither has ever been convicted of a crime. One, Carlo's son, runs trucking and other operations in the New York-New Jersey garment industry. The Tommy Gambino who flew to Vermont to see J. Leo Laramee is Carlo's nephew.

The deal that Falcone and Gambino came to Vermont to talk about involved Valley Lea Dairies Inc., a farmers' cooperative based in South Bend, Indiana. Falcone and Gambino had a contract to make Valley Lea's milk into cheese and sell it, and they persuaded Leo Laramee to run their operation again. Laramee was set up at a plant owned by Valley Lea in Hayfield, Minnesota, making Greek-style feta cheese for sale to a distributing company Thomas Gambino set up in West Haven.

At the same time, a Valley Lea mozzarella plant was opening in New Wilmington, Pennsylvania, with equipment owned by United Cheese Corp. of Brooklyn, which also received the plant's product. United Cheese was financially backed by Joseph and Vincent Falcone and their wives.

On November 13, 1975, Valley Lea filed suit in New York State Court, Brooklyn, against United Cheese and both Falcone families. In fifteen months of the mozzarella plant's operation, the dairy co-op's unpaid bills had mounted to $758,531.94. In addition to which, Valley Lea claimed $250,000 in other costs and damages. Valley Lea accused the Falcones of having "misappropriated" collateral and otherwise having violated their credit agreement.

The Falcones' response was familiar. In an answering affidavit, their lawyer contended that Valley Lea's plant "was infested with a bacteria which caused all of the cheese which was produced during this period of time to sustain a green mold which would render utilization of the cheese impossible." In fact, the lawyer contended that the Valley Lea dairy farmers actually owed the Falcones more than $150,000, instead of the other way around.

In the fall of 1976, the court forced the sale of the equipment and remaining inventory from the old Falcone Dairy facility, forcing that particular corporate entity out of business. The court received far less than the amount of Valley Lea's claim.

Meanwhile, the Greek cheese plant that Mr. Laramee was running in Hayfield, Minnesota, also turned out to be what you might call an ill-feta'd venture. Elmer Enstad, the manager, says the Gambino firm fell way behind on payments and had its credit cut off. Enstad says an agreement was worked out under which Tommy Gambino would gradually pay off a part of the debt that was defined as his share—about $26,000—in exchange for which he shouldn't be associated with the Falcones in their million-dollar problems with Valley Lea. Enstad says Gambino paid off the $26,000 and was let off the legal hook, though Valley Lea won't sell him any more cheese. "They kept him (Gambino) fairly clean on paper, though they were partners all the way as far as I'm concerned," Enstad says.

Having milked Valley Lea dry in the fall of 1975, the Brooklyn cheese merchants needed another source of supply, and found it in Luxemburg, Wisconsin. The Badger State Cheese Company there, a cheddar operation owned by a family named Koss, was in financial trouble and the Kosses were persuaded to sell 70 percent of the company to Tommy Gambino, his father Joseph Gambino (Carlo's brother), and some Falcone relatives. In came J. Leo Laramee to help convert the plant to mozzarella and run it.

The result was predictable. In August, 1976 (nearly six months *after* Joseph Falcone was convicted in Vermont), Badger State shut down, with debts estimated at $1.3 million, much of it in unpaid milk bills to dairy farmers.

In the early morning of July 6, 1977, two men lugged 210 gallons of gasoline into Giuseppe's Pizza Restaurant in Ambler, Pennsylvania. They apparently planned to light a fuse and watch the fireworks in the rearview mirror as they sped away in their '77 Buick LeSabre parked outside. Alas, however, they were working too close to the pilot light on Giuseppe's pizza oven.

Blooey.

There wasn't enough left of one body to identify it right away, but the other was quickly found to be that of Vincenzo Fiordilino of Brooklyn, the twenty-two-year-old nephew of Giovanni Fiordilino, whom police have long identified as a high-ranking member of the Bonanno Mafia family.

The arson in Ambler was only one of several dozen firebombings, torch jobs, and gas explosions that had been ripping apart pizza parlors in New York, Pennsylvania, New Jersey, and Delaware. A war seemed to have broken out over control of the pizza business in the northeast. Carlo Gambino, the boss of bosses, had died the previous October. Meanwhile, Joe Bonanno's top underboss, Carmine Galante, had been freed from a long prison sentence and was in New York working to resurrect the family, which had been in decline since the boss's two-year disappearance in the mid-1960s. Galante was murdered, gangland-style,

July 12, 1979, as he was relaxing with friends in a Brooklyn restaurant. The Bonannos were known to be pushing the Gambinos out of various rackets in 1977, and maybe the cheese industry was one of them.

The Gambinos *were* involved in the King of Pizza pizzeria in Dover, Delaware. Corporate records list Emmanuel and Giuseppe Gambino, both relatives of Carlo, as officers in the King of Pizza. On the night of November 5, 1977, someone put four bombs and a lot of gasoline on the parlor floor. Whoever it was proved almost as inept as the Ambler arsonists. The bombs and gasoline were still sitting there the next morning when employees at the nearby Pantry Pride supermarket smelled fumes and called the fire department. Just two nights later, however, patrons at a nearby bowling alley heard an explosion and saw smoke and flames. The arsonist had returned, and there was one less pizzeria in Dover.

Federal agents found that the Gambino pizzeria in Dover had been buying supplies from Ferro Foods, the operation run in New York by two Gambino relatives who were closely associated with the Falcones. They also found that the fastest-growing competitor in the industry in 1977 was Roma Food Service of South Plainfield, New Jersey. Roma is run by Louis Piancone, who says the operation is totally upright. He also says his brother Michael has no connection to Roma. In the early 1970s, however, Michael Piancone was also in the pizzeria business and shared an office with Roma. According to federal lawmen, he sold pizza parlors to aliens who would buy supplies from Roma. Back in the early 1970s, there was evidence that Michael Piancone was on good terms with the Gambino crowd. What the situation is now in that regard is a mystery.

It's no mystery, however, where Roma buys its mozzarella cheese. The cheese comes from Grande Cheese Products Inc. of Fond Du Lac, Wisconsin, the company taken over in 1941 by Al Capone and his friend—Joe Bonanno.

CHAPTER 7

THE TEAMSTERS

On a wintry night in 1976 I sat at the counter of a truck stop along Interstate 71 somewhere between Cleveland and Columbus. Next to me, still wearing his grease-smudged green winter jacket, was a lanky, craggy-faced, over-the-road (inter-city) truck driver from Akron.

I was in the truck stop as the result of a challenge from a long-time associate of James R. Hoffa, the former Teamster president who had disappeared the previous July and was by now generally presumed to have been murdered. Two weeks before he disappeared, my paper, the *Wall Street Journal,* had published a series of articles describing the theft of hundreds of millions of dollars from the union's biggest pension fund, and the resultant inability of many of the union's 2.3 million members to collect on their pensions. After the stories ran, tips started trickling in that the pension fund theft was merely part of a vast mosaic of corruption that costs the public incalculably. Then the Hoffa disappearance focused the whole country's attention on the Teamsters.

A search for clues led to the Hoffa associate who said that Hoffa had been a veritable saint compared to the current office-holder, Frank Fitzsimmons. He said that under Fitzsimmons's administration, the selling of sweetheart contracts and other rip-offs of the membership and the American public had achieved an open acceptance that Hoffa never would have tolerated. Without Hoffa around, the associate said, the Mob had unrestrained power. It could exploit its control of the Teamsters any way it wanted.

Because of what I already knew about Hoffa from my reading of the McClellan Committee hearings in the 1950s and the history of his federal trials in the 1960s, I found it hard to believe that any level of morality was operating in the union in those days, and even harder to believe that things were worse now. In 1967, when Hoffa's last appeals were turned down, he had handpicked Fitzsimmons to fill in as Teamster president until his prison term was over. Then, after Hoffa's parole in 1971, he had been outraged that Fitzsimmons refused to give back the power. So in 1975, Hoffa attempted the unthinkable—an open fight for the Teamster presidency in a campaign mounted around corruption charges against Fitzsimmons. And he paid with his life. That, it seemed clear, accounted for the far-fetched contentions I was hearing about Hoffa's sainthood. Finally, exasperated with my skepticism, the Hoffa associate issued this challenge: "Don't take it from me. Go ask the truck drivers. Go out to the truck stops along any of the interstates around Detroit or Chicago or Cleveland or Cincinnati"—admittedly Hoffa territory—"and ask the drivers what they think of Jimmy Hoffa and Frank Fitzsimmons."

I spent several days and nights doing the interviews. I learned that the Hoffa associate had been absolutely right about what the truck drivers would say. Hoffa had indeed become a folk hero to them. He may have been a crook, but he looked out for the drivers, they said. And as for Fitzsimmons, one twenty-year veteran from Akron said, "The guys are tired of Fitz, but we can't vote on him. Fitz is just a patsy between the government and organized crime as far as I'm concerned. The union's got down to the point now where they're not much good to us. They're just there to make money. It's a racket."

It is, indeed, a racket—perhaps the world's biggest.

Unlike the butchers' union, where racketeers mix with more business-like elements in a strange amalgam, the Teamsters' Union is totally, thoroughly, dominated by the Mob. It is by far the largest visible institution to be so dominated. It is, in fact, one of the most powerful institutions in the United States. It affects the price and availability of almost everything we buy. Thousands of meat packers are teamsters. Hundreds of thousands of government office workers are teamsters. So are the people who handle freight, including mail, at major airports, where the opportunities for organized theft are great. The Teamsters' Union holds mortgages on office buildings, hospitals, and small busi-nesses all across the country. The Teamsters have invested heavily in the insurance industry and have enjoyed great influence at many banks. They have bankrolled the better part of Las Vegas. In the 1970s the Teamsters have even moved into law enforcement and now control the working contracts for tens of thousands of city cops, state troopers, and sheriff's deputies. The Teamsters have bullied their way to influence over many other unions—the butchers, the bakers, and the Longshore-men, for example.

And there should be no mistake about one thing: the Teamsters are the crime Syndicate—not the individual truck driver or office worker or policeman who pays dues, but the union officials who control almost every facet of the national and regional administration. The Teamsters are an arm of the Mafia.

For several crucial decades through World War II, the union was run by Dan Tobin. Like Pat Gorman, in the butchers' union, Tobin was not a racketeer himself, but was totally unwilling and unable to keep a clean house. Tobin maintained the union's international headquarters in Indianapolis, which helped give it a low profile that was much to the liking of corrupt local leaders who ran their own fiefs as they chose.

Tobin was eventually succeeded by Dave Beck, a Seattle leader, who moved the union's headquarters to Washington. Beck was a totally venal man who had become a millionaire by helping himself to hundreds of thousands of dollars from union treasuries and "loans" from Teamster employers; he later went to jail for it. He certainly had neither the position nor the inclination to clean the Syndicate racketeers out of the Teamsters, and under his leadership their influence expanded.

It was during the late 1940s, however, that the Syndicate bought its ticket to eventual full control over the Teamsters. The Chicago Mafia, the old Capone organization, made a deal with a rising young union leader from Detroit—Jimmy Hoffa. The Mob would support Hoffa in his campaigns for Teamster power, and he would be their man. The first palpable benefit to the Mob was the huge insurance business that Hoffa's Michigan Conference of Teamsters began placing with agencies and insurance companies controlled by Paul "Red" Dorfman, long a key figure in the Capone labor rackets. After the deal with Hoffa, Dorfman's profits from Teamster insurance quickly ran into the millions of dollars, presumably spread around the Mob. Later, when Hoffa achieved regional and then national control, and created the vast Central States, Southeast, and Southwest Areas pension fund, the money rolling in to the Dorfman operation was almost uncountable. By the time Dorfman died in 1971, his son and partner, Allen, had long since taken over day-to-day command as the Mafia's trustee over the Teamster billions. In 1976 and again in 1978, despite an intervening prison sentence and repeated, well-publicized government investigations, Allen Dorfman was hired anew by the Central States pension fund to handle its vast insurance needs, and at this writing retains his open authority with the union.

The Mafia, meanwhile, had helped elevate Hoffa to power in the 1950s.

Having achieved control of the midwestern region with the help of the Dorfmans and other Capone mobsters, Hoffa needed support from another part of the country before making his assault on the union presidency. The East was the likely source of that support because the Mafia had so much power there. But a large faction in the dominant New York-New Jersey area Teamster apparatus was reluctant to go along. Many local leaders valued the loose-knit confederation of the international union because it allowed them independence. Hoffa's design was centralization; he dreamed of a national master trucking contract, a consolidated national pension plan, and a powerful international leadership that would speak for all the Teamsters with a single voice. For Hoffa, this was in part a sincere philosophy of unionism. He surrounded himself not only with the usual cadre of thugs, but also with some dedicated unionists. But the drive to centralize may have been part of his original deal with the Mafia—that by consolidating Teamster leadership, he could also consolidate and deliver the enormous potential graft.

Since it wasn't clear whether the majority of New York area locals supported Hoffa, the obvious solution was to create more locals— enough to establish a majority. In regional and national gatherings, Teamster locals are represented equally, regardless of their size. So Hoffa and the Mob set about to create a number of "paper" locals— locals with few if any members—that could swing the balance in New York area voting. To supervise this sham they needed someone who wasn't likely to be argued with. The clear choice was Johnny Dio, a member of the Lucchese Mafia family, a friend of the Dorfmans who was already a powerful influence in many unions, including the Amalgamated Meat Cutters.

Dio controlled what was known as the United Auto Workers-AFL (an organization totally unrelated to Walter Reuther's UAW, a CIO union). Eventually Dio's UAW-AFL changed its name to the Allied Industrial Workers Union, but under all of its guises it was no more than a shakedown operation that kept a lot of ex-cons in Cadillacs.

With the approach of 1957, the year of Hoffa's planned campaign to replace Dave Beck as president of the Teamsters, Dio engineered the creation of seven new Teamster locals. The extra supply of delegates from these locals guaranteed that Hoffa supporters would control the New York region delegation at the convention. According to testimony before the McClellan Committee, Dio created the new Teamster locals by chartering seven UAW-AFL locals and having them affiliate with the Teamsters. The locals were known as "paper locals," their tiny "membership" composed not of working people, but of friends and relatives of Dio.

So thorough was Hoffa's manipulation of the 1957 election that there are persistent rumors—never confirmed and occasionally denied—that Hoffa even leaked derogatory information about Beck to Robert Kennedy, before realizing that Kennedy was about to become Hoffa's own arch enemy.

Kennedy finished Beck all right, with a devastating series of hearings about financial double-dealing that would eventually put the Teamster boss behind bars. But just as quickly, Kennedy went to Hoffa's jugular, too.

It wasn't persecution, as some revisionist historians have charged. Hoffa deserved everything he got. His administration was fundamentally corrupt. The mobsters whom Beck had only tolerated became Hoffa's knights of the roundtable. Out of the shadows and into such respectability as the Teamsters could provide came the likes of local leaders Joey Glimco (twice arrested for murder) in Chicago, Anthony "Tony Ducks" Corallo (a figure in the Lucchese Mafia family probably superior to, though less well known than, Johnny Dio) in New York, and the murderous Anthony "Tony Pro" Provenzano in New Jersey, to say nothing of Hoffa's own brother Billy, a two-time convict.

When the law tried to stop them, the Teamsters provided, as they always do, the best legal counsel. Supposedly, the Landrum-Griffen Act, which grew out of the McClellan hearings, makes it illegal to use union money to pay for the criminal defense of an officer.

But the Teamsters have proven more adept at devising schemes to get around this rule than the government has proven in stopping them. In 1975, for example, William Bufalino represented several New Jersey Teamster officials who were under grand jury investigation; meanwhile he took a retainer from their union local to handle "union business." The crime the grand jury was investigating was the disappearance of Jimmy Hoffa.

With his high-priced defense teams and low-life maneuvering, Hoffa stayed out of jail for ten years after Kennedy began his pursuit of the Teamster leader in 1957. But it wasn't because Hoffa was innocent. He was ultimately convicted, twice, in 1964, and in both cases the evidence was overwhelming. The first conviction was for tampering with a jury that in 1962 had been unable to reach a verdict on yet another charge Kennedy had brought against him, with, again, overwhelming evidence.

Hoffa and his supporters later created the myth that the prosecution in the jury tampering case relied on the word of a lone witness. But the jury tampering was observed by a four-man FBI surveillance team. It was testified to by several relatives of jurors and others and was backed up by telephone records. Money had been offered and, at least in one case, handed out, and the husband of one juror, a policeman, was promised a promotion to sergeant. These were typical Teamster-Mafia tactics.

Hoffa's other conviction was for mail fraud involving $20 million of loans from Teamster pension funds and $1 million in related kickbacks. Some of the loans were to Mob-connected figures. The most prominent of the loans went to Sun Valley Inc., a Florida land development concern in which Hoffa personally had a large financial interest. The Sun Valley matter was exceptionally sleazy because the union helped Sun Valley sell retirement lots to Teamster members, and some of the lots were actually under water.

In the face of all this, it is sometimes difficult to understand why Hoffa, in death, holds the affection of many Teamsters, and the respect, though often grudging, of most. There may be several explanations. For one thing, a truck driver's daily routine is not likely to encourage respect for law enforcement—in fact, quite the contrary. He is hampered by seemingly unreasonable traffic laws, most particularly in recent years the widely-ignored fifty-five-mile-an-hour speed limit. Meanwhile, the laws supposedly designed to protect the driver's own health and safety—cargo limits, cabin design, rest schedules—are routinely flouted by trucking companies with the seeming complicity of federal and state authorities.

Moreover, corrupt as Hoffa was, and as much as he did to bring Mafia members into positions of power in the Teamsters, he stayed mindful of his constituency in the membership. He gave them at least the cosmetics of representation, and never forgot or let them forget his own days on the loading docks. While Hoffa's life was certainly not austere, and he did not lack for comfortable surroundings, neither was his standard of living out of line with his position. While he certainly sold out his membership in some very large ways for some very large amounts of money, he could never be accused of failing to put in a real working day in which he handled most union business rather effectively along the lines the membership would have expected him to. He was, in short, always a crook, but also always a Teamster.

Not so Fitzsimmons. On taking over when Hoffa finally went to prison in 1967, Fitzsimmons dramatically increased the perquisites of the union presidency and reduced its duties. Fitzsimmons's world is one of private jets, golfing resorts, and puffed-up salaries. His formless flab is quite in contrast to Hoffa's loading dock physique. Just hearing him speak one senses a noticeably lesser intelligence. He has delegated the time-consuming handling of union business to local and regional leaders—who, as often as not, are mobsters. Thus the Mob, under Fitzsimmons's casual rule, has tasted undiluted power—and has liked it. The Mafia can call the shots, as it prefers to do.

There are three real power bases in the Teamsters, all closely tied to the Mafia. One is the Presser organization in Cleveland. William Presser ran the jukebox racket in Cleveland in the 1940s. An associate of numerous mobsters, he became an early ally of Jimmy Hoffa. He has been convicted for contempt of Congress and for destroying subpoenaed evidence (the evidence was a payoff list prepared for a Cleveland distributing company; the list included not only Presser, but a federal judge and some political figures). He also has been convicted for misusing $590,000 in Teamsters' money. Nevertheless, federal judges in Cleveland have thus far seen fit to turn Presser back into the community without substantial punishment. Now in semi-retirement, most of his titles have passed to his son, Jackie Presser, also a pal of the politicians. Between them, the Pressers run the Ohio Teamsters and have a large influence in other unions. Jackie Presser may not be content with his father's backstage role, however, and is said by some to have designs on the international Teamster presidency.

Presser follows the common Teamster practice of holding down paying posts in many locals so that he can accumulate a salary of—according to his press agent—about $200,000 a year (some say it's more). He justifies this sum on the ground that he negotiates against "teams of $500-an-hour lawyers," and asks, "Are you saying as an educated person I don't deserve to get paid the same as those who negotiate against me?"

The second of the three sources of real power underpinning the Fitzsimmons regime is in Kansas City. The leader there, Roy Williams, is another possible candidate to replace Fitzsimmons when the Mob decides it's time for Fitz to go. Like Presser, Williams is a former close ally of Jimmy Hoffa, and the Labor Department study referred to earlier alleged direct ties between Williams and Kansas City Mafia boss Nicholas Civella. According to PROD, the dissident Teamster organization, Williams has been able to maintain various Teamster salaries aggregating around $100,000 a year. Three times the federal government has won indictments against him but each time he has been acquitted, or the charges have been dropped, twice after key witnesses for the prosecution were murdered gangland-style.

The third major Teamster power base is firmly controlled by the Genovese Mafia family in the East. Though some unsettling events occurred in the summer of 1978, the Genovese power has been, and still seems to be, exercised through another group of former Hoffa allies, a blood family named Provenzano, originally of New York but now of

New Jersey. Three brothers, Anthony, Salvatore ("Sammy"), and Nunzio Provenzano have controlled the New Jersey Teamster organization since 1961 through their control of Local 560, a 10,000- to 12,000-member trucking local based in Union City. The Provenzanos also control numerous smaller locals, run by stooges. Many of these locals are used to implement sweetheart contracts with wages and benefits so far below purported Teamster standards that the Provenzanos evidently feel embarrassed to bring them before the membership of their home local. Tens of thousands of members of these satellite locals are treated almost like slaves.

Anthony, usually called Tony Pro, has been identified before Congress as a member of the Genovese Mafia family, as has one of the Provenzanos' chief aides, Salvatore "Sally Bugs" Briguglio. Their power was cemented by the 1961 murder of Anthony "Three Fingers Brown" Castellito, boss of Local 560.

Some fifteen years later, an intensive investigation of the Provenzano organization was begun because of its presumed link to the Hoffa disappearance. During that investigation, the FBI stumbled on a witness to the Castellito murder who himself had gone into hiding shortly afterward. As a result, in 1976, Tony Pro and Sally Bugs were indicted for killing Castellito. In 1978, Provenzano was convicted.

Until the Hoffa investigation struck him in 1978, Tony Pro's power was so awesome as to preclude any meaningful challenges. Certainly his authority wasn't shaken by his 1963 extortion conviction, and the resultant 1967-1971 term he served at the federal prison at Lewisburg, Pennsylvania. Brothers Salvatore and Nunzio Provenzano simply played caretaker while the boss paid his debt to society. The Landrum-Griffen Act provided that Tony couldn't return to union office officially for five years after leaving prison for extortion, but when the ban expired in 1976 he quietly slipped back into the top job at Local 560.

Death seemed the only likely reward for anyone who contested Tony's power. Throughout most of the New York metropolitan area trucking zone, and on into upper New York State and down the Atlantic coast, not a contract was signed, not a pension fund dollar was invested, not a major grievance was pursued outside the imposing shadow of Tony Pro. The Teamster business office in Union City, New Jersey, operated as a headquarters for loansharking, counterfeiting and numerous other crimes, the most important of which was contract murder.

Provenzano became a leading suspect in the Hoffa case because Hoffa had told people that Tony Pro was one of three men he was going to meet at a Detroit restaurant at the time he vanished. Shortly afterward, Ralph "Little Ralph" Picardo, a former close associate of Provenzano's who had been convicted of murder, agreed to turn informer. He identified Sally Bugs and two other employees of the Provenzano organization as having gone to Detroit and murdered Hoffa.

Even so, none of this was enough to convict anybody of anything, and Tony Pro might have survived had it not been for a vigorous new determination that suddenly surfaced in the Department of Justice.

The FBI and Justice Department, scandalized by recent revelations of misconduct within, suddenly confronted their true mission. If Mafia guns could wipe out even the appearance of democracy and free speech in the Teamsters, then whose rights were safe? There might not be proof of who killed Hoffa, but the men believed to be responsible had committed many other grievous crimes. If enough energy, skill, and determination were applied, some of the cases could be proven—as they could have been all along.

More than any others, two men epitomized this tough new attitude. They are Kurt Muellenberg, head of the department's organized crime and racketeering section in Washington, and Robert C. Steward, who heads Muellenberg's special strike force offices in Newark, New Jersey, and Buffalo, New York. The drive they conducted resembled one begun 20 years earlier after another brazen Mafia attack on a public figure, the blinding of newspaper columnist Victor Riesel. The man who authorities believed was responsible for the Riesel attack was John Dioguardi— Johnny Dio—and although they couldn't prove it, they focused in so tightly on Dio that he has spent most of the intervening years in prison for other crimes. The parallel target in the Hoffa case was Tony Provenzano.

Late in 1975, five months after Hoffa disappeared, Provenzano was indicted for planning a $2.3 million pension fund loan involving a $300,000 kickback to mobsters and Teamster officials. Six months later came the Castellito murder indictment against Provenzano and his aide Sally Bugs. The kickback case was based on a hard-to-understand tape recording of a 1974 meeting about the loan; the tape, made secretly by an undercover informant, had been lying around the prosecutors' offices for eighteen months and had been regarded as weak evidence. Provenzano's words on it were few and vague. But with new testimony from Ralph Picardo—the informant who had talked about the Hoffa case—and with a brilliantly orchestrated trial in March, 1978, Tony Pro was convicted.

Two months after the pension fund conviction, which earned Provenzano a four-year sentence, a jury in Kingston, New York, told the stunned Teamster boss that he was also guilty of ordering the murder of Castellito. Tony Pro was sent immediately to the forboding New York State Prison at Dannemora. The Provenzanos still did not lose their hold on their Teamster organization, but the first signs of real trouble had begun to surface.

On March 21, 1978, while awaiting trial for the Castellito murder charge, Sally Bugs Briguglio was shot dead on Mulberry Street in Little Italy. Some federal authorities contend that Briguglio had betrayed Tony Pro and had conspired with another top Genovese underboss, Pasquale "Paddy Mac" Macchiarole, to take power in Local 560, either directly or through allies, if Tony Pro went to jail. One circumstance contributing to this theory is that Macchiarole was murdered apparently the same day Briguglio was. So (within a day or two) were at least two other members of the same gang. At the time Briguglio was being shot on Mulberry Street, Tony Provenzano—according to Justice Department sources—was dining at a restaurant very close by, probably within sound of the gunshots. His dinner partner was Matthew "Matty the Horse" Ianniello, the mobster who controls Manhattan's midtown bar and red light district and has underlings involved in commodities options frauds and other rackets. Some law enforcement officials believe that with the murders of March 21, in a scene reminiscent of the end of the movie *The Godfather*, either Provenzano or Ianniello had just established himself as operating boss of the old Genovese gang.

Whichever explanation for Briguglio's death is correct, it doesn't say much for the kind of people who control one of our largest and most vital industries. A week after Provenzano entered prison, he was replaced as head of Local 560—not by either of his brothers this time, but by his daughter, Josephine Provenzano. The local announced that Miss Provenzano, an office worker on the payroll in the past, had been elected by unanimous vote of the membership. Some observers suspect that this development indicates not unanimity, but discord; they believe Salvatore and Nunzio Provenzano yielded up the office to their niece because they regarded her as less likely to be shot by the opposition.

The Provenzano power base has been used as an open center for extortion, loansharking, counterfeiting, and murder. It is run by ex-convicts. Briguglio, a convicted counterfeiter who supposedly subsisted on a $31,000-a-year salary as Local 560 business agent, moved a few years before his death into a $125,000 house mortgage-free; records show that his wife (in whose name the house was registered) paid $105,000 cash down, and soon paid the other $20,000 so that the Briguglios owned the house free and clear. Another key figure in the local (though technically not an employee or officer), Thomas Andretta, through his wife bought Briguglio's old house for $90,000, also without having to obtain financing. Andretta, who has served two brief prison terms after convictions for hijacking, loansharking, and counterfeiting, is a former truck driver with no apparent legitimate occupation.

Briguglio's brother Gabriel, and Andretta's brother Stephen both have held various Teamster posts in areas where the Provenzanos dominate. All four men have been identified publicly by Justice Department officials as suspects in the presumed murder of Hoffa. The two Briguglios and Thomas Andretta personally killed him, according to the testimony of their former colleague Ralph Picardo. But at this writing none of them has been charged.

The Mafia has profited in many ways from its control over the international Teamster apparatus. The hiring capacity of the giant Teamster organization provides a perfect front. Mafia figures frequent the payrolls of Teamster locals with no-show jobs or at least irregular hours. Teamster members and employers are easy prey for Mafia loansharks or vice peddlers. Since trucking is involved in almost every aspect of American economic life, control over the Teamsters gives the Mafia leverage in almost any business it wants to muscle into.

But there have been two very immediate avenues to profitability for the Mob in the Teamsters' Union: pension and welfare fund fraud, and sweetheart contracts. Directly through the trust funds, and indirectly through the sweetheart contracts, the American consumer has been looted of money that must be in the many billions of dollars. The savage cost to Teamster members is even more easily discernible. But perhaps worse, in the long run, is the blow to the nation's morality; a large segment of business has been compelled to submit to corruption. Law enforcement has often been impotent, and at times complicitous.

CHAPTER 8

THE MAFIA'S PRIVATE BANK

Every week, $31 of the compensation paid to more than half a million North American trucking workers goes into a Teamster pension fund. It jumped to $37 a week in 1979. A million other Teamster members in other jobs are covered by varying contributions into the funds. The Teamster apparatus controls more than one thousand employee-benefit funds with reported assets of about $9 billion, growing by about $1 billion a year. The employees who purportedly benefit from this money don't see it in their paychecks; often, they don't ever see it at all. The employers who shell it out pass the cost directly on to the people who buy the goods that are being trucked. The price of practically everything rises. And the money flows steadily to the Mafia.

One of the largest Teamster funds—the Central States, Southeast, and Southwest Areas pension fund, operated from Chicago—has compiled a record of abuse that makes other landmark swindling operations look paltry by comparison. It is perhaps the biggest rip-off in history. Thorough records of the stealing have never been made available, but enough evidence has trickled out in various lawsuits and public filings to show that many hundreds of millions of dollars have been plowed into "loans" to racketeers or businesses related to them. The "loans" have never been paid back.

The overwhelming majority of the fund's investments—89.2 percent—were concentrated in real estate mortgages, mostly to small, speculative businesses. (According to the Institute of Life Insurance, most pension funds invested an estimated 10 to 15 percent of their funds in real estate.) Often the loans were for less than $1 million, which auditors consider too small to be worth the bookkeeping trouble for such a large fund. Moreover, the real estate involved wasn't exactly prime. Many of the investments were in second and even third mortgages.

Deals accounting for well over a third of the money loaned were listed as delinquent or already defaulted on, with the pension fund acquiring ownership of vast acres of questionable real value in lieu of hundreds of millions in cash. On thorough study, it's easy to guess that more than half a billion dollars in supposed investments were distributed to fund insiders, Mafia members, and their cronies. And this was only one of many suspicious Teamster pension funds.

The Central States fund has always prided itself on its apparent solvency, based on the fact that income from employer contributions exceeds pay-outs to retirees by $100 million or so a year. The trick, however, is that the pension pay-out has always been held far below what it should be. Reliable figures aren't available on how many Teamsters are getting retirement or disability pensions, and how many others are claiming pensions that haven't been paid. But when I went looking, I had no difficulty locating scores of Teamster members and former members who said they were being cheated.

Most often, the complainers had been victimized by technicalities that give the fund the right to withhold payment. Applied uniformly, these loopholes could destine hundreds of thousands of Teamsters to lose their pensions. Some of these abuses, though by no means all of them, were in theory cured by the "vesting" provisions of the federal pension regulation law, the so-called ERISA act, that took effect in 1976. Whether, in fact, ERISA has led to any real improvement remains to be seen. The law was designed to create uniform standards for well-intentioned pension operations. It wasn't designed to enable the policing of frauds.

Under the Central States pension plan, Teamsters are supposed to be able to retire at age fifty-seven for minimum benefits, or at age sixty or more for full benefits of up to $550 a month. But those Teamsters who expected to start collecting a pension on retirement often had to wait four to six months for the Central States fund even to respond to an application. And then a common response was a form that called on the individual teamster to prove he had twenty years of industry credits for a retirement pension, or fifteen for a disability pension. Few truck drivers keep such detailed records.

Trucking work by its nature involves frequent job-hopping among a myriad of small companies. "These trucking companies are very little," one Teamster complained after his case was lost. "They go bankrupt. They buy each other out. I doubt that 20 percent of the trucking companies are still doing business in the same form for twenty years. So records are simply not maintained. . . . The worker gets his paycheck indicating X-dollars were taken out [for pension fund contribution] but nobody ever knows whether the companies actually send in the money."

Constant transfers from one company to another and from one depot to another within the same trucking company caused an additional problem: the transfer of workers from one local to another. At any given time, hundreds of thousands of teamsters are represented by locals without reciprocal deals with the Central States pension plan. Many Teamsters frequently rotate into and out of these locals. I found in 1975 that Teamsters applying for pensions often are shocked to be told that they must have the minimum twenty years' service with one particular plan, even though they have been members of the same international union for many decades.

Even Teamsters who built up twenty years' total service with one plan sometimes found they had run afoul of the so-called "break-in-service" provisions. For example, the fine print of the rules that the Central States fund filed with the Labor Department says, "If a member did not work under a Teamster collective bargaining agreement requiring contributions to this Pension fund for three consecutive years, he cannot count years of employment before such a break in his total years of service for a pension." In other words, a service break would eliminate all prior credit. This provision has scuttled the pensions of many Teamsters who have been laid off during hard times in the trucking business, then several years later gone back to trucking. It also has scuttled the pensions of men who have been transferred into and out of union jobs not covered by the Central States pension plan.

What has happened to the $1.5 billion or so that Central States supposedly is administering, but regularly refused to pay out to retired Teamsters? Of all the men alive, Allen Dorfman probably knows best.

Few of the Teamsters whose employers contribute for them into the fund would be able to say exactly what Allen Dorfman has done for them over the years. But they have sure done a lot for him. And so have the rest of us whose purchase of trucked goods pays the cost of Teamster corruption.

Dorfman's official role as consultant to the fund—a job that has paid him as much as $75,000 a year plus expenses—has been only a small part of his profitable relationship with the union. That job was canceled in 1972 as a result of his conviction in federal court, Manhattan, for taking about $55,000 for recommending approval of a $1.5 million loan. But Dorfman stayed on at the hub of the circle of union leaders, company executives, Mafia members, and their lawyers and cronies who are the real beneficiaries of the pension plans. To the surprise of many, his power didn't seem to fade after the presumed murder in 1975 of his longtime ally Jimmy Hoffa.

In 1978, after a Labor Department task force had supposedly spent two years cleaning up the fund's operations, and had forced a reorganization of its board of trustees amidst ballyhoo that all the crooks were now kicked out, the board—almost incredibly—voted to extend Dorfman's contract! As uncovered by Jim Drinkhall of the *Wall Street Journal*, terms called for Dorfman to process claims for a fee of $450,000 a month, in addition to his other business, including the sale of "add-on" insurance to Teamster members and the sale of property and liability coverage for most of the pension fund's 500 borrowers. The fund in

1978 openly disavowed many other parts of its purported clean-up agreement with the Labor Department. But Dorfman is not the kind of man who needs a title or a salary to wield power and accumulate wealth, anyway. His father, Paul "Red" Dorfman, had been running a large part of the Mafia labor rackets in Chicago since Al Capone days, and had sealed the bargain that helped make Jimmy Hoffa international president of the Teamsters.

Through the efforts of his father, Allen Dorfman was appointed general agent for Union Casualty, a relatively small firm that handled insurance for the Chicago Waste Materials Handlers' union, which Red Dorfman ran as secretary-treasurer (in 1957, the AFL-CIO forced the elder Dorfman out of that job for misuse of funds and for entering into private deals with the employers).

In 1950, Allen Dorfman scored his biggest coup. The Central Conference of Teamsters—just taken over by Hoffa—threw out the low bid for its group insurance contract. Hoffa argued that the low bidder, Pacific Mutual Life Insurance Company, with assets of $377 million, had a history of financial trouble. Instead of Pacific Mutual, the union awarded its contract to the supposedly more stable Union Casualty Company, which had assets of $768,000. And so Allen Dorfman, Union Casualty's agent, went on the Teamster pad. Teamster business soon constituted more than 80 percent of his total income, with premiums running more than $10 million a year. Hoffa and the young Dorfman invested together privately in a lodge in Wisconsin and oil exploration in North Dakota.

In 1955, the Central States, Southeast, and Southwest Areas pension fund was born, and it didn't have to shop far for an insurance agent. According to Senate testimony in 1958, Dorfman charged his Teamster clients three or four times the normal rate of commission. Other witnesses said he paid the premiums of personal insurance policies he obtained for union officials, and helped spend hundreds of thousands of Teamster dollars on travel and entertainment.

Soon Dorfman and a few associates were running a complex of insurance agencies, which eventually was located in the same Teamster-owned building that housed the pension fund itself. In 1967, he got the job of monitoring the insurance coverage of the fund's borrowers—surely a convenient position for an insurance agent looking to pick up easy premiums. One Dorfman company acquired a Grumman Gulfstream (from Frank Sinatra) and leased it to the fund, which used it to fly Dorfman and other insiders around the country. The plane stopped frequently at Rancho La Costa, a southern California resort and land development where Dorfman and others acquired property.

La Costa was founded and is run by four men including convicted stock manipulator Allard Roen and former bootlegging and gambling figure Morris "Moe" Dalitz. It has been financed since 1964 with some $57 million in Teamster pension fund loans and commitments (according to 1972 records; the figure has been reported much higher, nearly $100 million now). Records showed that some $12.4 million of the loans had been paid back on schedule, but the team of auditors I consulted called the repayment schedule itself into question. Land development loans are considered relatively risky and short-term, the auditors said, and normally should be paid off completely in three to five years. Moreover, they pointed out, many of the loans at La Costa, as in other Teamster-financed projects, are third-party mortgages, which may indicate that new loans were made to pay off prior ones as they came due. "I don't know of any bank or real estate investment trust that's going into third-party takeouts of land development loans," one auditor said, as others laughed.

La Costa was far from the only business venture financed by the fund where Dorfman became personally involved. From 1964 to 1971, for example, some $13 million in pension money was poured into Beverly Ridge Estates, a California land development whose promoters transferred two parcels to Dorfman's name. The whole $13 million was still owing when the fund foreclosed on the property in 1972. A few years ago the fund sold the development for $7 million—about half of what it had previously mortgaged the place for—to one Allen R. Glick to whom it lent the entire $7 million he needed to pay for Beverly Ridge. The loan was for twenty-five years at 4 percent interest, far below what banks were getting for their money from prime customers. Even so, in December, 1977, the fund foreclosed on that loan, too. Once again, the pensioners apparently were saddled with a floundering real estate project while millions of dollars were given away.

Dorfman also acquired large blocs of stock in Bally Manufacturing Company, the slot machine people who are going into the casino business in Atlantic City, and whose operations have relied on some $12 million in Teamster financing. When Bally (then Lion Manufacturing Company) went into business in 1964, an important hidden owner was Mafia boss Gerardo Catena. More recent stockholders have included Frank Fitzsimmons, the Teamster president himself; Cal Kovens, a developer whose operations have been heavily financed by the pension fund and who has served prison time for defrauding the fund; and William and Jackie Presser, the Ohio Teamster leaders.

Another problem of the Central States pension fund is its concentration of investments in several speculative areas. Most spectacular is the Penasquitos land development project in southern California. By 1972, the fund had poured $116.7 million into Penasquitos and committed another $25.6 million for the future. One of the auditors who examined the fund's records informally commented: "Never before have I seen a single loan of this magnitude. If that goes bad, you own San Diego. Hell, you own half of California." Not quite—but the loan did go bad and since 1973 the fund has owned sixteen thousand acres, most of it undeveloped. If the project ever earns enough money to repay the loan, the fund, under an agreement made in 1973, will owe a 20 percent equity interest to the project's former co-owner, Morris Shenker, a St. Louis lawyer who has spent much of his long career representing James R. Hoffa. Shenker says he introduced the fund to Penasquitos in 1965, possibly through Hoffa. He says his 1973 agreement not only absolved him of all debts to the fund, but also "settled" millions of dollars in loans Penasquitos had made with fund money to other Shenker business interests. (Among these interests was Murietta Hot Springs, a purported health spa that was exposed on CBS's Sixty Minutes show as a rip-off of the elderly.) Asked if these other business interests repaid the money to Penasquitos or to the pension fund, Shenker says the situation is "too complicated" to explain.

During the 1976-1977 Labor Department investigation, several cosmetics were applied to improve the fund's appearance, but already by 1978 the warts were showing through again. Equitable Life Assurance Society of the United States was hired to manage the assets, but it was later revealed that important strings were tying Equitable hands, and the funds had withdrawn a promise not to fire Equitable without permission from the Secretary of Labor. The newly-hired firm of Arthur Young & Company, one of the so-called Big Eight accounting concerns, was just as quickly fired and replaced by a one-man auditing operation. The auditor was Harold Silverberg, and the operation had handled the fund's accounts for many years before the brief tenure of Arthur Young. It had formerly been a two-man auditing operation, but Silverberg's associate, David Wenger, had gone to prison after at least two convictions for misusing the fund's money.

And the professional actuary who had overseen the fund since its inception, A. Maxwell Kunis of New York, was rehired after being replaced in 1976-1977 by two much larger companies. Some twenty-five years ago, Kunis was actuary for Union Casualty Company, the small insurance firm to which Paul and Allen Dorfman steered the heavy business of Chicago unions and later of Hoffa's Teamsters. According to testimony at the McClellan hearings, Kunis once threatened an insurance executive with the loss of all Teamster business unless huge commissions were funneled to Dorfman, even after Dorfman's license had been yanked by New York State. Commented Robert Kennedy at the McClellan hearings, Kunis "serves the insurance companies, he serves the broker, and he also serves the Teamsters Union, which purchases the insurance." In 1978, he was awarded a new contract, to serve in place of two large actuarial firms that had been hired in *his* place during the Labor Department investigation.

CHAPTER 9

LET ME CALL YOU SWEETHEART

The term "sweetheart" was often associated with Teamster contracts in the Hoffa era. Robert Kennedy's investigations revealed many direct payoffs to Hoffa and his associates in and out of the union for the procurement of private deals. But under the reign of Frank Fitzsimmons, sweetheart contracts have enjoyed an open acceptance wherever local leaders want to sell them. The uncontrolled proliferation of these agreements, highly profitable to corrupt local leaders, could be one very important reason that the Syndicate was so intent on preventing Hoffa's return to leadership.

Sweetheart contracts naturally are more prevalant in so-called "commercial" trucking zones where Interstate Commerce Commission rules permit open rate competition among trucking firms. Outside these zones, competitive trucking firms must charge minimum rates set by the ICC, so there's less reason for them to try to save money by cheating their workers. The "commercial," or open-competition, zones are usually within large metropolitan areas.

There is an important exception, however, to the rule about non-competitive minimum rates existing outside commercial trucking zones. The exception is the so-called "private carrier"—a company that is mainly engaged in a manufacturing or retailing business, but which owns or leases its own trucks. One reason that many firms decided to carry their own goods rather than rely on common-carrier trucking companies is that private carriers aren't subject to ICC minimum rates. If they can cut costs, the shippers can save money. So sweetheart contracts are also common among private carriers, including some of the biggest companies in the country.

Trucking executives estimate that 80 percent or so of the trucking workers in the New York-New Jersey area are receiving pay and benefits below the National Master Freight standard. Even some Teamster leaders concede figures almost that high. A professional arbitrator who has been a respected figure in the New York trucking industry for many years says, "You can get any kind of contract you want. You make some kind of a deal with whoever's trying to organize. You'll find the same thing all over the country—St. Louis, Detroit. Chicago's a little better. Nobody's doing anything about it. They go to the international and the international sets up a committee to investigate and they give the committee to the same people that's doing it."

Fitzsimmons has received loud and persistent complaints from the more legitimate trucking executives, but the complainers get scant satisfaction. A joint union-management committee was set up to hear complaints in 1975, but soon afterward the appointed co-chairman from the union side quit, and the committee became mostly inactive. The co-chairman from the union was Salvatore Provenzano.

Becker's Motor Transport of Woodbridge, New Jersey, has hauled freight for such accounts as Coca-Cola, Owens-Illinois Glass, and Budweiser Beer. The contract between Becker's and Teamster Local 863 (dated January, 1971, amended July, 1973, to expire in 1976), as opposed to a master freight contract then effective, showed driver wages as low as $4.11 an hour instead of about $7 an hour, pension and health benefits of $28 a week instead of $56, and two weeks' vacation after two years instead of three weeks after one year.

The top officer of Local 863, who signed the Becker contract, was Joseph "Joe Peck" Pecora. Pecora and his brother, Thomas "Timmy Murphy" Pecora, both have been identified before Congressional investigating committees as members of the Genovese Mafia family, as is Tony Provenzano.

Salvatore Provenzano says there had to be substandard contracts because certain commodities are traditionally hauled at lower rates than others. Told that the national contract doesn't differentiate one kind of freight from another, he says that's the very reason he quit as the union co-chairman of the committee to investigate substandard contracts. "There's nothing in the contract saying what freight is," he says. "It's just what you think is morally right."

Law enforcement agencies are well aware of the substandard contracts. Their problem has always been to prove that a *quid pro quo*, or kickback, is involved. Trucking company owners who pay full freight allege that the kickbacks do exist, often in the form of union officers' relatives holding no-show jobs on trucking company payrolls, or even in the form of union people being secret owners of some trucking companies with substandard contracts. "The problem is, how do you prove it?" says the head of one large trucking company. For another, simple logic is proof enough that bribery of union officers is responsible for substandard contracts. "Why else would they give you one?" he asks. Teamster officials like Sammy Provenzano say there are other reasons, such as helping marginal trucking firms stay in business.

In 1977, the U.S. Government began an intensive coast-to-coast investigation of what may be the biggest organized sweetheart contract racket in history. The names of the employers involved read like a who's who of business: International Paper Company, J. C. Penney Company, GAF Corp., Iowa Beef Processors Inc., Crown Zellerbach Corp., Monsanto Company, Morton-Norwich Products Inc. (Morton's Salt), Avon Products Inc., AMF Inc., Inland Container Corp., Wheeling-Pittsburgh Steel Corp., Crown Cork & Seal Company, Westvaco Corp., and Continental Group Inc. (formerly Continental Can Company)—how many there are in all can't be determined. But every one of these companies, and more, have arranged contracts through Eugene R. Boffa, a convicted bank swindler from New Jersey who is an associate and, directly or indirectly, a benefactor of powerful racketeers in the union. Because contract terms needn't be disclosed publicly, it's impossible to say for sure whether all of Boffa's contracts are substandard, or whether some companies that have used him in the past have since dropped him. At this writing, the government has spent considerable time and money pursuing evidence, and has beaten back Boffa's attempts to win a court injunction halting the investigation (he says it's hurting business). But the government evidently hasn't found the evidence it thinks it would need to indict him or his companies.

I first encountered the Boffa operation late in 1976, while studying Iowa Beef Processors and its involvement in meat racketeering. Poring over Iowa Beef documents, I noticed reference after reference to checks for tens of thousands of dollars sent to Country Wide Personnel Inc. of Jersey City, New Jersey. What was Country Wide Personnel? I asked sources in Iowa Beef and in the butchers' union. They would only smile, and say, "You ought to look into that."

Boffa and a partner run two labor leasing companies—Universal Coordinators Inc. and Country Wide Personnel Inc.—which have demonstrated an amazing ability to hire truck drivers and handle Teamster officials while offering wages, benefits, and working conditions far short of master freight standards. For a fee of 8 to 10 percent over costs—which can easily mean hundreds of thousands of dollars a year from a single client—Boffa will insert himself as a buffer between a company and the Teamsters. The same drivers (more or less) will report to the same depots and take orders from the same supervisors as they did before Boffa was hired. But Boffa will send out the paychecks (with money he gets from the company that hired him). And the paychecks will tend to be smaller than before. Workers whom the company regards as troublesome can be dumped regardless of legal justification. And a company that hires Boffa can expect to be free of grievances, picket lines, and bothersome Teamster business agents.

In my interview in his office, Boffa said he went to work for Universal Coordinators in the early 1960s after becoming bored with his accounting practice. The labor leasing firm had been founded several years earlier by his partner, Louis Kalmar, a former truck dispatcher for International Paper, he said. Later, he said, in 1971, they founded Country Wide Personnel in an effort to forge a nationwide chain of franchised labor leasing companies.

The records tell a different story. Papers in the New Jersey Secretary of State's office show that Kalmar and his wife and Boffa started Universal jointly in December, 1960—right after Boffa had been indicted for swindling the Manufacturers Bank of Edgewater, New Jersey, which had just folded while he was president of it. Boffa was convicted in federal court, Newark, after a long trial in 1961, but was given a suspended sentence on the ground that his co-conspirators—two Pittsburgh men for whom he had approved large loans based on fraudulent documents—had run off with most of the loot to Brazil.

Boffa acknowledged in our interview that he had cordial relationships with Tony Provenzano, Mafia godfather Russell Bufalino, and his cousin William Bufalino, who is a Detroit Teamster official. But Boffa resents being asked about them. When Russell Bufalino's name came up, he

exploded, "Because I'm of Italian extraction every fuck who comes
through the door thinks I know this bastard. I worked like a goddamn
horse here for seventeen years and everybody says it's 'cause I'm
associated with him." He said his relationships with the Bufalinos come
strictly as a necessary part of his job negotiating Teamster contracts, and
that the same holds for Tony Pro. He acknowledged that he owned
another company that leases cars to Teamster leaders, and that he often
lends a Cadillac or Lincoln and a driver free to Teamster officials. "I'm
not adverse to doing people favors," he said. But he expressed anger
over suggestions that his success comes from anything other than being a
good labor negotiator. "Just because we have a leasing business and all
these bastards lease cars from me—nobody opens any doors for me," he
said. He flatly denied that he had ever had any personal business
dealings with, or had given money from his labor leasing companies to,
any Teamster or Mob people.

Again, the record proved a little different. In the Bergen County, New
Jersey, registrar's office, I found records of a $30,000 loan from Boffa's
wife, Marie, to Mildred Briguglio, the wife of Salvator "Sally Bugs"
Briguglio, the Mafioso and Teamster official who was murdered in
March, 1978. The loan was dated May 27, 1974, just days after Briguglio
had left prison on a counterfeiting conviction. Moreover, there were
records that this loan followed some neat legal maneuvering by which
Briguglio's property was conveyed from his name to his wife's. In return
for the $30,000, the documents showed, Mr. Briguglio gave Mrs. Boffa
a mortgage on the Briguglios' house. The mortgage was marked cancelled
a year later when Mrs. Briguglio sold the house. This was the sale, noted
earlier, to Mrs. Thomas Andretta. Briguglio and his brother Gabriel,
and Andretta and his brother Stephen, all have held various posts in the
Provenzano Teamster organization, and are regarded by the Government as prime suspects in the Hoffa case. In the spring of 1978, about
the time Sally Bugs and several of his friends in the Genovese family
were wiped out, Boffa discreetly took off for an extended trip abroad.

One case that produced enough of a public record to expose some of
Universal's dealings involved a Wheeling-Pittsburgh Steel warehouse in
South Brunswick, New Jersey. In 1970, the nineteen workers at the
warehouse managed to throw out a sweetheart contract thanks to the
support of two Teamster locals independent enough to fight the power
structure of their own international union. One of the locals, Local 169
of Philadelphia, had a standard contract with a Wheeling-Pittsburgh
warehouse in Philadelphia. Then, in 1969, that warehouse suddenly

closed and a new one opened in South Brunswick doing essentially the same work. As if by pre-arrangement, Universal showed up at South Brunswick to handle labor contracting and Teamster Local 84 showed up to sign a contract. Local 84 was run by the late Teddy Nalikowski, a close ally of Tony Provenzano. Before the bulk of the workforce was even hired, Local 84 signed a deal with Boffa containing the exact terms laid down earlier in a contract between Wheeling-Pittsburgh and Universal.

Soon, however, workers at the warehouse encountered members of nearby Teamster Local 701, a non-sweetheart local. They realized that Wheeling-Pittsburgh was paying much less than the standard Teamster contract called for. Moreover, according to affidavits filed later, the Wheeling-Pittsburgh workers were completely unaware that they were working under a contract signed by Local 84, which had never consulted them. So they petitioned for membership in Local 701, and a 701 business agent went to Wheeling-Pittsburgh to arrange a representation election.

The next thing the workers remember, according to their statements, someone from Local 84 and someone from Universal arrived together at the warehouse and announced that all employees would either sign Local 84 membership cards or be fired immediately. Protesting, the workers signed. But Local 701 filed a complaint with the NLRB. Salvatore Provenzano, Teamster executive for the region while his brother was barred from holding union office, immediately declared that Local 84 had prior jurisdiction. He ordered Local 701 to drop its NLRB complaint. International president Fitzsimmons backed Provenzano up with an implicit threat to put Local 701 in trusteeship and appoint new officers if the local persisted.

The cavalry arrived, however, in the form of Local 169 of Philadelphia, which had lost the Wheeling-Pittsburgh jobs when the company moved its warehouse to New Jersey. The Philadelphians had finally caught on that Wheeling-Pittsburgh was now paying $2.43 an hour for work still under contract to Local 169 at $3.01 and higher, with additional big savings on pensions and other fringes. So Local 169 filed its own complaint with the NLRB. Apparently sensing that Local 169, with its already signed contract, would open new and more threatening legal ground, the Teamster apparatus backed off and said it would allow Local 701 to organize the plant. Suddenly faced with a local that wouldn't sign a sweetheart contract, Wheeling-Pittsburgh decided that Universal's services weren't needed anymore. The company signed directly with Local 701 for higher wages and fringes. Asked for comment, Wheeling-Pittsburgh says that nobody involved in the decisions to hire and then fire Universal is still with the company, so it doesn't know why Universal's contract was ended. But the workers think *they* do.

The question arises: What is the obligation of large American corporations when they are offered the opportunity to sell out their own employees by making a deal with a convicted felon like Eugene Boffa who is financing the activities of hired killers like Sally Bugs Briguglio? Many of our largest, most respected corporations—and the list cited earlier in this chapter is quite certainly far from complete—obviously have decided that their obligation is to cut costs and increase profits. They know very well who they are really dealing with in these labor contracts, or if they don't, it's because they don't want to know.

CHAPTER 10

THE BANKS

Mafia bigshots always used to have politicians in their pockets to help them take care of their banking needs.

The crowd around Bayonne Joe Zicarelli had access to the Broadway National Bank of Bayonne through Congressman Cornelius Gallagher, who was a director of the bank and whose law partners owned controlling interest. Anthony "Little Pussy" Russo, a Vito Genovese underboss who ran the rackets along the New Jersey shore, did his banking in the 1960s through the politically powerful Wilentz family.

Democratic National Committeeman and former State Attorney General David T. Wilentz was director and legal co-counsel of First Bank & Trust Company of Perth Amboy (now the National State Bank), and his son Warren Wilentz, former county prosecutor and U.S. Senate nominee, was director and legal counsel of the Edison (New Jersey) Bank. The two banks financed Russo's land speculation with more than $800,000 in loans, with the Wilentzes' law firm acting as attorney. Most of the money was defaulted on. Russo did repay one $165,000 loan, but only after the State of New Jersey condemned some land and bought it from Russo for three times what he had just paid for it. One of the Wilentzes' law partners represented Russo (or his company) in these profitable condemnation proceedings, while Attorney General Arthur Sills, a former Wilentz partner whose name was still above the law firm's door, represented the taxpayers.

When the local newspaper tried to expose Russo's dealings, David Wilentz talked to the publisher. The story, which had taken six months to develop, was killed on the eve of publication. The reporter was fired. I was the reporter.

Nowadays, many of the old style urban political machines that produced these cozy banking relationships are disintegrating. But the Mafia has found new ways to break the banks. Where no politicians are available, there are still unions. What happens is this: the leader of a Mob-dominated union local approaches a fledgling bank whose officers are dreaming of the big time and drooling for a few heavy depositors to get them launched. The union leader offers to deposit hundreds of thousands of union dollars in the bank—money from pension or severance funds, or the union treasury. The interest rates are negotiable, which means the bank can pay less than top dollar to get the deposits. In return, however, the banker promises to approve loans for some new "customers" the union leader says he'll be recommending.

In 1976, the United States attorney's office and the FBI in Newark began investigating a series of Mafia banking raids that so far has caused the failure of at least four banks in New Jersey alone. Since 1973, at least $10 million and maybe much more had been lent out to, and not paid back by, a parade of characters whose names read like the index to the Valachi hearings, and there are clear indications that the same racket has been practiced in Ohio (where one bank closed) and elsewhere.

The "borrowers" have included loansharks, alleged murderers, and ex-convicts of all types. One borrower, a reputed Mafioso named Patrick Pizuto, actually got his loan from the State Bank (now closed) of Chatham, New Jersey, while serving a seven-to-ten-year sentence in Trenton State Prison. Pizuto came into the bank and applied for the loan one day while out on a work release program. Then, so he could spend the money he borrowed, he commuted his own prison sentence. To achieve this feat, he had an accomplice slip him a blank form of the kind used in Appellate Court decisions; then he forged three judges' names to it and mailed the "court order" for his release to the warden, who promptly released him. He picked up his loan money the same day.

Pizuto "borrowed" only $2,500. Most of his criminal colleagues took in the neighborhood of $30,000 to $40,000, because that tends to be the limit on an individual bank officer's authority to approve loans to one customer. Some hoods have incorporated themselves under a variety of phony business names so they could go back for numerous $30,000 to $40,000 loans. One set of loans from the State Bank (now closed) of Manville, New Jersey, reached about $750,000, all benefiting a firm run by Robert Gooding, a convicted extortionist and sometimes partner of Mafia enforcer Anthony "Tony Tumac" Acceturo.

When the banks fail, there are three sets of losers. First, there are the local small businessmen or professionals who have invested their savings to help capitalize a new banking venture in their community. Second comes the Federal Deposit Insurance Corporation, a government agency that has to bail out the depositors. And third are the union members whose aggregated dues or pension money may not be entirely reimbursable by the FDIC.

The Mafia, on the other hand, may be imposing its own sentences on figures in the investigation who have cooperated with the government, welched, or otherwise gotten out of line. The FBI reportedly has a tape recording of a conversation in which the former president of the State Bank of Chatham, Alexander Smith, who has pleaded guilty to misapplication of bank funds, was warned by a prominent lawyer, "We're gonna lay you out alongside Hoffa."

The lawyer who allegedly uttered this threat is George Franconero—living evidence that top New Jersey politicians bear links to the Mob, even in the late 1970s. Franconero is the former law partner of Governor Brendan Byrne. One client of the Byrne-Franconero law firm back in the early 1970s was mobster Thomas "Timmy Murphy" Pecora. He identified Byrne personally as his lawyer at the time. Pecora and his brother, known as Joe Peck, have been identified before Congress as members of the Genovese Mafia family. Joe Peck runs Teamster Local 863, whose pension fund had six-figure deposits in the State Bank of Chatham just before the bank went under because of bad loans in 1975.

Franconero pleaded guilty to submitting false data on a loan application. His sister, singer Connie Francis, came to court to support him. U.S. District Judge Herbert J. Stern sentenced him to probation after announcing that Franconero had agreed to give the government information about other culprits in the scheme. Judge Stern specifically noted, however, that Franconero had been exempted by the government from ever having to testify in court on these matters, which certainly limited his usefulness as an informant.

According to the uncontroverted testimony of others, Franconero had been the attorney for a purported leasing corporation, which issued

phony documents that were vital to the bank frauds. The docu
certified that the leasing corporation had delivered industrial equij
to various companies set up by the racketeers. Actually, the ind
equipment didn't exist, but the racketeers could use the phony
ments to collateralize loans, which they supposedly obtained to pa
the equipment. Through this method, mobsters and alleged mol
helped cause the loss of some $4.5 million by the Bank of Bloom
New Jersey. The bank was wiped out.

Franconero also is close to the key figure of another union local w
money most frequently has gone into banks at about the time mob:
have taken money out. That is Local 945 of the International Brot
hood of Teamsters, a large local that covers employees of (among o
things) the garbage collection industry, in which the Mafia has long b
involved. The key figure is Ernest Palmeri, whose title is only busir
agent, but who comes from a blood family that is prominent in
Mafia. According to the New Jersey Alcoholic Beverage Commissio
Palmeri and Franconero shared hidden ownership in a bar a
restaurant in Bergen County.

Palmeri's father, Paul, now dead, had a long arrest record ar
attended the famous Mafia convention at Apalachin, New York, in 195
indicating he was pretty high in the organization. Ernest's brother Fran
assisted Mob boss Jerry Catena in the Syndicate's attempt to monor
olize the supermarket sale of detergents. Ernest Palmeri's Team
ster local, 945, was put into trusteeship by its international in the lat
1950s because of a corruption scandal. To "clean up" the local, Teamstei
overlords sent in outside leadership: Mafia underboss Anthony "Tony
Pro" Provenzano. When Provenzano had Local 945 running to his
liking, he turned it over to the current leadership. Disclosure statements
of total bank balances and total interest income show that Local 945
keeps hundreds of thousands of dollars in low- or non-interest-bearing
accounts. Disclosure of the terms of specific accounts isn't required.

The individual shady bank loans that have turned up over the past few
years are far too numerous to set down. What follows is a brief account
of how one of the hardest-hit banks was moved in on.

The stockholders of the fledgling Bank of Bloomfield, New Jersey,
sealed their own fate in 1973 when they invited Robert Prodan to head
the operation. Prodan had been working at the much older and larger
Franklin State Bank in Newark. The Bank of Bloomfield's board
chairman happened to be a loan customer of Prodan's, and when the
president of the Bloomfield bank retired, Prodan was invited to succeed

him. Almost as soon as he arrived, Prodan set out to bring Bloomfield into the major leagues of banking. He went looking for big depositors, and pulled in at least $1 million from various Teamster groups, including Palmeri's 945. Then dozens of hoods, big-time and small-time, from New England to Michigan to Florida, lined up at the Bank of Bloomfield's door for loans that drove the bank into receivership with the Federal Deposit Insurance Corporation in December, 1975.

Much of what happened was the work of Arnold Daner, who had met Prodan in 1967. When Prodan took up a career with large New York area banks, Daner founded an import firm. Prodan invested heavily in Daner's import firm, which failed. Daner moved to Florida in 1972 and started a company that arranged financing for leases of industrial equipment. Daner says Prodan was his partner; Prodan has said he wasn't. Right about the time that Prodan took over the Bank of Bloomfield, however, Daner moved his business to New Jersey.

Daner has since pleaded guilty to conspiring with Prodan and their Mafia buddies to loot the bank. He agreed to testify against others, and was relocated by the government for his protection. He also got a two-year prison sentence. According to the government charges, both Daner and Prodan got tens of thousands of dollars in illegal kickbacks. The scheme worked this way:

Over nearly two years, the mobsters signed $6 million in equipment leases with Daner's firm. As they were signed, the leases were sold to the Bank of Bloomfield, which shelled out $4.7 million cash for the right to collect on them—the difference being the bank's interest on its money. This is common procedure. The trouble was, in the Bank of Bloomfield's case, millions of dollars of equipment that supposedly was being leased didn't exist. Equipment that did exist was inflated in value. So the lease money could be spread around among the crooks, and the bank had no collateral. Much of the phony equipment was in the garbage collection, disposal, and recycling field. The private cartage business has long been infiltrated by mobsters, so there were plenty of Mafia-owned garbage firms ready to file phony leases.

Two mobsters, Dominick Troiano and Charles Musillo, moved in as Daner's partners. Musillo and his son Michael financed a loansharking operation with vast sums taken in from leases on nonexistent garbage equipment. They pleaded guilty; Judge Stern sentenced the father to a maximum of four years in prison, the son to a maximum of eighteen months. Troiano helped bring in lease customers, including his relatives. He also pleaded guilty, and Judge Stern sentenced him to a maximum of

eighteen months. Among the many Bank of Bloomfield lease patrons familiar to law enforcement authorities were Thomas Milo, whose father Sabato, and uncle, Thomas Senior, were cited in the Valachi hearings as members of the Genovese Mafia family; Anthony "Buckalo" Ferro, identified as a Genovese soldier (Ferro had been observed earlier collecting cash payments from butchers' union leader Frank Kissel); convicted felons Joseph and William "Skippy" Scappatone; and a Detroit garbage firm, Central Sanitation Company, founded by Raffael "Jimmy Q" Quasarano and Dominick "Sparky" Corrado, whose respective narcotics and labor racketeering deals have been recounted at length in Congressional testimony.

According to Daner's undisputed testimony, Palmeri had a part in some of the leases, including one to Central Sanitation for $85,000, which involved real garbage disposal equipment. When Central Sanitation failed to make initial payments in the summer of 1975, the bank's outside directors became suspicious and the entire scheme was threatened. Still, the Central Sanitation lease wasn't paid, and the Detroit firm was in bankruptcy proceedings in 1977.

CHAPTER 11

STOCKS AND INSECURITIES

In its edition of August 30, 1968, *Life* magazine devoted twenty-seven pages to a relentlessly detailed account of the activities of a stocky, bullnecked cutthroat named John "Sonny" Franzese and the men around him. The article recounted Franzese's bloody rise to power in the Colombo Mafia family. When it appeared, Franzese, then forty-eight, had not yet begun serving a fifty-year sentence in federal prison for masterminding a series of armed bank robberies. He is serving it now. The article noted the bank robberies, but mainly concerned Franzese's trial—and acquittal—for the brutal murder of an underling, and how the laws of evidence cheated the jury out of hearing information that almost certainly would have convicted him.

One week after the article appeared, the Wall Street brokerage firm of Dean Witter & Company, now Dean Witter Reynolds Inc., second largest in the country, hired Sonny's nephew Joseph Franzese to fill a lowrung position on the executive ladder. Joseph Franzese was subjected to a routine background investigation, and received what Dean Witter says was "a favorable report" from "an independent business report firm"—despite the fact that the *Life* article was probably on the newsstands while the report was being made. As Franzese worked his way up that executive ladder, no one at Dean Witter knew that he was related to a notorious leader in a secret criminal organization that is built largely on blood relationships—or at least no one objected. After the FBI finally caught up with Joey Franzese and his multi-million-dollar securities fraud schemes in November, 1976, an official spokesman for Dean Witter told the *Wall Street Journal* he had never heard of Sonny Franzese.

The Franzese-Dean Witter case raises several interesting and important questions. Should there be guilt by association? How should business deal with Mafia kin who have no criminal records, or with employees who are known to befriend members of the Syndicate? The case—no isolated example—suggests an answer to these questions.

The answer is *not* that Dean Witter should have refused employment to a young man just because his name was Joseph Franzese. The answer *is*, however, that business ought to be aware of the high tendency of Mafia kin to follow the criminal path, and, when dealing with them, take a few unusual but relatively simple precautions.

Joey Franzese was leading a double life, but the dark side of it really wasn't hidden at all. Yet not until 1976, eight years after he had begun at Dean Witter, did an outsider view his other life and choose to expose it. By that time, Franzese had risen to a key managerial position.

The unlikely outsider who spoiled Franzese's racket was an immigrant British printing salesman named Peter Trott. Trott's task was to hunt up people who needed printing done and line them up with the printer best suited to their needs. In March 1976, a broker in the business introduced him to Imar Publications, a small firm that was about to cash in on the Off-Track-Betting craze in New York by publishing a new magazine called "Off-Track." Imar turned out to be owned and operated by one Jerry Franzese, whom Trott would later learn was a nephew of Sonny, the convicted bank robber, and a cousin of Joey, the Dean Witter executive. Trott hadn't heard the name Franzese before. He says Jerry Franzese offered the Off-Track Betting Corp. (a public agency) itself as a reference, and that OTB offices on Long Island told him they would distribute the magazine (which they ultimately did).

Granted, it would be hard to contemplate a better authority on off-track betting than someone from the Colombo Mafia family. Nevertheless, from Peter Trott's point of view, it was unfortunate that Jerry

Franzese was running the magazine. Trott signed Imar up with Holiday Press of Olive Branch, Mississippi, a subsidiary of Holiday Inns. After two issues, Imar still hadn't paid its printing bills, which had run up to $47,000. Holiday Press refused to extend more credit, and Imar became defunct.

Holiday Press was none too happy with its salesman, for Trott, by his own admission, was personally responsible for having talked the company into letting Imar work on credit. The printing firm, Trott says, directed him to stay close to Imar in hopes of discovering assets that could be seized by court order. So he repeatedly visited the Imar office on Forty-fifth Street near Sixth Avenue, and met with Jerry Franzese.

Finally, in August, Franzese told Trott that he was involved with a crime syndicate. He told Trott who Sonny Franzese was, and that Joey was his cousin. "I can do you favors—I'm connected," Jerry reportedly said. "I owe you a favor." So Jerry Franzese introduced the printing salesman to his cousin Joey, the Dean Witter executive, and promised they would bring Trott into "a good deal."

According to Trott's understanding, Joey was "manager of the margins desk" at Dean Witter's home office at 2 Broadway. "He functioned normally from nine to five," Trott says. "He had a nice wife and family. But he just didn't look at life like that. All he wanted was to make a big score so the money could go out and earn 'vig.' " Vig is short for "vigorish," or the weekly interest that must be paid on a loanshark account without reduction in the principal.

Trott began to find out what "vig" meant from his periodic visits to the New Hope Club, a Staten Island "social club," where the Franzeses hung out. The bigwig in the barroom seemed to be Tutti Franzese, a very large older relative of Jerry and Joey.

"The club is a dilapidated old house. It's very dark. There's a long bar. People came in and asked, 'Did you pick up the vig tonight?' I was told there were prostitutes operating by call from there. The place was full of young girls. They gave them mescaline, cocaine. There was a room with a bed in it, right off the main bar, and couples would go in."

By September, 1976, Trott says, "I realized I had new partners." Then the Franzeses explained "that Joey prepared computer programs at Dean Witter which controlled the record keeping of . . . customers' accounts. They explained that, because Joey occupied a primary position on the margins desk, he could generate accounts for nonexistent customers and negotiate fictitious transactions for these 'customers.' Joey assured [Trott] he was in a position at Dean Witter to effectively

293

control the . . . computer run-outs, and if necessary to destroy files in any fictitious account he generated, so that any illegal disbursements of Dean Witter's funds would either go undetected or, even if detected, could not be traced to him."

Joey told Trott that he had repeatedly managed to defraud Dean Witter's excess funds accounts in the past. (Excess funds are unclaimed accounts. Some persons, for example, may put money in the stock market without telling anyone, then die; after a given time, the money in the account reverts to the brokerage.) For obvious reasons, however, there are limits on how much one can steal from unclaimed accounts. So Franzese had thought up a new scheme, and it went like this:

Franzese would create an account in the name of Peter B. Simpson, and Trott would be supplied with a set of identification for Simpson. He was to go to a New York coin dealer with this identification, explain that he was in the process of divorce and wanted to hide his assets from his wife. So, Trott would say, he was planning to sell his large portfolio of securities through Dean Witter, and wanted to arrange with the coin dealer for an exchange of the Dean Witter checks for gold Krugerrands. The asset sale was to occur in two waves, each represented by a check. First Trott would swing a Krugerrand deal for about $285,000. And once credibility had been established, they would go for Big Casino— another $2.5 million in one check.

Trott was to open a post office box in Simpson's name. On November 2 or 3, he would receive the check at the box number. He would have it certified at a bank, exchange it for Krugerrands with the coin dealer and be picked up by Joey Franzese in a limousine. They would transport the coins to a bank on Staten Island. On November 1, as recounted in Trott's lawsuit, he "secured the mailing address-post office box number, made the preliminary arrangements with the coin dealer, and advised Joey that 'all systems were go.' "

There was one important thing the Franzeses didn't know about Peter Trott at this point. Several years before, a scandal had occurred at American Airlines. The executive who supervised the airline's in-flight magazine, *The American Way*, was convicted of demanding and taking kickbacks in the awarding of contracts for various things—including printing. And the name of the printing salesman who had turned the executive in to the government and started the whole scandal was Peter Trott. In that case, Trott had dealt with one of the top agents in the New York office of the IRS, Tony Lombardi.

Now, on the eve of a far bigger swindle, he went again to Lombardi, who didn't need much educating about who the Franzeses were. Lombardi explained to Trott that the Dean Witter scheme didn't involve tax dodging as the kickbacks at American Airlines had, and so shouldn't be investigated by the IRS. In a selfless move, Lombardi brought his valuable information to the FBI, which clearly had jurisdiction in the Dean Witter matter.

The check, which totaled $284,981.51, arrived at Trott's post office box at 8:30 A.M. November 3. By 8:45, it was in the hands of the FBI. Agents examined it, and told Trott to have it certified as Franzese had instructed. Trott was able to have this done at the Irving Trust Company. Two FBI men were loitering one hundred feet away. Then they rigged Trott up with a body tape recorder and microphone, and were listening in when Trott told Franzese the deal was set. Trott arranged additional conversations, so there was plenty of evidence against Joey Franzese when he was arrested the next day, before the Krugerrand deal was ever consummated.

U.S. District Judge Charles L. Brieant sentenced Joseph Franzese to probation, and fined him $1,000.

CHAPTER 12

THE DOCKS

In 1953, Budd Schulberg gave the world a classic exposé of corruption on the big city docks. It was a movie, *On The Waterfront*, a fictional work that confronted Americans with a stark and accurate view of a world they depend on but seldom see. It showed a tribe of muscular but utterly helpless men, assembling each day to beg work from bosses who were interchangeable, whether they came from the International Longshoremen's Association (the industry's major union) or from the stevedoring companies.

Ten years later, in a piece called "The Waterfront Revisited," Schulberg wrote: "Ties between political and waterfront leaders have always been close. To see how close, you only had to study the guest list of an I.L.A. president's testimonial dinner. There, prominent city officials and judges sat jowl-by-jowl with the 'labor leaders,' shipping executives, stevedore bosses, racketeers, and killers—one big happy family of despoilers gathered together in tribal ceremony, flaunting their power over the harbor and the city it serves and controls." Schulberg recited in his article a long list of high-ranking union officials and the various crimes they had been convicted of. He rattled off case after case of conflicts of interest, where union officials or their families got rich from the profits of stevedoring companies. And of the theft of cargo from the docks, he wrote, "The piers of the port are like supermarkets with no checkout counters."

Nevertheless, Schulberg saw a silver lining. For one thing, the New York-New Jersey bistate Waterfront Commission, which had been created largely in response to exposés by Schulberg and others a decade earlier, had survived political attacks by the union. It had imposed licensing requirements, changed the crooked and demeaning hiring hall procedure, and seemed to be making headway on other problems. Most of all, Schulberg seemed favorably impressed by Anthony Scotto, the new head of the New York Longshoremen and a growing power in the international union. At first glance, Scotto's background was a little alarming. He was only twenty-eight years old, and got where he was by marrying the daughter of his predecessor, Anthony "Tough Tony" Anastasio. Anastasio was the brother of Albert Anastasia (they spelled the name slightly differently), the widely-known Lord High Executioner of Murder Inc. Anastasio rose to power in the union via the Mafia, and he hand-picked young Tony Scotto as his successor. Scotto had married Anastasio's daughter in 1957, the same year Albert Anastasia was massacred in his Manhattan barber's chair. Carlo Gambino—head of Anastasia's Mafia family—had attended the wedding ceremony.

In Scotto's case, first glances may not have been deceptive. In 1969, a Justice Department list of Mafia figures was placed in the Congressional Record, and there on it, as a captain in the Gambino family, was Anthony Scotto. Reports based on Congressional releases identified Scotto's wife as the owner of the Englewood (New Jersey) Country Club, where numerous high-ranking Mafia figures including Thomas Eboli, Eugene and Jerry Catena, and Angelo "Gyp" de Carlo were said to come frequently.

In February, 1970, Scotto, by then an international vice-president of the union as well as its leader in New York, was given a chance to reply to all this in hearings before a New York State Joint Legislative Committee on Crime. When asked whether he was part of the Mafia, he declined to answer.

By 1977, word had swept the waterfront from New York to New Orleans that a mammoth federal investigation was underway. This was no narrow probe into a few particular instances of graft. Rather, the Justice Department had determined to try to end criminal control over the importing and exporting of goods from the United States. To a large extent, the waterfront investigation was the work of one FBI agent, Ray Maria, who had developed a reputation as a rackets-buster in Chicago.

Maria's investigation took a classic course, beginning with widespread electronic eavesdropping and undercover work, and then, when the secret could no longer be kept, a publicity phase in which tremendous pressure was applied to persuade suspects to become government witnesses. In the background was the long trial in federal court, New York, of Fred R. Field, Jr., vice-president and general organizer of the International Longshoremen's Union. Field was convicted in 1977 of shaking down officers of United Brands Company (formerly United Fruit Company) for $125,000 over several years to ensure the proper handling of the company's Chiquita brand bananas and other imports.

Once Maria's investigation became public, federal officials openly acknowledged that Anthony Scotto was a key target. At this writing, the government hasn't charged Scotto with a crime. The rest of the industry, however, hasn't come away so clean. In the first of what were expected to be several indictments coming out of the investigation, eleven executives of stevedoring or other dock-related companies, ten Longshoremen's union officials, and one accountant were accused of racketeering through the demand for and payment of hundreds of thousands of dollars in bribes. The 128-page indictment painted a grim picture of how business is done on American docks. Some twenty-one companies operating in the ports of Miami, Mobile, Jacksonville, Savannah, and Charleston were implicated in the gross manipulation of interstate and international commerce. Obviously, you couldn't ship unless you paid off. Among the union leaders indicted were four international officers of the ILA.

CHAPTER 13

STEINMAN

On April 25, 1970, a scruffy, half-literate little manipulator named Moe Steinman shuffled into a suite at the elegant Stanhope Hotel overlooking Central Park in Manhattan, pulled the blinds, and within a few hours assumed a stature that even the most celebrated racketeers in history hadn't dreamed of.

Other mobsters had gone only partway. Steinman had also gone partway—he had dominated the Fourteenth Street meat market. Some racketeers before Steinman had persuaded the heads of rival Mafia families to unite behind a single organized shakedown system. Thus had Steinman united racketeers from three powerful Mafia families, Genovese, Gambino, and Lucchese, and become the meat industry front for all of them. Other racketeers, before Steinman, had achieved nationwide control over certain specialty products, like mozzarella cheese, or over an atomized industry, like trucking.

But on this day, Moe Steinman, as a front for the Mafia, would achieve what no one else had achieved, even in the days of Al Capone or Lucky Luciano. Moe Steinman, who had risen from the gutter only by his lack of scruples, would tighten his fist around one of the biggest corporations in the country, a corporation that dominated a major national industry. It was an industry that Americans depended on every day. It was an industry—unlike trucking—clothed with all the garments of Wall Street respectability.

Into this darkened room at the Stanhope Hotel, Moe Steinman would summon Currier J. Holman, founder and head of Iowa Beef Processors Inc., by far the largest meat company in the world. Then, as now, Iowa Beef's sales were in the billions of dollars, and its food was on the tables of millions of Americans from Bangor to San Diego.

And Currier J. Holman, the tall, graying business genius who organized and ran this mammoth operation, was to come crawling all the way from the Great Plains with his co-chairman, executive vice-president, and general counsel, all at the beck of a foul-mouthed alcoholic hoodlum.

Iowa Beef, though founded only in 1961, already in 1970 dominated the meat industry the way few other industries are dominated by anyone. Since then, in partnership with Steinman and his family and friends, Iowa Beef has grown more dominant still. Moe Steinman and the band of murderers and thugs he represented had effectively kidnapped a giant business.

As a result of the meeting in the darkened suite at the Stanhope that day in 1970, Iowa Beef would send millions of dollars to Steinman and his family under an arrangement that continued at least until 1978. After the meeting, millions more would go to a lifelong pal of Steinman and his Mafia friends, a man who had gone to prison for using slimy, diseased meat in filling millions of dollars in orders and who wound up on Iowa Beef's board of directors. Consequent to the meeting in the

Stanhope Hotel, Iowa Beef would reorganize its entire marketing apparatus to allow Steinman's organization complete control over the company's largest market, and influence over its operations coast-to-coast. In 1975, Iowa Beef would bring Moe Steinman's son-in-law and protégé to its headquarters near Sioux City to run the company's largest division and throw his voice into vital corporate decisions. But, most important, a mood would be struck in the Stanhope that day—a mood of callous disregard for decency and the law. Iowa Beef would proceed to sell its butcher employees out to the Teamsters union, to turn its trucking operations over to Mafia-connected manipulators, and to play fast and loose with anti-trust laws.

Because of their hold on Iowa Beef, the racketeers' control of other segments of the meat industry would expand and harden. And as a result of all this, the price of meat for the American consumer—the very thing Currier Holman had done so much to reduce—would rise.

Moe Steinman is not impressive to look at. He is of average height, but seems shorter. He isn't fat, but there's something overweight about him. He has a sad, doberman-like face that is pockmarked and ruddy like a drunk's. Steinman is often drunk. His clothes are sometimes flashy, seldom tasteful. He is appallingly inarticulate, but everybody knows what he means.

Detective Bob Nicholson had been impressed the first time he heard Steinman's name, back in 1964 in the Merkel horsemeat scandal. When Merkel's boss, Nat Lokietz, wanted a connection in government so he could bribe his way out of trouble, he had called Moe Steinman. Steinman didn't arrange the bribe meeting—Tino De Angelis did— because Steinman was out of town. But after the bribery attempt backfired, Lokietz went to Steinman again in a last-ditch effort to keep Merkel afloat. In the spring of 1965, Steinman had met with Lokietz at the Long Island home of a Big Apple supermarket meat buyer, who acted as intermediary. The buyer was in Steinman's pocket; he would later plead guilty to evading income taxes on payoffs he took from Steinman. Through subsequent conversations that were wiretapped, police learned that Lokietz had asked Steinman to get the Mafia to rescue Merkel. Some money, some political clout, and Lokietz could be back on his feet again. Steinman huddled with Dio over the idea one night at the Red Coach Inn in Westchester County, but with the horsemeat scandal all over the papers and Dio involved in some promising new rackets, they decided to let Merkel go on down the drain.

As a result of these meetings, however, Steinman was called in for questioning before the Merkel grand jury. Nicholson was sent to serve the subpoena, and thus got to meet the racketeer for the first time. Immediately Nicholson saw the arrogant conniver that was Steinman, a man who thought he could wheel and deal himself out of anything.

Nicholson found Steinman at the Luxor Baths, the famous old establishment on West Forty-sixth Street where the wealthiest of New York's European immigrant community used to go. Nicholson remembers going into the lobby of the Luxor with his subpoena in 1965, and paging Steinman. The racketeer came down in his bathrobe and turned on his crude charm.

"Come on into the steam room. We'll have a nice bath," Steinman said.

Nicholson turned him down, but kept him talking. Maybe there would be an open offer of a bribe.

"After we have a bath," Steinman said, "we can talk. We'll have a few drinks, maybe we can go out to dinner."

Nicholson kept him talking.

"Do you have a girlfriend? Maybe I could get you a girlfriend. I'm a nice guy. You'll like me."

Steinman came to the United States at age eight. His father, a butcher, settled in Brooklyn. He quit school after eighth grade and ran off to work at the Chicago World's Fair in 1933. He returned to Brooklyn, where a young greengrocer named Ira Waldbaum had decided to lease out sections of his stores to meat dealers. This was, of course, long before Waldbaum's became the major regional supermarket chain it is today.

A dealer who had leased the meat departments in two Waldbaum's stores hired Steinman to run them, and the budding hoodlum was on his way. Steinman bought his first meat from Sam Goldberger, who would later go to prison for selling adulterated meat and bribing federal food inspectors. And Steinman made connections with two other Polish-Jewish immigrants, Max and Louis Block, who had just left their own butcher business to organize the Amalgamated Meat Cutters' union under rights obtained through mobsters Little Augie Pisano and George Scalise. Pisano and Scalise were of an older generation, but there was a younger, more contemporary Mafia figure whom the Blocks and Steinman and Goldberger began to meet—Johnny Dio.

Soon Steinman was expanding his meat counter operations to The Bronx and Westchester County. When the war came in 1941, Steinman quickly got himself classified 4-F, which allowed him to achieve fame and fortune while still in his twenties. From 1942 to 1945, Steinman was known among meat dealers throughout the five boroughs as "Black Market Moe."

"If you had meat during the war, there was no problem making money," recalls one prominent wholesaler. He and others say Steinman was almost certainly a millionaire by the time peace finally forced him to look for other rackets.

The racket he found was one he stayed with a long time. Essentially, it was a disguised way of taking kickbacks from supermarket chains for insuring "labor peace."

First, he would hire himself out as a supermarket executive who could handle "labor problems." Because all the chains were supposed to be competing with each other, for the benefit of the consumer, he could be a payrolled executive for only one of them (it was Shopwell Inc.'s Daitch-Shopwell chain). But in industry-wide bargaining, he would act as lead negotiator for the group of them. One chain alone, however, could not supply Steinman with all the money he would need for the required under-the-table payments to union leaders and Mafiosi, as well as for his own not particularly modest style of living. So it came to pass that the chains all bought substantial quantities of meat from a particular wholesale brokerage firm, and that the firm was controlled by Steinman. The firm would overcharge for its meat, and the overcharge would create enough money to provide for all the people who had to be paid off.

Steinman's wholesale meat firm would overcharge equally to all the supermarket chains, so that none of them would get a competitive advantage—even the chain for which Steinman was a salaried executive. The customer would pay through the nose for everybody's high living, but that was all right. If any upstart supermarket manager tried to offer the customer a better deal, he would feel the pain of the organization's cleaver in his back. Either the Block brothers' butchers or Johnny Dio's truckers would start making trouble.

Steinman has always needed a partner to mind his meat operations while he was out engaged in the real business of making payoffs, and manipulating the cost of food. In the original Mo-Jo wholesale meat concern, Steinman's partner was Joseph Weinberg. Court testimony later showed Weinberg's close connection to members of the Gambino and Genovese Mafia families, and perhaps it was Steinman who introduced them.

Paul "Constantine" Castellano was the brother-in-law of boss of bosses Carlo Gambino, and succeeded Gambino as head of the Mafia family when Gambino died in 1976. Like Steinman, Castellano was involved in wholesale and retail meat firms in Brooklyn in the 1930s. Others of his blood family also entered the industry, and the Castellanos now own many stores and distributorships in Brooklyn and Manhattan. They have a long record of welching on debts; of suffering suspicious hijackings; of selling goods that were later found to have been stolen off docks or trucks, and of cheating other firms by receiving the assets of companies about to go into bankruptcy proceedings.

One typical bankruptcy fraud revolved around Steinman's partner Weinberg. A veteran meat dealer, Weinberg was able to open Murray Packing Company in 1959 with a good credit rating. A few months later Joseph Pagano, a young Genovese henchman and convicted narcotics trafficker, became an executive at Murray Packing. Meanwhile, Gondolfo Sciandra, a Gambino soldier and relative by marriage, opened another new meat concern and it began buying supplies from Weinberg-Pagano company. So did the Castellanos' own company, Pride Wholesale Meat and Poultry Corp. But these favored customers always paid less than Weinberg and Pagano were charged by their own suppliers. For example, Weinberg's Murray Packing would buy hams for fifty cents a pound and sell them to Pride for forty-five cents a pound.

Murray Packing quickly stepped up its rate of buying meat, but fell further and further behind in paying its bills. Soon the "float" of unpaid-for meat had reached $1.3 million. At that point, in 1961, the creditors sued. Murray Packing was declared bankrupt and there were no assets around to pay the bills, because the Gambino-Castellano firms had received the meat.

The exceptional part of the Murray Packing case is that it was prosecuted (because the new U.S. Attorney in Manhattan, Robert Morgenthau, had an unusual interest in crimes of high finance). Joseph Pagano tried to take the entire rap himself by telling a federal court that he had withdrawn some $800,000 from Murray Packing illegally, and had lost it all gambling. The jury dismissed this story. Peter Castellana [sic], scion of the Castellano family, drew five years in prison; it was the only time in at least four similar bankruptcy cases that Castellana was brought to justice at all. Sciandra got eighteen months, and Weinberg, who contended he was just an innocent dupe, got one year. They were released after serving much less.

Pagano, however, was stunned by civil bankruptcy judge Sidney S. Sugarman, who also refused to believe the gambling story and ordered Pagano to jail for contempt of court until the $800,000 was repaid to

Murray Packing's suppliers. Finally, in 1970, after almost six years, the court accepted the Mob's offer of a deal. A lawyer appeared with $75,000—one can only imagine where it came from—and Pagano was released and forgiven the rest of his debt. Over the years, the court had collected just $8,244.30 from the others who helped steal $1.3 million. According to law enforcement reports, Pagano immediately was given command of a big Mafia move into the now illegal business of factoring Medicaid claims; members of Steinman's family also were heavily into the same business at that time.

Pride Wholesale Meat & Poultry Corp., the Castellano firm, had to go out of business as a legal entity in order to avoid civil claims in the Murray Packing bankruptcy. But Pride continues to be a trade name of the Castellanos, who are still major distributors of specialty meats and chickens, and occasional creditors in bankruptcy court. Among other things, Peter Castellana runs Ranbar Packing Corp., the region's largest distributor of Paramount chickens. Ranbar alone reports annual sales of $30 million.

The biggest Castellano racket, by knowledgeable accounts, continues to be loansharking. This high-interest emergency money lending isn't limited to the meat industry, but the Castellanos have used it there to increase the family clout. They are believed to control a large percentage of the independent meat companies in the Fourteenth Street market because of the debts owed to them.

From right after World War II and through the 1950s, while Joseph Weinberg was taking orders for Steinman's Mo-Jo meat firm, Moe Steinman was pursuing a rather unusual career as a supermarket executive. Exactly how his deal worked probably can't be learned at this late date, but clearly he was burning his candle at both ends.

At a court hearing once, he gave the following suspicious version of the story: after the war, he owned and operated eighteen independent meat outlets in Westchester County. In 1949, the owner of the Shopwell supermarket chain asked him to take over the chain's independently-owned meat concession by buying out the existing concession-holder. This Steinman did, for $65,000. Then (Steinman testified), in 1953, Shopwell decided to take over ownership of its own meat departments and bought Steinman out for Shopwell stock. The deal involved no cash, and so presumably left the thirty-five-year-old Steinman a major holder in the Shopwell corporation. He also became a salaried executive at about forty-five thousand postwar dollars a year.

The principal owner and manager of the Shopwell chain back then was Lou Taxin, who has long since retired. In an interview for this book, Taxin said he simply did not remember when or how Steinman became associated with Shopwell. He said he also didn't remember whether Steinman, while employed as a salaried meat buyer for the chain, was buying meats from his own wholesale firm. Old-time meat wholesalers say that's exactly what Steinman was doing, and that his unusual status was widely understood throughout the industry as a cover-up for graft. They also say the arrangement dated back to shortly after the war. When Steinman's name came up in criminal charges in 1973, Shopwell was quoted in the press as saying he had been with the company since at least 1947, not 1949 or 1953.

At any rate, the record is clear that by no later than 1953, Steinman had become Shopwell's director of meat operations. He also became its very first "director of labor relations." Everyone noticed that Steinman spent a lot of time with the heads of the butchers' union and the racketeers who controlled various unions. When Moe Steinman was involved in the contract talks, labor problems disappeared. The super-market chains he protected sometimes went more than a year without paying pension fund contributions for their employees, as the contract required, and the unions didn't object.

In 1956, Shopwell merged with Daitch Crystal Dairies to form the Daitch-Shopwell chain that is a leader in the eastern market today. Daitch's stock shares were traded on the public market, so shares of the merged corporation, which was known as Shopwell Inc., were also publicly tradeable. For many years they have been listed on the American Stock Exchange. In recent years, even before Steinman's 1975 "retirement," Shopwell's disclosure statements filed with the S.E.C. contained no reference to Steinman as a top officer or major shareholder. What has happened to the major block of stock he apparently once held in Shopwell can only be wondered at.

Whether Steinman helped engineer the Daitch-Shopwell merger wasn't learned either, but the merger was certainly fortuitous for him. Since 1956, the company has been headed by Herbert Daitch, who has been a staunch defender of Steinman throughout various troubles with the law. Daitch could hardly have been a more indulgent employer.

Moe slept late. Afternoons he spent with a girlfriend in a hotel, or in an apartment he kept in Queens. For his long-time girlfriend, Steinman picked the wife of an old friend. It was the subject of wide speculation in the industry whether the old friend knew about this liaison—especially after the old friend's name popped up on Steinman's illegal payoff list when it was made public as part of an indictment in 1973. Apparently the friend was getting $250-a-week "salary" from a Steinman brokerage firm while doing no work for the firm and while his wife, a busty, good-looking brunette, was sleeping with Steinman.

One law officer puts it this way: "All he [Steinman] ever did was drink, and eat, and fuck."

Well, not all. Steinman negotiated labor contracts with as many as eighteen different locals. Most of the terms were set over the telephone or across a bar table. Formal "negotiations" were staged later in hotel suites, but they hardly appear to have been conducted at arms' length. Steinman became lead negotiator in many labor dealings for a large group of supermarket chains, supposedly competitors, based in or near New York.

The membership in this clique of supermarkets was not fixed. Some chains showed more independence than others. But by and large they bought their meats, at least certain cuts, from whatever company Moe Steinman told them to buy from. And the extra money they paid for the meat kept labor problems away, and fattened their own incomes through kickbacks. The chains that supposedly competed with Shopwell, but which were later found to have executives on Steinman's payoff list, included Big Apple, Bohack, Food City, Sloan's, First National Stores (Finast), Foodarama, King Kullen, Shop-Rite, and, of course, Waldbaum's, Steinman's first employer. Food Fair, Grand Union, Great Eastern, Hills, and Key Food were other chains cited in court evidence as being under Steinman's influence.

While Steinman was passing out envelopes, his brother Sol handled meat buying for Shopwell. Moe's "boss," Herbert Daitch, evidently was content to settle for a pinch hitter if his last name was Steinman. Then, around 1961, while Moe's wholesaling partner Joe Weinberg was deep in the Murray Packing Company scandal, Sol left Daitch-Shopwell to take over another meat wholesaling operation, Trans-World Fabricators, Inc. More properly, Trans-World was a brokerage. From its office in the Fourteenth Street meat district, Trans-World took telephone meat orders from supermarkets (and other retailers) and made telephone purchases from meat processors to fill the orders. For the most part, there were no warehouses, where product was moved in and out. The firm just took "commissions" on what the supermarkets bought. And if the commissions weren't paid to Trans-World, often the meat couldn't be sold.

Trans-World had been started a couple of years earlier by Herbert Newman, who had been partners with Sol Steinman in another meat company in the early 1950s, and also at one point had been involved with Charles Anselmo, the bookie, loanshark, and chief supplier in the Merkel horsemeat scandal.

A couple of years after Newman started Trans-World, it was foundering. Newman, a heavy gambler and all-round big spender, effectively gave the company over to the Steinman brothers. True to expectations, the Steinman family brought Trans-World a quick upturn in business. Large orders were placed by major retailers, including, of course, Daitch-Shopwell, where the Steinmans, as official meat buyers, were all too happy to feather the nest of their own meat supply firm with money that belonged to Shopwell's public shareholders. Prices, as always, were puffed up to create a huge kitty for pay-offs to all concerned, including various Mafiosi. The shoppers paid for that. Soon, other commission companies were established under the same ownership, assertedly for tax reasons.

Back in the early 1960s even Moe Steinman probably didn't dream he could grab a commission on *all* the fresh meat that came into chain stores in a three- or four-state area. To accumulate money to handle his pay-offs, he claimed the right to commissions on certain easily identified specialty meat items. These included mostly the parts of the cow known in the trade as "offal": livers, oxtail, tripe, and flank, or "skirt" steak. All of this is meat that does not come from the four standard fresh-meat cuts—the chuck, the ribs, the round, and the loin. But the biggest specialty item by far for Steinman was the brisket.

At first, Steinman simply required that independent corned beef makers buy their briskets from him as part of his control of the offal market. Since corned beef requires processing, which is usually done locally, it was an easy item to control. If the processors didn't buy their briskets from Steinman, the supermarkets wouldn't buy the processed corned beef from *them*. This produced an easy $1 commission for every one hundred pounds of corned beef sold. But when Steinman saw how easy it was to control the corned beef market, he decided to nail the manufacturers both coming and going. "You don't sell to the supermarket anymore, you sell to me," he told them.

Steinman eventually testified, with his figures scrutinized by federal prosecutors, that he pumped from eight to ten cents a pound into the price of corned beef sold in a supermarket anywhere near New York.

To put it simply, by the late 1960s Moe Steinman had put a corner on the corned beef market for much of the northeastern United States.

It wasn't hard to figure out where Steinman's hold on the supermarkets came from. He controlled the unions. In the words of one meat dealer who started to lose his market until he joined the system, "The union personnel, the foremen, they made certain that nothing but Steinman meat was acceptable. I could sell Bohack meat at fifty cents a pound and it would be rejected. They had to pay Steinman fifty-five cents a pound."

In 1967, a big money-making opportunity arose for Steinman. It bore a prophetic similarity to the Iowa Beef Processors shakedown that began three years later. Holly Farms Inc. of Wilkesboro, North Carolina, hadn't been able to break into the New York market even though it was the nation's largest chicken producer. Holly Farms packaged its chickens by a new cryovac process that eliminated the need for re-packaging in the stores. This meant less work for butchers, so the butchers' union barred Holly Farms's product.

Steinman saw an opening. He arranged for Daitch-Shopwell to try the Holly Farms chickens for a few weeks. The union apparently "understood" and didn't complain. Daitch-Shopwell's president, Martin Rosengarten, was delighted, according to Steinman's testimony later: "He called me in and he told me, 'Here is a package that's great. It's beautiful. You can throw it in the case when it comes in. The only problem is, I don't know if the unions will allow it.' " He should have had more confidence.

Steinman immediately went to Al DeProspoe, the man Frank Kissel had selected to run Local 174 when Kissel went off to jail. They made a deal. As described later, the union would let in cryovac chickens if the supermarkets promised not to fire any butchers because of it. By the time Steinman broke the good news to Holly Farms, however, there was more to it. In his own words, "Now I turn around, when my president [Rosengarten] knew about it, and I said to my president that I want to ask them [Holly Farms] for the brokerage for the New York territory. He said, 'If you can get it, go ahead.' I didn't hide anything." Nor did Rosengarten seem to object to Steinman's design to sell the new product to all the chains in town, even though this would cost Shopwell—Steinman's employer—its competitive advantage. Steinman's commissions came first.

Holly Farms, of course, was delighted at what Steinman had pulled off, and was easily persuaded to let him have an exclusive brokerage contract—so much for every pound of Holly Farms chicken sold in or near New York. Details of the deal have never been made public. Rather than cut Newman in on the profits, Moe sidestepped Trans-World and set up a separate brokerage firm, Cedar Rapids Fabricators Inc., to receive the commissions from Holly Farms. Then, in his word, he "gave" Cedar Rapids to his son-in-law, Walter Bodenstein, to operate. Holly Farms also was somehow persuaded to hire Bodenstein, a lawyer, as its New York legal counsel, on substantial retainer. A similar practice would be followed three years later with Iowa Beef.

The deal with Holly Farms apparently continues to this day, though the amount of money it involves has been reduced, through no fault of the Steinman family. In the mid-1970s, Frank Perdue's catchy advertisements created a name-brand competition that cost Holly Farms its leadership. Holly Farms' chickens don't carry a brand name in the supermarket case. Perdue's chief brand-name competition comes from Paramount Chickens, the brand preferred by Pearl Bailey and Carlo Gambino, whose Mafia family distributes them.

In 1968, Frank Kissel was packing his bags for jail, which left a vacuum of bribery in the wholesale meat industry. After more than a dozen meat wholesalers had testified against Kissel and his union colleagues in 1967, union officials were getting edgy about taking money directly from the employers. So Steinman, who already had a lock on the retail (supermarket) end of the corruption, volunteered to fill the vacuum by becoming a middle man in the wholesale industry. "I'll deal with the companies, and you deal with me," he told the union officials.

The threat Steinman used over the wholesalers was not primarily labor trouble, but supermarket trouble. Sure, he controlled the unions, but he also controlled the buyers. Recalled one wholesaler later, "I was already in the chains. Suddenly Moe comes around to me and tells me I have to pay one thousand to this guy, fifteen hundred to that guy, five hundred to that guy. . . ." The wholesalers didn't know with certainty where the money was going. But a huge pool of cash was being accumulated, and problems were being taken care of.

The arrangement depended on phony sales to wholesalers by Steinman's Trans-World brokerage firm. "Moe would bill me for merchandise I didn't get," one wholesaler explained. "I'd pay with a check . . . I got 10 percent of the cash and Moe would distribute the rest in bribes."

Other wholesalers have explained the same pattern: wiretaps placed later by Nicholson's men confirm it. Of course, Moe kept a goodly share of the bribe money for himself and his Mafia friends. With the help of Steinman's supermarket network, the Mafia moved into waste hauling, soap distribution and even, of all things, the mass-produced bagel industry. First on the scene, as always, was Johnny Dio.

John Dioguardi was born in New York City April 28, 1914. He grew up on Forsyth Street in Manhattan's Little Italy. His father, Dominick, owned a bicycle shop. But young John apparently became closer to his uncle and neighbor on Forsyth Street, James "Jimmy Doyle" Plumeri, a prize fighter, racketeer, and Mafia member. By the time Dioguardi graduated from grade school in 1929, he had learned to terrorize pushcart owners by dumping their wares until they paid him.

Around 1954, after sporadic convictions on various charges, Dio became close to Jimmy Hoffa, as Hoffa sought New York support for his takeover of the Teamsters. Newspaper columnist Victor Riesel began writing about their activities, until, on April 5, 1956, he was permanently blinded in an acid attack outside Lindy's restaurant. Dio was accused of ordering the blinding, but was never convicted of it, although of the five men who took part in the attack, four were convicted and the fifth was murdered by his accomplices a few weeks after the attack. With one exception, those convicted served long prison terms, including years of additional time for refusing to testify against Dio.

In 1958, while in prison for a shakedown of stationery store operators, Dio went on trial again on similar charges involving shakedowns of the owners of electroplating shops. This time Dio was sentenced to fifteen to thirty years. But one year later, an appeals court overturned the first conviction, and, implicitly, the second, on the ground that Dioguardi never personally issued any threats. In a decision that seemed to legitimize the whole purpose of the Mafia, a divided court ruled that "Extortion cannot be committed by one who does not himself induce fear . . . but who . . . receives money for [the] purpose of removing or allaying . . . pre-existing fear instilled by others." Johnny Dio walked out of jail a free man on June 24, 1959.

In less than a year, the federal government yanked him back to court on charges that he failed to report taxable income from three dress manufacturing companies (all of them non-union) and two labor union locals. By the end of 1960 he was in the federal penitentiary in Atlanta, supposedly for four years. But two years later, in March, 1963, he was free again on parole, and in October he was discharged completely.

That was bad news for Kosher meat lovers. Dio's parole had been granted on the contention that he had a good job in legitimate industry—as a salesman for Consumers Kosher Provision Company in Brooklyn. Of course, no industry remains legitimate for very long with Johnny Dio involved in it. What had happened was that Dio and several fellow mobsters had managed to convince two rival kosher meat manufacturers that each needed its own group of mobsters to compete effectively with the other's group of mobsters. It was a trick that had worked decades earlier in the garment district. On Fourteenth Street, which supplies kosher meat coast to coast, it worked so well that the *Daily News* took to calling Dio and his colleagues the "Kosher Nostra."

Herman Rose, the owner of Consumers Kosher Provision, had let someone in the Dio organization know that he was desperate over the inroads recently made by his chief competitor, American Kosher Provisions Inc. Consumers had been losing many orders to American, which had clearly become lead brand in the supermarkets. It wasn't hard to figure out why. The year before, American had signed up two free-agent sluggers of real all-star class for its sales force: Max Block and Lorenzo "Chappy" Brescia. Who would say "no" to them?

Dio's son, Dominick Dioguardi, then about twenty-one, and James Plumeri's son, Thomas, thirty-two, convinced Herman Rose that in order to compete against the likes of Block and Brescia, Consumers would have to hire Johnny Dio himself—which Rose agreed to do in 1963 for $250 a week. This served, first, to get Dio his parole (the honest job) and, second, to give the Mafia power over not one but two kosher meat companies.

Herman Rose died in July, 1964. The Kleinberg family, which owned American Kosher Provisions, had already been shoved aside. In August, 1964, Dio announced that Consumers and American were going to merge. This allowed for a transfer of assets—namely meat—back and forth. Pretty soon, other firms were created or taken over—First National Kosher Provisions, Mizrach Kosher Provisions, Tel Aviv Kosher Provisions, Finest Provisions Company. Meat again was transferred back and forth. Supermarket chains went from one to the next as lead supplier. In instance after instance, a kosher firm's debts for meat purchased would climb, and then the income of the debtor company would be cut off by a switch in supermarket loyalties before bills could be paid. The suppliers—western cattle firms and unlucky local wholesalers—took a bath.

In January, 1965, Consumers' suppliers threw the company into involuntary bankruptcy proceedings. The very next month, Consumers was declared formally bankrupt, with tremendous losses. Within a year, American was in bankruptcy proceedings. A few months later, First National's remaining assets were sold at auction to satisfy judgments.

Mizrach became the lead Dio brand; its trade name was taken from a company that had been producing kosher salami, frankfurters, and baloney for forty years. When the original Mizrach went into reorganization under the bankruptcy law, it became an easy target for a Dio takeover. Milton Sahn, an attorney representing Mizrach's creditors, quickly accepted an offer from Dio whereby young Plumeri would sign on customers for Mizrach in exchange for 5 percent of the gross. Plumeri brought in more than $50,000 a week in new orders. (Sahn, the attorney who effectively approved Dio's takeover of Mizrach, now represents the wholesale meat industry trade association in New York. Sahn's co-counsel for the Mizrach creditors, Fred I. Zabriskie, later represented the Castellanos' meat interests.)

In April, 1966, the federal government filed bankruptcy fraud charges against Dio, his son Dominick, Tommy Plumeri, and David Perlman, a fifty-three-year-old kosher butcher without whose practical advice the racketeers might not have been able to slice a salami. In 1967, all but Dominick Dio were convicted of diverting some $200,000 in assets in the Consumers bankruptcy (the other bankruptcies weren't included in the charges). The men stayed free during four years of appeals.

That's the way the meat industry was in New York when Currier Holman rode in out of the west with the best idea a meat man ever had.

CHAPTER 14

HOLMAN

Currier J. Holman, the other meat industry leader in the darkened suite at the Stanhope Hotel that April day in 1970, presented quite a contrast to Moe Steinman. His features were even, his bearing distinguished. He looked like the very tintype of the midwestern business success that he had become.

It had been nine years since Holman, a veteran cattleman, had founded Iowa Beef Processors Inc. But he had spent a quarter of a century developing the vision behind Iowa Beef. In all that time, Holman had watched packing plants ship whole swinging carcasses of beef around the country, just as they had for a hundred years. Holman had sensed that butchering beef at the slaughterpoint, then shipping it out in boxes, would result in enormous economies. By 1970, he had built Iowa Beef into the largest meat processing firm in the world.

When Iowa Beef was founded, the industry was dominated by the so-called Big Five packers: Swift, Armour, Wilson, Morrell, and Cudahy. Before the end of fifteen years, Iowa Beef had become bigger than Swift, Armour, Wilson, Morrell, and Cudahy *put together*. It had even fostered a host of imitators, including the number two packer in the industry, MBPXL Corp. (originally Missouri Beef Packers), which also had edged ahead of Swift. In 1977, MBPXL was slaughtering thirty to thirty-three thousand cattle a week. This three-to-one ratio between number one and number two is among the biggest in any competitive industry in the United States today.

In an amazingly short time, Iowa Beef has changed the processing and marketing habits of an industry. It has influenced the eating habits of a nation. And yet, despite all of its innovations, and all of its genius, Iowa Beef found itself unable to stay in business at all without selling its soul to the Mafia.

Currier Holman was born in 1911 in Sioux City, Iowa, an area that his grandfather had helped pioneer. Holman's father had accumulated enough holdings in real estate and banks that neighbors considered the Holmans well-to-do, although family members insist they were poor-to-average. The elder Holman died in a flu epidemic in 1918. Currier moved with the rest of the family to California. His elementary school was Hitchcock Military Academy in San Rafael. After that he was packed off to prep school at Shattuck Military Academy in Faribault, Minnesota.

According to Holman's entries in *Who's Who in America*, his higher education was Notre Dame, '33. Notre Dame says it parted company with Holman for undisclosed reasons during his junior year in 1932. Grant Holman says his brother Currier quit college in disappointment after a broken appendix forced an end to his football career in 1932, but a roster of all Notre Dame football games ever played doesn't include the name Currier Holman. Yet decades later his speeches were peppered with recollections of his experiences on the team, and with comparisons between business at Iowa Beef and football at Notre Dame.

Even in the depths of the Depression, Holman found work. Swift put him in what was known as the "gut shanty," where his job was stripping the guts and offal from freshly slaughtered carcasses.

After several years, Swift put Holman into office work, but four months later he left. Armour had offered him the job he really wanted—buying cattle.

Holman saved his money and early in the war years he found an opportunity to buy into an established private cattle trading concern at the Sioux City stockyards. A few years later his partner retired and Holman went on his own. Halfway across the country a man known as Black Market Moe was starting a supermarket racket with his Mafia friends. But Holman had never heard of him. Holman was busy developing his own reputation as the biggest cattle trader in one of the biggest stockyards in the country.

For fifteen years Holman took phone calls from small slaughterhouses around the United States and bought cattle in the Sioux City yards to fill their orders. But through all that time he never lost the dream of one day starting his own packing company. Finally, in 1953, he began knocking on doors looking for financing. He managed to convince some twenty-five to thirty Sioux City burghers to lay out about $1 million, of which Holman himself put up about $50,000.

The new firm, Sioux City Dressed Beef, started operations in 1955. Though not nearly as revolutionary as Iowa Beef would be a decade later, Sioux City Dressed Beef cut an adventuresome style for its day. His backers accepted Holman's theory that beef and pork were two different businesses, and that the major packers were creating inefficiencies by trying to handle both products at the same time. Holman's packinghouse would concentrate on beef.

Sioux City Dressed Beef met with only limited success, both financially and technologically. One reason was that Holman had been unwilling to bet all his chips on it at the start. Instead of running the plant himself, Holman had his investors hire a manager while he continued full-time in his cattle-selling business. Within a few years, Holman and the packinghouse manager were feuding. Many of the investors sided with the manager. Holman and the investors who sided with him were bought out by their partners. After giving up on Sioux City Dressed Beef, Holman went back to ringing doorbells looking for money for a new packinghouse. Meanwhile, he had made friends with A. D. "Andy" Anderson, who had built a pork plant in nearby Dennison, Iowa, in the mid-1950s. Anderson shared Holman's opinions about the need to redesign the packing process to take advantage of modern technology.

They decided to found their new packing company together and by 1960 they got the money—mostly with the help of the investors who had sided with Holman in the split-up of Sioux City Dressed Beef. Iowa Beef Processors Inc. opened its first plant in May, 1961, in Dennison, Iowa, with Holman and Anderson as co-chairmen. Although the great technological leap forward was still in the future, even that first plant in Dennison represented an important advance. Holman bought the cattle directly from feed-lot owners near Dennison, thus thumbing his nose at industry practice. The rules of the stockyards said that all cattle had to be brought to Sioux City and sold there on the open market. Holman saw that this ritual postponed the slaughter for several days and caused a weight loss of up to 7 percent. Since Holman no longer was a member of the stockyards and was buying cattle only for Iowa Beef, he made his own arrangements with feed-lot owners. Cattle were brought in directly, just when the assembly-line process was ready to gobble them up. As little as two or three hours after the animal left the grain trough, the knife descended.

To make this system succeed, Iowa Beef needed a series of processing plants, each near a feed-lot center. So Holman and Anderson bought a second plant in Fort Dodge, Iowa, and remodeled it to their assembly-line system. It opened in June, 1962. (At this writing, Iowa Beef has ten plants and plans for more.)

In the early 1960s, Holman and Anderson knew very well where they were headed. If it made sense to reduce the carcass to quarters before shipping it out of the midwest, then it made further sense to reduce it to primal cuts (loins, ribs, chucks, and rounds) and eventually to smaller cuts known as sub-primals. That way, a supermarket would have to do no real butchering at all—just unpack a box, take each carefully trimmed piece of meat and slice it off like bread into individual cooking portions that would be placed in plastic trays.

Instead of receiving a swinging carcass, the purchaser would receive a box of what he wanted. A & P could hold a sale on chuck in New York while Safeway held a sale on rump roast in San Francisco. The butchering process would be much more efficient at a central location. By-products that the supermarkets couldn't use, such as bone (which can be ground up for animal food), fat, and hide, could be disposed of centrally, which benefitted both cost control and the ecology.

The first of these revolutionary plants opened in Dakota City early in 1967. It was capable at first of boxing only ribs and loins. Two more years were required to bring the plant up to where it could process an entire steer as Holman had dreamed. And by then, a second such plant was under construction at Emporia, Kansas.

By 1969, Holman and his associates seemed to have the technology well in hand. It would be only a few more years before their process was carried to its logical conclusion and they filled supermarket counters with their meat from coast to coast.

All their calculations, however, had omitted several factors that turned out to be just as important as technology: the butchers' union, the Mafia, and Moe Steinman. Holman never really admitted the *real* way his process saves money. He argued that pre-butchering the meat holds down shipping costs. But the expense of cutting, cryovacking, and sealing the meat largely offsets this savings. The one way that the Holman process indisputably saves money and sharply reduces the price of meat to the consumer is that it eliminates butchers' jobs in supermarket warehouses and stores. What the Iowa Beef formula really amounts to is replacing a large number of highly-skilled, highly-unionized butchers who receive big-city pay rates, with a smaller number of less-skilled, less-unionized butchers who receive rural pay rates.

So the butchers' union had a real cause for concern over the rise of Iowa Beef. It is the commonly accepted belief that the Mafia and Moe Steinman merely exploited that legitimate concern. But Robert Nicholson and others in and out of law enforcement have another theory: that some leaders of the butchers' union were, from the very beginning, part of a mammoth conspiracy to sell out their own members and shake down Iowa Beef as no major company had ever been shaken down before.

CHAPTER 15

THE CRIME

Iowa Beef came under siege in 1969. The developments were so swift and startling, and came from so many different directions, that at first shock it may not have occurred to Holman how they all related.

In approximately January, 1969, the Dakota City plant began to box whole steers. Until then, the plant had been able to handle only ribs and loins. The plant did have supermarket customers, but ribs and loins are used primarily by the so-called "HRI trade"—hotels, restaurants, and institutions. America's daily at-home diet is the chuck and the round, the shoulders and haunches of the animal, and the backbone of the supermarket meat trade.

Thus it was not until early 1969 that Iowa Beef could begin the mass marketing retail store campaign that Holman and Anderson had envisioned when they started out. Iowa Beef, it's true, was already at or near the top of the slaughtering business, but the company clearly was going to rise or fall on whether the new boxed beef program went over.

New York is easily the country's biggest meat market. The New York market traditionally includes everything within a wide sweep of the city—Moe Steinman had been defining his territory as everything within a 125-mile radius of Columbus Circle (at Fifty-ninth Street and Eighth Avenue). This 250-mile wide area is not only populous, but exceptionally carnivorous. Some 16 percent of all the meat consumed in the United States (according to industry figures) is consumed in this market. Moreover, the market takes in a lot of meat that is processed there and shipped elsewhere, including overseas. And California, the other major population center, has tended to be an island to itself as far as meat is concerned, with the big midwestern packers traditionally not shipping across the Rockies (though Iowa Beef is trying now to change all that).

At any rate, it is not unusual to hear meat men say that New York represents 25 percent of the total market they are shooting at. Clearly, Iowa Beef had to have New York.

To line up the market, Iowa Beef employed an experienced meat salesman, Lewis Jacobs. Under Jacobs, the company won orders fairly quickly from two major supermarket chains in the area, Pathmark (which is operated by Supermarkets General Corp.) and Shop-Rite (a cooperative of individually-owned chains that buy under the name Wakefern). Jacobs later recalled hearing that there was a clause in the butchers' union contract that might prohibit bringing in pre-butchered meat. Butchers' contracts all over the country had such clauses, some quite explicit. In New York, however, the clause was rather vague, and the Iowa Beef idea seemed good. So Aaron Perlmutter, chief buyer for Supermarkets General, decided to risk a purchase.

A half a dozen carloads (a carload is a tractor-trailer full, or about forty thousand pounds) were delivered and used. Then a shipment was rejected by Pathmark on grounds that it was no good.

Holman and Anderson flew to New York, barged onto the loading dock and opened the boxes at 4 A.M. "There was nothing wrong with the meat," Holman insisted. He went to Pathmark as soon as the doors opened that morning. He and Anderson spent eight hours arguing with underlings. Finally they fought their way to the boss's office. Milton Perlmutter ran Pathmark. At first, Perlmutter continued to argue that the Iowa Beef shipment had been of poor quality. Holman, knowing better, searched for another motive.

At last, Holman discovered that Milton Perlmutter indeed had a "hang-up—he wasn't going to buck the union. . . . He said, 'Look, our people on the dock won't unload that. Now it's as simple as that. I'm not going to force them to. I'll bring it up in negotiations.' "

For many months, Lew Jacobs couldn't sell any more meat to anybody.

In April, 1968, the butchers' union had begun a continuing campaign of diatribe against Iowa Beef and its new methods. Right on the heels of this campaign came the Moe Steinman-Iowa Beef shakedown. In the wake of the scandal, the union has contended that it never really opposed the concept of boxed beef at all, and that New York butchers rejected Iowa Beef's product in 1969 out of sympathy for a strike that their fellow butchers were waging over pay in the Dakota City plant. But Iowa Beef's meat was rejected in New York many months before there was a butchers' strike in Dakota City.

Throughout 1969, Iowa Beef continued desperately to try to sign up a major eastern supermarket chain. There was no success. The factory at Dakota City had a capacity for forty thousand cattle a week; yet production was down to six or seven thousand.

On a mid-summer morning of 1969, Benny Moscowitz, a meat dealer, sat down for coffee with Herbie Newman at a restaurant on the corner of Fourteenth Street and Ninth Avenue. Such meetings were frequent. Newman was the operating partner of Moe Steinman's meat brokerage business. Moscowitz was one of the meat dealers who had to pay bribe money to union officers and supermarket meat buyers through Stein-man. On this particular morning Newman managed to throw into the conversation the name of Currier Holman. That was interesting, Moscowitz said. It had been a long time since the two had talked, but Moscowitz used to know Holman rather well. Newman was ecstatic. He continued to pump the puzzled Moscowitz for details. The story began in 1945, when the Office of Price Administration had been trying to allocate scarce meat supplies. Moscowitz's stepfather, who was also in the meat business, had gone to Sioux City to try to find a source of cattle. Currier Holman knew where the cattle were, so Moscowitz back in New York began buying cattle through Holman. Holman would arrange for the slaughter at a nearby slaughterhouse, then ship the carcass east.

Over their coffee, Moscowitz told Newman this story, and couldn't understand why Newman was so interested. Moscowitz was strictly a small fry, and Holman was a thousand miles away. Yet Steinman's partner was bouncing around the restaurant booth. "Holman—oh, he's terrific," Newman exclaimed. Then he assured Moscowitz, "You'll hear from Moe about this."

Shortly afterward, on August 24, 1969, the Amalgamated Meat Cutters and Butcher Workmen of North America struck the Dakota City plant of Iowa Beef. Officially, the union said it was striking over pay and working conditions—very specific local issues—at the Dakota City plant. That made the strike easier to justify before the public and the government, and the local workers certainly believed it. Iowa Beef had never been a generous employer.

But the strike was heavily supported by the international union. The union's opposition to the whole concept of boxed beef had been too widely and repeatedly expressed for the issue to be confused now. Holman knew the strike was really over his basic concept. His mistake, if he made one, was to assume that Kissel and other international leaders were sincere in their undying opposition to boxed beef. He did not seem to consider at first that this giant international labor organization might just be setting him up for the Syndicate.

By October, the strike was beginning to hurt. Holman, undaunted, was still out looking for customers. One day, while he was in Los Angeles talking to officials of Young's Market, he got a message that an old friend from New York had been trying to reach him—Benny Moscowitz. Holman returned the call. "He said he wanted to bring a guy to see me."

A meeting was set up at the Rodeway Inn in Sioux City. Holman and Anderson "went up to the Rodeway, and, uh, Benny was sitting there, and he said he had some people he wanted me to meet." Unfortunately, Moscowitz's friends were late sleepers, and they weren't dressed yet. Holman had to wait for them. "I get up early," Moscowitz explained by way of excuse. "In the packing business, we're pretty early risers."

Finally Herbie Newman showed up in the lobby. He was a large older man with thick glasses, who, perhaps because of his vision problems, kept his head tilted back and tended to look down his nose at people. They chatted awhile.

"And then walks in a guy . . ." Holman paused, seemingly unable to describe Moe Steinman. "And so we're sitting in the middle of a lobby of a motel, and I said, 'What are you? What's your business?' "

318

"Er, I do a couple of things," Steinman replied. First, Steinman told Holman, he was a vice-president of the Daitch-Shopwell supermarket chain.

Holman: "I said, 'Well, that's interesting.' I said, 'We're trying to sell a lot of meat to the chain stores. We tried to sell your goddamn chain. Maybe you can help us.' "

"Maybe I can," Moe Steinman replied.

Then Steinman said, "I got a interest in another company, called Trans-World." Trans-World had been buying briskets (for corned beef) and other offal from Iowa Beef since the early 1960s. It still did not quite click in Holman's mind that he was looking at the man who, with Holman's meat, fed every drunk in the world's largest city on St. Patrick's Day.

"What do you want to talk about?" Holman asked.

"Well, we want to talk about buying some product from you. Newman's the one that wants to buy," Steinman said. "I'm here just, er, to help him."

Holman: "I said to him, I said, 'You know, you couldn't work for me.' I said, 'We don't countenance people doing two or three things on the side . . .' There was a conflict of interest someplace . . . Well, he laughed it off . . . He said he didn't consider it that."

At a convenient moment, Holman called Moscowitz aside and asked the reason for his visit, but Moscowitz didn't explain. Years later, Holman would give it more thought.

He did recall that at one point, Steinman said, "Maybe I can help you in New York City. Maybe I can help you with your labor problems."

"We can sure as Christ use all the help we can get," Holman replied.

Over the course of the fall and winter, the strike began to evolve into a war. Scabs were working at the plant and several of them or their relatives were shot. One woman died of gunshot wounds after rumors started that she had leaked information to company security guards. A bullet was fired through Holman's window while he was sitting in his office. (He kept the window with the bullet hole in it exactly as it was for several years afterward.) Police records indicate thirty-three instances of dynamite either found or exploded, but they don't indicate that anybody ever went to jail for it. The history of law enforcement in Sioux City would not have provided a threatened man much comfort.

While Holman saw his office become an object of siege, with bullets flying and dynamite bursting around the city, Benny Moscowitz kept reminding him of Steinman's visit. Moscowitz called several times and put on the phone people he said were former butchers' union vice-presidents; these men said they could help Iowa Beef resolve the strike. Holman evidently was slow to get the message.

To help deliver it, the Mob-bribed New York leadership sent fifteen hundred workers parading through the Fourteenth Street area urging the cutting shops there to refuse to buy even carcass meat from Iowa Beef.

Then P. L. Nymann's house blew up. "Gus" Nymann was Iowa Beef's general counsel. He lived at 3905 Sylvan Way in Sioux City. His neighbor on the left was Currier Holman. Said Holman later, "They burned our general counsel's house to the ground. It was intended to be my house, which is immediately contiguous to his, but they just missed . . ."

In all his statements, Holman managed to fuzz-over the question of exactly when he caved in and called Moe Steinman. He has also left fuzzy the date of another significant conversation. At some point in March or April of 1970, he called Fred Lovette, the head of Holly Farms, the nation's leading chicken producer. He knew that Holly Farms had run into problems with the butchers' union in New York just three years earlier, and appeared to have solved those problems by hiring Moe Steinman as a broker.

Holman: "I said, 'Fred, what, er, do you know anything about Steinman?' He said, 'Yeah, I know him, and, er, he's really responsible for our First National [Finast Supermarkets] business that you saw. I think he can help you in New York if anybody can . . . If you want to be successful with First National or the other retailers in New York City, it's my opinion that he can do a great deal for you.' "

By April, 1970, with the strike unsolved and the meat unsold, Iowa Beef showed a $9 million loss for the year so far. "The banks were becoming restless," Holman admitted.

Chemical Bank, the lead bank in Iowa Beef's $30 million loan line, wanted to talk it over. So Holman, Anderson, Howard Weiner (the treasurer), and Dale Tinstman (a Nebraska investment banker who was then handling Iowa Beef's securities and who is now president of the company) flew to New York April 10. As Holman recalled the meeting at the bank, Iowa Beef was told, "You people either put $15 million in equity in front of your line of credit, or we want to be paid off."

Two things happened then, apparently that same afternoon. A tentative agreement was reached in the butchers' strike. And Holman called Moe Steinman to arrange a meeting. According to Holman, the strike settlement came first. That leaves open the question of why Holman, knowing what he knew, would call Steinman immediately *after* the strike was settled.

The morning after the tentative strike settlement and the arrangement for a meeting with Steinman, Chemical Bank backed off from its demands. This gave Iowa Beef some breathing time. But everyone knew that sooner or later the boxed beef was going to have to come into the New York market if Iowa Beef was to survive.

Several days later the Dakota City labor accord was completed. On April 21, 1970, Iowa Beef's top executives were back in New York and settled in at the Stanhope Hotel for an afternoon meeting with Moe Steinman. At lunch beforehand, Holman explained the situation to Lew Jacobs, the company's unsuccessful New York salesman. As Jacobs remembers the explanation, Steinman had "indicated" that his Trans-World brokerage did business with the New York chains, and "would be the company that could best provide sales for the boxed beef product in the New York area."

Steinman arrived at the Stanhope with his brother Sol and partner Herbie Newman. Holman told him right off that Iowa Beef needed to sell the boxed equivalent of sixteen thousand carcasses a week in New York, more than had ever been sold by one company, and that he needed a "showcase" chain that would convert its meat program to handle Iowa Beef's product exclusively. By Holman's recollection, Steinman said, "I can help you with some of the retailers. I'm not sure I can help you with all." Then Steinman picked up a Yellow Pages and pointed out fourteen chains "that he thought he could help us with." Then Holman told Steinman about the union resistance, and Steinman said, "I don't know, but I think I can handle it."

Jacobs doesn't remember so much equivocating. He says Steinman declared that in exchange for a commission from Iowa Beef, "he would guarantee through his influence with union officials that metropolitan New York would be an open city insofar as receiving boxed beef products into the retail chain stores and warehouses."

That set the stage for the key Stanhope meeting the next day. The executives from Dakota City gathered in the suite where they had met the day before and they waited. Almost precisely at noon, they heard a knock on the door. Steinman led them down the corridor to another room where some men were waiting. "It was very dark," according to Holman. "The blinds were closed. I remember I couldn't even see. I was having trouble focusing on the guys' faces down the other end of the room." The faces were convincing testaments to Steinman's power. They belonged to:

• Irving Stern, international vice-president of the union and director of the New York region, who had emerged from Local 342, the main retail butchers' local in the area;
• Albert DeProspoe, the man Frank Kissel had picked to succeed him as head of Local 174, which dealt largely with wholesalers but also with some retailers;
• Irving "Izzy" Kaplan, also an international vice-president and head of Local 464, which covered most of New Jersey; and
• Frank Brescio, an official in DeProspoe's local and brother of Mafia labor extortionist Larry "Chappy the Dude" Brescia, the former bodyguard and driver for Lucky Luciano.

Also present, waiting for the Iowa Beef men, were two outside lawyers who were defending the union in civil lawsuits Iowa Beef had filed alleging Taft-Hartley Act violations during the strike. The lawyers had been brought to the Stanhope because Steinman promised that the lawsuits would be dropped as part of the overall settlement. But because he was an outside observer, one of the lawyers, Harold Cammer, was able to provide a delightful description of the meeting. He had never before seen Moe Steinman and didn't know who he was.

"He was just a furtive-looking character out of *Guys and Dolls*," Cammer says of Steinman. "I thought he was a messenger, or a coffee-getter—some greasy, sleazy-looking fellow who never looked you in the eye, who had a hang-dog look about him . . . I had no notion until later that he was a famous character. He looks like a worm."

"The Iowa Beef people," Cammer continues, "when they came in the room I thought they were Texas Rangers."

Stern had just come from the Black Angus where he and Steinman had shared an early lunch with lots of drinks and food and promises that the union's troubles with Iowa Beef would soon be over. Later, Stern would go to jail for tax evasion after being charged with taking bribes from Steinman. Now, on Stern's command, the two union lawyers and Nymann padded meekly back to the Iowa Beef suite to wait.

As soon as they were gone, by Holman's account, Stern demanded to know, "Okay, now, what is it? What's the deal?"

Holman replied that he wanted his boxed beef in New York, "and I don't want any more ass-aches like I got hit with out at Supermarkets General." Holman said he would drop his lawsuit against the New York unions if they would allow his boxed beef to come in.

"And there was silence in the room," Holman recalled.

Steinman broke it. "Okay, you guys go on down to your room and we'll come back to you," he said. Holman and the Iowa Beef crew left.

After about twenty minutes, there was a knock on the door. "Come on down," Steinman said. Holman and his men returned to the darkened room with the union leaders. "Mr. Stern was the spokesman. He was pretty cryptic. He said, 'Okay, if you do what you say you're going to do, you got it.' "

Thus the fate of Iowa Beef was sealed.

In May, Steinman arrived in Dakota City with his brother. Characteristically, he started intimidating his hosts before they could even begin to make any demands of their own. First, he dashed Holman's assumption, based on talks at the Stanhope, that he was going to do something tangible for his money, such as set up distribution warehouses for the meat in New Jersey, The Bronx, Manhattan, and Long Island. Holman had told his colleagues in Dakota City that Steinman would have to invest "some multimillion dollars" to establish his business. But when Steinman arrived, and Holman began to talk about the first distribution center, according to Lew Jacobs, the Steinmans immediately "rejected the idea on the basis that . . . it would entail too much money and they didn't want to get involved with the labor or the facility at that particular time." The executives nodded meekly. Moe wouldn't be handling any meat. Nobody asked Steinman just what it was that he expected to get paid for. Everyone knew.

Next came the discussion of the commission, which Holman had hoped to lower to the normal twenty-five cents a hundredweight or less. Moe immediately demanded fifty cents a hundredweight.

"For Christ's sake, I'm not going to pay fifty cents a hundred," Holman responded.

"Well," Steinman said (according to Holman's account), "look, I got to buy a union steward. You had trouble in Supermarkets General. I've got to buy a guy a broad. I may have to buy a chain store buyer and, er, I've got to pay in cash. I can do it for fifty cents. Take it or leave it."

Holman later recalled what went through his mind. "Anybody that's in the meat business in New York City is a crook . . . I finally agreed to pay him a half a buck."

Holman then told Steinman that Iowa Beef needed a "showcase" supermarket chain in New York. If one chain would turn its entire meat program over to Iowa Beef, other chains could see by example how Holman's new boxed beef concept saved money.

"The best one you can have is Waldbaum's," Steinman told him. "They sell the best meat in New York. They got the finest stores."

"What the hell," Holman replied. "Why don't you put it in your own goddamn store?"

"Herb Olstein, he ain't gonna buy boxed beef," Steinman said. Olstein—Steinman's friend and subordinate at Daitch-Shopwell—was and still is head of the chain's meat department. On the other hand, Steinman said, Aaron Freedman, the executive who supervised the meat department for Ira Waldbaum's chain, "is the kind of guy that's got an open mind in the meat business."

By November, boxed meat was flowing into the New York market without union opposition. Jacobs' reports back to Holman continued to reflect the one thing that was responsible for Iowa Beef's sudden new success: it was Steinman's behind-the-scenes talks with supermarket executives when Jacobs, the salesman, wasn't even present.

When Steinman's son-in-law, Walter Bodenstein, was brought into the Iowa Beef affair in December, 1970, his world was in transition. Johnny Dio had just gone to jail (in October) for the kosher meat frauds. On top of that, Dio and his Mafia overlord, godfather Carmine Tramunti, had just been indicted (in November) for the first of the J. M. Kelsey stock frauds.

Bodenstein says he had heard that his father-in-law was negotiating a contract with Iowa Beef, and he accepted Steinman's invitation to attend a meeting at the Hampshire House. Within days after the December 4, 1970, meeting, it developed that Bodenstein, not Steinman, would handle the day-to-day commission work for Iowa Beef's sales in the New York area. The operation, known as Cattle Pakt Sales (later shortened to C.P. Sales), would be handled out of Bodenstein's law office.

Early in January, it was Bodenstein who flew to Dakota City to finish details on the formal commission contract. But Holman insisted that Steinman's signature be on the contract, too. As Roy Lee, the president, remembers, Steinman "was a significant party to the agreement . . . It was my impression that he would not be part of the corporate structure, but he'd still be involved."

In the month between the Hampshire House meeting and the signing of the contract, the Iowa Beef executives went through the same kind of

handwringing they had gone through the previous April, when Steinman was originally taken aboard. Howard Weiner, the treasurer,
remembers Holman asking him right after the meeting December 4,
"How do they convert the money to cash?"

"I told him I didn't know," Weiner says. "I could guess." Weiner says
that on the corporate plane back to Dakota City he tried to tell Holman
how the money might be converted for a 10 percent kickback. He
remembers that Holman just kept repeating, "It's a shame that the 127th
largest manufacturing company in the country has to do business like
this. . . . It's a shame that the largest beef producer in the world has to
do business like this. . . ."

Gus Nymann, the general counsel, recalls that he told Holman, "This
is a dangerous situation." According to Nymann's testimony later,
Holman replied, "I know that you lawyers would tell us not to do this,
but I'm going to do it anyway."

Nymann also objected to putting a new lawyer, Bodenstein, on
retainer, as demanded by Steinman. He testified that he told Holman he
was pleased with the law firm that already handled occasional labor
matters for Iowa Beef in New York. Holman replied (Nymann testified)
that "if we had serious labor relations matters" Iowa Beef would still use
the other firm, but "it was important to have this retainer agreement"
with Bodenstein and "it was related to the commission agreement."

CHAPTER 16

THE INVESTIGATION

Seven years of investigating the New York meat industry had
produced a lot of informants for Robert Nicholson. On a hot day in
late summer, 1970, one of them called up.

"Have you got any idea what Moe Steinman is doing now?" the
informant asked.

Nicholson said he hadn't.

The informant suggested that Nicholson meet him at Pappas, the
popular Greek restaurant on Eighth Avenue and Fourteenth Street.

Within the hour, Nicholson was listening to the informant, a wholesaler, explain how big Iowa Beef was. Iowa Beef, the informant said, was
flooding New York with pre-fabricated meat, which was costing him and
other wholesalers a lot of money. And Moe Steinman was collecting half

a penny for every pound of meat Iowa Beef sold in New York. "They're trying to completely capture the whole meat market and force everybody in New York to buy from Iowa Beef, and they're using the union to do it," the wholesaler said.

Under Nicholson's prompting, he went on to tell how Trans-World Fabricators was arranging for the supermarket chains to pay huge overcharges for meat. He told how Trans-World kicked back money to chain store executives, union leaders, and mobsters. He told how wholesalers in the Fourteenth Street market were forced to make payoffs in order to get their meat into the supermarkets, and how Steinman would raise cash for bribes by billing wholesalers for meat that was never delivered. In an hour, the informant had laid down the entire bribery, extortion, and racketeering case that scores of law enforcement officers would spend years trying to prove.

Back at the district attorney's office, Nicholson proposed another mammoth investigation of the meat industry. He got a go-ahead. He also got Lou Montello, his old partner from the Merkel case, back, and a new partner, Detective Jack Carey.

To supervise the investigation, assistant D.A. Al Scotti assigned Franklyn Snitow, who had come to the office fresh out of law school only a month before. Bright but totally untested, Snitow still held the title of criminal law investigator; not until a few months later, in January, 1971, when he passed the bar examination, could he be sworn in as an assistant district attorney. Snitow hardly looked the part of a tough-as-nails prosecutor of the Frank Hogan mold. But despite his youthful face, adolescent voice, and inexperience, he quickly earned the admiration of the detectives. "The Iowa Beef Processors case would never have come about if it weren't for Snitow's persistence," Nicholson observed later.

In order to start throwing up wiretaps, Nicholson and his detectives needed probable cause that a crime was being committed. They figured the first obvious step was to start tailing Moe Steinman. That proved easier said than done. Steinman's behavior seemed calculated to be erratic. He left his apartment building by various doors. He would walk in various directions. Sometimes he would hail a taxi, and sometimes he would be picked up, and by various people, including, sometimes, a man the detectives recognized as Johnny Dio's son, Dominick "Nicky" Dio. Sometimes Steinman would ride from his building to another location, where he might be met by a second car.

The detectives changed strategies. As fall turned to winter—about the time the Iowa Beef deal was being formalized in writing—the detectives gave up on Steinman and began trailing his partner, Herbie Newman, instead. The switch proved fortuitous. While Steinman shrouded his life in the manner of some criminal genius from literature, Newman was a classic criminal klutz. While Steinman slunk unobtrusively in corners, Newman was a conspicuous six-foot, 235-pounder with a bulldog face, a shock of gray hair and big, floppy feet that gave him a funny walk. He wore coke-bottle glasses and kept his head tilted back at an unusual angle to see out of them. Evidently he was hard of hearing because he loved to shout; the cops discovered that they could overhear his half of a conversation from across the room.

Every morning, Nicholson, Carey, and Montello could depend on Newman's silver Cadillac to be parked near Trans-World's office at Gansevoort and Little West Twelfth streets in the meat district. Every morning between 10:30 and 11 A.M. he would leave on foot for the Manufacturers Hanover Trust branch at Fourteenth Street and Eighth Avenue. Inside the bank, Newman would proceed directly to his safe-deposit box. He could not have picked a better time for the police (or a worse one for him); 11 A.M. was the quietest hour of the day at the bank. And he always went to the same cubicle to open his box. Detective Jack Carey was always in the next cubicle, staring idly at his own empty safe-deposit box, which the police department had rented for him as soon as Newman's habits had been reported. The partitions between the cubicles reached only part-way to the ceiling, so a person in one cubicle could easily hear what was happening in the next one, especially if its occupant constantly talked to himself, as Herbie Newman did, in a loud, hard-of-hearing voice.

Every day Carey could hear Newman counting to himself, and the detective began to get the idea that hundreds of thousands of dollars in cash and securities were in Newman's box. Then, one day, Newman brought his son, Richie, into the cubicle with him and gave the young man an inventory, replete with denominations of more than $200,000 in bonds, and an accounting of so many shares of this and that.

After he left the safe-deposit box, usually with some big bills in his pockets, Newman would proceed to another bank. This was the one part of his routine that varied. He picked a different bank every day. Perhaps Steinman had cautioned him. At any rate, the detectives were able to keep up with him frequently enough to observe him handing a $500 bill to a cashier and receiving fives and tens in return, or a $1,000 bill and receiving twenties. Then he would go to another window, usually in the same bank, and change the smaller bills to a check, which he then might change elsewhere to cash, thus covering over the trail from his pocket money back to its criminal origins.

In the evening, he would meet Steinman at the Black Angus or the Bull and Bear. Since the Kissel case, when there had been evidence of electronic surveillance at the Black Angus, Steinman was spending more and more time at the bar in the Waldorf. The police could never get close enough to hear what Steinman told Newman at the bar table. But they didn't have to. Newman would immediately leave and go to the pay phone in the lobby. He would call union people, or the head of a meat company and say, "Moe says you gotta do this," or, "I just talked to Moe, and Moe said to tell you it's going to cost you . . ." or, "It's okay to fire so-and-so. Call me from the office tomorrow." Cops would stand behind Newman at the phone as if in line, holding dimes, listening. Once one of them tapped him on the shoulder and asked if he was going to be long.

Sometimes Newman would call people from his afternoon haunts, the race track or the Ozone Park Bar, to discuss meat sales. Over and over the police began hearing the phrase that would become ever more familiar in the coming year: "street." "It'll cost 75 cents plus third street," Newman would say. Or, "a dollar-ten plus eighth street." Eventually the cops would learn that "street" was the code word for the bribe. Seventy-five cents plus third street meant that the actual price of an order of meat was 75 cents a pound, but that the supermarket would be billed 78 cents. The other three cents would be the bribe money. Part would go back to the buyer, part would go to union officers, part to the Mafia, and part to keep Newman and Steinman in Cadillacs.

By the spring of 1971, the detectives had given Snitow enough to go to court with. Snitow got a wiretap order for the Trans-World brokerage office.

Eventually, there were orders to tap and bug Steinman's home, then his Queens apartment, Herbie Newman's apartment, and other likely sites.

In about July, 1971, the district attorney's office took what turned out to be a momentous step. It disclosed the meat industry investigation to the Manhattan office of the federal strike force against organized crime.

The strike forces had been set up in 1966 and 1967 in certain major cities with acute Syndicate problems. Originally the work of Attorney General Ramsey Clark, they were even more heavily relied on during the Nixon Administration. The idea was to throw concentrated expertise into Syndicate prosecutions.

In some locations, however, the appointed heads of the federal strike force, though the product of professional selection within the Justice Department, were themselves inexperienced or possessed of less than the soundest judgment. And that could mean trouble. Worse yet was the situation in a federal district like Manhattan after Morgenthau was removed by Nixon. The succeeding U.S. attorneys, Whitney North Seymour, Paul Curran, and Robert B. Fiske, Jr., though bringing to the office all the requisite integrity and legal skill, were by nature Wall Street lawyers, not gung-ho rackets-busters, and—judging from the evidence—were reticent about initiating investigations and seizing the offensive against the Syndicate. The presence in such circumstances of a strike force leader like William I. Aronwald led to real trouble.

Young Aronwald dominated the New York strike force for most of its existence, first as senior assistant and later as chief. He already had moved swiftly through careers as a college football hero, non-career Army captain and assistant district attorney under Frank Hogan. Determined to make headlines as a rackets-buster, he displayed the aggressive qualities that good cops and FBI agents dream of in a prosecutor, yet seldom find. He devoted his resources to daring and sometimes innovative investigations of the areas that most needed it. He achieved an impressive on-paper record of guilty pleas. Nevertheless, his biggest investigations failed to clean up anything. Key trials ended in debacles. The true villains escaped when they had seemed to be in real trouble. Other law enforcement agencies that Aronwald worked with became infuriated at him. But by the time he was done, in 1976, the well-known New York City crime writer Jack Newfield was remarking that Aronwald (along with the town's other special prosecutor, Maurice Nadjari) had inadvertently done more to further the cause of organized crime in the city than the heads of leading Mafia families.

Two explanations have been offered for why the district attorney's office brought its big investigations to Aronwald. Under oath, with Aronwald staring him in the face, Frank Snitow once testified, "With the advent of the strike force, we believed that our investigation would lead us to both state and federal violations and that it would be appropriate that we brought federal authorities in at basically the ground level."

Off the record, sources from the D.A.'s office tell a different story. "We were underfunded and without equipment," says one. "We needed tape recorders, lens equipment, cameras, general operation money. So, contrary to the desires of most of the people in the office, we were required to go to the strike force to obtain money."

The wiretap on Steinman's Sixty-fourth Street apartment turned out to be more frustrating than productive, although there were many intriguing calls.

There were lots of calls from the local meat dealers and buyers, but little in the way of incriminating discussion. The calls frequently ended with Steinman's admonition, à la Mae West, to "come up and see me." Then a strange thing happened. On a call to Newman's tapped telephone from a pay booth, Steinman told Newman, "I was down in Florida. I saw the people down there. They told me all about the investigation. I'll tell you when I see you."

What investigation? Nicholson's investigation? What people?

Then Steinman began telling callers not to talk to him on his home phone.

The constant admonition to "come up and see me" rang in Nicholson's ears. So the detectives bugged in Steinman's apartment. From industry sources who had been there, the detectives learned just where to put the microphone. "He took us into this room," one buyer had recalled. "It had a bar in there. Lounge chairs. He did all his business in there." So that's where the bug went.

Then another strange thing happened. As one detective later recalled it, "From that day that we put that bug in that room, he never went in there."

Despite the frustrations, the stepped up surveillance provided a lot of new insights and some hard evidence. Steinman was seen meeting regularly with Aaron Freedman, a Waldbaum's executive, at Patrick's Pub on Northern Boulevard in Queens. Sometimes, it was observed, Sal Coletta and George Gamaldi, meat buyers for the Hills supermarket chain, would join them. Steinman and Freedman would take long pleasure weekends in Florida. The wiretaps told how Steinman had just spent $5,000 refurnishing the Queens apartment he shared with his girlfriend most afternoons. Newman, too, liked Florida high-living. He had a $200,000 house on Normandy Isle off Miami Beach. He bought a thirty-four-foot boat for $65,000 and then ran it aground his first day out, wrecking it.

Other conversations made clear that Tommy Dio had good reason to go to bat for Steinman and Newman. Trans-World brokerage was paying him gobs of money—$78,000 in June and July alone, which Newman thought was way too much. When Newman complained, Steinman reminded him that in May they had paid even more. When Newman indicated that an accountant was asking embarrassing questions about these payments, Steinman suggested getting rid of the accountant by bribing him.

By Christmas, 1971, the investigation was ready to move on to a new stage. Whether or not the wiretap tapes alone could have proven a criminal case in court against any particular individual, the tapes were overwhelming evidence that a mammoth racket was going on. They would clearly justify judicial support for an expanded inquiry. Snitow and Scotti decided the next step would be to obtain a warrant to raid the Trans-World office, seize all books and records and try to trace various payoffs back to inflated meat prices.

A raid seemed all the more urgent because of certain signals Nicholson and his men were picking up that the racketeers might have become aware of the investigation.

On a cold, snowy January 7, 1972, detectives from the New York district attorney's office burst in on Trans-World's headquarters in an old several-story building on Gansevoort and Little West Twelfth streets. They presented their warrant, but it didn't get them much. The walls and floor of the office were scrawled with red paint. There were swastikas, and the words "Jew Bastard." There were not, however, any books and records. Someone in the office said they had been destroyed in a vandalism attack a few days earlier. And sure enough, the local police precinct had received a report a few days earlier of a vandalism attack on Trans-World brokerage.

Nicholson quickly reported back to Snitow, who accompanied the team of detectives to a meeting in the D.A.'s office with Harry Kurzer, Trans-World's accountant. Kurzer said that he, too, had seen evidence of the destruction after Sol Steinman had called him to report the "attack."

Snitow recalls, "We expressed our disbelief . . . of the circumstances surrounding the destruction of those books and records, and we stated that we had examined the premises, that it was curious that only the books and records of Trans-World Fabricators had been destroyed, in that Trans-World Fabricators shared space with, or locker space with, another firm at the same premises, and only those books and records belonging to Trans-World Fabricators had been sprayed with red paint, and the books and records of the other firm, which were located on a lower shelf, I believe, within that same locker, had been curiously left alone. We explained that we had reason to believe that in fact the material had not been destroyed and in fact it had been taken by Steinman so that we would not be able to conduct our investigation."

So Snitow and Nicholson proceeded to grill Kurzer himself for his recollections. They told him time and again, in Snitow's words, "that we knew what was going on and we wanted Mr. Kurzer to corporate, and we were willing to give him immunity, notwithstanding that he might have been involved in these crimes. We wanted Moe Steinman. And Mr. Kurzer declined to cooperate in any way, shape, or form . . ."

Nicholson had long ago devised the strategy for this investigation. The goal would be different from previous investigations. It was a new and more comprehensive goal. And Snitow shared it, and Al Scotti, the head of the rackets bureau, shared it, and Frank Hogan, the D.A., shared it. This time the object would be not simply to jail a few meat sellers, or meat buyers, or union officers, who would then return to business, or be replaced by others who would continue to be used as pawns in the great extortion game that robbed every meat-eating resident in a four-state area. This time the City of New York was out to bust the racket itself—to break the power of Johnny Dio and Chappy Brescia and Paul Castellano—to get the Mafia out of the marketplace.

The mobsters, of course, were well insulated. Except for Castellano's relatively small meat business, which was more or less just a front for his real activities, the mobsters didn't sell the meat, or buy it, or get on the phone to talk price with the people who did. Yet there was one man who tied the mobsters to every crooked deal in the meat industry, one man who could truly break them, and that man was Moe Steinman. Steinman had to be nailed so solidly that he would spend the rest of his life in jail if he didn't talk.

CHAPTER 17

THE SURRENDER

The books and records were gone. The accountant wouldn't talk. The wiretap tapes talked, but not enough. Secrecy and the advantage of surprise had been forfeited, as the "vandalism attack" at Trans-World made plain. The next step was to apply power, to try to make key witnesses talk by putting the screws to them. A grand jury was convened. Snitow called in a secretary and began dictating subpoenaes and, ultimately, indictments.

Before the cops could use Moe Steinman to work up to the Mafia, they would have to start with the lowest, sleaziest elements in the meat racketeering network and work up to Moe Steinman. And who was lower and sleazier than Herbie Newman? Subpoenaes were drawn for Newman and Sol Steinman.

Moe Steinman found out about it and told his brother and his partner to get out of town. Sol did. But Newman went instead to an apartment on Thirty-fourth Street and First Avenue. He had rented the apartment to bring girls to, but now figured it could serve as a hideout. The cops had been following him there for months, however, and now did so again, and immediately served the subpoena. So Newman went to Miami. There he bought a doctor, who mailed letters to the court saying Newman had contracted a fatal heart condition and couldn't travel. This allowed two lucky detectives to escape the New York winter by going to Florida so they could investigate Newman's health. When they returned with photographs of Newman painting his $200,000 house and hauling rocks onto his lawn, the judge ruled that Newman was well enough to come home and face the grand jury.

Newman testified on fourteen separate occasions. Then he was indicted for criminal contempt of court for giving "conspicuously unbelievable, evasive, equivocal, and patently false answers."

After his indictment for criminal contempt, Newman went back down to Florida. When the time arrived for his trial, another doctor wrote that Newman was suffering from terminal cancer. This time, the doctor was telling the court the truth. Newman died in 1974, protecting Moe Steinman's secrets with his last breath.

As soon as the District Attorney's office saw that it would get nothing out of Herbie Newman—though it continued to offer Newman every opportunity to commit perjury—the office tried another avenue. The whole Moe Steinman investigation had started eighteen months earlier with the Iowa Beef incident. Maybe the investigation would end there. Iowa Beef was fifteen hundred miles away, but it did business in New York, and it had conspired in New York, and Iowa Beef and its officers were subject to the New York courts.

Out in Dakota City, doubts about the Steinman deal still smouldered in the minds of subordinate executives, ready to ignite if the District Attorney's office threw off the right spark. Then, in March and April, 1972, a flurry of grand jury subpoenaes arrived from New York, throwing Iowa Beef's sleepy midwestern headquarters into a turmoil. The D.A.'s office figured that somewhere in a company the size of Iowa Beef, there had to be an honest man—or at least a disgruntled one.

Maybe all the subpoenaes would produce a cooperative witness.

It wouldn't be Currier Holman. Holman immediately went looking for criminal defense counsel in Manhattan, and hired Richard Wynn and Jeffrey Atlas, two former assistants in Hogan's office who had recently gone off on their own to do defense work.

The week of May 15, 1972, Wynn and Atlas flew to Dakota City to begin preparing a defense against the inquiries being made by their former boss, the district attorney. Holman maintained his complete innocence. But his stonewall began to crumble almost immediately, for the subpoenaes had indeed found some honest men. The first was Howard Weiner, the treasurer. When Wynn and Atlas interviewed him, he laid the whole story on the line.

Howard Weiner flew to New York with his private lawyer and told the grand jury his story. It was perhaps the biggest break in the whole Moe Steinman investigation. With the information that Weiner supplied, Snitow was able to summon other officers from the firm and ask them for details—not just their own colored accounts of what went on, but precisely whether so-and-so said what Weiner said he said, or, if not, what actually happened.

By the time Holman himself came to New York July 21, the dam had broken. Everyone at the D.A.'s office expected that Holman would now cooperate. They expected him to testify that Moe Steinman had shaken him down for huge payments to support the continued bribery of supermarket executives and (more important, because the law provided much greater penalties for this) union officials. With Holman's testimony, Steinman could be indicted, and so could every union officer who had been at the Stanhope.

What the D.A.'s office still hadn't realized, however, was that Currier Holman's primary concern was and always had been selling his meat. And no matter how many lawyers and detectives Frank Hogan could marshal, Moe Steinman still controlled the New York meatmarket. Holman was not about to cross him.

Back in their own huddle, Snitow and Scotti agreed they couldn't charge Holman or Iowa Beef with a substantive crime—not unless somebody came forward with evidence showing that commissions to C.P. Sales had actually gone to pay bribes. And it was quite possible that Steinman had arranged the deal carefully enough that the connection didn't exist, and that the bribe money really *was* paid entirely from other funds. Morally, that might not amount to much of a distinction, but legally, it was everything.

Still, there was another road that the prosecutors could follow. They could charge a *conspiracy* to bribe—there was plenty of evidence of intent. Not only did they have the testimony of the subordinate officers at Iowa Beef, but they had secretly recorded Holman's own interview at the District Attorney's office. And while Holman on tape didn't exactly admit a conspiracy to bribe, he did admit that Steinman repeatedly told him there would be bribes paid. And he did admit that his own mental state at the time was one in which he believed that "everybody in the meat business in New York is a crook."

So the rackets squad would charge Holman and Steinman with conspiring with each other, and try to build from there.

In New York State, where a junkie can be sent up for life, the maximum penalty for conspiracy to bribe labor union officials—the worst thing Holman and Steinman could be charged with—carries one year.

That charge alone certainly wouldn't put Steinman as deeply into the corner as the prosecutors wanted him. On the other hand, the year would have to be served at a place like the Rikers Island jail, alongside pimps, junkies, and muggers. And Nicholson had a gut sense that Steinman was terrified of such a place. Moreover, if a year wasn't enough to impress Steinman, it might be enough to impress Holman. The mere threat of a plausible conspiracy indictment might impress him. And with Holman's cooperation, the D.A. could pin an extortion rap on Steinman that would carry a fifteen-year prison stretch.

Finally, there was the power of the federal government. As far as Scotti's men were concerned, Bill Aronwald and the strike force were on their team in this case. All sorts of federal anti-racketeering statutes carried penalties of up to twenty years, including interstate travel to break state laws.

Steinman had been to Iowa at least twice to see Holman, and Holman had come to New York at least three times to see Steinman. Moreover, bribery usually results in violation of income tax laws. So the D.A.'s men once again brought their laboriously assembled case to Aronwald.

In August, 1972, Aronwald assigned several Internal Revenue Service agents attached to the strike force to start questioning the man Nicholson figured was the best prospective witness regarding tax violations: Harry Kurzer, the accountant for Trans-World and other Steinman-related brokerages. In several meetings in late summer, Kurzer consistently denied that anything untoward had taken place in connection with the meat businesses. In an effort to end his reluctance,

335

Aronwald arranged a complicated deal under which Kurzer could receive immunity from prosecution if he incriminated himself while telling any story that turned out to be the full truth. But the denials continued. Finally, however, Kurzer agreed to throw them a bone.

The books of some of the brokerages contained long lists of employees who were relatives of Steinman, or of his fellow senior executives at Daitch-Shopwell supermarkets. Kurzer acknowledged that these were not bona fide employees of the brokerages. He said he had warned Steinman repeatedly that listing relatives on the employee payroll was a possibly illegal tax dodge, and that if Steinman wanted to give money to his relatives he couldn't deduct it from his corporate taxes as a business expense. He said Steinman had promised to clean up the books, but that Kurzer later discovered that Steinman had merely transferred the relatives to the books of a new firm that received cash from the other firms. The new illegal payoff firm happened to share an address with Walter Bodenstein, who was its principal officer.

In addition, Kurzer conceded to the feds that he had warned Steinman about some other "business expense" deductions that the IRS men had already grown suspicious of: the posh Steinman pad in Florida, for example, and big cars for everybody—and heavy bills at the Black Angus Restaurant and the Tammybrook Country Club, which was operated by an ex-convict meat dealer Steinman was friendly with. All this tax chiseling was petty stuff, of course, compared to the union and supermarket bribery the cops were after. But it was illegal, and carried potentially stiff penalties. The case was moving in the right direction so long as Steinman was being backed into a corner, a corner he couldn't get out of without turning on his Mafia friends.

On March 12, 1973, a joint federal-state press conference announced some indictments that shook the meat industry coast-to-coast. The People of the State of New York had charged Currier Holman, Moe Steinman, and Iowa Beef Processors itself with conspiring to commit commercial and labor union bribery. The federal government charged Holman, Steinman, and C.P. Sales with conspiring to violate a state anti-racketeering law and with interstate travel to carry on unlawful activities. The United States also charged Moe and Sol Steinman, Walter Bodenstein, and Herbie Newman with filing fraudulent tax statements in connection with the phony employees.

For the D.A.'s office, it was only the beginning. A new round of grand jury hearings was begun immediately, in an effort to build on the terror that had suddenly seized the meat district. Among the first witnesses to be called were Jules Tantleff and George George, both of whom had been implicated by wiretap evidence in 1971 in a Steinman scheme involving union payoffs. Like Newman before them, Tantleff and George each knew that if he pleaded the Fifth Amendment and refused to answer, he might be given immunity from prosecution: That would mean he would have to tattle on Moe Steinman, or else go to jail indefinitely for civil contempt of court. So both Tantleff and George took the Newman alternative: obfuscation.

On May 31, 1973, both men were indicted for criminal contempt of court, as Newman had been, for giving "conspicuously unbelievable, evasive, equivocal, and patently false answers," and Tantleff faced an additional charge of first degree perjury.

The indictments of Tantleff and George scared Moe Steinman, Nicholson's sources reported. Right now, Steinman faced just a year on the conspiracy charge. But if Tantleff and George were convicted and decided to talk rather than go to jail, they could testify to extortion, which carried up to fifteen years in a state prison.

Moreover, Nicholson had located Nat Meyerson, Steinman's other son-in-law, who had been involved with Bodenstein in a shady Medicaid factoring business and who had kept accounts for some Steinman-connected brokerages. Meyerson's marriage to Steinman's daughter Helene was breaking up, and Meyerson was feeling no particular love for the Steinman clan. He might testify. The meat buyers, too, were beginning to quake in the aftermath of the spring indictments. Six years before, industry leaders had come over en masse to testify in the Kissel case, and now perhaps, it could happen again. After all, the small cutting shops of Fourteenth Street were being hurt, not helped, by Steinman's ploy with boxed beef.

Also, the District Attorney's men still viewed the strike force as an ally. Trans-World was handling huge amounts of cash. If the federal government would lay claim on Steinman for back taxes, the bill could run in the millions and overwhelm him.

It was summer, now, 1973, and Nicholson knew exactly what he wanted Steinman to do. It would be more than just talk. Nicholson wanted Steinman to wear a hidden tape recorder in conversations with Tommy Dio, Chappy Brescia, and various members of the Castellano family. The recordings would provide conclusive back-up evidence in court.

Moe Steinman had been scrapping for nearly half a century in New York. He knew better than to leave himself without a way out. In

337

January, 1972, about the time Trans-World's books were destroyed by "vandals," Steinman had found himself a brilliant criminal lawyer, Elkan Abramowitz. Like Currier Holman, he had gone for his defense to a former assistant U.S. Attorney.

Steinman made the better choice. While Wynn and Atlas led their client, Holman, into the wired-up lair of the District Attorney to make an on-the-record confession, Abramowitz played the prosecution like a violin. He knew the feuding that sometimes goes on between rival law enforcement agencies. He saw the presence of both state and federal agencies in the meat investigation, and was able to turn the other side's superior numbers to Steinman's advantage (though he modestly denies now that this was his intent).

On one side was Frank Snitow, inexperienced and relying heavily on Al Scotti and Bob Nicholson. Scotti and Nicholson had been chasing the Mafia for years. They had already achieved too many false victories through plea bargaining. This time they were hunting bear. They had an unmistakable bloodlust for Steinman and the higher-ups. If somebody was going to leave a door open for Steinman's escape, it would have to be Aronwald.

Within days of the time the joint federal-state indictments against Steinman were filed in March 1973, Abramowitz dropped by Aronwald's office "to talk preliminarily about discovery and other matters." Marvin Sontag, the IRS agent assigned to the case, sat in on the meeting. The subject of Steinman's possible "cooperation" came up. But Abramowitz says he left the office telling the strike force team that Steinman probably wouldn't want to cooperate because the mobster thought he could defend himself successfully.

Nevertheless, there's evidence that Steinman was secretly preparing even then to deal with the federal prosecutors by squealing on selected bribe recipients, while protecting his true friends. Certainly he would not turn over information on anyone with independent ties to the Mafia—only on those whose criminal dealings were done exclusively through Moe Steinman. That way they couldn't spread the investigation further if they were to start squealing themselves. And the Mob wouldn't be angry.

Irving Stern, the regional butchers' union leader, was just the kind of man Steinman was likely to turn on. Steinman couldn't stand Stern personally. Stern had been a leftist labor organizer at one time, and still preached the language of militancy. Now he was dealing in dirty money, like the others—and yet not like them. Stern seemed out of place as a racketeer, and was privately derided by Steinman and the butchers' leaders Steinman was closest to.

By May, 1973, word of the investigation had spread to every bar on Fourteenth Street, and Stern was visibly scared. A lot of people noticed it. Nicholson got an anonymous phone call saying that Stern had cashed a large amount of bonds, supposedly around $200,000 worth, in an effort to hide his bribery hoard. During this period, Stern foolishly went for legal advice to Walter Bodenstein. Bodenstein welcomed Stern to his home in Westchester, then secretly tape-recorded the proceedings as the union leader worried out loud about the loot he had stored up from Moe Steinman. The recording confirmed what Nicholson had been told about a large amount of bonds. Later it became a valuable tool in Moe Steinman's arsenal. It put Stern in a bag that Steinman could deliver at will.

Justice takes a holiday in August. Almost all judges go on vacation the whole month, and if there are no judges there are no courts, and so lawyers often take the month off, too—including prosecutors. As a rule, no business is considered so urgent that it can't wait until September. Frank Snitow assumed it would be no different in August, 1973. When the courts closed, Snitow cleared Moe Steinman from his mind and took his wife to Europe.

For Elkan Abramowitz, however, the August doldrum offered a brilliant opportunity to strike. He called Aronwald's office. Aronwald was on vacation, but Abramowitz got Sontag, the IRS agent. Abramowitz said he wanted to find out what kind of deal he could get if Steinman would give the government some very big cases. Sontag reached Aronwald, and the federal prosecutor agreed to come back from vacation the next week to talk with Abramowitz. Not one word of this was breathed to anyone else, particularly not anyone from the District Attorney's office.

It so happened that the Internal Revenue Service had been working for some time on an investigation into suspected violations by supermarket chains of the wage and price control act then in effect. Two years earlier, President Nixon had launched his surprise inflation-fighting program by freezing prices and wages. There had followed several "phases" during which prices and wages were allowed to move a little bit according to the strictures of Washington. (Ironically, Irving Stern was appointed by the Nixon Administration to a wage-price board that supervised the controls for the food industry.) In June, 1973, a new freeze was announced, which was to end August 13. There would follow another "phase," and then, finally, prices and wages would go back to being determined by the people who were buying, selling, working and hiring. The problem was that a lot of people had really been operating that way all along, even when it was illegal. And the IRS, which was charged with finding and punishing these people, was having a tough time of it.

The IRS knew good and well, for example, that something funny was going on in the meat business. Despite its suspicions, however, the IRS apparently didn't want to assign accountants, lawyers, computers, and clericals to fish for months among meat purchase records with uncertain result. So, with the price freeze now due to expire in a week or two, the IRS still didn't have a case to take to court to punish the food chains. Legally, indictments could be filed after the freeze, but practically, they would have lost much of their appeal.

Suddenly, in absolute defiance of coincidence, in walked Elkan Abramowitz and Moe Steinman with an offer of sworn testimony and documents to show that under-the-table agreements existed between New York area supermarket chains and wholesale meat dealers. The excessive part of the payment was to be deferred until after controls went off. Thus the effective wholesale prices were actually higher than the ones posted, which explained why retail mark-ups looked excessive. And Steinman could name a score of supermarket chains that had participated in such deals.

Twenty supermarket chains indicted for overcharging customers! Aronwald had to take note. "He saw the cameras rolling," a lawyer at the D.A.'s office later remarked.

Would Steinman also tell his story of bribery in the meat industry, Aronwald wanted to know? Abramowitz said that Steinman would name some buyers and union officials, but wouldn't identify them until after he got his deal in writing. Would Steinman also agree to testify against any Mafia people? Steinman didn't have any dealings with organized crime people, Aronwald was told. Steinman liked to be seen in their company, and pretended to be friends of theirs, but only because it made people afraid of him. If Aronwald wanted his supermarket indictments he would have to agree to take Moe Steinman's word for that. No Mafia. Aronwald agreed.

And, Abramowitz went on, not only would Aronwald have to come across with a sweet deal closing out any existing or prospective federal charges against Steinman, he also would have to get the state off

Steinman's back, too. In order to get the supermarkets, Aronwald would have to deal with Scotti on Steinman's behalf to make sure the mobster was protected on all flanks. And still more: Abramowitz said all charges would have to be dropped against Sol Steinman and Walter Bodenstein.

Abramowitz said he also would like charges dropped against Steinman himself in exchange for the supermarkets. But they all knew that Scotti would never agree to dismiss the state's pending charge against Steinman in the Iowa Beef Case. Scotti would insist that Steinman plead guilty to the Iowa Beef indictment or its equivalent as part of any kind of deal. But the state charge carried a one-year maximum sentence, and the state would not be able to charge Steinman with any other crime if he put his story on the record under a broad grant of immunity.

So how would it be if Steinman also agreed to plead guilty to one federal tax count? Aronwald could then promise to recommend in court that Steinman's federal sentence be made concurrent with the state sentence. As Abramowitz well knew, a one-year concurrent federal sentence would actually be to Steinman's benefit, because Steinman could then serve all his time in a relatively comfortable federal detention center with other tax cheats, and could avoid the ungodly world of pimps, junkies, muggers, and hold-up men to be found in state prison.

Aronwald took the bait. Justice was indeed taking a holiday in August, 1973.

During the second week of August, Aronwald called Scotti. Steinman had agreed to plead guilty and cooperate fully, he said. But a formal deal had to be signed immediately, because the price freeze act was about to expire. Scotti, startled, explained that it was Snitow's case, and Snitow would be in Europe for another week. Aronwald insisted it couldn't wait. The deal would be sealed the following Monday, August 13, in Abramowitz's office, and the D.A. was invited to send a representative. Aronwald insists he explained the whole deal to Scotti over the phone and that Scotti had agreed to it.

Scotti says he told Aronwald that he wouldn't intervene in an assistant's case, and begged Aronwald to wait one week for Snitow to return. Aronwald wouldn't do it. At the same time, Abramowitz says that Aronwald was beseeching him to make a separate deal for Steinman with the strike force, leaving the state out of it, but Abramowitz wouldn't do that.

Scotti tried to get in touch with Snitow. Snitow couldn't be reached at his hotels, because his wife, who preferred the charm of small pensiones, had changed their tour arrangements. Scotti went to Interpol, the international agency that was created to aid cooperation among police departments of various countries. Interpol agents began a bizarre manhunt for Snitow across Europe.

Nicholson also was on vacation. Lou Montello was sent to Abramowitz's office August 13 without authority to agree to anything. Apparently he didn't participate in any negotiations, but, as instructed, brought back a copy of the deal worked out by the lawyers. Aronwald says he got a call later that day from Paul Vitrano, head of the D.A.'s detective squad, saying the deal had been approved by Scotti. Says Vitrano, "I don't recall having made that call, and I wouldn't have had the authority to do it. If anybody made a call it would have to have been Scotti." Everyone agrees Scotti didn't make it.

The next day, August 14, 1973, Aronwald signed the agreement on behalf of both the state and federal governments. The agreement was explicit on that point. Abramowitz says that Aronwald told him the D.A.'s office had approved the deal, that Montello's presence led him to believe it, and that once his client Steinman started talking, there could be no further state or federal prosecution beyond the guilty pleas Steinman had agreed to make.

Nicholson—back from vacation in midweek—and Montello went to Abramowitz's office, anxious to find out what Steinman would say, disbelieving it would be the whole truth. They found Aronwald, Sontag, some other federal officials, and Abramowitz. They did not find the guest of honor, who chose to be more than an hour late. And when Steinman finally did come through the office door, Bob Nicholson was more disgusted than surprised.

"He'd been drinking," Nicholson recalls. "He walked in with a quart bottle of Dewars in his hand and slammed the bottle on the table."

Nicholson felt himself filling with rage. The racketeer from the gutter had successfully intimidated the head of the federal strike force and all his men. They were supposed to be ridding society of people like Steinman. Yet Steinman was putting on an act designed to cow them, to put *them* on the defensive. And it was working. Nicholson looked around the room at Aronwald and the IRS men, all waiting obediently for Steinman to tell them as much or as little as he cared to. And if Steinman was really going to open up about the Mafia, Nicholson wondered, why hadn't Aronwald invited any FBI men to hear it?

The racketeer with the bottle in his hand launched into his life story. "I was a poor boy from Poland. . . . I had nothing. . . . I got to be a big man. . . . I got a lot of money. . . . I'm doing this for my family. . . ." He carried on about his daughters, about how much he loved them. He complained that investigators had been bothering the girls ever since their names had been found padding his payrolls. "I'm not like you people," he rambled on. "I drink. I carry on. I know you all think I'm associated with organized crime and the Mafia," he said. Then he denied it. He said he just "set out to live my life to give that impression." He wanted to be seen with them. But he didn't really know them.

"But I do know about bribery," he said. "I do know about meat buyers, union officers, wage-price . . ."

Nicholson: "He was naming the companies, and whetting everybody's appetite. And I sat there listening to him and the only thing I could think of was, 'You're a liar.' He was dominating the conference. He was running the whole show. The government officials were there joking with him."

Steinman returned a cold stare. "He didn't like me, and I had no love for him either," Nicholson says. Nobody spoke. And then Nicholson and Montello fully realized that the federal men were taking Steinman's side. The two detectives, who had been investigating the meat industry for more than nine years, sat looking at the newcomers who were suddenly pulling their carefully woven carpet out from under them. Everybody in the room seemed to believe what Steinman was saying—everybody but Nicholson, Montello, and, of course, Steinman himself.

"You say you're going to give names, dates, places on bribery," Nicholson said. "How are we going to know you're telling us the truth."

"You can get other people in," Steinman said. He said he would provide corroborative witnesses if the government would grant them immunity. There was his brother, and his son-in-law. "I got books, records," he added.

Then Nicholson asked the kicker: "Would you be willing to wear a concealed tape recorder and have conversations with these people about these instances?"

Steinman looked nervously at Abramowitz. Abramowitz showed no expression. Nobody spoke.

"Yeah," Steinman finally said. "I would."

"Then let's go right from this meeting down to our office and get started," Nicholson said. That would leave no time for Steinman to tip anybody off, or to rig any conversations. It would leave no time for second thoughts. There would be instant proof.

It was Aronwald—not Abramowitz—who leapt up. He went out to the hallway. Nicholson followed, and this is his version of what happened there.

"Steinman isn't going to wear a wire," Aronwald declared. "It would cause too many problems. Problems with the Justice Department. I got to go to Washington to get permission to let him wear a wire."

"*We* don't have to go to Washington," Nicholson told him. "We [the D.A.'s squad] could do it easily. We can wire him this very day."

"No," Aronwald responded. "That means we'd be making new cases and this thing will drag on forever. The wage and price violations are urgent. We need his testimony. He couldn't testify and wear a wire at the same time."

"I know this man," Nicholson pleaded. "I've had him under investigation for the better part of ten years. This man never told the truth in his life. You have to have some kind of control over him. Send him out with a wire and you'll know soon enough whether he's telling the truth or not."

Aronwald stared back at Nicholson. "I believe him," he said.

Nicholson didn't believe Steinman, and he didn't believe Aronwald believed Steinman, either. "He knew as well as I did that if Moe Steinman went out with a wire we'd have a new investigation going within twenty-four hours. What happened was, he just saw the case slipping away from him and becoming a New York County District Attorney's case again."

Montello and Nicholson agree with this description of the meeting. Sontag says he, too, agrees that the strike force sold out Nicholson's investigation; then he indicates that he's being sarcastic, and tells an interviewer to believe anything the interviewer wants to believe; then he hangs up. Aronwald denies that Steinman ever agreed to wear a wire when talking to Mafia figures. He says the district attorney's office in its wiretap investigation "produced absolutely no evidence of any criminality whatsoever against Moe Steinman or anyone else." About the more general changes that he blew the Steinman investigation, Aronwald says, "I don't care to respond . . . You're trying to deep-six me."

Later that day, Interpol caught up with Snitow on the canals of Venice. Racing to the nearest phone, Snitow called his office. Told what had happened, he was furious. He offered to fly home immediately, also at his own expense, to try to straighten things out. He was told it was too late for that. Bill Aronwald's signature was already on a letter agreement with Steinman. The racketeer was already confessing under a grant of immunity. It would be impossible to make further cases against him.

It seemed the news couldn't get worse for Snitow, but it did. When Snitow returned on Monday, August 20, 1973, Nicholson and Montello gave him an account he could scarcely believe. He remembers Nicholson was "livid—we were on Moe Steinman's turf, and Moe Steinman seemed to be controlling things." Snitow asked to be included in the interviews, figuring there might be a way to salvage the situation. Now that it would be forever impossible to use testimony from Currier Holman to convict Steinman of extortion, as originally planned, at least Snitow might try the reverse. He might get Steinman to help convict Holman in the Iowa Beef case.

So for two or three days of interviews, Snitow probed for Steinman's story—and was shocked to find that it backed up Currier Holman's story. Steinman insisted that he had never intended to use Iowa Beef's commissions to bribe anyone. He insisted that Holman had never believed Steinman would do such a thing. In fact, Steinman insisted that his books and records would show that all his bribes were paid with money from other brokerage deals. The money that went to C.P. Sales could all be legitimately accounted for.

By the end of the first day, Snitow and Aronwald were having words. By the end of the third day, the whole deal had blown up in an explosion of tempers. The D.A.'s office was claiming Steinman was lying, which would have abrogated the agreement. But the deal Abramowitz and Aronwald had drawn up required a mutual decision by federal and state authorities that Steinman was lying before the deal died. Aronwald stuck with Steinman. Abramowitz gallantly tried to make peace during an afternoon at the D.A.'s office, but failed. Sources who were there recall "an almost violent confrontation" during which Scotti—who Aronwald insists had approved the whole deal—called Aronwald "a liar," and accused him "of allowing Steinman to run the investigation."

The D.A.'s men should have expected as much. Walter Bodenstein, Steinman's son-in-law, whose indictment for tax fraud had just been dropped in exchange for Steinman's "cooperation," was still operating under a contract with Iowa Beef that would soon be worth $1 million a year or more. In fact, just at the time of the Iowa Beef investigation, when Steinman's testimony could have been deadly to Holman, the C.P. Sales contract was being extended for another five years. For that kind of reward, Steinman was not about to turn on Currier Holman.

Says an important figure in the case from the D.A.'s office, "Steinman absolutely boxed us in because of the unwillingness of another law enforcement agency to stand up to him with us. Once Steinman knew Aronwald was willing to believe him, he didn't need us anymore. Rather than get support [from the strike force], we were told, if you don't want to go ahead with it, okay, they believe him, they'll go ahead. It was made to appear as if we were sabotaging the investigation. Aronwald thought he would really get these guys. Moe supposedly would produce and he didn't."

"The effect it had," said Nicholson, "was that we never again got a chance to talk to Moe Steinman."

As a final irony, the Justice Department in Washington vetoed the prosecution of the wage-price cases Aronwald had been attracted to. The department decided it wasn't worth trying a crime that would no longer be a crime when the trial occurred. Aronwald has argued since then that the wage-price cases weren't the most important part of the Steinman deal anyway—"just the most pressing."

CHAPTER 18

THE SCRAPS

In the spring of 1974, in advance of the pending Iowa Beef trial, the D.A.'s men made one last effort to get Moe Steinman's cooperation. Snitow brought the mobster before Judge Burton Roberts to make the guilty plea the Aronwald deal committed him to make. Normally when a judge takes a guilty plea, he requires the accused person to put on the record a full confession of whatever deeds he is pleading guilty to. This record in Steinman's case might create evidence against Holman. But under questioning from Judge Roberts, Steinman steadfastly refused to concede that he or Holman had ever planned to bribe anyone with commissions paid by Iowa Beef. Faced with this, Roberts refused to accept Steinman's guilty plea, and ruled that the state would have to prove the charges at a trial, infuriating Snitow more than ever.

The Iowa Beef case came to trial in June, 1974, and the state had problems. Not only was there no evidence from Steinman, but the case was open to question morally. Holman had conspired to bribe his way into the New York market, all right, but who could argue that Holman and his boxed beef didn't have a right to be in the New York market in the first place? Can you convict a man for what he does with a gun at his head, even if it's only a financial gun?

346

On the first day of trial, the defense lawyers, Richard Wynn and Jeffry Atlas, made a tactical blunder that may well have cost them the case. They waived a trial by jury, and asked Judge Roberts to try the case himself. They reasoned that consumers were so angry over high meat prices, a jury would want to hang any meat producer it could get its hands on, and that no housewife could give Currier Holman a fair shake. What they ignored was that Holman's only hope for acquittal was the flexibility by which juries can depart occasionally from the legal straight and narrow to allow for moral right and wrong. A jury might be persuaded that Holman had no real choice but to break the law and pay Moe Steinman, that any other man might have done the same thing. Judge Roberts had no such flexibility. His only real option was to rule that Holman had broken the law, and was therefore guilty. And that's exactly what happened.

Actually, there should have been little doubt that he would convict. Indeed, the decision was about as favorable to Holman as anyone had a right to expect. Roberts all but made the executive into a martyr.

"IBP's dire financial position made it imperative to him that the fastest and surest way of opening the lucrative New York market to boxed beef be utilized," Judge Roberts wrote. "There are very few people in American business who would have acted differently in these circumstances," the judge continued. "In a certain sense, this court will always consider you a victim of the extortionate practices" of union officials and supermarket executives in New York. And he gave Holman an unconditional discharge—no punishment.

After thus writing off the major product of the three-year investigation by Nicholson and the rackets squad, Roberts angrily and blindly lashed out at the massive injustice of it all. But he picked the wrong targets. Incredibly, he attacked Snitow and the District Attorney's office.

Rising from the bench in a rage, Roberts castigated the District Attorney's office for making a deal with Steinman, whom he called "a barracuda," to convict Holman, whom he referred to as "a minnow." He accused the D.A.'s office of cooperating in the federal deal to give Steinman no more than a year in jail in exchange for his testimony. He cried that the deal was so outrageous he had been "sorely tempted" to acquit Holman "in the interest of justice" just to show his contempt for the extortionate villainy of Steinman.

Moe Steinman served a grand total of six months in relatively comfortable circumstances.

This was the thanks Nicholson got for eleven years.

BEYOND REASON

A Condensation of the book by

MARGARET TRUDEAU

In Cassis, in southern France, I filmed my second picture—
Guardian Angel—*finished this memoir, and learned of the
suicide of Yves Lewis, my distant love.*

PROLOGUE

One sunny Wednesday in August 1969, I caught the ferry from Vancouver to the Sechelt Peninsula. It was a brilliant blue morning, with a slight haze over the mountains, promising perfect beach weather. I was off to see my maternal grandmother, Rose Bernard, in her cottage at Robert's Creek, deep in the cedar forest—the scene of my happiest childhood days. It was no accident. I regarded that little house—with its tar-paper roof and robin's egg blue window frames, its neat garden of roses, fruit trees and vegetables carved from the great forest that stretched miles about and beyond—as the only possible place to go. I was a fully-fledged flower child of twenty, in tinted granny glasses and peasant clothes.

I was not so much a hippy as a failed hippy, a hippy without a cause. I had gone through the North American adolescent experience—sixties high school graduate, university with the student activists, rebellion against my parents, seven months on the hippy trail in Morocco—and come out the other end with even less idea about what was to become of me than when I had begun. It wasn't entirely my fault. I embarked on my search for mysticism and freedom because I fell in love with Yves who was the apotheosis of that world and insisted his mate should be the same. I tried. I smoked pot with the best of them and came to love it; I shed all my bourgeois belongings and came home with nothing but a small knapsack containing two pairs of jeans, and a collection of fashionable, white embroidered cotton shirts; I frizzed my hair; I found a diet so extreme that people actually died on it—the Oshawa Zen macrobiotic diet of brown rice and a few, carefully selected but none too nutritious, vegetables.

351

But Yves Lewis, my liberated lover, was not impressed. Returning smug and soulful I had presented myself to him at Berkeley, California—only to be turned down. I wanted to bake whole wheat bread and talk love and peace; Yves and his friends had their minds on war. He wanted to show off his arsenal of rifles and hand grenades (for the Symbionese Liberation Front? I never did discover); I wanted to settle down and have babies. I fled the tear gas and the revolutionaries of Berkeley in horror. And rejected.

Vancouver, with my healthy, sane parents, was clearly out. Who could stand a father who had been a cabinet minister and was now chairman of a prospering capitalist enterprise, the Lafarge cement company? Or a doting pretty mother, who cooked roast beef and chocolate mousse? Or, come to that, four normal, obedient sisters who had the temerity to laugh at me? It was insufferable for me. I was insufferable for them. With what dignity I could muster I settled on my grandmother's peaceful home as a balm for their mockery and denseness; a sparkling escape from Vancouver with its Coca-Cola advertisements and gas fumes which repelled me.

Robert's Creek is a beautiful place, and perfect for self-indulgence. Grandma's house stood on a bluff overlooking the Howe Sound, a wilderness of wild roses and hedge flowers where I could sit and day-dream, watching the endless passing of tugs towing the log booms down to Vancouver. Occasionally I stirred myself sufficiently out of my reveries to wander down the wiggling path to the sea.

Some days I didn't feel like yearning for Yves, or dwelling on Morocco, so I basked in sentimental nostalgia for my childhood summers. I wallowed in memories: the sweet smell of grandma's loganberry pies and buns stealing into the dormitory I shared with my sisters; the shivering dawns when she harried us out of bed and we sat warming our toes by her wood stove; the nights we slept out on the veranda overlooking the bay, where the bats came whirling through the porch, sending shivers of delight down our spines as we hurled ourselves under the bedclothes.

As the days of this peaceful existence became weeks and the weeks threatened to become months, I began to wonder what would become of me. Join a commune in the wilds? Teach handicapped children? Become a nun? My wounded sensibilities could clearly stand no violent exercise or excessive noise. If there was one thing that shone out it was that never, under any circumstances, would I join the despicable bourgeois world of bridge clubs and whiskies before dinner. I would never fall to that level of "respectability." I felt ashamed and saddened for my friends who had forsaken the true path for such misguided values.

I was moping happily one day in the garden when the telephone rang. It was a party line: three long and one short ring meant it was for us, a rare occurrence. Grandma answered: it was my mother, doubtless with some trivial and prosaic questions for me. Was I eating well? Had I thought what I would *do?* I mooched ungraciously to the phone.

"Margaret," my mother was trying, and failing, to sound casual, "an old boyfriend of yours has just called, someone we once met on a holiday who took you waterskiing. He wants to take you out on a date."

I was outraged.

"Mother, I don't want a date with *anyone.*" My tone sounded as if she proposed something indecent. She was suitably crestfallen. "Aren't you even interested to know who it is?"

A prickle of unseemly curiosity stirred inside me. I tried to beat it back. I failed.

"Well," it came out at last, with extreme bad grace, "who then?"

"Pierre Trudeau."

CHAPTER 1

GROWING UP

My first memory is of my younger sister Betsy's birth—sitting in the drawing room waiting to decide on a name, when I was four years old and used to being the baby myself. I cannot truly remember how I felt. My next image is far more revealing. My father came home from a trip—What trip? Where to? The details have gone—and he brought me a pair of blue sunglasses. Gingerly, with infinite care at handling such a precious object, I put them on. I have this vivid memory of astonishment: "These are for *me.* Just for me—all by myself." Amazed that in a family of five girls I was going to possess something that was just mine, and that my father had actually thought of buying something specially for me.

My next memory comes later, though the concern is the same. I am going to school and I am extremely excited. My three elder sisters— Heather, Janet and Rosalind—attend Rockcliffe Park public school already, and now, after so much waiting, I'm at last to go with them each morning. In the playground the teachers line us up and discover that I am, by several inches, the smallest. It's an honor, clearly, being the smallest in the school and I try to take it as such, but I have misgivings. Is it right to be so small?

Injustice figures next in the line of childhood reflections. My memory produces a music lesson with a redfaced teacher wearing bright purple lipstick. She is getting us to produce words to the scales. "What do these notes sound out?" she asks, and sings, "Da, *da*, da." The little girl sitting next to me puts up her hand. "I *love* you." The teacher beams. "And what about: da, da, *da*, da, da?" Trembling with my own cleverness I raise my arm and chant: "I do *not* love you." I was snatched out of my wicker chair and ordered to stand in the corner while the teacher summoned the principal to tell me what a wicked, cruel child I was. I was too upset to explain, too shocked to cry.

Until I was nine my father was a minister of fisheries in Lester B. Pearson's cabinet. A big, energetic man, he worked late into each night and we didn't see much of him. But his influence, the unmistakable stamp of his authority, was on everything we did. The childhood friends, the fads and passions of my early years, pale into a shadowy insignificance today beside his towering presence. My mother, whom we all adored, was a tall woman with hazel eyes; she was a worrier, but she seldom judged and she was never vicious.

Dad was the eldest son in a family of five, and the Sinclairs emigrated from Scotland soon after his second birthday. His father, also James, had been a schoolteacher in Granges, Banffshire, and having struggled and totally failed to make enough of a living to feed four children—the fifth was born later—decided to seek his fortune in the colonies.

He chose Canada quite simply because his passion was fishing, and he knew that one of the greatest salmon rivers in the world runs along the west coast of Canada. Every penny of their savings went on the boat crossing, and the first years in Vancouver, then a small fishing port filling up fast with immigrants, were a struggle.

They never regretted the move. Vancouver is green and lush with mountains running down to the water, and the fish were like no fish Jimmy had ever seen. He prospered so excellently with his teaching career—later pioneering new training colleges—that before long he had saved enough to buy a cottage up the coast, build his own smokehouse for the salmon, and indulge a passion that never dimmed. When I was a child I often sat on the steps of the cottage, listening to his stories of the move from Scotland and of great fishing sagas, or singing sea shanties with him. When my grandmother, who disapproved of such things, was away from home, he would brew me up a special treacle from a secret recipe—in a flat pan he would melt down butter and sugar that turned as hard as stone. His accent remained strongly Scottish until the day he died.

My father inherited not just the Scottish inflections—which come back even to this day, particularly when he embarks on one of his more colorful stories—but the dour outlook of a Presbyterian Scot. An excessively strict upbringing had left its mark. There was no question but that he must excel at school, and he did, getting a place at the University of British Columbia and later becoming a Rhodes scholar at Oxford. He met my mother, Kathleen Bernard, daughter of a modest Vancouver railwayman, when like his father he became a schoolteacher; Kathleen was his brightest mathematics pupil. There were twelve years between them, and very properly he waited for her to finish school and study as a nurse before proposing.

We did everything as a family: my father called us the Brawling Sinclairs and took pride in the racket and the standing of such a respectably large group, even if we *were* all girls. My sister Betsy was his favorite, with her blond hair and her close resemblance to my mother; she was his dream daughter and he had a joke about how when Betsy grew up he was going to turn my mother in and marry her. Betsy conformed, but retained her wonderfully dry sense of humor. Heather, seven years older than me and the eldest, was a redhead with a freckled face and blue eyes and a strong will. She went her own way. Janet, two years her junior, was a gawky and awkward child who kept lizards in jars and picked up stray dogs and was only saved from being the continual underdog herself by forming a particularly close bond with my maternal grandmother. Lin, fifteen months my senior, probably had the loneliest of childhoods. Because I was a quick learner and skipped grade three, she and I found ourselves in the same class. At one time she became fat, wore glasses and took refuge in harlequin romances. It was not to last—Lin became Miss Simon Fraser University, and then Miss Radiology.

As for me, I was my father's son, the boy he never had. My sisters were all going to succeed in their own particular ways, but I was the one singled out, the one with the extra spark, the child most like my father. My mother considered me the most selfish of the family—and she was probably right.

Culture for me, long into my teens, was rock music. I was fourteen when the Beatles hit Canada. Lin and I would sneak out to the garage and listen to their songs on the car radio. We weren't allowed too much music in the house.

If we lacked culture we got the open spaces instead. When John Diefenbaker brought the Conservatives back into power my father left politics. He bought an old log cabin up Vancouver's most northern mountain, Hollyburn, with no running water or electricity, deep in the forest surrounded by fir trees, pines and blueberry bushes. There were mountain lakes all around and deep snow in winter which we had to gather in buckets and melt down for water. We named the cabin "High Hopes," and every weekend either took the chairlift up the mountains or, when that was out of order, as it often was, we hiked up, the provisions on our back. It took two hours. During the daylight hours we built, dug and swam. At night we played cards—Hearts, Whist, Crazy Eights, Cribbage—and Monopoly. My father loved Scrabble.

My father's son, I played the part. I was a tomboy—I built forts in the woods, and had adventures on the lakes. These were happy times: a great converted dormitory for us and our cousins in the attic, an oil stove with a perpetually simmering pot of soup for children as they came in cold from outdoors. That cabin was the best gift my father ever gave me: much later the outdoor life was the very one I tried so hard to create for Pierre and the children.

When I was sixteen I was chosen by Delbrook Senior High to represent them on the teen fashion council of the Hudson's Bay Company store in the center of town. One girl from every school in the neighborhood came and spent Saturday mornings listening to a model talk about grooming and poise and charm; the afternoons were devoted to helping out in the different departments. The idea was to train potential managers. I loved those days; when I got to university I spent my first long summer vacation working in the store full time. It was then that the manager asked me to switch from sociology into commerce so as to prepare for a future job on the staff. I would, he told me, make an excellent manager. They even offered me a full scholarship. I was flattered, but it never really occurred to me to accept.

I graduated in the summer of 1965. A couple of years ago I saw that a television series had been made about my generation: *Whatever Happened to the Class of '65?* They had a point, treating us like a social phenomenon. We really were the last of the innocents, the end of an era—middle-class kids who never rebelled, girls who wouldn't have dreamed of wearing jeans to school, whose greatest dream on earth was to become a cheerleader.

I was given the choice of going on to the University of British Columbia, a traditional conservative university with high academic standards, or of going to the brand new university of Simon Fraser, then barely completed. I, of course, wanted Berkeley in California, but that was out of the question. My father, in his inimitable way, helped me make the decision: he announced that if Lin and I opted for U.B.C.— both universities were some half hour's drive from my parents' house— then we could make our own way there. If on the other hand we agreed on Simon Fraser, he would buy us a car. The friendly persuasion worked, and we acquired a Volkswagen.

Simon Fraser had been built on top of a mountain overlooking Vancouver: the long, curvy road that led up to it added to a sense of isolation and remoteness. It was all concrete and glass and, because Vancouver is a rainy city, it was gray, always gray. My first year was simply an extension of my schooldays: a continuation of middle-class respectability. I was a good student; I dated a football player; I excelled in sociology and won myself a first-class scholarship.

Student activism in Canada was born my second year, 1966. I was studying political science, sociology and anthropology, and my education took place continuously both inside and outside the classroom. The dean of my department was Thomas Bottommore, a Marxist scholar who influenced me deeply. There were Maoists and Liberals, Conservatives and Trotskyites among us and we talked and talked and talked. Stuck up on that rainswept mountain arguing was a formative way in which to spend a year. It changed me.

I started to date Philip, an English teaching assistant who was in Canada to study for his Ph.D. on revolutions. A gentle, serious man, he dictated that our dates should be spent mainly studying together. A good Saturday night for us was a bottle of wine, classical music on the record player and talking politics. This was the start of a new rebellion at home. My father, never appreciative of any boyfriend, was downright rude to Philip. Somewhere along the way he had become antagonistic toward radical Englishmen, and he sensed in Philip, quite wrongly, an agitator. His hair was a bit long. He wore a beard. And he was small—he had had rickets as a baby during the war. And my father, who could perfectly well tolerate a dim football player, couldn't stand a mild revolutionary.

My involvement in politics throughout, apart from my personal battles

357

over Philip, was a curious one: that of a spectator, but never that of participant. Just as I had always turned away at the last moment from becoming cheerleader at school, so now I didn't join the students in their sit-ins. What did happen to me was that I began to question things in a way I never had before, and the form that took made my father yell at me that I was an insolent little girl. We tried a reconciliation scene at Waikiki Beach in Honolulu on a peace-offering family holiday, but that was a total failure. On our return I packed my bags and moved out.

My efforts at lodging and sharing apartments formed the next decisive step in my education. I took as little as possible in the way of allowance from my father and soon found myself installed with a professor, Michael Mulkay, his wife Lucy, who was a fashion designer, and their three-year-old daughter. I learned a lot from them.

Michael and Lucy taught me to listen to music and to look at pictures and, having heard me moan and grumble over my courses, suggested I try some English ones instead. It was through them that I came upon the Romantics, William Blake, Coleridge and Keats. I got obsessed with the idea of freedom, and choices of ways of living, with materialism and greed, with the influence of pop music and revolt. They were good months for me. In the last two semesters Marx was definitely dead. I began to listen to Timothy Leary and Buckminster Fuller; here were my new gods. (The summer after I married Pierre, Buckminster Fuller came to lunch. I asked the cook to prepare something especially delicious for my hero. He came in, sat down, refused lunch, saying he had no time to waste on food, spoke incomprehensibly and without interruption for an hour and a half, and then told me that he was painting a tapestry of careful thought and I was not to interrupt. When he left I cried.)

The last two years were crowded with new emotions. A group of university friends introduced me to pot in a cottage facing the sea, where we sat on the beach for hour after hour listening to "Penny Lane" and "Strawberry Fields Forever" on our cassette tapes. When it rained, we retreated indoors and watched the spray hitting the window panes, and had intense conversations about cabbages and kings. Pop music meant a great deal to me—Janis Joplin and her rasping, pleading voice; the Beatles, who seemed to stand for good; and the Rolling Stones, who stood for bad. Because I was the newest arrival, I cooked the meals, choosing to ignore all that Kate Millett had taught me in *Sexual Politics,* preferring a life of dependency and discovery. It was easy to get marijuana. We grew it in our gardens in the summertime or bought the grass that came up cheap and plentiful from Mexico and California. I drank it all in—the music, the drugs, the life. I jibed only at opium, scared off by Coleridge, and though some of my friends tried L.S.D., there was no cocaine about. I did try mescaline one day, and spent eight hours sitting up a tree wishing I were a bird.

It was in this bewildered though cheerful cast of mind that I set off for what my father announced was to be our last holiday together as a family. Heather stayed behind because she had married Tom; Janet didn't come because she was in France. The rest of us packed our cases for the island of Moorea in Tahiti. It turned out to be a paradise—wild, tropical, with none of the shoddiness of Honolulu. We stayed at the Club Méditerranée.

On Christmas Eve I met a handsome Frenchman named Yves Lewis, waterskiing. His father was the man who first dreamed up the Club Méditerranée, and Yves had come to Moorea to teach waterskiing, at which he was the local champion. He had been on the island a year and a half, a beautiful, almost god-like man, with silvery hair bleached to the color of sunshine, with eyes as green as the water he skied on. He was also a gifted flautist and had a degree in sociology from the Sorbonne—a yogi with astonishing humility about his own achievements. In the evenings he sang his own songs, laments about banality and greed, and danced the Tahitian national dance, the *tamourai*, with such skill and dexterity that even the Tahitians stopped to watch him. Who could have resisted him? I fell in love. But I also received a nasty shock; from my experiences with grass and sex and political activism, I thought I was quite something. Yves made me see I had a long way to go.

One hot, lazy afternoon after I had been waterskiing I stayed out on the raft, resting and gazing at the white beach and the very green palms. There was a man skiing in the bay; I followed his progress idly, more than a little impressed by the ease of his performance. When later he came over to my raft we started a "What are you doing here?" and "What do you study?" conversation that soon, casually, led to student rebellion, and Plato and revolution.

My mother had been sitting on the beach watching. "Do you realize who that was?" she asked, as I climbed out of the water alongside her.

"Oh, Pierre someone or other," I said vaguely. She laughed.

"That's Pierre Elliott Trudeau, the justice minister—the black sheep of the Liberal party."

Oh no, not another politician, was all I thought at the time.

I saw him only once again before our first date. That was when my father took us to the Liberal Convention when Pierre was chosen as party leader.

CHAPTER 2

ON THE HIPPY TRAIL

After the discoveries and the passions, the rebellion and the days in which not a moment seemed to pass without some new experience, my last months at Simon Fraser were something of an anticlimax. It was like a battery running down. Tahiti and Yves had made such an impression on me that I took a semester out of school, and spent it sleeping the time away. Yves had changed me and he had also made a mark on my soul—he had become a symbol for me, a romantic fantasy I was never to quite shake free of. When I returned to Simon Fraser my friends were all ahead of me; somehow the spark had gone. I indulged my newfound passion for the Romantics, taught for a while in a free school run in a couple of empty rooms on the campus, and moved into a hideous basement apartment in the ugliest of Vancouver's suburbs, Burnaby.

Like many of the luckier middle-class Canadian students, I was offered a holiday in Europe after graduation. My parents had fixed Janet up with a family in Aix-en-Provence, and wanted to do the same for me. Typically, I wanted no plans. All I would tell them was that I would be leaving the day after Christmas, 1968. "Where will you go?" asked my mother anxiously.

"I have no idea. I will fly to Geneva—and then who knows?"

Fate, or possibly perversity, took me to Morocco. My father had fought in North Africa and told such appalling tales of white slavery, poverty and pestilence that I was probably drawn there simply to spite him. In Geneva I paired up with Ross, a friend from schooldays. He had a shiny new Ford Cortina and we bickered all the way across France and Spain and down through Morocco until we reached Agadir where we suddenly put the brakes on and stopped. We had found sun and the sea and an agreeable hippy commune of sorts, sharing showers with a tourist camp.

I was well provided with money by my anxious parents, and my first action on arriving in Agadir among the hippies was to get myself a house of my own—a ten-dollar bamboo house on the beach complete with charcoal burner, cooking pots and a sleeping mat. It took me days to overcome my shyness with the other hippies; I felt square, critical and much, much too clean. But when Ross left, which he did after a couple of weeks, I had no option but to throw in my fate with the others, learn to play the guitar; eat what food there was; throw away my conventional notions of sexual morality; and live. For the first time in my life I had the sensation of peace, tranquility and utter freedom.

Finally the German tourists who shared our camp rebelled. We were a dirty, scruffy, disorganized lot to them, and what was worse, we were scroungers. They asked the police to move us on, which they duly did, very politely, to a new and far more beautiful camp north of Agadir. I took down my house and reassembled it under the trees of our new home, with the help of four Japanese boys who had become the heart of the community: four straight, industrious, inventive boys who cooked delicious Japanese meals and remained impassively polite.

Too much money rather than too little was my problem. How not to depend on it, and live like the others? After a couple of weeks I moved on again, this time totally on my own, to Essaouira, the old sea town of Mogador, up the coast, where I had heard of a Moroccan family who took in paying foreign guests.

I soon became an established part of the North African hippy circus. Old friends from Agadir drifted through and we would exchange experiences and joints before they moved on again—only to meet up again somewhere else a few months later. There were a lot of North American boys, draft dodgers from Vietnam, dozens of French kids, some Japanese and Germans. Most of us were in our late teens or early twenties; a few had been living the life for years. It was an inexpensive and harmless existence. Occasionally, telling no one, I would sneak off for a night to an expensive hotel, with a real bathroom and a good meal in a restaurant.

After a month in Essaouira I crossed the mountains to Marrakesh in an ancient bus, sitting next to a sheep trussed up by its four legs. The bus stopped in the main square of Marrakesh, enormous, crowded, menacing after my months of subdued village life. I was terrified. This seemed an altogether new challenge. Jolted in the bustle and the dark, startled by the snake charmers and the persistent beggars, I was suddenly rescued by a young European boy who led me off silently down narrow streets into the Arab quarter. I had no time to resist.

Fate again seemed to be taking a hand. I found myself in a hostel, a halfway house run by two young Christians—Ricky, an English girl, and her Dutch husband. The house was full of foreigners like myself. Ricky organized us all with the minimum of fuss and the greatest of kindness: she allocated each of us tasks, charged a small rent, and in return fed us and gave us mats to sleep on. Only keef was tolerated. There was no sex.

One of my contributions to the household was a cheap, portable record player and eight highly coveted record albums—The Beatles: "White Album," The Rolling Stones: "Sympathy For The Devil," Steve Miller Band: "Sailor,"—tunes of our generation; the voices of our collective soul.

I left Marrakesh the day I could stand the lice no longer. Every morning my companions, particularly the men, would sit intently picking the nits out of each other's shoulder-length hair, grooming themselves like monkeys. The goody-goody atmosphere and the lice; I'd had enough. My Japanese quartet had turned up and I joined them for a trip into the mountains, to an orange grove and a flowing river outside a village called Eureka. There in the moonlight, among the ruins of a crusader castle, I took my first L.S.D. trip. Yves would have been proud of me. I was moving nicely up the ladder of enlightenment.

Soon I returned to Marrakesh and a hostel of my own. It was in the Jewish quarter, two blocks from the spice market, so that when the wind blew my way the air was sweet with cloves and cinnamon, myrrh and incense. I had decided to run a house like Ricky's, only without the religion. No junkies and no speed freaks—I hated the way they seemed to grow old before my eyes, their skin wrinkling, their teeth rotting. It was as well that I felt so strongly. Opposite was another hostel like mine—but this one run by a Charles Manson character named Paul who dealt in heroin, and thrived on a drug-induced hippy hypnotism, gloating over his new and often female addicts. He was about forty, older than the rest of us, with matted, filthy hair, and a maniacal look in his eye: a big man, a cheap guru. He loved what he called his "mind games" when he turned his inmates into Christs and Mary Magdalenes and ordered them around like zombies. He made a bid to get me to join the fun, but some vestige of self-preservation and sanity remained and I became a fervent crusader against him, forbidding anyone from my own household back into the hostel if they crossed his threshold.

By now I had been in Morocco five months and was fast growing bored with the promiscuity and the emptiness of the hippy life. When a friend suggested we go back to Essaouira to meet up with Leonard Cohen and his girlfriend Clare I fell in happily with the plan. I was sick of being so thin, so perpetually ill, so kicked around. Women's liberation hadn't hit the hippy kingdom: women had their place—barefoot and pregnant. As a girl you were expected to take care of the boys, sew patches on their jeans, do their marketing and make love with whomever asked you.

I wasn't out of it yet, however. I joined Leonard and Clare and traveled with them to Tangier where I stopped taking drugs, rented an apartment in the European quarter and planned to work with a fashion designer friend for a couple of months while I tuned in again to normal life. My first morning in the workshops I felt a stab of pain in my left hand. A young French doctor diagnosed a break in a small bone at the back, and put it into plaster. Instead of getting better, the pain grew, throbbing jerks of agony that drove me screaming back to him a couple of days later. He was far from sympathetic. Wait, he said; give it a chance. Have a tranquilizer. That night, my entire arm by now quite numb, I wandered out into the streets of Tangier almost frantic. A Moroccan lady driving past in a car slowed down and asked me what was wrong. I showed her my hand. In a second we were on our way to the Spanish hospital, where the surgeon on duty removed the cast and discovered that far from a break I had osteomyelitis in my hand. It was already withered and a gray-blue color. I was told later that for the first forty-eight hours I spent in the hospital, much of the time delirious with pain, ripping my sheets, and quieted only by the morphine that I had so adamantly rejected in the streets of Marrakesh, the surgeon believed he would have to amputate my hand.

I couldn't seem to escape the hippy world, however hard I tried. When I returned to my once beautiful, clean apartment from the hospital I found the place had been defiled by junkie friends using the bathroom for a clean fix. I changed the lock. Then I was induced—no, lured is the better word—to meet Ahmed, the drug king of Tangier. He courted me as if I were a queen, invited me to a sumptuous meal, tried to shower me with dresses, which I refused, flattered me and showed me priceless jewelry. His strategy, I assumed, was to install any European girl in a villa or apartment that he paid for himself, provide her with whatever drugs she liked to take, and press her to give parties for her friends, at which they, in turn, tasted, got hooked, and ordered through Ahmed. The more I refused to become involved the more Ahmed persisted. "Would you like a house? Shall I get you a flat? A villa?" One day he appeared and threw a bunch of keys into my lap.

"Here you are. It's yours. A villa. No strings attached. I won't come near you." I kept my head and threw them back. Like Paul in Marrakesh, Ahmed had to be fought. I saw it as a mission to go around warning new arrivals about him.

Soon after this episode I was convinced it was time to go home. I would leave at once, miraculously undamaged by an experience that had made victims of many other girls precisely like myself. More than that: I was not only undamaged, I had grown up. I had learned about generosity and freedom. Now was the moment to try it out on Vancouver and return to Yves to show him how truly worthy of him I had finally become. Reaching home I paused with my parents for no longer than it needed to convince them that an already troublesome teenager had turned into a weird, vegetarian, mystical flower child, and I was off again to find Yves in Berkeley. My relationship with Yves was like falling asleep on a train and endlessly overshooting a country station, only to have to return once more on a second train and then fall asleep and miss it again. Desperately trying to reach him, I always found I had unconsciously missed my goal. This time I had not only become liberated and relaxed: I had gone too far. Before, I had been too bourgeois. Now I was too hippy. "You're living in a hippy dream," said Yves, eyeing with contempt my frizzy hair and granny glasses as well as the faraway gleam in my eyes. "Come back when you've learned something about *life*." Even I realized that this was becoming a crazy exercise. Crestfallen, confused and now totally without a plan for the future, I set off for my grandmother and the Sechelt Peninsula.

CHAPTER 3

A SECRET COURTSHIP

When I look back on it now I can't help being a little ashamed of the speed with which I shed my hippy certainties. One day I was staring out to sea from a clifftop near my grandmother's home, luxuriating in the romantic ideals of happy brotherhood. The next I was on my way back to Vancouver by ferry, to meet my mother for a shopping spree. Yves and flower power were relegated to the back of my heart; at the front was only one thought: "I've got nothing to wear for the prime minister."

It had been all too easy to persuade me to accept the date. I kept up my fashionable nonchalance for just the time it took to buy a dress. In a French boutique called Armagi, I found the ideal garment—gabardine, white, short sleeves with fine stitching around the seams.

I woke next morning to a chilly premonition that I had really let myself in for something. My sisters bounded into my room—it was like a birthday, being looked at and fêted. I had been persuaded to go to the hairdresser, and my hair was now wound up in a sleek brown knot, the jagged ends lopped off. Janet lent me makeup, and Mother pinned a diamond brooch onto my dress; Heather filled me several glasses of sherry. I was ready far too early.

At seven I heard a car in the drive. I was terrified: not only did I have then—and indeed have now—a great awe for people of importance, but Trudeaumania was still at its height and I was part of it. What was I doing with the prime minister of Canada? Why me? And what was this formidable man really like? If I was honest all I could remember was a nice looking middle-aged man with funny old-fashioned shorts and a stripy T-shirt.

When Pierre came through the door I liked the look of him immediately. For one thing he had such an air of fun, such a charming, teasing expression that he made us all laugh. Being late summer he was tanned, which looked good against his white shirt, blue blazer and colored ascot. He had dark glasses, and wore a flower in his buttonhole. He was confident, flying high, a good first year as prime minister behind him with the country at his feet, and the polls predicting great things for him. I liked the charm, the boyish ways, and couldn't stop myself sneaking a look at his legs: Pierre was once given the award of being the man with the most beautiful legs in the world. He, on the other hand, could hardly have been pleased with what *he* saw: what all the grooming and dressing up had done to me was to turn a flower child into a Barbie doll.

I got him out of the house as soon as I could—unable to stand the nervous gigglings of my sisters, nor the feigned relaxation of my mother. A blue Pontiac stood in the drive. The two plainclothes officers were dressed to look more like chauffeurs than policemen, but the muscles and the air of security were unmistakable. We set off to catch the sky-ride up Grouse Mountain to what Pierre and my father had agreed was the most appropriate restaurant in town, the Grouse's Nest, perched on the mountaintop with a spectacular view over Vancouver. We made polite, stilted conversation.

The awkwardness vanished by the time we stepped into the restaurant. Within just a few minutes I had blown my cover. The little French dress was a sham, and I couldn't keep all the small talk up. We talked about student revolution and I told him about Berkeley and the tear gas, the arsenal and Morocco. It all came pouring out. I had found a friend at last.

I told him about my unhappiness, about my grandmother's peaceful cottage by the sea, about my shattered plans. He listened, kindly, more father than friend. Over dinner he suggested that I should leave Vancouver and get as far away as possible from the things that seemed to weigh so heavily on me: my family, my background, my friends.

As we danced again, I realized that I was feeling increasingly drawn to this intense, wiry man, the antithesis of Yves Lewis and all I thought I believed in. He didn't strike me as old. In fact it was an immediate pleasure not to be battling with a young man's ego. I never stopped to wonder what possible future there could conceivably be for two people so obviously unsuited to one another—one cerebral, clearheaded, rational, devout and almost fifty; the other confused, scatty, certain of only one thing and that was to avoid all possible formality and social responsibility, and barely twenty. "If you come to Ottawa," Pierre said, as he dropped me back at my house with a brotherly kiss, "do let me know. I'd love to have you come for dinner."

At that instant I decided that I wanted this man for myself.

The next morning I was on the beach having a picnic on the pebbles when I saw his helicopter overhead on its way to Whistler Mountain where he was due to open the Garibaldi Park Reserve. Already, in just twelve hours, my mind was made up. I would put Yves and his unattainable ideals behind me and take up Pierre's suggestion, move to Ottawa, find a proper, serious job, and, who could say—I might even look him up.

I went east with some trepidation. My first sight of Ottawa was not reassuring: a busy city center full of office blocks and blue-suited businessmen. I didn't much care for what I saw. But I was soon swept up in my new job, as junior sociologist in a branch of the Department of Manpower and Immigration, working under a Czech called Dr. Celovsky at six hundred dollars a month. A prince's salary. I was at least rich.

It took me two weeks to build up the courage to call Pierre. By the time I got through I was convinced he wouldn't even remember my name. I had signed my contract that morning, and dared myself to do it by way of celebration. Pierre's voice was warm, faintly amused. "Come over for dinner tonight," he said when he had taken in what I had done. "Be warned though. It's only spaghetti." It could have been dog food for all I cared.

The prime minister's residence, 24 Sussex Drive, familiar to me from so many press photographs and news bulletins, is a large stone mansion set in acres of perfect lawn. It was October, a warm early autumn evening, with a few fallen leaves marring the unbroken expanses of green. I approached the door with some hesitation. It was opened instantly by a cheerful woman who welcomed me into the library. I was sad when she left me. The room itself was bleak—shelf upon shelf of art books and volumes of philosophy, political treatises and leatherbound theological tomes. "The prime minister will be down shortly," Verna had announced portentously, leaving me to browse. It was like waiting for the king.

It needed only Pierre's voice to convince me that I had been right to come—there is no more cheery and flirtatious manner in the world than his. Dinner was the sort of meal a would-be wife dreams of: course after course of insipid, colorless food, each more bland than the last until it became a matter of guess-work alone as to whether we were now eating cauliflower, cheese or crème caramel. Always on the lookout for a task, I had an immediate picture of myself supervising delicious little snacks, under the by now miraculously smiling faces of the Trudeau ancestors.

Once again I did most of the talking, but I managed to get him to reveal something of his own past. I discovered that his father had made a small fortune by buying into service stations during and immediately after the Depression; that he had been a funny, boisterous father to have around even if highly ambitious and extremely demanding for his eldest son. Pierre was brought up in luxury, transported by chauffeur to his Jean de Brébeuf classical college in Montreal each day. He had had to overcome a shy, even gentle nature by taking boxing lessons. His mother, Grace, was Scots by origin, his father French Canadian. The Trudeaus spoke French at home, but Pierre was soon bilingual in English. He was a bright scholar, getting with no trouble a law degree at Montreal University and following this effortlessly with a master's in political economy at Harvard. After this he did a spell at the Sorbonne in Paris, and then went to the London School of Economics.

It wasn't until 1962 that he became a teacher of constitutional law at the University of Montreal. From then on things happened very fast. Against all odds he was nominated for parliament by a principally Jewish community for saying: "If I were one of you, I wouldn't vote for me, but for one of your own." He became minister of justice in the Lester Pearson government only a couple of years later. He spent two years in that job, making a name for himself with sweeping reforms of the judicial system, championing fair play and human rights and becoming the beloved black sheep of the Liberal party. His informal approach, which included the sandals he wore in parliament on stuffy summer afternoons, was greeted with both affection and distaste, but never indifference.

I was beginning to discover that behind this silky, charming manner and the absolute confidence that had given him such a reputation for arrogance, was a curiously solitary figure. He appealed to me as a romantic who paid pretty compliments and loathed vulgarity and, as he couldn't prevent himself from saying, all the profanities of my generation.

When I told him that I had just signed a six months' contract with the government a look of unmistakable panic crossed his face. "My God," I saw him thinking, "this lady's moved into town!" After dinner he proposed a stroll in the garden. I was a little cold. Across the river, in the crisp autumn air, we could just see the lights of the distant shore. Pierre gently kissed me. My future looked even more promising.

Things never happen to me in moderation. Floating along next morning in a state of romantic euphoria, I was startled out of my fantasies by a letter from Yves. "I'm going to buy a sailboat," it said. "Please come sail around the world with me. Now I have something precise to offer you." I took this to be the marriage I had pressed for. "Darling Yves," I wrote back hastily. "Your letter has come too late. I'm beached in Ottawa. I'm contracted into the very society you urged me to join—remember?" My letter wasn't entirely lacking in smugness.

I now settled down to the inflexible routine of the civil service. My job, I discovered, consisted of finding ways of helping misfits "rejoin the mainstream of Canadian economic life." The chronically poor, the hippies, the unemployed were all placed under our scrutiny as under an enormous magnifying glass. I wasn't totally happy with our way of going about things: living in our fluorescently lit, wall-to-wall carpeted offices, drawing our generous salaries, and having remarkably little contact with the people whose lives we were supposed to be magically transforming.

I soon finished what I took to be my first assignment, handed it to the director and waited to be told what to do next. Nothing. That *was* my job, they told me. The trouble was that I had done it too fast. So while they fished around for new ideas I sat at my desk with my pencils, notepads and government directories lined up neatly in front of me, reading Doris Lessing and writing adolescent poetry. I was bored.

It was just as well that I had Pierre. During these autumn months, our meetings were beginning to preoccupy me more and more. By Christmas we were confessing to each other that we were unmistakably in love, though we both were still full of doubts, Pierre far more than me. It was ludicrous, he kept saying. "I am simply *too* old. How can you take up with a man two years older than your mother?" During the moments his doubts were at their most acute he fought me off and returned to his social life of pretty ladies. I saw pictures in the papers at dinners and balls with other women—and like anyone in love suffered agonies of jealousy. One woman in particular seemed to pose a serious threat, a professor of French literature at Carleton University called Madeleine Gobeil, for Pierre frequently sought out her company. They were old, intimate friends, Pierre reassured me. No danger there. Another rival was a French Canadian actress, a sultry, pouting girl. I kept coming across pictures of her arm in arm with Pierre. None of this was quite as troubling, however, as the day he flew Barbra Streisand up to Ottawa to accompany him to a gala at the Arts Center. They had had, so my morning papers told me next day, a candlelit supper at 24 Sussex. It was romance. Every paper carried it. For the next few days my pique and jealousy was such that each time Pierre rang I slammed down the phone: "Go back to your American actresses!" I yelled at him.

By Christmas, though, the worst was over, and we settled down to a pattern. We met for dinner once or twice a week, when Pierre's chauffeur collected me at seven, and Pierre walked me home around 10:30, when he had to get back to work. The dinners were fun, but agonizingly short. But we had the weekends. Not every weekend, but many. It was then that we took off for Harrington Lake, his country residence, where we feigned great house parties and messed up all the beds for the Monday morning maids. We never in fact took anyone with us. Even better were our trips to his remote log cabin and square mile of land at Morrin Heights in the Laurentians. It was on these occasions that I really came to admire his self-sufficiency, the way Pierre did things because he wanted to do them, and not for social conventions. "Choose your own life," he kept repeating to me. "Do what *you* want to do." We sat by great log fires: Pierre cooked steaks and prepared salad while I told him about "High Hopes" and my childhood holidays on the Sechelt Peninsula, my Moroccan adventure and Yves.

It was an often lonely life. My work was boring. I had no friends. But for him I would have packed and caught the next flight home. In any case, when I was with him my gloom miraculously vanished. I simply forgot how very lonely I was the rest of the time. As we became happier and happier in each other's company, so I lived only for our evenings and dinners alone together.

Then came the day when Pierre asked me to a costume ball at the National Gallery. It was our first public outing. We had always agreed that I would be bored at receptions at the governor general's or at diplomatic dinners, but this would be a livelier occasion. He told me that he would be going in black tie, since he hated dressing up, but pressed me to go ahead with my plans for a Juliet costume. I dug out a red velvet hippy dress, with sleeves that fell to the ground, and had my hair pinned up under a net of pearls. When I got to 24 Sussex, Pierre was charmed and in good spirits; I by then was distinctly nervous. I had good reason to be.

From the instant I stepped out of the car to the flashing of photographers' cameras, to the moment I got home, I was in hell. It wasn't only that we were gaped at, shoved, and cut off from one another, but that every group we joined fell silent on our arrival; jolly laughter froze and jokes were broken off midway—"Here comes the prime minister." Wandering around in what seemed to be a lonely, aimless way I could sense people whispering, "Who *is* that dopey looking girl?" When we danced, people stopped to stare. As soon as we got into the car I burst into tears.

If I had needed additional convincing that we were not cut out for public occasions I received it a few weeks later. Pierre was not going to be put off by one attempt. One evening he asked me whether I would like to accompany him to the house of some old friends of his, the Porteouses. It turned out that I had met Wendy before, and there would only be her and her husband, Timothy, and a couple of other old friends of Pierre's. I was delighted and flattered. Was he perhaps finally beginning to think of me seriously?

The night of the dinner came around. I had made a special effort to look pretty. The first question that Wendy put to me was: "Do you speak French?" Pierre didn't give me a chance to reply. Unwittingly, for we had never discussed my languages, he said: "With a good old French name like 'St. Claire,' what do you expect?" "*Ah bon*," said Wendy. And, despite the fact that both she and her husband were English-speaking, and that the other guests spoke it perfectly, the whole dinner was conducted in French. The terrible thing was that I didn't understand a word—I couldn't speak French at all. The moment at which I should have told them passed by. Then the laughter and the jokes were such that all I could decently do was plaster a grin on my face and pretend to be following them. No one spoke to me. They were only interested in Pierre and in their own lives.

At 10:30 Pierre had to go back to parliament. Rudely brushing aside all offers of dessert I fled from the house after him, wailing at him in the car that I had never felt so insulted, so betrayed, in all my life. Pierre looked helpless, but it was then that we made a firm resolution: no more social experiments. Which is why, when we married eighteen months later, the event came as such a total shock to the world. "My country mistress," Pierre used to call me.

After Easter I quit my job—I had had enough of sitting in front of an empty desk. I began to think seriously of child psychology, and was accepted as a graduate student in the psychology department of Ottawa University, to start in the fall. I had six months to fill. During this time, after a most romantic, flirtatious holiday with Pierre, I realized that I no longer wanted to be Pierre's country mistress. I wanted more. I wanted to live with him. I wanted his children. And as Pierre sensed my growing closeness he seemed to shy nervously farther away from me again, as if he were simply accepting the inevitable: that a dizzy, distracted girl twenty-nine years younger than he would in the very nature of things sooner or later leave him.

The end came one weekend when Pierre was holding a caucus party up at Harrington Lake. I was staying in the house, but since there were workmen around all day setting up marquees I had to stay hidden indoors. Chafing at the absurdity of it, alone, in hiding, I suddenly found that I couldn't stand the futility a moment longer. I packed and left. I saw Pierre once again as I was leaving Ottawa for the west. The airport was closed because of a major plane crash and in that rather heightened mood of fear and nostalgia for a lost love, I went to call once more at 24 Sussex Drive. I was dressed up for the part of romantic heroine, since I had decided to fill in the waiting hours by attending a garden party for Prince Charles being given by the governor general. I found Pierre in as sad and emotional a state as I was. We both cried. "I can't press you to stay," Pierre told me. "You're too young and too romantic. And in any case I don't believe you would be faithful." I went off, full of renunciation, and was immediately charmed by Prince

Charles who looked at me closely and said: "Are you an actress?"

"No."

"Well, then you should be," and he moved on.

I settled down once again with my long-suffering parents and prepared to spend the summer with old friends, forgetting Pierre. The plan worked for a while. I had fun. Then one day I realized what a charade it all was and hurried to the phone. Pierre's immediate warmth put me on my guard. "Will you come scuba diving with some friends?" he asked, as if nothing had happened. I was furious.

"What for? More pain? I can't go on playing this sort of life." I was the one who always waited by the phone, I thought crossly. It was Pierre who played all the shots. To my surprise, he sounded confused.

"No, I've done some serious thinking. Come and we'll talk about it." He was about to pass through Vancouver on his way to the Williams Lake carnival and rodeo, so I hitched a lift with him back to Ottawa on his official plane.

We always argue about what happened next. As I see it we spent the weekend at Harrington Lake. One boiling afternoon, sitting down by the water, Pierre said reflectively: "Well, Margaret, perhaps we should talk about getting married?" It was a question. Not, says Pierre, a proposal. But I chose to take it as such. In a second I was on my feet and flinging my arms around him.

"When? Tomorrow?"

It was the first time the word had been mentioned. Pierre laughed, "Hey, take it easy." I was so excited I leaped from the rock I was perched on and into the lake where I swam around and around in circles like a frenzied dolphin. When I was calmed down, he put his conditions to me. I had to convince him, he told me, that I would be a good, faithful wife to him; that I would give up drugs, and stop being so flighty. He made it sound as stark and bald as he could.

"You must realize that you are not marrying just anybody. I am the prime minister of Canada. My job means a lot to me, and it won't be an easy life for you. It wouldn't be an easy life, even were I not prime minister. I'm fifty years old, I have never lived with any woman for long, and I'm extremely solitary by nature." I paid no attention to his words, only to his proposal.

We set off for the promised scuba diving trip in a state of considerable excitement, managing with difficulty to keep our plans from the friends who accompanied us, Joe and Debby McInnes. We went to Andros, an island close to Nassau, where the diving was superb. We lived in a derelict shack on the beach and dived all day, spending romantic and exhausted evenings pacing the sand while Pierre questioned me minutely about my past. He needed to know everything, he said, in case anyone in the future blackmailed him about me. *Everything*. It was sometimes funny, sometimes painful telling him, but I didn't really care. Occasionally he said, almost sadly: "I know you'll leave me one day."

"Never, never," I replied passionately, furious that he could think of such a thing.

"Let's test it," he said finally. "You go back to Vancouver and keep our plans a secret. I don't want a circus of it. We'll have a quiet wedding when we think we're ready."

CHAPTER 4

PREPARING FOR THE WEDDING

Pierre had set me some tasks, and I was anxious not to fail him. In Vancouver, three thousand miles away from him, under the watchful eye of my mother, and my sister Lin as my other confidante, I would prove I was worthy of him. The first challenge Pierre had offered me was to demonstrate that I was capable of fidelity—particularly fidelity a long way away from him and in the company of close friends of my own age. The second was to stop smoking marijuana. Not just because it was illegal and a prime minister's wife simply cannot smoke grass and get away with it, but because Pierre was convinced that I was merely using it as an escape; a childish way of refusing to face up to reality. We had had heated arguments about it, with me begging to be allowed a few joints from time to time. Pierre was adamant. I had to give it up, or no marriage.

At the same time I set myself a couple of other, secret goals. I had decided to become a Catholic. I felt that it was essential for our happiness that I should at least be able to understand and accept the rules of his faith, as well as some of its traditions.

I also wanted to become a first-class skier. Pierre is a remarkable all-around sportsman—though he won't play a single competitive game—and while I couldn't canoe, or play golf, or do judo, I could at least ski. I had no intention of watching Pierre waiting impatiently at the bottom of every slope, while I picked myself out of a snowdrift.

Then there was the little matter of the French. If there was one thing that my embarrassed and unhappy evening with the Porteouses had taught me, it was that never again in my life was I going to come across to anyone as quite so dumb. Languages, I had come to see, played a central part in his life. He was not only fluent in German, French and English, but loved speaking them whenever he got the chance, official or otherwise, taking great pleasure in his excellent accent and wide vocabulary.

Arriving home in Vancouver that September I threw myself into my tasks. I found a small language school that had opened recently in the center of the city, called the Alliance Française. With considerable pride, and enjoying the deception greatly, I explained to my teacher that I needed to learn French because I was marrying a French Canadian, a young lawyer from Montreal called Pierre Mercier, and that I would be traveling constantly around Canada with him. The web of fantasy was growing.

Next I turned to the most demanding task, converting to Catholicism. It wasn't as simple as I had hoped. British Columbia is a mainly Anglican and Lutheran province and I couldn't find the sort of church I was looking for. My searches revealed just two Catholic churches in our neighborhood, a grand, social one which I shunned, and St. Stephen's, a hideous, modern building, more like a gymnasium than a church. With a sigh, I settled on that. My priest, Father Schwinkles, was obviously devout and deeply sincere, but he was an anxious, timid man and not always easy to reason with. I used the same story about marriage as I had at the Alliance Française, adding that Pierre Mercier was a practicing Catholic.

During these months I was also concentrating on the more mundane and practical side of preparing to become the wife of the prime minister of Canada. Did I look right? Was my hair cut well enough? What clothes was I going to need? I had to have a fairly extensive trousseau as I knew that soon after the wedding we would be paying an official visit to Russia for which, Pierre informed me, teasingly, I would need extremely ladylike clothes. None of my favorite shawls and beads but suits and dresses. At the same time I didn't want too many, since I planned to get pregnant as soon as I could.

During the long winter evenings, when darkness fell at four, I was learning to sew once again as I was determined to sew my own wedding dress. I went to evening classes with Mrs. Rees, certainly the best teacher of *haute couture* in Vancouver. I had decided it was to look as little like a wedding dress as possible, yet not be so plain as to be pointless. I settled on a caftan, made out of a loosely woven white material, with angel sleeves, onto which, the last morning, so that no one but I saw it before the ceremony, I was going to stitch a hood. As I sewed I dreamed about the life to come.

After six weeks at home I went back east to spend Thanksgiving with Pierre in Ottawa. It was an exceptionally good visit. Pierre could see for himself that I had taken his tasks to heart, and had already made progress. I had given up marijuana and was showing no signs of a romantic fling with another lover. We had never been closer or more loving. It was then, sitting at 24 Sussex, after the turkey and the cranberry pie, that we fixed a date for the wedding. We settled for March 4, 1971.

Whatever doubts Pierre may have had about me as a suitable future wife were abruptly removed by a tragic incident through which I was able to support him. One of the reasons why I had wanted to be with him for Thanksgiving was that terrible things were happening in Canada. The F.L.Q., a small group of heavily armed terrorists, had launched what were all too soon seen to be the beginnings of a radical and violent separatist movement in Quebec. Until then the F.L.Q. had been going in for bombing letterboxes. In November 1970 they changed tactics.

Two cells of highly organized terrorists, among them young, educated students, kidnapped James Cross, a British diplomat, and then the Quebec minister, Pierre Laporte. Overnight a national crisis was declared. Naturally I wanted to be by Pierre's side: his loneliness in the days to come brought his position home to me in a way nothing, no pomp or glory or officialdom, had managed to before.

Pierre's reaction to those terrible days will go down in history. From the first phone call announcing the kidnappings his mind was made up: the Canadian government would not give in to terrorism. There was to be no bargaining, there would be no deals. Even though Pierre Laporte was a valued friend, no bargain was to be struck to save him. He did not believe it to be morally right to give in to fanatics whose declared aim was to overthrow the system through violence and terror.

When I reached Ottawa I found him in a state of great turmoil, though his absolute unshakable conviction that he would not be blackmailed gave him tremendous strength. He needed it.

The tragic news came suddenly. The phone rang at one o'clock on Monday morning. We were asleep. I heard Pierre say: "Oh, my God." Then: "Where did they find him?" And I knew that Laporte was dead. Pierre put down the receiver; I heard him crying. Tears pouring down my own face, I tried to comfort him. I knew that my strength for him lay in my innocence, my ignorance of politics. I couldn't understand the political implications, but I could love him. That night brought us very close together. He was a shaken man: I watched him grow old before my eyes. It was as if Laporte's death lay on his shoulders alone: *he* was the one who wouldn't negotiate, and *he* was the man who would now have to take responsibility for the murder of an innocent man. It gave him a new bitterness; a hard sadness I had never seen before.

The events in Quebec not only bound us closer than ever before; they altered, in a matter of days, our whole way of life.

Before the final blow fell there had already been some changes around Pierre. They had repelled me instantly. When I arrived in Ottawa I was met at the airport by Pierre's driver and told that we were to go straight up to the prime minister's house on Harrington Lake. It was late autumn, and a gentle mist was rolling in over the water. I looked out eagerly for the view I loved so much: the open fields, the solitude and wilderness. They had vanished. In their place were army tents, tanks, men with rifles. Before that moment Pierre had never had bodyguards. After it he was never without them. Suddenly there was around-the-clock security.

Pierre and I knew, although I was only there for that one weekend, that it was never going to be quite the same for us again. Our days of freedom and pure, unsullied romance were over forever. From now on everything we did would be under police supervision. A rebel against authority anyway, I think that moment triggered in me the feeling that was later to break my spirit, when I was still struggling to remain Pierre's wife: the feeling of an omniscient police presence. It started that day, Thanksgiving 1970.

I got back to Vancouver in time to break the news to my father that I would be going back to Ottawa at Christmas to stay with Pierre. He was furious. "Christmas," he said, "is the time to be with your family." I realized the time had come to tell him the truth. "Dad, Pierre and I are going to get married." I have never seen a happier man, first dumbfounded then ebullient with joy. "Well, my God, how wonderful," he kept repeating, again and again. My marriage to Pierre, the prime minister of Canada, was to be the fulfillment of his own failed political

376

dreams. He hadn't made it to 24 Sussex; I would be there in his place. He had always joked that the only thing he wanted in life was to see his five daughters all married, and what better match? I swore him to total secrecy.

Pierre and I drove down from Ottawa to Montreal together. As we were loading the car I noticed that he had packed just one suitcase. "Where are the presents?" I asked him.

"There are no presents," replied Pierre, surprised at my question. "We don't give presents at Christmas."

Coming from a family which takes its celebrations very seriously this was a nasty shock to me. When Pierre caught sight of my horrified expression he laughed. "O.K. Let's go and see what we can scrounge from the official gifts upstairs." In the attic we came upon box after box of rich spoils. I fell on them with delight: it was like Hudson's Bay Company, Eaton's and Holt Renfrew all rolled into one, and free. When we set off for Montreal the car was overflowing with Christmas presents.

When we got there the first thing we did was go to tell Suzette, his sister, and Charles, his brother, the news. No, I'm wrong. We didn't actually tell them we were getting married. We didn't have to. It was absolutely apparent. Never in his life before had Pierre brought a girl home for Christmas, and never had he treated a woman so attentively in their presence. He rarely left my side.

Pierre's sister, with whom we were spending the holiday, lived just down the street from his mother. It was from Suzette, a docile but stubborn woman some three years older than Pierre, whom I liked immediately, that I learned something of Pierre's childhood, and the very powerful part his mother had played in it. As Suzette made ready for Christmas, she and I chatted, and I started putting together a picture of this happy, prosperous family struck down tragically by Pierre's father's death when he was just fifteen.

The only sadness that Christmas was that Pierre's mother, Grace, was already very frail and her behavior almost childlike, but with rare moments of lucidity. She appeared as a fragile, birdlike figure, bearing little trace of the elegant woman she had been in her heyday. Only a certain fastidiousness remained, a love of good clothes and things correctly done, and the piercing blue eyes of a young girl. She conveyed her approval of me silently, clasping my hand tightly as I sat by her bed.

Pierre was a devoted son to Grace and lived with her much of the year long after he was grown up. On her insistence Pierre went to the best universities, and it was because of her enthusiasm and encouragement that he set off on his many travels. She had always encouraged Pierre to read, to argue, to develop his mind, and I believe that it was largely because of her that Pierre has turned out as generous, tolerant and understanding as he is.

When she died the sad task came of distributing among the family her possessions, and making sure that every one of them had those things they best remembered. We discovered hidden away in one of her bureaus a complete handmade trousseau of the finest silk, embroidered in Paris, wrapped in blue tissue and never used. Being the only member of the Trudeau family small enough, I acquired the trousseau. When I had time to examine the chest's contents more fully I found that I had inherited the most delicate of silk slips bordered with lace, exquisite nightdresses in georgette satin and chiffon, and gossamer fine handkerchiefs. I wore them for occasions which mattered, like the days I lunched with the Queen, or the nights I hoped to conceive a child. And once used they would be lovingly handwashed at 24 Sussex, so that they are in as fine condition today as when I first acquired them.

As March 4 grew nearer, Pierre became increasingly agitated. Every night our phone in Vancouver rang. "Are you quite *sure* you want to go ahead with this?" came his anxious voice down the line. If anything, as the weeks crawled by, my certainty grew.

In January came the day to make the wedding cake. By now, through dint of hints and guesses, like an elaborate parlor game of innuendo and forfeit, most of my family knew what was about to happen to me. Everyone, that is, except for Betsy, who was away, and Janet, whom I dared not tell: I love her dearly, but she is the wickedest gossip alive.

I chose that day to break the news to my grandmother, who came down from her cottage on the cliff to spend a few weeks with us. Her first reaction was one of total horror. "Oh, no, no, good lord no, you can't mean that," she said, without pausing to think how much it would upset me. I had made a point of preparing her because I wanted to give her time to go shopping with my mother and buy something new to wear for the wedding, but my mother had warned me that with her anti-Liberal, anti-marriage, anti-playboy views, there was bound to be trouble. She was a devout Protestant, to boot.

Pierre won the day. He could charm anyone. I warned him over the phone that grandma wasn't too happy. "Leave it to me," he said. When he arrived at the church for our wedding he saw my grandmother standing drawn up near the steps. "Hey, Mrs. Bernard," he called out.

"What are *you* doing here? Don't you know Protestants can't come into a Catholic church?" She frowned, then her face creased with laughter. From that day on they were firm friends, with grandma flirting with my husband in the most outrageous way.

As February wore on Pierre became, if anything, still more nervous and jittery. Some days I even thought he might have called the whole thing off if it hadn't been for my rock-hard determination. Even his friends began to see that something was wrong, but when they questioned him he brushed them off brusquely.

It wasn't long, however, before his jumpiness exploded in public. In all fairness, I have to take the blame for it; I was the one who used coarse language, not Pierre. One night, a couple of weeks before the wedding, Pierre was in the House of Commons in an unusually distraught and distracted mood. As the session wore on tempers became heated and one Opposition member in particular seemed to be directing needling cracks at him. Suddenly he could bear it no longer. Leaning over the bench, he mouthed, extremely distinctly, "Fuck off." There was an uproar. Instantly Pierre, very red in the face, explained that he had been saying "Fuddle duddle" to the honorable member.

No one was fooled. Within hours it had become a *cause célèbre* in Canada, and "fuddle duddle" a national slogan. It started a mania for T-shirts printed with the words, and cartoons in all the papers and magazines. It was even raised as a question of privilege in the House. Does a prime minister have the right to tell a member of the Opposition to fuck off/fuddle duddle?

Throughout this period I had been working toward my Catholicism. The final conversion took place just one week before my marriage. I knew then that I had to come clean with my priest because he would be officiating at the wedding.

I went through a quiet service with two close Catholic friends and afterward approached Father Schwinkles very earnestly. "Now I'm a Catholic I would like to confess," I told him. "I want to get all my past misdeeds out and be forgiven." Father Schwinkles was somewhat surprised by my sudden religious zeal but gave me an appointment.

Next morning, suppressing my laughter, I knelt down behind the red curtain. "Father, I have disobeyed my parents. I have had premarital sex. And I have occasionally told lies." I could see his head nodding, scarcely attentive to my words. "I'm afraid I lied to you." I sensed a sudden keenness in his attention. "I'm not marrying Pierre Mercier. I'm marrying Pierre Trudeau." There was a long silence. I started giggling on the other side.

Finally there came a low gasp, and in a strangled voice Father Schwinkles pronounced: "Go down on your knees, and say the Lord's prayer. Do three Hail Marys for your sins."

When we emerged from our adjoining booths I found Father Schwinkles white and shaking, saying in a quavering voice that he must go and talk to the bishop. Before he scurried off, muttering to himself, I stopped him. "Father, we want *you* to officiate. We want a quiet and very simple wedding."

March 4 dawned clear and chilly, with bright sun and early spring flowers pushing up through the snow that still lay deep on the lawn. The wedding was fixed for 5 P.M. Given the time difference, we had planned that a late afternoon wedding would give Pierre time to leave Ottawa at 2 P.M., still do a morning's work, yet also give us enough leeway to get away to the mountains that night.

Then, as I was putting the last touches to my dress, and packing up the suitcase I was taking with me into the mountains, disaster struck. Without warning, the worst snowstorm in recent Canadian history hit the east. Ottawa airport was closed. When Pierre asked them to keep it open for him he met firm resistance. What was the point in the prime minister risking his life for a skiing holiday? For such, officially, was his plan.

For an hour things looked bleak. A white blanket of snow settled over Ottawa, and the weather forecast promised more. Then, by one of those miraculous twists of fortune, the sky lightened, just long enough for Pierre to dash to the airport and take off. We had been listening to the forecast from Vancouver with horror. Then came his call: "Don't worry. We're off. Wait till I call you from the airport." And he was gone.

The call came at 5:30. Pierre had made it. It was a beautiful clear early spring evening, with the light just fading. There had been a soft fall of snow in the morning but through it you could see the crocuses and daffodils. We drove up to the church, my father at the wheel, Lin and I in the back. There was a car blocking the way. A policeman stepped out from behind it and said rather haughtily to my father: "I'm sorry, sir, no one can come in here." "Get that car out of the way," replied my father, laughing. "I have the bride in here."

We had done it. No one but our families knew anything. There were no crowds, no reporters. Pierre had achieved his sacred ceremony, even if it was held in a church that looked more Protestant than Catholic and was so shabby that it even lacked real pews. To make up for it we had splashed out on the flowers: freesias, daffodils, tulips and cornflowers, nothing but spring flowers, banked up in all the bays and window sills and on the altar, and with sprigs of wheat in the posies (the Virgo sign for fertility). It looked more like a flower shop than a church.

After the wedding service we drove off to the Capilano Golf Club, where my father had booked a private room for his sixtieth anniversary celebration. The food was superb: smoked salmon, *filet de boeuf* with Béarnaise sauce, wedding cake and champagne.

That dinner was the first inkling of what was to come, the first realization that I had done a truly incredible thing. I hadn't just married the man of my dreams: I had married the prime minister. The waiters were all shaking with nerves because they had not been prepared for this. Even my parents were respectful. "That's the way it's going to be," I thought. "People are in awe of him. In time they will be in awe of me."

As we left for the mountains we were pelted with buckets of rice, our eyes blinking in the crisp air and the yellow glare of the arc lights set out in a fan all around the drive. We were driven up to our honeymoon cabin in the back of the police car, the two officers in front, tactfully chattering away to each other, their eyes fixed firmly in front of them, while Pierre and I held hands and whispered in the back. I was happy and proud to be the prime minister's wife.

Because of the difference between eastern and western time, it was very late for Pierre by the time we reached the cabin after a two-hour drive. Then, at 6:30 A.M. next morning the telephone rang. It jarred us out of a dead sleep. Pierre leaped out of bed in a frenzy as this was an unlisted number, and he had told his switchboard to put no calls through except in an extreme emergency.

"Hello, hello," I heard him say urgently into the receiver.

"Oh hello," came the laconic reply, "I called to congratulate you." It was President Nixon, calling mid-morning from Washington to tell us how happy he and Pat were.

Later that morning we went out skiing. It was a brilliant sunny morning and I was looking forward to the day. I soon discovered that in the long months during which I had been preparing myself so diligently for marriage, in one field at least I had overprepared. We set off from the top of the mountain and within seconds I was out-skiing Pierre completely. He spent the next few years catching up with me.

CHAPTER 5

ON BECOMING CHATELAINE

On March 7, our absurdly short three-day honeymoon in the mountains already over, Pierre and I flew to Ottawa. I had been dreading our arrival at the airport. I knew that there to meet us would be cabinet ministers and their wives, as well as close friends and relations of Pierre's who had heard the news over the radio and wanted to be the first to welcome us back. We stepped through the glass doors into pandemonium: congratulations, embraces, warm handshakes—all eyes on us, beaming smiles everywhere. Photographers, reporters and curious onlookers thronged the hall, pressing in on us until I felt dazed. Dazed, but not unhappy. It was a wonderfully warm welcome, and I longed to tell them all how happy I was and what a success I was going to make of it. The pictures taken that day show a shy but eager girl; a brand new blushing bride.

The day we came home to 24 Sussex Drive there had just been a fresh snowfall and an air of stillness and magic lay over the scene—the immense white garden, the big windows lit up cheerfully to welcome us. In the back of the car I hugged Pierre: this was to be my home. We turned into the gates, the guards came to attention and saluted, and we swept up the drive to the front door. I found the whole household waiting to greet me in the hall, a long file of smiling people eager to say hello. I already knew most of them, of course, because of my eighteen months of surreptitious calls on Pierre. But my arrival at 24 Sussex as his bride was quite a shock to them, particularly since only three days before they had no idea that Pierre was even planning to marry. Now here he was with his bride. This was a very different matter from a casual, eager-to-please girlfriend. They finally had a mistress of the house, a twenty-two-year-old girl whose reputation as a hippy and flower child was known to every one of them.

My married life had begun, and with it the long, arduous task of learning to be chatelaine of 24 Sussex Drive. There was so much to learn. Not merely the protocol, how to receive guests and what to talk about to important visitors, but the entire organization of an enormous household, which had been running well for years without me.

My immediate problem was not so much the space and grandeur, as simply getting used to having so many servants, so many strangers bustling around my house. I kept waking up in the early morning and wondering what all the noise below was, and whether someone had broken in. It was an effort to stop doing things for myself and accept being waited on.

The halcyon days didn't last terribly long. The effusiveness and warmth that I basked in during my first weeks as the prime minister's wife didn't survive the long Canadian winter. Before the snows had melted it was clear that there would be friction between me and almost everything I touched. The glossy façade began to crumble. The rot started with the servants and it provided me with a sour, if symbolic, taste of things to come.

My first battle was with the cooks. There were two of them, Margaret and Rita, when I arrived, neither one with any gourmet pretensions, but both of the plain, old-fashioned, English school. Given my taste for brown rice, and my fastidiousness, I wasn't going to put up with the extraordinarily drab and unvaried meals that I had eaten during my earlier evenings with Pierre—one long round of steak pie, chicken pie, meat loaf and chocolate chip cookies. Two days after the honeymoon was over I started work on the menus.

I set to work, fired by a crusading zeal to get Pierre eating a proper balanced diet. From a dozen new cook books I drew up a series of healthy, nutritional and, to my mind, delicious menus. Then, braving the wrath of the cooks, I insisted on being present when a new dish was tried out, and refused to order anything for a formal dinner party until it had been well tasted among ourselves. It wasn't easy. Rita was charming and gentle, and eager to please me, but I soon discovered that Margaret was a tyrant, the kind of woman who was as sweet as cloying sugar to my face, yet harried and tormented the other servants behind my back.

Margaret and I just couldn't hit it off. It was hardly surprising: it would be hard to imagine two women less alike. I was slight, thin, determined and in a position of authority; she was fat, lazy and domineering. One of us had to go. But it took me ages to find a replacement.

The fact that I was so immediately engrossed by the details of our food and servants gives some idea of how lonely those first months of marriage were. After the dry, mild weather of Vancouver even the climate was alien to me.

My isolation was increased by the fact that Pierre had decided that there was no need for me to get involved in politics. He put an embargo on me. I was absolutely taboo, not only for his office, but for everybody.

No one was to come near me, no one was to pester me, or ask me questions. I was to give no interviews. No one dropped in: who does drop in on a prime minister? I had grown up in a house full of busy, gregarious people, where friends came and went all the time, and at first I begged my friends to do the same at 24 Sussex. But they were daunted by the police checks, however friendly, and that distinct aura of formality that lay like a shroud over the house.

During those first months I also had a hard time transforming myself from a peasant-skirted, Indian-shirted hippy into a gracious lady. None of it seemed to come very naturally to me, though I did find that being hostess at parties, where I was often the youngest person in the room by twenty years, was aging me with frightening speed. At the tea parties and luncheons for the wives of visiting heads of states I sometimes felt more like their youngest daughter than their host's wife.

They put me down continuously, nicely but continuously. It was as if they couldn't help it, but I felt very small. And I soon found that I didn't have much in common with most of the wives of Pierre's colleagues; partly because they were all so much older than I was, and partly because I am, by nature, indiscreet and I had to protect myself by not becoming involved.

The one political wife who was immensely kind to me from the day I moved to Ottawa was Mrs. Michener, wife of the governor general. She was a perceptive, if somewhat regal, woman, and once I had become accustomed to her formal airs and astonishingly high standards I grew to love her dearly. Soon after we were married she gave a party for us in the governor general's residence: it was to be the wedding reception we had never had, and Pierre invited all his close friends. (The dress I wore that night was the one that later got me into such trouble in Washington on my last official engagement as the prime minister's wife. It had been made especially for the party, a fine white wool dress studded with pearls and fitting like a glove, which to my romantic eyes seemed more like the real wedding dress than my caftan ever did. Washington accused me of slumming.)

A few days after the ball my phone went again. It was Mrs. Michener; would I care to take tea with her? Somewhat flustered, I made my way across the street, and then proceeded to be given my first lesson in How To Be The Perfect Prime Minister's Wife. She wasted no time. No sooner were we sitting around her immaculately laid tea tray with its bone china and thinly sliced cucumber sandwiches, than she started listing some of the things I must do.

aid gallantly: "We like our women *big*," and proceeded to pile
huge mound of dumplings onto my plate, while helping me
from a passing dish of meat. I found all the food heavy and rich,
re was much too much of it. I struggled away at my task, trying to
each mouthful swallowed as another mark in Mrs. Michener's
hen came the day when I was presented with the great Russian
ty: horse. That was nearly the end of me.
re we left for Moscow we had been warned by Pierre's office that
ild undoubtedly be bugged the entire time, and to behave
re with some caution. "Oh come on," I said laughing to the man
d us. "What's all this cloak-and-dagger stuff? Don't tell me they
prime minister of Canada." He looked patronizing. "Just you
d see."

second day in Moscow his point was proved. We were installed in
te in the official guest house, an austere, dark set of rooms with
lmost drab furniture relieved only by touches of luxury all the
emarkable for being so rare: gold silk bedspreads and carved
ards. I decided to test out the bugging story. We had been
around the city looking at the sights and I was exhausted. As we
bedroom door behind us, I said loudly and distinctly to Pierre:
rre, what wouldn't I give for an ORANGE! My kingdom for an
GE, one fresh orange." Five minutes later came a knock at the
utside stood an expressionless waiter, holding a tray in his hands.
at a banana, an apple and, in the middle, occupying pride of
n orange. He placed the tray ceremoniously on a side table and
carving up the orange, which he then presented to me with a low
ot a word was said.

re long the charms of our permanent eavesdropper began to pall,
rre and I found ourselves retiring constantly to our bathroom,
–both taps running so that we wouldn't be overheard—we
d in furious arguments about Russia. I complained that it was all
edibly drab and dingy, while Pierre defended it. When the
opper took the form of my interpreter Tanya, a dumpy,
hirted, black-skirted lady who stalked so close to my side that she
ays bumping into me, my irritation grew. Her unreasoning
sm also drove me mad. Her lines were quite something. One day
ed a park with three decrepit benches, a moth-eaten patch of
nd one solitary tree. This, so Tanya informed me, was no
y park. It was a rest-and-recreation area donated by the
g government, so that the People of Russia could relax. Another

"If you have a president's wife, or someone wl
do—and this applied particularly to royalty—an
cigarette, then you must pick up a cigarette y(
comfortable."

Since I didn't smoke, I laughed. Naively, I ex
joke—how could I possibly light up a cigarette
frowned.

"That, my dear, is just the point," she saic
learning all the things that you have to do howe
unnatural and trying."

I felt suitably chastened, but my heart sank at

This was the first of many such teas. Mrs. Mic
make me good, and for all our differences I
hard to her lessons. I set to work to become n(
Minister's Wife, but the *most* perfect wife in th(

The day my pregnancy was confirmed there
Canada. I've done it, I thought, I've done it. T
worked it all out on his plastic calendar, looke
"Your baby is due on December 25."

Shortly after we got home from the Caribbea
official visit as wife of the prime minister, and a
was to Russia, a grueling program of seven ci
couple of days in Siberia. I was almost childishl
anxious to do well: now had come the moment
Mrs. Michener's lessons.

The only person who knew I was pregn
daughter, Mrs. Gvyshiani, a gentle, tactful, v(
whom I grew very fond. I had confided in her
appear rude at official banquets by not eating o
and also to explain why I wasn't as eager as I mi
every morning with a full day's schedule of h
visit. I begged her to keep it a secret. If the l
early it would be a long wait for the Can
touchingly kind and considerate, and foun(
stopping my morning sickness by carrying a le
and giving me slices to suck in the car between
She couldn't do much for me at the official
usually found myself stranded miles away down
night I was placed next to an important gentlem

day she took me to the Tretyakov Gallery in Moscow, hurrying me past the masterpieces of pre-revolutionary Russian art and coming to rest with a reverential sigh of admiration before a row of paintings of great buxom ladies with their sickles and vast haymaking machines. "These are the *great* paintings," she informed me. "But it ain't art," I replied.

But I did try very hard to be pleasant. I made friends with Premier Kosygin, whom I found gentle, considerate and graceful—a man whose soft eyes had a charming twinkle to them. Obviously a family man, he talked to me for hours on end about his family and his grandchildren, what they had studied and where they worked. He spoke English to me because he knew how much I hated going through an interpreter. I was struck by his well-tailored clothes, his manicured hands and rather austere good looks. Mr. Brezhnev was quite a different proposition. From the moment I set eyes on him I was reminded of faceless civil servants and politicians the world over, in their navy suits, preferably pinstriped, their light blue shirts and ties, like insurance salesmen at conferences. He gave the impression of being a hard, brusque man—burly like a great, sleek bear. Neither of us could think of anything beyond banalities to say to the other. To him I was just a wife. (I wasn't the only person who found Brezhnev hard. Several years later Rostropovich, a close friend of Pierre's, whispered to me at a concert: "I luff your husband. I luff Willy Brandt. Brezhnev is a shit.")

I shouldn't have been all that sorry to leave Russia. My complete lack of briefing had made me an ill-equipped and ignorant visitor, my morning sickness had spoiled my sightseeing, and for young lovers hating to be apart, the protocol was terribly confining. It was my first taste of enforced segregation. Every time the official cortège set off, Pierre traveled in front with Brezhnev and Kosygin in one car, while I was stowed away in the second surrounded by ambassadresses and their incessant "quack, quack, quack" of small talk.

The official "goodbyes" were said on the red carpet at the bottom of the steps to our plane but for me the visit did not end there. Mr. Kosygin broke with protocol and followed us up the steps to our own territory. He understood my emotional state—saying goodbye is never easy. Dismissing his entourage of aides, K.G.B. and ambassadors, he boarded our plane and in the crammed quarters provided for the Canadian Air Force men who traveled with us, he hugged me farewell. Both of us wept openly. In a world so full of divisions, political maneuvering and protocol, I felt our tears were an unspoken prayer for peace and friendship: please, no more borders!

If there was one thing that I learned faster than anything else, it was that a prime minister's wife has an extraordinarily varied life. One minute I was firing a cook, the next discussing ice floes with strange, non-English-speaking geologists; one day sitting at home watching television, the next, in full regalia, waltzing with a head of state. There is no studying for the part, no understudy to take over when confidence fails. In the first year I had a taste of almost everything that would come my way during my marriage to Pierre: a state visit abroad, a number of receptions at home, a household to reorganize, official and formal clothes to buy, a style of life to master, even a pregnancy. It had two other major events: a journey inside our own country and along our borders, which gave me a chance to see something of Canada, and a visit from Queen Elizabeth, certainly for the wife of a Commonwealth prime minister the most daunting and fearsome of engagements.

It needed all Pierre's understanding and sympathy and many rehearsals of Mrs. Michener's lessons to prepare me for my first encounter with the Queen. It came in July when she visited Vancouver for the British Columbia centenary celebrations, an occasion I had been both dreading and longing for. It was my first really frightening social engagement, and my first visit to my home town as the prime minister's wife.

My immediate reaction on seeing Queen Elizabeth on the steps of her private airplane was one of shock and incredulity: her dress and coat were simple, even dreary. Where was the regal aura I had been dreading? As she came down the steps toward me my terror began to fade; her expression was genuinely friendly and as I curtsied she gave my hand a warm squeeze. As we stood talking, a gust of wind swept the hat I had so carefully chosen from my head. I caught it as it flew off. A lady in waiting appeared as if by magic at her side with a hat pin, and the Queen showed me how to secure my wretched hat firmly to my hair, her very blue eyes gleaming with amusement.

The three days of her visit passed smoothly, professionally and without incident, a tribute to the extraordinary polish of her official machinery. I did my bit, a cog that gave no trouble. I felt I had been simply swept up, carried along on a sea of goodwill and exemplary manners and deposited gently down again at the other end, before the magic carpet whirled up and away on its next engagement. I was delighted and very pleased when Pierre told me that she had seemed pleased with his choice of wife. When it was all over I received a letter from my Aunt Jessie in England, who had seen the official reception on television: "I'm proud of you," she wrote. "You did that like a lady."

CHAPTER 6

FAMILY LIFE

Behind the officialdom and the formality, the show and the façade, Pierre and I led a very quiet life. Anyone reading the stories published in the newspapers and magazines about our glamorous high life, our exotic parties and expensive tastes would have been amazed if they had seen what really went on at home. Pierre is a shy, unsociable man by nature, and I spent much of the first few years either pregnant or nursing a new baby. Apart from the glittering official receptions, when I scrambled out of my jeans and hurried off to the hairdresser, and my afternoons with old girlfriends, we saw very few people. That was the way we wanted it: ours was a private affair.

From the day I entered 24 Sussex Drive as Pierre's wife I knew I had to establish one room that I could call my very own. I told Pierre that I needed a corner that was out of bounds to everyone else in the house, a place where I wouldn't be disturbed by domestic problems or put on show. Pierre understood perfectly. "Take one of the attic rooms, then you'll be really out of the way," he said at once. He had asked me whether I would like a piece of jewelry as his wedding present. "What I would *really* like," I told him, "is a sewing machine." It may sound funny but that's the way it was: in those days I simply couldn't imagine anything in the world that I wanted more.

The sanctuary I chose was on the third floor, a charming, sloping attic room, with a fine view that allowed me to gaze out over the gardens and down to the river. It was the room into which Pierre had unceremoniously bundled all the presents he had received from official visitors. The bulk of it was real junk; expensive, ornate objects, but junk nonetheless, the sort of acquisitions you can never find a use for, yet are just too valuable to throw into the garbage.

It took weeks until the day came when my room was bare. I looked round with pleasure: now what? Should it be basically a sitting room, with squashy chairs and a hi-fi set? A little study, where I could work? I settled on a sewing room, and gave my Ferrari of a machine pride of place. It stood on a plain pine table which I had made in the government workshops. I splashed out on the walls, and had them painted a bright canary yellow, a color I love, with white, lacy curtains. Here I was to spend many happy and tranquil hours.

The sewing room was invaluable, not simply because it provided me with a sanctuary: it was the room in which my growing wardrobe took shape. Since I wore jeans and sweaters about the house, spending so much on a formal wardrobe seemed a shocking extravagance. But here Mrs. Michener took a hand. At one of our early teas she intimated that I didn't have *quite* the right afternoon gown, or quite the number of long evening dresses required. And what about hats? And gloves? Having youth on my side, she said sternly when I protested that no one would notice because I was so young, was not enough. Wasn't it a challenge to become one of Canada's best-dressed women?

Soon my cupboards were overflowing with morning suits, tea dresses, cocktail dresses and ball gowns. The situation wasn't helped by my growing family. One month I was size eight, six weeks later, I could barely scrape into a ten. I became a local lending boutique for all my friends. A size twelve ball dress? I had one in pink tulle or one in flowered silk. A size six tennis dress? I owned just the thing. Size ten ski pants? In navy and beige. I had so many unwanted clothes that I soon started dressing our maids from my cupboards. I laughed when I saw them waiting at table or opening the door in dresses that I could remember myself wearing at the Elysée in Paris or on the Great Wall of China.

When I first arrived at 24 Sussex the weather prevented me from exploring the grounds, but after a couple of months a thaw set in and I was able to turn my attention to the gardens. 24 Sussex, as Pierre soon informed me, comes under the National Capital Commission. The job of planting out the formal beds, and keeping the flowers in full bloom, falls to them. As the snow thawed, a team of government gardeners appeared in their heavy aprons and leather gloves like purposeful gnomes and set to work. Within hours platoons of bulbs were in place, then, just as I was getting used to them, the gnomes would be back. With military precision, the beds were stripped and replanted with something else. There would be rows of tulips, serried ranks of stems, six inches apart, same height, same color, same shape; the next week there would be beds and beds of pink impatiens, same height, same color, same shape. And so it went on. I started a campaign against the system, begging for a little spontaneity, a little mixture. The gnomes eyed me warily but the next time they came I found more color, a few lupins and dahlias, some snapdragons and stocks, injected into the platoons of regulation buds.

Though the house from the outside appears enormous it had curiously few habitable rooms. For a nursery I had to take one of the guest rooms on the second floor. I turned it into the most charming baby's room imaginable. I bought an antique rocking chair and table, scoured the handcraft shops for a patchwork quilt, and had a plain pine crib carved and upholstered. Everything was in the palest robin's egg blue.

When I went to the hospital for my five-month checkup I discovered to my outrage that fathers were not allowed to be present at the birth. I protested and threatened to move to another hospital. There was no question of going through it all without Pierre. Finally the doctor relented, and applied for permission from the directors of the hospital, particularly when I told him stubbornly that if he did not agree I would have my baby at home. The rules were changed for all fathers-to-be at the Civic Hospital and a promise given that Pierre would be with me.

Just before Christmas the phone rang late one evening. It was Jill Turner, the wife of a minister in Pierre's cabinet.

"John and I know that you're not going to be able to join your family at Christmas because the baby is due so soon. Would you like to come and have Christmas dinner with us?"

"How kind," I said, touched by her thoughtfulness. "But I'm afraid there's no question of that. I'm having my baby on Christmas Day."

Pierre and I had worked it all out. We'd go to mass at midnight on Christmas Eve; sleep in on Christmas morning; open our presents, have lunch; then go and have the baby. It all went according to plan. When I woke on Christmas morning something was definitely happening. We opened our presents, had lunch and called the doctor. Like Jill Turner he laughed increduously, but to humor us came over to check. He didn't laugh so much when he had examined me.

"Take that Labrador for a walk," he suggested, "and bring the baby on a bit."

Pierre had given me the puppy months before on the doctor's advice that I should take constant exercise, and I had walked miles with him, cutting paths through the deep banks of snow right up until the last day. So we set out, Pierre with his stopwatch to time the contractions, me hanging on to the leash with one hand and Pierre with the other. I was perfectly calm: I felt fit and happy and confident. It was Pierre who was getting increasingly agitated—particularly when he put down the stopwatch somewhere and couldn't find it—despite the fact that he and I had discussed the event at length, and Pierre had even attended the fathers' pre-natal class.

Justin's arrival was as uncomplicated as the nine months he had spent inside me. Pierre, who is a fanatic about drugs, had convinced me after reading every book on the subject he could find to go through natural childbirth with no artificial help at all. To please him I agreed, despite the reluctance of my doctor. My midwife was a sensible, reassuring woman, and I had no more than twenty minutes of what could be described as real pain. I didn't even have to ask what sex he was. I had known it was going to be a boy. Pierre and I hugged each other. Justin had come, and it was Christmas Day.

When I learned that I was expecting Sacha we converted a second spare room alongside Justin's room, creating a new guest room in the attic. At the same time we decided to have a private sitting room for the family on the second floor, a room that would be absolutely out of bounds to all strangers. Justin saw it for the first time when he was nearly two, and the room still without any furniture. A cheerful, bright, manically energetic little boy, he peered around the door, broke into shouts of pleasure, and started racing around and around it in circles, yelling at the top of his voice: "Freedom, freedom." He had picked up the lines of a song by Richie Havens, which I often sang for him at bedtime: "Sometimes I feel like a motherless child. A mighty long way from home. Freedom! Freedom! Freedom!" From that day on, our sitting room was the "freedom room."

In the autumn of 1973 I was in the last months of my second pregnancy. I had had a lot of trouble with the baby, who was lying in a slightly awkward position giving me twinges of agonizing pain. I was also far larger than I had been with Justin, and could scarcely heave myself about the house. As Christmas approached, my efforts to give Justin a special day on the twenty-fifth, for after all it combined his second birthday with the first Christmas he was really conscious of, redoubled. I combed every department store in Ottawa to find the plastic motorcycle he had been begging for.

We ate Christmas dinner on Christmas Eve, so that the staff could spend the holiday with their families. My mother was staying with us, as was my sister Janet. Just as I raised my glass of wine to Pierre's toast I felt a strange, familiar twinge. It went away. After dinner I stretched out on a sofa to watch television. The pains started again. This time there was no mistaking what they were: contractions.

Soon after ten, Pierre came to take me to midnight mass and was amazed to find me lying down. "Pierre," I said, laughing. "I don't think I'd better come with you. This baby's coming."

He roared with laughter. "Trust you to imagine yourself into a second Christmas baby," he teased me. "You couldn't *possibly* have two babies on

Christmas Day. Come on, get your coat on. It's just false labor."

I dragged myself up and called Tara, the Jamaican maid we had brought back with us from our vacation there. She was a Catholic and had decided to come to midnight mass. I told her what I thought was happening. It made the service a somewhat comic event, particularly when a procession of choirboys filed past. One of them was bearing a plastic bread basket with a plastic doll to represent the baby Jesus. "If they don't watch out," I whispered to Tara, "they're going to have live entertainment soon." We giggled again at "Hark the Herald Angels Sing," for by then I was really going into labor, clasping the seat to suppress a groan when the contractions came.

Sacha's birth was a long and painful one. It took all the rest of the night. Again, prompted by Pierre, I refused to take all analgesics and in the end I was proud I held on. He was born as dawn came, a rather weary and angry baby. I fell in love with him at once, and our shared painful night was the start of a special bond between us. There was also something quite uncanny about the date; not just one Christmas baby but two. And Yves Lewis was born on Christmas Day as well.

With two children in just under three years of marriage Pierre and I found that our basically strong earlier physical attraction for one another was being seriously undermined. I got fat and preoccupied and was unrecognizable from the carefree, sexy girl he had married.

The honeymoon had by now vanished under a blanket of diapers and small babies, and Pierre and I settled down to an untroubled domestic life, broken only by the trips abroad we absolutely could not avoid making. We spent what time we could up at the lake, and even in the city saw as few people as possible. It was a way of life that suited Pierre as much as it did me; he is a conscientious and loving father and much given to routine. The days sped by, scarcely altering.

Our third son, Micha, arrived on October 2, 1975. Throughout my pregnancy I had been convinced my new baby would be a girl. By now I was getting into the knack of childbirth: no more ridiculous inhibitions. As he popped out I gave a bloodcurdling yell; you could have heard me down on the parking lot. My immediate reaction on seeing another boy was bitter disappointment. I wanted nothing to do with him. It was a wily nurse, who remembered me from Sacha and Justin, who got round my rage. She brought him to me to feed when I had relegated him to the nursery; as he started sucking so I fell in love.

Pierre and myself and the babies: we were a happy, intimate family when we were allowed to be. There was also something very cloistered about my existence, particularly when Pierre was away on a trip, and the chef, the only man in the house, had gone home for the night. Eight women and three small children living together, retiring to our own cells at night, like a secluded nunnery. It was then that I felt more like a mother superior than a prime minister's wife, doing the rounds of my postulants and worrying about their souls.

CHAPTER 7

SAVED BY PROTOCOL

There was no escaping official life—it was there all the time, lurking. It emerged in frenetic bursts of entertaining and dressing up; catching planes to new places and talking to strangers through interpreters, only to be switched off again just as suddenly, leaving me washed up in my privacy and peace.

It wasn't long before my childhood habit to be secretive, to split myself into separate isolated parts, each carefully locked away from the other, began again with a vengeance. I became two different people. In the background at 24 Sussex and up at the lake I was Mrs. Trudeau, an ordinary suburban Canadian housewife who liked to bake bread and cross-country ski. The moment officialdom struck I was transformed into the wife of the prime minister; it was all rather like Cinderella and her pumpkin. And how does a twenty-two-year-old girl, with no experience of protocol, formality or procedure, learn the rules? One thing was clear; I had to learn them, and I had to learn them fast.

"Protocol will protect you," Mrs. Michener, my mentor, kept repeating. "If you get that right, you won't have to put *yourself* on the line. You will be judged by your manners."

I believed every word. The problem was how to absorb it all. By keeping his staff away from me, and not thinking to provide me with an assistant, or even an experienced social secretary who could have guided me along, Pierre effectively kept me in the dark far longer than I need have been. He meant it kindly, but it was a mistake.

I learned the hard way, by watching and listening to the other wives when they came to visit us, or I went to them, and imitating those whom I judged masters of the art. Everywhere I went I kept muttering rules and advice to myself: "Remember to offer Mrs. So and So orange juice, because she doesn't drink alcohol. Remember to carry the carnations sent by the principal's wife when you visit the school. Talk to General X about sailing. Don't mention religion to Mrs. Y. . . ." And so it went on. To my astonishment it soon dawned on me that I wasn't alone in my revulsion against the tedium of official life. Almost everyone seemed to loathe it, and some were driven nearly insane by it. And this realization, in a sense, was to prove my downfall, for I now set out, singlehanded, to change it all. I had a mission, a crusade. I was going to make official life fun.

First there was the issue of the presents. From the day Pierre and I arrived in Moscow I was showered with presents. One day Mr. Kosygin gave me a magnificent amber necklace; the next, the government presented me with a bone china tea set. Then the foreign minister's wife, Mrs. Gromyko, produced an interlocking set of Russian dolls and lacquered boxes. Mrs. Gvyshiani gave me boxes and pins and ornaments. Then came the day for our return present giving; I had been counting the hours until I could return some of their generosity.

I asked the external affairs secretary to send over my present for Mrs. Gvyshiani so that I could wrap it up beautifully before presenting it. To my consternation, and total disbelief, there appeared a meager plate silver maple leaf, costing probably no more than thirty-five dollars. "But this," I moaned to Pierre, "is what I ought to give Tanya, my interpreter, *not* the prime minister's daughter." From that day on I made presents *my* business.

The presents were, of course, a two-way business. In the United States all official presents belong to the state; in Canada they belong to the recipients. I soon found myself showered with things of immense value and beauty. Just after we were married the governor of Newfoundland offered me an otter coat, and the commissioner of the North West Territories a Mackenzie mink—Pierre made me refuse them, saying they were too costly. But there was little he could do about the sunburst gold Andrew Grima brooch covered in diamonds given me by the Queen, nor the Inca pink clay adobe with tiny carved figures given me by Mrs. Perez, nor the four crates of Japanese tableware, nor Mrs. Gandhi's silk saris, nor Mrs. Nixon's Bartlett print, nor Mme. Giscard d'Estaing's marble jewelry box—24 Sussex was filled to bursting with the tea sets, boxes and lacquered trays, though Pierre put his foot down at a sealskin kayak and presented it to the Museum of Man.

The gifts under control, I now turned to the more awkward question of briefing. Having been humiliated in Russia by the full depth of my ignorance of everything from simple geography to the identity of the people to whom I was introduced, I begged Pierre to make certain I had written notes in good time before a visit. In the early days this would merely consist of another copy of the collection of notes that went out to the press. Later on, after I had seen how thorough and elaborate the American briefing books are, with photographs of all the people you are likely to meet, and a brief resumé of their tastes, I became more demanding. Sometimes I even got my hands on Pierre's notes, which were far more amusing. . . . "Perhaps you should not get too heavily involved with X," they would read, "because having evaded tax for six years, he is about to be impeached."

Of all the official visits I paid, the one to France in the autumn of 1974 was the most difficult and the most redolent of protocol. It wasn't made easier by the fact that I wasn't long out of the hospital following serious emotional stress. By then the contradictions of my life were really beginning to tell on me.

There is no doubt that the French can be the rudest, most arrogant people in the world. This was our first state visit to France since De Gaulle had made his "Vive Québec Libre" statement in Montreal during Expo '67 and so effectively cut off relations between France and Canada for almost a decade. We simply had to do well. It wasn't going to be easy: we had to open the door of good relations again, yet at the same time assert that France could not treat Quebec as a separate, independent country.

My first function without Pierre (he was at an official, men only, lunch) was a reception given by Mme. Chirac, the prime minister's wife, a chic woman with a sharp nose. The food was superb. The guests were all women, the wives of cabinet ministers, diplomats and members of parliament, and, oh boy, did they condescend to me. I was the youngest by twenty-five years, and they made me feel like a stupid, ill-informed, clumsy, illiterate child. Outwardly all was civility and good breeding; inside I was seething.

The hostility oozing out of these French women toward me grew more intense as the days went by. I had one afternoon off. Savoring every minute of it I decided to go to a fashion show. It was at the time when St. Laurent was changing his neat, tailored look and presenting wild Russian peasant costumes in his collections. I was eager to see them. Mme. Chirac, on hearing my plans, pressed me to go to an *haute couture*

At sixteen I was chosen to represent my high school on the teen fashion council of the local Hudson's Bay Company store. We learned charm, poise and basic store management skills. Here I am, in the center of the group.

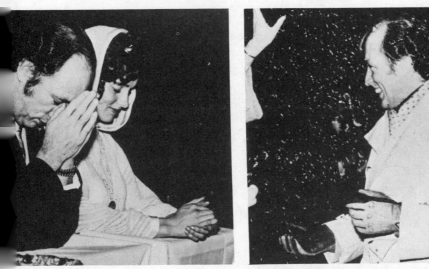
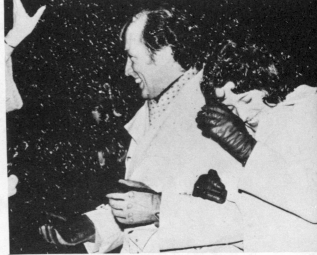

Pierre and I were married in the midst of the heaviest snowstorm in recent Canadian history, in a small church bedecked with spring flowers. We wanted a small, quiet ceremony, and astoundingly, we managed it: no one outside our families knew of the wedding until it was a fait accompli.

Justin, my perfect Christmas son, three days old at above left; right, Micha and I both snug in hand knits from my mother. Below, our happy family at Harrington Lake, my favorite of our residences.

Above, a happy moment in the Rocky Mountains. Pierre carried Justin, and Sacha "rode" with me. Below, walking with Micha (in my arms) and Justin, on a visit to my parents in Vancouver.

Clockwise from upper left: I found England's Prince Charles to be among the most engaging and down-to-earth of my state dinner companions. Being eight months pregnant didn't prevent me from touring the Great Wall of China on our visit there. On my only official trip to the United States, I met the Carters—and my "short" dress caused a minor scandal. I always enjoyed escorting the charming Prince Philip on royal visits.

Clockwise from upper right: While Pierre admires his impeccably coutured wife, I am lifted from a near fall by my gracious Queen. My visit to the Louvre with Mmes. Giscard d'Estaing and Chirac unnerved me so that I passed out cold in the museum. It was a great honor to meet Prime Minister Golda Meir. I arrived in Havana, Cuba with my dress blood-spattered, but Premier Fidel Castro seemed not to notice.

Above left, Margaret Trudeau walks off the Today *television program after the show's interviewer, Jane Pauley, became persistent in attempting to get Mrs. Trudeau to speak about her private life. Above right, Margaret as the object of celebrity hounds. Below, having a good time at Studio 54. Right, with a friend in the south of France.*

G. SPITZER

fashion parade by a more conservative designer. I protested: "No. I really want to see St. Laurent." They demurred. Finally, with sighs and considerable bad grace, Mme. Chirac insisted on accompanying me to St. Laurent.

Clothes were so immensely important: if I felt correctly dressed it gave me that initial boost in confidence that enabled me to cope. If my shoes were even slightly scuffed I felt distracted and self-conscious. I had begged to be able to take a maid to France with me, but my request had been turned down as pretentious. On the night of our grandest dinner during the tour, held at the Elysée, I had a pink silk organdie Valentino dress with painted peonies to wear. It was a very low cut dress which I kept for only the grandest occasions. To show it off at its best I decided to have my hair done by Alexandre, who opened his salon especially for me. His makeup men took three-quarters of an hour on my mouth alone. I came out radiant: my hair cut severely across in bangs, the "mandarin look," white and black and impassive. But it was not the hairstyle nor the face to go with a fluffy pink décolleté dress, as I soon discovered back before my own mirror. I scrubbed most of the lipstick off my mouth, but had no time left to do much about my eyes which had almost totally disappeared under more layers of greens and grays than even Elizabeth Taylor puts on. In despair I realized I would have to abandon the fluff for something far plainer; something stark. I settled on a white silk shirt and a long black evening skirt. No sooner had I stepped inside the Elysée when I saw my terrible error: there was not a woman present who was not wearing *haute couture*. Alone, I looked out of place.

My worst gaffe in France happened on the day that Mme. Giscard d'Estaing took me to the Louvre. I was with a crowd of French ladies and we passed in front of what seemed to me to be every single picture in the building, pausing for a few seconds, while the ladies kept their eyes riveted upon me to check my reaction. My French was still atrocious (adequate accent but horrendous grammar) and I felt that they were testing me. I took a cowardly if unpremeditated way out. I passed out cold on the floor. The dear wife of the French ambassador to Canada, Mme. Viau, threw herself forward to break my fall, but I collapsed all the same in a heap on the stone floor, I now believe entirely under the pressure of feeling myself on the defensive and sneered at.

Fainting was an unconscious escape I often took on formal occasions, particularly when very nervous or pregnant. When the Queen spoke in Charlottetown and was halfway through her address I disappeared under my chair on the podium. On another occasion I was sitting next to Mr. Michener and across the table from President Tito during his state visit to Canada, toward the end of a seemingly week-long meal of interpreters, cigars and goodwill. Just as Mr. Michener rose to his feet to offer the official welcome toast, I had to stumble out of the room before fainting.

Possibly the most successful and certainly the most unusual trip we made was to China in the autumn of 1973, a "getting-to-know-you visit" of the old fashioned sort made more important by the fact that we were the first western nation to visit China officially. I was seven and a half months pregnant with Sacha. I went to my doctor for my monthly visit in October, bewailing the fact that I was going to have to miss this trip. I was astonished to hear him say: "Why ever don't you go? There's absolutely no reason not to." All he insisted was that I take along someone to help (which was a godsend, for it set a precedent and in future, especially when ill or pregnant, I was allowed a companion).

It was mid-October when we arrived in Peking. The weather was perfect, warm by day and cool at night, which was just as well since I had had very little time to prepare suitable clothes for the trip, and was in any case a very awkward shape. I was amazed by the beauty of Peking and the way that the capital of the most populated country in the world still looks like a sprawling country town, with single-story buildings made of sticks, clay and bamboo poles. Everywhere there was green. Mao's order that for every Chinese born a tree should be planted had taken fruit by the time of our visit: huge trees lined every street, turning Peking into a restful, gentle city. When we went south we found orange blossom out, jasmine trees smelling sweetly, and cassis flowers everywhere.

My most appropriate visit while in China was to Peking's one maternity hospital. It was a very comic occasion. I went surrounded by a great gang of journalists and at the door we were enveloped in big white coats, and sterilized masks, hats and slippers. There was lots of laughter and jokes. After a tour of the wards we went on to the case room, which, to my Canadian eyes, looked like a relic from one of our history museums. Forceps, a bucket and a rickety old table. Mischieviously I asked the doctor where the mirrors were to let the women watch their babies being born. He looked shocked. "Oh yes," I insisted, "you know, mirrors where Mommy and Daddy. . . ."

"Daddy," came a horrified cry, "Daddy in here . . . ?"

Since I had myself had a blood problem with Justin I asked my interpreter to find out what this hospital did with cases of RH incompatibility. The doctor in charge looked puzzled.

"What do you mean? The babies die, of course."

It was my turn to be astonished. "They don't need to die. That's a disease of the past. There's an injection you can give within two hours of the birth of the first baby." And I described the inoculation that had been discovered in Winnipeg at the RH Disease Center and what it had done for me. The Chinese doctors were very interested and when I saw our deputy minister of health that night at the hotel he agreed to put the Winnipeg center in touch with the Peking hospital, and get them to send vaccine and information. Even Pierre was impressed. And it was uphill work impressing Pierre.

At every stop in China we were met by a vast, enthusiastic crowd. To my western eyes they were all identical. I became convinced that the crowds plus costumes and bands were moving with us, because wherever we were, they were—the same little girls doing the same dances in the same clothes with their faces painted, tassels in their hands, and little black shoes on their feet. And they always chanted the same song, a verse which, roughly translated, means "Long Live Friendship between Canada and China." Unfortunately it sounded exactly like "Goddamn Whistle: Canada-Peking." Once I had told Pierre, neither of us could hear it any other way, so our paths were lined with little girls leaping into the air singing "Goddamn Whistle: Canada-Peking."

For all our marvelous travels, I did miss one encounter I had much looked forward to: a meeting with Mao. By then Mao was already weak. No appointments could be made to see him; it was simply a question of waiting and seizing the good moment. That moment came just at the time I was visiting a kindergarten, so Pierre went alone.

Missing Chairman Mao was a terrible disappointment, but compensated for by a fascinating encounter with Premier Chou en Lai. The year we visited China he was seventy-six, a handsome, thin, elegant man with prominent cheekbones and warm brown eyes. I had had several unremarkable conversations with him in the course of our many receptions. Then came the day we were due to leave Peking. Pierre and I had a free lunch to ourselves. Since, despite the series of delicious meals we had eaten, we seemed to have missed out altogether on Peking duck, I asked our Chinese guide whether there was a restaurant in the city we could visit to eat it? Then I thought no more about it.

That morning we were in the Great Hall where Pierre and the

premier were signing documents. When the formal ceremony was over, and we were preparing to take our leave of him, Chou en Lai took my hand and said, with old fashioned courtesy: "I have heard you want Peking duck. It will be my privilege to have a Peking duck lunch for you and your party."

The feast was prepared as by a magic genie. No more than what seemed like minutes later we were summoned back into the dining room at the Great Hall. At the door the Chinese maître d'hôtel started, Chinese fashion, sifting the men from the women, so that all the women in the party were directed to sit at one side of one huge round table, and the men at the other. Chou en Lai stopped him and my translator told me what he had said: "Mrs. Trudeau doesn't like protocol of this kind. As it is her lunch she is sitting next to me."

What followed was undoubtedly the most curious and fascinating discussion in all my five years of official banquets. Our entire talk was conducted in English, despite the fact that Chou en Lai usually made a point never to speak anything but Chinese in case his words were misinterpreted. He broke his rule for me, I think, because I was just Pierre's pregnant wife.

We began by talking about my coming child. "I have very strong views about illegitimacy," the premier began. "I think it is a terrible thing for women to have to give up their babies, or have abortions, because they aren't married." He paused. "I have been thinking about this for many years, and I'll tell you why. Just after the Revolution a woman got on a train with her baby. When she got off at the next station, she left her child in a basket on the seat with a note which said: 'Please take this baby to Chou en Lai and let him bring up my beautiful boy. The social stigma against me because I am not married is too great to bear.'"

"Did you keep the baby?" I asked immediately. "What happened to him?"

Chou en Lai replied: "My wife and I already had a family of our own, so we couldn't adopt him. But we put him with good people."

"And have you followed his progress?"

"Yes," he replied, smiling with obvious pride, "indeed we have. He's turned into a fine boy."

His next topic was even more unexpected. "I imagine you think Chinese women are liberated?" he asked me.

"Well," I said cautiously, "they appear to be working side by side with the men. Economically they seem to be liberated. They're a main part of the working force."

"Ah," he said. "You're wrong. They are not liberated. You are liberated."

I was astonished. "Me? I'm pregnant. I don't work. I am a mother and a housewife."

"Yes," he said. "But the Chinese women are extremely embarrassed by their femininity and you are not. Let me give you an example. I had what you call a Girl Friday in my office, a girl who was really indispensable to me. I also liked her very much. Then one day she didn't appear. I assumed she was ill. After a week of embarrassed silence from everyone it finally emerged that she had transferred jobs—because she was pregnant. She had left word that she would return when this embarrassing state was over. She couldn't stand the thought of facing me in so humiliating a state." I was immediately conscious of my huge belly. I grabbed a napkin off the table and covered it. Chou en Lai laughed. "Oh dear, no, no, you have come to terms with yourself as a woman. You are proud. To watch you walking as proud as a queen with your big belly is the happiest sight to see because you are so proud of it. Chinese women are still feudal in their attitudes toward their own femininity, their own bodies, their own sexuality. They have just become versions of men." I was so astonished by his words that I managed to swallow down the only course in the entire meal that I found repellent: snippets of the ducks' intestines floating around in broth. In a true Peking duck dinner you eat the whole bird.

During my six years with Pierre we paid one or two major visits abroad each year, and we traveled around inside Canada almost continuously—Pierre was usually away from home for a trip at least every couple of weeks. The Canadians, I soon found, don't really like their prime minister traveling despite the fact that internationally Pierre has put Canada on the map. The picture I got of these trips from reading the newspapers was a slightly malicious one, as if they hoped to catch him being absurd, or on a joyride at the taxpayers' expense.

Our staff, on the other hand, loved them. All seven women and the chef would be lined up on the steps of 24 Sussex when we set off on a visit, and the maids in particular reveled in the new clothes and the tales I brought home. It demeaned them to have a prime minister's wife in jeans; they hadn't joined the staff for that. They were much more respectful to me when I put on my silk dresses and floppy hats. God knows I did so often enough. For every trip abroad, we hosted at least six at home.

Of the dozens of official visits I hosted, a few stand out with particular vividness; they are usually those which ended in disasters, or near disasters. President Bhutto's visit in 1976 is such a one.

We were scarcely settled after returning from a visit to Mexico where rose petals had cascaded daily on our heads, little girls had dressed up in peasant costumes and serenaded us everywhere, and there had been endless singing and laughing—a warm, delightful visit. It was midwinter in Canada when we got home and the morning we met President Bhutto and his wife it was bitterly cold. The reception took place in an icy military hangar, where the president was to review the guard. As we went to leave the hangar and climb into waiting cars, the huge doors slid open and a massive shower of huge icicles came crashing down, denting the tops of the cars. It was a miracle that President Bhutto wasn't killed.

While all the crashing, shouting and chaos was going on I felt a terrible giggle rising up in my throat. I clamped my hand over my mouth. As we left the hangar, a journalist came up to me. "Mrs. Trudeau," he said slyly, "I couldn't help noticing that you found it very amusing that there was nearly a terrible accident."

"No, no," I said hastily. "I didn't find it a bit amusing. It was just that I couldn't help thinking of the contrast between Canadian hospitality and Mexican hospitality. When we arrived in Mexico we were showered with rose petals. When guests come here they're showered with icicles."

My official chore at home, once the prime minister's dinner was over, was entertaining the wives. I usually gave a luncheon, generally for eight women, chosen, like our official guests, from different professions and from different parts of Canada. These lunches weren't always much of a success. I sometimes found myself surveying the table with loathing and irritation: what in the world can I possibly find to talk to these crows about?

After lunch was over, I would dream up ways of entertaining them—take them to day centers or a city school, or simply for a drive into the countryside. I soon discovered on my own travels, getting to know the wives and the official circuit, how very little any of us actually wanted a heavy official program of visits to places in which we had not the slightest interest. Frankly, I just wasn't interested in dental hospitals, or zoos, or centers for adult education. They bored me almost to tears. They bored all the other wives too. I cannot see a picture of a prime minister's wife opening a new hospital or civic center today without conjuring up for myself the murderous thoughts that must be going through her head under the widebrimmed hat. Wives, just like me, just like any woman, wanted to get their hair done, sleep in late, and if they were lucky, visit a picture gallery or go to the theater. They simply didn't want to review the entire Brownie pack at 9:30 A.M. So I quickly organized a whole new system for visiting wives, cut down their schedule to the bare minimum that I would have wanted myself and tried to introduce at least some informal time.

On their arrival in Ottawa I offered them a choice—either a relaxed tea with myself and the children in the gardens of 24 Sussex when the weather was good, or in the freedom room when it was bad, or a formal tea party. The formal occasion would be complete with hats, and one of my by now impressive selection of tea sets, and we would be waited on by a maid.

Those tea parties provided some of my best official moments. Freed from the constraints of their husbands and the other ministers, some of the wives revealed comic and unexpected sides to their natures. In Moscow I had formed no very strong impression of Mrs. Gromyko, other than of a large and obviously intelligent woman. A very different person came to tea in Ottawa. To my surprise she had opted for a simple afternoon with the children and I was somewhat nervous when her official car drew up at 24 Sussex. Would Justin dribble all over her? Had the cook remembered the cake? She couldn't have been easier, chattering away and plying me with advice and hints about how to bring up the children. As she left, to my astonishment she said to me: "Do you realize that you live in *paradise?* No country in the world has the luck and the opportunities that you have here."

As I went along, watching and listening and learning, so I came to admire the women who put up with this life, and particularly those who handled it with style and dignity; women like Queen Alia of Jordan who later became a real friend. No one, however, impressed me more than our Queen, with her warm friendliness and utter dedication. I have reason to be grateful to her. On one of our first encounters I was wearing a brand new *haute couture* suit I had bought in Rome, with very high heeled shoes. I was extremely nervous. As I sank to the ground in a deep curtsy it became crystal clear to both of us that I was not going to make it up again. Without altering her expression by as much as a flicker, the Queen strengthened her grasp, tensed all the muscles of her right arm, and drew me up to my feet with a grip of iron, smiling impassively the while.

CHAPTER 8

ON THE CAMPAIGN TRAIL

Not long after we were married I was approached by the ladies of the Liberal Association: would I become their honorary president? All previous prime ministers' wives had accepted; it never crossed their minds that I wouldn't follow suit. Would I care to be on various Liberal committees? Play a part in the parliamentary wives' meetings? To everyone's amazement, I refused. I agreed to help out on special occasions, but said that at this stage I didn't wish to get involved in any work I could not give myself up to completely. If I took a job on, I wanted it to be not a token, but a proper one.

The political ladies took my excuse in good heart. They put it all down to youth and timidity. What they didn't realize was that I had a very different reason for refusing, and they would have been shocked had they learned what it was. I didn't get involved with their activities because I didn't *feel* involved. I never had been a card-carrying Liberal. I couldn't seem to summon up any party fervor—indeed, I sometimes felt that there were as many "nincompoops" in the Liberal ranks as there appeared to be in the Conservative and National Democratic parties. A heresy, I know. And with that sort of attitude it would have been worse than hypocritical to become a fake Liberal lady.

However, when the Liberals got back in again at the election I allowed myself to be drawn closer into the fold—but always in a social, never a bureaucratic, capacity. I gave caucus parties up at the lake, barbecue lunches by the waterside, to which candidates and members brought their families. One night we even held a candlelit barn dance up there; the flares from the marquee reflected in the still black water of the lake. I soon observed, and began to revel in, the great difference in style between the parties, particularly between our party and the Conservatives. It brought out both the best (a longing to excel) and the worst (a taste for malicious teasing) in me. I passionately wanted the Liberals to dress better, look better, do things with greater taste and panache; at the same time I dearly wished to poke fun at our rivals.

Though I spoke in public myself as little as possible, pleading everything from pregnancy to a sore throat, there was no escaping it altogether. I was agonizingly nervous the first couple of times, my knees trembling so violently that I couldn't see how I would avoid keeling over on my way to the stage. Sometimes I didn't even get any warning of what

411

was about to hit me. I would be daydreaming in the front row, wishing I were at home reading a book, or hiking in the mountains with Pierre, when a tag end of a sentence would impinge like a hammer on my thoughts: ". . . and now I will call on Mrs. Trudeau." There was nothing for it then but to ad lib, which invariably got me into trouble with the sorts of things I came out with.

One day in Vancouver, at a meeting in the area where my parents live, I suddenly found that I had a microphone in my hands. There was silence all around; just row upon row of expectant eyes. The room swam before me. Fearing that unless something could be forced from my lips I would take my easy way out and faint, I said the first thing that I could think of: "Pierre has taught me everything I know about loving." It was quite true, but I didn't mean it quite the way it came out. There was an enormous guffaw from the audience and a good deal of smirking. I turned crimson and got deeper into the mess. "No, no," I said hastily. "I mean about being a loving person." Ha, ha, ha, they all roared.

But I got better. The day even came when I gave a speech of Pierre's for him. He was called away suddenly to a summit meeting in Germany on the day he was to receive an honorary degree from Ottawa University. I read out his words and just hearing them come out gave me a heady rush of confidence.

In those first few years Pierre and I handled that awkward balance of political and home life reasonably happily. I felt lonely, yes, but not left out. That was perhaps due to Pierre's tact and the way that whenever someone interesting was in town, like Marshall McLuhan or Richard Burton, he made a point of having me at the lunches he gave for them. When something really bothered him then he did discuss it with me: he knew that, because I kept my distance from the other political wives, I was perfectly safe. If it was just some old wheat policy speech he kept it to himself. I was grateful: nothing could have bored me more, though my attitude would have scandalized the other political wives.

In the spring of 1974 Pierre called an election. It was only eighteen months since the last one, but he had had such a very close shave that time, with barely a working majority, that he dared not wait any longer. It was now or never. A bid for a real Liberal victory.

Yet it wasn't going to be easy. The dwindling majority, said the political pundits he consulted, came not because of Liberal policies but because of Pierre himself. His manner with the public, they told him, was too dry, too professorial, his voice too hard and cold. They expected rousing rhetoric; what they got was a boring, highly intellectual lecture. People simply thought him arrogant and aloof, a brilliant but cold man, abrupt and remote.

I am probably the only person alive who really knows how very unjustified this reputation is: Pierre is one of the gentlest of men, a loving father and a very loyal friend. But he is also painfully shy, a genuinely private person, quite incapable of expressing his feelings at all convincingly. I had a hunch that if I fought the election by his side, demonstrating on every platform and in every convention hall of the country just how happy we were together and what a devoted family man he was, then Pierre would have a better chance to convince people that he was the man to lead them.

My immediate problem was that I couldn't get Sacha, then just four months old, to accept a bottle, however much I tried. I was also secretly troubled by the thought that having fed Justin for six months I should do the same for Sacha. So if I went, the baby would have to come too.

Pierre took some persuading. I pleaded, I bullied, I begged. In the end, reluctantly, fearing that Sacha would fall ill, and I would grow bored, Pierre gave in. And once he agreed, he appeared delighted to have me along—we had one of the best times of our marriage.

We decided—for by now I too was part of the decision-making team, a team that really worked well together—to handle the 1974 campaign quite differently from previous ones. We weren't going to court the press, and we weren't going to canvass in the traditional big cities any more than we strictly had to. Instead we resolved to make for the wilds, for the villages, for the small towns, attend local rallies and fêtes, picnics and meetings and get to know as many people, in a totally informal way, as possible.

It was a grueling life: up at dawn, in the air seven or eight hours a day, then new arrivals, new crowds, new speeches. It wasn't surprising we got on one another's nerves. Ivan Head, an old adversary of mine and Pierre's special assistant in international relations, was along as Pierre's speech writer and did his best to ease me out, creating an indefinable but unmistakable aura that I was totally redundant to the trip. He was always smiling, always whispering something in Pierre's ear, and I felt moments of pure childish jealousy. To fight back, I worked.

As the campaign progressed, it became increasingly clear that Pierre had to adopt a new, relaxed, intimate style and I worked away at him. He needed to be down to earth, emotional, committed—not rational. It was quite a battle. Ivan Head had views of his own about Pierre's style, and even stronger views about my role, or, perhaps lack of a role, in the campaign. And though I had my friends in the informal camp, Ivan Head was powerful and my cries about how terrible Pierre's speeches had become, full of heavy rhetoric and ponderous, interminable paragraphs meaning nothing, fell on deaf ears.

Then I got a lucky break. Pierre was to give a wheat policy speech at Humboldt, up in Saskatchewan, and a small group of us flew up there early one morning by private plane. A great crowd had turned out to see us. After greetings and cheers Pierre stood up and embarked on one of the longest, most tedious of speeches, written by the very minister in charge of the Wheat Board who was sitting complacently on the podium with his wife. I looked out across the sea of faces with pity and fury: "These people are bored rigid. They haven't come here to listen to this," I said to myself. Worse was to come. The last five minutes of the speech were a highly embarrassing eulogy of Pierre, and even he looked ill at ease as he delivered the fulsome words. He sat down, to muted applause, and I was called to the microphone.

I was too cross to be tactful. In any case I was made more courageous by the great roar of welcome that went up from the crowd. "I must apologize," I started, feigning contrition, unable to prevent the malice rising in me, "but neither the good minister here, nor his lovely wife, have been kind enough to write an elegant speech for me to make. So you will have to make do with plain, honest words." And I went on to talk about the new programs for women and children which the Liberals were embarking on, reminding them of things we had done and trying to inject a note of sincerity into the proceedings. Behind me, I felt the podium stiffen with rage. The people, however, loved it, and laughed and cheered.

I returned to my place and looks so hostile that I could almost feel them. All the way back to Ottawa I was in disgrace; no one spoke to me, no one came near me. Typically Pierre just laughed. He thought it was wonderful. And from that day on he *did* change his tactics. He asked his ministers to prepare bald policy statements that could be given out to newspapers, and he simply used the words as the basis for his own speech, a real, heartfelt, interesting, imaginative speech that people could follow and even enjoy. He stopped being a professor, and started shouting out the words with real emotion. The effect was dramatic.

As May became June, then June July, so our exhaustion grew stronger and our enthusiasm more forced. After forty rallies every one blurred into the next and seemed the same; the speeches were the same; even the people were the same. We were kept going only by a growing sense of victory, a swelling tide of success.

The political touchstone in the country is Toronto, an ethnically mixed, fickle, and changeable city. If Toronto didn't want Pierre, then neither would Canada. We left it till last.

It was a marvelous, blue, unclouded day. One hundred and fifty thousand people had brought their picnics to Toronto Island to eat on the grass and hear what Pierre had to say. When he stood up there was a hush. He talked for about twenty minutes, clearly, calmly, radiating confidence. When he sat down you could have heard the ovation twenty miles away. Then I got up to speak. I talked about motherhood, my children and the family, and before long all the moms in the crowd had tears trickling down their cheeks.

When I finished, others spoke, and the atmosphere grew better and better. From that moment I had no doubts that we would win, though everyone kept repeating that we wouldn't.

When we got home that night tension was growing. It was only then that I realized that I had never in the last two-month dash paused to consider what we would do if we lost. Was I going to have to pack up my two babies and the entire house next morning and move out? On the one hand I wanted out, badly; but then why had I worked so hard to stay? Pierre, I knew, had no doubts; he still has no doubts today. But I was really torn. And when, at midnight, the news of our success came, my tears might have been those of pain or pleasure.

Next morning was a brilliant sunny day and I sat having my breakfast on the porch of the freedom room watching the white sailing boats in the sparkling bay. I waited for a phone call of thanks, of praise, of something, from someone. I waited; and I waited. It was absurd of me—everyone was exhausted, why should they have thought of me? But something in me broke that day. I felt that I had been used.

CHAPTER 9

IF YOU CAN'T PLEASE EVERYBODY, PLEASE YOURSELF

My rebellion started in 1974. From then, until the day I walked out of 24 Sussex three years later, it built up momentum in fits and starts. It took many different forms; a sad ending of my love for Pierre; a return to the inner turmoils and confusions of the weeks after Morocco; a sense of mounting claustrophobia that had, like some enormous bubble, to burst soon.

The first visible explosions were all directed at the official life, by sad irony the very life of protocol and formality that I had finally and so painfully mastered. By 1974 I had become good at it; very good at it. But it was too late and I certainly hadn't managed to make it fun.

Absurdly, Pierre had been and still was my staunchest friend in my efforts to reduce the protocol, and when really grotesquely formal occasions were forced upon us, we joked about them together, laughing, often hilariously, over narrowly averted disasters or comic incidents. More and more often, though, the laughter turned sour: Pierre began to find my rebellion heavy-handed and tedious (and so did the Canadian public). My outbursts didn't strike him as quite so funny, nor my independence quite so endearing. A split appeared in the ground between us and it widened with each episode—episodes that every newspaper reporter who wrote about us was by now on the alert for. What *will* Mrs. Trudeau come out with next? Everyone, it seemed to me, was watching me, longing to find a good juicy story for the front page.

Micha, the last baby, came in October 1975, and in the January of 1976 Pierre was going to Latin America, a big three-week, three-country trip to Mexico, Cuba and Venezuela. A very important trip in terms of Canadian-Latin American relations, particularly as it was the fruit of Pierre's attempts to expand Canada's ties with the Third World. It was made all the more important by the fact that the United States was still entirely cut off diplomatically from Cuba.

We flew first to Mexico. It was like coming home—magic and drugs, all my old stomping grounds. We stayed in a luxurious hotel in the center of Mexico City where the butter was brought to our table molded in the shape of a bunch of roses. Mexico seemed to me like the center of the sun. The places we went to, the things that we did, the warmth and hospitality we encountered everywhere made me feel excited in a way I hadn't felt for ages.

I felt so good in fact that my normal caution began melting in the sun. One day Pierre and I were taken on an official trip to Palenque, the Mayan ruins in the jungle not far from Mexico City. All the way from the airport to the ruins the roads were lined with posters reading: "*Bienvenido Pierre Trudeau.*" When we got there I found two old friends

od and stone, kept cool by channels of water, across which
n huge, flat stones. Every window opened onto tropical
visit to Cuba marked a change in me, almost a reversal to
ays. During my years with Pierre I had coached myself
litics, so that when people abroad asked me what party I
sed to reply, half joking, "I'm a monarchist," which let me
Now, looking around Cuba, hearing about Che Guevara
ring all the stories in the Canadian press about how the
sts who were flown there in exchange for Cross's release
remely unhappy, I felt a resurgence of political conscious-
ong they were. This is the answer to Utopia, I said to
g out over the flowers, the tropical paradise all around me.
lution, it is truly marvelous.

assed by all too quickly; never had an official visit seemed so
or so completely devoid of stuffiness. One day Pierre and
nced they were going off for an evening's private talks at
ed destination. I was to stay in Havana with Micha and
an dance troupe give a performance. Ivan Head, who
in with us, informed me that I couldn't accompany Pierre
ecause there would be nowhere for me to stay, and my
ld only embarrass our Cuban hosts. That day, at lunch,
next to Castro. "Why aren't you coming with us?" he

owed to," I replied sourly.
not?"
ey tell me it would be an imposition with Micha and that
g."
at me scornfully. "I thought you were a photographer. You
rking." Then he went on. "I am not inviting any press up
. You shall be our photographer and, of course, you must
because there's no one else who can fulfill his needs."
n visit showed up more sharply than ever before the
s between what I felt happy doing and what I was actually
do. The two, I was beginning to see, were just not
Next morning we were to visit a chemical plant and Castro
at I stay on in my jeans and keep photographing. I was
new I would get jostled around with the other photogra-
ed out an old T-shirt from my suitcase and off we went. It
et" stamped across the back; unfortunately it also had a
logo on the front alongside the Canadian flag. And this

waiting: they had seen news of the
security cordon and lain in wait fo

And when one of them whisper
for you," I didn't protest. I left my
car while I went to look at the ru
hurried up to me. "I think you shou
has slipped something into your b

"Thank you so much. Those mu
And, opening my bag, I drew ou
breakfast table. What he didn't rea
little plastic sack of peyote mushro
myself a secret taste. It made me l

From Mexico we flew on to Cu
regalia: a beautiful silk dress I h
shoes, hat and handbag. Just befo
Havana I went to consult Pierre, w
plane, about whether I should w
matter carefully. "How about that d
took the pin from its box and just
plane lurched, embedding the tip
the front of my dress. Since by n
runway I had no time to change
Trudeau, on the first Canadian off
her clothes.

It was very hot when the plane
blanket of steamy heat that hit us in
on the runway. I was immediately n
with incredibly beautiful eyes, and
made him physically very attractive

He endeared himself to me fro
Micha. At the airport, in his speech
glad to have the distinguished prin
wife and his intelligent entourage, b
am concerned, as far as the peopl
important visitor today is Miche." (
that moment on Castro had Micha
pictures of Micha slobbering over
even went so far as to have special b
Trudeau, V.I.P. Official visitor of t

Pierre and I were staying in a cha

in natural wo
we stepped
gardens. Thi
my student
away from p
supported, I
off the hook
and rememb
F.L.Q. terro
were now ex
ness. How w
myself, looki
If this is rev

The days
enjoyable—n
Castro anno
an undisclos
see a Canad
was once ag
and Castro
presence wo
I was sitting
asked.

"I'm not a
"Why ever
"Because
you're worki
He looked
should be w
there tonigh
bring Miche

The Cuba
contradictio
expected to
compatible.
suggested th
delighted. I
phers so I fi
had "Marga
little Liberal

made people angry; very, very angry. To wear a scruffy old T-shirt on an official visit was bad enough; but to wear a Liberal T-shirt when I was meant to be representing not the party but the country was sacrilege. Murmurings were heard in Ottawa. Nor did the press much like me around. They wanted me up there on the receiving end of the photographs, not down there with them.

Our next stop was Venezuela. As part of my briefing mania I had already been in touch several times with Mrs. Schwartzmann, our ambassador's wife, an extremely conscientious woman who had sent me details of Mme. Perez's work with day care programs, and informative notes about the sort of people I was likely to meet. I was all set to like her. On arrival I discovered that she was a Cuban émigrée—and there is no one in the world who hates Cuba more. My enthusiasm about what I had seen fell on not just deaf, but decidedly chilly, ears. I also soon saw just why the briefing notes had been so informative: people, social people, were her life. Their rank and pedigree were the spice of life to her, not some dreary chore to master. We weren't destined to get on; I was not in the mood for silly pretensions. Nor was I in the mood for all the tedious lunches and cocktail parties she had laid on for me.

Mme. Perez changed all this. I had asked to see her day care program in operation and been told that it was out of the question, that Mme. Perez ran it from an office in the city and never went near the poor areas herself. I felt bolshy. "O.K.," I said to Mrs. Schwartzmann, "why don't Mme. Perez and all the ladies around her go and get their hair done and I'll take a taxi down to the slums and have a look for myself." Consternation. Very sourly Mrs. Schwartzmann said she would see what she could do.

I hadn't, until now, really spoken to Mme. Perez, beyond the initial civilities. When I met her to discuss her work I was immediately charmed. Here, I found, was a delightful, warm figure with a great sense of humor and sparkling eyes, who, far from never visiting her centers, went there five days a week, and kept the whole thing going by cajoling rich Venezuelans to part with their diamond earrings and ruby necklaces. She was only too happy to show me how it worked.

We set off in a private coach, Mme. Perez in a simple white dress, sturdy shoes and a plain gold cross around her neck, me in a safari suit and slung around with cameras. We took Micha with us. When the bus drew to a halt, I happened to look behind at the other ladies—Mme. Perez's entourage and various diplomatic wives. An identical expression of dismay and distaste was on all their faces. The clothes these women were wearing were the most inappropriate I have ever set my eyes on: high-heeled crocodile shoes, silk Pucci dresses, heavy gold jewelry, suede handbags. They were terrified: what had they let themselves in for? They could scarcely get off the bus, let alone walk along the rough, unmade roads.

Mme. Perez herself blossomed among the ghetto children. All the families we called on seemed to know her very well, and the children crawled up onto her lap with cries of pleasure. The sight touched me profoundly, actually finding one of these social figures—and who more protocol-ridden, one would have thought, than Mme. Perez?—engaged in an extremely demanding job of her own, with no self-publicity and no fuss. So profoundly, in fact, that I decided to make some special gesture toward her. I had a sudden urge to write her a song, and sing it to her myself. We were due to have a final dinner, just the four of us, the Perezes, Pierre and me, and my plan was to sing it afterward. Pierre was all for it.

Then our program got switched around. I find the memory of the scene almost too embarrassing to describe. Instead of our informal little dinner, the evening turned into a massive reception, possibly the most formal and pretentious dinner I ever went to in all my years as Pierre's wife. The whole of smart Caracas was there, in full evening dress, with tiaras and medals. I had half decided to abandon my plan but Pierre (to tease me? in malice?) persuaded me to go ahead with it. So when the plates were cleared away I rose unsteadily to my feet and delivered my little aria:

> *Señora Perez, I would like to thank you.*
> *I would like to sing to you.*
> *To sing a song of love.*
> *For I have watched you*
> *With my eyes wide open,*
> *I have watched you with learning eyes. . . .*

I hardly need to describe the effect. Half the guests were so embarrassed they kept their eyes riveted to their plates. A few of the Venezuelan women seemed touched and smiled their support. The Canadian delegation, to a man, was horrified. This, in the eyes of people like Ivan Head, was the last straw. Mrs. Trudeau had gone *too* far. I could see a smirk from ear to ear.

The episode was to have its repercussions. The first morning we were back in Ottawa, having reached home late the night before, I set my clock radio to wake me at nine. It was an Arctic cold morning. I was lying snugly under the quilt half asleep when suddenly I heard an outraged voice saying: "I think she is an absolute disgrace to this country. She is a disgrace to every Canadian woman. She has no right at all to sing ridiculous songs in official company."

This was followed by a second, more reasonable voice, a man this time: "Well, no, I don't quite agree with you. She's *trying* to be honest at least." In an instant I was as frozen inside the bed as the air was outside; I wanted to crawl to the bottom of that bed and never come out. My instinct was to switch off the sound, but then I forced myself to listen.

A caller came on: "Hey Margaret, if you're out there listening, just you keep doing it. You are a gift to us."

This friend was a friend indeed, but there were all too few like him. The next six callers had nothing but venom and spite.

At this point the interviewer chipped in. "I doubt you are listening, Margaret Trudeau, but if by any chance you *are*, why don't you give us a call. Here is the number. The lines are now free. Call in."

I shot up in bed, seized the phone and dialed. "I meant no insult to anyone," I said stoutly in my own defense, stirred out of my terror by what I felt was monstrous misunderstanding. "I admire Mme. Perez. I don't only think she's an excellent prime minister's wife, but she's working very hard for her own people in her own right. I wanted to sing a song in admiration."

The critics were momentarily silenced. But that phone call started a whole new area of criticism. Should the wife of the prime minister of Canada phone in to talk shows?

The following week I was offered a phone-in show of my own on the local Ottawa early morning show. Luckily, Pierre was away, so he wasn't in a position to forbid it. I decided to accept the invitation simply because I had reached the breaking point. I was sick to death of all the sneers and criticism that I was never allowed to answer. My sharp tongue, it seemed, got me into trouble whatever I did. I was tired of hearing people say: "How can such a lovely girl say such terrible things?" Now I was really going to give it to them.

The presenter, Michael O'Connell, opened the show by asking: "Now Margaret, is there any song that you would like us to play to start the program?"

"Yes," I replied immediately. "A song called 'Garden Party' by Rick

Nelson." (It was about how he went to a garden party and everyone was either rude or unpleasant to him. In the song he sings: "If you can't please everybody, you might as well please yourself.") Then the phone calls started. Many, I was relieved to find, were friendly, and they grew friendlier as the show went on, and as I put across some of my own feelings and difficulties without having them misrepresented by the press. A few were censorious, like sharp-tongued nannies. A couple were outright hostile. I tried to be as reasonable and calm as I could.

My rage was really with the press, not with the public. I felt that there had been a growing campaign among the more malicious newsmen to put me in as bad a light as could be found and distort everything I did or said. The battle had reached its peak on our return flight from Venezuela. That day, prompted by a feeling that we had, after all, spent a frenzied three weeks of hard work all together, and yet scarcely met, I decided to leave our suite in the front of the plane and go back and talk to them. It was the first time I had done so, and I was taken aback by the boozing and jollity I found. Nonetheless, I made my way somewhat awkwardly to where my photographer friend, Rod McIvor, was sitting and sat chatting with him about the song in Caracas. "Will you sing it to us?" asked one of the reporters in a friendly manner. I hesitated. Then I thought it would seem standoffish to refuse, so in a wavering voice I obliged. Meanwhile another man had handed me a bottle of good Cuban rum, and though I don't drink, I took a swig to play my part. That was my error. The papers next day were full of stories about my carousing with newsmen and swigging back booze straight from the bottle, and transcripts (they had, it turned out, switched a tape on) of my song circulated around Ottawa for weeks. I felt shattered, totally betrayed. And that was enough. I didn't go with Pierre on his next official visit to Britain and Germany. I simply refused to go. I felt too scared.

I wasn't let off the hook for long—1976 was official year *par excellence*. No sooner was one case unpacked, it seemed to me, than I was back up in the attic dragging it down again for the next round of parties, receptions, airports and pleasantries.

It was Olympics year. Pierre and I received the whole world in Montreal. I was looking forward to it enormously; for once formality was to be mixed with fun, and dozens of people were coming through Canada whom I had wanted to meet for years. Before moving up to a suite at the Queen Elizabeth Hotel in Montreal for two weeks, we had a series of informal lunch parties at Ottawa.

The sailing events were being held in Kingston, and when the Queen arrived on *Britannia* she invited us for dinner to watch the final heats. It was a horrible evening, blustery, raining hard, the sea as gray as the sky. Pierre and I were accompanied by the lieutenant governors and premiers of all the provinces and their wives. We were picked up from shore by the Queen's barge.

I was deeply disappointed by what I found on board. I had expected luxury and style; instead I found overstuffed, faded chintz sofas, bland, wishy-washy colors and a total lack of elegance. It was like finding the Queen herself in an old cotton print dress. The main salon looked more like the drawing room of an English country house than a luxury liner. The sheer lack of pretension verged on the shabby. None of this extended to the staff, however, who were immaculately turned out in starched white and waited on us with naval promptitude, nor to the china and linen. Nor to the food, which was superb. As the Queen swept down the massive staircase in the main salon—which made the boat more like a house than ever—she imposed her own grandeur. It was my first taste of that curious blend of the shabby and the very grand.

A few nights later, installed at the Queen Elizabeth Hotel, I found myself unexpectedly receiving Prince Charles for dinner. This wasn't my first real encounter with the Prince. That had come years before when I was pregnant with Justin. As he led me out to dance in my décolleté Valentino dress I had caught him peering down the front. He blushed.

"My father always told me to look into my partner's eyes when she is wearing a low-cut dress," he said laughing.

"Feast ye while ye may," I replied. "If I wasn't three months pregnant, there would be nothing to see."

That night at the hotel we had a marvelous time, so wonderful and full of jokes that a photographer caught us giggling together behind a shared menu and splashed the picture across the papers. Prince Philip reprimanded his son for monopolizing my attention.

In late August King Hussein and Queen Alia of Jordan invited us to spend a holiday with them. It was a tricky situation, because of the politics involved, but since I wanted to go so badly, and Pierre felt it would do me good, we solved the diplomatic hurdle by saying we would spend one week in Jordan, and a second week in Israel, thereby offending no one. Actually we were delighted. Both Pierre and I had dreamed of a biblical pilgrimage to the Holy Land.

Our week in Jordan was delightful, and Alia, whom I had first met and got to like in 1974, became a closer friend than ever. But from the moment we hugged goodbye at the Hussein bridge on the Jordan side and walked across into Israel everything changed. A smartly dressed business delegation was waiting to greet us; ambassadors were lined up and bowing; from that second on, protocol reigned. We were never alone. We were pressured and propagandized and lectured and harassed. I was so furious that my manners got worse and worse. Pierre went as far as to call me a "detestable" traveling companion. He was incensed at my atrocious behavior, and felt it reflected badly on me, on him, and on Canada generally.

CHAPTER 10

THE DREAMS GO SOUR

There is no doubt at all that for much of the time I lived with Pierre I was deeply unhappy. There was so much that was good—the babies, the all-too-rare moments that Pierre and I had totally alone, the trips abroad and the holidays—but there was also a lot that was rotten. The honeymoon was over much too soon. As Pierre settled down to married life and no longer felt he had to court me, so he returned to spend more and more time at his work, leaving me alone. I waited, and waited, and waited all day for him to come home, devoting the last hours to putting on my makeup and my prettiest clothes so as to look beautiful for him. When he appeared he took *off* his best clothes and climbed into old, baggy slacks. When I told him how bored I was, he looked disgusted: "How *can* you be bored when life is so full, when you have so many options?"

There were of course happy patches. The chronicle of our crumbling love affair would be false without them. I made a few intimate friends, with whom I could laugh about the official life, and briefly forget how much a prisoner I was. Queen Alia of Jordan was the closest of these.

I met her and King Hussein for the first time when they came to Ottawa for an official visit, immediately after the 1974 election. We took to each other at once. Alia was magnificent to look at: a mass of striking blond hair, green eyes, an irresistible smile. She arrived when I was at my lowest ebb, exhausted and feeling somehow betrayed by the election campaign; despite our victory, or perhaps because of it. Within hours she had taken me in hand, forced me to laugh about our lives, poked fun at my fears.

There was no formality between us: despite her being a Palestinian born on the West Bank, and me a politician's daughter from Vancouver, we were just two girls, sitting and giggling in her bedroom, me in jeans, she in her invariably magnificent clothes, with trunks of silk lingerie and boxes of priceless jewels scattered about the floor. The fact that she understood what I was talking about was enough to comfort me. "You're lucky, don't you understand," she kept repeating. "Pierre will eventually leave politics and you'll be free. Mine is a life sentence."

When we went to Amman on holiday in June 1976 I found her just as exuberant. Once again we talked, we gossiped, we comforted each other. We even made plans to share a little London house where we could escape to spend holidays together; she had a fantasy that we would join the European jet set and decorate our Chelsea home with all the taste she complained was lacking in her modern Amman palace. She wanted to buy Georgian furniture. She was quick, she was sharp, she was witty. She made me laugh with her stories.

Our friendship was cemented in the marvelous present of cameras she gave me, which became my third eye, an excuse to leave the house and go walking, the means of being not merely a participant, but a fly on the wall at official functions, as I was in Cuba. I saw her far too seldom, but it was enough to know that she was there. Our relationship became almost telepathic. The days I was most depressed were always those on which my phone rang: "Margaret, are you all right?"

Later that year I got involved in the U.N. Conference on Human Settlements in Vancouver and campaigned with Barbara Ward for clean water. "You're like a lovely pot of honey, all those busy bees of the press come rushing to you whenever the lid is off," Barbara Ward said to me somewhat fancifully. "Why don't you find a message and push it?" So I carried buckets of water with the best of them and started talking about pollution and the environment and not whether or not I would be wearing my pink Valentino dress to a dinner with the Queen.

Even so it had begun to be clear to many Canadians that I was not temperamentally suited to the job of First Lady. Not long after Pierre and I were married the strains of the life had begun to show. I became nervous, jittery, unpredictable. Even my children could not always distract me from feelings of acute tension. My actual "breakdown," when it came, was almost a relief, phony as it was.

After the 1974 election, when Queen Alia had been to Ottawa and gone home again, I took off for one of my more adventurous "freedom trips"; this time without consulting Pierre, who had taken Justin off fishing in the St. Lawrence. I was desperate. I phoned him from the airport.

"I'm off to Paris," I told him, "I want to practice my French."

Characteristically, he said at once: "Yes, by all means, off you go."

I had forgotten my passport, but bluffed my way through Orly airport without one, using a special paper given me by the airport authorities, only too happy to be of service. Once I reached Paris I booked for a night into the Hotel George Cinq.

So far so good. Next morning my real freedom trip began. Leaving the press reporters lounging in the front hall I sneaked out of the back door with my suitcase and moved to a small hotel by Notre Dame, overlooking the Seine. I spent several happy days taking photographs, walking around the parks, eating in student cafés.

But I couldn't go on fooling myself for long. I hadn't come to Paris just to recuperate; there was more to my visit than that. I have to have a fantasy in my life; I can't long survive without one. And my fantasy was Yves. I had come to Paris clutching a screwed up corner of paper on which I had written down his last known address: Rue de Blanc Manteau 35. One fine, sunny morning I made my way there and, trembling with anticipation, struck the enormous copper gong that hung alongside the entrance. I heard steps, the key in the lock. The massive door swung back. There stood a middle-aged woman with frizzy, red hair. My heart sank.

"I'm looking for Yves Lewis," I said hesitantly, in my poor French. She looked blank. I tried again. "How long have you lived here?"

"Four years."

"Has someone called Yves Lewis left a forwarding address?"

"No."

Slow tears of frustration started trickling down my face. I had had no idea I cared so much. My frizzy-haired companion was moved almost to compassion.

"*Le monde*," she said, shrugging her shoulders in a not unfriendly way, "*ça change*."

I walked the streets of Paris for the rest of the day trying to put my life together again. By nightfall I had decided to move on again. But I still had no proper passport. I called on our Paris embassy and asked them to provide me with one in the name of Margaret Sinclair.

Armed with my new credentials I caught a plane to Athens. Greece had a shrine of sorts for me: I went to see the village where Yves had been at school. Then I moved on to Crete. There was nothing sinful or sinister about my trip: I simply needed to be on my own. In Crete I rented a car and drove about the island. I swam, took photographs and had only a knapsack for luggage and a blanket to sleep in. It was precisely what I wanted. I passed the days in a romantic reverie, a soothing daydream of almost adolescent romance. It was like Robert's Creek all over again. After two weeks I was ready to go home.

I caught a plane back to Paris, called Pierre, who had begun to worry about my mysterious disappearance, and told him I was coming home. "Fine," he said, "why don't we go to the Celebrity Pro Tennis Tournament in New York?"

That proved my undoing. I arrived home in that curiously high and edgy state that comes from being too much alone: anxious to make it all up with Pierre, yet resisting every effort on his part. The night before the Tennis Tournament I fell in love. I hadn't looked at another man in four years; it was sudden; it was fantastic. He was a high-powered American; a charming Southerner whose name is of no importance. I became like someone possessed. We danced all evening. I cried all night. When we got back to Ottawa next day I raced up the stairs to our private refrigerator and drank off the half bottle of vodka I found there. Pierre, who caught me at it, was appalled.

"Have you been unfaithful to me in Paris?" he kept on asking. "Have you? Have you?"

We passed a nightmare weekend up at Harrington Lake. Pierre never left me alone. "I know you've been unfaithful. I know it. Otherwise why be like this?" Late Saturday night, exhausted, frantic, I seized a kitchen knife from the table and rushed out into the snow, where I started tearing off my clothes to find a bare spot to plunge the blade in.

"O.K.," I screamed at Pierre. "O.K. I've fallen in love." The confession shocked us both into silence.

"You're sick," was all he said at last.

If I wasn't sick then, I soon became it: frightened, lonely and very mad. When the children ran up to kiss me, I shrank back. When the maids asked for instructions, I panicked. Pierre kept urging me to seek psychiatric help. Finally, my own will worn so thin that I was happy to take anyone's advice, I checked into the Montreal General Hospital under a Dr. Boz. Wendy Porteous drove me—the same woman who that dreadful evening so long ago had put me down about my French. We had an extraordinarily giggly, happy drive down to Montreal: a delicious lunch, lots of wine. I couldn't really believe I was mad. Then she left me.

I had expected the psychiatric wing, and was half curious to meet my fellow inmates. Because of the security, the need for police at that stage to guard me even inside a hospital, I was shown instead into a suite in the urology section, where aging businessmen came to have prostate operations. It reduced me to tears at once. "I want to go with the others," I wailed. They arranged for me to have a round-the-clock shift of private nurses.

Dr. Boz explained the treatment he had in mind for me. "I want to bore you," he said. "I want to make you sleep. Relax."

It was all a bit like *Alice in Wonderland*. "I feel paranoid. I feel everyone is watching me," I said to him.

"Everybody *is* watching you. That's not paranoia. That's reality."

"I feel hostile. I have illusions of grandeur. I think I'm somebody."

"You *are* somebody."

I had come down here to get away from Pierre and think about my marriage in peace. I found myself constantly watched by nurses and fed pills that made my tongue swell and my mind sag.

Though not my lover, my American friend called me every day. I sometimes felt that only he and Alia could understand what I was going through. Gradually I began to take a tentative hold on myself. I weaned myself off the tranquilizers and flushed my daily dose down the lavatory, thus clearing my mind to think. I kept sane by questioning the nurses about their own lives, and brewing myself up little pots of what Dr. Boz, smugly seeing recovery in my domestic chores, took to be tea but were in fact sweet potions of marijuana. I took photographs in the hospital grounds. I wrote to Alia. One Sunday the hospital priest came to talk to me. His words electrified me. "Whatever are you doing here?" he asked contemptuously. "You should be home with your children."

That settled it for me. I called Dr. Boz, and asked him whether I was committed. "No," he replied reluctantly. So I summoned my policeman and prepared to leave. But not before I consented to make an appearance before the journalists who had been thronging the hospital grounds like vultures since my arrival, reporting that I was in hospital for an abortion. I was thin, disheveled, gaunt. "Why don't you leave me alone?" I asked them. "Can't you feel any compassion for me? I don't know how long I shall be here, but I am suffering from severe emotional stress. Please go away." They went, and rather to my surprise my statement brought me sympathy, encouragement and flowers from every corner of the country. The Mental Health Associations praised me for my honesty, and fellow sufferers wrote with understanding. I received three thousand letters.

Pierre seemed pleased to see me, and I was there in time to accompany him to France and Belgium for the N.A.T.O. summit. It wasn't an easy trip. Pierre continued to eye me with doubt, and I took refuge as frequently as I felt I dared to in quick puffs of marijuana. When I got back to Ottawa the psychiatrist whom I had agreed should visit me took Pierre's side: I must get off drugs. Week after week I lay speechless and furious on his couch. Finally I could stand it no longer. I smoked not one but two strong joints before setting out for one of my regular appointments. No sooner was I settled in his office than I began to talk. I told him about my dreams, my childhood, my marriage. A look of profound self-satisfaction spread across his face. "You see," he said at the end of our hour, "you can do it, you know, without drugs." I laughed. I never went to him again.

Meanwhile, on the doctor's advice, Pierre had consented to allow me to fly down to the United States for a brief clarifying meeting with my friend. Both of them agreed that it was merely an unhealthy obsession, best cleared up. The arrangement was that I should have dinner with my friend, agree never to speak or meet again, sleep the night with friends and fly home. It didn't quite work out that way. When I flew home next day I swore to myself that I would never see him again—or that if I did I would leave Pierre. I kept my word.

These were not happy times for us. Pierre, jealous and brooding, took it out on me by leaving me even more often on my own, and treating me coldly, even with hostility. When we spoke, it was almost always about the children, and even then often words of reproach. Pierre, quite rightly, said I was too harsh, too distant with them. That I wasn't pulling my weight at home.

I reacted in the unkindest way I could. I went back to smoking marijuana more or less openly in front of him, sometimes, if I was desperate enough, as much as four joints a day. (Though never before, then or later, did I smoke when pregnant or nursing a baby.)

The end came in a series of inexorable steps. We had a bleak Christmas on the island of St. Lucia, the prettiest of all the Caribbean islands, like Tahiti, volcanic and lush, with crumbling old colonial buildings. It could have been marvelous. Instead Pierre and I lived locked in our own private nightmares, made all the starker by the luxury around us. We swam, lay on the beach, played with the children. I read Carlos Castaneda and wrote pages and pages of letters to Yves, letters I never sent.

I did see my Southerner one more time. And once more was enough. I realized that it wasn't he who had destroyed my marriage—simply that I had used him to escape my own unhappiness.

I returned to Ottawa for two days, then turned round and entered the United States as the wife of the Canadian prime minister on a state visit. Our meeting with the Carters, on the White House lawn, was informal and relaxed. That night, for the official dinner, I put on my white pearl dress, the one I had made for the Micheners' ball after my wedding, and had long considered my favorite dress. It came to three inches above the ankle. (Unknown to me, there was a run in my sheer stockings.)

Next morning there was an uproar in the newspapers. "Mrs. Trudeau and her gaffes!" "Margaret does it again!" My dress, it transpired, had been a disaster. How dare I attend a White House banquet in a dress that didn't reach the ground and in laddered stockings?

A few days after our return to Ottawa, moody, undecided and fretful, I went to a cocktail party held by an old friend of mine in honor of Premier Bennett of British Columbia. I was talking to a group of journalists when a man I knew slightly came up to me.

"Hello, Margaret. Have you heard the news? Hussein's wife Alia has just been killed in a helicopter crash."

He could have had no clue what his words meant to me. I started shaking. Tears poured down my face. A friend drove me back to Pierre. Later we discovered that Alia had been killed on the return flight from visiting a man in the south of Jordan who had written to her complaining that he was not receiving proper treatment at the local hospital. She had flown off with Colonel Zasa, King Hussein's closest aide, to pay him a visit. They crashed in a sudden rainstorm.

It was all too much for me. It made a mockery of all our conversations, the way Alia had kept on insisting that everything would turn out well for both of us. Pierre and I discussed our future calmly, with none of the aggravation of the previous months. We both agreed that nothing should happen precipitately. I would leave for a ninety-day trial separation—and we would take it from there.

CHAPTER 11

TAKING OFF

In the eyes of the world my weekend with the Rolling Stones was the freedom trip to end all freedom trips. No one but Pierre knew I had already left him for a temporary separation. To the rest of Canada, to the journalists and newspapers of the world, my escapade was yet another example of what a wicked wife I had become, flaunting my infidelities in Pierre's face.

It was all a ghastly mistake: the truth of that Toronto weekend makes dull reading for anyone who saw the newspapers at the time. It began innocently and entirely by accident. Pierre and I reached our decision to part on Friday March 4—our sixth wedding anniversary. I was packing my cases to leave for New York when a call came from Penny Royce in Toronto. "How about dinner with the Rolling Stones?" she suggested, half joking.

"Why not?" I replied a little bitterly, "I'm free. I've just left Pierre."

On my previous visits to Toronto I had always stayed at the Windsor Arms, a small, quiet hotel in the center of the city. When I reached the airport that Friday, however, I found that Penny had checked me into the far larger Harbor Castle Hotel, because, as she explained in the car on our way into town, the Stones were staying there and we could sneak more discreetly into their suite for the dinner she had arranged. My first meeting with the Rolling Stones was over drinks. Mick Jagger was polite and charming. We drank wine. There were no drugs about.

The Stones had come to Toronto to make some live recordings in the El Mocambo, a small nightclub—a sort of beer cellar that reminded Mick of his first London club appointments. To discourage mobs of hysterical fans, the El Mocambo management had kept their visit a secret and simply announced a booking of the April Wine. When the Stones appeared on stage there was a riot among the tiny audience. It was a spectacular, memorable evening, and it was an honor to be there. Afterwards Penny and I went back to the hotel on our own and had a drink.

Next afternoon, about to leave for New York, I bumped into Ronnie Wood, the Stones' guitarist.

"Hey, where are you off to? Aren't you coming to tonight's session?"

I hesitated. "I'm not a groupie. I can't possibly."

"Why don't you work, then? Take some photographs."

It seemed the perfect solution. What was I going to do in New York anyway? And wouldn't this be a fine start to my new career? I put on my jeans jumpsuit and snapped away hard with my cameras all evening.

Next afternoon I prepared once again to leave Toronto. This time I heard a timid rattling on my door handle. Outside stood a skinny, pale little boy wearing a jogging suit. He was in tears. It was Marlon, Keith Richards' seven-year-old son. "Where is everybody? Where are they?" he sobbed. "Dad's lying on the floor crying. What shall I do?"

I went with him up to the Stones' suite and found that Anita Pallenberg, Marlon's mother, was out shopping, and that Keith was indeed curled up on the floor in a fetus position, moaning. His case, for possession of heroin for trafficking, was due to come up the next day in court. Marlon and I dragged him off the floor, laid him as best we could on his bed, and I covered him with a blanket. I couldn't just abandon the child, so, clearing a space among the dirty plates, empty bottles and garbage that littered the room, I settled down on the floor to help him glue together a model airplane.

When Mick and the others came back we discussed what could be done for Keith. I was loath to get involved, but since I had good contacts with the various Canadian mental health associations I offered to find a psychiatrist who could at least give evidence for Keith at the trial. They were delighted, and having phoned an acquaintance at the M.H.A., Penny and I went to Ward Island, the hippy community across the water from the hotel, to talk to friends who might be prepared to take in Marlon if both Keith and Anita had to go through a period of rehabilitation.

By this time it was too late to leave for New York that night, so I went off to eat with Ronnie Wood and the Stones' drummer, Charlie Watts. They dropped me back at the hotel before midnight, saying they were off to a recording session. At 5 A.M. I got a call from the lobby. "It's us. We're back. Can we come up? How about a game of dice?" For the Stones day is night and night is day. Slightly bemused, I climbed into my jeans, and hastily made my bed before the whole group clattered into my room, in high spirits and drunk with the euphoria that comes from an all-night working session. We settled down to drink, play dice, smoke a little hash. Mick and Keith disappeared into a corner to work out a new number. It was fun; I was happy to be part of it. At nine o'clock we drew back the curtains on a cold gray morning and ordered coffee. One by one the Stones departed to their own rooms to sleep. Ronnie was the last to leave.

By the time I reached New York the scandal had exploded: "Prime Minister's Wife and Rolling Stones," "Margaret in Hotel Corridor in White Pyjamas," "Sex Orgy in Canadian Prime Minister's Wife's Suite." There was no stopping the rumors, many of them emanating from Paul Wasserman. Too late did Mick ring and warn me: "Don't talk to

Wasserman, he's our press agent and is trying to get publicity for us. But he's an arsehole."

If it was bad for me, it was worse for Pierre. People in Canada yelled "cuckold" when they saw him pass in the streets. Stony faced, he pretended nothing was wrong. When I got back to Ottawa I was in disgrace, total, unredeemable disgrace. It was hardly surprising. Pierre forced me to listen to a tape of the Michael O'Flattery interview; a free-lance journalist, O'Flattery had trapped me on the phone, protesting undying friendship. It sounded truly terrible. I protested; I explained what had happened step by step. It was no good. That night we went to a performance of *Romeo and Juliet* at the National Arts Center. I wore my ill-fated Washington dress; I had a black eye.

My "independent career" was not quite all that it might have been. Work wasn't easy to come by. I was inundated by offers—but every enterprise I got involved in turned out to be a con of one kind or another, usually people luring me on and then exploiting me in return for some "exclusive story." *People* magazine offered me work—in exchange for an interview. I took some pictures for them, but the interview was sexy and sensational, a travesty of everything I said. They fooled me again by telling me that Elizabeth Taylor had agreed to have me to tea on her farm at Middleburg, Virginia, to take some pictures of her. When I got there, she was furious. There had been no such deal.

The greatest con of all was the *Good Morning America* show. It was June 4, 1977. I had been told that my appearance on the breakfast show, presenting a selection of my own photographs, would act as public audition for the job of presenter on the program. When I got to the studio I found that my fellow guest was Anthony Quinn and that we were to be interviewed by a blond, hardbitten woman, a typically plastic Miss Chicago. She was heavily and theatrically made up, her hair a bulletproof helmet of hairspray.

I began by describing my photography. Miss Chicago beamed. "Now Margaret. You talk with such love about your children. You always say Justin is a prince, Sacha very brave, and Micha an angel. I have to ask you a question that must be on the mind of every one of our twelve million viewers this morning. Have you abandoned your children?"

I had to restrain myself from jumping up, rushing over and messing up her odious straw hair. It almost started what would have been the most popular catfight on American television. I controlled myself. "How could you," I asked back. "How could you possibly ask such a question?"

433

A "hard" and "selfish" career girl, capable of "neglecting her children," were not the only insults hurled at me. 1977 was a bewildering year for me; a hard year; the beginning of my new life.

On a trip for *People* magazine to Paris, a promotion tour for Perrier, I found myself sitting next to Bruce Nevins, the company's president, on the plane. I was cross at the unaccustomed discomfort of a long flight, tourist class, and pulled my eye mask sulkily over my face. It wasn't until we landed that I realized who he was. Bruce befriended me in Paris and on our return to New York I started dating him regularly, though he was diametrically the opposite of any man I had ever dreamed of falling in love with: West Point Military Academy, instructor in guerrilla warfare for the commandos in Vietnam, president of Levis in Hong Kong, strong Nixon supporter. But he was a good friend, a strong, big-shouldered man, with the warmest brown eyes a woman could hope for. We had Sunday brunches at the Tavern On the Green in Central Park, reading the newspapers, and sober, cozy dinners at Elaine's and Nicola's. He worked hard and we shared a warm love. It was some months before I realized with sadness that Bruce, whatever else he may be, is a confirmed lifelong bachelor.

It was while I was with him that I started acting classes. Mornings were given over to private lessons with Bob MacAndrew to prepare me for movie parts. It was a struggle but I grew better and still cherish the day when Bob declared that my best talents as an actress lay in "innovation." Afternoons were more daunting: I had been allowed to audit Wynn Handman's advanced acting class—something of an honor for a total newcomer since Wynn's classes were widely regarded as the finest in contemporary theater. His studio, an old fashioned, run-down series of rooms, was above a laundromat on West 56th Street. Classes started at 4:45 every afternoon. For the first months I watched in awe as the professional actors and actresses tackled parts that ranged from Beckett to Shakespeare. I thought my future was made the day he gave me a chance at Erma Bombeck—though I was so overwhelmed by Katharine Hepburn's performance in *Philadelphia Story* that I couldn't stop aping it.

Those were the serious times. Mostly I racketed around New York, getting involved in scenes I couldn't cope with, and people I couldn't understand.

There was my weekend in Las Vegas. I was invited there by a wealthy businessman who groomed his crinkly hair with a blowdryer. He first took me to La Grenouille on St. Valentine's Day and over lunch suggested we go to Las Vegas for the Muhammed Ali fight.

"How can I possibly come to Las Vegas?" I said flirtatiously, "I've got nothing to wear."

And indeed I hadn't. Charmer that he was, he presented me with the best Valentine's present that ever came my way—carte blanche at my favorite store, Ungaro's.

The romance of the present was in sharp and crazy contrast to the actual weekend. The fight was bloody and brutal. The hotel suite where I stayed was quite outstanding in its vulgarity: cupids spouting water, paintings on velvet, a bar with golden stools, polyester rugs and wall to wall mirrors.

There was my cowboy with whom I played pinball until six in the morning. There were my nights in Studio 54, New York's most exclusive club, and favorite territory of Truman Capote, Andy Warhol, Bianca Jagger and Halston. One night the air reeked of the sweet chemical stench of amyl nitrate and a jerky, stoned blonde was parading about shoving a bottle under people's noses, saying: "Sniff."

I came to my senses at last after one truly sleazy evening. The party was over; the last of the misfits had wandered off. I was alone, aching. Empty tequila glasses were scattered around the room, and there was a faint smell of stale grass. I tried to sleep, but found myself pacing the room in a growing panic of desolation, willing the cold black world outside to wake and share the misery with me. Looking out of the window as dawn came up all I could see were the garbage cans in the basement area eleven floors below me. I covered sheets of papers with a desperate scrawl: "Help me please."

The lost year was over.

I went to bid it farewell at the anniversary party of Studio 54. The whole of smart New York was there—two miles of solid traffic. On the way through the pouring rain, wearing what Joan Crawford called "fuck me shoes," I saw a dog turd floating past on the rushing water in the gutter like a little boat. I sat in the balcony high above the stage, looking down on all the things I was giving up: the anxious days, the drug-high nights, the phony glamor, the botched friendships, the betrayals. They were none of them worth it.

EPILOGUE

My thirtieth birthday has fallen as I finish this. I'm in Cassis in the south of France making my second movie, *Guardian Angel*. The

435

Good Morning America fiasco didn't get me a job as presenter—I was told that I didn't quite seem to represent the middle American housewife— but it did secure me a part in my first film, *Kings and Desperate Men*. I may never make a good film actress or a gifted photographer, but I'm going to try.

I've changed a lot in the past year. Leaving Pierre was like stepping out into Beelzebub's Chaos. I spent a lot of time sinking. I think I'm on the way up again.

Perhaps there comes a moment in life when you understand how really alone you are. My mother warned me early: "Life is a lonely affair. You may share companionship from time to time with those you love, but you are always in the end, alone." Not me, I triumphed indulgently. I have three beautiful sons, who will always be part of me. I had my one romantic fantasy, my ideal: Yves. It doesn't matter that I was never with him. It was enough to know he was there.

One bright September morning in Cassis my leading man, Francis Lemaire, a fine comedian, appeared in the make-up room looking sad and wretched. "Charles Boyer committed suicide yesterday." Micheline, my make-up girl, and I commiserated, but privately I couldn't feel too shaken: Boyer was eighty, and his wife had died two weeks before.

"I had even sadder news this morning," Francis went on as I went back to my make-up, only half listening to him. "My best friend's son has also committed suicide." I looked as sympathetic as I could, thinking he would feel better if he talked about it. "You wouldn't know him," he went on. "The father—my friend—was the man who invented the Club Mediterranée."

I froze; waited. And then it came. "His name was Yves Lewis."

Being me, the dramatics were spectacular: I pulled my hair, I raved, I screamed, I cried, I refused to believe him. A great emptiness, like a merciless cold wave, broke over me. That morning Francis and I had our most important scene in the film together; it took all the courage I had to go through with it, and only because I knew that my real Guardian Angel was there could I face what was the cruelest reality of my life. In the image of Christ to the last, Yves had hanged himself at the age of thirty-three and a half. My search for him is finally over; but unlike Yves I shall go on surviving.

I see my children for five days every two weeks when I go back home to Ottawa to share with Pierre a life we never had before. I take them to the dentist and buy their shoes. Only now can I love them as they should be loved.

Since I left the warm protection of 24 Sussex, Pierre has given me all the moral support he can muster. He has not helped me at all financially, partly because of my stubbornness about being independent, partly because he is loath to aid me to live a life that is apart from him and our sons. Mommy *has* to work.

It is quite possible that Pierre and I could never have made a life together. It wasn't his age or my inexperience, or even the fact that he was prime minister. Pierre likes his life programmed: the good, Christian philosopher-king who wants to live his life by his will, not by the vagaries of fortune. I spent an awful lot of time trying to please him, yet could never quite escape from my own romantic fantasy or the desire for a life very different from the one I was expected to lead. Quite simply, I preferred being his country mistress; I began to detest being his wife. Now I prefer being alone.

Is it beyond reason for me to hope for a peaceful life, or has my past put me beyond reach of such a dream?

I don't, I realize, come out of this story very well. I have tried at least to be honest.

Priscilla Davis poses next to the large double portrait of her and Cullen, which Cullen commissioned from the artist, Wayne Ingrams.

A Condensation of the book by

GARY CARTWRIGHT

BLOOD WILL TELL

AUTHOR'S NOTE

The high stakes and the rich excitement of the plot first drew me to the story of Cullen and Priscilla Davis. It has those ingredients in abundance. It also has something to think about: how the legal system works when the man accused is a multimillionaire, can afford the best lawyers, and cannot be bankrupted by the need to defend himself.

I do not mean to imply that justice miscarried. Cullen has consistently maintained his innocence of the crimes he has been tried for; in one case he was acquitted and in the other the jury was unable to agree on a verdict. Cullen's lawyers did establish reasonable doubt in the first trial, and until a verdict is reached in the second case, Cullen rightly enjoys a presumption of innocence. That's as it should be. The facts are the facts, and I have stuck to them. But had the facts been exactly the same and had the accused been poor, would the trials' outcomes have been different? And would that have been as it should be?

CHAPTER 1

In the beginning no one thought of it as a mansion, much less *The Mansion*. That would come later, as the empire that financed it was shaking at the roots. To the thousands who drove by it every day, wondering but never knowing who was up there or what was happening, the big house off Hulen Street looked more like a museum than a mansion.

It stood alone on the knob of a hill, its 181 acres of manicured lawn bordered to the north by the Clear Fork of the Trinity River and to the south and west by the Colonial Country Club golf course. A quiet residential lane named Mockingbird came to a dead end at the mansion's southeast gate, which was technically the main entrance but always seemed like the rear entrance to the estate. Hulen Boulevard, a major artery connecting the old silk stocking area called Arlington Heights with the newer pocket of upward mobility known as Tanglewood, ran for nearly a half-mile along the western edge of the mansion grounds. Old-timers sometimes referred to the land as "the old dairy," though it hadn't been used as a dairy since well before the early 1940s when Fort Worth oil millionaire Kenneth W. Davis, Sr., purchased the tract.

In late 1968 a gang of workers appeared with bulldozers and backhoes and enough equipment and supplies to build a shopping center. A foundation was poured over thousands of feet of high ground. Gradually and without fanfare, the eye-popping sprawl of trapezoids and parallelograms and oddly sloping white walls that would come to be called The Mansion appeared and took life.

It was said that the mansion covered 19,000 square feet, though that figure was probably exaggerated, and was constructed at a cost of $6 million. That figure included the lavish furnishings and collection of paintings, bronzes, and gold and jeweled knickknacks, but not the land itself. It was difficult to calculate the true value of 181 privately owned acres along the river just southwest of downtown Fort Worth. It wasn't the size or cost of the mansion that made it such a showpiece, but the fact that it was so highly visible, located as it was on the highest knoll of the choicest piece of land.

What sort of person would build such a home? People found it hard to imagine. Obviously, someone who wanted to call attention to himself: to those who knew the story, this was the strangest part of all. The mansion at 4200 Mockingbird was the carefully planned, meticulously supervised dream home of Kenneth Davis's middle son, T. Cullen Davis, a man who, until the moment he moved in, was lost in the shadows of his family name.

Although the Davises had lived in Fort Worth for almost fifty years and were counted among the richest families in town, the name was so obscure that no society editor or gossip columnist was likely to recognize it, much less accord it any special meaning. There were many rich and ostentatious families in Fort Worth, third- and fourth-generation oil and cattle people, but the Davises weren't among them. The *Fort Worth Star-Telegram,* founded by the city's patron booster Amon Carter, knew so little about the Davis family that it hadn't even bothered to maintain a separate file on the family in the reference room. Alice Bound Davis, wife of the oilman and mother of his three sons, had donated the money to construct the Noble Planetarium at the Fort Worth Children's Museum but had intentionally allowed people to forget her contribution by naming it for Miss Charlie Noble, longtime astronomy instructor. Ken Davis, Sr., was a contemporary of Sid Richardson, Clint Murchison, Amon Carter, and other legendary Texas wheeler-dealers, but hardly anyone below the rank of bank president thought of him that way, or thought of him at all. He was known, not affectionately, as Stinky Davis. "He was a short, robust man, no more than five-six," a longtime business acquaintance explained. "But he wasn't the sort of man you'd call Shorty." No one used his nickname in his presence, of course, but the mere mention of Stinky Davis caused quakes and tremors in the boardrooms of a number of large financial institutions.

Stinky Davis raised his three boys, Kenneth Jr., Cullen, and Bill, to be frugal, protective, diligent, hard-nosed business types. All three graduated from Arlington Heights High School and Texas A & M. They were sent to Texas A & M because, as a family friend put it, "it was the cheapest, hardest place the old man could find." In those days, the late 1940s and the first half of the 1950s, Texas A & M was sometimes called "West Point on the Brazos," referring to the river that cut through and isolated part of central Texas where the institution was located, and to the compulsory military training that the all-male student body had to endure. Aggies were a breed apart, the dirt and guts and fingernails of higher education in Texas.

When the old man died in August of 1968, the three sons took over the family-owned conglomerate known as Kendavis Industries International, Inc. The old man had literally built it from nothing, starting with four employees in 1929 and expanding it in his lifetime until it had thousands of employees and offices and subsidiaries all over the world. Yet hardly anyone, not even the old man's most trusted advisers—perhaps not even the sons themselves—had a true concept of Stinky Davis's net worth. What the old man left his sons was an equal and undivided share of a business worth in excess of $300 million. In the ten years after the old man's death, Kendavis Industries (sometimes known by its logo, Kiii) quadrupled in value, and still only a handful of people had any real concept of its reach and wealth. This was because Stinky Davis had doggedly refused to sell shares of his companies to the public. With one exception, all the companies under the Kiii umbrella were wholly owned by the old man and later his sons. It was and is without question one of the largest privately held conglomerates in the United States—it has been estimated that fewer than 5 percent of *all* companies in this country are as large. By 1977 combined sales of the eighty-plus Kiii companies exceeded $1.03 billion.

It was not apparent at the time, but the wall of secrecy that Stinky Davis so carefully constructed around his empire began to crumble on August 29, 1968, the day he died. It was also the day that T. Cullen Davis, his middle son, married Priscilla Lee Wilborn, a sexy, twice-married platinum blonde who came from so far on the other side of the tracks it wasn't even the same railroad. Though the date of the death and the marriage appeared to be coincidental, it had a strategic value. Since Cullen's brothers were both divorced, it was agreed that the newlyweds would move into the old family home on Rivercrest in Arlington Heights. Thus Cullen Davis, who had just inherited an equal share of the family fortune, became a little more than equal. No one knew it at the time, but Cullen was already drafting plans for his mansion.

To say that the marriage shocked Fort Worth society would be to overestimate the esteem in which Cullen was held back in 1968. But the wedding did cause some tongues to wag. People who had never paused a moment to consider Cullen considered him now and asked *why her*? Priscilla was an outsider and went out of her way to show it. She was a tiny, striking figure with a cascade of silver-blonde hair and an affinity for gowns cut spectacularly low. At Cullen's urging, one of Priscilla's first expenditures as a member of the Davis family was for silicone breast implants. She came to the marriage with, as they say in Fort Worth, "a good balcony," and after the breast implants she snapped heads every time she walked through the lobby of the Colonial or River Crest Country Club. Cullen's first wife, Sandra, had been known among the social set as a plain, unadorned woman who made her own dresses and kept her place, but Priscilla knew little and cared less about such places: in her experience, women who knew how to operate sewing machines were likely to spend their whole life behind one. Priscilla's notion of a fine gown required a bare minimum of material, yet she thought nothing of spending $20,000 a month on clothes. Her favorite piece of jewelry was a gold necklace that spelled out RICH BITCH.

Once so formal and reserved that even his father complained that Cullen dressed like "some kinda popinjay," Cullen now lived vicariously through Priscilla. He began to shun high society in favor of discos and classy honky-tonks, and he squandered huge sums of money on indulgences that must have had the old man spinning in his grave. Not the least of these was the $6 million mansion. It was hardly the place Stinky Davis would have built, but of course that was the point.

It was said that Cullen built the mansion to immortalize his marriage to Priscilla, and maybe in the beginning this was true. But other forces played just below the surface. For whatever reason, the marriage was not as solid as the mansion. Although Cullen adopted Priscilla's oldest daughter, Dee, and gave her his family name, Dee Davis and her new step-father were far from compatible. Dee wasn't accustomed to harsh discipline, but Priscilla said Cullen whipped her frequently and some-times severely. On one occasion when Dee forgot to lock the kitchen door, Cullen broke her nose and slammed her kitten on the floor until it was dead. Priscilla's other children, Jack Wilborn, Jr., and Andrea Wilborn, continued to live with their father and visited the mansion only occasionally. Andrea, a tender and sensitive girl, came to fear Cullen and finally refused to visit the mansion at all. Priscilla, too, seemed to bring out a dark side of Cullen Davis. Priscilla complained to friends that Cullen demanded either too much or too little; the couple couldn't seem to find a happy medium. Cullen accused her of having illicit affairs, and when she denied the affairs, he broke her nose and on another occasion her collarbone. Other times he snubbed her or humiliated her in public. In the early years of the marriage Cullen and Priscilla traveled extensively to Europe and South America, but gradually Cullen started traveling alone, and when he did, Priscilla's alleged affairs became more than a figment of Cullen's imagination.

In August 1974, almost exactly six years after the death of Kenneth Davis, Sr., and the simultaneous and shocking marriage of his second son to an overt outsider, Priscilla filed for divorce and Cullen moved out of the mansion and into a motel. It was to be a bitter, protracted divorce struggle. Each side hurled charges of deceit and treachery, and each time they seemed close to a settlement, one or the other found a reason to delay the final resolution. At the same time something else was happening that upset the equilibrium of the family fortune. Three months after Priscilla filed her divorce papers, the youngest brother, Bill Davis, filed suit against his two older brothers, charging that they were conspiring to squeeze him out of his inheritance. There had been numerous disagreements among the brothers, but two things in particular inflamed Bill Davis. First was Cullen Davis's "extravagant and wasteful business expenditures and investments" in the management of Cummins Sales and Service, one of the major Kiii subsidiaries that Cullen headed. Second, Bill objected to "the use of the [company] personnel, banking relations, deposits and credit . . . to obtain [personal] loans for T. Cullen Davis." According to Bill Davis, Cullen had turned Cummins from a moneymaking concern into a business that was $46 million in debt. What is more, Bill Davis charged, Cullen had run up personal debts of at least $16 million since the death of their father. Perhaps the most damning part of the suit was the charge that Cullen and Ken Jr. manipulated stock in Stratoflex, the only major Kiii stock available to the public, for the purposes of tax fraud. This last charge smacked of criminal intent and threatened to provoke an investigation by the Securities and Exchange Commission.

As the months wore on and the battle raged between husband and wife, and among brothers, Cullen settled in for a long fight. He had a new girlfriend, an attractive young divorcée named Karen Master, and instead of in a motel he now lived in her home in the Edgecliff section of Fort Worth.

Priscilla, too, was finding it unpleasant to live alone and invited a strange procession of people unknown to Fort Worth society to share the mansion. The first was a former motorcycle racer named W. T. Rufner. Priscilla started seeing Rufner several months before she filed for divorce, and when Cullen moved out of the mansion, Rufner and a consortium of his friends moved in and stayed for six months or longer. T-man, as Rufner was known in the Fort Worth drug world, eventually wore out his welcome and was forcibly evicted from the mansion. At the same time Priscilla began carrying on with a six-foot-nine former Texas Christian University basketball player named Stan Farr. By the spring of 1975, Farr was sharing not only the mansion but the master bedroom.

After many delays the divorce trial was finally scheduled to begin on July 30, 1976, but again there were problems. This was Priscilla's thirty-fifth birthday and she was a nervous wreck. Her lawyers once again filed a motion to delay the divorce trial, using a letter from Priscilla's doctor as evidence that she was in no condition to endure a trial. Domestic Relations Court Judge Joe Eidson promised to rule on the motion in a few days.

Three days later, on Monday, August 2, Cullen and Ken Jr. and their chief financial adviser, Walter Strittmatter, were meeting with attorneys to discuss the lawsuit brought by Bill Davis. As Strittmatter recalled, they were sitting in the fifth-floor executive room of the Mid-Continent Building when word reached corporate headquarters that Judge Eidson had granted Priscilla's request. Eidson not only granted another delay in the divorce proceedings; he also ordered Cullen to pay a lump sum of $52,000 for maintenance and attorneys' fees and increased support payments from $3,500 to $5,000 a month. It was claimed that Cullen took this latest bad news in stride, but Ken Jr. was upset and said so in no uncertain terms. It wasn't the money. What galled everyone at the meeting was the continuing problem of having to go through Judge Eidson in order to make any sort of corporate transaction. Judge Eidson reserved for himself the right to tell Cullen how to run his business. What chapped Cullen was still another order by Eidson, this one prohibiting him from visiting the mansion or otherwise hassling his estranged wife. Cullen no longer pretended that he built the house for Priscilla. It was *his* mansion. "She's just a guest there," he snapped. Cullen claimed that just prior to the marriage Priscilla had signed a prenuptial agreement disclaiming any right to the family fortune.

Cullen worked until nearly 8:00 P.M. on August 2. For the next four or five hours his whereabouts were unkown.

It was about midnight on that hellish August night when Priscilla and Stan Farr returned to the mansion. Someone had tampered with the security system, but Priscilla dismissed the warning as she moved through the kitchen turning out lights. Andrea was spending the night, and Priscilla speculated that her twelve-year-old had carelessly deactivated the security system. If so, it was the last thing she ever did: the girl lay dead in the basement utility room, a bullet hole through her chest and her eyes open as though death had come before she could blink. As Priscilla walked to the stairs leading to the master bedroom, a man in black stepped from the laundry room, said "Hi," and shot her once through the chest. Stan Farr raced downstairs and the killer shot him four times, then dragged Farr's enormous body down the hallway to the kitchen, toward the basement where Andrea's body was hidden. Terrified, clutching at the bleeding wound in her chest, Priscilla escaped through the courtyard and down the hill to the home of a neighbor she had never met. She banged on the door, screaming: "My name is Priscilla Davis. I live in the big house in the middle of the field off Hulen. I am very wounded. Cullen is up there killing my children. He is killing everyone. . . ."

CHAPTER 2

Priscilla threw a party to celebrate Cullen's moving out of the mansion, and it lasted through the fall of 1974 and most of the winter of 1975. From all accounts it was some party. The guest of honor was a highly improbable figure named W. T. Rufner who arrived at 4200 Mockingbird almost as soon as Cullen departed and stayed until Priscilla, with the help of some friends, evicted him six months later. In the meantime a varying number of drifters, musicians, and drug dealers camped out at the mansion on a semipermanent basis. While there was enough drunken laughter, loud music, and backfiring motorcycles to terrorize a medium-sized town, hardly anyone in Arlington Heights, and least of all T. Cullen Davis, was aware that the mansion had gone underground.

Actually, Cullen had once met the guest of honor. He'd driven Rufner home from the airport. This was in March 1974, five months before Priscilla filed for divorce. Friends David and Judy McCrory had moved to Boston, and Priscilla had flown up for a short visit. When she returned, Cullen met her at the airport. Priscilla was accompanied by a man with daffy green eyes, shoulder-length hair, and a scraggly beard.

a part of the hijinks in the Winnebago. That other virtue of the times—sex—was also in abundance. Marazzi testified that "W. T., Larry, Priscilla, that guy from Oklahoma City I didn't know, and his girlfriend" all got naked on the trip to College Station and indulged in some group sex. Valerie was no novice to group sex, either. At roughly that same period of time the pretty Arlington Heights teenager found herself in Larry Myers's bedroom with Myers, Rufner, and Priscilla. Valerie recalled that they were all naked in bed when Rufner suggested that the men switch partners. The switch was made, and Valerie and Rufner sat on the edge of the bed and watched as Priscilla and Larry Myers got it on. According to Valerie, Rufner changed his mind when he observed that Priscilla was enjoying the experiment. "He apparently got jealous and poured a drink on her," Valerie said. This ended the fun and started a fight, but Valerie Marazzi recalled that the group remained friends. Priscilla denied any part in such salacious behavior.

In late August, several weeks after Cullen moved his things into a motel, T-man brought "some cutoffs, a couple of T-shirts, and some jeans" to 4200 Mockingbird and began spending the night. By September he was living full time at the mansion. That same month Sandy Guthrie Myers and a woman friend also moved in with Priscilla and Dee Davis. A few days later, Larry "Squint" Myers joined the group in residence at 4200 Mockingbird. Still others added themselves to the protracted live-in party. From time to time the residents at the mansion were said to include Dee's boyfriend and musician Delbert McClinton and his wife, Donna Sue. McClinton, a well-traveled writer and singer who got his education in the dives along the Jacksboro Highway, was regarded as a genuine star in his field.

From all accounts Priscilla was a magnanimous hostess. Though several of the guests who later testified against Priscilla told of fights and broken furniture and acts of blatant indiscretion, Priscilla must have gone out of her way to provide a pleasant environment. She paid legal fees for Sandy Myers and for Rufner and gave T-man, who wasn't working regularly, gifts of clothes, jewelry, and boots. She threw a surprise birthday party for Sandy Myers, which was attended by more than one hundred, including David Jackson and some of T-man's motorcycle companions. Sandy said that there was cocaine, pot, and pills "all over the house." Rufner slept in the master bedroom with Priscilla, while Sandy occupied Andrea's room—when Andrea came for weekends, she shared Dee's room. Most of the guests had moved on by January 1975 (Larry Myers had moved to the state prison at Huntsville), but Rufner stayed until May and Sandy Myers until July. From time to time Dee Davis's friends Valerie Marazzi and Bev Bass also visited the mansion, as did Priscilla's longtime friends Larry and Carmen Thomas and David and Judy McCrory, who had returned by now from Boston. There were times, too, when W. T. Rufner's dog was in residence at the mansion.

Though he was a lovable fellow, there were moments when T-man's behavior was more than Priscilla bargained for. Rufner and Skipper Nitschke got in a fight and broke a valuable statue. Another time Rufner got zonked on Percodan, a powerful painkiller that Priscilla had been taking since a skiing accident, took out his knife, and ripped the stuffings out of one of the teddy bears that Priscilla kept on her bed. That same night, while the McCrorys were visiting, T-man pushed his way into her bathroom while Priscilla was relaxing in her sunken tub. Not finding the conversation to his liking, he crowned her with a potted plant. Rufner recalled later that Priscilla screamed for him to "take your goddamn junk and get out of here," but then she had told him that on several occasions. It was T-man's impression that she was habitually overwrought. "Talk's cheap," he said, "pussy and whiskey cost money." Several days later Priscilla allowed him to return, though with not as many clothes as before. Another time Priscilla asked her friend Pat Burleson, a karate expert, to evict Rufner. All in all, Rufner's life with Priscilla was not dull. "There were mornings when it was total harmony," he said, "and mornings when it was total hell."

Priscilla remembered it as "a time of great loneliness in my life. I might have fallen for a number of people. It just happened to be T." Priscilla remarked that Rufner was never "physical" in her presence. Of course they had lovers quarrels. Friends told of the incident when T-man ripped open her silver fox bed covering after a quarrel over which TV program to watch. There was another altercation in which Rufner is supposed to have taken out his knife and cut off Priscilla's bra and panties. But the one that broke it off for keeps was when Rufner wrecked Priscilla's Lincoln Continental.

This happened in May of 1975. Rufner had already moved out of the mansion, but he continued to date Priscilla. Rufner probably didn't know it, but Priscilla already had plans to replace him. A few months earlier she had met a six-foot-nine former TCU basketball player named Stan Farr. Known around town as "the gentle giant," Farr was pleasant and noncombative, the type who was careful to mind his language and open doors for ladies. Priscilla had enjoyed her sabbatical away from

Fort Worth society, but now she missed it, missed her old friends and trips to Colonial and River Crest and wearing furs and jewelry. One thing that made Stan Farr so attractive was his enormous presence. At six-nine he more than filled an average door, and in boots and cowboy hat he dwarfed Priscilla the way a St. Bernard would dwarf a toy poodle. Priscilla could well imagine walking through Colonial on Stan Farr's massive arm. She could picture the looks of envy. Farr was much on her mind when Priscilla went out for the last time with W. T. Rufner.

The argument started as Rufner, Priscilla, and Rufner's friend Virgil Davenport were driving to the Old San Francisco Saloon. T-man, who had been washing down Percodan with Scotch and beer, was already thoroughly ripped, and he launched into a harangue about Priscilla's new friends. Actually, they were *old* friends, though Priscilla hadn't seen much of them in recent months. When Priscilla stopped her Lincoln Continental in the parking lot in front of the saloon, T-man announced that he had changed his mind about going in. They argued for a few more seconds, at which time Rufner threw the car into reverse and stomped on the gas. "When I did that, she hit the brakes," he recalled. "I believe we snapped the drive shaft." Priscilla rushed inside, leaving Rufner and Virgil Davenport with the damaged automobile. Shortly, Priscilla reappeared with Larry Thomas and his brother, Jerry Thomas, and several other friends. They had words with Rufner; then T-man and Davenport left in a cab. Rufner directed the cab to 4200 Mockingbird. He no longer had a key to the mansion, so he rang the bell. Andrea opened the door and admitted Rufner and his friend. Rufner was helping himself to a drink when Priscilla arrived with Larry and Carmen Thomas, Jerry Thomas, and others.

There are several versions of what happened next. Rufner said that he tried to apologize to Larry Thomas for wrecking Priscilla's car but Thomas told him, "The best thing for you to do is go home and sober up." Instead, Rufner went to the kitchen and mixed another drink. This time *Jerry* Thomas, former Golden Gloves heavyweight champion of Texas, told him to leave. "You're in this lady's house and she wants you out," Thomas said.

"Basically, I was about ready to leave," Rufner said. "But when Jerry Thomas said he was gonna throw me out, I told him which way hell was."

Jerry Thomas recalled that Rufner said something about going for his gun. When T-man reached for his hip pocket, Thomas floored him. T-man struggled to his feet and Thomas floored him again. "At one point," Thomas said, "he nearly bit the end of my finger off." After a few more blows, T-man decided it was time to go home. The party that began nine months earlier was definitely over.

In a few weeks Priscilla had a new bed partner, Stan Farr.

Meanwhile, there was also a new love in the life of Cullen Davis. A month or so after he moved out of the mansion, Cullen began dating Karen Master, a twenty-six-year-old divorcée and the mother of two handicapped children. Within a year he had moved into Karen Master's home in the Edgecliff section about six miles south of the mansion.

At first Karen Master seemed an unlikely choice as the new woman in Cullen's life. She was attractive but certainly not striking, and her manner was so mild and unobtrusive that she suggested one of those housewives you see in why-can't-I-make-good-coffee commercials. A high school dropout at age fifteen, she had moved through a series of mundane jobs, selling shoes at Thom McAn, working part time in a boutique, working nights at Stripling's Department Store. Later she returned to night school at Fort Worth Technical High School. The highlight of her life was being elected Miss Flame of 1965 by the Fort Worth Volunteer Fire Fighters Association. She recalled with nostalgia being invited to cut the ribbon for the opening of the new Carpenters Union Building. As one Arlington Heights socialite put it, "Stick a wad of chewing gum in her mouth and she'd definitely pass for a carhop."

But in the months after she met Cullen Davis, Karen began to look like a new woman. Her mousey blonde hair was coiffured and dyed platinum. She had silicone breast implants. Her plain pipe-rack wardrobe was replaced with originals from Neiman Marcus and with gifts of furs and jewelry. It was the old "Pygmalion" pattern. Some thought that Karen was trying to look like Priscilla: the differences between Priscilla and Karen were more a matter of style than appearance. An Arlington Heights socialite told of her mild amusement when Karen interrupted a small cocktail gathering at the Rangoon Racquet Club and inquired meekly if Cullen planned to be home for dinner. "We were talking business when she came in. She had her hair in curlers and had left her two kids in the car outside," the socialite said. "Cullen was very understanding. He asked if she'd like to join us." It was difficult to imagine Priscilla cooking dinner, much less rushing into the RRC with her hair in curlers and asking if Cullen would care to join her at home. No one could picture Priscilla scrubbing a skillet or operating a vacuum cleaner, just as no one could imagine Karen wearing a RICH BITCH necklace. The platinum hair and silicone breasts went with Priscilla, but Karen wore the trappings like a uniform.

Karen Master seemed more like Cullen's first wife, Sandra. There was even a confusing likeness of names. Sandra's maiden name was Masters and her younger sister was named Karen. The similar names—Karen Master and Karen Masters—had some people believing that Cullen was living with his ex-sister-in-law.

A few days after her eighteenth birthday, Karen married Walter Master. They had two children, Walter Adrian Master III, nicknamed Trey, and Chesley Joseph Master, born three years later and named for a distant relative that Karen's mother had uncovered in her tireless search of old courthouse records. Both were normal, healthy boys, but in 1971, when Trey was four, and Chesley was six months, Walter and Karen Master and their two boys were driving home from Sunday services at the Assembly of God Church when a drunk driver hit them head-on. Karen was almost killed—she suffered a fractured skull, a fractured jaw that caused facial paralysis, a burst eardrum, and an arm broken in three places. It was five weeks later when doctors decided that Karen was well enough to be told that both of her children had suffered permanent brain damage. Even then doctors had no concept of the extent of the damage.

By the fall of 1975 Cullen was like a member of the family. He had moved into Karen's modest home in Edgecliff and become a father figure to her two children. Cullen's two sons, Cullen Jr., who was now twelve, and Brian, who was nine, were frequent visitors. Chesley was enrolled in a class for the multiple handicapped at Tarrant County Regional School for the Deaf. With Cullen's encouragement, Karen began working with the parent/professional section of the Texas Association of the Deaf. Naturally, Cullen assumed financial responsibility for Karen and her children. He gave Karen between $3,000 and $5,000 a month for household expenses and bought her tens of thousands of dollars' worth of jewelry and furs.

CHAPTER 3

Fort Worth was just Stan Farr's kind of town. From the first day he walked across the campus of Texas Christian University he could feel the sweet vibrations. There were no strangers at TCU. The first week in September was called "Howdy Week." The men greeted him with the obligatory "Howdy" and inquired, "How's the weather up there?" Coeds sized him up as though he were 240 pounds of sausage in a display case. Down the hall from his room in the athletic wing he could hear the laughter as a group of jocks tumbled the soft drink machine down the stairs. Someone had thought to install a special seven-foot bed in his room, and as he lay back, his boots almost touching the footboard, he must have been thinking that he had arrived at the Promised Land. Like it said on the bumper stickers: *Fort Worth, Ah Luv Yew!*"

After an uneventful basketball career at TCU, most of it spent watching from the bench, Stan operated a variety of businesses—a pizza house, a swank supper club, a topless hamburger joint. They all went bad. He moved to Kansas City and worked for a brewery. He married for the second time (his first was a brief marriage in high school), then returned to Clifton, Texas, sixty miles south of Fort Worth, to join his father and younger brother Paul in the construction business. In the early 1970s Paul was killed in a car wreck. The business just seemed to fall apart after Paul was killed.

Like a nearsighted moth attracted to the only flame it had ever seen, Stan Farr returned now to Fort Worth, where an ex-jock, even one who failed to distinguish himself, was something special. A beer distributor who liked his looks hired Farr to hang around bars, buying drinks and pitching the product. By now most of the Jacksboro Highway dives had fallen into ruin; now the action was the new and fashionable bars near TCU and along Camp Bowie Boulevard. In a sense Hell's Half Acre had moved uptown, or more accurately, to Arlington Heights. In the course of a day's work, Farr visited the Rangoon Racquet Club, the Old San Francisco, the Sea Hag, the Round Up Inn on the rodeo grounds, Colonial, Western Hills, Green Oaks, the Carriage House, the Merrimac, anywhere the swingers were likely to gather. His job was to create goodwill and he was good at it. On several occasions in the early 1970s he ran across Cullen and Priscilla Davis, but the relationship was only a nodding acquaintance.

Farr tired of buying beer and playing shuffleboard and watching the afternoon crowd in its relentless pursuit of sexual adventure. The dream of owning his own quick-profit business was never far from his mind. The hot venture of the moment was constructing cheap apartment complexes and selling them before the walls began to crack. When a Dallas promoter approached him with a proposition, Farr borrowed all his credit allowed and signed on, but the business folded before they could put up the first "For Rent" sign and Farr was flat broke again. Farr claimed the Dallas promoter stiffed him, but the banks that he had borrowed from demonstrated no sympathy and several lawsuits were forthcoming. Billy Gammon said: "It was typical of Stan's luck that he got into the quickie apartment game ten months after the fire went out." Farr's sister, Lynda Arnold, added: "My brother was the all-time nice guy, but he was amazingly gullible. Right up to the end, people he trusted were still doing a number on him."

In the winter of 1975, as he was struggling to pay off his debts, Stan met Priscilla. The attraction was mutual and instant.

By summer Stan Farr had moved into Cullen Davis's mansion and was contemplating some serious changes in his life. He decided to grow a beard and exchanged his suits and sport coats for cosmic cowboy wear. The cosmic cowboy fad had swept across Texas some five or six years earlier, but, characteristically, Stan was slow to see its potential. By 1975 the cosmic cowboy industry had spread across the country. That could mean only one thing—that the fad had peaked and would soon be replaced by something else—but Stan Farr didn't see it that way. Not long after he moved in with Priscilla, Farr invested in a new business venture, a pseudo-western discotheque called the Rhinestone Cowboy.

Unlike the clandestine affair with W. T. Rufner, Priscilla made no secret of her love affair with Farr. By the summer of 1975 Cullen knew that Farr was living in the mansion, as did many others in Arlington Heights. Priscilla went out of her way to show off her new lover. They were seen regularly in the night spots and country clubs, the six-foot-nine jock in his boots and beaver hide buffalo-hunter's hat and the five-foot-three "rich bitch" in her flimsy blouses and hip huggers. As though Farr were not sufficiently conspicuous, Priscilla bought him a silver and turquoise genuine bear claw necklace that would have looked like a logging chain on anyone else. Priscilla affected the style of the cosmic cowgirl, frequently going barefoot and wearing nothing but a skimpy halter and very brief Levi's cutoffs. In any crowd they were certain to stand out. Priscilla said: "Being married to a celebrity like Cullen, I naturally attracted a lot of attention. But being with Stan took the limelight off of me, which I enjoyed. Stan and I had an agreement that when we went into a place we wouldn't separate. Otherwise the men would attack me and girls would attack him."

Stan Farr was five years younger than Priscilla, and they were telling years—the difference between a man of thirty and a woman of thirty-five. This was no doubt one reason Priscilla enjoyed the company of those much younger, particularly Bev Bass, who was in Dee's 1976

AHHS graduating class. Bev and Dee had been friends since the seventh grade and frequently spent the night together, and after Cullen moved out, Bev spent a good deal of time at the mansion even when Dee was away. The daughter of two professional educators, Bev Bass was an exceptionally pretty girl with honey-blonde hair and hazel eyes. She was a good student and athlete—she ran the hurdles on her high school track team. Bev seemed to enjoy the company of older women. Before she started dating Gus (Bubba) Gavrel, Jr., she was a close friend of Gavrel's mother. "We'd go shopping a lot, or have lunch," Bass recalled. "I went over to the Gavrel house a lot for dinner." So while Bev and Dee Davis remained close friends, it seemed natural that Bev and Priscilla would become friends and confidantes. When Bev Bass learned that she was pregnant in the summer of 1975, the first person she told was Dee and the second person was Priscilla, who quickly arranged for a secret abortion.

In her role as confidante and surrogate mother, Priscilla was fulfilling her self-image—*good old Mother Davis.* Many of Priscilla's private conversations with Bass concerned Dee Davis. Dee was definitely a problem. A marginal student, she had frequent disciplinary problems at school, and when Priscilla tried to correct her, the result was a shouting match between mother and daughter. Priscilla was relieved when Dee began dating Brent Cruz, a popular boy from a good Arlington Heights family, but Dee had other friends who were less exemplary and it was this group that concerned Priscilla. Andrea, too, was a problem, though of a different nature. Since the girl's unfortunate encounter with Cullen, Priscilla seemed unable to reach Andrea. In this respect, Bev Bass became a surrogate mother to Priscilla's youngest. Andrea would sometimes talk for hours with Bev, telling her things she discussed with no one else. Andrea expressed her special feeling for Bev by making her a bracelet with charms that spelled "I Love You 2." Bev helped Andrea with her lessons, combed her hair, picked out her clothes, and took her to favorite places—mostly pet shops. Bass recalled, "Andrea would look at the animals in cages and wish she could let them all out. She was the sweetest, most innocent, beautiful child you've ever seen. She really didn't like to be around people as much as she liked to be around animals." In the dirty torrent of charges and countercharges that followed, Andrea Wilborn would be the forgotten person. One of the low points of the murder trial was when lawyers for the defense tried to establish that Andrea kept a small marijuana plant in her room at the mansion.

CHAPTER 4

As the summer of 1976 approached, Fort Worth society played out
its ritual of debutante functions, charity balls, golf tournaments,
graduations, and class reunions.

In mid-July, Farr was "terminated" from his position at the Rhinestone Cowboy. Priscilla seemed relieved. She wanted him to run for
political office—she thought county commissioner would be a good place
to start—but Stan had other ideas. He was talking to investors about
buying Panther Hall, Fort Worth's honky-tonk of honky-tonks.

On July 28, Priscilla went to the office of Dr. Thomas Simons, the
surgeon who had removed cysts from her breasts. She complained of
new lumps on her left breast and of flare-ups from her ulcer, but there
was a more pressing matter she wanted Simons to consider. The divorce
trial was now two days away, and she wanted Simons to write a letter to
Judge Eidson stating that she was in no physical condition to endure the
ordeal of a trial. In Simons's waiting room Priscilla had a chance meeting
with Sandy Myers. According to Myers, Priscilla seemed terribly
distraught. "Something heavy is coming down," Priscilla supposedly
whispered. Priscilla didn't elaborate, but Myers had enough experience
with drugs to recognize rampant paranoia. So did Dr. Simons. He had
been prescribing Percodan, Valium, and other drugs for Priscilla for
some months. In his judgment the pills were being dispensed in safe
quantities, yet Priscilla demonstrated the symptoms of an addict—
irrational fears, dark, unexplained forces, a world crashing around her.
Simons didn't know that Priscilla was juggling doctors and pharmacists
to obtain many more Percodan than were reflected in his records. There
was no physical reason she couldn't face the divorce trial, but her
emotional state was another matter. The following day Simons drafted a
letter to Judge Eidson stating that the patient was "in no emotional
condition" to appear in court.

On Friday, July 30, the letter was read into evidence, to the
astonishment and dismay of Cullen Davis and his attorneys. Cullen's
lawyers argued that another delay would cause serious financial conse-
quences, not only to their client but to Kendavis Industries and parties of
unnamed creditors. Eidson was unsympathetic. The judge noted that
Kendavis Industries' profits for the previous year were $57 million, *after*
taxes. Cullen Davis didn't strike him as a man on the verge of financial
disaster. The judge announced that he would rule on Priscilla's request
for another delay the following Monday, August 2.

Monday afternoon, as Cullen, Ken Jr., and Walter Strittmatter were meeting at corporate headquarters, word of Judge Eidson's decision arrived by messenger. The judge had granted the delay; worse, he had increased support payments from $3,500 to $5,000 a month and ordered Cullen to cough up another $52,000 for maintenance of the mansion and attorneys' fees. Ken Davis, who was already upset by the latest turn of events in their legal battle with the younger brother, was furious and made no effort to conceal it. But Cullen seemed to take the news in stride.

Earlier that day Cullen had lunch with his adopted daughter, Dee Davis. They talked about the fact that she would soon enroll at Texas Tech, and about Andrea, who had been in Houston visiting her grandmother. Jack Wilborn had planned to drive to Houston over the weekend and bring Andrea home, but there had been a change of plans. Dee told Cullen that she had gone to Houston instead and that Andrea was spending the night at the mansion.

Dee had not the slightest intention of staying home that night. It was one of those strings of hellishly hot summer days when Arlington Heights kids sleep till noon, devote an hour or less to suntan mainte-nance, take a dip, nap, and reappear just after sunset. From Dee's point of view, lunch with Cullen had already spoiled her day.

Bev Bass slept till noon, dressed, and drove to the mansion in her 1972 Skylark. She planned to shop for her father's birthday gift, and Andrea was going along. When Bass arrived at the mansion, Dee and Brent Cruz were listening to the stereo and Priscilla was propped up on her giant bed, watching three TV programs at once and talking on the telephone. As usual, Andrea hadn't dressed or combed her hair. Bass selected a brown tube top and skirt for Andrea, brushed the kinks out of the girl's long silky brown hair, and hurried her to the car. At a department store on Camp Bowie, Bass bought a golf shirt for her father's birthday. She also priced waterbeds; her own had developed a leak. They visited two pet shops. Andrea fell in love with a pygmy goat, but Bass pointed out several sound reasons why a goat wouldn't be happy at 4200 Mocking-bird, where Priscilla already had an impressive collection of stray dogs. Bev and Andrea cruised Arlington Heights for a while, stopping to visit several friends, then circled by California Leather Cleaners to see what plans Bubba Gavrel had made for the evening. Bubba told Bev that they were having dinner with friends. He'd pick her up around 6:00 P.M. Bass told him to pick her up at the mansion. She kept several changes of clothes at Dee's house and didn't feel like going home.

459

Bev and Dee made plans for later in the evening. After dinner they would all meet at Brent Cruz's house, where Dee promised to gift-wrap the golf shirt and accompany Bev while she delivered it to her father. Since Bass's waterbed was in bad shape, it was agreed she would spend the night at the mansion.

Despite the good news from Judge Eidson, Priscilla was feeling rotten. Everywhere she turned there was turmoil. Dee was bitching about not having enough spending money, and Andrea had trashed the kitchen attempting to bake a cake, which she never got around to finishing; Priscilla found a bowl of abortive goo stashed in the freezer. Then there was Stan Farr. He seemed preoccupied and petulant. Farr no longer felt comfortable in the mansion. Priscilla reminded him that the divorce was sure to be final in another four months. She had to stick it out that long. "In a few months we can get married and build our own place," she told him. Farr didn't reply. Friday had been Priscilla's thirty-fifth birthday, but she hadn't felt like celebrating. But now it was Larry Thomas's birthday and Judy McCrory's wedding anniversary, so she reluctantly agreed to a small celebration that night. She already regretted it. Judy and David McCrory were having marital problems, and Priscilla felt it was foolish to be celebrating a marriage that was about to end. Next to Cullen, David McCrory had become Priscilla's least favorite person. She hated his big mouth, hated his constant yammering about this or that big deal, hated the theatrics and the way McCrory had of making an obvious failure appear to be part of his grand plan for success. Priscilla had a word for David McCrory. He was a *nerd*.

Cullen's activities on the afternoon of August 2 were predictable, up to a point. After the meeting with Ken Jr. and Strittmatter, Cullen went to his own office and worked until after 5:00 P.M. At 5:30 P.M. Cullen walked to the garage where his blue and white Cadillac was parked, but instead of the Cadillac he drove away in a company pickup truck. Thirty minutes later, according to a security guard at Mid-Continent, Cullen returned to his office and stayed until 7:50 P.M. Whatever his plans, they didn't include dinner at home. Several hours earlier Cullen's secretary telephoned Karen Master and told her Cullen would be home late. Cullen claimed later that he left his office at 7:50 P.M., had dinner alone, and went to a movie. But there was no one to support the story. The only persons who claimed to have seen Cullen from the time he left the Mid-Continent Building until after midnight were the three witnesses to the shootings.

Around 9:00 P.M. Priscilla and Stan Farr left the mansion to meet their friends. Priscilla kissed Andrea and activated the security system as they walked out the door. As Priscilla anticipated, dinner was a disaster. McCrory prattled on about his newest get-rich scheme, a karate school that his friend Pat Burleson had let him manage. Stan hardly spoke. After dinner they stopped by the Rangoon Racquet Club, where things weren't much better. Bubba Gavrel and Bev Bass were at the RRC when Priscilla's party arrived, and Priscilla motioned for Bass to join them. Bass recalled: "Priscilla leaned over and whispered to me that she'd gotten what she wanted in court that day. I told her I was gonna spend the night with Dee, and she said, 'Good. I'll tell you about it later.'" Even though it was only a little after 11:00 P.M., Farr kept looking at his watch and yawning.

Andrea was alone in the mansion at least as late as 10:30 P.M. That's the time when she talked on the telephone to Stan's sister, Lynda Arnold, and to Lynda's fourteen-year-old daughter, Dana. The only person who knows what happened next is the killer. Sometime after 10:30 P.M. the killer entered the mansion, either with a key or with Andrea's consent. Someone deactivated the security system. As police reconstructed it later, the killer took Andrea to the basement, stood facing her, then shot her just below the left breast with a .38 Smith & Wesson. The killer must have been only a little taller than Andrea. The girl was five-foot-seven, but the bullet, which entered her chest and exited with no deviation two inches to the left of the midline of her back, dropped two inches in its flight. The killer stood no more than six feet away when he fired the shot. Since there was no sign of a struggle, it was speculated that Andrea knew and trusted the person who took her to the basement. Only the killer knew if she screamed or pleaded for her life or even recognized danger. Her body was discovered in one of the large utility closets in the basement. She was on her back in a pool of blood; the brown tube top that Bev Bass had selected was stained from the breast down, the skirt hiked up to her waist. There was blood on her arms and on the top of her head, suggesting that she fell face down but that the killer turned her body over to make certain she was dead. Her eyes were open, expressionless and permanently frozen as though death had come instantly. Traces of blood found at the top of the basement stairs augmented speculation that the killer handled the body.

He was hiding in the laundry room just to the right of the mansion's main entrance when Priscilla and Stan Farr returned home about midnight.

Priscilla was not alarmed when she noticed that the security system had been deactivated. This was the sort of carelessness she expected from both Dee and Andrea. Priscilla knew that Dee was expecting Bev Bass; as it turned out, Dee spent the night at Brent Cruz's house, but Priscilla had no way of knowing this at the time. Andrea was especially careless about admitting visitors. Priscilla remembered the time she'd opened the door for W. T. Rufner and his friend. It would never occur to Andrea that anyone who rang the front bell was anything less than friendly. As Stan Farr started up the stairs to the master bedroom, Priscilla walked through the kitchen, turning off lights. This is when she noticed that someone had left on the light at the top of the basement stairs. When Priscilla got close to the door at the top of the stairs, she saw what appeared to be a bloody palm print on the door facing. She called out to Stan Farr, who couldn't hear her, then started toward the stairs leading to the master bedroom.

In statements to the police and later in court Priscilla described what happened next: "Cullen stepped out from the direction of the laundry room. He was dressed all in black. His hands were inside a black plastic bag and he had on a shoulder-length curly black wig, the kind colored people wear. I remember thinking *how ridiculous*. He said, 'Hi,' . . . and then he shot me. I felt the blood and the big hole in my chest. I screamed to Stan, 'I've been shot! Cullen shot me! Stan, go back!' But I could hear Stan coming downstairs. I was lying on the floor but I could see Stan at the bottom of the stairs . . . he had pushed the door shut and was holding it from the inside and Cullen was, you know, pushing from the outside. Cullen fired through the door and I could hear Stan . . . he said something like *Uh*! and I knew he'd been shot. Then Cullen pushed the door open. Stan grabbed him and they wrestled around and then Cullen jerked back and fired again. Stan turned and fell and was kind of, you know, looking at me. He was kind of on his side with his chin up. Cullen stood at Stan's feet and shot him two more times. Stan made a gasping sound, sort of a gurgle. Then Stan just kind of laid his head down—he closed his eyes and laid his head down and died. . . ."

By all reasoning Priscilla should have been dead: she had been shot from almost exactly the same position and in nearly the same part of her chest as Andrea, but the bullet miraculously missed her main artery. The killer must have thought she was dead or dying, because he paid no attention. Instead, he took Farr by the feet and began dragging his body down the hallway, leaving a wide trail of blood all the way to the kitchen . . . toward the basement where Andrea's body lay.

Priscilla testified: "That's when I decided to try for the back door and I unlocked it, you know, and he heard me unlock the door and I ran out, you know, onto the patio part . . . and he came after me, and, anyway, I tripped and fell down."

The man in black caught up with her in the patio courtyard, near the marble statue of Aphrodite. He grabbed her arm and started pulling her back inside. "I was pleading with him," Priscilla said. "I was saying, 'Cullen, I love you. I didn't . . . I have never loved anybody else. Please, let's talk. Please, Cullen . . . you're hurting me.' " The killer relaxed his grip but continued to pull her toward the house, saying very softly, "Come on, come on." Priscilla asked the question for which there was no answer: "Why are you doing this?" She could see the gun muzzle sticking through the plastic bag: the wig kept slipping, and the killer used the gun hand to push it back in place.

Many times, as she recalled the story, Priscilla saw it in slow motion, like a dream with a plot that never changed.

"I remember things," she said. "I couldn't understand why he wouldn't shoot me again. I was thinking at the same time—what is he holding onto that *wig* for? You know. No matter what is going on, you are still thinking. I guess it's somewhere in my mind too. What's so important about holding onto that wig? He thinks he is hiding from somebody. Then he got me to the back door and . . . now that's when I don't know why he turned loose of me."

It's only speculation, but the killer must have believed that Priscilla was too badly wounded to escape. His priority seemed to be dragging Stan Farr's body to the basement. Perhaps he intended to return for Priscilla and take her to the basement too, take her to the bodies of Andrea and Farr, and then, his revenge complete, finish Priscilla with the one remaining bullet in his .38. But the killer failed to reckon with Priscilla's tenacity, her well-honed survival instinct. As soon as the killer had resumed dragging Farr's body, she literally dove into the bushes behind the marble statues. She could hear him coming after her, then she heard something else. She heard voices from the driveway. She hadn't heard the Blazer—her ears were still ringing from the gunshots—but now she heard a man and a woman. It was Gavrel and Bev Bass, but Priscilla didn't consider that at the time. Her first thought was *It's Dee! She's come home! He'll kill her too!* Later Priscilla realized that in those unbelievable seconds she had allowed herself to think the unthinkable. It wasn't until the following day that they told her Andrea was dead, but somehow she already knew.

Priscilla's testimony continued: "I ran . . . I remember thinking I was going to try to run to Jim Morgan. He owns those condominiums next to the property . . . then I decided I had better not try to go that far, so I decided to cut across to one of the houses. It was like, you know, a dream . . . or a movie. You know, every time I have seen any movies and see these stupid women fall down, I just . . . well, I thought about it and I fell flat on my face.

"I heard a shot. Screaming. More shots, just a bunch. But I kept going. Then I fell again, and I scratched my head up here and my knee and everything. Anyway, I got up and thought . . . I was really thinking maybe I should walk, that I would last longer. Then I thought, no, Priscilla, just run and stay calm. Don't panic, Priscilla. Stay calm. You know, I was trying to keep from . . . not going into any form of shock. I was trying to breathe through my diaphragm. I was really going through all of this. Just holding my skirt real tight [up around her chest] to keep from bleeding so much. My heart was pounding and it was pumping more blood. That's really what I was trying to keep in my mind more than anything."

The next thing she recalled was banging on the door of a neighbor's home, screaming and banging and finally ringing the doorbell. This was the home of Mr. and Mrs. Clifford Jones, and the thoughts that they must have registered at that moment were never expressed. They could hear a woman's voice screaming, "My name is Priscilla Davis. I live in the big house in the middle of the field off Hulen. I am very wounded. Cullen is up there killing my children. He is killing everyone!" Clifford Jones and his wife had never heard of Priscilla Davis, nor were they about to open the door, but they called out to the woman that they had telephoned for an ambulance and for the police. They still refused to open the door until police arrived.

In sworn statements and court testimony Bubba Gavrel and Bev Bass supported Priscilla's story.

Gavrel, who at five-foot-ten was about five inches taller than Bass, was first to see trouble. As Gavrel closed the door of his Blazer, he could see something Bass couldn't—over the courtyard wall, he could see a man and a woman in some sort of struggle. The woman was blonde, but in the dim light he identified the man only by his voice. The woman was pleading, "I love you! I've always loved you!" and the man was saying, "Come on, come on." Bass recalled that as she stepped down from the Blazer, she heard a woman's scream from inside the house, then a noise like a gunshot or something breaking. It occurred to her that someone was having a fight, but she said nothing to Bubba.

Like Priscilla, the killer probably hadn't heard the young couple arrive; the echo of screams and gunshots must have been ringing in his ears too. The killer disappeared into the house—this was the moment when Priscilla dived into the shrubs. A moment later the man reappeared. He no longer wore the wig. His head was bowed, and his hands were concealed in a shiny black bag. Gavrel recalled saying, "What's going on? Where is everybody?" Bass said that the man was stealing something from the mansion, but before this could sink in, Gavrel saw the man at the courtyard gate and heard him say, "They are right this way. Follow me." Gavrel still didn't recognize the figure, only that it was a man dressed in black. The man led the couple along the front of the garage and around the corner, along the walkway toward the breakfast room door, the mansion's main entrance. The lights over the garage flickered from a short in the wiring; Gavrel still couldn't see much, but he followed close behind the man, and Bass walked just behind Gavrel. When the man was a few feet from the well-lighted breakfast room, Bass suddenly recognized him.

"Bubba!" she called out. "That's Cullen!"

In one movement the man turned around and shot Gavrel in the stomach. "It felt like a horse kicking me," Gavrel said. He fell backward. For a moment the killer stood directly over the husky young man, pointing the gun at the victim's head. By now the .38 was empty; it's not clear whether the killer knew this as he stood over Gavrel.

Bass said: "Then Cullen looked at me. I was scared he was gonna shoot me, so I started running." She ran back along the pathway, hurdling a low retaining wall, zigzagging down the hill and the rough driveway toward the Hulen Street gate. Somewhere in there she lost one of her Dr. Scholl's sandals, but she kept running and zigzagging, expecting that at any moment the pursuing man would fire. She could see the man over her shoulder, and she called out, "Cullen, please don't shoot me! It's Bev!" She called this out eight or nine times. When she was almost to Hulen, Bass looked around again and the man was no longer pursuing her. She flagged down a passing motorist and jumped into his car.

While the killer was chasing Bass, Gavrel was looking for help. But he was paralyzed from the waist down; there was no feeling at all in his legs. Using his thick arms for support, Gavrel dragged himself to the breakfast room door. It was locked. Through the glass panels he could see the wide trail of blood along the hallway where the killer had dragged Stan Farr's body. Bubba took off a shoe and tried to break the glass. Realizing he needed something heavier, Gavrel dragged himself back along the pathway and tried to pry loose a stone. When he heard the killer returning, Gavrel curled up and played dead. He heard the man run by, then saw him at the door. When the gunman discovered that the door was locked, he reloaded his pistol and fired three times, shattering the glass panel. He kicked out the remaining glass and disappeared inside the house. A few minutes later, Gavrel heard the killer returning. He walked over and looked at Bubba's motionless body and said, "Oh, my God!" That was the last anyone saw of the man in black.

When Gavrel was sure the man had gone, he dragged himself through the broken glass and into the kitchen. He managed to reach a telephone, but it wasn't working. "I was feeling bad . . . real weak," Gavrel said. "I just leaned my head up against the wall and closed my eyes."

Later, there would be much controversy over exactly what time all this was happening. John Smedley, the second person to see Bev Bass after she escaped from the killer, put the time of their meeting at exactly 12:47 A.M. Smedley was a patrolman for Homeguard Security Company, and he had just checked out the service station at the corner of Hulen and Bellaire, the nearest intersection to the mansion. He was reporting to his dispatcher—that's how he remembered the exact time—when he heard a woman's loud whistle. It was Bev Bass, who had caught a ride with motorist Robert Sawhill. Smedley had parked his patrol Jeep. Sawhill had already telephoned police and then called for an ambulance when Bass spotted the patrol Jeep. She put her fingers in her mouth and let out a whistle that could be heard for several blocks. When Smedley looked up from his radio log, he saw a young woman across the street, whistling and waving her arms. Smedley wheeled his Jeep around and pulled across to the Mr. M Food Store. The young woman ran out to meet him.

"She was very excited . . . out of breath," the private patrolman said. "She said in a loud voice, 'You've got to help me. My boyfriend's been shot and he's dying.' There was a man [Sawhill] there and I told him to call the police, but he said he'd already called them. The girl said, 'Be damn sure the police have been called.' I radioed my 314 [call letters] to my dispatcher and asked him to also notify the Fort Worth PD that we had a signal 37 [shooting]."

Bass interrupted Smedley, shouting, "You don't *understand*! There's been a shooting! My boyfriend has been shot and he's dying. I saw him get shot!"

466

"Where?" Smedley asked, trying to calm the girl.

"At Priscilla's!"

Smedley recognized the name; he'd once worked security at the mansion, and friends of his had attended parties at Priscilla Davis's house.

"The big white house on the hill," Bass continued, words tumbling from her mouth almost quicker than Smedley could unscramble them. "My boyfriend is dying. I saw him get shot. I saw him do it."

"You saw *who* do it?" Smedley asked.

"It was Cullen. Cullen did it!" the girl screamed. "I saw his ugly fucking face. He's trying to kill me too. He chased me all over the place!"

Bass pleaded with the private patrolman to take her back to the mansion, but he told her to wait for the police. Within a few minutes two Fort Worth police cars pulled into the Mr. M's parking lot. Bass ran to the first patrol car, jumped in, and screamed, "Just go! I'll tell you on the way!" By the time the first patrol car reached the mansion, at least eight people had been told of the shootings, and at least five of them heard Priscilla or Bev Bass name the killer as Cullen Davis. The first report had come from Clifford Jones. Police logged the call at 12:42 A.M. Two minutes later, Sawhill made the first of two calls to police headquarters; after that Smedley's dispatcher called. At almost the same time, an ambulance had reached Priscilla. She repeated the story that Cullen was killing everyone, and the ambulance drivers reported the name of the suspect to police en route to the emergency room at John Peter Smith Hospital.

Officers Jimmy Soders and J. A. Perez were patrolling the Tanglewood area in separate squad cars when they were dispatched to the Mr. M Food Store less than a mile from the mansion. The time of the call was 12:45 A.M. Soders recalled that the woman he knew later as Bev Bass leaped into his car, told him her boyfriend had been shot, and directed him to the Hulen Street gate. On the way, Soders asked the girl who shot her boyfriend and she told him, "Cullen Davis did it. I saw him do it. I know him."

Perez and Soders both drew their pistols and ran toward the door that Bass pointed to as the main entrance. Bubba Gavrel was no longer where Bass had seen him fall, and she ran and pushed ahead of the cops. "I grabbed her and made her come back and sit by the wall," Perez said. "She was highly excited. I had to be very stern with her." The two cops led the girl back to the private patrolman, Smedley, who arrived just behind them; they told Smedley to keep her outside.

His pistol cocked and ready, Perez entered through the broken panels and saw Gavrel leaning against the wall, holding a telephone. "Damn thing don't work," Gavrel said. The two cops moved slowly; it seemed likely that the killer might still be inside. Soders followed the trail of blood down the hallway to the kitchen where he discovered Stan Farr's body. Farr was on his stomach, his head turned to the right. His eyes were closed, and dark, matted hair covered part of his face. The broad back of his white cowboy shirt was stained with blood.

By now two more officers had joined the search, and at least two dozen more were on their way to 4200 Mockingbird. Perez, Soders, and two others made a quick search of the twenty-room mansion's main floor. It was Perez who discovered a blood smear on the door leading to the basement. Blood dotted the glass window near the basement entrance. More cops and police dogs were arriving at the mansion as Perez and Sgt. J. D. Tigert moved cautiously down the basement steps. The basement was dark, and Perez beamed his flashlight from side to side. Sergeant Tigert checked the right side of the room, and Perez worked the opposite wall, where several utility closets were located. Perez flashed his light on a door and opened it. The small room was filled with lawn furniture. He moved along the wall to a second door. "I had my flashlight in my left hand, the gun in my right," Perez said. "I pressed against the wall. The door opens out, and I held it open three to four inches and looked in. And I saw some feet . . . laying down, toward the door. I closed the door and motioned for Sergeant Tigert. I shined my light in the little room. Sergeant Tigert had his gun drawn. He went inside."

In the beam of Perez's flashlight Sergeant Tigert saw the body of Andrea Wilborn, lying on her back in a dark pool, her eyes open and looking at him. In his dozen years on the police force, Tigert had seen many bodies, but the body of the young girl was something he wasn't prepared for; he was trembling as he backed out of the room. All he could say to Perez was "Find the light switch." Perez had already turned away and was running the beam of his light along the basement wall. Upstairs, they could hear the dogs and the movement of many sets of feet.

Upstairs, Soders and others were attempting to question Gavrel, who was so befuddled from shock and loss of blood he couldn't even tell them where he had been shot, much less who fired the bullet. Gavrel kept telling Soders, "Get an ambulance."

Outside, Bev Bass watched the ambulance arrive. More numb than hysterical now, she followed the ambulance attendants to the door, watched as they loaded Gavrel on the stretcher, then followed them back to the ambulance. Paul Goheen, one of the ambulance attendants, also recalled that Gavrel didn't know where he'd been shot or who shot him. "Just get me out of here," Gavrel told the ambulance attendants. "He's going to come back and get me." Who? Hell, Gavrel didn't know *who*. Just get him out of here fast. Goheen would also say that as they loaded Gavrel into the ambulance, the victim handed him two Baggies of what appeared to be marijuana. "Get rid of these," Gavrel supposedly said. Another ambulance arrived, and Bass watched as they carted out the body of Stan Farr. "I wanted to see if they had found Andrea," Bass said. "Then they told me she was dead too. All I said was 'Let's go.'" Apparently Bass said several other things. She told the police that Cullen Davis was living at Karen Master's house and gave them the address and telephone number. She also told them that Cullen had a private airplane at Meacham Field. It occurred to her that Cullen might be attempting to escape in his Learjet. Then something *else* occurred to her. "You better get somebody out to Bill [Davis] and Mitzi's house," she said. "He might try to kill them too."

The same thought could have passed through the mind of Bill Davis. When he heard news of the killings a few hours later, he telephoned the sheriff and asked for protection, then herded his family to the attic and sat guarding the attic door with a shotgun until the deputies arrived.

Ken Davis, Jr., had also heard of the murders. Shortly after 4:00 A.M. he telephoned Cullen at Karen Master's home. Cullen told his brother he hadn't heard about the killings and that he'd been home "most of the night." He didn't seem particularly upset.

"What are you going to do about it?" Ken Davis asked.

"Well, I guess I'll go back to bed," Cullen replied.

Karen Master recalled that almost as soon as Cullen hung up from the conversation with his brother, the telephone rang again. It was an Officer Ford from the Fort Worth PD, asking to speak to Cullen Davis. Cullen spoke briefly and hung up. Karen telephoned her mother, and while they were talking, the operator cut them off and said the police had an emergency call. It was Officer Ford again. He asked to speak to Cullen again.

Ken Davis telephoned a second time, then the phone rang again, and it was Officer Ford calling for the third time. This time Ford told Karen to "remain on the line."

Karen recalled: "We had both started getting dressed. I held the phone to my ear. Every few minutes Officer Ford would come back on the line and say, 'You still there?' He wouldn't let me hang up until Cullen was completely dressed and outside in the yard."

By now Karen Master's house in Edgecliff was surrounded by police cars. In one of the cars sat David McCrory, who had intercepted cops at the hospital and led them to Master's house. At 4:30 A.M. Cullen walked outside and surrendered. His Cadillac, which had been seen as late as 11:50 P.M. at the garage downtown, was parked in the driveway—the pickup that Cullen had driven from the garage earlier was now parked in another downtown garage. Before police took him downtown, Cullen led them to four pistols stashed in his Cadillac and a fifth handgun inside the house. As it turned out, none of the five guns was the murder weapon.

In the massive investigation that followed, Tarrant County Sheriff Lon Evans recalled a curious connection. In June, less than two months before the murders and at roughly the same time Cullen was attending his high school class reunion, two teenagers playing on the banks of the Trinity at the edge of the Davis estate discovered a Colt .45 automatic equipped with a silencer. The gun didn't appear lost, it appeared *abandoned*. It had been recently cleaned, inside and out, and there was no trace of fingerprints. The sheriff had pretty much dismissed the .45, but now he thought again about it and asked federal Alcohol, Tobacco and Firearms agents to attempt to trace its ownership. They traced it to Roy Rimmer, Jr., Cullen's best friend.

CHAPTER 5

For most of his thirty-eight years District Attorney Tim Curry had prepared himself for a career in law, but nothing in his background anticipated the case that was dropped in his lap on the morning of August 3. Curry grew up in Arlington Heights. He'd known the Davis family for years, though not well. In the late 1950s when he was attending AHHS, Curry's world orbited around places like River Crest and families like the Davises. Curry was nearer the age of Bill Davis, but he knew Cullen by name and reputation. "Cullen was the kind of guy nobody paid much attention to," Curry said. What one did pay attention to was the family name. Stinky Davis's son . . . accused of murder? Tim Curry wasn't ready for that.

From the beginning, the case against Cullen Davis seemed open and shut. Though both Priscilla and Bubba Gavrel remained in intensive care and had been unable to make statements, it seemed likely they would corroborate Bev Bass's story. Meanwhile a team of police and DA's investigators was collecting an impressive amount of physical evidence from the mansion. It all seemed to be there—the motive, the means, the opportunity. It seemed apparent to Curry that Cullen's best defense would be insanity. He recalled the 1966 J. Lloyd Parker murder case in which the heir to the Parker oil fortune was convicted of murdering his father, then sent to Rusk State Hospital for psychiatric treatment. Parker had recently exhausted his appeals and surrendered to authorities, but for ten years he had avoided prison. Curry thought that this sort of example should not be repeated in Fort Worth, and he moved quickly to have Cullen examined by Dallas psychiatrist Dr. John T. Holbrook. Just as quickly, Cullen's lawyers stopped him. Although Cullen had been in jail only a few hours, he had been visited by a number of attorneys including Cecil Munn, Hershel Payne, and Bill Magnussen. Curry had heard that famed Dallas attorney Phil Burleson, one of the defense lawyers in the Jack Ruby murder trial, had agreed to represent Davis.

Curry's next priority after the abortive psychiatric examination was to decide on the charge and recommend bond. That afternoon he gathered with his chief assistants, Joe Shannon, Tolly Wilson, and Marvin Collins, to discuss the case. Collins, the best constitutional lawyer on Curry's staff, brought up the possibility of charging the multimillionaire with capital murder. Under Texas law, a capital crime is a murder committed while in the act of another specified felony—robbery or burglary, for example. Collins noted that Judge Eidson had signed a restraining order almost two years before, barring Davis from "coming on or about the premises at 4200 Mockingbird." Collins argued that Eidson's order could be construed to mean that Cullen Davis committed an act of burglary and therefore an act of capital murder. Curry had serious doubts about the theory. He felt that the law might not be construed this way. Their only recourse was to file the lesser charge of murder, which carried a possible life sentence.

On Curry's recommendation, Justice of the Peace W. W. Matthews set bond at $80,000, twice the normal amount. Cullen paid the full amount in cashier's checks and walked out Tuesday afternoon, about sixteen hours after the murders.

Joe Shannon, Curry's best criminal prosecutor, took charge of the investigation at the start. A former state legislator with a reputation for dogged conservatism, Shannon had also grown up in Arlington Heights, though he had never socialized with the wealthy families. For the next fifteen months Shannon devoted at least 90 percent of his time to the Cullen Davis case. But on August 3, the morning after the murder, Shannon found it difficult to connect the pieces. All he had to work with at the time was Bev Bass's sworn statement and the statements of the Clifford Joneses and the security officer, Smedley.

"The big problem for the first two days was trying to find out from Priscilla what happened inside the mansion," Shannon said. "Nobody had been able to talk to her. We talked to Gavrel very briefly that night [August 3]. His memory wasn't too strong. He was still pretty doped up after the surgery. He was saying, 'Yeah, I think it was Cullen Davis,' but not unequivocally. I had already talked to Bev Bass so I just assumed Bubba would make the same positive identification, but now I had my doubts."

The only people who had been allowed to visit Priscilla were Judy McCrory, who had relayed simple messages back and forth to investigators, and a priest, who had told Priscilla what she had instinctively known—that Andrea was dead. "There was a ton of evidence at the mansion," Shannon said, "but we couldn't make heads or tails of it. [Detective] Claude Davis's first theory was that Stan Farr had crawled around to the kitchen, leaving that line of blood. I disagreed because the trail of blood was too smooth. We had fingerprints, bullets, shattered glass, shreds of plastic, rivers of blood, and a nine-foot door with a hole in the center, but we were only guessing what happened."

It was a miracle that Priscilla Davis was even alive. The bullet that entered her chest made an unexplained turn to the left, barely missing the aorta, the main artery leading from the heart, as it passed through her body. Bubba Gavrel was hurt more seriously. The bullet had entered the left side of his abdomen, below the ribs, and was lodged near his spine. The bullet severed a vein attached to Gavrel's kidney, and he nearly bled to death before he reached the emergency room. Surgeons had stopped the bleeding but decided to leave the bullet lodged near the spine rather than risk the delicate surgery necessary for its removal.

On August 5, Priscilla was well enough to talk to investigators. Though she was still groggy and tubes were running out of her arms and chest, she told the story graphically, in that same slow-motion, highly detailed manner she would use many times in recalling the nightmare. Now investigators had a story to match the physical evidence. As they combed the mansion's 19,000 square feet, what they found was a perfect match. Every piece of the puzzle fit, just as the three witnesses described it. Crime scene investigators found fragments of the plastic bag at the spot where Priscilla said the man in black was standing when he shot her. More fragments were discovered near the door the gunman fired through to hit Farr, and still more in the basement utility room where Andrea was killed, on the sidewalk where Gavrel was shot, and near the breakfast room door, mixed there with the shattered glass. Everywhere the witnesses said shots were fired, investigators found plastic fragments. The plastic bag was discovered on the second floor near the master bedroom. The killer's final act before escaping had been to run upstairs. Why? The logical theory was that he was looking for Priscilla and understood her enough to realize that in moments of trauma she always retired to her bedroom.

All of the bullets were accounted for. One was in the basement under Andrea's body. It was theorized that the killer reloaded after killing Andrea. Priscilla was shot once and Farr four times—two bullets were removed from Farr's body, and three more slugs were discovered near the spot where the two shootings took place. One bullet was in Gavrel's spine. Gavrel said that the killer had reloaded before shooting out the glass (these were the shots Priscilla heard as she ran down the hill), and three slugs with traces of glass were recovered in the breakfast room. A total of ten, all in place. An autopsy done on Farr's body corroborated Priscilla's story of his final desperate gasps for breath—one bullet penetrated his larynx, causing him to suffocate on his own vomit. Investigators also discovered part of Farr's bear claw necklace at the foot of the stairway where Priscilla had described the struggle. The pieces fell into place so neatly the investigators didn't look for any other theory.

More than forty fingerprints were lifted from the scene, but the only ones that were identified belonged to the maid and to Det. Claude Davis, who supervised the crime scene investigation. The thing that puzzled investigators was that none of the prints belonged to Cullen Davis. In fact, none of the physical evidence directly connected Cullen Davis to the crimes. With three eyewitnesses, it didn't seem to matter.

If anything worried Tim Curry, it was the lack of a murder weapon. They knew it was a .38 Smith & Wesson, but they didn't have it and, as it developed, never would. Curry knew about the Colt .45 with the silencer found abandoned on the riverbank two months earlier. "That silencer is a first-class job," Curry said. "It's no easy job to build a silencer for a .45. It's got to screw inside. A silencer has only one purpose, to kill someone."

Priscilla had reported a burglar at the mansion about the same time that the .45 was discovered, but that didn't help Curry's case. Nor did the fact that the gun had been traced to Cullen's friend Roy Rimmer. Even before the weapon was traced, Rimmer told the sheriff that he'd heard someone found a gun similar to one stolen in a burglary of his home. Evans showed Rimmer the gun with the illegal silencer, but Rimmer said he didn't think it was the same gun. Digging through old reports, investigators discovered that Rimmer reported a burglary of his home in January 1972. Rimmer reported extensive losses, including seven other weapons, but he failed to report the mysterious .45. Rimmer explained that he apparently overlooked the .45 in filing his burglary losses. Later, investigators questioned an inmate in the state prison about the burglary. "He didn't deny the burglary of Rimmer's home," Sheriff Evans said, "but he denied taking the gun." Curry knew that Roy Rimmer was heavily in debt to Cullen Davis, but that didn't explain why Rimmer's gun was left on the bank of the river a few yards from Cullen Davis's property. Rimmer's gun would remain one more mystery in a crazy quilt of unresolved mysteries.

Cullen apparently didn't know it, but Curry's men had him under constant surveillance; the DA hoped that the defendant might lead them to the murder weapon, and Curry didn't entirely dismiss the thought that Cullen might run for it. But Cullen resumed his life as though nothing had happened. He went to the office every morning, usually had lunch at the Petroleum Club, shot a little pool, and went home early to Karen's house. A model citizen, in most respects. Now that the initial outcry was subsiding, time was in Cullen's favor. A majority of those in Arlington Heights couldn't bring themselves to believe he had done it. A majority of those at the Rangoon Racquet Club were already formulating the theory that Priscilla was trying to frame him. "If Cullen wanted those people killed, he would have hired a hit man," an oilman at the RCC pointed out. Bo Rankin, who had known the Davis family since childhood, added that Cullen wasn't *crazy*. "I believe any man's capable of anything," Rankin said. "But if I were he and wanted to kill my wife, I would have been in Mexico City when it happened." "Or at least headed that way a few minutes later," another regular observed. It was all too improbable. *Impossible*.

Bev Bass had gone into seclusion. For several days after the killings, her parents kept her at home, and a few weeks later they drove her to Lubbock and enrolled her at Texas Tech. After that, about the only people who ever saw Bass were her parents and the Gavrels. She became more than Bubba's girlfriend; she became his nurse and his strength.

As the investigation continued through the second week of August, Tim Curry began to reconsider Marvin Collins's arguments for capital murder. Collins was a sturdy advocate; not a day went by when Collins didn't collar Curry or one of the assistant DAs with some new case history he'd dug up in support of his theory. The theory was this— Cullen Davis entered a habitation with the intent to commit another felony, *murder*. There was no dispute that it was his own house. But he was under civil injunction not to enter that property. The question was this: *was he in fact the owner?* The law broke the question into three parts. An owner is, number one, the person who has title to the property; or number two, the person who has possession of the property, whether lawfully or otherwise; or number three, the person who has greater right to possession of the property. Number three was the key to this case, Collins believed. Gradually, Curry and Tolly Wilson came to agree. Joe Shannon was the last holdout. Shannon recalled: "My thinking was, it just ain't right. The legal aspects ain't good."

By the third week of August, Collins had finally convinced Shannon that the theory was legally sound, but Shannon was still reluctant to reindict Cullen Davis on charges of capital murder. As Curry listened to Shannon's objections, it occurred to him that there was yet another, overriding argument in favor of *Collins's* position—by charging Davis with a capital crime they could probably hold him without bond. As long as Cullen Davis was in jail, Curry could be sure that the defense would cause no great delay in the trial. A fast resolution would be to everyone's advantage. By now Phil Burleson and one of his associates, Mike Gibson, had taken charge of Cullen Davis's defense. They had hired an ex-FBI agent to head up their own investigation and gave every indication of spending whatever amount they thought necessary to free their man. Curry heard rumors that Davis was considering hiring famed Houston trial attorney Richard "Racehorse" Haynes. Even if the rumor was false, it was apparent to Curry that Cullen's men intended to play hardball.

Still another assistant DA, Jim Bennett, had come around in support of Collins's theory, and now Curry and his staff stood four against Shannon's one in favor of capital murder. What happened next made the vote academic. On the morning of August 20, one of Curry's investigators reported by radio that Cullen was in his Cadillac headed for Meacham Field where his Learjet was serviced and ready for takeoff.

"Maybe he's flying to Brazil for the sun," Tolly Wilson speculated.

"Not on my ulcers he ain't!" Curry said. The DA had already received an attachment from the court ordering Davis to appear before the grand jury, and Curry instructed his men to use the attachment and haul the defendant downtown. By 10:00 A.M. Davis was charged with capital murder and was back in jail, where he would remain for the next year.

On August 27, without comment, Judge Tom Cave denied bond. Trial lawyers all over Texas were shocked when they heard that Judge Tom Cave had ordered Davis held without bond. One lawyer who wasn't especially surprised when the state appeals court rejected Cullen's efforts to get out on bail was Phil Burleson, the head of Cullen's swelling team of highly paid defense lawyers. Burleson wasn't surprised, but he wasn't worried either. One of the best criminal lawyers in Texas, he knew from experience that cases such as this weren't won or lost in these early skirmishes. The word generally used to describe Phil Burleson was *ruthless*. Burleson called himself tenacious, but whatever the word he didn't deny it. Burleson knew that hard work and imagination could win the Cullen Davis case. "Anytime you have what purports to be eyeball witnesses, you have problems . . . until you *interview* those witnesses, put them to the test," Burleson said.

Burleson, therefore, was less concerned with the three eyewitnesses than with the physical evidence, or lack of it. He was sure that the state had more physical evidence than it had shown in the bond hearing, but he couldn't find out what it was. Fingerprints? Bloody clothes? Traces of hair? Footprints? A gun? Another witness who saw the defendant near the mansion that night?

"There had been nothing in the papers, no speculation at all," Burleson said. "I thought that was strange. While Cullen was out on bond, the DA asked us for a copy of his fingerprints, to which they were entitled. We took Cullen down to the police station to be printed, and while we were there, this crime scene officer Jim Slaughter must have thought we were detectives. He blurted out, 'Why do you want all these prints? You got three eyewitnesses.' At that point the real detectives were getting us out of the room fast, and I was beginning to think the prosecution didn't have all that much in the way of physical evidence. They were counting on the eyewitnesses to carry them through."

The eyewitnesses did appear to be a formidable factor, certainly to the public. There had never been a case in Fort Worth exposed to so much publicity. In the glare of daily media accounts, Cullen seemed as good as convicted. Burleson and Mike Gibson anticipated that at some point the publicity would begin to work in their favor—a witness might come forward, for example, to confirm Cullen's alibi—but so far the only news had been bad. The two Dallas lawyers decided their only course was to ride it out.

Tom Cave originally set the trial date for October 11, but because of a delay in the bond appeal the trial was soon reset for February 21. Meanwhile, Domestic Relations Court Judge Joe Eidson scheduled final hearings in the divorce case for January 17, though no one except Eidson seriously believed that the divorce would be finalized while the murder case was still pending.

Priscilla was back in the mansion, recovering from her gunshot wound and other medical problems and trying to deal with the complications of her new status as principal witness in Fort Worth's most famous murder case. Mostly, she sat on the double queen-size bed with the silver fox spread and the stuffed animals and yellow-haired rag doll with the pink dress, using the bank of telephone lines to talk to her friends Judy McCrory, Carmen Thomas, and Lynda Arnold. Judy had filed for divorce from David McCrory and frequently spent evenings and weekends at the mansion. Sometimes Priscilla played Scrabble or backgammon with Rich Sauer, the new man in her life. Sauer had played basketball with Farr at TCU. There was always an armed guard downstairs, and the panel of lights on the bedroom wall told Priscilla that all locks were secure. Nevertheless, she kept a loaded .32 under her pillow. The master bedroom was just like before, except now there were dozens of laminated photographs of Stan Farr, the gentle giant, and of Andrea, Dee, and Jackie Wilborn, and of course of Priscilla herself. Dainty little signs saying things like "Love is being able to let go" were mounted among the photographs.

Priscilla seldom left the bedroom. She had been advised by her divorce attorneys to "stay off the street," and when she did go out, usually late at night and only with her bodyguard and close friends, Priscilla wore the silver-plated .32 strapped to a custom-made holster on her right boot. For the most part, life outside her bedroom had been reduced to a single ritual: every evening as the sun set, Priscilla ventured downstairs and activated the controls that automatically slammed shut the mansion's many drapes, as though shielding out the night was her final measure of security. Friends marveled at her tenacity; how could she stay there in that museumlike chill, surrounded by art treasures and pursued by ghosts of that incredible night? They didn't understand; she had no choice. It was like a fairy tale, only in reverse. Rich little poor girl, a prisoner in her own castle. After all that had happened, the price she had paid, Priscilla was not about to walk out now. The memories sustained Priscilla and strengthened her resolve. When she went downstairs to close the drapes, she passed the door with the pink heart and the words ANDREA'S ROOM. For weeks after Andrea's murder, Priscilla would open the hotel-size refrigerator and discover small concoctions, cookies, or half-baked cakes that Andrea had stored for a time that wouldn't come.

Dee came home from Texas Tech and personally supervised Thanksgiving dinner. Jackie Wilborn came to the mansion for the holiday. In some ways, Jackie had taken it harder than Dee. Jackie was only fifteen and had never lived under Cullen Davis's roof; it was difficult for Jackie to understand why Priscilla had not stayed with his father. All this wouldn't have happened. It was a valid question, one Priscilla couldn't touch. Priscilla's seventy-one-year-old mother came for Thanksgiving, and so did a niece and other relatives. What was there to talk about? With the help of a half-dozen TV sets and a blitzkrieg of football, Priscilla survived the family gathering. Her mother was already talking about *Christmas* for god's sake. Priscilla wanted to ask her: what makes you think there is even going to be Christmas?

Priscilla laughed when she heard that they were dropping her name (but not Cullen's) from the *Fort Worth Social Directory*. She didn't give a damn about that. A group of "prominent citizens," including publishing heir Amon Carter, Jr., and power broker Babe Fuqua and some leading bankers, had petitioned to have Cullen released on bond. This was no mere act of charity or friendship; it was good business. They had a sizable stake in the welfare of the man who owed many millions of dollars and still controlled, even from his jail cell, one of the city's great conglomerates. For the first time in memory the subject of prisoners' rights had a majority of advocates at Colonial.

CHAPTER 6

In his private cell downtown, where he conducted daily business meetings and had at his disposal a color TV and a bank of telephones, Cullen had reached a major decision. He had decided to add to his team of attorneys Richard "Racehorse" Haynes, the legendary Houston lawyer who had successfully defended plastic surgeon John Hill on charges that he had murdered his Houston socialite wife by poisoning her with French pastry doctored with cultures of human pus and excrement. Cullen had read about Racehorse Haynes in *Blood and Money*, the best-seller written by his AHHS classmate Tommy Thompson.

Even before he was asked to join the defense, Racehorse Haynes was intrigued by the Cullen Davis case. Haynes's own life-style befit his flamboyant reputation—a lavish home in Houston's exclusive River Oaks section, a forty-foot yacht, a Cessna, a $40,000 Porsche Turbo Carrera, a replica of the classic Excalibur motorcar, and enough motorcycles to kill himself eight times over. There wasn't anything in Racehorse Haynes's life that wasn't a challenge, or the fruits of a challenge. He was a skydiver and a motorcycle racer and a champion of the hopeless cause. When he'd had a drop too much Scotch, he'd been known to race his motorcycle through motel lobbies. He once talked his way out of a drunk driving ticket by performing a back flip off the bumper of his Porsche. A man whose ego seemed to be on a permanent collision course with his courage, Haynes was absolutely convinced that with enough time and money he could win any lawsuit anywhere. If Nixon had hired him, Haynes once remarked, the man would still be in office. He could probably get Hitler off on a reduced charge of malicious mischief.

It was late September when Haynes first met Cullen Davis. Tom Cave's ruling denying bail was being appealed, and Davis had been locked up about four weeks. The bond appeal was taking up a lot of time, and they had only two months to prepare for pretrial hearings.

While Haynes, Burleson, and Mike Gibson worked on the legal aspects of the defense, young Steve Sumner worked the streets, gathering fragments of information, pursuing tips and leads, and interviewing potential witnesses. With a staff of five full-time investigators and anywhere from fifteen to twenty part-time investigators, Sumner quietly descended into the netherworld of the Fort Worth drug culture.

From the beginning Sumner demonstrated an aptitude for hard work and practical logic. He quickly proved good at gathering evidence and screening witnesses, but what impressed Cullen Davis was Sumner's ability to *connect* the bits and pieces. The bits and pieces continued to collect, but by early December, less than two weeks before the beginning of pretrial, the defense didn't have a workable scenario. Sumner had an ambulance driver willing to testify that Bubba Gavrel didn't know who shot him, yet was sufficiently lucid to dispose of a marijuana stash before being taken to the hospital. And they knew by now about Bev Bass's abortion, including the fact that Priscilla paid for it and that the two women conspired to use Bass's sister's name on the clinic records. But only Cullen, with his engineer's mind, could connect these facts with the murders.

A few days before the start of pretrial hearings, Sumner asked Cullen if the name William Tasker Rufner rang a bell.

Cullen said it didn't.

"How about Larry Myers? Or Sandy Guthrie?"

"They don't ring a bell," Cullen said. "What does it mean?"

Sumner said he didn't know. At that point they were just names.

By the time jury selection began on February 20, Cullen Davis had been in jail six months. Though he had a private cell, Cullen hadn't exactly been alone. Jailhouse records revealed that during the months of November, December, and January, Davis received 399 visits to his cell. Sheriff Lon Evans denied that Karen Master had been allowed to visit her boyfriend, but he defended frequent visits by Davis's business associates. "You're talking about a man who owns eighty-three companies," the sheriff said, "not some convict up there. People come in every day with papers for him to sign and blueprints to look at. He's a busy man."

After eight weeks of jury selection, only eight jurors had been seated. Cave had sequestered the jury, which meant that as soon as a juror was selected, that juror became a prisoner of Tarrant County—sequestered jurors had even less freedom than the defendant, who was at least allowed to confer with associates and talk freely on the telephone. Sequestered juries are a problem under any conditions, but in a case where it might take four months just to fill the jury box, the situation was fraught with danger. On April 13, six weeks to the day after the first juror was seated, the whole thing blew apart. It was revealed that the fuse had been burning since March 7, when the second juror chosen, Elizabeth Panke, requested permission to visit her terminally ill father in Elmhurst, Illinois. Cave granted the request. Though Mrs. Panke was accompanied by a court bailiff, she made several unauthorized telephone calls outside the bailiff's presence. Cave received information that in at least one call she discussed the Cullen Davis case. Mrs. Panke denied this, but it placed Cave in a tenuous position. Since none of the other seven jurors knew about Mrs. Panke's conversation, many attorneys felt that Cave could merely dismiss Mrs. Panke and continue the process of jury selection. But Cave wasn't sure. He announced from the bench that he wanted to study the case law overnight.

The next morning Cave brought with him a copy of the Texas criminal code. To the hushed crowd in the courtroom the judge read a passage that declared a new trial must be granted in felony cases "where a juror had conversed with any person in regard to the case."

Solemn-faced and trembling, Cave said, "It therefore becomes the clear duty of the court to declare a mistrial of this case at this time."

At this stage, Tom Cave wasn't waiting for someone to file a motion for change of venue. Cave could do it himself. He had concluded that there was no way the trial could continue in Tarrant County. He was already looking for another city in Texas, preferably one far from his doorstep. Cave found that city. It was Amarillo, in the Texas Panhandle, some 350 miles northwest of Fort Worth. The new trial date was set for June 27, 1977.

CHAPTER 7

Amarillo was a randy, bull-headed, good-humored cowtown, the kind of town that Fort Worth used to be, back before the time of Cullen Davis and his generation. Fort Worth called itself "the place where the West begins." Amarillo *was* the West, if not the heart, then surely the spirit.

Amarillo was isolated, self-contained, and conditioned to independent thinking. Buck Ramsey, a local poet and philosopher who had been a working cowboy until he was crippled a few years ago, described Amarillo as "a place where they send their daughters east to be educated and keep their sons at home to learn how to be bastards like their daddies."

Amarillo was the perfect place to try Cullen Davis.

Tim Curry wasn't just trying to boost morale when he extolled the qualities of Amarillo and told his staff, "This is the best place in the country we could try this lawsuit." People here weren't likely to be intimidated by Cullen Davis's wealth, least of all Judge George Dowlen, a longtime prosecutor appointed to the bench less than two years before.

While the prosecution spoke in quiet, confident terms of victory, the defense said hardly a word. They were about to make up for lost time, however. Racehorse Haynes had already sent out some local feelers and was in the process of assembling a staff of behind-the-scenes specialists the likes of which Amarillo or few other places had ever seen. Cullen Davis had spent almost a year behind bars, but the long delay was a kind of blessing. "We thought we were ready for trial before," said Steve Sumner, the lawyer in charge of investigation for the defense, "but we've received an incredible amount of new information in the last few weeks."

By August 2, the anniversary of the slaughter at 4200 Mockingbird, most of the panelists had been selected, from a group of about 150 prospective jurors.

The jury consisted of nine men and three women, ages ranging from twenty-six to sixty-four. Three were Catholic, three Baptist, three Methodist, one Church of Christ, one unaffiliated Protestant, and one with no religious affiliation. Most of them were working people, men and women who were used to listening and taking orders. "Look at them," a Potter County attorney said. "They're people who've been stomped every way but flat, but they're good people and they'll be fair." Another lawyer observed: "You'll notice that a lot of them are overweight. Overweight people are docile and submissive. They'll hate Priscilla because of her flashy dress and her living with Stan Farr. People in Amarillo don't appreciate that sort of behavior." If they dislike Priscilla, would it follow that they would appreciate Cullen? "Don't matter," the attorney said. "Racehorse won't let it get to that."

An Amarillo attorney, Dee Miller, joined the team for the purpose of helping remind the jurors who were the good guys and who were the bad. Miller was about as good as you could get in Amarillo. All twelve jurors knew him either personally or by reputation. Dee and his twin brother, Oth Miller, headed one of Amarillo's most prestigious law firms, and an older brother, G. William Miller, was known to everyone in the Panhandle as the chairman of the Federal Reserve Board. Not a week went by that the Amarillo media didn't use some sort of national story quoting G. William Miller on the state of the economy. Dee Miller was a director of the North State Bank, past president of the Amarillo Country Club, and a cog in the local Democratic party. One of his law partners explained: "Dee has a large following in town. If there's anyone in Amarillo he doesn't know personally, he knows someone who does. Dee's greatest talent is knowing how to make friends and keep them." Miller was regarded as an adequate criminal attorney, but his legal reputation was no factor in his selection to the Cullen Davis defense team. He questioned no witnesses, offered no objections, argued no pleadings; his function for the next five months was to be seen sitting at the defense table close to Cullen Davis. For this Dee Miller collected the largest fee of his career.

There was one important order of business to be completed before testimony could begin. Dowlen would have to rule on several hundred motions filed by both sides.

The state knew that Cullen's attorneys had subpoenaed a number of witnesses who were prepared to describe episodes of drugs, sex, and violence at the mansion and asked that the court require defense attorneys to demonstrate relevancy before blurting it out to the jury. "We want to make sure a whole bunch of skunks aren't thrown into the jury box," Assistant District Attorney Joe Shannon told Dowlen. The judge granted this motion and instructed the defense to make no references to drug use, sexual hijinks, or "specific acts of misconduct" other than felony convictions without first taking it up with the court outside the presence of the jury. Dowlen stopped short of saying such testimony would be inadmissible. He reserved the right to rule on each issue as it came up. He also granted a prosecution motion prohibiting the characterization of Priscilla's friends as "dope fiends, pillheads, traffickers in narcotics, prostitutes," and various other derogatory expressions, unless supported by evidence. "If they don't admit it, we won't call them that," Haynes smiled to the judge. "We'll let somebody else call them that. We do not intend to engage in name calling, but there are prosecution witnesses who have referred to other prosecution witnesses in such terms." The state also asked Dowlen to forbid references to Priscilla's relationship with W. T. Rufner and restrict questions about her conduct at social events. Dowlen hedged on these motions, however. He would have to wait and view them in context.

The defense renewed its request that Cullen Davis be released on bond. Although a dozen district, state, and federal judges had already denied bond, Dowlen promised to hear new evidence and review the motion, even though Judge Tom Cave retained the final voice in all bond matters.

Dowlen unexpectedly granted the defense's motion for bond. Defense attorneys posted certified checks totaling $1,650,000 in Fort Worth and Amarillo, and Cullen Davis was temporarily a free man. As TV cameramen and reporters clogged the parking lot outside the Potter County Courthouse, Cullen walked to his chauffeured Cadillac, carrying a portable color TV set and wearing a smile wider than a Panhandle sunset. Karen Master walked beside him, smiling and waving to the cameras. Cullen's two sons by his first marriage were en route from Dallas for an emotional reunion. Cullen told reporters that all he wanted to do was "talk to my kids, go eat a seventy-two-ounce steak, visit my employees in Potter County, and sleep in a good bed." By the time testimony began the following Monday, Judge Cave would have revoked the bond and ordered Davis returned to jail. For the moment, however, the man who had everything just wanted to savor freedom and exult in victory. He had been a long time without either.

On Sunday, August 21, as Cullen secluded himself in the Hilton Inn with his family, friends, and attorneys, Priscilla arrived at Amarillo International Airport. The state's star witness was technically on leave from Fort Worth's St. Joseph's Hospital and carried with her a letter from doctors stating that she would probably have to go to Pittsburgh in a few weeks for major surgery to repair nerve damage incurred in the shooting. Priscilla looked pale but determined. She had waited more than a year to tell her story to the jury, and now her time had come.

A few minutes later she too checked into the Hilton Inn. For the first time since their separation in the summer of 1974, Cullen and Priscilla spent the night under the same roof.

CHAPTER 8

Long before George Dowlen called the court to session on Monday afternoon, all fifty-two seats were taken and people jammed the hallway clear back to the stairs.

"What's she wearing?" asked a shapeless and badly used Panhandle housewife with her cheeks heavily rouged and her hair tinted raven black. The woman had driven more than fifty miles that morning, not realizing that dozens of other housewives would likewise be eaten up with curiosity. These were soap opera addicts, and they did not miss the chance to see the real thing. They filled the courtroom and spilled into the corridors—from which, ironically, they watched the proceedings through a glass panel about the size of a small TV screen.

"Look at her!" another housewife said.

"I can't see. What's she wearing?"

"I can see. I can tell she's guilty just by looking."

Priscilla's guilt or innocence wasn't an issue in the case, of course, but that didn't faze the housewives, the majority of whom were already convinced that the Priscilla Davises of their experience were responsible for the evils of mankind. This seemed strange because at this point they knew nothing at all about Priscilla except the little they'd read and heard two months earlier when she appeared at a pretrial hearing. They didn't remember what she'd testified, but they recalled vividly what she wore—an expensive outfit with frills of virginal white lace and a tiny gold cross dangling between her silicone breasts. The women who swarmed the courtroom instinctively concluded that Priscilla was a woman without shame. They were incensed by the story of an Amarillo newspaper reporter who accidentally encountered Priscilla carrying a Bible and walking down the hallway of the Hilton Inn. "I think that image of Priscilla with the Bible and gold cross hurt the state more than any single thing," Hugh Russell said later, months after the trial ended. "There are a lot of sincerely religious people in Amarillo, and they were turned off by that. A lot of [prospective jurors] mentioned it in voir dire. They saw her as a Bible-toting phony."

What wasn't reported by the Amarillo newsman was that Priscilla was *also* carrying a suitcase—she was caught in the act of changing rooms. Nor was it mentioned that the gold cross was the same one that had been found in her purse just after the shooting of August 2, 1976. None of the cameras and prying eyes could see the agonizing pain that Priscilla continued to endure even as the predators hacked at her: doctors had implanted a catheter in her back to drip medication to raw nerve endings shattered by the passage of the bullet.

The gaggle of spectators had to wait for Priscilla's entrance on Monday, however, because the state called Judge Joe Eidson as its first witness. Eidson's testimony was intended to establish the motive for everything that happened. The state quickly developed the point that on the day of the murders Eidson had given Cullen Davis some bad news, then turned the witness over to Racehorse Haynes for cross-examination.

Haynes walked briskly to the witness stand and read the divorce judge a list of ten names. Eidson said he didn't recognize any of them. Racehorse smiled and said that was a shame because it was a list of ten men and women, many of them known felons, who were living at 4200 Mockingbird while Cullen and Priscilla were in the act of divorce. For the present, however, the name Racehorse wanted to pursue was that of one Stanford Farr. Eidson didn't seem able to place the name, so Haynes cleared it up for him: "The man was living there! She was buying him things such as boots and cars and paying his business expenses. Are these circumstances for which it is necessary to increase alimony?"

Eidson replied that he didn't know about Stan Farr, but if he had: "I might have granted the increase, I might have left it as it was, or I might have terminated it."

"You might have terminated it because there was no statutory authority to support continued alimony for a woman supporting another man?" Haynes asked, holding his hand to his ear as though he anticipated a very soft answer.

"That could have been the grounds," Eidson admitted.

On redirect questioning, Joe Shannon fired back, asking Eidson if he had been told that Davis was living with Karen Master.

Shannon: Do you recall any confession [from Davis] that he was using any funds from community property to support Karen Master?

Eidson: No.

Q: Do you recall any confession or representation that he was using any funds from community property to support the children of Karen Master?

A: No.

Eidson did seem to recall that Davis was one of two principal owners in Kendavis Industries International, Inc., the eighty-three-corporate business empire.

Q: Do you recall what the profits of Kendavis Industries were after taxes in 1975?

A: I believe $57 million.

"The number $57 million is one you can recall," Haynes observed.

"Well, I think it's rather impressive," Eidson shot back.

Shannon asked Eidson about the restraining order barring Cullen Davis from 4200 Mockingbird, the one necessary to their contention that Davis was a burglar as soon as he entered the mansion intending to kill his wife.

Shannon: On August 2 and August 3, 1976, did Priscilla Davis have a greater right to possession of the residence at 4200 Mockingbird than the defendant, Thomas Cullen Davis?

Phil Burleson jumped up to object, but Dowlen overruled.

Eidson: Yes.

Eidson and Priscilla passed in the hallway as she prepared to take the witness stand, but the judge apparently didn't notice her. He must have been the only one in the courthouse who didn't. The corridor sounded like a chicken yard at feeding time as Priscilla moved through, smiling and nodding.

Joe Shannon had cautioned Priscilla several times about her appearance in court. He had told her, "Wear something like you'd wear to church." Shannon didn't want the state's key witness to appear in pigtails and pinafore, but neither did he want her in the plunging necklines that had become her trademark. Taking Shannon at his word, Priscilla spent $25,000 on a new wardrobe. The outfits that she selected had high necklines, low hems, and an abundance of lace and ribbons. Shannon looked at the new wardrobe and approved. "It wasn't what I'd want my wife to wear," he said, "but I thought it was in good taste." What did surprise Shannon was that in her eleven days on the witness stand, Priscilla never wore the same thing twice.

Racehorse Haynes had anticipated that the state would use Joe Shannon to lead Priscilla through direct examination. She was certain to supply the most dramatic testimony, and of all the prosecutors on Tim Curry's staff Shannon had the best flair for drama. Instead, Tim Curry elected to question Priscilla himself. Racehorse watched with new interest as Curry took her around the course in his easy, low-key, what-next style.

Right away he got her to acknowledge that she and the late Stan Farr had been lovers. In fact, Farr was living with her at the mansion while she was in the process of divorcing Cullen Davis. There was no use sparring about these points because Racehorse Haynes had already developed them when he cross-examined Eidson.

Priscilla began to shake when Curry asked her about her three marriages and children. Before the trial Joe Shannon had repeatedly warned her: "Just tell the truth." That's what Priscilla was trying to do, but she had anticipated the next question would be about Andrea, a name that often brought tears to her eyes.

Q: Do you have any other children [besides Dee and Jackie Wilborn]?
A: Yes, sir.
Q: And what was that child's name?
A: Andrea Lee Wilborn.
Q: How old was she?
A: She was twelve.

Curry then led Priscilla through the nightmare of August 2-3. How Andrea was left home alone for the evening while she and Stan went out to dinner to celebrate birthdays and anniversaries of close friends. How Priscilla had locked the back door manually and activated the electronic security system. When they returned about midnight, the door was still locked but she could see by the panel of lights inside that the security system was no longer activated. With Curry leading her gently, Priscilla described finding the bloody handprint, calling out to Farr, and her astonishment when Cullen stepped out of the laundry room, said "Hi," and shot her between the breasts. She told about Cullen's struggle with Farr, and how Cullen stood directly over her lover to squeeze off the last two shots. About trying to escape, about Cullen coming after her and how she pleaded for her life, about Bev Bass and Bubba Gavrel driving up and how she took that opportunity to run—the whole story exactly as she had told it many times before. Curry was pleased; no matter how many times Priscilla told the story, she told it the same way, down to the hand gestures and tears as she recalled a particularly painful moment. She was a damn good witness, Curry thought.

Racehorse Haynes thought Priscilla was a little too good and objected repeatedly that the witness was expanding her answers outside the scope of the questions. During his own questioning Haynes bore in, marveling that Priscilla couldn't seem to recall how many times she had "rehearsed" her testimony with lawyers for the state, and repeatedly referring to "your version" of the murders. Priscilla interrupted him at one point and blurted out: "You keep saying my version. I want to make it clear what I said is what happened."

At the end of the day Cullen lingered in the courtroom and talked with reporters, as he would many times in the days that followed. Priscilla's tears were as phony as the rest of her story, he said, then asked, "You've never seen a person who could turn tears on and off like a water faucet, have you?"

By midmorning of the third day Curry had completed his direct examination and turned the witness over to Haynes. Racehorse intended to waste no time with amenities. Whatever the jury or the crowd in the courtroom may have thought of Priscilla before, she had been impressive under direct examination. Haynes's whole case was based upon discrediting her as a person and as a witness. In the week that followed he did that and more.

Introducing into evidence photographs of three drinking glasses found at the crime scene, the lawyer spoke of his list of "phantoms" and implied that three glasses proved that Andrea had not been alone at the mansion between 9:00 P.M. and midnight. He questioned Priscilla about the security system and about a burglary that had taken place at the mansion in the months just prior to the killings. He followed with a series of questions designed to show that a number of people might have had keys to the mansion during the months after Davis moved out.

Priscilla first claimed that the only people who had keys to the main entrance were herself, Farr, Dee Davis, and two maids. Later, she admitted that a number of live-in guests might have had keys from time to time, but this was before she had the locks changed. This was the opening Racehorse was probing for, and now Priscilla was forced to acknowledge his mysterious list of "phantoms." They included W. T. Rufner, country and western singer Delbert McClinton and his wife Donna, Jan Scurlock, Sandy Guthrie Myers and her husband, Larry Michael Myers, a convicted felon. Priscilla admitted that each had lived in the mansion for periods ranging from several weeks to several months. In the days that followed, this list of phantoms increased, but for now Haynes was content to use only four names to challenge her identification of Cullen Davis as the killer.

Q: Was it [the killer] Horace Copeland?
A: No, it was Cullen Davis.
Q: Was it Robert Downing?
A: Who? . . . No, sir, it was not.
Q: Do you know a Robert Downing?
A: No.
Q: Was it David Hack?
A: No, sir.
Q: Do you know a David Hack?
A: Yes, sir.
Q: When was the last time you saw David Hack before August 2, 1976?
A: I really couldn't tell you.

The jury had heard the name Rufner before, but this was the first mention of David Hack or Robert Downing. As the case developed, their names remained obscure, but Horace Copeland, who had been shot to death in a Fort Worth apartment only a few weeks before, emerged later as a central figure. The defense planned to contend that Copeland and Stan Farr had been partners in a drug deal that went sour shortly before the killings and that Copeland had threatened to kill Farr. But for the moment the phantom that Haynes wanted to implant in the minds of the jurors was the rogue motorcycle racer, W. T. Rufner. The jury had already heard Rufner's name but didn't yet know that Rufner had moved in shortly after Cullen moved out and at roughly the same time of his own drug bust. Now it was time for the jury to take a look at Rufner, and Racehorse had a dramatic visual aid—a photograph he wanted to introduce as evidence.

He had it printed poster-size on paper so thin it was nearly transparent. Casually, Haynes approached the bench. As he unfurled the photograph for the judge's inspection and displayed it so that the flourescent light in the courtroom ceiling clearly illuminated it for those in the jury box, all four prosecutors jumped to their feet. "You can see right through it!" Tim Curry protested. "He [Haynes] did it deliberately!" Racehorse protested his innocence, but you could see the smirk on his face. In previous testimony outside the jury's presence Priscilla testified that she didn't recognize the picture, and on this basis Judge Dowlen refused to admit it into evidence. But the damage was done. Everyone in the jury box, in fact everyone on that side of the courtroom, could see that the color blowup was a picture of W. T. Rufner and Priscilla. Priscilla wore a low-cut halter top and hip-hugger slacks, and T-man was buck naked except for a red-and-white candy-striped Christmas stocking covering his genitals. They posed with arms around one another. Dowlen ordered that a piece of cardboard be taped to the back of the photograph before permitting Haynes to continue grilling Priscilla.

Priscilla repeated that she'd never seen the picture before and in fact believed it to be a trick manufactured to embarrass her. Haynes challenged this and asked, "Have you ever seen W. T. Rufner in a social atmosphere when he was running around without his clothes on?"

"I don't recall that I have," Priscilla said.

"You have never seen W. T. Rufner naked as a jaybird with his you-know-what in a sock? You do recognize the man in the photograph as W. T. Rufner?"

"Well," Priscilla said, studying it again, "I recognize the face. I don't recognize the sock."

Haynes turned to the bench and told Dowlen, "I have a difficult time believing anyone could see W. T. Rufner in that attire and not remember it."

"So do I," Priscilla shot back. "That's how I feel about it exactly." The jury snickered.

Later, the defense tried to introduce two other sexually explicit photographs. The pictures were blurred and the subjects had their backs to the camera, but it appeared to be a man and a woman, both naked, cavorting about in the shallow water of a lake. Haynes tried to connect the photographs with a trip that Priscilla, Rufner, and some others took to the Willie Nelson Fourth of July Picnic in 1974, a few weeks before Priscilla and Cullen separated. Again, Dowlen refused to allow the photographs into evidence, but this did not prevent Haynes from pursuing his line of questions designed to show that Priscilla was messing around with Rufner even before the separation.

"It is true, is it not, that you knew W. T. Rufner before you separated from Thomas Cullen Davis?" Haynes asked. Priscilla said it was true.

As Joe Shannon stood to object, he again had that creepy feeling that Priscilla, the strength of their case, the one eyewitness who could connect the bizarre events of August 2-3, could in fact be their weak point. Priscilla had assured the prosecution that her relationship with W. T. Rufner was purely platonic until well after the separation, but now Shannon wasn't so sure. The defense was continuing to harp on the July 4 Winnebago trip to the Willie Nelson Picnic in College Station. If Priscilla had really been just a mother hen chaperoning her daughter Dee and the other teenagers, then how could she explain those naked people cavorting in the photographs? The jury had not yet been allowed to view the pictures, but Shannon knew that Racehorse Haynes had not given up trying. Sooner or later the defense was bound to find a witness who would admit being there and verify the pictures into evidence. Sooner or later the defense was bound to question her about the trip with W. T. Rufner to visit the McCrorys in Boston. Sooner or later they would trip her on that one too. He had repeatedly told Priscilla to tell the truth. "If you've done something bad in your life," he had instructed her, "just pony up to it like a little soldier. Just say, well damn it, I guess I did. People will forgive you for making a mistake, but they won't forgive you for lying." Shannon was less concerned about what the jury might be thinking than he was about what Priscilla's testimony might force from the court. A witness who volunteers false information automatically opens the door for what lawyers call *collateral impeachment*. The defense could attack or impeach a witness on matters relevant to the case, but not on collateral or secondary issues. Unless, of course, the witness lied about some of those irrelevant issues. Priscilla believed that her private life was in no way related to the issue in this case—the murder of Andrea Wilborn—and the prosecution fully agreed. So did Judge Dowlen, up to this point. But the judge had already allowed the defense to stray into an area whose relevancy was suspect: if Priscilla insisted on lying or even leaving false impressions with the jury, the defense would be permitted to dredge up all the sordid details. Up to this point Priscilla had left the impression that she barely knew W. T. Rufner. Because of this, it was entirely possible that the court would allow the defense to demonstrate collaterally just how well she did know him.

It was Priscilla's fourth day on the witness stand when Haynes began to probe her drug habits. Outside the presence of the jury, Haynes announced to the court that Priscilla had used LSD, cocaine, heroin, and marijuana for the past several years and asked permission to question her about the drugs. Prosecutors objected strongly, but Dowlen ruled that the defense could pursue this line of questioning as long as the jury did not hear. Racehorse opened by asking about cocaine. Priscilla replied that she had never used it.

Q: You've never snorted it? Did you ever snort a white powder when you didn't know what it was?

A: I don't do things just because they seem to be fashionable.

Q: Have you ever in your life taken LSD?

A: No, sir.

Q: Have you ever in your life snorted heroin?

A: No.

Q: How about speed?

A: I have tried diet pills.

Q: Have you ever used marijuana?

A: I have tried it—when I was a teenager years ago.

Assistant DA Tolly Wilson objected as Haynes began to drift into other topics, declaring that the only purpose of these questions was to get the witness on record "so they can come back tomorrow with the daily copy [transcript] and find some small inconsistency." Haynes replied that it was his intention to provide "independent proof that the fidelity of this witness's answers are questionable."

When the jury had returned to the courtroom, Haynes began questioning Priscilla about her use of the prescription painkiller Percodan, the suggestion being that the drug might have impaired her ability to recall the details of August 2-3. Priscilla told the court that she first took Percodan in 1973 after breaking her ankle skiing, but added that she took the drug only occasionally until after the shooting. Before the shooting, she said, her prescription for Percodan was limited to twelve tablets. Later, as the pain from the bullet wound became unbearable, her personal physician, Dr. Thomas Simons, and the surgeon who operated on her the night of the shooting, Dr. Charles Crenshaw, wrote prescriptions for up to 200 tablets a week.

"Did you have any idea at all that the continued use of Percodan could be habituating?" Haynes asked the witness. Priscilla said she didn't.

Q: No physician ever told you that?

A: I've been told it's possible to become addicted to Excedrin. I've been told that if you overdo it, it can have bad side effects.

Q: Have you been told Percodan is addictive?

A: I've never been told I was addicted, nor am I.

Judge Dowlen called a recess at this point, and the prosecutors huddled with their witness in one of the back rooms. The defense had already subpoenaed prescription records from two Fort Worth pharmacies. Although Priscilla was claiming that she used only small amounts of the powerful painkiller in the months prior to the murders, the records showed that she refilled her prescription every month from September 1975 through July 1976. The prescriptions hadn't been for twelve at a time, as she had said under oath, but for fifty. Not fifty a month, but fifty a week. During the month of July, for example, records showed she got fifty tablets each on the sixth, twelfth, seventeenth, twenty-third, twenty-seventh, and twenty-eighth.

Tim Curry felt that the defense hadn't yet damaged his witness with the questions about the illicit drugs, though it was possible they might be able to impeach her collaterally later. But now Haynes was moving into a dangerous area. The subpoenaed pharmacy records would prove beyond a doubt that Priscilla had received enough Percodan to addict several people.

"Are you addicted to Percodan?" Curry asked in his soft, professional voice. "Just tell me the truth."

Priscilla hesitated, then answered, "I guess I am."

"Then don't lie about it," the district attorney told her.

When Haynes resumed his questioning after the recess, Priscilla was ready to pony up.

Q: And are you saying you were not addicted to the use of Percodan?

A: No, sir. I don't mean to mislead the jury.

Q: You are addicted to Percodan, aren't you?

A: Yes, sir, there's a possibility.

Q: Don't you know it to be a fact?

A: It's highly possible.

Q: How many Percodan were you taking a day?

A: Due to the pain from the gunshot, I was taking far more than 100 a week.

Q: Were you taking more than *200* a week?

A: That may be closer to it. I was having to take four every couple of hours.

Priscilla went on to explain that her doctors had become concerned about her addiction and had her admitted to the hospital in July, even as the jury selection was proceeding in Amarillo. "It got to the point where

I couldn't take the pain anymore," she said, looking at the jury now. "I went into the hospital for spasms in my back and had a nerve block."

The court recessed for the day.

CHAPTER 9

Friday, August 26, was the birthdate of Lyndon Johnson, and the court was recessed for the holiday. Nobody talked about LBJ that day, but the entire Panhandle crackled with gossip about the trial. A local TV reporter called it "the biggest thing to ever hit Amarillo." In every bar, restaurant, and department store the major topic was Cullen and Priscilla.

Outside the courtroom Priscilla couldn't stop talking about the trial. After two days of grueling cross-examination, she was more determined than ever to get "the truth as I know it" to anyone who would listen. During the Friday recess she told reporters: "I'm not saying I'm Miss Goodie Twoshoes, but their only defense is to destroy my credibility. It is obvious they don't have a case if the only thing they can do is destroy my credibility. To insinuate that I had some big drug orgies is absurd. They are dragging a bunch of dogs. It doesn't matter if I was the biggest hooker, doper, or what have you. It has absolutely nothing to do with what he did. . . . They are trying this like a smutty divorce . . . while in reality it is a murder. A twelve-year-old child was killed. They seem to forget that. I never will. They say the truth died with Andrea. It didn't."

Cullen was talking too. If Priscilla was the wanton hussy that the defense lawyers were claiming, reporters wondered why Cullen married her in the first place. Priscilla changed, Cullen told them. "I knew she was taking a lot of drugs, but only in retrospect did I realize how seriously they had affected her. During the past year of investigation I have discovered that Priscilla has caused my home to make Sodom and Gomorrah look like Petticoat Junction." Earlier in the summer Davis had appeared edgy, haggard, and depressed, but now that the trial was under way, he seemed calm, even jovial. "Many people have been wondering how I could be so well adjusted after so long in jail," he said at one point. "Possibly the answer can be found in the old saying, 'If rape is inevitable, relax and enjoy it.' "

While those with time on their hands indulged in gossip, the real in-fighting was taking place in the judge's chambers. One issue concerned an affidavit signed by a Joe L. Crow who claimed to have overheard a telephone conversation in which W. T. Rufner threatened to kill a girlfriend, Carmey Green, unless she agreed to supply him an alibi for the night of August 2, 1976. According to the affidavit, Rufner told Carmey Green, "I'll kill your ass," unless she swore in writing that he was with her on the night of the murders. The affidavit didn't say who Crow was or how he happened to overhear the conversation. Court papers filed by the prosecutors claimed Crow used an illegal wiretap. Also at issue was a defense affidavit signed by Sandy Guthrie Myers, this one to the effect that Rufner had once threatened the lives of both Priscilla and Stan Farr.

Dowlen ruled that testimony regarding alleged threats and violence was immaterial at this point of the trial, but once again he didn't rule out the possibility that it could become relevant later. On these grounds he allowed the defense to probe the stormy relationship between Priscilla and Rufner outside the jury's presence.

Although the prosecution objected repeatedly, Racehorse Haynes bombarded Priscilla with questions about Rufner's alleged penchant for violence.

Q: Do you recall an incident at 4200 Mockingbird when W. T. Rufner was choking you so hard that you thought you were going to die and the only reason he stopped was a cigarette was burning a hole in the bedspread?

A: W. T. was not physically violent with me ever.

Hardly allowing the witness time to catch her breath, Haynes asked her about other incidents—had Rufner once pulled a knife and sliced her dress from waist to hem, had he once cut off her bra and panties, had he once fought over her with Larry Myers? Priscilla denied each allegation. She did recall a time when T-man threw a potted plant at her as she was taking a bath, but she denied Haynes's contention that Rufner had also pulled a pistol. She verified the story about the time he had wrecked the transmission of her Lincoln Continental Mark IV outside the Old San Francisco Saloon and how when she returned home that night with ex-boxer Jerry Thomas, Rufner was waiting inside the mansion.

The following morning Dowlen permitted Haynes to question Priscilla in front of the jury about the incident outside the Old San Francisco Saloon.

Q: Was W. T. Rufner unhappy with you?

A: I guess you could say that.

Q: Was he unhappy about the fact you were dating Stan Farr?

A: I don't know that he was. I was also dating several others.

Q: How did he get into the house?

A: Andrea.

"*Andrea* let him in?" Haynes asked, as though he could hardly believe his ears.

"Yes, sir," Priscilla said evenly. "They were just talking." She went on to explain that she asked Rufner to leave, and when he hesitated, Jerry Thomas "was on him instantly . . . just pulverizing him. I had to break it up."

Q: After that time did Stan Farr tell you W. T. Rufner threatened to kill him?

A: No, sir.

Q: Did Stan Farr say he was going to Florida to kill the person who took money from the Rhinestone Cowboy?

A: No, sir.

It was at this point in the trial that members of the press became privy to the defense's master plan. Whether inadvertently or on purpose, defense lawyers conveniently left a memo on the table next to exhibits already admitted as evidence. It was no secret that reporters checked the contents of this table during recesses. According to the memo, it was the defense's plan to show (1) "Priscilla Davis knew something was about to happen that night"; (2) "Beverly Bass could not see who shot Gavrel"; (3) "The person who did the shooting was, in fact, after Stan Farr and did not intend to shoot Priscilla."

Confronted with the memo, Phil Burleson admitted to reporters that the memo was "substantially correct" and that the defense also planned to prove that there was a conspiracy between at least two people to put the blame on Cullen Davis. Burleson wasn't yet ready to name the two conspirators, but it was apparent that he meant Priscilla and Bev Bass. If the defense had intentionally arranged for reporters to see the memo, the question was *why*. It appeared to some that, even very early on, the defense intended to take the offense. At this point their only shots had been at Priscilla's credibility. The jury might believe that Priscilla was a liar and a tramp, but it was asking a great deal for jurors also to believe she would deliberately conceal the true identity of the person who killed both her lover and her twelve-year-old daughter. The defense's plan appeared to have two edges: it would supply a motive for the murder of Stan Farr (revenge) and Priscilla's cover-up (greed), *and* it would take the focus off the murder of Andrea Wilborn.

Still, leaking this strategy to the press and getting it to the jury weren't the same thing. Or were they? There had been a number of reports that the jurors were receiving unauthorized visitors. There were also rumors about unchaperoned visits from jurors' spouses. If the rumors about conjugal visits were true, God knows what had been said or conjectured. Maybe they had even played Cullen and Priscilla.

When Priscilla had taken the witness stand for the seventh straight day, Racehorse Haynes fired off a barrage of questions designed to establish that both she and Farr suspected trouble in advance of August 2. This was exactly the line of questioning the prosecution feared, and Shannon objected heatedly that it wasn't relevant. Dowlen overruled him and permitted Haynes to proceed.

Q: Do you recall seeing Sandy Myers in the office of Dr. [Thomas] Simons a few days before August 2, 1976?

A: I recall seeing her one time in the waiting room when I had an appointment.

Q: Was it just a few days prior to August 2?

A: I don't recall the date.

Q: When you did see Sandy Myers, did you tell her you wanted to talk to her?

A: No, sir.

Q: Did you tell her "Something heavy is coming down?"

A: No, sir. I did not say that.

Q: You don't remember what you said.

A: I remember what she said to me.

Q: You don't remember what you said?

A: I don't believe I told her anything.

Haynes wanted to pursue this conversation, but the state objected again and this time Dowlen cut Haynes off. Haynes then asked Priscilla about the .357 magnum that Farr carried in his black Thunderbird. Didn't this indicate he feared for his life? Priscilla replied that Farr carried the pistol only when he transported large sums of money for the Rhinestone Cowboy. Racehorse treated the jury to his mystic smile; he wanted them to remember this later when he developed the fact that the pistol was still in Farr's car on the night of the murder, several weeks after he was terminated from his job at the Rhinestone Cowboy.

"Were you present [at the Rhinestone Cowboy] when Stan Farr told Horace Copeland, 'Get the hell out of here'?" he asked quickly. Just as quickly, Priscilla replied: "Stan did not talk that way to anyone. Not in my presence." Earlier in this same cross-examination, Haynes was questioning Priscilla about her ambulance ride to the hospital when he asked abruptly, "You knew at the time, did you not, that Andrea Wilborn was dead?" Priscilla had answered, "No." Race thought now about returning to the question but decided that the implication might do more harm than good. He'd rather not attack her motherhood just yet. He had again insinuated to the jury that Farr had poor relationships with both Rufner and Copeland; that was enough for now.

"We have no more questions for this witness at this time," Haynes announced suddenly at the end of the day.

Priscilla's ordeal was nearly over. That night Tim Curry and his assistants considered their own strategy for the redirect examination. It was becoming obvious that Cullen Davis would never take the witness stand. The prosecution therefore decided that the jury needed to be educated about the man whose fate they would judge, his impulsive spending habits, his fondness for guns, his well-documented temper tantrums. Dowlen wasn't likely to admit testimony concerning isolated episodes of rage, but he would have to entertain questions along these lines if they pertained to the victim, Andrea Wilborn.

The state got an unexpected break the following morning. As Curry was asking questions about Andrea's relationship with Cullen, leading up to the revelation that the girl had been so frightened of Davis that she finally refused to visit the mansion, Priscilla blurted out how Cullen had once kept Andrea awake most of the night working on her math. Before the defense could object, Priscilla told the jury that Cullen had kicked at the girl and called her stupid. Dowlen ordered the attorneys to approach the bench, but even as they argued, Curry knew his side had won a point. Despite objections by the defense, Dowlen now allowed the state to question Priscilla about the occasion a few months before the separation when Cullen ordered her to telephone Andrea and instruct her to come to the mansion for the weekend.

Priscilla told the jury: "He [Cullen] told me to call Andrea and tell her to get over this weekend. And I told Cullen I wouldn't lie to her. He said, 'Damn it, I said call her and get her over here.'" Again the defense objected. Curry cautioned his witness, "Now don't tell me what Andrea said. That would be hearsay. Just tell me what you said to her."

Priscilla continued: "I said, 'Hi, Andrea. Why don't you come see us sometime. We sure do miss you. . . . Andrea, you know you need to work on your math. Cullen just wants you to work on your math. I wish you would come over.'"

That's when Davis jerked the telephone from her hand. Priscilla then revealed what Cullen had said to Andrea.

"He said, 'Goddamn it, Andrea, I want you over here this weekend.' Then he said, 'I don't give a goddamn what your plans are, I want you over here. . . . All right, goddamn it, you're not welcome over to this . . . house again until you're ready to do exactly what I tell you. And furthermore, you're to return everything I ever gave you. I don't give a goddamn what it is, you are to return it.' "

"After the phone call," Curry asked softly, "did Andrea Wilborn ever return to 4200 Mockingbird while the defendant was living there?"

"No, sir," Priscilla said, tears welling in her eyes, hands and lips trembling.

"How old was she at the time?"

"She was ten."

When Curry questioned her about the guns that Cullen kept around the mansion, Priscilla told about the frequent times she had watched Cullen shoot target practice at the family home at Eagle Mountain Lake. He was a very good shot, she recalled.

Q: How many handguns did he own?

A: I don't know. He had several.

Q: Where have you seen them?

A: Under his bed, in the closet, on a shelf in the old house, on a shelf in his dressing area in the new house, on the floorboard on the driver's side of his automobile, and in the trunk of his car.

Priscilla wept as Curry delivered his final volley of questions.

Q: Mrs. Davis, did W. T. Rufner shoot you and Stan Farr on August 2, 1976?

A: No, sir.

Q: Was it Horace Copeland who shot you and Stan that night?

A: No, sir.

Q: Tell the jury, Mrs. Davis, who it was that shot you and Stan that night.

A: It was Cullen Davis, the defendant.

Most of the defense's final assault came while both Priscilla and the jury were out of the courtroom. Haynes argued that he should be allowed to question Priscilla about her divorce litigation with Jack Wilborn, about how she had lured Wilborn into sexual encounters, then screamed rape. It was all a part of her long-established pattern as a "greedy schemer," Haynes told the court; she used sex to skin Jack Wilborn, now she was trying murder on Cullen. Haynes claimed this line of questioning went to the very heart of the matter. "The motive for fabricating a story against Cullen Davis was this woman's personal greed and design to obtain his fortune," Haynes declared. The prosecution argued that testimony from a divorce case that was ten years old was both irrelevant and highly prejudicial. Dowlen agreed, but he made one concession to the defense: he permitted them to ask questions about Priscilla's current divorce suit against Cullen.

Haynes was hell-bent on establishing that Priscilla had signed a prenuptial agreement and damn well knew she signed it; that's why she had to frame Cullen. Priscilla stuck to her claim that the agreement had been obtained by fraud. Haynes claimed the agreement was witnessed and notarized by Cullen's secretary, Fern Frost, two days before the marriage, but Priscilla testified that she had never seen Frost until the very day of the marriage, in the hospital reception room as Stinky Davis lay dying. Haynes launched one final foray. He wanted the jury to believe that the reason Priscilla spent $20,000 a month while she was married to Cullen was to accumulate separate property for the time when she planned to dump him. Priscilla didn't deny spending $20,000 a month, but as to the suggested motive she responded, "I never gave it any thought."

When Haynes questioned her about the Davis family property on Eagle Mountain Lake, Priscilla referred to it as "our lake house."

"That is the editorial *our*?" Haynes inquired, looking down his half-moon glasses at Priscilla.

"Well, it would be kind of foolish to run around saying everything was Cullen's," Priscilla replied in that little girl's don't-be-silly voice she used on such occasions.

"Everything was Cullen's, wasn't it?"

"Not to my way of thinking."

"Yes, ma'am!" Haynes declared, looking hard at Priscilla, who shook her head and returned his glare.

After eleven grueling days on the witness stand Priscilla was excused and allowed to return to Fort Worth. Both sides reserved the right to recall her as a witness, but as it developed, neither side exercised that option. Instead, for the next two months Priscilla remained the trial's major offstage character, maligned almost daily by the defense and defended by other state's witnesses as they corroborated her story of the events of August 2-3.

"I don't think they laid a glove on her story about the murders," Tim Curry said that night as he shucked his cowboy boots and prepared to relax with a few beers. "They came at her with everything they had, but she came through it very well." Certainly the defense had soiled her reputation and would continue to. She had been less than truthful about her relationship with W. T. Rufner and her drug habit, and Curry was reasonably sure that the defense would bring forth witnesses who would swear that Priscilla knew she was signing a premarital document. Priscilla had also denied mentioning her divorce case when she talked to Bev Bass at the Rangoon Racquet Club in the hours just before the killings, but this seemed like small change in a high-stakes murder case. What pleased the district attorney was that the defense hadn't been able to shake her story about the night of the murder.

Although he didn't admit it at the time, even Racehorse Haynes agreed that Priscilla had made a better witness than he anticipated. "I thought it was a stroke of genius the way Tim Curry handled her," Haynes said later. "He brought her to the end in super style. I'd have to give him an A."

As the final spectators crowded out of the courtroom on September 7, sated by nearly two weeks of testimony detailing Priscilla's love affairs, drug addiction, and association with numerous rogues, felons, and phantoms, members of the press clustered around the accused killer, Cullen Davis. In a scene reminiscent of a football locker room after a tough game, there was an almost self-conscious reverence in the questions put to the dapper, cool-mannered defendant. Whatever sins had been laid at Priscilla's doorstep, reporters agreed among themselves that she was very convincing when she identified Cullen as the killer. Nobody who had followed the case believed that Cullen would take the witness stand and deny the accusations, but that seemed to be the only question anyone dared ask.

Cullen answered straight out: "I am not particularly looking forward to getting on the stand, but I wouldn't hesitate to do it for one minute. I am not going to get up and get in a liar's contest. I don't care to get in a liar's contest with someone over such unscrupulous lies. It makes me cringe and disgusted that she says things like I kicked Andrea and called her stupid. She has no one to back that up, and Andrea is not here to confirm it. I am the only one left alive to confirm that that is not true."

That night over cocktails at Rhett Butler's, Judge George Dowlen admitted that it had been the most harrowing two weeks in his career. "Cullen and Priscilla are the only ones who know the truth," he said. "And one of them is lying. Every once in a while their eyes make contact. And they *know*. Nobody but the two of them. God, it's a strange deal."

The next major witness for the state would be Bubba Gavrel, but first the prosecution called a series of witnesses to corroborate parts of Priscilla's story.

Mr. and Mrs. Clifford Jones, who owned the home next to the Davis estate, substantiated almost word for word Priscilla's story of how she had beaten on their door that night, bleeding from a hole in her chest and shouting that Cullen was up at the mansion shooting everyone. Ambulance driver Thomas Southall told of picking up a terrified Priscilla at the Joneses' home and later helping remove the bloody corpse of Andrea Wilborn from the mansion. Southall had also heard Priscilla identify Cullen as the killer.

It was toward the end of the third week of testimony when Bubba Gavrel hobbled into the courtroom on crutches and was sworn in. Like the other state's witnesses, Gavrel confirmed key parts of Priscilla's story and filled in details as he had in previous statements. Joe Shannon began by asking Gavrel if he had worn a watch that night—there were some uncomfortable time discrepancies in the various statements, and Shannon wanted the jury to understand that the witnesses were only approximating time to the best of their recollection. Gavrel replied that he didn't have a watch and was therefore guessing at the time.

After telling the jury that he and Bev Bass had talked with Farr and Priscilla for about forty-five minutes at the Rangoon Racquet Club, Gavrel told about first driving by his parents' house, then heading for 4200 Mockingbird where his date planned to spend the night with Dee Davis. He estimated that it was between 11:25 P.M. and midnight when he parked his Blazer in the guest parking area near the mansion. Shannon asked what happened as Gavrel and Bev Bass stepped into the driveway.

"I heard a woman screaming, 'I love you. I've always loved you.' I looked toward where the screams were coming from." Pointing to the courtyard on the diagram near the witness box, Gavrel said he saw a man pulling a woman by the arm. The man was saying, "Come on. Come on." Gavrel couldn't recognize either, but the man wore dark clothes and the woman was a blonde. As he and Miss Bass began walking along a wall that separated the driveway from the courtyard, Gavrel said the man walked to the courtyard gate. "He was wearing dark clothes and he had a garbage sack," Gavrel said, demonstrating for the jury how the man held the sack in front of his abdomen. "I asked him, 'What are you doing?

Above, Priscilla Davis and Thomas Cullen Davis. She introduced her wealthy husband to new high-living ways of spending his fortune. Below, "The Mansion" at 4200 Mockingbird Lane, Fort Worth, Texas, where two murders occurred.

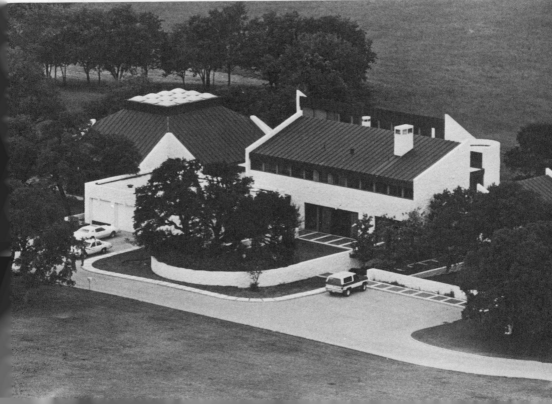

Tiny Priscilla Davis, at 5'3", enjoyed the spectacle she and former TCU basketball player Stan Farr made when they appeared in public together. Here, his 6'9" frame towers over her at the Colonial Country Club, Right, Priscilla in a wheelchair following the near fatal shooting attempt on her life in The Mansion.

GENE GORDON

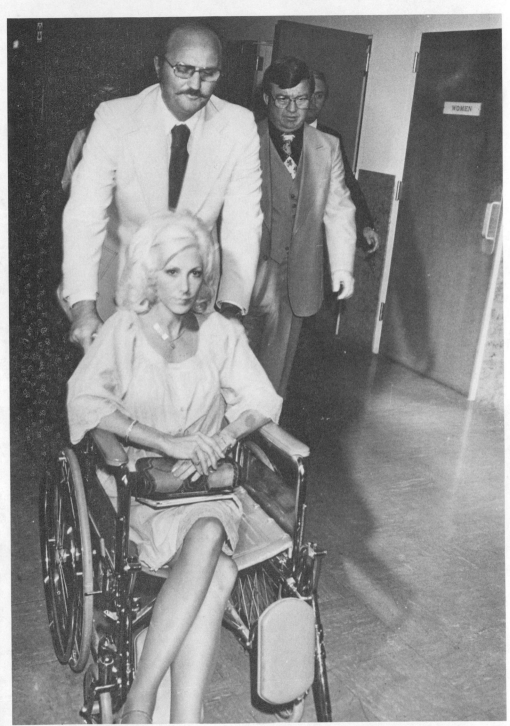

RON HEFLIN

Above, District Attorney Tim Curry. Right: Cullen is flanked by his famous attorneys: Phil Burleson, at left, from Dallas, and at right, Richard "Racehorse" Haynes from Houston. Below, left to right: Cullen under arrest for murder; Stan Farr's body loaded into an ambulance; Cullen and his girlfriend Karen Masters, after acquittal, waving good-bye to it all as their car leaves the Potter County Court House in Amarillo.

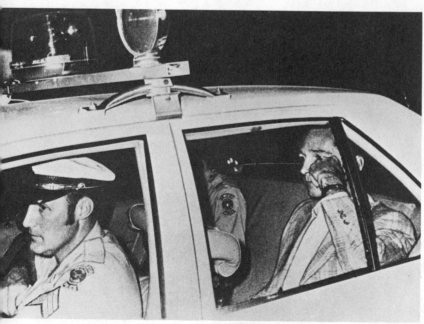

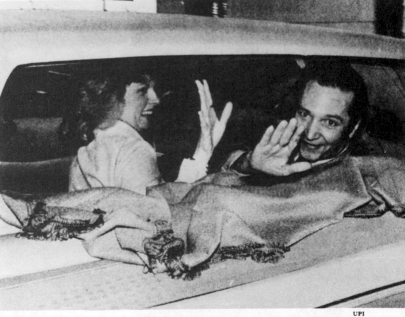

Cullen Davis and Racehorse Haynes swap post-acquittal congratulations at a popular Amarillo singles' bar called Rhett Butler's. Haynes' flamboyant courtroom manner followed him to the party, where he sang and mugged (below).

*T. Cullen Davis with his longtime girlfriend,
Karen Master. In May, 1979, Cullen and
Karen were married. The marriage took
place within an hour after Cullen's divorce
from Priscilla became final. Karen had been
a key alibi witness in Cullen's first trial.*

What's going on?' and he said, 'Let's go in.'" The man in black led the couple in front of the garage to the walkway leading to the mansion's main entrance. The courtroom was dead silent as Shannon asked what happened next.

"That's when he shot me," Gavrel said in a cold monotone. "She [Bass] said, 'Bubba, that's Cullen,' and that's when he turned and shot me."

"At the time he shot you," Shannon asked the witness, "did you have an opportunity to observe him?"

"Yes, sir," Gavrel said. He looked at the defense table and pointed to Cullen Davis.

Gavrel told about being paralyzed from the waist down and crawling to the front door as Cullen chased after Bev Bass, about trying to open the front door and looking through the window at the blood-smeared floor, about playing dead as the man in black returned, and watching as he shot out the windows and disappeared inside the mansion. A few minutes later, Gavrel said, the man came back through the windows and started down the sidewalk. "He looked at me and said something like 'Oh, my God!'" Gavrel told the jury.

As Bubba Gavrel recounted the rest of what he could remember from that bloody night, Phil Burleson's mind was racing ahead. As the defense lawyers had anticipated, there were some inconsistencies between the story Gavrel was telling now and sworn statements he had made on previous occasions. The exact position where he first saw the man dragging the woman, for example. In one statement Gavrel had indicated the sidewalk, and in another, the courtyard. It seemed like a little thing, but Burleson was looking for little things; Gavrel's veracity as a witness in this case was none too good, and it would get worse with each inconsistency that the defense could bring to the jury's attention. By the time most of the state's major witnesses reached Amarillo, they had already given statements to the police, testified at the bond hearing, and given depositions in various civil suits. Once they had undergone direct examination in Amarillo, their version would be on record at least four times. One of Burleson's jobs was to match carefully each of the four versions before beginning the cross-examination. The lawyer had devised a sort of storyboard using index cards and colored markers to indicate points in dispute.

Since court was about to recess for the weekend, Burleson decided to save his loaded questions for Monday morning.

As the fourth week of testimony began, Burleson quickly established several things designed to show that Gavrel was less than a fair and impartial witness. He got Gavrel to acknowledge that his family had filed a $13 million lawsuit against Cullen Davis, and he asked if Gavrel and Bass had drunk and smoked marijuana on the night of August 2. Gavrel said they had a few drinks but denied using grass. Burleson let that hang for a minute while he questioned the witness about inconsistencies in previous statements.

Q: Did you ever say he [the man in black] turned to the left?
A: Yes, sir.
Q: But you're telling the jury now that he turned to the right?
A: Yes, sir.

After leading the witness through various inconsistencies, Burleson asked abruptly if Gavrel had ever heard the name Paul Goheen. Gavrel stiffened slightly as he admitted that he had heard Goheen's name. In an affidavit for the defense, Goheen, the ambulance attendant who escorted Gavrel to the hospital, said that Gavrel didn't know who shot him and that en route to the hospital Gavrel gave the attendant two Baggies of marijuana.

Q: During the time you were in the ambulance, you say you don't remember [anything]?
A: I remember the ambulance guy in the back telling the driver to slow down. I told them to go faster.
Q: Anything else?
A: I remember the guy in the back cutting my shirt off.
Q: Do you remember giving the attendant anything?
A: No, sir.
Q: Do you remember giving the attendant two Baggies of marijuana?
A: No, sir.
Q: Do you recall [Fort Worth policeman] J. L. Soders asking who it was that shot you and you saying, "I do not know the man?"
A: No, sir. I don't remember talking to him.
Q: Do you remember telling police the man who shot you was much shorter than you are and about thirty-four years old?
A: No, sir.

Later, Burleson tested Gavrel's memory regarding conversations with his parents in the hospital.

Q: Do you recall your father saying, "Well, that girl out there said it was Cullen Davis so if anyone asks you, you say that's who it was?"
A: No, sir.
Q: Do you remember Tommy Jourden?

A: No, sir. I know what he says and all that but I don't remember him.

Burleson's small points were beginning to make an impression. Gavrel's testimony was beginning to look too neat, his memory too selective. Burleson finished his cross-examination feeling that the jury had its doubts about Gavrel—and in a criminal case, reasonable doubt was all the defense needed. The witness was handed back to the prosecution for redirect examination.

The prosecution spent the next several days trying to establish that Gavrel and Priscilla were both too badly wounded to "conspire" against Cullen Davis. Dr. Michael Heard, the intern on duty the night they brought the two gunshot victims to the emergency room of John Peter Smith Hospital, testified that Gavrel was in shock and had lost four pints of blood, about one-third of his body's capacity, by the time he was carried into the emergency room. Within a matter of minutes he was anesthetized for the three hours of surgery that followed. Under the skillful questioning of Marvin Collins, the doctor described the anesthetics used to "crash" Gavrel. One was an LSD-type drug that sometimes caused patients to hallucinate. After surgery, Gavrel was given Demerol, which, like the pre-op anesthetic, could explain the young man's temporary memory loss.

Dr. Heard's contention that Gavrel was in shock was a clear setback to the defense, and they objected repeatedly, but Dowlen allowed Collins to continue.

Heard went on to explain that after surgery both Gavrel and Priscilla Davis had tubes connected to respirators inserted in their windpipes. They were placed in different rooms. During the three days before her transfer to another hospital, Heard continued, Priscilla Davis made no attempt to walk, and of course Gavrel couldn't walk. The doctor added that the bullet lodged in Gavrel's spine remained there to this day.

For the next two days Racehorse Haynes attacked Heard's testimony, but with very little success. What was worse from the point of view of the defense, the jury now had expert testimony explaining Gavrel's curious loss of memory.

As the trial entered its second month, the prosecution paraded before the jury a number of police officers and crime scene investigators. The state's strategy at this point was to bolster the testimony already given by Priscilla and Bubba Gavrel and to prepare the jury for their third key witness, Bev Bass. It was time, one DA investigator explained, "to get all the bodies, all the bullets, and all the bloodstains in place."

The leadoff witness for this segment of their case was Officer J. A. Perez, one of the two Fort Worth cops that Bev Bass led back to the scene of the murders. Since the defense had challenged Gavrel's identification of Cullen Davis partly on the contention that the poor lighting conditions would make it impossible to recognize the gunman, Joe Shannon opened by asking Perez if there was enough light outside the mansion that night to read a newspaper.

"Yes, sir," Perez said. "You could read a newspaper or any other book there. There was a lot of light."

There was an eerie silence in the courtroom as Perez described approaching the mansion that supercharged hot August night. Through the broken window Bev Bass spotted Gavrel lying bloody and motionless on the breakfast room floor. "She tried to push past me," Perez said. "I grabbed her. I made her come back and sit behind the wall." Perez and Officer Jimmy Soders drew their sidearms and moved slowly toward the broken window and into the mansion. At this point they thought the killer might still be inside. While Perez looked after Gavrel, Soders followed the broad trail of blood to the kitchen and found the body of Stan Farr. By now several other officers had arrived, and more were on the way. After a quick search of the twenty-room mansion, the officers returned to the kitchen. That's when Perez noticed a blood smear on the facing of the door leading to the basement.

"Right here on the stairway there was a smear of blood that appeared to be a handprint," Perez said as he pointed to the diagram of the mansion interior. There were also dots of blood on the window near the basement entrance.

With his flashlight in one hand and his gun in the other, Perez led Sgt. J. D. Tigert down the steps and into the basement. In the beam of light the officers could see several doors along the basement walls. Moving to his left, Perez opened a door and stepped back quickly. He didn't know what he was expecting, but all he found was some lawn furniture. Very slowly, he moved to the next door and opened it. "I pressed against the wall. The door opens out, and I held it open three to four inches and looked in. And I saw some feet . . . laying down, toward the door. I closed the door and motioned for Sergeant Tigert. . . ."

What Tigert saw was the body of Andrea Wilborn, lying on her back in a pool of her own blood. More blood stained her face and arms. Her eyes were open, but she was clearly dead.

Meanwhile, upstairs there were at least twenty-five Fort Worth cops inside the mansion and possibly that many again outside. By some estimates there were maybe eighty cops at the scene, though nobody seemed to know for sure. This inability to determine just who was at the scene immediately after the murders was particularly handy to the defense. Racehorse Haynes complained: "The same thing that made this a sensational case in the press prevented the cops from doing a good job at the scene."

For the next several days the state introduced a wide variety of physical evidence, much of it bloody and gruesome and all of it designed to reinforce testimony already on the record. This evidence included:

—The nine-foot door with the bullet hole through which Stan Farr took the first of four shots.

—Morgue photos of the bodies of Stan Farr and Andrea Wilborn. There were four views of Farr, each displaying a different gunshot wound. There was one of Andrea Wilborn's naked chest, showing a gunshot wound just below one breast.

—The blood-soaked, striped tube top Andrea had worn the night of her murder.

—Stan Farr's bloodied shirt.

—A dozen blood samples and photos of bloodstains taken from the basement utility room where Andrea's body was discovered and from the entrance leading to the basement.

—Bloodstains removed from the breakfast room area where Priscilla and Farr were shot, from the hallway along which Farr's body had been dragged, and from the patio walkway Priscilla had described in her first escape attempt.

—Bev Bass's sandals and purse.

—Two bullets, one found on the stairway where Farr was first shot and the second outside a glass door which could have been penetrated by bullets that Gavrel said Cullen Davis fired to regain entry into the mansion. Earlier in the trial, the state had produced five more bullets, one discovered under the body of Andrea Wilborn and four from the breakfast room. Two more bullets recovered from the body of Stan Farr would be produced when the state called Fort Worth crime lab director Frank Shiller to testify. The remaining bullet was lodged near Gavrel's spine. The ten bullets fit the state's scenario exactly. The gunman had executed Andrea Wilborn, then reloaded as he waited. That was one. The second bullet wounded Priscilla. Bullets three, four, five, and six killed Farr. The seventh bullet wounded Gavrel. This also explained why the killer had chased but not shot Bev Bass. He would have been out of bullets. Gavrel testified that the gunman reloaded before firing three shots through the window and entering the mansion.

—Fragments of the garbage bag found in the breakfast room, on the stairs where Farr was shot, and in the basement utility room. The plastic bag itself, which was found upstairs in the master bedroom, had already been introduced, as had other fragments.

—Synthetic fibers from a wig found on the plastic bag.

Detective Gary Nichols, Greg Miller's partner, had been called to identify most of the physical evidence. In cross-examination, Phil Burleson zoomed in on the three drinking glasses found in the kitchen, the ones that were supposed to prove that Andrea Wilborn wasn't alone between the hours of 9:00 P.M. and midnight. Burleson asked whether any liquid had been discovered in one of the glasses. Nichols replied that it had, but it wasn't tested.

Q: Were you not trained to preserve liquids from a crime scene as a member of the crime scene search team?

A: We're trained to use our own discretion.

Q: Well, what did you do with the contents of the glass? Did you throw it away? Did you drink it?

A: I poured it down the sink.

In rapid-fire questioning, Burleson asked Nichols if he had taken footprints in the area around the house, or vacuum samples from carpeting and upholstery, or fingerprints from Farr's shoes, and finally if he had found any "plastic bags with a white powdery substance in them in the home."

In each case, Nichols answered that he had not.

Farr's stained shirt and Andrea's bloody tube top and the other pieces of evidence were placed on a table near the jury box where they remained throughout the trial. As each new item of evidence was introduced, it was added to the gory collection. It was like watching someone dress a stage.

CHAPTER 11

As the Cullen Davis trial moved from summer into autumn, the Panhandle wind shifted to the north, kicking up dust devils on the plains and releasing trapped layers of heat from the broken sidewalks of downtown Amarillo. The year seemed to begin here with autumn.

There was a new punch in the air. The trial still dominated conversations, but now there were other topics to consider—livestock prices, winter wheat, football. Shoppers who patronized the fading downtown stores paused to examine new fall fashions. But from time to time the spell was broken, and people would stop and stare as two bailiffs herded a pitifully isolated group of nine men and three women between the Executive Inn and the courthouse. The Cullen Davis jurors had the loneliest job in town. *They* were the prisoners.

From his cell at the top of the courthouse, Cullen looked down at the elms reflecting a brilliant yellow in the lowering fire of daylight. As jail life went, things weren't all that bad for Cullen Davis. The jail was so overcrowded that many prisoners slept on the floor, but Cullen enjoyed a private double-bunk cell. He had his color TV—his favorite program was "The Fugitive." Cullen said he liked it because "you know he's innocent, but the cops can't catch him." Cullen joked with reporters about the jailers "taking away our peanut butter privileges," but most of his meals were catered. The only luxury really out of reach was freedom. Cullen was always freshly groomed and immaculate in his expensive business suits, very much the corporate president, collected and in control. Most evenings at 6:00 P.M. a deputy brought a fresh change of clothes and drove Cullen to see his chiropractor. There was a popular image of Cullen as a man alone, abandoned to the cold-steel world of jailers, lawyers, and hard rules, but that was not the case at all. Karen Master was always close by, as were Cullen's corporate subordinates, crisp, efficient men trained to stay out of sight and ahead of the game. A vice-president of Mid-Continent visited him every other day, bringing corporate news and papers to sign.

In many ways Cullen had never enjoyed so much attention, so much popularity. The Menopause Brigade, as one bailiff called the housewives and groupies, fawned over him like loving aunties, resolving to do anything they could to see that he stayed comfortable. They scolded Deputy Sheriff Al Cross for not seeing to it that his bed linens were changed properly. They brought him cookies and pies and flocked around him at every opportunity. They brought their children and grandchildren to meet him and—for some strange and convoluted reason—had him autograph their copies of *Blood and Money*, the best-seller about the famous John Hill murder case in Houston, a case in which a commoner husband was accused of scheming to murder his fabulously wealthy wife. One had him autograph her neck brace, and another offered to iron his shorts and socks.

Why did they do it? They didn't merely acquit the man that three eyewitnesses had placed at the scene of a brutal murder—they *adored* him. It was as if he were someone to whom they were beholden, someone born to royalty, whose very birthright, courage, and fortitude set him above the struggling masses. In some inexplicable way, Cullen promised meaning to their own lives. "The Cinderella's Sisters Syndrome," you might call it. Why did the Prince pick *her*? And where did Priscilla Lee Childers Wilborn Davis get off acting high and mighty? He had given her everything, and what had she given him? Betrayal!

During each recess Cullen moved freely among his admirers, shaking hands, posing for pictures, exchanging pleasantries, talking football or finance. Cullen's people (as they were eponymously called) had installed a telephone in the judge's outer office, and it was common to see the defendant making corporate decisions on long distance. The housewives loved this aura of power and the plain-spoken, almost boyish manner that went with it.

Not all the groupies were shapeless and middle-aged. There was a nifty, dark-haired young morsel who enjoyed getting Cullen in the corner and discussing sociology. And there was a stream of young beauties, most of them escorted from Dallas or Fort Worth by Cullen's subordinates, who frequently decorated the seats behind the defendant. They shared catered luncheons with Cullen and Karen and at night visited the better clubs around town, the Hilton Inn or Rhett Butler's or other places frequented by the movers and shakers of Amarillo. One particularly striking young woman was Rhonda Sellers, a Dallas Cowboys cheerleader and the former Miss Metroplex of Dallas—Fort Worth. Rhonda was the daughter of one of Karen Master's best friends. Cullen had sponsored Rhonda in the Miss Texas Pageant. Members of the jury probably didn't know her name, but they would not forget her face. *She* was for Cullen Davis. It seemed unthinkable that this lovely, openly wholesome young woman would support Davis if he were a cold-blooded killer.

On September 22, 1977, Cullen celebrated his forty-fourth birthday, his second straight birthday in jail. Karen surprised him with a new painting. It was done by one of the courtroom artists in the style of the highly publicized painting of Cullen and Priscilla that hung in the mansion, only this one portrayed Cullen and Karen with all their children spaced around them like satellites. Cullen's first wife, Sandra, who had been in virtual seclusion since the murders, flew to Amarillo for the occasion with their sons, Cullen Jr., fourteen, and Brian, eleven.

Though Cullen no doubt knew about this "surprise" in advance, there had to be a lump in his throat as his two boys came bursting into the courtroom, hugging him and crying and saying how much they missed their daddy. As reporters gathered close, Cullen Jr. was heard to sob, "Daddy, I just want to be with you alone." It was hard to say what Cullen was thinking; he wasn't much for expressing emotions. Maybe he was thinking about his own daddy.

Haynes had to feel that the trial was going well. If, as he claimed, he couldn't yet read the jury, he could certainly decipher the mood of the community. Those who weren't pro-Cullen were at least anti-Priscilla. A month after Priscilla's testimony, people still spoke of her in tones normally reserved for vermin. Judge Dowlen's own secretary seemed unable to bring herself to speak Priscilla's name, referring to her as *that woman*, and had joked that she might write her own book about the case and call it *Silicone and Sex*. That's how *she* saw the issues. Things looked better by the day. With luck, they would all be home by Thanksgiving. Cullen had already made Thanksgiving reservations at a Colorado ski lodge. It made Racehorse happy to see his client happy.

In the next couple of weeks, several things happened that dampened the defense's enthusiasm and reflected poorly on the client. There had already been talk about lax security, but the rumbling got louder when a convicted murderer on his way to the state prison at Huntsville was left unguarded in the hallway while a deputy sheriff looked in on Cullen Davis. Upstairs in the jail, while Cullen continued to occupy a private cell and watch his private TV, an eighteen-year-old prisoner in a cell with eight others was viciously gang-raped.

The defense was naturally concerned about security—in a case this sensational there was a possibility that some crazy could walk into the courtroom and, before anyone saw what was happening, blow away Cullen Davis—but now there were grumblings about other types of security. It was not uncommon to see Cullen, a man charged with capital murder, walking unguarded along the hallway. One day, accompanied only by an attorney, the defendant who could not qualify for bail walked out of the courtroom and took an elevator to the ground floor. He didn't try to escape, but he could have.

The ripper came the first week in October when Cullen was observed chatting privately with the mother of juror Marilyn Kay Haessly. Miss Haessly had been sequestered since June 29, but like the others she had been permitted telephone calls and visits by her family. These visits were supposed to be monitored by bailiffs, but that didn't turn out to be the case. Now it came out that married jurors were being allowed *conjugal visits,* unsupervised naturally, originally without Judge Dowlen's knowledge but later with his permission. The judge reasoned that the jurors were already under enough hardships and that denying them normal sexual recreation bordered on a cruelty he was not prepared to dispense. Of course, there was the possibility that husbands and wives could make love without speaking of Cullen and Priscilla, but, as someone pointed out, what else was there to talk about?

After the incident with Marilyn Kay Haessly's mother, Dowlen announced that new security guidelines would be forthcoming. "And," he added, "they will be followed." Even as courthouse observers were discussing shutting the barn door after the horses are into the next county, yet another revelation reached the public. The Tarrant County auditor sent a query to Amarillo asking *who is going to pay the jury's liquor bill?* Until then it had been assumed that members of the jury took nothing stronger with their meals than Dr. Pepper.

When it came time for Bev Bass to take the witness stand and tell her story, Phil Burleson was ready. Though Bass portended to be the state's strongest witness, the tall, silver-haired Dallas lawyer saw any number of holes in her story. At the heart of it all was the *curious relationship* between Bass and Priscilla Davis. Burleson didn't for a minute believe that it was a mother and friend-of-daughter thing, as the state contended. Nor could he swallow the older sister-younger sister relationship. No, it was something more. No one ever used the term *bisexual* in the courtroom, and no one introduced any actual proof of bisexual conduct, but the defense's many innuendoes and repeated allegations of their *special relationship* planted the idea in the minds of many.

Later, Burleson explained his personal theory like this: "Priscilla knew who the killer was and struck a deal. Bev's mind was on Cullen that night—she and Priscilla had talked about the divorce at the Rangoon that night. Remember, Priscilla's involvement [in the divorce trial] that Friday was not *lightly* done. She had gone to a great deal of trouble to convince a doctor to write a false report. She had spent time posturing, so that the following Monday, when they got a report on the judge's ruling, she wanted to tell someone. Bev says she was going out there that night to spend the night with Dee. Hell, she knew Dee was shacked up with her boyfriend. Bev wanted to know exactly what had happened in court that day. I really think they got together . . . somehow that night they got together and decided to name Cullen as the killer. Maybe they knew the real killer, or maybe they didn't, but they decided to put it on Cullen."

As the pretty teenager with the honey-blonde hair took the witness stand and began telling her story, no one listened more intently than Phil Burleson.

Bass told of driving her own car to the mansion earlier on the crucial day of August 2. As she recalled, it was about noon when she arrived at 4200 Mockingbird. Andrea had just returned from vacation Bible school in Houston the previous day, and Bev had made plans to take the girl shopping. The image of Andrea as an innocent child, trusting and dependent on the judgment of older friends and family, was reinforced by Bev Bass's recollection of how she'd helped Andrea pick out a blouse and get dressed. Tim Curry felt that it was vital that the jury get some sort of *feeling* about Andrea, that they picture her as a soft, artistic, sensitive girl enchanted by the simple beauty of life and so delicate that she could train her bird and cat to coexist. As things stood, all they knew about the girl was that she was twelve and dead. In her civil depositions, Bass had touchingly described that afternoon with Andrea, how the girl had talked about the Bible school and how Andrea had lingered for a long time at a pet shop, not to buy anything but just to talk to the animals. But, of course, the defense had studied the same deposition, and when Bass got to the part about the pet shop, Haynes successfully argued that the testimony was not relevant and so the jury never heard it. It was somewhere around 4:00 P.M. when Bass and Andrea returned to 4200 Mockingbird. Priscilla, Dee, and Dee's boyfriend were there. They talked for an hour or more; then Bubba Gavrel arrived.

At the very beginning of Bev Bass's testimony, Tim Curry established that the young woman had known the Davis family for seven years and was therefore not likely to be mistaken in her identification. The district attorney asked about the several stops that Bass and Gavrel had made earlier on the evening of August 2, about the accidental encounter with Farr and Priscilla at the Rangoon Racquet Club, leading her skillfully to the murder scene. Bass recalled that they left the club about 11:30 P.M., twenty minutes or so after Farr and Priscilla. Like Gavrel, she was not wearing a watch and could only approximate the times. She told of arriving at the mansion and, as she climbed from Gavrel's Blazer, hearing what sounded like a scream "coming from the house."

Bass supported Gavrel's version almost point by point. In the courtyard she could see the man in black, and her first thought was that they had stumbled on a burglar breaking into the mansion.

"And what if anything did Bubba Gavrel say to the man?" the district attorney asked.

"He said: 'Hey, what's going on? Where is everybody?'"

The man told Gavrel, "They are right this way. Follow me." Bass said that Gavrel followed the man and she walked toward the door leading to the breakfast room, the main entrance to the mansion.

Q: At the time you got to the [well-lighted] area how close were you to the man?

A: Well, Bubba was about three feet behind him, and I was right behind Bubba.

Q: Did you ever recognize the man in black?

A: Yes, sir, as he was turning the corner.

Q: At the time he turned the corner did you say anything?

A: Yes, sir. I said, "Bubba, that's Cullen!" He turned around and shot. Bubba screamed, and he stumbled and fell in front of me.

Q: Well, what did the defendant do?

A: He leaned over Bubba with his hands out.

Q: When he leaned over, how close was he to [Bubba]?

A: About two feet. I screamed, and he [Cullen] just stood up and looked right at me. I turned and ran . . . and he followed me.

Q: How long did you stand there face to face with him?

A: A few seconds.

Q: Did you say anything?

A: I said, "Cullen, please don't shoot me! It's Bev!" I just kept screaming, "Cullen, please don't shoot me! It's Bev!"

Bass testified that she hurdled a small retaining wall and ran in the direction of Hulen Street, zigzagging between the grass and the gravel driveway, thinking that at any second the man would fire at her. "I kept turning around and watching him," she said, her voice unsteady and her hands trembling as she looked across the courtroom at Cullen Davis. "I saw the garbage bag in his hand, and I knew he had a gun in it. I couldn't tell if he was shooting at me because my ears were ringing . . . and I kept screaming, 'Cullen, please don't shoot me, it's Bev!' When I got about three-fourths of the way [to Hulen Street] . . . I turned around and he was there. I couldn't tell if he was standing or running. He kept raising the sack . . . I was afraid he was going to shoot me, so I kept running back and forth on the road and over the grass. And then I looked back again and he was gone. He just disappeared."

At this point the jury was excused while Curry questioned Bass about statements made to motorist Robert Sawhill, who picked her up on Hulen, and later to security guard John Smedley and the two police officers who arrived shortly. The district attorney was attempting to establish that the young woman was still under the emotional impact of the shooting and that therefore her testimony should be admissible under the hearsay guidelines.

Although all the prosecutors felt that Bass had told her story well, Curry knew that on at least one point they had problems. According to Bass, she had identified Cullen Davis as the killer to the first four people she encountered—Robert Sawhill, the motorist who first picked her up on Hulen; security guard John Smedley; and the two cops. But in the weeks of investigation following the killings, the state hadn't made much of an effort to locate Sawhill—Bass hadn't been able to remember the name of the motorist who picked her up on Hulen, and Sawhill didn't immediately come forward. To Curry's embarrassment, it was a newspaper ad placed by the defense that finally located Sawhill, and now the man who should have been able to corroborate part of Bass's story was a witness for the other side.

Later in cross-examination, the defense would ask Bass about "the newspaper article" in which she first learned the name of Robert Sawhill. Dowlen wouldn't allow her to answer that question, but Curry knew that the defense would eventually call Sawhill and that his story wouldn't support all the things Bass recalled telling him that night. That was a bridge they would have to cross when they reached it. Right now Curry had only two more questions for his witness. First, he solicited testimony that after their accidental meeting at the Rangoon Racquet Club, Bass didn't see Priscilla Davis again "for three or four days."

Curry had one final question for Bass, and the DA knew it was going to be a shocker. His face was grim as he walked back to the table and took something from an envelope, then whirled and shoved it in front of her. "Can you identify who this is?" Curry asked bluntly. Tears seeped into Bass's eyes as she looked at the frozen-in-death body of Andrea Wilborn lying on the floor of the utility room. "It's . . . Andrea . . . ," Bass said. Then she broke down completely and was led sobbing from the courtroom. After a thirty-minute recess, Dowlen announced that the witness was in no condition to continue and adjourned for the day. It was a cruel but necessary ploy for the prosecution; Curry wanted the jury to dwell at least overnight on Bev Bass's story before the defense began attacking her.

The unexpected recess also gave the defense a chance to review the inconsistencies in Bass's various statements. By the following morning Racehorse Haynes was snorting fire and brimstone as he hurled questions at the young witness. To everyone's surprise, Bass maintained herself fairly well. At times she came across as a spoiled rich girl and at other times as a silly teenager, but the defense was never able to shake her on the one key point—that she recognized Cullen Davis as the gunman in black.

Instead, Haynes concentrated on showing that Bev Bass was something less than an innocent, wide-eyed teenager accidentally caught up in a murderous web and just trying to tell the truth as best she could recall. In early testimony the district attorney had asked what Stan Farr was drinking that night at the Rangoon Racquet Club. Bass had once said that Farr drank bourbon, but now she couldn't remember. Wasn't it *Chivas?* the prosecutor inquired, to which Bass answered rather naively, "What's Chivas?" Curry told her it was the brand name of a Scotch, then hurried on to the next question. But now it was Haynes's turn, and he called her attention to that same question.

Q: Miss Bass, you are acquainted with alcohol, are you not?

A: What do you mean?

Q: You weren't trying to suggest to the jury that you are so naive that you thought Chivas was *bourbon,* were you?

A: I'm sorry, I didn't know what it was.

Haynes asked several questions about "your personal problem" and "your special relationship with Priscilla Lee Davis," then he directed her attention to the gathering at Brent Cruz's apartment an hour or so before the meeting at the Rangoon Racquet Club. Tempering his cutting edge with a fatherly smile, Race wanted to know who was there "in that little room." He was especially interested in Brent Cruz's thirteen-year-old sister. "Was she there all the time or just part of the time?" the lawyer wanted to know. And what were they doing "in that little back room?" Now Bass was on the verge of tears. It wasn't so much what Haynes said, it was the way he said it.

"I don't understand what you're trying to do," she said, her voice trembling badly.

"The truth is," Haynes said, leaning in close to the witness, "the group of you were all alone in that little back room, were you not?"

A: I don't remember.

Q: You didn't have any sort of mood modifier while you were back there in that little room, did you?

A: No, sir.

Q: And you didn't see Gus James Gavrel put anything in his undershorts, did you—a green vegetable substance in a plastic bag?

A: No, sir.

For the next hour or more Haynes led the witness over an almost minute-by-minute account of her activities before and after the murders, pressing her for exact times and places, who did what and went where. The lawyer had a large blackboard carted into the courtroom, and as Bass attempted to answer each question, Haynes listed the answers chronologically in chalk letters easily visible from the jury box. Every time the witness answered, "I don't remember," Haynes wrote I.D.R.'s for the jury to consider, a list that would remain visible throughout the remainder of the trial. Just as the prosecution had dressed the set with the bloody clothes of Farr and Andrea, Haynes had his own props and his own method of dressing the stage.

Referring to Bev Bass's deposition taken in October 1976, about two months after the murders, Haynes grilled her about her conversation with Robert Sawhill.

Q: So, on October 16, 1976, you didn't say that you told the man [Sawhill] that Cullen Davis had shot your boyfriend, did you?

A: No. It was my first deposition, and they didn't ask me things in as great detail.

Q: You were trying to be truthful, weren't you, ma'am?

A: Yes.

Q: Well, the fact is you don't really remember what you told the man in the car, do you? You either said it was Cullen Davis or the man who owns the big house on the top of the hill, didn't you?

A: I don't remember which.

Q: And now you remember. Your memory has improved, has it?

A: I just now calmed down where I can sit down and remember it.

Haynes produced yet another statement, the one that Bass made to Det. C. R. Davis in the early morning hours of August 3. Passing close to the jury box to make certain he had everyone's attention, Haynes read a passage in which Bass stated: "While we were walking on the walkway, I heard loud noises coming from inside the house. I heard a woman scream. I think I heard one shot. A man was walking in front of me and Bubba. . . ."

Haynes looked over the rim of his half-moon glasses as he phrased his next question.

Q: Is it your testimony now that the man in black was *not* walking with you and Bubba at the time you heard the shot?

A: Yes, sir.

Q: So what you said in the statement of August 3 is not true?

A: It's out of sequence. Will you not let me explain it?

Q: You want to say that when [Det. C. R.] Davis typed it up, he typed it out of sequence?

A: If you're asking me if I'm lying, the answer is "No, sir." But you're making it very difficult for me to answer.

Q: You say you heard a noise that *sounded* like a gunshot?

A: I'm not sure what kind of noise it was.

However inconsequential the questions, Bass became increasingly frustrated, and Haynes appeared increasingly suspicious of her flawed memory. At one point she said, "I have an explanation if you'll just let. . . ."

"I'm *sure* you do," Haynes said, taking off his glasses and walking away from the witness stand as if to say that he had heard all the lies he could stomach for one day. "I'm *positive* you do." Several members of the jury smiled and exchanged glances. But Racehorse wasn't done yet. He continued to question her about the noise she claimed to have heard.

Q: Are you saying that the noise was comparable to the sound of gunfire?

A: What does comparable mean?

This time several jurors laughed out loud. It was Racehorse Haynes at his best. Suddenly, without warning, Haynes slammed a briefcase on the table. You could hear the noise at the opposite end of the hall.

"Comparable," Haynes said, treating the witness now to his condescending smile. "Did that sound like a gunshot?"

Bass didn't answer, but the look on her face said it did.

In its efforts to impeach Bev Bass and tar her with the same brush already used on Priscilla Davis, the defense was counting heavily on Bass herself. They were certain that somewhere along the way she would either lie or leave a false impression with the jury, and that would open the door for collateral demonstrations, just as it had with Priscilla.

Earlier in the cross-examination, Haynes had probed Bass's relationship with Priscilla.

Q: The relationship between you and Priscilla Lee Davis was a personal relationship, was it not?

A: I don't understand.

Q: She was more to you than just Dee's mother. You and she discussed your own personal situations, did you not?

A: A few times, yes, sir.

Q: When you had this problem of a personal nature in August of 1975, you went to Priscilla Lee Davis, did you not?

A: Yes, sir.

Q: In reaching a resolution to this problem, you used the name Priscilla Lee Davis, did you not?

A: I don't remember.

That was the opening Haynes sought. He now produced a document to refresh her memory and had Bass identify both her own handwriting and the name of Priscilla Lee Davis. When he was satisfied that Bass fully recognized the document, Race resumed questioning.

Q: So Priscilla Lee Davis accompanied you to the place where you solved your problem?

A: Yes, sir.

Q: And she extended financial assistance to you, didn't she?

A: She loaned me some money.

Q: And how old were you at the time?

A: Sixteen.

Although Dowlen had ruled that the defense could not actually use the word *abortion*, he permitted questions concerning previous statements. "Just enough rope to hang her," one lawyer observed. It now developed that Bev Bass had tied the noose herself almost a year earlier in a deposition taken in December 1976.

Haynes waited until Bass's fourth and final day to spring the trap. Using records subpoenaed from Pregnancy Control, Inc., he began by asking about a "consultation" she had had with a doctor in August 1975. Bass didn't remember it.

Q: Do you recall when you were giving testimony in December 1976 you were asked if your health was good and you indicated it was good and had always been good?

A: Yes, sir.

Haynes adjusted his glasses on his nose and read from the deposition.

Q: Question. "Have you had any operations in the last five years?" And your answer was, "I've had my wisdom teeth out, that's about all."

A: Yes, sir.

Q: Now that answer you gave in December was not truthful, was it?

A: No, sir. It was something I wanted to forget about, and I had forgotten it.

Before Haynes could ask his next question, Bev Bass started crying. In a voice choked with tears she asked Dowlen, "Could I please take a break?" Dowlen called a recess, and the prosecution hustled Bass to a back room. Curry told her the same thing he had told Priscilla: just tell the truth. Curry felt that the defense had pretty much fired all its shots by now. Bass had been smeared by her association with "the Queen Bee" (as Haynes was now referring to Priscilla), but her basic story hadn't been challenged. When Bass had stopped crying, she returned to the witness stand resolved to make the best of it. Haynes tempered his tone accordingly.

Q: You had consulted with a medical person back in August 1975, hadn't you?

A: Yes, sir.

Q: So when you said no, you had just forgotten about the consultation, isn't that right?

Bass didn't immediately reply. She seemed again on the verge of tears as Haynes rephrased his question.

Q: The truth of it is, you hadn't forgotten about that incident. You had just decided that it wouldn't be discovered.

A: No, sir.

Q: You had used your sister's name in seeking a resolution to your problem, hadn't you?

A: Yes, sir.

Q: So your *sister's* name now appears on that record, isn't that right?

A: Yes, sir.

Q: And after Priscilla Lee Davis testified [at the same hearing], she told you about this line of questioning and that she had lied, didn't she?

A: No, sir.

Q: And you were prepared to forget about that incident again until yesterday when you found out those records had been subpoenaed, weren't you?

A: No, sir, Mr. Haynes. I told you, I tried to block that from my memory and I had.

Bev Bass was about to break down again, but that was all right. Haynes had finished with her.

By now there had been thirty-five days of testimony, not counting weekends and holidays and other recesses, thirty-five days of steady shelling by the best witnesses the state had in its arsenal. Race decided that though he deserved a drink, he didn't need one. He was high enough on his own accomplishments. He was certain they had shot down two out of three eyewitnesses, or would just as soon as they started calling their own witnesses. Bev Bass he wasn't sure about. If she hadn't already soiled herself in the eyes of the jury, it was probably too late. The district attorney was out there now telling the press what a solid witness Bev Bass had made. It pained Haynes to admit it, but it was entirely possible the DA was correct. Bass's testimony had obviously not supported the defense's conspiratorial theory.

But Haynes was not about to abandon his theory of conspiracy. Conspiracy wasn't something he had to prove, only a seed for the jury to warm over when they finally wrestled with the question of *reasonable doubt*. Haynes knew from experience that the jury could believe that Bass was telling the truth and *still* believe that she conspired to blame Cullen. If Bass left one indelible impression with the jurors, it was her loyalty to Priscilla, coupled with an open hostility toward Cullen. This was the impression Haynes wanted the jury to take with them when it came time to deliberate the verdict.

As the prosecution questioned security guard John Smedley the next morning, Haynes, Burleson, and Mike Gibson were looking ahead to another trouble spot. As expected, Smedley supported Bass's story all the way. The most damaging part was Dowlen's ruling that Smedley could repeat for the jury what Bass told him in the passion of the moment. She told him: "It was Cullen. Cullen did it. I saw his ugly fucking face. He's trying to kill me too. He chased me all over the place." After Dowlen's ruling, there was very little the defense could do to challenge Smedley.

The state had reached the homestretch, and soon it would be time for the defense to present its case. The final two prosecution witnesses would be Dr. Feliks Gwozdz, the Tarrant County medical examiner who did the autopsies on the bodies of Stan Farr and Andrea Wilborn, and Frank Shiller, director of the Fort Worth crime lab, who had been assigned the very important task of explaining the physical evidence. In the final analysis Shiller's job was to prove the state's circumstantial case—namely, that the bullet that killed Andrea Wilborn was fired from the same gun that killed Stan Farr.

Racehorse had looked forward to matching wits with Dr. Gwozdz, though he was aware of the risks. They talked about expert witnesses; none was more expert than the Tarrant County medical examiner, and few were as ingratiating in the eyes of a jury. For some days now Haynes had been mulling over a theory that Andrea Wilborn was killed somewhere other than the basement utility room. If Gwozdz was as good as his reputation, he might be able to confirm this, thus punching a large hole in the prosecution's version of how things had happened that night. "I felt like it was a critical spot in the trial," Haynes said.

There was a detectable queasiness in the courtroom as Gwozdz told about examining the bodies of the two victims. The girl, he said, had two wounds—an entrance wound in the right chest and an exit wound in the left back, two inches below and three inches to the left of the entrance wound. The bullet penetrated Andrea's aorta, the doctor said, producing shock and massive bleeding, probably causing death in a very short time.

When it was the defense's time to cross-examine, Racehorse went straight to what he considered the critical part. Looking at Gwozdz's own report, he asked why there was no mention of a urine specimen from the body of Andrea Wilborn. The doctor answered that the girl's bladder had collapsed, and there was no urine to examine.

Exactly! "Isn't it true, doctor," Racehorse asked, "that people who die traumatically have an involuntary emptying or voiding of the bladder?"

Gwozdz acknowledged that this was usually the case.

"And is it not also true that within *moments* of voiding, the bladder begins to fill up again?"

Gwozdz made several remarks about bladders and their strange workings, but he never got around to answering Haynes's question. Racehorse repeated the question several times, still with no results. No one in the courtroom, least of all the jury, understood this line of questioning, and Haynes was finally forced to drop it. He explained later: "I'd been through this sort of testimony with doctors before and I *knew* that it was true . . . that as soon as a bladder is empty, it begins almost at once to fill up again. Andrea's bladder was empty. Yet there was no trace of urine in the utility room. No one mentioned the smell of urine on her panties, or on the floor. Urine has a very distinctive odor that any trained crime scene investigator would have to notice. Involuntary bladder function at the scene of a homicide is not at all unusual. Crime scene investigators see it all the time. But it was *not* there. That suggests just one thing—that she was killed somewhere else. The empty bladder proved that she had an involuntary bladder function within a minute or a minute and a half of the killing; otherwise the bladder would have filled up at least a little. But for some reason I never could get Gwozdz to acknowledge it." Haynes considered calling in his own expert, but he sensed that the jury was becoming impatient and decided that on this he had reached the point of diminishing returns. All he could really hope to prove was that Andrea wasn't killed in the place that the prosecution contended and that the cops had once more botched the investigation. Besides, Haynes had bigger things on the line. What would later become known as the "Ordeal of Frank Shiller" was about to begin.

Shiller, an intelligent, articulate, soft-spoken man who directed the Fort Worth crime lab, was to be the final and in many ways the most important witness for the state. In his opening remarks to the jury almost two months earlier, Tim Curry had acknowledged that the state's case was circumstantial but promised that testimony would be presented proving that the gunman who killed Stan Farr also killed Andrea Wilborn. It sounded easy. But even as Shiller was being sworn in, the jury looked across the courtroom at a preview of the ordeal to come—Racehorse Haynes, a splendid figure in his three-piece suit and handmade cowboy boots, sat puffing on his pipe as he examined *each tiny piece of evidence with a magnifying glass*. It was probably an illusion, but to those who had watched the magnificent lawyer for many days now it even appeared that he had bleached his temples for the occasion. Like any great courtroom lawyer, Racehorse was part detective, part actor. It was impossible for the jury to know where the one role ended and the other began. Haynes himself probably didn't know.

Point by point and item by item, Shiller's testimony substantiated the testimony of the three eyewitnesses concerning how and where the massacre of August 2 took place. As each bullet was labeled and offered into evidence, Shiller told where the bullet was found and in what condition. Some of the bullets were too badly damaged to make accurate comparisons, Shiller told the jury, but the bullet removed from Farr's body matched a bullet found on the breakfast room floor. This bullet in turn matched the bullet that killed Andrea Wilborn. And all three of these bullets matched the bullet found behind the stairway door. There was no doubt at all that this was precise and accurate, Shiller said. The crime lab director was about to tell the jury that no fewer than three experts hired by the defense had examined these same bullets and reached the same conclusion when Haynes's objection cut him short. By now Shiller had been on the witness stand for two and one-half tedious, excruciatingly slow days.

On Monday, October 17, as the trial entered its ninth week, Haynes went to work on Shiller. First, he muddied the water by bringing up "the judge's bullet," a mysterious projectile that had arrived by mail weeks before. From there he went on to establish the hypothesis that any ten bullets fired from the same gun would each show "dissimilarities" because of the residue each would leave in the gun barrel. No one had ever produced the murder weapon, he reminded the jury, but several other guns had appeared. In addition to the Horace Copeland gun, still another .38 now known as the September 15 gun had come into the hands of the court. ("Some nut from Wichita Falls sent it in," one of the prosecutors explained.) This gun, too, was a red herring, but Haynes used it effectively. Shiller had test-fired the September 15 gun, and now Haynes solicited his admission that even though Shiller *knew* that the test bullets were all fired from the same gun, he couldn't prove it by ballistics examination.

During one barrage of questions the defense discovered the titillating bit of information that for a short time just after the killings the clothes of the victims along with other evidence had been stored in an unlocked cabinet at the Fort Worth police station. Maybe this didn't seem important to some people, but "locker thirteen," as it soon came to be called, fascinated Racehorse Haynes. He asked Shiller repeated questions, referring to "the celebrated locker thirteen." Tolly Wilson objected angrily to Haynes's use of the word *celebrated,* and Haynes demurred. Thereafter, he referred to the "unique and unlocked locker number thirteen."

As the trial dragged into its forty-third day, half the seats in the courtroom were empty. One juror dozed for minutes at a time, and the others seemed less than interested in the proceedings. There had been several heated arguments among jurors, and if someone didn't get on with the trial, there would be many more.

Nevertheless, the ordeal of Frank Shiller continued. The tempers of the lawyers weren't much better than the jurors', though the lawyers at least pretended to know what was being said. After a grueling session in which Haynes questioned Shiller about his opinion that Andrea Wilborn had been shot point-blank from a distance of less than five feet, reporters asked the lawyer *why!* Why was he going *on and on* like this?

Haynes replied, "I'm only showing that they tailored the distance to fit their own configurations."

When Tolly Wilson heard this, he exploded: "I'll tell you what it shows. It bloody well shows the killer knew who he was shooting. It bloody well shows it was intentional. And it bloody well indicates that the son of a bitch was looking a twelve-year-old girl square in the eye when he shot her!"

By the seventh and final day of Shiller's ordeal, even the groupies had left. Haynes asked a last series of questions of Shiller, this time about the filaments of the wig and how they were recovered from the scene. When Haynes was done, Tim Curry got to his feet and almost offhandedly said, "May it please the court, the state wishes to call no more witnesses at this time."

It did please the court; it pleased damn near everyone. A kind of collective sigh of relief went through the courtroom, though Cullen seemed not so much relieved as defiant. You could see the old Texas Aggie spirit boiling over. They had made it a little rough, but now it was his turn.

CHAPTER 12

There was a full house as Racehorse Haynes delivered his opening remarks for the defense. The housewives in the hallway jostled one another to get a glimpse of the famous Houston attorney, and W. T. Rufner moved among them, trying to hawk autographed T-shirts for $100 a copy. They were being modeled by a trained chimpanzee named Racehorse. The picture on the T-shirts was not the same one that the defense had blown up to poster size; Rufner denied any knowledge of the famous photograph, backing up Priscilla's claim that the whole thing was a trick engineered by Cullen's people. But the similarity was unmistakable. In this one, T-man posed alone, naked except for the Christmas stocking covering his genitals. Below the picture were the words "Sock it to 'em, W. T." T-man realized that at $100 a pop he wasn't likely to sell many T-shirts, but as he told a Dallas television crew, "I'm here for the exposure."

The packed house included a newspaper editor and several out-of-town lawyers who had flown to Amarillo just to watch Haynes in action as he outlined for the jury the case that the defense planned to present.

He started with the motive, which the state had contended was Judge Eidson's ruling ordering the defendant to increase alimony payments. The defense planned to demonstrate that what the state claimed was motive was in fact the very antithesis of motive. "We will prove that Priscilla Lee Davis knew of the prenuptial agreement," Haynes said. "That she knew she couldn't get into his separate property—the family estate. The lack of motive is this—Cullen Davis was *saving* money. It is true that the court ordered him to pay $5,000 a month, but she was spending $20,000 a month before [the separation]."

Haynes promised the jury that "we will bring in Robert Sawhill to show that Miss Bass took liberty with the truth. And we will show the relationship between Priscilla Davis and Beverly Bass. We will show that Priscilla Davis stood to profit if Cullen Davis was found guilty. We will show that Bubba Gavrel stood to profit and that he in fact said, 'I don't know who shot me.'" Haynes pointed out that the state had conveniently neglected to call Officer Jimmy Soders, one of several witnesses who claimed to have heard this denial. The state argued that Gavrel was in shock at the time, Haynes said, but the defense would show that he had enough presence of mind at the scene to ask an ambulance attendant to dispose of his stash of marijuana.

"We will show you a different picture of Stan Farr," Haynes said. In the weeks before his murder, Farr carried a pistol. He had failed in business, and there were a number of judgments against him. "The type of people with whom Stan Farr was doing business," Haynes continued, "were not the type to resort to the courts to collect debts." Farr had, or claimed to have, more than $100,000 at the time of his murder, Haynes said, and Horace Copeland knew this. The defense would show that Copeland was a man worthy of Farr's fear. Regarding W. T. Rufner, the purpose of his testimony would not be to disparage the character of Priscilla. "In that regard," he said, looking up from his notes, "I think Priscilla Lee Davis stands on her own." Instead, the purpose of his testimony would be to establish that for a period of time he had a key to the Davis mansion, as did a number of other people of questionable character.

Finally, the defense would show that Stan Farr was the target of the assailants. Haynes used the plural, indicating that he believed more than one assailant was involved. He repeated his contention that the assailants were "persons who do not resort to the courts to collect money owed." Andrea Wilborn, Haynes concluded, was "an accidental victim." Priscilla herself was not the primary target, nor was Bubba Gavrel, who happened to stumble onto the massacre.

Haynes added one final, intriguing footnote: "Maybe at the conclusion of the defense's case there will be some development that will surprise you . . . some development that at this juncture is not foreseen."

This final note about future unforeseen developments caused much speculation in the media, and perhaps some second-guessing among prosecutors, but all it really reflected was the defense team's faith in its own ongoing investigation. Steve Sumner was beginning to connect the hundreds of bits and pieces of miscellaneous information his investiga-

only in holding on to his substantial fortune. Dowlen ruled that there could be no mention of the bitter litigation with his brother Bill Davis, but permitted the state to ask limited questions about documents filed in that suit. Papers from that suit contended that Cullen's personal debts were $16 million, not $11 million. Corporate debts in a single company, according to Bill Davis, ran to $46 million. Bill Davis further contended that Cullen used corporation funds to back other loans, thereby "recklessly increasing the indebtedness of the corporation to sums in excess of $150 million." The way Tolly Wilson interpreted it, Cullen's financial problems were something more than "minimal." The court records jolly well proved that Priscilla had him by the sore place; Wilson questioned Munn at length about the August 2 meeting with Cullen and Ken Davis, pointing out to the jury that Bill Davis was specifically *not* invited. Munn testified that before the meeting, Cullen had lunch with his adopted daughter, Dee Davis.

"Did Cullen Davis tell you [at the meeting] that Andrea was back in town?" Wilson asked the witness.

Munn said he didn't recall.

"And when he heard the results [of Judge Eidson's ruling] there was no reaction?"

Munn answered that he couldn't recall any reaction from either Cullen *or* Ken Davis. Certainly Cullen demonstrated "no hatred," Munn repeated.

"Would you describe killing a child's cat in front of that child an act of hatred?" Wilson asked before anyone could stop him. Racehorse Haynes bolted out of his chair like his pants were on fire, angrily objecting to the question. Dowlen called all the attorneys to the bench for a cooling-off period. There was no doubt in Tolly Wilson's mind that the question was out of order. But he didn't regret it. It would very likely be the only time in the trial that Cullen Davis would be accused of any misdeed prior to the murders.

For the next several days the defense focused its attack on Bubba Gavrel. Doris Costello, a clerk in the emergency room at John Peter Smith Hospital on the night of the shootings, testified that Gavrel was "conscious" when they brought him in and was sufficiently lucid to give his name, address, and telephone number and to sign a consent form. The state countered by asking Costello if Gavrel had seen Priscilla Davis that night. Costello said that he hadn't to her knowledge.

Ambulance attendant Paul Goheen testified next, telling the jury that when he first entered the mansion, Gavrel was seated on the floor, holding a telephone. When the ambulance attendant asked the victim where he had been shot, Gavrel answered, "I don't know. Get me out of here." When Goheen asked *who* shot him, Gavrel gave the same answer: "I don't know. Just get me out of here." Moments later, as Goheen was attempting to remove the victim's trousers in the back of the ambulance, Goheen testified that Gavrel produced two Baggies of marijuana and said, "Get rid of this." Goheen said he threw the Baggies out of the ambulance window. Bev Bass was "cussing . . . she was very excited," Goheen continued. "Her eyes looked glassy . . . consistent with using drugs." Goheen told the jury that he no longer drove an ambulance—he was now a policeman in a Fort Worth suburb.

There was a hollow ring to parts of Goheen's story, but prosecutors failed to point this out to the jury. Even as attendants loaded Gavrel into the ambulance, it must have been apparent that some sort of major criminal activity had taken place. Didn't Goheen know that marijuana was illegal? Didn't he realize it was evidence? Then why did he throw it out the window? *How* did he throw it out the window? Did the rear of the ambulance have roll-down windows? Which window did he use to dispose of the marijuana? These were all legitimate questions, but the prosecution didn't ask them.

Prosecutors had to be embarrassed when the defense called its next witness—Fort Worth police officer Jimmy Soders. The reason that the state had neglected to call this key witness became apparent when Soders admitted that Gavrel told him, "I don't know the man" when asked who did the shooting. The state won the point back in cross-examination. When Soders asked Bev Bass who shot her boyfriend, she replied: "Cullen Davis did it. I saw him do it. I know him."

The big gun in the defense's assault on Gavrel was Tommy Jourden, who shared a cubicle with Gavrel after the shootings. Even before Jourden took the stand, it became apparent the big gun might backfire.

Jourden was a calculated risk. There were aspects of Jourden's life that might cause him to appear less than worthy to a jury—he had been unemployed for more than a year, had applied for welfare on the grounds that a back injury made him totally disabled, and had more than a passing acquaintance with personal injury suits—he had been involved in three, one of which was still pending. However unfair the judgment might have been, Jourden *appeared* to be a hustler. Racehorse Haynes was confident, however, that these matters could be kept from the jury. Weighed against what Jourden claimed to have overheard, it was a risk they had to take.

Jourden testified that on August 3, the day after the murders, Gavrel's father visited the intensive-care cubicle. According to Jourden, the conversation between father and son went like this:

Gus Sr.: Do you know who shot you?

Gus Jr.: No, sir, I don't. It all happened so quick and it was dark and I didn't see who it was.

Gus Sr.: It was Cullen that done it. A girl out there [Bev Bass] said it was, so if anybody asks you, you say it was Cullen. Someone is going to pay for doing this.

After Gus Sr. left, Jourden continued, he engaged Bubba in a conversation in which the victim again denied knowing the gunman. Jourden said that he then told Gavrel: "You know, if this rich man shot you, you're going to be a rich man yourself. You can file suit on him."

Jourden quoted Gavrel as replying: "I guess you're right. I hadn't thought of that."

Cross-examination brought out the curious fact that Jourden had waited four months before reporting the hospital conversation. The witness denied the prosecution's claim that he finally came forward "for the purpose of bettering yourself [financially]." Jourden, who appeared to consider himself a good witness, didn't appear shocked at the question.

When Jourden had completed his testimony, both sides claimed that he had helped their case. This was in keeping with the defense's strategy, part of which was to implant in the minds of the jurors that the state had called only the witnesses who fit their concept of what happened. Burleson, for one, believed that the state was in danger of becoming complacent; that they had lived with their concept so long they failed to notice its inherent flaws, or appreciate the new flaws that the defense was preparing to explore. "They think we're scatter-shooting," Burleson said. Burleson was positive that if they kept scatter-shooting long enough, they were bound to hit some nerves.

One of their next witnesses, Robert Sawhill, was a case in point. Since Sawhill was the first person Bev Bass encountered as she fled for her life, why had the state not called him? It might be assumed that Sawhill would contradict part of Bev Bass's testimony, and this was true. Bass claimed that as she jumped into Sawhill's car, she identified the gunman as either Cullen Davis or "the owner of the big house on the hill." Now it was Sawhill's turn to deny it. The only time Davis's name was mentioned, Sawhill testified, was when the girl told him, "You know there's a divorce case going on up at the Davis estate." But as Burleson continued to question Sawhill, something emerged, something that was not obvious in the beginning but would grow much larger in the minds of the jurors as the case progressed. There had already been some confusion about the exact times that everything happened, but Sawhill was very sure that when he telephoned the police that night it was 12:20 A.M. He remembered that when he and some business associates left the Ramada Inn, someone pointed out that it was uncivilized to close the bar at midnight. Sawhill remembered looking at the clock in the lobby and then at his own watch—it was exactly 12:05. The distance from the Ramada Inn to the place on Hulen where he first saw Bev Bass was precisely 9.5 miles—he had checked it later to be certain—and taking into consideration one detour on Interstate 20, driving at his normal speed, it would have taken him thirteen minutes. He estimated that another two minutes elapsed from the time he picked up Bass until he called the police. Therefore, he called the police at exactly 12:20. According to police records, this was twenty-two minutes before they received Sawhill's call (and at least twenty minutes before Priscilla was beating on the door of a neighbor's house, screaming for them to call the police). The conflict of times became more apparent when it was recalled that security guard John Smedley, who arrived just as Sawhill was calling the police, placed the time at 12:47. Records kept by Smedley's dispatcher confirmed this.

The next witness for the defense supplied yet another mystery to the time and events of that night. John Brutsche, general manager of a moving and storage firm, told the jury that as he and his wife drove along Hulen and passed the mansion that night, they saw a large, expensive, late-model car turning slowly into the driveway of the Davis estate. He couldn't tell the color of the car, only that it was a single color (unlike Cullen's white-on-blue Cadillac which was supposedly parked in a downtown garage). Brutsche guessed that the time was 10:50 P.M. He based his guess on the fact that as he and his wife left the parking lot of a downtown church, they looked at the clock on the Continental National Bank Building and observed that it was 10:33. He remembered that they had promised the baby-sitter to be home before 11:00 P.M. and stopped at a convenience store to get some change. So it had to be around 10:50 when he passed the Davis mansion. This would have been at least an hour before Stan Farr and Priscilla arrived. As Racehorse excused the witness, he walked by the jury box with that *who do you suppose was in that car?* expression, scratching his head and rolling his eyes.

The defense had made its point. There was considerable doubt now about what time things took place. There was a gap of twenty to fifty-seven minutes, an insignificant amount of time measured against all that had happened but enough time to allow for a conspiracy. The large car seen entering and leaving the mansion grounds needed some clarification, and the defense called its next witness to establish that Cullen Davis was driving his pickup on the night of the killings. Jake Smith, night cashier of the parking garage in the Continental National Bank Building where Cullen parked both his pickup and his white-on-blue Cadillac, testified that Davis had left the garage at 5:30 P.M. on August 2, driving the pickup truck. Jake Smith could say for a fact that Cullen's Cadillac was still in its parking place at midnight when he got off duty. "I could see it from my booth," Smith said positively. "Mr. Davis's car stayed right there!" To support his memory, the night cashier produced his log from the night of August 2—a list of the license numbers of all the cars still at the garage when Smith checked out at midnight. "Yep, there it is right there," Jake said, pointing to the list. Smith added that he didn't see Cullen or the pickup again that night.

"Hell, what does that prove?" Joe Shannon said during the recess. "Does anyone believe that Cullen Davis didn't have access to another large, expensive car?" During cross-examinations, the prosecution used the garage records to trace the comings and goings of Cullen's two vehicles in the days just prior to the murders. On the evening of July 29, Jake Smith recalled, Cullen parked the pickup behind the Cadillac, removed something from the Cadillac trunk and placed it in the pickup, then left in the pickup. The following night, July 30, the pickup was in its parking place when Smith made his check at 11:15 P.M., but it was gone the following morning when the day cashier made a new check. Since this was a weekend and the garage didn't keep logs on weekends, there was no way to show how many times the two vehicles entered and left on Saturday afternoon or Sunday. Smith had already told about Cullen leaving in his pickup on Monday, August 2. On the morning of August 3, the pickup was parked in *another* garage across the street, and the Cadillac was parked in the driveway of Karen Master's house. What did it all mean? Only that sometime after midnight, Cullen or someone returned the pickup and took the Cadillac.

It was Halloween Eve when Haynes, Burleson, and the other attorneys met and decided the time had come to present Cullen Davis's alibi—Karen Master. Karen would testify that in the early morning hours of August 3, she woke up at 12:40 and saw Cullen asleep beside her. She had gone to bed around 9:00 or 9:30 P.M. and couldn't say what time he came home, but she was sure he was there at 12:40 A.M. She remembered looking at the digital clock on the nightstand. As with some of the other witnesses, the defense knew it ran a calculated risk by putting Karen Master on the witness stand. She would have to admit to the jury that Cullen had lived at her house from September 1975 until the morning of August 3 when he was arrested. Having made much hay of the fact that Priscilla was shacking up, it might be embarrassing to shed some light on *Cullen's* private love life. It was difficult to explain why many of the same people who thought Priscilla so shameless for bedding down with assorted characters saw nothing wrong with Cullen shacking up with Karen, unless it was the fact that Karen was ten years younger than Priscilla and not nearly as independent. Who could tell, in ten years she might *be* Priscilla. People talked a lot about the money that Priscilla spent on clothes, but nobody thought it curious that Karen was always the model of fashion in suede and leather and fine furs. They envied her, but there was nothing malicious in their envy. A man might perceive Priscilla as a threat, but not Karen. Something else bothered the defense attorneys—when Karen had testified before the grand jury and again at the bond hearing shortly after the killings, she said nothing about waking up at 12:40 A.M. Though Haynes hadn't yet joined the defense team at the time Karen appeared at the two hearings, he had an explanation for her failure to supply an alibi that might have spared her live-in lover many months in a jail cell. "Back then 12:40 didn't do us any good," he said. "They were playing games with the times then. We knew that grand juries ask loose, sloppy questions and play fast and free with numbers—'When did you kill your grandma and do you drive a 1948 Ford?' That's the sort of thing grand juries ask. It was only after we nailed them down on times that Karen's testimony had any meaning."

To those who had endured two months of jury selection and more than two months of testimony, Karen Master was an object of fascination, possibly because it was so difficult to assess her role in these bizarre happenings. Karen was a mature and no doubt courageous woman who had cared for her two handicapped children with a minimum of complaint, but in many ways she seemed painfully dependent on those around her. She was pretty in the way that a doll is pretty, with bright sunflower eyes and a smile as innocent as fresh paint. Because she was a potential witness, Karen wasn't allowed in the courtroom, and yet she always seemed to be there—chatting in the hallway and in the judge's waiting room with secretaries, reporters, friends, looking after things, caring for her children, preparing elaborate lunches that she would share with Cullen and his people, always waiting for something. Day after day, *waiting*, her composure and her faith seemingly unshaken, Karen's very presence in Amarillo gave force to a twisted logic in defense of the man she loved. The wife of a local attorney, who specialized in education for the handicapped and had worked with Karen's younger son, said, "I *know* Cullen didn't do it because I know Karen Master. She is a wonderful mother. A woman like that wouldn't live with a killer."

As she took the witness stand and began to tell her story, Karen was almost a caricature of sweetness and composure. Hands folded in her lap, she listened attentively to each question that Racehorse Haynes asked, then turned in exaggerated slow motion and smiled to the jury as she answered. One cynic of the press declared that she had obviously been rehearsed for this once-in-a-lifetime role.

With Haynes feeding her the questions, Karen described the events of August 2–3 as she recalled them. It was a normal morning, she said. Cullen left for his office around 7:30 or 8:00 A.M., driving his Cadillac. She took her two children to school and spent the remainder of the morning and part of the afternoon at a new beauty shop she'd heard about. Late in the afternoon she took the children to a snow-cone stand. Somewhere around 5:00 P.M. Cullen's secretary called and told her he would be late, which wasn't unusual; Cullen often came home after Karen and the children were asleep. Her friend Sherry Jones telephoned around 6:30 P.M., inviting Karen and Cullen to dinner. Karen recalled telling her friend: "No, it's already prepared. It's in the oven. He's going to be late for dinner." Sherry Jones called again about 8:30 P.M. Karen didn't remember what they talked about. (One of the many rumors that circulated was that Sherry Jones called a third time, around 11:30 P.M., at which time Karen told her she was worried about Cullen and wanted to go look for him. But Karen denied this.) Somewhere around 9:00 or 9:30 P.M., Karen continued, she took a sleeping pill and went to bed. This was earlier than her normal bedtime, but Karen remembered feeling tired.

"And what is the next thing you recall?" Haynes asked.

"I awoke very briefly at 12:40. I raised up and looked at the digital clock. Cullen was in bed. He appeared to be asleep. He was wearing just his shorts and was half uncovered. I went back to sleep."

The next thing she knew, Karen told the jury, it was about 4:00 or 4:15 (she apparently didn't look at the clock), and the telephone was ringing. She walked around to the other side of the bed and answered. It was Ken Davis, wanting to talk to his younger brother. She recalled that the conversation between the brothers was brief, no more than three minutes. She heard Cullen say, "Oh, no! My God! Really! Who was shot?"

Q: And what did you do next?

A: I got up. I walked to Cullen's side of the bed. He was awake, laying down. I sat down on the bed. We looked at each other. The phone rang again immediately. I picked it up. It was a male voice. Officer Ford of the police department. He asked to speak to Mr. Davis.

Just to clear the air, Racehorse then asked, "Has and does Cullen Davis assist you financially?" Karen turned to the jury as she answered yes. In conclusion Racehorse asked, "Are you in love with him?" And again Karen turned in slow motion, smiled at the jury, and said, "Yes."

Joe Shannon opened his cross-examination by inquiring why Karen Master kept turning and smiling at the jury. Karen turned to the jury, paused, smiled, and said: "I have not had an opportunity to look at the jury until now. I think they are very interesting people, don't you?" Shannon was immediately sorry that he had asked, and he moved on to other questions about her activities both before and after the killings, leading her to August 12, 1976, the day she appeared before the Tarrant County grand jury. Yes, Karen remembered the day. Shannon opened a copy of the grand jury transcript as he considered his next question; theoretically, in fact legally, Karen Master should not have disclosed to the defense *anything* said in the grand jury room, but Shannon was fairly certain she had. He didn't intend to make an issue of it. It was much more important that the jury concentrate on the questions he was about to ask. Approaching the witness with the transcript in his hands, Shannon asked: "And do you remember being asked the question: 'Between midnight and 4:00 A.M. what is the first thing you remember?' And do you remember answering: 'I do not remember the time. The phone rang and both of us woke up'?"

Karen pursed her lips as though trying to think hard, then shook her head; she didn't remember the exact question and answer. Without waiting for a reply, Shannon asked if she recalled telling Det. C. R. Davis, "The first thing I knew, the phone was ringing." Karen answered with an emphatic "No!" Well, Shannon said, holding up another document, she certainly didn't tell Detective Davis that she woke up at 12:40 and saw Cullen in bed.

Q: Did you tell Sherry Jones on the morning of August 3, "He took off his clothes and lay down on the bed and went to sleep"?

A: No, not in those exact words.

Q: Did you tell her, "I thought he came home between 12:30 and 1:00"?

A: Not that I recall.

Q: Were you less precise with Sherry than you are with this jury now?

A: That is correct.

Very early in the trial Dowlen ruled that it would be improper for the jury to know that the defendant had been denied bail; therefore the state was not allowed to mention the bond hearing nine days after the murder. It was therefore incumbent on the prosecutor to ask his questions gingerly, referring only to "your previous testimony." Shannon went about his business in a clear, professional manner, establishing that on at least three occasions when authorities had asked about that night, Karen had not once mentioned waking up and seeing Cullen in bed at 12:40. She had told her friends Rosemary Mabe and Sherry Jones about 12:40; wasn't it curious that three times when she had opportunities to clear Cullen's name—she had not *once* mentioned the alibi?

Shannon turned her attention now to the night of August 4, to a conversation she had with Cullen Davis outside Schick Hospital in Fort Worth. Shannon was curious about the nature of this conversation.

Q: Did you tell the grand jury that you had to satisfy yourself what time Cullen got home?

A: No.

Q (reading from the grand jury transcript): "Well, of course Cullen prefaced our conversation with the fact that his attorneys advised him not to discuss the case. But I asked him to satisfy in my own mind what time he got home, and he said a little before 11:00."

Karen didn't answer, but neither did she appear shattered by the apparent contradiction.

Q: Wasn't the reason that you had to satisfy your own mind that you didn't wake up until 4:00 when the *phone rang?*

A: That is not correct.

Q: In that conversation outside Schick Hospital, didn't Cullen tell you that he had worked at the office, then gone to the chiropractor, then back to the office to work another two or three hours? Then he went to eat. Then he came home. He got home a little before 11:00.

A: Yes, I told the grand jury that.

Q: But now you deny it?

A: I was confused.

Q: When was the first time you told any lawyer for Cullen Davis that he was home with you at 12:40?

A: About the same time I talked to the grand jury. I can't recall exactly.

Shannon wanted to ask her forbidden questions about the bond hearing, but he knew that violating court orders could blow their whole case. As it turned out, he didn't have to; Karen did it herself. Apparently confused by his repeated references to a "prior court hearing," she finally blurted out, "Are you referring to the bond hearing?"

The words were hardly out of her mouth before Haynes was on his feet requesting permission to approach the bench. By now it was late afternoon. The jury looked tired. Shannon had time for one more question before Dowlen recessed for the weekend. His question was, "Isn't it a fact that you didn't take the stand and testify even though your attorneys knew you had this information?"

"That's true," Karen acknowledged.

But *why?*

"It didn't seem relevant," she replied.

On Monday morning, October 31, Shannon again directed Karen Master's attention to her testimony before the grand jury, nine days after the shooting. Again, Karen answered that it didn't seem relevant to tell the grand jury about waking up at 12:40. Besides, she said, "The grand jury did not ask me that."

Shannon proceeded to quote from the grand jury transcript.

Shannon: Question: "Now between the hours of 12:00 midnight and 4:00 A.M., *when* is the first thing you remember and what time was it?" Answer: "I do not remember the time. The phone rang and both of us were asleep."

Karen: I understood the question to mean in effect, "When is the first thing you remember hearing?"

Shannon continued to grill Karen Master about her testimony before the grand jury, and Karen continued to insist that she had told the truth.

Karen: At that time 12:40 didn't prove guilt or innocence either way. It had no relevance. It didn't seem significant.

Q: And you told the grand jury the whole truth?

A: Yes, I told the whole truth.

Q: And you didn't know on August 12 the time of the murders?

A: No, sir.

Q: And that's the very reason, is it not, why you didn't tell the grand jury about that man, Thomas Cullen Davis, lying in bed with you . . . because you didn't *know* what time it was supposed to be!

A: No, that's not true.

And why, Shannon demanded to know, hadn't she apprised Det. C. R. Davis of this piece of pertinent information?

A: I found out later that C. R. Davis had been hired by Priscilla Davis to do personal work for her. I didn't think it was appropriate [to tell him].

Shannon pointed out for the jury that Karen was also misinformed on this point. Priscilla hired several off-duty policemen as bodyguards, but C. R. Davis wasn't one of them.

There was one final segment to Cullen's alibi. The defense called James Mabe, a business and social acquaintance, who testified that on the night of the murders Cullen called his home and discussed a trip to Mexico that Mabe and his wife, Rosemary, had planned with Cullen and Karen. Mabe recalled that the phone call came at 12:15 A.M. The witness could not say for certain that Cullen telephoned from Karen Master's home, only that that's where Cullen said he was calling from. As Joe Shannon pointed out later, the call to Mabe was not only suspiciously "convenient," it sounded downright phony. Mabe said that Cullen called to ask about travel visas for the trip. Cullen Davis would have qualified as an expert on travel visas; he must have known that all the documentation needed to enter Mexico was a passport, a birth certificate, or even a Texas voter registration certificate. So why would he be calling Mabe after midnight *except* to create an alibi? Shannon's cross-examination of Karen Master and James Mabe didn't totally destroy the alibi, but it shot it through with large holes.

Cullen later supplied his own version of the alibi to members of the media, contradicting Karen's story that he told her he arrived home "a little before 11:00." Cullen told reporters that on the evening of August 2 he worked late, ate alone, went to a movie, and arrived home at 12:15 A.M.

CHAPTER 13

It was early November when the first swirling snow blew down the Great Plains, snarling traffic at Amarillo Airport and at times obliterating highways. Lawyers, reporters, and witnesses attempting to reach Amarillo had to deplane at Lubbock and travel the final 100 miles by bus. It was a spectacular and frightening experience: when the wind blew, as it did almost constantly, it was impossible to distinguish the highways from the endless track of white swirling powder. Under the best conditions the Potter County Courthouse could charitably be described as cozy, but now that winter was approaching, the narrow hallways and dim offices resembled a refugee camp.

W. T. Rufner returned to Amarillo.

To set the stage for Rufner's appearance before the jury, the defense first called Jerry Thomas to describe the fight that he and Rufner had at the mansion in May of 1975. Thomas testified that he hit Rufner only after T-man appeared to be reaching in his pocket for "a knife or a gun." Next, a Fort Worth pharmacist told the jury that in the weeks just prior to the murders Priscilla ordered hundreds of Percodan and Percoset (a similar painkiller) from the Summit Park Pharmacy. In the six weeks before the killings, pharmacist Daryl Spence said Priscilla filled prescriptions for 450 Percodan. Another pharmacist, Ollie Chote, who worked for Whitten Pharmacy, showed that Priscilla had juggled doctors and pharmacies to obtain still more painkillers. In the four weeks prior to August 2, she had filled a prescription for 250 Percodan at Whitten Pharmacy—this in addition to the 450 pills she got from Summit Park Pharmacy.

Dr. Thomas Simons, who along with the surgeon who had operated on Priscilla prescribed most of the painkillers, testified that in addition to Priscilla he had also treated Stan Farr, W. T. Rufner, and Sandy Guthrie Myers. The doctor kept no independent records to show how many Percodan he had prescribed for Priscilla, but he recalled that the prescriptions began in July 1975. The period that most interested the defense, however, was July 28–30, 1976. The defense contended that on July 29 Sandy Myers ran into Priscilla in Dr. Simons's waiting room. This is when Priscilla supposedly told Sandy Myers, "Something heavy is coming down." On the morning of July 30, a few hours before the scheduled divorce trial, Priscilla visited Dr. Simons's office to pick up a letter that he had prepared stating a medical justification for again delaying the divorce proceedings. "She told me she was in no condition to appear in court," Dr. Simons testified. "After examining her, I agreed."

"But isn't it a fact that you agreed to write the letter even before she came to your office?" Racehorse Haynes asked the doctor.

"Yes, based on her emotional state at the time," Dr. Simons admitted.

On the morning that he was to begin testifying, W. T. Rufner woke in his Amarillo motel room pursued by dark visions and surrounded by unsold T-shirts. Though he had reduced the price from $100 to $10, T-man had many more T-shirts than customers, and though the promised interrogation by Racehorse Haynes seemed sure to punch up his business, there were other, more serious problems to consider. Not the least of these was the fact he was still on probation from his drug bust of March 1974. T-man knew that some of the questions he would be asked might not sit well with his probation officer, particularly since Haynes was likely to concentrate on the months *after* he was placed on probation. T-man had never seen the inside of a prison, but he knew that he might if Haynes established that he violated the terms of his probation. On advice of his attorney, Rufner decided to take the Fifth Amendment on any incriminating questions. To settle his nerves, T-man downed a handful of Valium with a few slugs of Scotch. He looked around the cluttered room for his pocket knife, then remembered that a deputy had taken it away from him the previous day as he sat in the judge's reception room peeling an apple. Damned if he wouldn't rather be somewhere else.

Haynes opened by asking Rufner's occupation. "I'm a union electrician," T-man responded. "I also work on motorcycles. I'm also in the T-shirt business." Several jurors smiled when he admitted the T-shirts were "a relatively new enterprise." Apparently some of the jurors had already got word.

Q: Are you in love with Priscilla Lee Davis?

A: I'm in love with a lot of women. Some of them I haven't even met.

More smiles from the jury.

Haynes had never met Rufner until that morning, but he wasn't surprised at the answers. He anticipated that T-man would milk the jury for a few laughs. Haynes was content to guide the witness through the ups and downs of his tempestuous relationship with Priscilla, particularly the parts about feuding, fighting, fornicating, and getting stoned. In a way, Rufner's candor worked for the defense. In her own testimony Priscilla had portrayed the Boston episode as an accidental meeting and had described Rufner as "obnoxious," but that wasn't how T-man remembered it.

Q: While in Boston, Massachusetts, were you paired up together?

A: I don't know what you mean by paired up. We weren't tied up together.

Q: You weren't tied up. Did you keep close quarters, though?

A: I had a place to sleep. She had a place to sleep.

Q: There was not mutuality? You didn't share the same couch, so to speak?

A: Yes, we shared.

It was hardly necessary for Haynes to point out to the jury that the sharing of a couch in Boston took place at least four months before Cullen and Priscilla separated. T-man declined to answer about narcotics at his three-day birthday celebration in June or the July 4 Winnebago trip to College Station, but again it was apparent that Priscilla and Rufner continued to frolic behind Cullen's back. Haynes wanted the jury to share his understanding of the Winnebago trip, the cast of characters assembled by Priscilla, the Queen Bee, how she had not only allowed but encouraged her daughter Dee and other teenage girls to travel in the company of men twice their age, men who had records of drug arrests and no qualms about soliciting sexual favors from available nymphets.

Shortly after Priscilla filed for divorce on July 30, 1974, W. T. acknowledged that "we fell in love." By early September he was spending the night at 4200 Mockingbird.

"You moved in, did you not?" Haynes asked.

"I had some of my clothes there," Rufner admitted. "Several pairs of cutoffs, a few T-shirts, a pair of jeans." Rufner added that "I've always had more than one lady in my life." But in September he started dating Priscilla "exclusively." Within a week or two, Rufner continued, he had stashed most of his wardrobe at 4200 Mockingbird. Haynes established that Dee Davis continued to live at the mansion, and in short order Sandy Myers, Larry Myers, and a number of others took up more or less permanent residence.

The defense attorney went on to establish that Rufner usually had a key to the mansion and that he was familiar with the security system and knew the locations of both the upstairs and downstairs safes. In fact, Haynes continued, hadn't Rufner boasted about his knowledge of the security system and even given several friends, including Danny McDaniels, a tour of the basement where the elaborate panel of electronic instruments was located? Rufner admitted that "out of professional curiosity" he once showed McDaniels and others the basement wiring. Haynes asked if Rufner knew a man named Horace Copeland and if he once demonstrated the security system for Copeland. The witness answered that he didn't know Copeland "much" and had no recollection of showing him how the security worked.

Haynes questioned Rufner about other out-of-town trips in the company of Priscilla. How about the trip to the motorcycle races in Ontario, California? Yes, T-man recalled. And the trip to Waco, and the trip to Houston. He recalled those too. And hadn't they also made a trip to Oklahoma City?

"If I'm not mistaken," Rufner said, nodding his head.

"How could you be *mistaken* about going to *Oklahoma City* with *Priscilla Davis*?!" Haynes demanded to know. If Rufner was playing for the jury, Haynes felt he could do no less. It pleased him that the jury seemed amused by his last observation.

Calling Rufner's attention to yet another altercation with Priscilla, Haynes asked, "Didn't she tell you at that time to take your junk and get out?"

T-man smiled as he told the jury, "She told me that more than once."

"And so you took your several pairs of cutoffs and jeans and moved out. But you returned, did you not?"

"Not with as many clothes," Rufner replied.

Haynes established that this pattern of feuding and making up continued until the incident of May 1975, when Rufner wrecked Priscilla's car in front of the Old San Francisco Saloon and later got creamed by Jerry Thomas. Wasn't this the last straw, so to speak? Yes, Rufner remembered it well. Rufner said, "It didn't feel like home to me anymore. I felt more comfortable with my mother and my dog."

By now the jury must have had a degree of sympathy for W. T. Rufner. He was a rogue, but a rogue with charm. Several jurors smiled when T-man summed up how it was, living with Priscilla: "There were mornings when it was total harmony. There were mornings when it was total hell." Rufner didn't come across as a killer. On the contrary, it must have appeared to the jury that he was the one usually in danger of getting killed. The defense had failed to prove that Rufner had any kind of relationship with Stan Farr or Horace Copeland; in fact, Rufner had pretty much dropped out of the scene by the time Farr moved in. The only unanswered question was why in the weeks just after the murders he had moved with such determination to establish an alibi, cajoling and perhaps threatening Carmey Green to sign a statement swearing he was with her on the evening of August 2.

When his first day on the witness stand ended, T-man and two reporters rushed straight for the bar at his motel and ran up a $96 tab, which Rufner insisted on charging to Cullen.

While W. T. Rufner was unwinding and sampling the pleasures of Amarillo, Joe Shannon was jogging down a dusty road behind the Holiday Inn, contemplating his cross-examination. Shannon had decided that the trial was a perfect time to lose weight. By dieting and jogging four or five miles each night, the assistant DA had lost thirty pounds. Shannon was now in charge of the prosecution. Tim Curry had gone back to Fort Worth to supervise prosecution of a multi-million-dollar fencing operation and generally sort through the backlog of cases that had accumulated during the Cullen Davis trial. But he was leaving Cullen's case in the hands of his three top assistants, Shannon, Tolly Wilson, and Marvin Collins.

For all their setbacks, Shannon still felt their case was going well. Rufner's testimony had done a fair amount of damage, but nothing like the prosecution expected. Some of the damage could be repaired in cross-examination. Shannon couldn't do much about the lies Priscilla told regarding her sexual adventures with Rufner, but he could clear up the part about Carmey Green and the alibi that Rufner had worked so quickly to obtain. In fact, Shannon saw an opportunity to make a point of his own in the cross-examination of Rufner.

T-man appeared considerably more composed when Shannon began his questioning the following day.

Q: Were you afraid for your life in late 1976 and early 1977?

A: Yes, sir.

Q: And were you afraid that one of these days you would wake up dead with a certain pistol in your pocket?

A: Yes, sir.

Q: Had you heard there was money on the street and there were people who would assist in making you a patsy in this double homicide?

A: Yes, sir.

Q: Did you ever hear that the defense was planning to pin this whole deal on you?

A: Many times.

Q: And was that your concern when you went to Carmey Green?

A: Yes, sir.

Q: Did you hear that it would be easier for the defense if both of you [Rufner and Green] were eliminated?

A: Yes, sir.

Q: Did you communicate this to Ms. Green?

A: I did.

Q: Did you hear that the plan of the defense was to try to lay this whole thing on a dead man?

A: I did.

Q: And did you hear that dead men tell no tales?

A: I know that to be a fact.

Shannon knew that the defense would continue pointing the finger at Horace Copeland, but the point that he wanted the jury to keep in mind was this: *dead men tell no tales*. Rufner's alibi was at least as good as Cullen's, and Copeland couldn't defend himself. That night as he jogged along the road behind the Holiday Inn, Shannon had another thought. "Their case really boils down to ABC," he told investigator Rodney Hinson. *"Anybody But Cullen."*

The defense had squeezed all they could from Rufner, but Haynes wanted to leave the jury with one final reminder of how the Queen Bee operated. He called ex-teenagers Becky Ferguson and Valerie Marazzi. Valerie, who was seventeen at the time, described the free use of drugs and open sex aboard the Winnebago.

For the next several days the defense called a series of witnesses to establish that Priscilla had been less than truthful in her testimony about Stan Farr and that Horace Copeland had a motive for killing Farr. Dowlen had postponed ruling on the admissibility of Sandy Guthrie Myers's testimony about the accidental meeting with Priscilla in the doctor's office, but now the judge viewed it in a new light. Since this part of Sandy Myers's testimony was offered as impeachment of Priscilla's earlier denial, Dowlen let the jury hear Myers's version of the conversation two days before the murders.

Myers said that Priscilla started the conversation by inquiring how Larry Myers was doing in the state prison. "Then she became very intense and said, 'Something heavy is coming down,'" Myers recalled. "I asked if it had to do with the divorce and she said no, but she couldn't discuss it with me at the doctor's office." At this point Dowlen excused the jury, taking the sting out of the remainder of Sandy Myers's recollections. Earlier, when Haynes had asked Rufner if he ever threatened Priscilla or Stan Farr, T-man replied angrily, "That's a lie!" But Sandy Myers recalled a morning in March 1975 when she and Rufner were in the kitchen of the mansion and Rufner appeared badly upset by the prospect of being replaced by Stan Farr. According to Myers, Rufner told her, "I'll get that tall son of a bitch and I'll get that cunt." Myers also remembered running into Rufner at Dr. Simons's office a few weeks after the murder, at which time Rufner supposedly told her: "They aren't gonna stick me with this one. The threats I made about Priscilla and Stan, I've got a good alibi."

In support of their contention that Priscilla was extremely nervous, and apparently expecting trouble before August 2, the defense called Sylvia Meek, a private investigator, who told the jury that Priscilla apparently had a "premonition" of impending danger because she tried to hire Meek as a bodyguard on July 5. Debbie Patton, a friend of the family, testified that on July 31 Priscilla "seemed very worried . . . upset . . . nervous." Debbie Patton was a regular patron at the Rhinestone Cowboy in the spring and summer of 1976, and she told of seeing Stan Farr and Horace Copeland talking "in the back room" of the bar on more than one occasion. About that same time, Debbie Patton continued, she opened Priscilla's purse to borrow her lipstick and saw a silver-plated pistol.

Becky Burns, a Fort Worth barmaid, told of walking into the kitchen of the Rhinestone Cowboy and observing Farr and Copeland snorting cocaine with country music star David Allan Coe. Burns testified that on several occasions she saw Farr and Copeland with large sums of money. She knew that the two men had a "gambling activity" at the Pelican Bay Yacht Club in the spring of 1976.

"Did you know that in addition to his other activities, Horace Copeland engaged in trafficking narcotics?" Haynes asked Becky Burns.

"Well, I knew he was dealing in narcotics," she answered.

The defense then called another former Rhinestone Cowboy waitress, Polly Ware, Horace Copeland's onetime girlfriend, who had caused much confusion early in the trial when she called her attorney, Charles Baldwin, and said she thought she could produce the murder weapon—Copeland's R & G Industries .38 pistol. The gun hadn't checked out, but it had created sensational headlines, as had Baldwin's comments to the press that Farr feared Copeland was planning to kill him. Until Ware took the witness stand, the jury knew nothing of these allegations.

Polly Ware told the jury that she lived with Copeland from October 1975 until January 1976. A month or so after they broke up, Ware said, she learned that Copeland was married. In July 1976 there was an incident in the Rhinestone Cowboy in which Copeland grabbed her and roughed her up. That's when she asked attorney Baldwin to seek a civil injunction against her former lover.

Baldwin, who followed Ware to the witness stand, told the jury that he subpoenaed Farr as a witness in the legal proceedings, but Farr refused to testify because he feared reprisals from Copeland. Baldwin testified that Farr told him: "You don't know Horace. If he won't do it, they will." *They* apparently referred to the friends and associates of Horace Copeland.

By now the defense had clearly established a relationship between Farr and Copeland, contradicting Priscilla's contention that the two men were only casual acquaintances. Priscilla had told the jury that Horace Copeland never visited the mansion, but the defense called another witness, former TCU football player Randy Garmen, who said he accompanied Copeland and Copeland's son, Rick, to a party at 4200 Mockingbird. Garmen didn't remember any drugs, but at one point in the party he saw "Horace and Priscilla Davis go in this small room and close the door." It must have appeared to the jury that Farr and Copeland had *something* cooking—there was the trip to Mexico, the white powdery substance that several witnesses saw them put in their noses, and the large sums of money that Becky Burns recalled. Other witnesses had testified that Priscilla thought Farr had referred to Priscilla as "my meal ticket" and "my investment." Then, too, there were stories about money missing from the till at the Rhinestone Cowboy.

Ronnie Bradshaw, co-owner of the Rhinestone Cowboy, took the stand to support much of the previous testimony. He testified that Horace Copeland was a regular at the club and that Farr was fired about two weeks before the murders and after the cash shortages were discovered. He also recalled Copeland's troubles with Polly Ware. It was about that time, Bradshaw told the jury, that Farr asked him to return a gun that Bradshaw had locked in his desk drawer. "He told me he needed the gun back because he was scared of Horace Copeland," the club co-owner said. "He told me, 'Ronnie, I've got to have the gun back. I've been subpoenaed to testify in the Horace-Polly thing.' He said he didn't think Horace would get him, but he might have somebody else do it."

The prosecution scored an unexpected point in cross-examination when Bradshaw admitted that Farr had also expressed fear that "he would have some trouble with Cullen Davis." Whatever Farr's reasons for wanting the gun, he never had a chance to use it. The gun was found under the seat of his Thunderbird after the murders.

To nail down their theory that Stan Farr was the primary target, the defense had one more witness—Farr's sexy nineteen-year-old secret lover. If Kimberly Lewis's appearance in Amarillo came as a surprise to the prosecution, imagine Priscilla's reaction when news reached Fort Worth. The ex-TCU coed with the long, light brown hair and cover girl face told the jury that she and Farr were keeping secret rendezvous from March 1976 until the day of his murder. They would usually meet at the housing project that had become Farr's latest venture. Lewis testified that in the week before the killings Stan carried a gun in his car. "He said he needed it because people were after him," she said. When Kimberly Lewis last spoke to Farr a few hours before the shooting, "he sounded very nervous."

Haynes and Burleson felt that their case had about reached the point of diminishing returns. Unless their investigators could track down the potential witness they had code-named Mr. Dynamite, the defense had shed about all the light on the subject that the jury could tolerate. The trial was in its eleventh week. The jurors had sat through sixty days of testimony. It had been more than four months since the judge had sealed off the fourth floor of the Executive Inn, and even though the jurors continued to receive limited family and conjugal visits, it was apparent that the twelve people chosen to decide Cullen Davis's fate were approaching the breaking point. Without normal sexual and social outlets, emotional tension was bound to erupt into personality clashes among the jurors. Studies of such cases proved that people "tend to make decisions out of desperation." The one thing nobody wanted at this point was a divided jury.

The season's first major blizzard was roaring down from the north that second week in November when the defense team gathered in its apartment compound for a final review of strategy. Steve Sumner, who had been on the road again, had nothing encouraging to report. Sumner had at least fifty new witnesses on his string, but their tales of drug dealings and back-alley intrigue added very little to what the jury had already heard. The investigators still hadn't cornered Mr. Dynamite. Worse yet, of the hundreds of people that Sumner and his detectives had interviewed, there wasn't a single witness who remembered seeing Cullen Davis on the night of August 2. It appeared that Karen Master would be the only witness who could establish an alibi for the defendant. In another two weeks it would be Thanksgiving, and all the lawyers agreed on one thing; they didn't want the jurors celebrating Thanksgiving locked away from their families.

The way Haynes saw it, there were only two more witnesses necessary to the completion of their case. Racehorse wanted the jury to hear testimony from Katherine Brooks, Horace Copeland's former business partner, who would tell about Copeland's comings and goings on the night of the murder. And he wanted to call to the witness stand a nationally known drug expert to reinforce their "two-worlder" theory. If Sumner hadn't uncovered a bombshell witness by then, the defense would rest its case. Both sides would still have an opportunity to call rebuttal witnesses. If the state wanted to hold the jury all the way through Christmas, let the state assume the risk of a jury mutiny.

But Sumner called their attention to one final item on the night's agenda—the disturbing and recurring story that on the night of August 2 someone else had visited the Davis estate. For several weeks they had heard the rumor that a would-be burglar about to enter the mansion was frightened off by the unexpected appearance of a car or a person. Sumner had relegated the rumor to his nut file, but it wouldn't stay down. "It's coming now from four different sources," Sumner told the others. Now they had a *name*, along with a sketchy report—it seemed that a Fort Worth nurseryman who had been pressing Priscilla for an overdue bill had secretly visited the estate on the night of the murders. The way Sumner heard it, the nurseryman, Uewayne Polk, had ridden his motorcycle down the hike and bike trail that ran along the Trinity River bottom adjacent to the estate. He parked his bike and crossed the river on foot, then crept across the mansion grounds. His intention was to take back some of his plants. The mysterious nurseryman was about to enter an unlocked door beside the swimming pool when he was frightened off by something or someone. "Unbelievable!" Burleson said. "But I don't see how we can ignore it." Burleson was certain that the prosecution had also heard the story. A Fort Worth attorney who had been contacted by Uewayne Polk believed that the story had also been leaked to a Fort Worth newspaperman. "Get on the phone to that lawyer," Haynes told Sumner. "Tell him to get Mr. Uewayne Polk up here. Get him here tonight!"

Later, Burleson described what happened that night: "Steve and Mike and Race and I stayed up most of the night talking to Polk. We pounded on him, asking questions about every aspect of the case. There was no way we were going to put a bombshell witness on the stand at that stage of the game if there was any chance he would blow up in our face. Even after questioning him all night, we still didn't know whether to believe him. We told him to go back to Fort Worth while we checked out his story."

Haynes asked Sumner for an opinion. Was Polk's story logical?

"I don't know," Sumner admitted. "It doesn't fit with any of our other information. I think we've got to consider this as separate and apart from the rest of the defense."

Burleson decided to fly to Fort Worth and check Polk's story himself. To the lawyer's surprise, it seemed to check. Burleson even walked down to the river bottom to determine for himself if it was possible for a person to cross on foot. "The water was only two or three inches deep when I checked it," Burleson said. "I called the Corps of Engineers.

Their records showed that it would have been about that shallow on the night of August 2."

Burleson collected other evidence—a photograph of Polk's motorbike and a copy of a business receipt the nurseryman had presented to Priscilla—then hurried back to Amarillo to confer with the other lawyers. Burleson still felt that Polk's story was unbelievable, but he recognized an even greater risk. What if they refused to call Polk to the stand? What if the *state* called him? And what if Polk suddenly changed his story and remembered that the man he saw creeping up to the mansion that night was Cullen Davis? Either way, Burleson was sure that the story would break in the *Fort Worth Star-Telegram* in the next day or two.

"If we're going to call him," Burleson said, "we better do it fast."

The next morning as Uewayne Polk and his attorney met with lawyers behind the closed doors of Judge Dowlen's chambers, rumors of a "bombshell" witness spread through the courthouse. From time to time reporters caught a glimpse of the mysterious, neatly dressed, bearded man and his attorney being quickly escorted along the hallway, but nobody could predict the testimony that would follow. "Is this your dynamite witness?" someone asked Sumner. "All I can tell you," Sumner said, "is hold on to your seat." Even reporters for the *Fort Worth Star-Telegram*, whose paper had agreed to hold the story for another day, had very little warning of what was about to happen.

Behind the closed doors of Dowlen's chambers, Haynes made a formal request: "Since we don't have a grand jury like the prosecution does, can we put him under oath in here?" Dowlen agreed that it was better to air Polk's testimony in secrecy, and Haynes proceeded to question the witness under oath.

"It was probably the most traumatic moment of the trial," Haynes said later. "Polk described the fellow he saw that night at the mansion, and it didn't sound like Cullen, but we didn't have a good picture of Cullen to show him. We decided to call Cullen into the judge's chambers. He wouldn't say anything . . . he'd just walk in, do a front, a left, and a right profile, then leave. That's what happened. Then I asked [Polk] the question: 'Well, is that the man you saw or not?' Just as I asked the question, my blood went cold. What if this was a trap set up by the prosecution? What if the SOB said *yes!*"

Polk played with a button on his vest, then answered firmly: "No."

There wasn't a vacant seat in the courtroom, or a square foot of unoccupied space in the hallway, as Uewayne Polk poured out his bizarre story to the jury. He began by explaining that he was a landscaper and part owner of the Wedgewood Nursery in Fort Worth. In the spring of 1975, Priscilla Davis called him to 4200 Mockingbird and asked him to draw up preliminary designs for both interior and exterior work on the mansion. Polk told the jury that he completed the designs but didn't hear again from Priscilla until May of 1976. She was planning a party and needed the work done as quickly as possible. Polk did the work on schedule and on June 7 presented her with a bill for $677, which she failed to pay. Polk said that he returned to the mansion in late June but again failed to collect his money. In July he tried two more times, both without results. Priscilla claimed that she lost the bill. Polk told her he would return with a new one.

Polk testified that he again appeared at 4200 Mockingbird on Monday, August 2, bill in hand. He remembered it was about midday when the maid let him in. Priscilla didn't come downstairs but agreed to talk to him on the telephone.

"At this point I got pretty mad," Polk said. "I could have talked to her by phone from the nursery. Priscilla said she was going to see Cullen in court that day."

On Priscilla's instructions, Polk said, he tacked the new bill to the bulletin board above the kitchen telephone. He decided that he would come back that night and take the plants that rightly belonged to him. Through a panel of glass he could see the two maids working in the kitchen. They had their backs to him. Polk unlocked the sliding glass doors separating the pool from the mansion lawn. Having supplied himself an entrance, he walked back toward the kitchen and departed by way of the breakfast room door.

Polk told the jury that it was about 7:00 P.M. when he arrived at his home near Eagle Mountain Lake. He ate dinner with his wife and read the evening paper. Around 9:00 P.M. he filled his trail bike with gas, loaded it in his truck, and drove to where the Loop 280 Bridge crosses the Trinity River, a spot about two miles from the Davis mansion. Wearing jeans and a dark shirt and carrying a burlap bag, Polk followed the trail as far as the Hulen Street Bridge. There he hid his bike in the brush, removed his shoes, and crossed the shallow stream heading in the direction of the mansion.

"I had my tow sack with me," he continued, explaining that he intended to use the bag to repossess his plants and shrubs. "I sat down under a tree to dry my feet and put my shoes on. I looked at my digital watch. It was 11:11. I remember thinking this was my lucky night."

While he was drying his feet and putting on his shoes, Polk saw a man with a sack over his shoulder walking toward the Hulen Street Bridge. "I thought he was a hobo," Polk told the jury. "It's close to the tracks, and a lot of hoboes hang around down there."

Polk testified that the man walked toward him. When he was about eight feet from where Polk sat, the man squatted, took out a cigarette lighter, and lighted a cigarette. That's when Polk got a good look at the man. He was five-eight to five-ten, chunky, and had very big eyes. "I could see white all around the pupils," Polk recalled. The man had no beard but wore his curly hair short. His face was round and his cheekbones were high. When the man finished his cigarette, Polk continued, "he headed toward the Davis mansion. The same direction I was headed."

For a few minutes Polk lost the man in the darkness, but as the nurseryman was approaching the northwest corner of the mansion, the corner nearest the pool area, he again caught sight of the man. "He was squatting down on his knees," Polk told the jury. "He put something on his head and walked toward the front of the house. I ran back [to some hedges] where it was dark. Then I saw a figure *inside* the pool area. I froze behind a palm. It was the same man I'd seen by the river."

At this point Racehorse Haynes asked his bombshell question: "Was the man you saw Cullen Davis?"

"He was definitely not Cullen Davis," said Polk, looking at the defendant.

"And what did you do then?"

"I ran back toward the river. I got back on my bike and went home."

Haynes asked Polk why he had waited more than a year to tell this strange and disturbing story.

"Out of fear," said Uewayne Polk. "Fear for my business. Fear of the man who really did it. Fear of Priscilla Davis's friends. I had built up a really good clientele. I couldn't see dragging it down."

Even before Dowlen could call a recess, reporters bolted for the door, scattering the groupies in a mad dash for the few telephones. It was like a scene out of *Front Page*. Those who were not burdened by deadlines stood numbly in the hallway, trying to digest the implications of what they had just heard. One of the first things that came to mind was the obvious contradiction over the security system: if Polk had unlocked the sliding door as he testified, Priscilla would have noticed the light on the security panel as she and Stan Farr left that night. Then there was the apparent impossibility of Polk attempting to carry away all those plants in a burlap bag. During the recess several new facts about the mystery witness emerged. "He told his lawyers he didn't want to talk to the state," Marvin Collins said. The state had known about Polk for at least a week and had also checked his story. "It's an insult to the intelligence of the jury," Tolly Wilson claimed. The state's investigation had revealed something else about Uewayne Polk's past—in January 1969 he had pleaded guilty to armed robbery and been sentenced to ten years' probation.

Joe Shannon used fewer than ten minutes to cross-examine Polk.

"How much have you been paid to come up here and tell that cock-and-bull story?" the outraged assistant district attorney demanded to know.

"Not a red penny," Polk replied.

"You just came here as a fair, good-hearted citizen?"

"I was worried about a man losing his life."

"And so you waited sixteen months to tell your story."

"I wanted to forget it."

"I have no more questions for *this* witness," said Shannon, taking his seat at the prosecution's table.

It had been weeks since anyone in Amarillo had talked to Priscilla, but at the lunch break several reporters telephoned her from Stanley Marsh's office. She had just heard Polk's testimony on the noon news and was enraged. "He's a lying goddamn mother fucker!" Priscilla said. "Did anybody ask him *how* he planned to repossess all those plants? They were all inside. There are ten or twelve plants around my bathtub . . . a little plant by the guest bath downstairs . . . three ming trees in the hallway. Maybe one by the pool. Isn't it just perfect that all these people are coming forward with their stories? Karen . . . James Mabe . . . after all these months they're coming forward. And that story about Stan skimming money at the Rhinestone Cowboy. Stan got fired because he knew who really was skimming."

After Uewayne Polk, the defense's final two witnesses were, to say the least, anticlimactic.

Katherine Brooks, who was in partnership with Horace Copeland in a bar called The Eyes of Texas, told the jury that on August 2 Copeland arrived at the club about 6:00 P.M. "He went directly to the office and locked the door," she said. "He stayed in the office about an hour. Then about 7:00 P.M. he came out and left. I didn't see him again that night." Brooks testified that when she again saw Copeland the following night, "he wouldn't talk" about the murders at the Davis mansion. In cross-examination the prosecution established that Katherine Brooks and Horace Copeland had dissolved their partnership in October 1976, eight months before Copeland was killed. "It was not a friendly breakup," the witness admitted. At the time of Copeland's death she was suing him, alleging that Copeland put his name on a deed of land belonging to her and used it to borrow $45,000 from a bank. The defense had one final question: what kind of car was Copeland driving on August 2, 1976? "A 1975 silver Cadillac," she replied.

On Friday afternoon, November 11, twelve weeks after the first witness appeared in Amarillo, the defense called to the stand Dr. Robert Miller, a nationally recognized expert on dangerous drugs. At considerable expense, the defense had brought him to Amarillo to detail the evils associated with the habitual use of the opiate-based drug Percodan. The jury seemed especially attentive as Dr. Miller described the devastating effects of the drug on a person's memory as well as that person's ability to perceive reality. When mixed with alcohol, Miller told Haynes, the drug had a "potentiating effect."

Q: Would that person [who mixed Percodan with alcohol] actually believe that a fictitious episode was true?

A: Yes. But it depends upon the individual. Some are more prone to do it than others.

On Monday morning, the prosecution called Uewayne Polk's estranged wife as a rebuttal witness.

Answering questions directed to her by Tolly Wilson, Paige Polk immediately defused the bombshell. It was true that Uewayne Polk made a mysterious, late night visit to the Davis mansion, she told the jury, but it wasn't the night of August 2.

"A few days before the murders, Uewayne told me he had been to the mansion that night but had not taken anything," Paige Polk testified. "He said he drove the truck in and took the dirt bike out of the truck and drove it to the riverbed . . . then went on foot through the trees toward the pool area of the house. He was outside and was considering messing with the glass, and then a few cars came up the driveway, so he left."

Even if the date had been correct, it would have been impossible for Polk to look at his digital watch and determine the time as 11:11 P.M., she added. Polk's watch hadn't worked for several months, not since Polk fell out of a boat and into the water. Finally Paige Polk said that she spoke to her husband by telephone the previous Wednesday, just before he left for Amarillo. A divorce court judge had ordered Polk to pay his estranged wife $75 a week, but he was "about $350 behind." Paige Polk said that she asked him about the money.

Q: What did he tell you?

A: That he was going to Amarillo, and as soon as he got back, he would pay me.

At this point the state requested a recess. While the prosecution was reviewing final strategy, Steve Sumner was eating a packaged sandwich on the courthouse steps. As Sumner was finishing his lunch, Rod Hinson, one of the investigators for the Tarrant County DA's office, came rushing down the courthouse steps.

"What's the hurry?" Sumner asked.

"Haven't you heard?" Hinson grinned. "We just rested our case."

Sumner took the courthouse steps four at a time, almost running down a groupie as he sprinted to the fifth floor where Haynes and the other defense lawyers were holding a secret caucus.

An hour later, Racehorse Haynes stood up, looked at Cullen, then at the jury, then at the judge, and announced, "At this time, the defense rests."

Shannon had guessed some weeks ago that the defense would not put Cullen on the witness stand, but Tolly Wilson and Marvin Collins were stunned. "I can't believe a defendant would come to West Texas and not get on the witness stand himself," Collins said. "If you're gonna try to float an alibi," Wilson remarked, "you sure as hell better take the witness stand." Racehorse Haynes claimed later that it was one of the hardest decisions of his career, but the consensus among defense lawyers was that "Cullen is very poor witness material. He doesn't emote. It's doubtful he could look sincere and honest." A skeptic might argue that Cullen didn't *have* an alibi, but perhaps he didn't need one. Of the entire cast of characters who had appeared with their sordid tales of duplicity and foul deeds, the only one who remained a total stranger to the jury was Cullen Davis.

As the lawyers closed themselves off in Dowlen's chambers to begin drawing up the charge that would be read to the jury on Wednesday, someone asked Cullen what he was thinking.

Cullen replied that he was thinking about going skiing. In fact, he had already made reservations for the Thanksgiving weekend.

On Wednesday, November 16, as the attorneys prepared to deliver their final arguments, Judge George Dowlen read his charge to the jury.

In charging the jury, it was necessary for Dowlen to explain the complicated statute of capital murder by which this case was being prosecuted—in order to find the defendant guilty of capital murder, the jury had to agree that he had first violated the state law against burglary. If the jury did not find the defendant guilty of capital murder, it would then consider the lesser charge of murder. But the key phrase in Dowlen's charge was "reasonable and moral certainty." In order to return a verdict of guilty, the jury would have to reach a reasonable and moral certainty that the defendant committed the crime, to the exclusion of all other possibilities. In other words, if any one of the twelve had a *reasonable doubt,* it was that juror's duty to bring in a verdict of not guilty.

Dowlen had allowed each side three and a half hours for closing arguments. By law, the state would both begin and end the arguments, but each side was permitted to allocate its time according to its own wishes.

Tolly Wilson opened for the state, reviewing in detail that bloody night at the mansion and pointing to Cullen Davis as the man in black who came there with the premeditated intention of "killing the source of all his troubles [Priscilla] and anyone else who got in his way." First, it was necessary to kill Andrea Wilborn. His second bullet was reserved for Priscilla, Wilson told the jury. Cullen assumed Priscilla was dead or dying when he dragged Stan Farr's body to the kitchen, but Priscilla was able to run into the courtyard. Cullen caught her, but the unexpected appearance of Bubba Gavrel and Bev Bass diverted his attention, and she was able to escape. "If Bubba Gavrel and Bev Bass hadn't arrived when they did," Wilson continued, "we'd have three unsolved murders . . . three bodies in the basement, and a bushy-haired stranger driving off." After apparently killing Gavrel and chasing Bass until it was obvious he couldn't catch her, Cullen then returned to look for Priscilla. Discovering the door locked, he reloaded and shot out the window and raced to the place he was certain she would be hiding—the master bedroom. Unable to find Priscilla and realizing that the police would soon be alerted, he dropped the plastic bag used to conceal his fingerprints and made his own escape.

As for the defense's claim of a conspiracy, Wilson said, the contention that two women running in opposite directions, one seriously wounded and the other frightened for her life . . . "the very idea is so far beyond human experience as to be ridiculous." The defense had made a great fuss about discrepancies in time, Wilson pointed out, but the main discrepancy was in the testimony of Robert Sawhill. Wilson had an explanation for this. "Sawhill was wrong," he said. Sawhill had *also* testified that while Bev Bass was seated in his car, she took out a cigarette and lighter, and yet "her cigarettes and lighter were found back at 4200 Mockingbird." Regarding the alibi, Karen Master had destroyed her own credibility by not telling it to the grand jury. And the testimony of Uewayne Polk was hardly worth rebutting. "Can you believe that he intended to put all those plants in that tow sack, get on his motorbike, and go back home?" Wilson asked the jury. "But . . . if just one of you twelve believes Uewayne Polk . . . if you have a *reasonable doubt* . . . then Polk did his job."

The defense selected Mike Gibson to lead off. Gibson pointed out that the state had called twenty-three witnesses and the defense had called forty-four, and the sum of the testimony "showed you the true color and character of Priscilla Davis." Just look at Priscilla Davis, Gibson challenged the jury: "All those young people around her . . . massive amounts of Percodan . . . illegal drugs. Priscilla claimed her relationship with W. T. Rufner was platonic, but W. T. called it love. And why was W. T. trying so hard to get an alibi?" Because he had a good idea who really did the killing, Gibson contended. He connected three pieces of seemingly unrelated testimony for the jury's consideration: (1) the allegation that shortly before the murders Stan Farr was flashing a large roll of money; (2) the testimony that two of Rufner's pals, Danny McDaniels and David Jackson, once watched Priscilla open the upstairs safe and take out a bag of cocaine; (3) and the fact that the killer had left the plastic garbage bag upstairs where the safe was located. "David Jackson or someone who did the killing was going for that safe upstairs," Gibson claimed. He again reminded the jury of the many dope dealers and convicted felons who lived at the mansion with Priscilla. "The flow of substances through that house and through that lady was *phenomenal*," Gibson said, shaking his head at the mere thought.

Sandwiched between the arguments of Gibson and Racehorse Haynes, Phil Burleson's closing statements had a practical, matter-of-fact, almost cutthroat quality. He reminded the jury that neither Bev Bass nor Bubba Gavrel knew who killed Stan Farr, only what happened to them—"that someone was up there they thought was Cullen Davis." As for Priscilla, it hardly seemed reasonable that she could remember anything with all that Percodan and alcohol churning in her head. "How many times have you heard the words 'I don't remember' from their witnesses?" he asked. "From *their* witnesses, but not from ours." Burleson added that "the absence of rebuttal witnesses by the state proves that our witnesses were truthful. We brought you the real facts." Priscilla had told the jury that when she first heard Bev Bass's voice in the driveway that night, she thought it was Dee. Burleson pounced on this. "Why didn't she call out, 'Dee, run!' if she thought Bev Bass was Dee?" Burleson wondered. "Either she lied, or she was totally unconcerned for the safety of her own daughter. Here is a woman so selfish—so concerned with her own self—she will do anything." Burleson reviewed the lies that Priscilla had told on the witness stand, then posed this key question. "If she wanted you to believe this one thing [that Cullen did it], why didn't she tell you the truth about everything?"

Now it was Racehorse's turn and no circus-tent evangelist ever approached his subject with more righteous indignation.

"They brought you the very best case they could," Race opened, thumbs in his vest, "and it fell woefully short." Haynes told the jury that he had no doubt the state would accuse him of "endeavoring to assassinate the character of their witnesses." It was an accusation, he would have the jury believe, that cut to the quick. "I only wish [Bubba Gavrel] could see the light," Race said. "I do feel sorry for the Bubba Gavrels of this world . . . [but] I can understand why he got into it; there were others behind Gus Gavrel, Jr." Race paused to allow the brimstone to heat properly. "But I do *not* forgive him for lying, nor should you. Because when you raise your hand to God, things like parents or peer group pressure mean nothing at all. No, the person I hold hostility against is Priscilla Lee Davis, that corruptor of young people, the Machiavellian influence behind this whole thing."

Haynes put Priscilla aside for the moment to assail the investigative job done by the Fort Worth police. Haynes reviewed a long list of apparent foulups on the part of the investigators; about the only thing he could find for approval was the fact they found none of his client's fingerprints at the murder scene.

A man of evangelical zeal, Racehorse saved his best for last. *Everything* . . . every bit and piece of the state's case . . . "is predicated on the testimony of Priscilla Lee Davis, who is not worthy." Race could hardly find words to describe Priscilla, but the ones that came to mind were "the Queen Bee" . . . "the Dr. Jekyll and Mrs. Hyde" . . . "the other-worlder" . . . "the lady in the lah-dee-dah pinafore" who rubbed elbows with socialites and hobnobbed with known criminals. It was difficult to keep from smiling when Haynes told the jury in a soft, wondering voice, *I didn't understand Priscilla Lee Davis until Dr. Miller explained her."* Pounding his fist on the railing of the jury box, Haynes said, "Dr. Jekyll became Mrs. Hyde . . . using that big house to bring in

those people . . . those scalawags and thugs . . . skuddies, rogues . . .
brigands . . . Sandy Myers . . . Larry Myers until he went to prison . . .
all those people that Priscilla Lee Davis in her other life associated with.
Don't you wonder . . . why would a grown woman permit her own
daughter to associate with those people? Because she was in that other
world!"

As Joe Shannon sat listening to Haynes's final remarks, he could also
hear the occasional wails and sobs from the back of the room. Without
looking around, he knew that Jack Wilborn was breaking apart inside.
Days and sometimes weeks had passed without a single mention of
Andrea Wilborn, whose tragic ending was the whole reason they were
here. The jury had no real feeling of Andrea as the warm, sensitive,
unobtrusive child who had become the almost accidental victim of
wanton violence and illegal skulduggery. Because of legal restrictions,
the jury had heard none of the bond hearing testimony about Cullen's
previous acts of violence, the threats, the beatings, the broken bones, the
mutilated kitten. Shannon wondered if the jury could look through
Cullen's cool, poised, high-born demeanor and recognize a man capable
of murdering a twelve-year-old girl. The state had considered calling
Jack Wilborn as a rebuttal witness. Wilborn was prepared to tell the jury
that Andrea was terrified of Cullen Davis. It was too late now for
second-guessing. The defense seemed shocked that the prosecution
hadn't called Priscilla back to Amarillo, but Shannon dismissed that
thought with a firm conviction. "All Priscilla could have done is get up
and deny all the things those skuddies and rogues said about her,"
Shannon reasoned. No, it was too late for second-guessing. The
prosecution would stand by its case. Regardless of the lies, Shannon felt
they had two things going for their case. First, there was a great deal of
physical evidence to support the stories of the three eyewitnesses. They
were solidly in line with the physical evidence. Then there were the
statements made by Priscilla and Bev Bass in those crazy moments just
after the shooting—what lawyers call *resgestae* statements. *Excited utter-
ances,* Shannon called them. If the prosecution had done its job, the jury
would believe that when the two women ran from the estate telling
everyone that *Cullen did it,* they spoke only the passionate truth of new
believers. It didn't seem reasonable to Shannon that Priscilla and Bass
had a motive, much less time, to construct elaborate lies.

As Shannon took the floor and began to address a courtroom that was
deathly silent except for the periodic wails of Jack Wilborn, he knew one
thing for sure—this was it. This was the last dance.

Shannon took a photograph from the evidence table, but he held it against his chest so that nobody could see. He started on a low note, talking for a while about the physical evidence and sometimes the lack of it. "What difference does it make that we don't have a photograph of the bullet in the basement?" he asked the jury. The jury followed Shannon with one eye as he began talking about Uewayne Polk . . . "a self-confessed would-be burglar who just happens to beat burglar No. 1 to the mansion . . . just happens to note that it is not T. Cullen Davis. I'm surprised burglar No. 1 didn't wear a name tag that said W. T. Rufner."

Wasn't it curious, Shannon asked the jury, that Haynes failed to ask Uewayne Polk if the man he saw was *Horace Copeland*?

Glancing at his famous adversary at the defense table, Shannon reminded the jury that "a good defense lawyer is a master of illusion. Illusion No. 1—W. T. Rufner. He's a free spirit, but does that make him a killer? No, it just makes him a patsy. Illusion No. 2—Horace Copeland. Copeland and Stan Farr were in fact friends. As a copout they call Bradshaw to testify that Farr was afraid of Copeland. You may also recall that Bradshaw told you Farr was afraid of *Cullen Davis*. This illusion is climaxed by the fact that dead men tell no tales. Illusion No. 3—there is no evidence that Farr owed Copeland any money, as the defense promised to show in their opening remarks. Not one shred of evidence to show any peculiar relationship between Bev Bass and Priscilla Davis. You must know by now that Priscilla paid for Bev Bass's abortion. Let's get it out in the open . . . *abortion,* that's what everyone has been talking about. I'm sure you've figured that out. Was that the motive for Bev Bass to lie, because she owed Priscilla a favor? Illusion No. 4—Uewayne Polk."

As Shannon approached the jury box still clutching the photograph to his chest, he reminded the jury of Polk's testimony, the part in which the witness told of tacking his bill of $677 to the kitchen bulletin board on the afternoon of August 2.

"I would like you to look at this picture labeled Defense Exhibit No. 10 and tell me if you see a bill tacked to that bulletin board," Shannon said matter-of-factly, as he placed the photograph on the railing of the jury box. Shannon surely had to resist the temptation of a broad smile. The photograph of the kitchen bulletin board taken only hours after the murders had been one of a number of pictures introduced by the defense very early in the trial. Nobody seemed to remember why. But the picture was as clear as the implication; there was no nursery bill on the bulletin board.

"If we were here trying the murder of Stan Farr," Shannon continued, "this case wouldn't be circumstantial. The only circumstantial evidence is that the same gunman who pumped four shots in Stan Farr also shot Andrea Wilborn. If you believe that T. Cullen Davis killed Stan Farr, you have to believe that he shot Andrea."

Shannon reminded the jurors of the sequence of witnesses. "Thirty percent of this lawsuit has been devoted to trying a divorce case," he estimated. "Another 50 percent has been Priscilla's association with those skuddies that Mr. Haynes told you about. The remaining 20 percent has tried to answer the question who killed Andrea Wilborn. It really doesn't matter what you think of Priscilla. What in the world did Andrea Wilborn have to do with any of this business?"

The defense had claimed that Priscilla was gooned out on Percodan, but the prosecutor reminded the jury that Priscilla didn't start heavy doses of the drug until *after* the murders.

It was important to keep in mind, Shannon continued, that the gunman reacted and shot Gavrel only after Bev Bass said, "That's Cullen!" Shannon posed this question: "Would Horace Copeland have reacted to this or just kept on walking? [The gunman] was luring them into the house, but he turned and fired at the mention of the name Cullen Davis."

In an evangelical tone every bit as righteous as that employed by his adversary, Shannon also reminded the jury that the defense had even attempted to smear Andrea Wilborn by suggesting that she had "a little bitty marijuana plant behind the door of her room."

Shannon turned and looked straight at Cullen Davis. "What you've seen in this court," he said, "is an attempt to run over everyone that gets in this man's way. Just like on August 2 . . . People were in his way and he *fixed their twats*—that's exactly what he did . . . Their whole defense has been ABC—*Anybody But Cullen!*"

Shannon could see Dowlen glancing nervously at the clock: time was up. He had already reviewed the physical evidence, so Shannon went straight to what he considered the heart of their case—the *resgestae* statements of the two women witnesses. They were terrified and running in opposite directions, he repeated, and yet they told the same story. *Cullen did it.* "When people are excited and shook up," Shannon told the jury, "they tell the truth. That's why it is admissible as evidence."

The prosecutor avoided looking at Jack Wilborn as he reached once more for the color photograph of Andrea Wilborn's body. By now everyone in the courtroom knew that the man weeping was Andrea's

Reporters pushed through the mob in an attempt to question Cullen, but deputy Al Cross, his pistol drawn and ready, hurried the freed man to the jail downstairs where he would be formally released. Those reporters who did not face an immediate deadline rushed three blocks to the Executive Inn where the jurors were already packing and being reunited with their families. All except Freddy Thompson. The split second that Dowlen told the jury they were dismissed, Freddy literally leaped out of the jury box and disappeared.

Every single juror who agreed to be interviewed used two phrases from Dowlen's charge to explain how they resolved many months of legal haggling in such short order. The phrases were "moral certainty" and "reasonable doubt." "I'm not sure we all thought he was innocent," said Karl Prah, the Braniff agent. "But there was room for reasonable doubt, and that's what we were told to find." Prah and others made it absolutely clear that the source of their doubt was the mouth of Priscilla Davis. "I didn't believe her," Prah said. Juror James Watkins agreed: "Some of the things she said I didn't believe. I think maybe she didn't lie to us, but she didn't tell us enough of the truth." Toying with a beer at the Surf Room bar, Mike Giesler wondered if the verdict would have been the same if Priscilla had openly confessed that she was addicted to Percodan, that she slept around as it pleased her, and that she selected a procession of unsavory bed partners and house guests. "They pretty well had her pegged," Giesler continued. In his twenty-eight years, Giesler said, he'd had experiences with women like that. On the prosecutor's master list of jurors there was this notation beside Giesler's name: "been divorced, bitter as to way treated . . . wife had somebody else's baby, took as his own. Felt 'used' when found out later. . . ."

"I don't think Priscilla's as bad as ol' Racehorse made her out to be," said Walter Jones, "but I think most of the jury felt she had lied to them about a number of things, so they couldn't take her word about anything."

Jury foreman Gilbert Kennedy told reporters, "I don't think the defense did all that much to shake her story about the shootings, but there were so many things she denied about herself that were later brought out. We didn't give much credibility to her testimony as a whole."

Curiously, the rumor that circulated the previous night that the jury stood ten to two for acquittal was totally accurate. On the first ballot Kennedy and Jones voted guilty. Jones told *Fort Worth Star-Telegram* reporter Glenn Guzzo that he couldn't swallow the defense's theory of conspiracy. He initially voted guilty because the independent accounts of Priscilla and Bev Bass were almost identical. "I couldn't find any way to let them get their stories together," Jones said. When Jones marked his first ballot, he thought he might be the only juror voting guilty. Even at ten to two, Jones admitted he felt overwhelmed. "When ten people jump up and say, 'Not guilty,' you wonder if there was something you didn't see. If it had been closer, we might still be there." Neither Kennedy nor Jones put stock in the defense's contention that Stan Farr was the killer's real target. Their reasonable doubt was not predicated on their belief that Horace Copeland or someone else committed the crimes. They changed their votes based on discrepancies in times and on the entrance and exit of the large, expensive car that two witnesses saw at the mansion about the time of the murders.

None of the jurors believed Uewayne Polk's strange tale, and most of them had grave doubts about the credibility of Tommy Jourden and Karen Master. All of the jurors looked on Bubba Gavrel as an innocent victim who didn't know who shot him, and all of them seemed to believe Bev Bass. And yet, by some convoluted logic, they refused to accept Bass's identification of Cullen Davis *because* it matched Priscilla's story.

As *Star-Telegram* reporter Guzzo discovered a few days later, the juror who exercised the most influence on the deliberations was Karl Prah. In those long nights of isolation, Prah had dwelled on Racehorse Haynes's suggestion that eyewitnesses can be badly mistaken without really lying, and he had formulated his own theory to explain how two women running in opposite directions at the same time could compare stories. Prah labeled his theory "coincidental conspiracy."

In a special section of the *Fort Worth Star-Telegram* devoted entirely to the Cullen Davis affair, Guzzo wrote: "Prah's theory of 'coincidental conspiracy' seemed rather simple to him; he was surprised no one else had thought of it. And it explained how Priscilla and Miss Bass could get their stories together without implicating Miss Bass in a plot to frame Cullen Davis.

"Prah recalled that Priscilla said her flight across the field after she had been shot was a long one. While she ran, she heard a shot, then screams and a series of shots. The time span between the first shot (at Gavrel) and the series of shots (which Gavrel saw fired through the glass) could have been a minute or several minutes, but either way it was a long time to be running. The suggestion was that Priscilla could hear the very loud noises in that dead night air no matter how far away from the mansion she got. If she heard the screams (of Miss Bass) then she also may have heard the words the voice was shouting, over and over again: 'Cullen, please don't shoot me, it's Bev.' Eight or nine times Miss Bass said she had repeated her desperate plea to the killer she thought was the man she had come to know well over the past five years."

The more Prah thought about it, the more certain he became Bev Bass's cries sparked the coincidental conspiracy. "That's where Priscilla could have gotten Cullen's name, even if she knew it was somebody else who did it," Prah suggested. Why would Priscilla conceal the identity of the person who had just murdered her daughter and her lover? Prah had that figured too. "At that time Priscilla did not know her daughter was dead," Prah told Guzzo. "When she fled, it was convenient to blame Cullen, so she could be safe from the real killer if the shootings were drug related. Once she found out Andrea was dead, it was too late to backtrack."

When defense attorney Steve Sumner heard Prah's theory he observed, "God, that's so bizarre we wouldn't have dared try it on a jury!"

Minutes after the reading of the verdict some of the jurors congregated in the Surf Room bar where Ray Hudson, Karen Master's father, was buying drinks. At Hudson's invitation four of them were chauffeured across town to Rhett Butler's, where Cullen's victory party was commencing. On Roy Rimmer's instructions, Cullen's people had taken over Amarillo's favorite watering hole for a celebration that Texans would talk about for months, not always favorably. At first the party was limited to Cullen's people and the attorneys, but gradually five jurors, three bailiffs, a few select groupies, at least a dozen reporters, and even Judge George Dowlen himself would be a part of the party.

The judge had spent almost all his evenings for the past four or five months at Rhett Butler's. The demands of the trial had been especially hard on Dowlen—among other things, his girlfriend had broken off their relationship—and so on this particular night Dowlen did what he did every night: went straight to Rhett Butler's and started ordering Scotch and celery sticks. He didn't join the party, *the party joined him.* "I guess what I should of done is got up and leave when Cullen and his people came in," Dowlen said later, "but, damn it, I didn't have anywhere to go."

As the party grew, it resembled the dressing room of a Super Bowl winner. Flashbulbs popped, people hugged and kissed and laughed and cried and flashed victory signs, and normally intelligent newspaper people milled about like teenyboppers at Graceland. Dee Miller, who hadn't questioned a witness, drank a toast to the largest fee of his career;

573

and Racehorse, whose own fee was rumored to be astronomical, proposed a toast to all the money spent on photographs of investigators taking photographs of investigators.

You could see Racehorse glowing like a long-smoldering forest fire. The illustrious Houston attorney was well into his cups and having abstained for so long was in no mood to stop now. Race was the Vince Lombardi of trial lawyers: he hated to lose, but God, did he *love* to win. Considering the publicity and the fee and the test of endurance, this would be his biggest. Now it was over. Race was persuaded to sing a couple of verses of his favorite Willie Nelson song. Then Race and Cullen moved into the glare of TV lights and did the kind of slap palms-bump-asses number you would expect from two rookies who had just combined on the winning touchdown. An Amarillo television man had pushed through the crowd to Haynes. They were doing the nightly news *live* from Rhett Butler's, and they wondered if Race would mind making a statement. The attorney ordered another drink and said he wouldn't mind at all. Race took himself downstairs, thrust his chin toward the camera, and made a statement that he probably regretted the next morning.

In a strident evangelical crescendo, the famous lawyer told the television audience about Priscilla Lee Davis. "She is the dregs," he said. "She's probably shooting up right now. She is the most shameless, brazen hussy in all humanity. She is a charlatan, a harlot, and a liar. She is a snake, unworthy of belief under oath. She is a dope fiend and an habitué of dope. She is the most sordid human being in the United States, in fact the world. Someone ought to put up a barbed-wire fence around her and keep her there."

At 4200 Mockingbird the mansion was overlit, as it was almost every night, bright and silent as a ghost ship motionless on the horizon. Lynda Arnold, Stan's sister, was there, and so were a few other close friends, but Priscilla wasn't receiving. James McDaniels, a chauffeur and body-guard, told inquiring reporters that Priscilla was in "a state of shock" and in no condition to make statements to the press. Lynda Arnold was openly enraged by the verdict in Amarillo. "I hope all the money it took to buy all the lies gives those people a lot of joy," she said bitterly. "I hope all the people who lied can live with it." Later, Priscilla talked to two reporters who called from Amarillo. "I know the truth. I know he did it," she said. "But he can't hurt me anymore. Now he'll have to answer to God. That's one he can't buy." There was a long silence, then Priscilla added: "It looks like everyone won today except me. Cullen has his freedom, Racehorse has his million dollars, you guys have your stories, your books, and your movies. The cost has been tremendous. Just remember one thing: it cost me a child I loved very much. That's the part that nobody wants to talk about."

For the first time in almost sixteen months Cullen Davis went to bed that night a free man. Technically, he still faced murder charges in the death of Stan Farr and charges of attempted murder in the shooting of Priscilla and Gavrel—he would remain under bond totaling more than $1 million—but the chances he would be tried on the remaining charges were poor. He was still front-page news across Texas, but now the stories had a fluffy, gossipy society slant, as witnessed by this opening paragraph the following day on the front page of the *Amarillo Daily News:*

"He sat there, slowly sipping his wine. After thinking for several seconds, the defendant in the longest murder trial in Texas history said the trial would not prevent him from resuming his life."

On Saturday night, two days after the verdict, Stanley Marsh 3 came through with his promised party at Toad Hall. He invited the whole cast including Cullen and Karen. Cullen appeared less jubilant than he had at the victory luncheon. Too long had he been a martyr; now he conducted himself with the quiet, relaxed dignity of a hero. There were people at the party who had never seen Cullen wear anything except a business suit, but tonight he came casual in an Ultrasuede shirt, slacks, and loafers. It was like chatting with one of the boys, as Cullen joked about his ordeal and predicted that Priscilla would end up working in an all-night doughnut stand in Waco. Stanley asked Cullen about Priscilla. If she was such a hussy and harlot, why had Cullen married her? When someone asked Stanley later about this conversation, the Amarillo millionaire explained: "Cullen told me she changed for the better after they were married. But when Fort Worth society refused to accept her, she went back to her old ways. Well, I told him, a tiger can't be expected to change her spots. Cullen corrected me. He pointed out that tigers have stripes."

A reporter wondered what Stanley thought of Cullen now.

"Let me put it this way," Stanley said. "I don't think Minnesota Fats would have enjoyed drinking with Cullen."

"Can I quote you on that?"

"I insist," Stanley said. "Fats was just a pig, but he had standards. Blood will tell, I always say."

EDITOR'S NOTE

Nine months after his acquittal on murder charges Cullen Davis was jailed for the second time. This time he was accused of putting out a contract on the life of his divorce-court judge, Joe Eidson. The trial ended in a hung jury. In the retrial Davis was found not guilty. Less than two hours later District Attorney Tim Curry dismissed all of the murder-related charges against Davis.

On May 24, 1979, Cullen Davis and Karen Master were married in Fort Worth. The marriage took place within an hour after his divorce from Priscilla became final.